web by design

THE COMPLETE GUIDE

web by design

THE COMPLETE GUIDE

Molly E. Holzschlag

SYBEX®

San Francisco • Paris • Düsseldorf • Soest

Associate Publisher: Amy Romanoff
Contracts and Licensing Manager: Kristine Plachy
Acquisitions Editor: Suzanne Rotondo
Developmental Editor: Maureen Adams
Editor: Kim Crowder
Technical Editor: Will Kelly
Programming and Technology Advisor: Aaron Bertrand
Lead Research Assistant: Lee Anne Phillips
Book Designers: Patrick Dintino and Catalin Dulfu
Color Reference Designer: Amy Burnham
Graphic Illustrator: Andrew Benzie
Desktop Publisher: Franz Baumhackl
Production Coordinator: Theresa Gonzalez
Production Assistants: Beth Moynihan and Rebecca Rider
Indexer: Matthew Spence
Cover Designer: Carol Gorska
Cover Illustrator: Susan Gross

Sybex Inc., 1151 Marina Village Pkwy., Alameda, CA 94501

Library of Congress Card Number: 97-81251
ISBN: 0-7821-2201-9

Manufactured in the United States of America

10 9 8 7 6 5 4 3 2 1

For Scott.

"When you part from your friend, you grieve not; For that which you love most in him may be clearer in his absence, as the mountain to the climber is clearer from the plain."

KAHLIL GIBRAN

ACKNOWLEDGMENTS

I have been blessed with the extraordinary support of many people who worked with and cared for me along the way. I take this opportunity to thank them here.

Lee Anne Phillips, assistant and researcher, is central to helping me and my books in countless ways. Her humor, spirit, and seemingly endless energy are not only treasured gifts, but necessary sustenance.

Aaron Bertrand, technical assistant and programming coordinator, is a rare find. Enthusiastic and gifted, his guidance of the program-oriented chapters and program sections of the Design Studio Web site have been invaluable.

Amy Burnham, graphic design consultant, developed the spunky color palette and swatches found in the color reference of this book. Thanks Amy, for your friendship and talent.

Gregory Gooden and Annex.com generously set me up with interactive chats and newsgroups for the Design Studio.

Sanford Selznick assisted with Macintosh issues and delivered screen shots with fervent Mac devotion.

Thanks also to author and designer Lynda Weinman for the 216 safe color palette from which the one in this book was inspired, and for the CLUT and related palette graphics made so courteously available via the Design Studio site.

For being a generous mentor to me, I thank Harley Hahn. Thanks also to Wendy Murdock. Our walks through eucalyptus groves and along California beaches soothed my soul and prepared me for the journey of this book.

My agent, David Fugate of Waterside Productions provides expert, committed service. But his value extends far beyond the scope of the job as he always lends an ear, shares wisdom, and guides me with humor and insight through the maze of computer book publishing.

Advice has been generously shared with grace and kindness from general attorney Larry Deckter, contract attorney Bill Rogers, and trademark and copyright attorney Claire Wudowsky.

Sybex is a rare phenomenon, intensely dedicated to the quality of individual books as well as the care and feeding of its authors. I'd like to thank Suzanne Rotondo for her faith in me and this book; Amy Romanoff for her enthusiasm about this project; Maureen Adams for her easy-going but ever-wise input; and Kim Crowder for our great talks and all the support as I learned to embrace my tendencies to overextend myself beyond wear and tear. As individuals you are each exceptional, as a group your vision is unequalled.

I'd like to express my gratitude to Will Kelly, whose technical edits are regularly insightful, occasionally ruthless, and always keep me honest; for production wisdom and concern for excellence: Theresa Gonzalez, Franz Baumhackl, Molly Sharp, Dave Nash, and Scott McDonald. Artist Susan Gross is responsible for the exceptional cover illustration, and Carol Gorska for cover design.

To the Web Training Team at MSN: Ira Goldstein for so generously sharing his optimism, business acumen, and flash (you'll pardon the pun). To Jody "Internet Baglady" McFadden, the brightest gem among gems. Vito Ciavarelli, a quiet friend in dark times and light.

Imagine three highly spirited racehorses running neck and neck—not for the finish line but because it feels so good! That would be me and my comrades in Web design arms, Matthew Straznitskas of BrainBug and Wil Gerken of DesertNet and the Weekly-Wire. You are my classmates, brothers, and beloved friends.

To the following generous network administrators, programmers, writers, editors, designers, business owners, and graphic artists for teaching and inspiring me: Matthew Bardram, C. Scott Convery, Beverly Eppink, Doug Floyd, Nathan Hendler, Dan Huff, Alex Lapin, Katie and Russ Magnuson (and baby Alexandra), Brock N. Meeks, Joel Neelen, Eric Picard, Dr. Joel Snyder and Jan Trumbo of OpusOne, Phil Stevens, Danny Vinik, Zak Woodruff, Ruth Zaslow.

Thanks to the Web Design list and its denizens for always providing terrific assistance day or night.

To my loving family who lends not only down-to-earth support, but their vibrant personalities for the color samples in the color reference of this book: Phillipa Kafka, Ph.D., Ole Kenen, Linus Holzschlag-Kafka, Esq., and Morris Kafka-Holzschlag. Personal friends and life-support: Michelle Armitage, Esq., Patty Sundberg, Patricia Hursh, Ph.D., Jeff Rogers, Andrea Morken, Susan Lee Benson and Susan Fleming, M.D., John George, Jonathan Young, Jason Hellwege, and Claire Wudowsky, Esq. (who deserves a medal for visiting while I was writing part of this manuscript). Your love and care of my mind, body, and spirit have helped me survive and thrive. I love you all.

CONTENTS AT A GLANCE

TABLE OF CONTENTS

INTRODUCTION

Web by Design is unlike any book I've ever written. It is based on a vision I call *holistic Web design*.

I've made stabs at describing this vision as both a professional designer and as an author. The central ideas regarding holistic Web design appear in all my books, in articles, and are expressed in my work as a consultant, designer, and instructor within the field.

Web by Design undeniably looks at each component of design: HTML, space, graphics, typography, and programming. This book is unique in that the viewpoint is a holistic one, and it is with this book that I've matured enough to express this vision with greater clarity.

Holistic Web design seeks to combine the many separate facets of design and look at them not for the strength or faults of individual aspects, but for the power that appears when these parts are combined. It also takes into account that we, as Web designers, are the parents of a new and changing medium. That's a sensitive position, and one I am confident *Web by Design* supports.

Like most Web designers, this book is unflaggingly optimistic and embraces the challenges of the field by turning them into triumphs.

Why Another Design Book?

The literal and virtual shelves are filled with books on how to design this and how to program that. Some of these books are meant for newcomers, others for experts. Most of these books are broken up into the specific technologies of graphic design, HTML, and Web programming.

But what of the gestalt, the whole, the entirety? There exists today a need for a book that gathers the many eggs of the industry and puts them in a single basket. That's what *Web by Design* is designed to do—take the many aspects of Web design and apply them in a realistic manner to the whole of the industry.

Web by Design assumes a certain amount of knowledge on the reader's part. Certainly, any reader will benefit from the broad-spectrum wisdom within this book, but the chewy stuff is best suited for the practicing Web designer. Furthermore, *Web by Design* seeks to serve a plentiful helping of theory and practice of a Web site's design in totality—how it looks, how it feels, how it works, and how it acts and interacts with the most important aspect of its existence, the Web site visitor.

Web by Design is a guide. It takes you on a journey through the pieces of design and provides a context in which to see those pieces as a whole. Whether you are a technologist who wants to strengthen your design knowledge or a designer who wants to apply design principles to technology, this book serves as the bridge between both worlds.

Organization

Web by Design contains twenty-five chapters and is divided into seven parts. Each part examines a specific aspect of design, looking at both concepts and practical applications of those concepts, and concludes with a review chapter. Complete with quizzes, tasks, and summaries, the review chapters allow you to try techniques on your own, as well as test your knowledge of the information shared in the book. You can also use the review chapters as a quick-reference when looking for main concepts rather than detailed discussion on specific Web design topics.

Part I: "What Every Web Designer Must Know" (Chapters 1-4) provides a safe approach to Web design via accessibility. From there, HTML techniques that will serve to enhance your productivity are discussed. Interface, an essential element in the design of all interactive media, is explained and exemplified. Part I wraps up with a review pulling examples from the Design Studio's Front Office area.

Part II: "Designing for Success" (Chapters 5-8) lays the foundation for success in design. Areas stressed include planning, managing information, working with the logistical issues of a Web site, and a wrap-up that involves actively mapping a Web site.

Part III: "Inner Space: Designing for the Screen" (Chapters 9-11) is a series of chapters that deal with the spatial issues of the Web. Web real estate is limited; these chapters tell you how to open up the screen and use the available space effectively.

Part IV: "Total Control: Web Page Layout" (Chapters 12-15) teaches techniques using standard HTML, tables, and frames to structurally lay out pages. The chapters include examples and exercises as well as many design tips and tricks for laying out pages with lasting punch.

Part V: "Bright Sites: Designing with Color and Graphics" (Chapters 16-18) zooms in on Web color and Web graphic technology. From scanning to working with Web-safe color to optimizing graphics for speed and beauty, this section is a powerful resource for any Web designer.

Part VI: "The Fine Art of Fonts: Web Typography" (Chapters 19-21) is a section dedicated to looking more closely at classic typographic techniques and applying them in the Web environment.

Part VII: "Dynamic Media: Multimedia and Web Programming" (Chapters 22-25) delves into interactivity, audio, video, and the wide variety of Web programming techniques that are available to bring life to your Web sites. Exercises that will strengthen your understanding of multimedia and programming as they exist today complete this part.

At the end of *Web by Design* you will find two appendices: a complete HTML reference and a cross-browser reference guide. In addition, a color reference has been included in the center of this book in order to bring life to the color issues discussed here. The color reference is a 32-page guide to Web-based color, complete with a 216 safe-color palette, 24 color combinations derived from that palette with associated usage examples, a color wheel, and several color screen shots depicting the companion Web site to this book, the Design Studio (http://www.designstudio.net/).

Conventions Used in This Book

This book uses a variety of conventions designed to get you to important information with ease.

To indicate that you choose a menu command, the symbol ➤ is used. For example, to instruct you to select the Open command from the File menu, the text says, "choose File ➤ Open."

To highlight important information, you'll see Notes, Tips, and Warnings throughout the book:

NOTE

Notes give you further commentary or "by the way" information pertaining to the discussion at hand.

TIP

Tips offer practical and often technical comments to enhance what is being taught.

**W**ARNING

Warnings alert you to important problems to avoid or procedures that you *must* follow to achieve desired results.

Not So Conventional Conventions

I've also added a few unconventional additions to the standard list. These are:

Inside Info—Quotes from Web design professionals, philosophers, and other relevant individuals. These quotes either support the teaching within the book or offer a different opinion to show you how design is ultimately a subjective experience.

"All Inside Info quotations are set aside in a quote, like this."

Online! Sidebars—These sidebars contain information about Web-based exercises or resources.

ON line!

Information is set aside in a sidebar, such as this one.

Offline! Sidebars—These sidebars contain examples, activities, or resources that you'll find *off* of the Internet.

OFF line!

Much like the Online! sidebar, the Offline! sidebar appears like this.

About the Design Studio Web Site

The Design Studio Web site is meant to serve as a helpful example for many of the concepts contained in this book. The Web site, which is available at `http://www.designstudio.net/`, is divided up similarly to this book, but with additional resources appropriate within the Web environment. Included is a newsgroup, chat rooms, and links to a range of sites. A design tip of the day is provided on the site's main page for your regular enjoyment.

An interesting facet of the Design Studio is that it isn't just *my* site, or limited to the breadth and scope of this book. You get to participate! Post your quiz answers to the newsgroups, submit tasks, and most especially, share your tips and ideas about Web design with other designers.

 NOTE

As with all Web sites, the Design Studio goes through visual as well as structural changes. Therefore, don't be too terribly surprised to see redesigns, changes to HTML, or additions to the site. After all, that's one of the advantages of a Web site—it can be updated and shaped to meet the needs of the present.

About the Author

Photo Credit: Balf Walker

My entrance into Web design wasn't even close to intentional. It came about as an indirect results of a holiday gift given to me by a friend. The gift? A 300-baud modem.

I attached that modem to my Commodore 64, and before I knew it I was communicating on BBSs and now-defunct commercial online services such as Q-Link. The Internet wasn't an option for those of us with home-based, 300-baud modems. It was still reserved for institutional organizations.

It didn't take much time for me to get hooked on this world of communication and cool file downloads. And the more time I spent online, the hungrier I became for new stimulation.

I wasn't disappointed.

The technology grew to fulfill my need for faster downloads and better computers. A few years passed, and through them paraded 1200-baud modems, then 2400-baud modems (oh, we thought *that* was fast!), and 14.4, and 28.8, until one day I found myself sitting at a T1.

By then, my computer of choice had changed from the Commodore 64 (which I remember with great fondness) to a DOS-based XT, then a 286-MHz processor, and then a 386, and then a 486. 4 meg of RAM, 8, 16, 32, 64. Windows 3.1 to Windows 95. And even though I am a "Windows" person, it's more by history than design. I love computers. I can sit at a Macintosh, a PC, and on the fortunate occasions I've had to play with SGI machines, well—I get palpitations just thinking about them.

And to think, I was once so cool. A hip chick, a party girl. And now?

Nerd city.

Blame it on the Internet—which I was cruising as soon as it was even remotely available to the public. I used to borrow a friend's hacked password to get into the local medical library and do research using the Gopher system. I saw the Web when it was a brand-spanking new text baby and HTML was truly a simple markup language. I built my first Web site without graphics because there *were no graphical browsers*!

The point is that I've been in love with some form of the Net since it was a little child in the eyes of the public. I've had the pleasure of watching it explode into this multimedia *event* right before my eyes.

It was only natural, then, that my love for communication, design, and technology should end up right here with Web design. This field, like no other of which I am aware, so naturally blends the scientific and the artistic, the verbal and spatial, the linear and the tangential. It's really a very balanced place, and I feel balanced and fulfilled within it.

That small holiday gift changed my life more drastically than anything else quite so specific. My education and profession have been built up around the wonders I found in the intangible world of the ethers, and many of my most profound friendships have resulted from or are able to continue because of the Internet.

Academically, I hold a BA in Communications and Writing, and an MA in Media Studies. I have worked professionally for a number of private, commercial, and corporate companies as a systems operator, coder, and eventually, a Web designer. Included in this list are GEnie, DesertNet, and The Microsoft Network, where I am still involved as a contractor in community development. I maintain relationships with several design firms where I act as a consultant and freelance designer. It keeps my chops up!

In the past two years, my interest has turned toward writing and teaching. I have written four Web design and Internet technology books prior to this one, contributed to many others, and have written several popular columns.

I teach classes in Web design, writing, and communications and am adjunct faculty for the New School University, the University of Phoenix, and Pima Community College. I have done corporate training for The Microsoft Network, developed a Web design course for DigitalThink, and developed testing for a professional screening company, Background Knowledge.

Well, enough about me! It's time to explore *you*.

As readers of my work you are the final judge as to the quality of the experience provided in this book. Please visit my personal Web site, http://www.molly.com/, e-mail me your thoughts, or share them on the Design Studio Web site.

See you online!

PART I

what every web designer must know

chapter 1

APPROACHING DESIGN

CHAPTER

1

APPROACHING DESIGN

E very time you laugh at a joke, or cry at a tragedy, you are responding not only to the emotional impact of the moment, but your own personal experience that enables you to identify what is funny or what is sad.

Being a Web designer is not just about being a trendy artist or a flavor-of-the-month technologist. Web site design is an extremely creative and technically challenging field, and if it is to be done well it demands depth from its creators. This depth is drawn not from aesthetics or binary data, but from the life experiences that inspire and attract individuals to the field in the first place.

That's a pretty serious way to start out a book intended to be an upbeat learning experience. This reasoning is important, though, because I want to impress upon Web designers that they are, in fact, architects of the future. The media that you work with every day is bigger than you—and it has the potential of literally changing the way the world communicates. The field has an energy that is palpable, and if you've ever been at a large computer and communications convention like Comdex or Internet World, you've undoubtedly felt that energy.

Approaching Web design is the same as approaching a convention hall filled with that energy, with the latest and greatest in technology, with people flying high on the rapid pace of the industry and their related success. The approach should fill you with excitement, but it should also present you with a sense of respect at its sheer magnitude.

From that excitement you will draw inspiration and energy to learn how to design better, more competitive, and highly successful sites. Pause for a moment and consider how the designs you create will impact your world; put yourself into the shoes of your potential visitors—if you don't, you may leave out entire populations who not only deserve, but need to be in that world.

> *" . . . this new medium has an amazing potential to*
> *enlighten, empower, and educate."*
>
> KATHY E. GILL, Internet Columnist and Webmaster

Accessibility is the term we will use to define the right of passage into your Web world. In Web design, accessibility is the ability to pass from the mundane, linear, and tactile world into the virtual, non-linear, and highly imaginative one that you create. For those who visit your sites, accessibility is an entrance into your content. The Web worlds which you create can, when shared, become a powerful and interactive experience.

Whether the objective is to sell, to entertain, to inform, or to express, the impact of that experience is at a maximum when you bring the panorama of your experience to the virtual table and that depth is met by today's sophisticated, enthusiastic audience.

Accessible design means, in a technical sense, that *any* individual visiting your site is going to be able to access it. It should not matter which type of computer hardware, software, or browser type and version he or she is using. Hopefully, the social, economic, or geographic environment in which an individual lives will not prevent access to the information and recreation the Web has to offer. Finally, if an individual has a visual or other physical limitation, he or she will ideally be able to get to the information you're providing on your site because you've had the foresight to provide that information in an accessible format.

This chapter will show you:

- What a computer platform is
- Why computer platforms are directly related to accessible design
- What Web browsers have to do with accessibility—and how it came to be that way
- That *standards* and *conventions* are different things, and both will affect you as a Web designer
- How all of the preceding issues can be practically addressed by Web design techniques
- Examples of how accessibility can be achieved

Certainly, some of the issues listed above are out of the designer's immediate control. A client with a product to advertise will logically focus on an advertising campaign— possibly overlooking the opportunity to offer something back to the community.

You might often be in the position to make suggestions as to how an advertiser can provide philanthropic projects on a Web site, perhaps devoting a page or two to the company's charitable and community-oriented activities. This adds to the quality of the relationship between the company and the people visiting the site. To add this information increases awareness and interest in the site, resulting in a desire for access to that site. Combine this with technical accessibility, and the results are enhanced public relations and product viability.

There will also be times when you will choose not to make your designs accessible, or to make them only partially accessible. These choices will depend upon who you are designing your site for, and why you are designing that site in the first place.

These choices should never be entered into lightly—which is why this book begins with issues of access. A common notion is that it's best if you know the rules before you choose to break them. To be confident that your choice is an educated and thoughtful one is something that should be practiced as a rule.

Cross-Platform Considerations

The definition of the term *computer platform* is fairly vague. Many technical terms fall in to popular culture and roll off of people's tongues far too casually, like so many bad jokes at an office party, oftentimes skewing the meaning. I'm guilty of it myself, it's an occupational hazard.

When you think of platform, you probably think of a *type* of computer. While that's accurate, what's more accurate is that platform relates to the type of programming interface a computer uses. To keep it simple, the most critical aspect of platform for the Web designer is the *operating system* used by that computer.

ON line!

The following Web sites offer helpful information on platforms and operating systems:

- **PC Webopaeida:** This site is a virtual storehouse of any and all information about personal and general computer information, http://www.pcwebopaedia.com/.
- **Microsoft:** This corporate giant has one of the most jam-packed Web sites on the Net. Check it out at http://www.microsoft.com/.
- **Apple:** To learn more about the Macintosh, visit Apple's site at http://www.apple.com/.
- **Digital Equipment Corporation:** An extremely interesting site for DEC computers, which many UNIX- and VAX-based operating systems run on, http://www.dec.com/.

There are a variety of operating systems (OS for short) that must be considered by Web designers. Because of the different programming interfaces used by such systems, the software designed to work with them can vary significantly. To make a Web site run identically, or as close to identically as possible, no matter what platform is interfacing with your Web site, it is important to keep in mind *cross-platform* considerations, or how to make your Web site accessible to all platforms.

The Platforms

The most common platforms for public users of the Internet appear to be the Macintosh and the PC. Another platform of significance is UNIX. Within each of these three groups there are distinctions.

While the hardware for these platforms do in fact have differences, the real challenge comes up with the software that's been written for their individual programming interfaces.

Here are the three primary platforms, what they do, and what some of their subsets include:

- **PC**—Literally, *PC* stands for *personal computer*. While a Macintosh can be a personal computer, the common meaning excludes Macs and refers to any computer with an Intel or Intel-style microprocessor. Operating systems that fall under the PC's domain include DOS, Windows (all versions including Windows 3.1, 95 and above, and NT), and OS/2 (see Figure 1.1).

- **Macintosh**—Developed by Apple, the Macintosh uses a different type of microprocessor and different file formats than PCs. The OS in a Macintosh is always the proprietary Mac OS (see Figure 1.2). Macs have historically been popular computers for the public as well as the desktop publishing and graphic design industry, and therefore carry a lot of weight in the Web design world.

- **UNIX**—Unlike the PC and Macintosh, UNIX has never been dependent on a specific piece of hardware, such as a microprocessor. In fact, it was built specifically to be portable and flexible, and to function in a multi-user environment. Until recently, UNIX had the distinction of being the leading operating system for workstations. The Internet's infrastructure demanded the kind of power UNIX offers, and many computers and computer users are still on the UNIX platform.

FIGURE 1.1

The Windows 95 OS

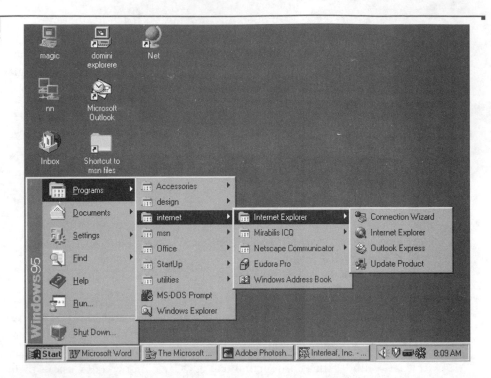

FIGURE 1.2

The Macintosh OS

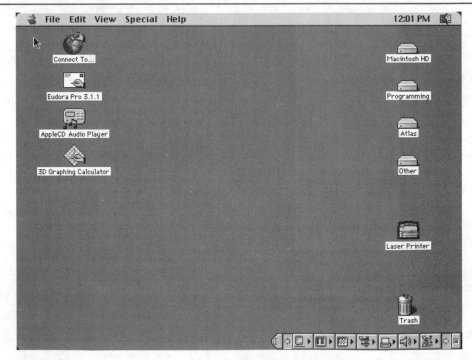

It's important to mention several other platforms, including VMS (Virtual Memory System) which runs on DEC's VAX minicomputers and workstations (found with some frequency as Internet servers); Sun Microsystems and SGI (graphics-intensive systems from Silicon Graphics); and LINUX, a takeoff of UNIX that is freely distributable and runs on a number of hardware platforms (LINUX has a very enthusiastic user base). Of course, there are other platform minorities.

Because platform has so much to do with the software that is developed, and the software is what determines the *user interface* or how you view the Web, being familiar with these platforms, and their differences, will be very helpful to Web designers interested in creating accessible Web sites.

While Web developers will need to know a lot about the delivery mechanisms involved with servers, the focus of this book is how platforms interact with design-specific issues.

The software you'll be most concerned with is the Web browser. Web browsers have a fascinating, if not disturbing, history that impacts Web designers on a daily basis. Understanding the origins of this problem makes you better prepared to work within the limitations of the interfaces resulting from platform differences among your users.

Battle of the Browsers

Web browsers are the user interface to the Web. Their evolution has been rapid and confusing—especially to the designer who wants to make a site accessible but still embrace the new technologies offered by each new version of a browser.

Nature shows us that when environmental conditions are unstable, newly introduced attributes can become commonplace very quickly. Natural selection seeks to keep those attributes that are strong and will allow for survival of the fittest. If you apply this metaphor to the evolution of Web browsers, it's obvious that many of the attributes developed in the unstable environment of the Web are in fact strong, while others are weak.

Furthermore, the "fittest" doesn't necessarily translate to the best. In the case of Web browsers vying for market position, it's a really tough call to say which is a better browser versus which strategies used by the corporations behind the browsers have been more clever.

The two browser developers that have made it to the top of the heap, Netscape Communications Corporation and Microsoft Corporation, are engaged in a battle of market savvy and technological one-upmanship in an attempt to survive the rigors of the Internet climate. Both are striving for domination, yet neither has the full spectrum of attributes required for that survival.

> *" . . . there's a market exploding. And we know that to stay ahead of that market, we have to run really fast . . . it's a very Darwinian thing."*
>
> MARC ANDREESSEN, Vice President of Technology, Netscape Communications Corporation

The problems with Web browsers stem not only from the rapid-fire pace of growth and competition, but also from platform problems and the diversity of hardware that exists. You'll see the specific browser and platform issues unfold throughout this book. Figures 1.3, 1.4, 1.5, and 1.6 demonstrate a taste of this—two platforms, two different browsers, the same page. The most obvious differences between the platforms (comparing Macintosh to PC) are the differences in font size, style, and visible area of the page. When you compare the browsers themselves, you can see differences in interface design, which is most obvious in the use of icons and toolbar size and design.

In order for you to make a site completely accessible, you'll need to step very far back from recent trends and follow standards that might not apply to the latest technology. Doing this may help you find clever and creative ways to bridge the gaps.

The history of browser battles is an interesting one, and the following short overview should help you to gain a better understanding of how and why browsers are as limited—and as dichotomously powerful—as they are today.

Browser History

The Web began as a hypertext-based environment viewable only by text-based browsers such as Lynx (see Figure 1.7). But in 1993, Marc Andreessen (now Vice President of Technology, Netscape Communications Corporation) and Eric Bina developed a *graphic user interface* (GUI) at the National Center for Supercomputing Applications (NCSA). The Mosaic browser, shown in Figure 1.8, can be cited as the single most important factor in the shift of the Internet to widespread, commercial use. Its interface was easy to use, and the fact that it could display graphics was an attractive feature.

FIGURE 1.3

*Macintosh plat-
form, Internet
Explorer*

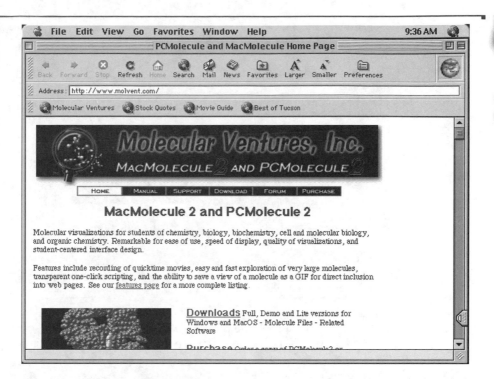

FIGURE 1.4

*Macintosh plat-
form, Netscape
Navigator*

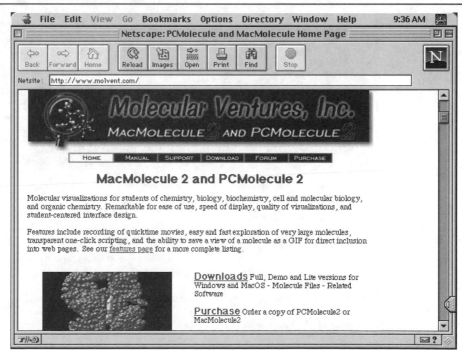

FIGURE 1.5

*Windows 95 plat-
form, Internet
Explorer*

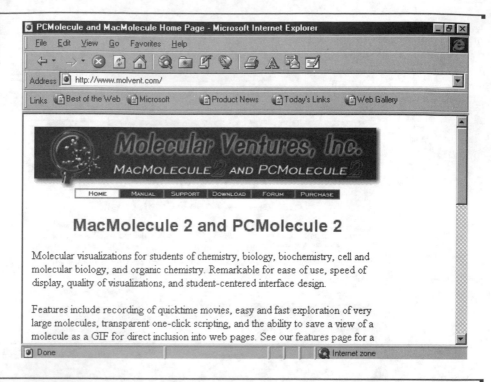

FIGURE 1.6

*Windows 95 plat-
form, Netscape
Navigator*

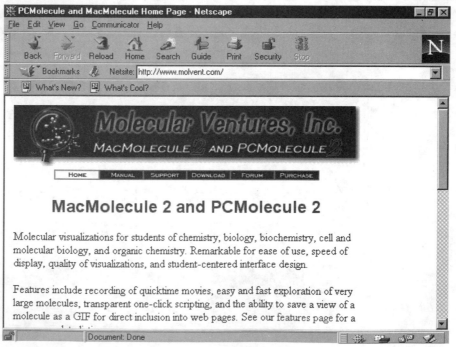

FIGURE 1.7

Lynx is a text-based browser.

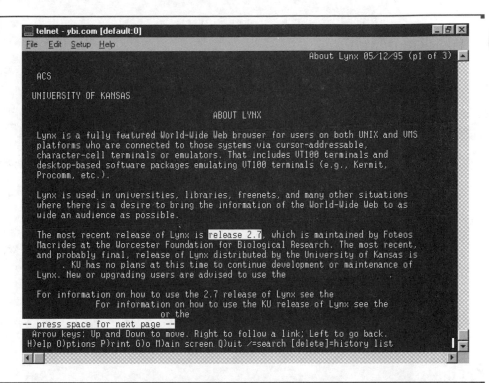

FIGURE 1.8

Mosaic was the first graphical Web browser.

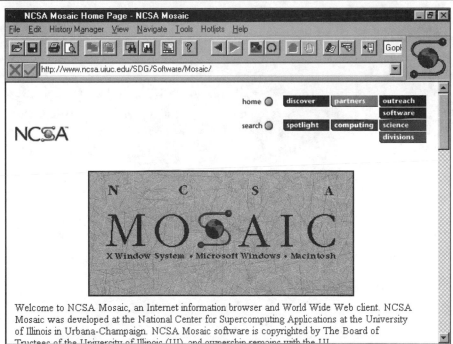

Mosaic took only three months to develop, yet broke the ground for the growth of a new medium, a new industry, and an environment of challenge and change. Very quickly, a medley of Web browsers began to pop up, including Cello and eventually, Netscape Navigator—a cousin to Mosaic. Netscape released its first version of Navigator in 1994, barely a year after the first graphic browser entered the scene.

The Netscape browser moved quickly to the forefront both because of its constantly expanding features and cross-platform interoperability. Essentially, Netscape used Mosaic's gift of visual—and therefore commercially inviting—Web browsing potential and took (and continues to take) it to the next level. Features such as background colors and graphics, plug-in technologies for video and audio, and the foundations for the development of new software languages such as Java and VRML moved the browser from a tool to the seed of an industry.

Enter Microsoft. With monetary, technical, and support resources unequaled in any market, Microsoft began its quiet penetration of the browser market. By procuring the early code of Mosaic, and then embracing current Netscape conventions, the Internet Explorer browser was born. Microsoft then added dissident functions, including inline video, support for background sound, marquee, and several new HTML tags, and to top it all off, decided that this browser would be free.

ON line!

Check out the latest news in browser technologies:

- **Microsoft's Internet Explorer:** News, product downloads, and general information, `http://www.microsoft.com/ie/`.

- **Netscape Navigator:** Product information, version downloads, white papers, `http://home.netscape.com/`.

- **Other browsers:** C|NET keeps up with trends and changes in the browser industry on their special browser site, `http://www.browsers.com/`.

The battle lines were drawn. Microsoft and Netscape have been fierce competitors for the last two years, each one attempting to outdo the other in terms of functionality, cross-platform interoperability, and new technologies. And, of course, dominate the market share. While the actual dollars spent on the browser itself might not garner monies, the money spent on and by third-party developers, computer hardware manufacturers, and purchasers of operating systems and other necessary equipment to *run* the browsers skyrockets.

NOTE

So who's winning the browser war? It's hard to say, really. Statistics are often skewed due to the latest trend or the statistical source. Furthermore, many people (like me) use both browsers regularly. Browser statistics are typically drawn from servers that identify browser types coming in to a given site. For example, Mecklermedia's site reports at this writing that Netscape Navigator owns 65.6 percent of the market, Internet Explorer 25.0 percent, and other browsers make up the rest of the pie. C|NET reports these statistics by the number of times each browser is downloaded, showing on the *same day* that Internet Explorer was downloaded 1,512,672 times, topping Navigator at 120,660! It is generally thought that Netscape holds the realistic share at a falling 60% or so.

In a way, this competition is very healthy because it's forcing each browser developer to be accountable for its actions to some degree. On the other hand, it's very frustrating for designers who have to figure out ways of dealing with the idiosyncrasies born out of this battle.

Standards and Conventions

So what's to protect designers from total chaos? For one thing, there are HTML and Web standards. HTML stands for *Hypertext Markup Language*, and most readers of this book will be at least somewhat familiar with the language. HTML's linguistic origins are related to SGML, or *Standard Generalized Markup Language*, a digital document format language. HTML uses SGML foundations and allows users to format Web documents.

HTML began with simple tags such as those necessary for paragraphs and headers. The original HTML specifications were authored by Tim Berners-Lee at the birthplace of the Web, the European Laboratory for Particle Physics (CERN), in Geneva, Switzerland. In a few short years, HTML has gone from a simple formatting language to one with powerful layout and programming controls.

In order to help keep some consistency over the rapid growth of HTML and related technology standards, an organization called the World Wide Web Consortium (W3C) evolved (see Figure 1.9). Members of the consortium range from major corporations such as IBM and Sun Microsystems to smaller independent companies, and of course, browser developers such as Netscape and Microsoft.

This consortium publishes regular papers that try to document the emerging technologies and changes to HTML. At various intervals, new specifications are published. These are considered the *standards*.

OTE

December 18, 1997 marked the passage of the HTML 4.0 standard. This is an advanced standard that browsers have yet to fully implement. As a result, designers will continue to work with a 3.2 standard as well as adopting the features of 4.0 that they can use, where they are able to use them.

FIGURE 1.9

The W3C's home page

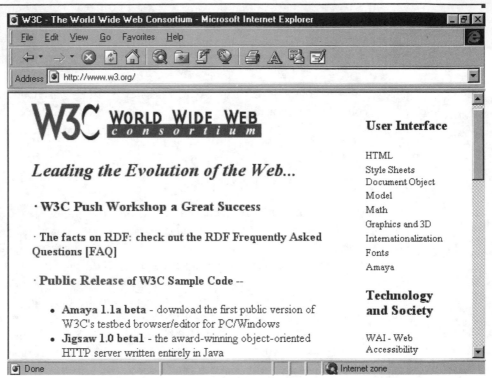

 line!

Check out the World Wide Web Consortium's extensive Web site. The entire history of HTML standards can be seen here, as well as abundant lists of links to relevant information. The W3C also supports a number of e-mail lists and newsgroups that you can join to keep up with various HTML and design issues at http://www.w3.org/.

However, standards are not to be confused with *conventions*. This distinction was pointed out during a discussion with *Internet World* columnist and network guru Dr. Joel Snyder, who stated that it's Web designers and browser companies who don't pay attention to standards. This renegade behavior is what causes the disparity. In other words, what you do *conventionally* as a designer may or may not have anything to do with what is considered standard.

OFF line!

Here's an exercise to get you thinking about standards and conventions.

In your field of work or study, is there anything that is considered a *standard* and anything that is done *conventionally*?

A personal example is when I'm cooking. From time to time I might use a recipe, which calls for a standard measurement of specific ingredients. But rather than measure a teaspoon of salt, or a $1/4$ teaspoon of paprika, I simply add these to taste. This is a convention—and one that most people follow. Even the best gourmets deviate from the standards and go with what they've done conventionally because it works better for them.

Personalize the concept of *standards versus conventions* by finding what it is in your own life that operates on this basis.

Snyder's point is well taken, but it's also necessary to be a renegade—it's what pushes the limits of the technology and forces change to come about. Here's the rub: Designers live in a world where their obligation is to create accessible design that simultaneously demands more of the technology. It's a catch-22, and it is not something that will be immediately resolved.

So what do you, as a designer, do to make a Web site accessible? There are access conventions that will help you make choices about the way you design. How much of a renegade or conformist you decide to be will always depend on the nature of the project you're doing.

I've designed this book's companion Web site, the Design Studio, to be accessible to anyone interested in visiting it. While I obviously want to make it visually attractive, and there are certain areas that require technologies that might not be accessible to everyone, there are a number of things I'm doing with that site so that it is as broadly accessible as possible. You'll see these techniques described within this chapter and throughout the book as we examine the making of the Design Studio site.

On the other hand, the sites I've developed for the Microsoft Network sit on a proprietary platform. In other words, you have to be a member in order to access the information, despite the fact that it is built upon the Internet's infrastructure and uses HTML and related technologies as its delivery mechanism. *Everyone* who accesses those sites is using Windows 95 and Internet Explorer or its derivative, the MSN Program Viewer. The accessibility issues are answered in the project—other platforms or browsers are not an issue since the parameters for technology, geography, status, and varying abilities have already been set by MSN.

In the next section, we're going to take a closer look at what makes a site accessible, giving you the tools to build or fix your Web sites. We'll wrap up this chapter with a comparative demonstration between the two sites just mentioned. This will help you see how the type of project you are working on will guide you as a designer, and how your awareness of accessibility and choice will help you create attractive and successful Web sites.

Equal Access Sites

Equal access can be gained by using a combination of techniques when coding and designing your sites. By following these concepts, you add a new level of accessibility that you might have otherwise overlooked.

HTML and graphic design issues are covered later in this book, and some of the methods described and some of the code demonstrated might be unfamiliar to you. Fear not. By introducing these concepts now, you gain a strong foundation upon which to build your future as a Web designer. What's more, if you're already familiar with HTML coding and related techniques, you'll be able to apply these techniques immediately.

> *" . . . As we move towards a highly connected world, we must ensure that the tools for working in that world are usable by anyone, regardless of individual resources, capabilities, and disabilities."*
>
> Proceedings, the Sixth International World Wide Web Conference, Stanford University

Remember, it's you—the designer—who must work to evaluate the project in the context of accessible design. If you have learned these concepts well and find that you are unable or do not want to make a particular site fully accessible, that's your choice. It's not an issue of good or bad, but of having the foresight to make educated decisions about your work.

Accessibility Techniques

The central issue to making a Web site accessible means making it readable in a text-based browser such as Lynx. Sites with advanced HTML technologies such as tables, frames, style sheets, sophisticated programming, and multimedia are going to choke those browsers. The first thing you have to decide is whether the information in a given site is important to people who cannot for some reason access that site with a contemporary, graphic-based browser; this is *readability*.

A more subtle issue is *contextual appropriateness*. What this means is that everything you employ as a designer should have some purpose. It doesn't always have to be a functional purpose—it can be an aesthetic one. But don't do something just because you *can*; do it because it makes sense. A deaf or hearing-impaired individual might be able to see your design, but will he or she understand the design if you have an audio clip on a page and start out the text with a reference to the audio? That individual is going to miss the reference. You can avoid a problem like this by thinking carefully about *context*.

Finally, you want your sites to function. If someone is visiting your site on a 14.4 modem connection from a remote country with faulty technology and a text-based browser, you can bet that person is going to be frustrated if they can't fill out an order form for a product they need. Providing alternatives to forms and other interactive devices is simple enough to do, and can help immeasurably. This is *functionality*.

If you pay careful attention to readability, context, and functionality, you're three steps ahead of the game!

Now we'll look at some specific problems, and demonstrate solutions.

Readable Design

One problem that comes up in regards to readability is the fact that images are so pervasive on today's Web sites. Here are some guidelines when working with images:

1. **Use the** alt **attribute.** This attribute allows you to place a description of individual graphics in the HTML code. The description will then show up on the Web page in the place of the graphic. Descriptions should be clear and concise:

   ```
   <img src="myface.gif" alt="Photograph of Molly">
   ```

   Sometimes graphics aren't photos or artwork, they provide a functional purpose. Bullet graphics or clear graphics used as spacers are perfect examples. In cases like this, you can use a description or a symbol such as an asterisk to denote the bullet:

   ```
   <img src="bullet.gif" alt="*">
   ```

   or

   ```
   <img src="spacer.gif" alt="spacer">
   ```

By doing this, your pages become sensible when graphics are unavailable or turned off (Figure 1.10).

FIGURE 1.10

Alt tags in action

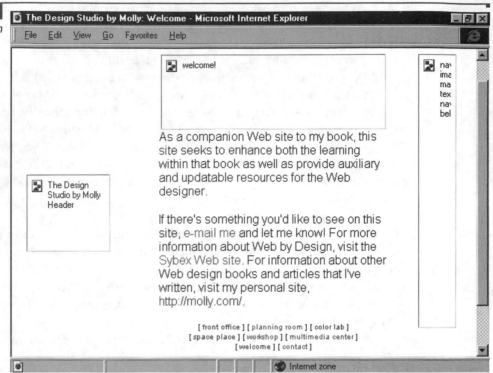

2. **Avoid text on graphic images or provide alternatives.** As you'll learn in later chapters of this book, typography on the Web has some limitations. In order to get around these limitations, designers will create graphics with the text they want to set in a specific type. The way to deal with this is to either avoid it completely or provide alt attribute elements as described above.

3. **Pages with image maps or non-standard navigation require alternatives.** If you're using an image map, an alt attribute can only go so far. You need to provide text-based link alternatives. You can use the alt attribute in the image, and for client-sided maps, in the individual image areas as well. An example from the Design Studio site is shown in Figure 1.11.

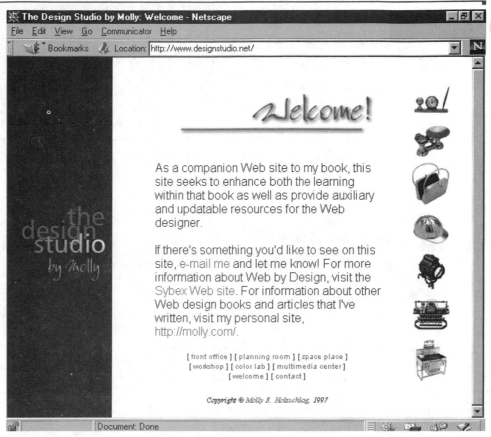

The following code sets up the image map that you see on the Design Studio Web site. The image:

```
<img src="images/navmap3.gif" width="50" height="395" border="0"
alt="navigational image map, text navigation below" usemap="#navmap3">
```

The Map data:

```
<map name="navmap3">

shape="rect" coords="0,0,57,46" href="office.htm">

<area shape="rect" coords="0,48,57,98" href="planning.htm">

shape="rect" coords="0,100,57,160" href="space.htm">
```

```
<area shape="rect" coords="0,162,57,214" href="workshop.htm">

<area shape="rect" coords="0,216,57,275" href="color.htm">

<area shape="rect" coords="0,278,57,330" href="type.htm">

<area shape="rect" coords="0,332,58,393" href="media.htm">

<area shape="default" nohref>
```

The alternative text navigation is shown here. This is the code that supports text-only access to the page, working around the graphic-based image map:

```
<!--begin text navigation-->

<div align="center">

<font face="arial" size="1">

[ <a href="office.htm">front office</a> ]
[ <a href="planning.htm">planning room</a> ]
[ <a href="space.htm">space place</a> ]
<br>

[ <a href="workshop.htm">workshop</a> ]
[ <a href="color.htm">color lab</a> ]
[ <a href="media.htm">multimedia center</a> ]
<br>

[ <a href="index1.htm">welcome</a> ]
[ <a href="contact.htm">contact</a> ]

</font>
</div>
```

4. **Provide alternative HTML or text-only downloads for all unreadable pages.** This is a particularly potent method of handling accessibility issues. It frees you up from constraints and allows the bulk of information on your site to be available via a download or another avenue for text only. Table and frames-based sites are especially good candidates, since they are notoriously inaccessible. Newspapers, magazines, information services, and other content-rich sites that make extensive use of these technologies should consider these options as a first-line defense.

Contextual Design

To deal with contextual issues, follow these guidelines:

1. **Use anchor references to empower your visitors, rather than confuse them.**
Obviously you don't want to clutter your pages with a lot of descriptions about
where your links are going, but you can work these descriptions into the context
of your page. Links that say "click here" aren't clear enough. Here's an example:

```
My favorite type of baked potato is from an old recipe. Click
<a href="potato.htm">here</a> for the details.
<p>
```

A better way to do this:

```
My favorite type of baked potato is from an <a href="potato.htm">old
recipe.</a>
<p>
```

2. **Follow contextual linking into multimedia components.** When you have
audio, video, or other advanced programming available, make the link descriptions sensible:

```
Welcome to Molly's Music Emporium! All of our selections are available for
your listening pleasure in Real Audio format. Here are some:
<p>

<ul>

<li>The Courage Sisters: Life as a River.
<br>

Enjoy this <a href="life.ra">Real Audio clip</a> of this uplifting folk/rock
composition.
<br>

<li>Don Reeve: Amanita Muscara.
<br>

Frightening yet at times joyous, <a href="am.ra">listen to a 45 second
clip</a> from this guitar virtuoso.

</ul>
```

The anchor references here are clear. Also, I've set up the context by first introducing
that clips are in Real Audio. Each anchor describes the link, and people who cannot

access Real Audio won't bother with the link. If I hadn't set this page up, this link might make less sense:

```
Frightening yet at times joyous, <a href="am.ra">Amanita Muscara</a> is a
powerful tune from this guitar virtuoso.
```

3. **Minimize the number of links on a page.** Am I saying don't link? Of course not—this is the Web after all! But think about each of your links. Are they necessary? Do they make sense? By making navigation as straightforward as possible you'll avoid confusion for everyone.

Functional Design

If you are going to use interactive ordering forms for a product, it is extremely helpful to offer a print-based option. Whether it's simply letting people know that the page is printable, or that there's another link for the full text ordering form, you've enhanced the accessibility of your site immeasurably. Another option is to provide a telephone number (preferably a 1-800 number) and any other method of contact you might have available.

Here's part of a page of code from The Gadabout Salon page. Notice how there is a fully functional form, calling for a number of input boxes including text boxes, check boxes, and submit buttons. This form looks great, as shown in Figure 1.12, but it could be completely inaccessible to a variety of individuals.

```
<form method="post" action="http://www.gadabout.com/htbin/mailto">
<input name="from" type="hidden" value="gadabout@bitbucket.opus1.com">
<input name="subject" type="hidden" value="Order Via Gadabout">
<input name="version" type="hidden" value="Form version is 2.0">
<input name="to" type="hidden" value="gadabout@worldnet.att.net">
<input name="success" type="hidden"
value="http://www.gadabout.com/spa/thankyou.htm">
<input name="failure" type="hidden"
value="http://www.gadabout.com/spa/failure.htm">

<pre>
Name:    <input type="text" name="Name" size="25">
Address: <input type="text" name="Address" size="25">
City:    <input type="text" name="City" size="25">
State:   <input type="text" name="State" size="5">
Zip:     <input type="text" name="Zip" size="10">
Phone:   <input type="text" name="Phone" size="15">
Fax:     <input type="text" name="Fax" size="15">
```

```
email:    <input type="text" name="email" size="15">
</pre>
<p>

<input type="checkbox" name="Order" value="Spa Menu">Please send me your
current spa menu.<br>
<input type="checkbox" name="Order" value="Mailing List">Please put me on
your mailing list.<br>
<p>

Message:
<p>

<textarea name="Message" rows="5" cols="35"></textarea>
<p>

<input type="submit" value="Send your Request">  <input type="reset" value="
Clear ">
</form>
<p>
```

FIGURE 1.12

Gadabout's inter-
active form

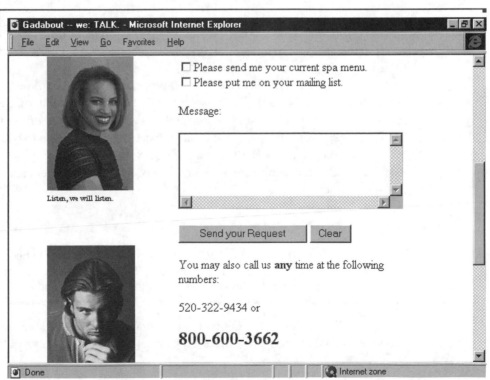

For individuals who might not be able to access this page, the Gadabout Salon designers included a 1-800 number alternative as well as specific locations for their salons:

```
You may also call us <b>any</b> time at the following numbers:
<p>

520-322-9434 or

<h2>800-600-3662</h2>

Gadabout offers four locations.  Please visit, we'd love to see you!
<p>

<ul>

<li>East – 6393 East Grant Road
<li>El Rancho Center – 3382 East Speedway Blvd.
<li>St. Phillip's Plaza – 1990 East River Road
<li>Canyon Ranch –  8600 East Rockliff Road

</ul>
<p>
```

This is functional design. It means that the functionality of the Gadabout form is not impaired because of an inability to reach audiences who do not possess the means to deal with a functional element.

Another functional problem is advanced programming and multimedia. There are applications that fall into this field that currently have very little alternatives available other than the designer creating a completely separate site. A good rule of thumb—both in the context accessible design *and* good Web design in general—is to be sure that everything you put on a Web site has a purpose. Sometimes that purpose will be aesthetic, and other times the element is a necessary aspect of that site, such as a search engine interface.

Don't put anything on a page that is simply meant to wow people because it sports the latest technology and makes you look cool. It doesn't. You look cooler by designing with care and consideration and well-thought-out function and aesthetics.

There will be functional issues that you will rarely (or ever) be able to make fully accessible, and that's okay. Just think about what you're doing, why you're doing it, and if you can truly afford to lose the people who aren't able to reach your site because of geographical location, physical limitations, or any number of other accessibility restrictions.

These responsibilities and choices regarding accessibility can best be exemplified in a personal design experience. When designing sites behind the firewall of the Microsoft Network, the parameters have essentially been set for me. Everyone viewing the pages is using Internet Explorer and related technologies. This design environment can be compared to an *intranet*, which many designers reading this book are required to work with on a daily basis.

However, just because the parameters are pretty clearly defined doesn't mean that accessibility issues can be entirely ignored. MSN in general is quite GUI-specific and makes extensive use of frames and programming such as JavaScript and VBScript so that a large number of individuals can't access the network in the first place. Members visiting the DisAbilities Forum on the Microsoft Network have any number of issues that can prevent them from enjoying the Forum's maximum offerings—which for obvious reasons should be as accessible as possible.

ON line!

These sites will help you with further information and resources on accessible design:

- **The World Wide Web Consortium Accessibility Developments:** This site offers news, updates, and links to related articles and materials, http://www.w3.org/WAI/References/.

- **WebABLE:** The "authoritative Web directory for disability-related Internet resources," includes a vast accessibility database, http://www.yuri.org/webable/index.html.

- **Sun Microsystem's Enabling Technologies Program:** Offering information on Sun's influential accessible platform development, http://www.sun.com/tech/access/.

- **Apple's Disability Connection:** http://www.apple.com/disability/welcome.html

Figure 1.13 shows the front page of the DisAbilities Forum. The main navigation is an MSN standard. It, or one like it, must be used with all Forums within the *Communicate* section of the network.

FIGURE 1.13

The DisAbilities Forum on MSN

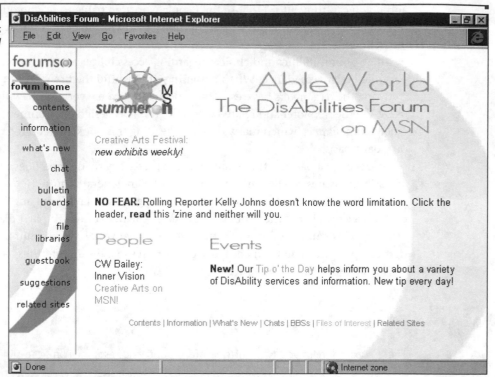

OTE

These examples were taken from sites developed in the summer of 1997. The Microsoft Network seeks to keep content fresh and interesting, so it may have changed considerably by the time you read this book.

The navigation, shown on the left of Figure 1.13, is created with Macromedia Flash. However, one problem with Flash is that it has no accessibility features. This means that anyone requiring a text alternative to the site is out of luck, unless the designer has the foresight to include those options (which she did). Here's the code:

```
<a href="contents.htm">Contents</a> |
<a href="info.htm">Information</a> |
<a href="whatsnew.htm">What's New</a> |
<a href="chatmain.htm">Chats</a> |
<a href="bbsmain.htm">BBSs</a> |
<a href="libmain.htm">Files of Interest</a> |
<a href="linksmain.htm">Related Sites</a>
```

OTE

Macromedia Flash is a great little animation program that we'll discuss in detail in Chapter 23.

Other problems with the DisAbilities Forum include the use of GIF animation, such as the header in the upper-right corner of Figure 1.13. While the animation can't be seen, certainly the `alt` tag can be used, which I did in fact employ, as shown in the main page code:

```
<img src="images/dis-ani1.gif" width="300" height="100" border="0"
alt="DisAbilities Forum Animation: AbleWorld - No Pity, No Limits, No Fear">
```

Finally, portions of the site, such as the Rolling Reporter Magazine, use Real Audio. In Figure 1.14, you'll see the underlined link where contextual accessibility has been employed, using the word *hear* in order to clearly state that if you click that link, the results will be auditory.

From this example, you can see that even with set parameters, there are still issues you must consider when designing the site. You may not achieve total accessibility, but you can come close.

FIGURE 1.14

*Real Audio link on
The Rolling Reporter*

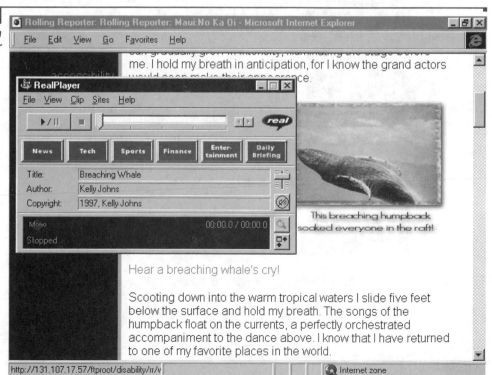

Case Study: The Design Studio

The Design Studio Web site (http://www.designstudio.net) that accompanies this book has been designed to be broadly accessible. One constraint is the use of tables to lay out the site. Most designers require tables to achieve today's contemporary designs, but I did some interesting things with tables in this site that I'd like to draw your attention to. Figure 1.15 shows the main page with table borders turned on so you can see the table structure.

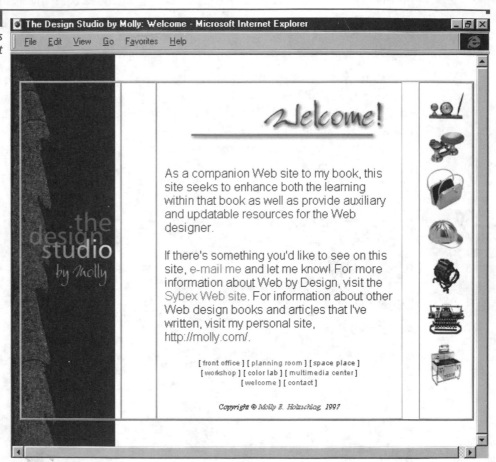

First, notice that there are five table cells. Only three columns are used, the other two provide spacers. Here is the code for the first column:

```
<td width="125">

<img src="images/dsh.jpg" width="112" height="102" border="0" alt="The
Design Studio by Molly Header">

</td>
```

You can see that the only information in this table is graphical, and it has an associated alt tag.

The second table is a spacer, which I've used to gain better control of the layout:

```
<td width="25">

<img src="images/clear.gif" width="25" height="1" border="0" alt="spacer">

</td>
```

The next table cell creates the text column—including the body text, the text-based navigation, and the copyright information:

```
<td width="320" bgcolor="#FFFFFF">

<img src="images/welcome.gif" width="300" height="100" border="0"
alt="welcome!" align="right">

<br clear="all">

<font face="arial">

As a companion Web site to my book, this site seeks to enhance both the
learning within that book as well as provide auxiliary and updatable
resources for the Web designer.
<p>

If there's something you'd like to see on this site,
<a ref="mailto:molly@molly.com">e-mail me</a> and let me know!
For more information about Web by Design, visit the
<a href="http://www.sybex.com/">Sybex Web site</a>. For information about
other Web design books and articles that I've written, visit my personal
site, <a href="http://molly.com">http://molly.com/</a>.
<p>
</font>

<!--begin text navigation-->

<div align="center">
<font face="arial" size="1">

[ <a href="office.htm">front office</a> ]
[ <a href="planning.htm">planning room</a> ]
[ <a href="color.htm">color lab</a> ]
<br>
```

```
[ <a href="space.htm">space place</a> ]
[ <a href="workshop.htm">workshop</a> ]
[ <a href="media.htm">multimedia center</a> ]
<br>

[ <a href="index1.htm">welcome</a> ]
[ <a href="contact.htm">contact</a> ]

</font>
</div>
<br>

<!--begin copyright and mailto-->

<div align="center">
<font size="1">

<i>Copyright &copy; <a href="mailto:molly@molly.com">Molly E.
Holzschlag</a>, 1997</i>

</div>
</font>
</td>
```

You can see there's a lot of data placed in this third cell—it's where the most important information lies. If you were to throw out every design technique, you would still want the information available that describes the site's purpose and resources. Special care has been taken to make sure that this is as accessible as possible.

If you see HTML code or other data that you don't understand—don't worry—we'll cover these techniques in Chapter 2.

The fourth table cell is simply a repeat of the second: a spacer cell to ensure white space and fixed placement of information. Finally, the fifth cell contains the image map that was noted earlier:

```
<td valign="top" width="50">

<img src="images/navmapt.gif" width="50" height="362" border="0"
alt="navigational image map, text navigation below" usemap="#navmapt">

</td>
```

Figure 1.16 shows the page in DosLynx, a text-only program. As you can tell, the information is intact, despite the table layout.

FIGURE 1.16

The Design Studio table layout is accessible in Lynx.

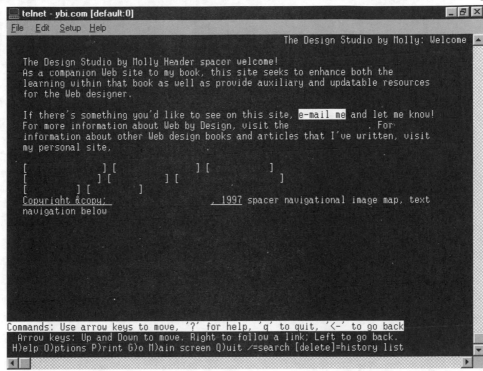

Next Up

This chapter introduced you to platform considerations, browser history, issues of standards and conventions, and a number of design techniques—all intended to get you thinking about accessible design. For some, this information will be old hat, for others, it will be important to how they evolve as designers.

Whether or not you choose to make your site accessible is, once again, an issue that will be determined both by the environment and your assessment of your site's needs. The primary message is that your choices should be based on a foundation of knowledge rather than the hearsay so pervasive among self-taught Web designers.

Chapter 2 gears you up to learn critical HTML tags and helpful tricks that will enable you to create your own sophisticated HTML style.

chapter 2

HTML
ABSOLUTES

HTML
ABSOLUTES

TML is inseparable from Web design. Just as our skeletons provide the framework for our bodies, HTML provides the structure of a given Web page. While you should study HTML as a separate piece of the larger design, there are helpful HTML methods that this book will teach you used by developers and designers who build Web pages every day. As a designer, you need to know about the tools, methods, and options available to help you create successful Web sites.

We will focus on the following issues in this chapter:

- General HTML guidelines
- HTML tools
- Common design tags and attributes
- META tags
- Custom templates
- The future of HTML

While you'll learn more advanced HTML techniques throughout this book, this chapter provides the foundation upon which you will place a strong personal or company directive. The idea is to know the *absolutely* most important foundations of HTML for the working Web designer.

General Guidelines

HTML is a formatting language. It was never intended to become the nuts-and-bolts language of interface design and programming layout, but it is rapidly evolving into just that.

In the first version of *Teach Yourself Web Publishing with HTML in a Week* (Sams.Net, 1994), Laura Lemay made the comment that HTML " . . . is not a page description language like PostScript, nor is it a language that can be easily generated from your favorite page layout program. The focus of HTML is the content of the document, not the appearance."

My, how times have changed! That comment was written only three years before this book, and a better description of HTML is that it *is* in fact becoming a page description language, *is* very easily generated from page layout programs, and *is* focused on the appearance of a document as much as the content.

So, as you can see, the first rule with HTML is to *keep up*! Changes are made to the language frequently and you can remain savvy with regular visits to a number of Web sites, listed in the following Online! sidebar.

ON line!

Tracking changes in HTML is easy if you know where to go to stay in the know. The following three sites will be of tremendous value to you in your quest for HTML information:

- **The World Wide Web Consortium:** You'll recall we learned about the W3C in the discussion of browsers in Chapter 1. This meta-organization tracks and attempts to regularly formalize additions to HTML standards, `http://www.w3.org/`.

- **Netscape's DevEdge Online:** Developers will be especially interested in this informative publication on all that is new in the world of Netscape development. `http://developer.netscape.com/`.

- **Microsoft SiteBuilder Network:** One of my all-time favorite design resource sites which includes plenty of HTML information, `http://www.microsoft.com/sitebuilder/`.

Tags and Attributes

HTML is actually a logical language. Even a novice can look at standard code and discern some meaning from it. HTML is made up of two primary features: *tags* and *attributes*.

Tags

A tag is the HTML command that alerts the browser that a new type of information needs to be interpreted. Typically, a tag begins with a left angle bracket, contains the tag's name, and ends with a right angle bracket:

```
<body>
```

Tagged sections within an HTML document are generally closed with a companion tag. The closing tag uses a left angle bracket, a forward slash, the tag's name, and a right angle bracket:

```
</body>
```

There are exceptions to the HTML tag rule. Some HTML tags do not require a closing companion tag, and others work in a slightly different fashion.

Attributes

Within tags you'll find commands that give a specific tag an attribute, or a variety of attributes. For example, if you wanted to have the body of your page have a background color of red, you could use the following code to make that happen:

```
<body bgcolor="red">
```

Most tags support multiple attributes:

```
<body bgcolor="red" text="white" link="blue" vlink="green">
```

This HTML page will appear in the browser as having a red background, white text, blue links, and green visited links.

A tag plus one or more attributes is referred to as a *string*. Note also that attributes are never placed in a closing tag. Appendix A lists all major HTML tags and attributes.

Structural Guidelines

My grandmother wasn't an educated woman, but she was very wise. Her legacy taught me, among other things, the following three concepts that have helped me keep my life in order:

- What you open, close.
- Neatness counts.
- Everything in its place.

Little did I know that these concepts would have vast impact on the work I do as a Web designer! These snippets of wisdom, when applied to HTML coding, will help you work faster and avoid common pitfalls.

What You Open, Close

As I demonstrated in the previous section, HTML tags typically have a companion closing tag. So keep in mind, if you open a tag, you must close it where it is appropriate to do so. Forgetting to do this could very well make your page unreadable.

Neatness Counts

I'm a stickler for neatness—I like to see neatly organized pages and typically flush most critical tags to the left, adding spaces between certain tags for readability. Remember, you or someone on your team will often have to make changes and updates to HTML pages. If the code isn't neat, you compromise speed and accuracy. Keeping code neat helps individuals navigate that code easily.

A messy section of code looks like this:

```
<html><head><title>My Home Page</title></head><body bgcolor="white"
text="black" link="blue" vlink="green">Welcome to my home
page!</body></html>
```

A neat section of code follows the simple guidelines of flushing most tags left and adding spaces between groupings of tags:

```
<html>

<head>
<title>My Home Page</title>
</head>

<body bgcolor="white" text="black" link="blue" vlink="green">

Welcome to my home page!

</body>
</html>
```

There are no hard and fast rules regarding the way tags are arranged on a page. Some coders like to indent sections of code; others, like me, prefer to keep their code flush left. WYSIWYG (What-You-See-Is-What-You-Get) editing software tends to be pretty haphazard. As a general guideline, flushing tags left and placing a hard return between critical sections and comment lines is a good way to go if you don't yet have a suitable method of your own.

There is no right or wrong way to make a page neat. Each coder develops their own methods. Some indent certain pieces of code, others, like me, have a habit of grouping tags and adding spaces as you see in the above sample. My style is not necessarily the style that's going to work for you. The objective in this case is to impress upon you that developing a style is important. As long as the code ends up readable and easy to navigate for you and for your company members, you're on the right track.

Everything in Its Place

This concept is an offshoot of the first two, and suggests that all the code you create should be stored neatly in its own container. Put into specific HTML terms, develop a work method based on this concept that helps you speed up your creation and maintenance of code; this process can be called the *container method.*

By creating "containers" using HTML tags, you can work on code without getting confused or frustrated as it gets more complex. You'll notice that a need for such a method is going to become especially important as you work on tables, which often have numerous components.

To begin using the container method, simply remember that when you enter a tag, also enter its companion tag. First, enter the code that defines the page as HTML. This is the first container.

```
<html>
</html>
```

Now, add the second container, *within* the first:

```
<html>
<head>
</head>
</html>
```

The third:

```
<html>

<head>
<title>My Home Page</title>
</head>

</html>
```

The fourth:

```
<html>

<head>
<title>My Home Page</title>
</head>

<body bgcolor="white" text="black" link="blue" vlink="green">

</body>
</html>
```

And now the text:

```
<html>

<head>
<title>My Home Page</title>
</head>

<body bgcolor="white" text="black" link="blue" vlink="green">

Welcome to my home page!

</body>
</html>
```

Each container builds upon the first, and creates its own container. Remember those decorative boxes, you'd open the large one and within it was a smaller one, and so forth? Each box acts to contain the next, and whatever *that* box contains as well. This is the container method in action.

T I P

You'll notice color names in body tags are used in the early chapters of this book. I did this for clarity. In professional HTML, you should avoid this use and work instead with hexadecimal color codes. Such codes give you a much greater range of color to work with. More information on hexadecimal color can be found in Chapter 16.

Use these basic concepts when working with HTML, and you're sure to improve your coding skill, style, accuracy, and speed with little effort. The rewards are certainly worth it.

HTML Tools

I once moved into a new apartment and couldn't find my hammer. All I had was a screwdriver and nails, and I needed to get a nail into the wall. I picked up the screwdriver and figured "Hey, I can use this." Well, I didn't do a very good job at getting that nail into the wall. What I did end up with was a really bad bruise from whacking my thumb so hard!

In order to avoid the painful experience of using the wrong HTML tool, make educated choices when it comes to the virtual hammers and screwdrivers of Web design.

Which tools are the right ones? This isn't an easy question to answer, because there are so many individual situations with just as many unique variables to consider.

It is easier to make better choices when you have reliable information about which tools are available, what their advantages and disadvantages are, and how much they cost. This section will examine not only the *way* in which HTML code can be generated, but *why* one type of tool might be more appropriate for your needs than another.

A busy designer or design firm is ideally going to have a number of tools available, because different jobs require unique approaches. Still, the bottom line is you need to know the code. While you might find yourself working with a software package such as NetObjects Fusion, you'll want to have the coding skills and a text-based editing environment to make changes or additions not available within the software package.

Text-Based Coding

Text-based coding is coding by hand in a plain-text editor. The HTML coder types in the HTML to their specifications and then saves the file using an .htm or .html extension to denote the file as being HTML.

This method of HTML coding from "scratch" is for designers who want to have total control over their design. While you will want to employ a variety of HTML tools, being able to compose code in this fashion pays off immeasurably.

Typically, people who share this perspective learned HTML in a text-based environment. Text environments force you to learn HTML, and learn it well. You become a true coder, not a software slave. And, much like the shopkeeper who could add faster and more accurately with her abacus than her tourist visitor could with his calculator, coders who learned within the text environment tend to work quickly and skillfully.

OTE

I'm not the only code purist—out of 10 designers polled for this chapter, half of them said that despite all of the other tools they might use in a given day, they still rely on their own skills within a text environment.

Nowadays there are literally hundreds of fancy editing options for HTML. I'll look at many of them here, but before I do, I want to stress a few of the advantages of text-based coding:

- **Total control**—If you know HTML thoroughly, *you* determine how your code will look and act. You can keep your HTML as simple or as complex as you choose, without having a program dictate style and method for you.

- **Creative freedom**—The better you know HTML, the more creative you can be with the language. Progress in HTML code, and subsequently, Web design, is made when people understand the environment and push its limits. Finding creative workarounds and innovative solutions for long-standing problems can only be done by people who know the code.

- **Independence and up-to-the-minute options**—HTML software programs such as FrontPage or NetObjects Fusion are bound by fiscal limitations, meaning that new code information isn't added to a program until the next release. If you want to use a newer piece of code than your fancy program allows, you may find yourself in an argument with the software—wasting time, money, and precious energy.

- **Troubleshooting**—If you've ever had car trouble while driving on a hot desert highway, you appreciate the significance of *why* knowing how to get under the hood and fix a problem is such an advantage. Instead of waiting for someone to come and get you out of trouble before the vultures start landing, you can quickly troubleshoot problems and get back on track. Save time, money, and total frustration when HTML begins acting up by knowing how to get under the proverbial hood and fix the problem.

- **Easy portability**—If you know how to code in HTML, you're going to be that much more skilled with other HTML software options.

- **Cost**—All operating systems offer a native text editor that you can use to code HTML. This means you spend nothing—zero, zilch—on what could be your primary HTML tool.

Each platform has at least one, if not several, text editors available.

PC

For people working on the PC platform, there are a number of native editors that can be used to create HTML documents.

- **DOS**—Simply type in **EDIT** at any DOS prompt to pull up the DOS-based text editor. This is a perfectly acceptable editor in which to code HTML.

- **Notepad**—Windows Notepad in both the 3.1 and 95 versions is a favorite among text-coding fans (see Figure 2.1). Charles Convery, a software specialist at Sunquest Infosystems, says it all boils down to one word when it comes to HTML programming: Notepad.

```
bbsmain.htm - Notepad
File   Edit   Search   Help
<body bgcolor="#FFFFFF" text="#FFFFCC" link="#FFCC99"
vlink="#9999CC" alink="#FFFFCC" background="images/bak2.jpg">

<table border=0 width=500 cellpadding=10 cellspacing=0>

<tr>

<td width=500 valign=top align=right colspan=2>

<img src="images/bb-hed.gif" alt="" width=300 height=50>

</td>
<tr>
<tr>
<td class=2 width=500 valign=top>


The DisAbilities Forum offers the following Bulletin Boards (BBSs). Simply cl
to read and post to the BBS of your choice will be launched.  Enjoy!
</td>
</tr>

<tr>
<td class=3 width=5oo valign=top>


<a class=p href="news://MSNnews.MSN.com/MSN.forums.disabilities.general"><b>D
```

Macintosh

The Macintosh operating system comes with a text editor called SimpleText which can be used for programming HTML (Figure 2.2).

FIGURE 2.2
Coding HTML in SimpleText

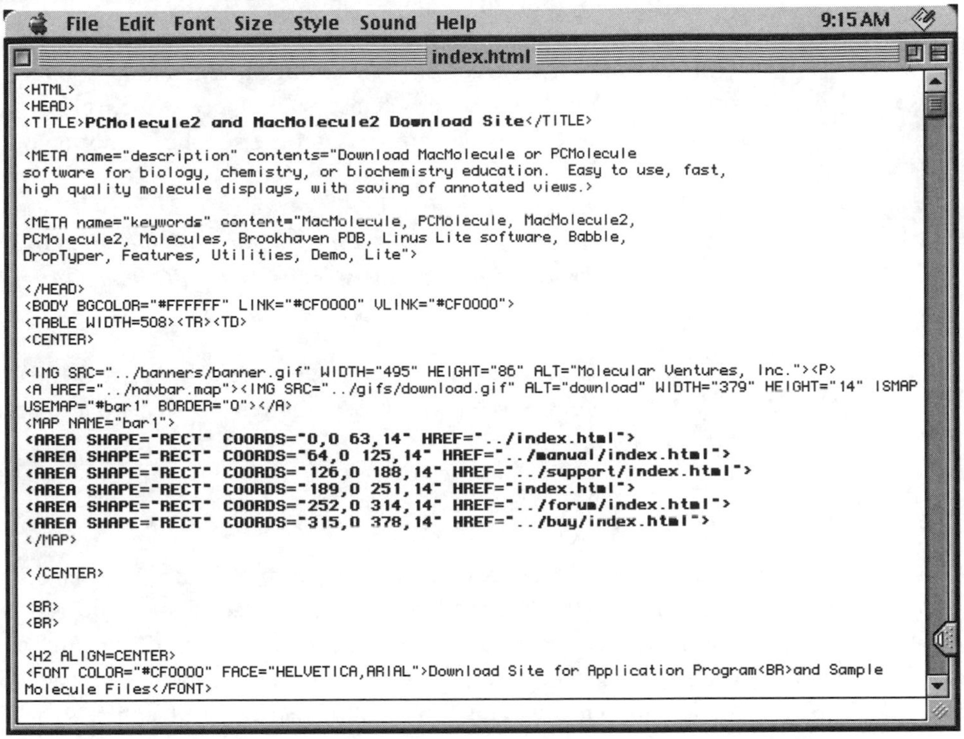


```
<HTML>
<HEAD>
<TITLE>PCMolecule2 and MacMolecule2 Download Site</TITLE>

<META name="description" contents="Download MacMolecule or PCMolecule
software for biology, chemistry, or biochemistry education.  Easy to use, fast,
high quality molecule displays, with saving of annotated views.>

<META name="keywords" content="MacMolecule, PCMolecule, MacMolecule2,
PCMolecule2, Molecules, Brookhaven PDB, Linus Lite software, Babble,
DropTyper, Features, Utilities, Demo, Lite">

</HEAD>
<BODY BGCOLOR="#FFFFFF" LINK="#CF0000" VLINK="#CF0000">
<TABLE WIDTH=508><TR><TD>
<CENTER>

<IMG SRC="../banners/banner.gif" WIDTH="495" HEIGHT="86" ALT="Molecular Ventures, Inc."><P>
<A HREF="../navbar.map"><IMG SRC="../gifs/download.gif" ALT="download" WIDTH="379" HEIGHT="14" ISMAP
USEMAP="#bar1" BORDER="0"></A>
<MAP NAME="bar1">
<AREA SHAPE="RECT" COORDS="0,0 63,14" HREF="../index.html">
<AREA SHAPE="RECT" COORDS="64,0 125,14" HREF="../manual/index.html">
<AREA SHAPE="RECT" COORDS="126,0 188,14" HREF="../support/index.html">
<AREA SHAPE="RECT" COORDS="189,0 251,14" HREF="index.html">
<AREA SHAPE="RECT" COORDS="252,0 314,14" HREF="../forum/index.html">
<AREA SHAPE="RECT" COORDS="315,0 378,14" HREF="../buy/index.html">
</MAP>

</CENTER>

<BR>
<BR>

<H2 ALIGN=CENTER>
<FONT COLOR="#CF0000" FACE="HELVETICA,ARIAL">Download Site for Application Program<BR>and Sample
Molecule Files</FONT>
```

"Would you be surprised if I, as a graphic designer, told you that I want an Apple PowerMac computer with, of course . . . PhotoShop 4.0.1, GIFBuilder, and this may sound strange, SimpleText! Yeah, I don't use any software to create Web pages. I know the source and I prefer to type it myself and have control over any tag."

JOEL NEELEN, Graphics and Web Designer, NextDada, Belgium

UNIX

UNIX fans typically enjoy using one of the following three editors:

- **vi**—This UNIX text editor is extremely popular among hard-core coders from the very "old school" of HTML coding.
- **Pico**—This basic, no-frills text editor can be used for generating HTML.

- **Emacs**—This is another popular editor used on the UNIX platform (it's also very prevalent among VMS users). It's more complicated than vi or Pico, so much so that it comes with an online psychologist called Meta-X-Doctor to help you endure the psychological problems you will face while using it. It is considered to be very powerful, and many programmers prefer it to other options.

> *"Hands down, no question or moment of doubt in my mind, I'd use Emacs on a UNIX system to code HTML. If for some reason I found myself all alone in a room without a UNIX terminal, I'd use BBEdit on a Macintosh."*
>
> NATHAN HENDLER, Web Engineer, DesertNet

While you will certainly find that other methods of working with HTML will provide different advantages, there simply is no better way to learn and understand the code than by doing it from scratch.

HTML Editing Environments

HTML editing environments are steps away from plain-text editors, but miles away from *WYSIWYG* (What-You-See-Is-What-You-Get) editors. The difference is that all of the advantages ascribed to text editors exist in an HTML editing environment. By the time you get to the more complex WYSIWYG environment, those advantages are lost.

At this point in my own development, I feel the HTML editor is the *ideal* environment for the types of jobs I do. The reason is because an HTML editor provides a perfect balance between hand-coding (my preferred method of coding) and numerous power tools, such as automatic image sizing. If you know HTML pretty well, but are looking for some power options to help you work more efficiently, HTML editors might just be the answer. Here are some advantages to help get you thinking about the value of HTML editors:

- **A text environment with enhancements**—Whether it be templates, toolbars that automatically insert specific tags, or—one of my favorite options—image wizards that automatically size an image and create the width and height values, you maintain total control of text-based coding with valuable alternatives at your fingertips.

- **Spell and syntax checkers**—Most registered versions of HTML editors come with spell checkers and HTML syntax verification software. These enable you to output a cleaner product—both in terms of your content, and your code.

- **Tag colorization**—To add user-friendliness and make code navigation easier, many HTML editing environments colorize specific tags. This way, if you're looking to make adjustments to tags related to tables, you look for a color rather than the smaller, potentially less-noticeable tag.

- **Multi-file search and replace**—Perhaps one of the most powerful features of HTML editing environments is that you can update hundreds of pages of code automatically.

- **Cost**—HTML editing environments tend to be affordable, typically around $75 to $150 per license.

Some of the more popular HTML editing environments are described in the following sections, including additional resources so you can get more information and updates on these and other software selections.

PC

Editing environments for the PC are abundant. Here are a few favorites:

- **Allaire HomeSite**—This editor has become my personal favorite (Figure 2.3). It's got all of the best features an editing environment should have, plus a very customizable interface. Check it out at `http://www.allaire.com/`.

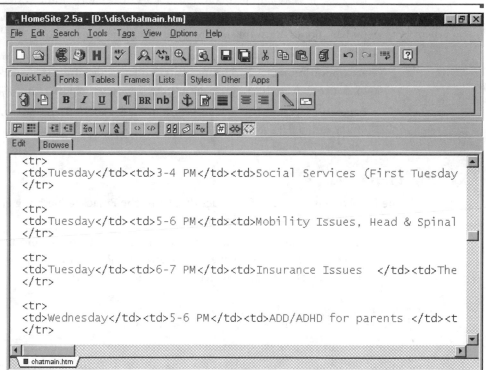

FIGURE 2.3

HomeSite's editing environment

"Allaire's HomeSite 2.5 is unmatched as a text-only authoring tool. With every release, the program keeps up with the latest in HTML, including style sheets, and you don't need a blow-'em-away system to run it."

IRA LACHER, Contributing Editor, Web Publisher Magazine

- **HotDog Pro**—Once my personal favorite, I came to prefer HomeSite's user interface. However, this is a powerful and popular editor, and I recommend it highly. You can download a demo at `http://www.sausage.com/`.

- **HTML Assistant Pro**—This very competent HTML editor has the distinction of being one of the first available HTML editing environments for the PC. The pro version has come a long way since those early days. For more information, check out `http://www.brooknorth.com/pro97.html`.

Macintosh

While many Macintosh editing environments have been created, only a few have stayed tried and true over the years. They include:

- **BBEdit**—This program is a favorite among Macintosh programmers because they use it as a plain text editor, too. Recent versions and a variety of tools and extensions have helped enter it into the class of HTML editing environments. By Bare Bones Software at `http://www.barebones.com/bbedit.html`.

- **HTML Editor**—This editor offers pop-up menus for standard HTML tags, as well as supporting tables and forms. Author Rick Giles offers it as shareware; download a copy from his home page at `http://dragon.acadiau.ca/~giles/`.

- **PageSpinner**—I've had Macintosh friends gush about this award-winning editing environment. It's available for demonstration download at `http://www.algonet.se/~optima/pagespinner.html`.

UNIX

The following is an add-in for Emacs that turns the Emacs text-editing environment into an HTML editing environment:

- **Emacs Package**—By adding an HTML mode to the text-environment of Emacs, UNIX users have an effective editing environment. `http://www.tnt.uni-hannover.de/~muenkel/software/own/hm-html-menus/overview.html`

HTML Converters

Converters are software applications that take a word-processed or spreadsheet document and automatically convert the formatting into an HTML page. They're a convenient tool to have on hand, and are particularly advantageous in the following situations:

- You have large amounts of data to process quickly, such as multiple news articles or long research documents.

- You're not too terribly concerned about the consistency or quality of code. Perhaps the documents are not going to be in the public eye and will only be used by you or several of your colleagues at your place of work.

- You have the ability and/or resources to hire someone to create or modify existing converters to your specifications.

 NOTE

Many editing environments, including Allaire's HomeSite and Sausage Software's Hot Dog, contain HTML converters. If you only require a converter from time to time, and already have a good editing environment, check to see if it has conversion capabilities.

PC

The following converters are available for the PC platform:

- **Microsoft's Internet Assistant**—This converter integrates word processing, browsing, and Web document creation. Its understanding of HTML is very limited and development of this product stopped in 1995. However, because the integration of Internet Assistant conversion is included with programs such as Word and Excel, savvy developers have written more extensive macro-based, customized add-ins to make the program a powerful contemporary contender. http://www.microsoft.com

- **The Ant**—This program consists of a set of HTML conversion utilities for MS Word documents. http://telacommunications.com/ant/

"For serious editing, I would go with Microsoft Word 95. Word 95 is not only an amazing text editor, but an unbelievably powerful programming language too. I've written the code to 10,000+ page sites all managed and maintained in Word. It's one hell of a groovy editor."

WIL GERKEN, CEO, DesertNet

Macintosh

Internet Assistant and The Ant are both available for the Macintosh running MS Word.

UNIX

There is one HTML converter for users of UNIX systems worth mentioning:

- **Interleaf**—This program provides code conversion from many word processing and publication utilities, including MS Word, WordPerfect, and FrameMaker. It requires Motif runtime. `http://www.interleaf.com/`

WYSIWYG HTML Editors

Growing in popularity, WYSIWYG editors can be extremely powerful—or extremely problematic. WYSIWYG software allows you to design your page without ever learning HTML. You lay out the data—images, text, and so forth—and the software creates the HTML.

Choosing to use WYSIWYG software truly depends upon your individual circumstances. If you're a professional designer, you're likely going to use it in concert with other tools. A WYSIWYG all by itself is best used by people with no HTML experience who need to get *something* onto the Web and can't afford or do not wish to hire a professional designer.

While WYSIWYG software will eventually become a more sophisticated, first-choice tool among designers, the haphazard code generated by software packages of this nature combined with the fiscal issues create problems for professionals at this time.

Advantages of WYSIWYG editors include:

- **Learning curve**—WYSIWYGs are visually-based user interfaces and therefore the learning curve is fairly low.

- **Consistency**—If you have a lot of people that need to work on pages, WYSIWYGs are the way to go. The reason is that everyone working on a page will generate the same code idiosyncratic to that particular software package.

Disadvantages of WYSIWYGs:

- **Lack of control**—Software in this category will often override your personal styles or decisions.

- **Extraneous code**—Most WYSIWYGs are not as intelligent as good HTML coders. A lot of extraneous code can be thrown in. This code is left alone by amateurs, but most professionals will want the option to go in and streamline, alter, or update it, which means having to fall back on a text editor.

- **Fiscal limitations**—As mentioned earlier, major software packages can only be released at various intervals. Tags or methods that you want to employ might not be available to you until an upcoming version. Also, because the software might override something it doesn't recognize, you don't have the power to alter or troubleshoot problems in the WYSIWYG environment.

PC

Again, the PC market is filling up fast with a wide range of WYSIWYG editors. Here are some of the most well-known:

- **Microsoft FrontPage**—This is probably the most popular WYSIWYG program for the general public. Designers use it, but not to the extent that people who want to build pages and not put a lot of time into learning the product do. My personal experience with it hasn't made me a fan, largely because of the lack of precise code it generates. There are typically extra <font> tags, unnecessary <blockquote> tags, and non-breaking spaces. Furthermore, trying to improve the code of a novice who has used FrontPage to generate it can be a time-consuming nightmare. Recent improvements to the software are starting to turn my head slightly. More information can be found at their Web site, http://www.microsoft.com/frontpage/.

  "I like FrontPage for quick tables and layout. The environment makes previewing and development of applications and databases a breeze too."

  ALEX LAPIN, Programmer, BrainBug

- **Claris HomePage**—I like this WYSIWYG more than FrontPage. It's less cumbersome and the code is a little cleaner. Check out Claris' Web site, http://www.claris.com/.

- **NetObjects Fusion**—A more popular choice for designers, this program offers excellent layout templates. http://www.netobjects.com/

- **SoftQuad HotMetaL Pro**—One of the originals, now known for tables and frames support. http://www.sq.com/

Macintosh

Macintosh WYSIWYGs are becoming very popular, which may be due in large part to the many desktop publishers who are familiar with WYSIWYG layout programs such as QuarkXPress. The following editors are big among Macintosh users:

- **Adobe PageMill**—The main advantage to PageMill is its integration with other programs within the Adobe suite. Many designers use PageMill, although it carries the limitations of all other WYSIWYG software packages. http://www.adobe.com/

- **Microsoft FrontPage for Macintosh**—Once again, a popular choice among non-designers. http://www.microsoft.com/frontpage/

- **SoftQuad HotMetaL Pro, Version 3.0**—HotMetaL is available in a Macintosh version. http://www.sq.com/

UNIX

Many of the popular WYSIWYG packages for PCs and Macs have been made available on the UNIX platform as well. These two are choice options for UNIX users:

- **WebWorks Publisher**—Combine this package with FrameMaker for a full WYSIWYG package by Quadralay. http://www.quadralay.com/

- **SoftQuad HotMetaL Pro, Version 3.0**—HotMetaL is also popular with UNIX users. http://www.sq.com/

A full reference of HTML tools with links is available on *Web by Design*'s companion site, the Design Studio, at http://www.designstudio.net/.

Common Design Tags and Attributes

While HTML is far too complicated a language to teach in one chapter, there are specific tags and attributes that you should be introduced to now. Many of you will already know them, but not necessarily in the context of Web design.

You'll get the HTML basics in this chapter. Later chapters will delve further into layout and specific design concepts, and the HTML will become more complex.

If you are new to HTML, it's important to study it thoroughly if you intend to be a good HTML coder. For the novice, Sybex offers *Mastering HTML 4.0*, by Deborah S. Ray and Eric J. Ray (1997) and *HTML 4.0: No experience required* (1997) by E. Stephen Mack and Janan Platt.

Standard Page Tags and Attributes

Every HTML page has specific tags that *absolutely* must be in place. Beyond that, there are standards in terms of page formatting and linking that are important to mention here.

Page Must-Haves

All HTML pages must have the following tags:

<html> . . . **</html>**   The beginning <html> and ending </html> tags announce to the browser that an HTML page is about to begin or end.

<head> . . . </head>   The <head> tag includes header information such as titles and, as you'll see later on, special commands and scripting information.

<title> . . . </title>   Title tags allow you to name your page. This information will be displayed in the browser's title bar. Titles are essential for page identification, so don't forget to name your pages appropriately:

```
<title>The Design Studio by Molly: Welcome</title>
```

<body> . . . </body>   The <body> tag determines the basic attributes of a page, including the background color and/or graphic to be used, and the text color variables. More specific information on using <body> tag attributes to achieve sophisticated design can be found in Chapter 16.

Figure 2.4 shows the source code for a standard HTML page, with a little text thrown in for good measure. Figure 2.5 demonstrates that the results are indeed readable in a standard browser.

FIGURE 2.4

The code of a standard HTML page

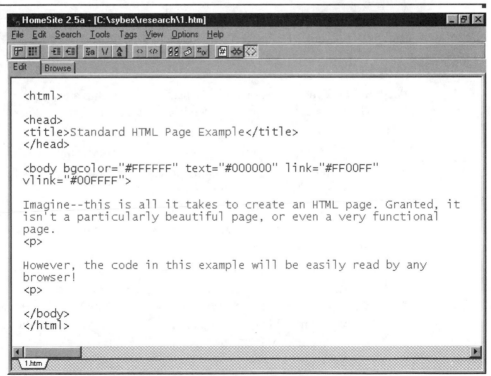

```html
<html>

<head>
<title>Standard HTML Page Example</title>
</head>

<body bgcolor="#FFFFFF" text="#000000" link="#FF00FF"
vlink="#00FFFF">

Imagine--this is all it takes to create an HTML page. Granted, it
isn't a particularly beautiful page, or even a very functional
page.
<p>

However, the code in this example will be easily read by any
browser!
<p>

</body>
</html>
```

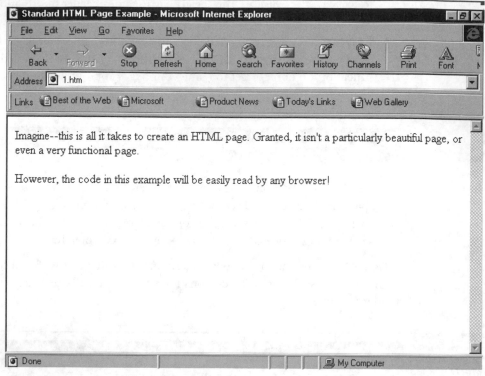

FIGURE 2.5

The same code viewed with Internet Explorer 4.0

Anchors

Anchors allow you to link to a specific page or spot within a page. An anchor requires the anchor tag, `<a>`, along with a reference attribute, `href`, and a closing, `</a>`, tag. Here's an example:

```
<a href="MyLink.htm">Here's a link to my publications list.</a>
```

Standard Linking   To link to another page, you must be certain that your reference links to that page. There are two methods to do this:

1. **Absolute Linking.** This method requires that you use a complete URL in the reference. Use Absolute Linking when you are linking to a page that resides on another server:

   ```
   <a href="http://www.sybex.com">Visit the Sybex Web site</a>
   ```

2. **Relative Linking.** When you are linking to a page that resides on your own server, you can link to it without using an absolute URL. If I'm linking from my welcome page to my contact page, and both pages reside in the same directory, the code on my welcome page will look like this:

   ```
   <a href="contact.htm">Go to the Contact Page</a>
   ```

But let's say the page resides in another directory. For example, you want to link to a poem in your poetry directory. You are going to have to define that directory. Here's how the code will appear:

```
<a href="poetry/poem1.htm">My best poem yet!</a>
```

If you want to link back up to the root directory from a sub-directory, you can use the standard ../, which denotes root:

```
<a href="../contact.htm">Back to the Contact Page</a>
```

For more information on anchor tag usage, be sure to refer to Appendix A.

Intra-Page Linking   Not only can you link to other pages, but you can link to points, called *targets*, within a single HTML page. This is done by naming a particular section of text (or a graphic, object, or other media) and then referencing that target. At the top of the page you might have a series of link selections that reach down farther into the page. An example would be:

```
<a href="#selection3">The Third Rule can be found here</a>
```

The target would appear as:

```
<a name="selection3">The Third Rule:</a>
```

Click the first link, and you will end up at the target, as demonstrated in Figures 2.6 and 2.7.

Text Formatting

Simple text formatting, such as bold, italic, and underline, can be achieved with these easy tags:

**** . . . ****   Bolds text

<I> . . . **</I>**   Italicizes text

<u> . . . **</u>**   Underlines text

Other text formatting absolutes include:

<p>   This is the paragraph tag. It has two standard uses. The first is to place a single <p> at the end of a paragraph, which will command a carriage return and one line space, as follows:

```
Here is a sample paragraph of text.
HTML coders can select from two
methods to control paragraph formatting.
This is one of the methods.
<p>
```

FIGURE 2.6

The anchor link

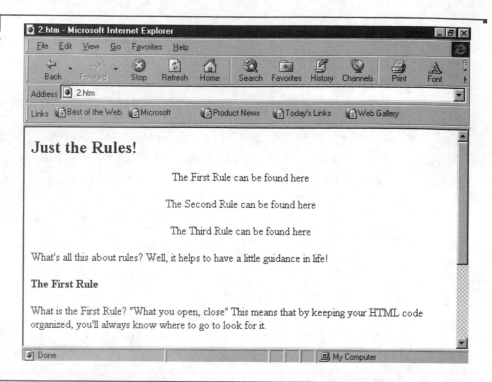

FIGURE 2.7

The anchor target

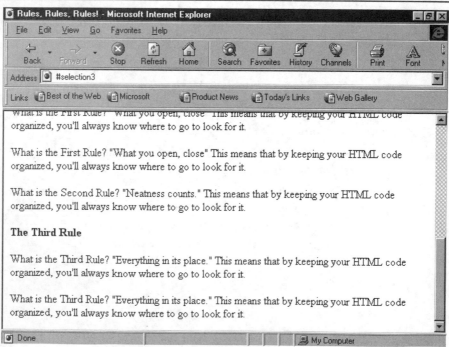

You'll notice in the above example, there is no closing </p> tag. However, paragraphs in HTML can also be coded using the standard open/close method, which is the second standard use:

```
<p>
Here is a sample paragraph of text.
HTML coders can select from two
methods to control paragraph formatting.
This is the other method.
</p>
```

**
** This is a line break. No additional lines are added after the break. This tag is helpful when formatting text that requires you to break a line, such as in an address:

```
Cool Stuff Limited<br>
P.O. Box 000<br>
Anywhere, Anyplace<br>
```

OTE

Which is the best method to code paragraphs? Either the single end paragraph tag <p> or beginning <p> and end </p> paragraph tags are acceptable. Since the opening <p> tag allows for alignment attributes (see Chapter 9) and style sheet attributes (see Chapter 20), there are distinct advantages to using the open/close method. However, you'll note that the simple, single <p> method is used in most cases.

With these simple tags, you can create a complete text document in HTML. Figure 2.8 shows the code and Figure 2.9 shows the results.

Lists

Designers typically reach for two types of HTML lists—ordered, which are numeric lists, and unordered, which are bulleted lists.

Lists are made up of two components, the tag that denotes ordered or unordered, and the <li> tag, which command for the number or bullet.

<ol> . . . </ol> This is an ordered list. Each <li> will call for the subsequent number to be shown.

```
<p>
<ol>
<li>Ten pennies.
<li>Two nickels.
<li>One dime.
</ol>
```

Figure 2.10 shows how the browser interprets a numbered list.

FIGURE 2.8

The code of a complete text document.

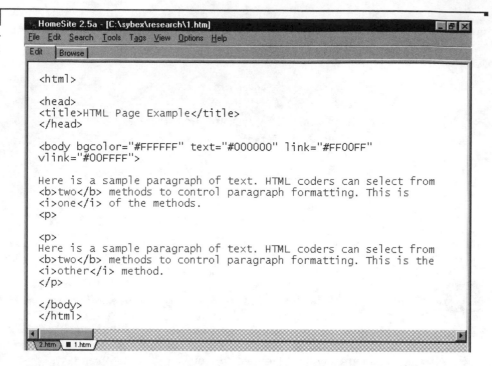

FIGURE 2.9

An HTML page with text and paragraph formatting.

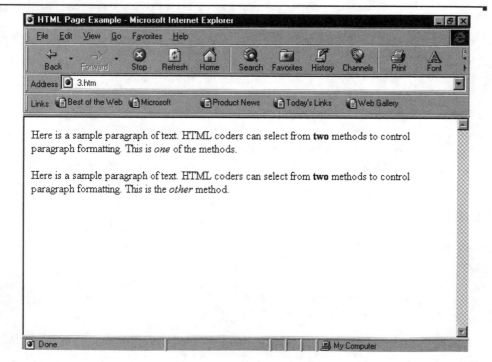

FIGURE 2.10

A numbered list

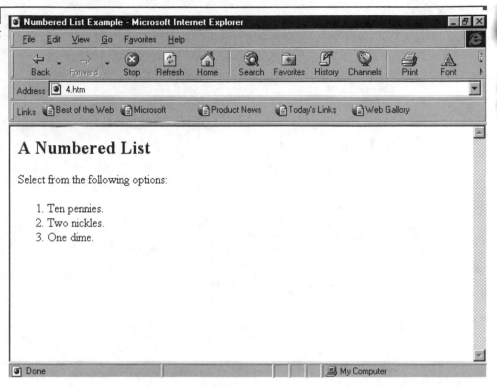

\<ul\> . . . \</ul\>   This is an unordered list. It works essentially the same way, but places bullets in place of the numbers.

```
Ms. Tery is considered a candidate for promotion because she has:
<p>
<ul>
<li>a strong willingness to learn.
<li>professional relations with co-workers.
<li>excellent mid-year reviews.
</ul>
```

Figure 2.11 demonstrates the bulleted list.

FIGURE 2.11

A bulleted list

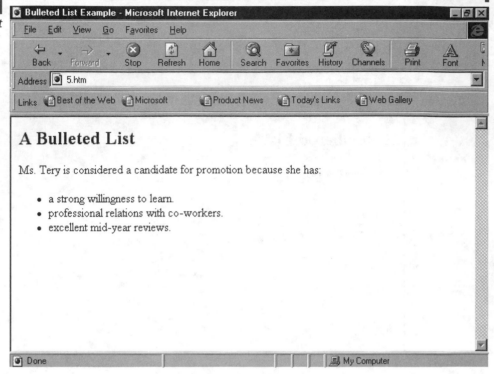

> **A Bulleted List**
>
> Ms. Tery is considered a candidate for promotion because she has:
>
> - a strong willingness to learn.
> - professional relations with co-workers.
> - excellent mid-year reviews.

Image Tags

Images are critical to design, making the image tag one of the most frequently used by Web designers. Image tags don't require a closing tag, but they do have a number of important attributes.

OTE

Additional tags that you'll need or want to use will be discussed in later chapters, and you can always refer to Appendix A for more information on the image tag and its various attributes.

Image tags are made up of the tag, <img>, and the image source, src:

```
<img src="myface.gif">
```

As long as the image `"myface.gif"` is in the same directory as the HTML page that is calling upon it, this is all the code *required* to render that picture. However, you should include the following attributes in *every* image tag you code:

width="x"   This defines the width of the image.

height="x"   This is the height of the image.

border="x"   The value of "x" in this case determines how much of a border the browser will draw around an image. For the truly accomplished Web designer there will rarely, if ever, be a case where your border value is going to equal anything other than "0".

alt="x"   As we explored in Chapter 1, the importance of the `alt` attribute is significant—it makes your pages accessible.

Adding the information to the earlier image example will result in this code:

```
<img src="myface.gif" width="150" height="150" border="0" alt="A
photographic face shot of Molly">
```

Why is it so important to add attributes to the `image` tag? By defining width, height, and border, your browser can prepare the layout for that image in advance. This can improve speed and visual continuity as the browser retrieves the page and the image. And, of course, the `alt` attribute allows for accessibility.

Special Tag Considerations

A number of special considerations need to be addressed so that you, the designer, will benefit from a growing body of wisdom for those working with HTML daily. These considerations will enable you to work more efficiently.

Comment Tags

One of the most helpful methods of keeping track of a complicated HTML page and allowing for multiple people to work on the same page consistently is to use comment tags.

Long ago and far away, this was done by a more traditional looking `<comment>` tag. However, this tag never really got used much, and another method came to the forefront. A contemporary comment tag looks like this:

```
<!-- this is my comment -->
```

Anything that is placed within the opening <!-- and closing --> won't be displayed by the browser.

The primary use of comment tags is to help define sections of the page, as follows:

```
<html>

<!-- begin header information -->

<head>
<title>My Home Page</title>
</head>

<!-- begin body -->

<body bgcolor="white" text="black" link="blue" vlink="green">

Welcome to my home page!
<p>

<!-- begin text navigation links -->

<a href="info.htm">Information About Me</a> .
<a href="contact.htm">Get in Touch!</a>

</body>
</html>
```

You can see from this simple example that comment tagging can help group information, making it logical and easy to locate.

Another very helpful use of comment tagging is to provide instructions and directions to other coders:

```
<html>

<!-- Mike: Please include header information here -->

<head>
<title>Happy House Incorporated</title>
</head>

<!-- Mike: change color to hex, please -->

<body bgcolor="white" text="black" link="blue" vlink="green">

Welcome to Happy House Incorporated!  We provide the best in all your
household good needs.
<p>

<!-- Mike: add the graphical navigation before the text-based -->
```

```
<a href="info.htm">Information About Happy House</a> .
<a href="contact.htm">Get in Touch with Happy House!</a>

</body>
</html>
```

Now Mike knows what to do with this page, every step of the way.

Still another use of comment tags is to hide information in the page's code until you want the public to see it. Say you want to alternate a different image for each season. You can leave the code information on the page, simply putting comment tags around the data you don't want to have appear in the browser:

```
<html>

<head>
<title>Time of the Season</title>
</head>

<body bgcolor="white" text="black" link="blue" vlink="green">

<!--
<img src="autumn.jpg" width="300" height="100" border="0" alt="autumn
header">

<img src="winter.jpg" width="300" height="100" border="0" alt="winter
header">

<img src="spring.jpg" width="300" height="100" border="0" alt="spring
header">
-->

<img src="summer.jpg" width="300" height="100" border="0" alt="summer
header">

Welcome to Time of the Season.
<p>

<a href="info.htm">Read about Time</a> .
<a href="contact.htm">Contact Time</a>

</body>
</html>
```

Figure 2.12 shows this HTML code as it should appear. In Figure 2.13, the comment tags were removed—and look what happens.

FIGURE 2.12

The comment tags hide the graphics.

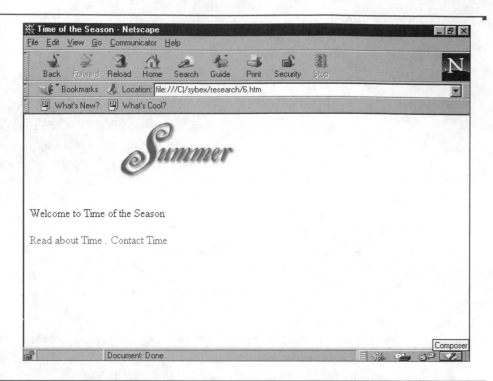

FIGURE 2.13

Remove the comment tags and all of the graphics appear.

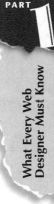

Finally, comment tags are a terrific way to put information about the page's authors, designers, and contacts into the code. Here's an example from The Weekly Wire, a premiere alternative news site located at `http://www.weeklywire.com/`. The Weekly Wire identifies all of its pages using comment tags:

```
<!-- Site by DesertNet Designs . sales@desert.net -->
<!-- DesertNet . 326 S. Convent St. Tucson, Arizona 85701 -->
<!-- Phone 520.622.3039 . Fax 520.206-0354 -->
<!-- Web Engineers . Wil Gerken . Nathan Hendler -->
<!-- Art Director . Amy Burnham -->
<!-- Administration . Doug Floyd -->
<!-- Online Editor . Zak Woodruff -->
```

Comment tags are a way to get maximum power out of your pages, and enable you, the designer, to have plenty of consistency and control in your HTML code.

Page Identity, Copyright, and Contact

Site identity and clear communication are an integral part of interface design. Identifying sites by name and any branded symbol such as a logo is key, both because it helps keep a user oriented, and because there are legal and professional considerations a Web site should address. Some of these considerations include copyright information and making the site's owners and Web management available through a contact method. It's important to clearly identify who is behind the Web page. This is an integral part of interface design, as you'll see in Chapter 3.

In terms of HTML, there are three things to make a habit of on every page. The first is to use the `<title>` tag, mentioned earlier in this chapter, to appropriately identify both the site and the page's identity. Many designers like to add the same information to what is essentially the footer information of a page.

Footer information can, and should, include the page's copyright notice and an e-mail link so visitors can contact the site's management in order to ask questions about the site. If you have extensive contact information, you can use that link to go to a full page where the information is presented in detail.

Copyrights use the special character code `&copy;` to achieve the © symbol.

Here's an example of a simple footer:

```
<!-- begin footer -->
&copy; 1997, So And So Industries, Inc.
<br>
<a href="contact.htm">Contact Us!</a>
</body>
</html>
```

You can also link the copyright information to a separate, more extensive copyright, trademark, and contact page, as the Weekly Wire does:

```
<a href="http://weeklywire.com/copyright.html">&copy; 1995-97 Weekly
Wire</a> . <a href="http://weeklywire.com/info/">Info Booth</a>
```

ON line!

The following sites will help provide you with more information on legal issues on the Net:

- **U.S. Copyright Office:** This is a very helpful starting point for copyright information, `http://lcweb.loc.gov/copyright/`.
- **The Internet Law and Policy Forum:** This site keeps up with various legal issues of concern to the Net community, and works to create " . . . a neutral venue in which to develop solutions to the challenging legal and policy questions of the Internet." `http://www.ilpf.org/`
- **The World Wide Web Consortium's Policy Page:** This site is a great jumping-off point for a variety of up-to-date information on legal and policy issues such as intellectual property rights. `http://www.w3.org/Policy/Overview.html`.

If you have legal questions about copyright, it's important to discuss them with an attorney as legal issues on the Net are in a state of constant flux.

META Tags

Another helpful tag for designers is the META tag. While it has many uses, including page and author identification, the primary reason to discuss META tagging is for designers working with commercial Web sites. A META tag offers information that will be used by servers to carry out a variety of actions as specified by the user.

The META tag offers several attributes that, once defined, are picked up by search engines and Web worms crawling through the Web and storing URLs and related information in their databases. Search engines and Web worms are intelligent agents that monitor the Internet for newly added information, taking any newfound data back to a home base for cataloging. Thorough designers will ensure that META tags are in place for the post-production phase, ensuring that the site will be ready for indexing with various engines, and prepared for those worms that come sneaking around.

Using the META tag for this purpose is pretty straightforward. There are two attributes that you want to be certain to include. The first is a short description, defined by the description and content attributes; the second is keywords, done in the same fashion. Here's an example of a properly defined META tag:

```
<head>

<!-- Site by BrainBug -->
<!-- http://www.brainbug.com -->
<!-- brainbug@brainbug.com -->
<!-- (860) 278-2200 -->

<!-- Copyright 1997, BrainBug -->

<title>BrainBug: Creativity That Works.</title>

<META name="description" content="BrainBug is a provider of digital media
communications for business.">

<META name="keywords" content="graphic, design, world, wide, web, internet,
advanced, media, digital, communications, cdrom, print, connectivity,
BrainBug, intranet, audio, marketing, registration, online, animation,
sites">
</head>
```

As you can see from this example, there is no closing META tag. The information is simply put into a sentence or string of words and then the tag is closed. You'll also note that the code in this example is very clean, with comment tags to add additional information to the code's page.

 **OFF line!**

Spend some time writing a description for your Web site project. Get away from the computer for a bit and brainstorm clever and catchy yet sensible paragraphs. Keep your writing down to about 25 words total. Then, work on keywords. With keywords, you need to anticipate what people who are looking for your site will be thinking.

Custom Templates

Creating custom templates is a powerful way to ensure that your Web sites have all of the elements you want them to. Your sense of coding style, comment tags, META tags, and any other personal touches can be named and claimed by creating templates.

How you do this will depend upon the software you're using. I develop templates in HomeSite by creating a clean file including the absolutes I want to see on every page of a given site. The template can then be opened up by anyone, and because I've already got my containers and elements the way *I* want them, the end results will be that much more consistent.

Case Study: The Rolling Reporter

One of my favorite ongoing Web projects is the Rolling Reporter 'zine on the Microsoft Network. I work with Kelly Johns, a T-6 paraplegic who travels the world over, skiing, scuba diving, journeying into the wild and unruly corners of the world. Kelly's job is to write articles and take photographs (Figure 2.14) on her excursions; my job is to make sure the site gets coded and designed.

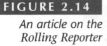
FIGURE 2.14

An article on the Rolling Reporter

Here's an example of a custom template I've prepared for Kelly using the various absolutes mentioned in this chapter:

```
<!-- Site Concept by Kelly Johns -->
<!-- Design Director: Molly E. Holzschlag -->
<!-- Contact: Kelly_DF@msn.com -->

<html>

<!-- begin header -->

<head>

<title>Rolling Reporter: Place title here</title>

<meta  name="description" content="Explore the world of possibilities for people
with disabilities. Limits were made to be broken!">

<meta  name="keywords" content="disabilities, disabled, handicap, sports, fitness,
travel, access, accessibility, rolling, reporter, kelly johns, molly holzschlag,
kelly, molly, disabilities forum, microsoft network, MSN,  the microsoft network">

</head>

<body bgcolor="#000000" text="#000000" link="#FF9933" vlink="#9966FF"
alink="#9966CC" background="images/rr-bak.gif">

<!-- end header -->

<!-- begin navigation -->

<table width="600" cellpadding="0" cellspacing="20" border="0">
<tr>

<td valign="top" align="right" bgcolor="#000000" width="110">


<div align="center">
<img src="images/globe.gif" alt="globe graphic" width="100" height="109">
</div>
<p>

<font face="arial,helvetica">

<a href="about.htm">about the rolling reporter</a>
<p>
```

```
<a href="articles.htm">travel articles</a>
<p>

<a href="sports.htm">sports and fitness</a>
<p>

<a href="access.htm">accessibility reports</a>
<p>

<a href="contact.htm">contact</a>
<p>

<a href="default.htm">home</a>
<p>

<a href="http://forums.msn.com/disabilities">visit the disabilities forum on MSN</a>

</font>

<pre>

</pre>

<hr 50% noshade>
<p>

<font face="times" size="2" color="#FFCC66">

<i>Place Pull Quote Here</i>

<pre>

</pre>

<i>Place Pull Quote Here </i>
<pre>

</pre>

<i>Place Pull Quote Here </i>

<pre>

</pre>

<i>Place Pull Quote Here </i>
```

```
<pre>

</pre>
<i>Place Pull Quote Here </i>

</font>
</td>

<!-- end navigation -->

<!-- begin content -->

<td valign="top" width="450">

<div align="right">
<font size="5" face="times" color="#9966FF">Place Article Title Here</font>
</div>
<pre>

</pre>
<font face="arial,helvetica">

<!-- begin article text here.  after each paragraph place a <p> to indicate paragraph
end -->

<!-- end of page 1 -->

<!-- end article -->

<!-- begin footer -->

<div align="right">
<a href=".htm"><i>continued . . .</i></a>
</div>

</font>
</td>
</tr>
</table>
<p>

<div align="left">
<font size=-1>&copy; 1997<br> the rolling reporter</a>
<br>
<a href="contact.htm">Contact Information</a>
```

```
</font>
</div>
<p>

<!-- end footer -->

</body>
</html>
```

OFF line!

Here's an exercise for you—visit the Design Studio Web site. From the Front Office, you can download the graphics and template for this example. Open it in your preferred editor, and add some text to see how easy and powerful custom templates can be.
http://www.designstudio.net/

While pages within a site will certainly be different than others within that same site, maintaining consistency is very important—as you'll learn in Chapter 3. Not only do custom templates enable you and others to work on the same code quickly and with few problems, they keep your design on-track.

Next Up

A technical author and HTML coder named Laura Lemay (quoted earlier in this chapter) wrote an HTML book just as the Web began to take off commercially. It gave millions of people new to the Internet what they were hungry for: a simple, easy-to-use reference guide to HTML.

In an online discussion in September of 1997, Laura shared these comments regarding the future of the Web and, more specific to this chapter, HTML: "Probably the best way I can think of to describe the future of the web is simply 'more.'"

Some of the things the future holds in terms of *more* include:

- More control over presentation, with style sheets for formatting, and element positioning so that you can control where every single element goes on a page

- More programming control over pages, such as the use of JavaScript, VBScript, and Dynamic HTML

- More multimedia, audio, and video capabilities

- More—and better—authoring tools

To support the increasing fascination and demand for these Internet design techniques and Web technologies, the structure beneath the Internet is gearing up. Across the world, money and effort is being put into creating an even more powerful, faster foundation for this medium to rest upon. How this will conceivably impact HTML, much less our potential in every area of life, is unpredictable.

HTML will inevitably change. It *is* changing, all the time. But it will change more—becoming a lot more like a programming language than the format script language it once was. This is evidenced with *Dynamic HTML* (DHTML), which is mostly the incorporation of programming into the HTML environment. Whether HTML will still be called HTML or turn into something vastly different is almost irrelevant. What is relevant is that knowing HTML today gives you a better chance at understanding the changes as they come down the pike.

The possibilities are currently limitless, or limited only by our imagination. Either way, the future of the Internet should not be considered lightly, especially by those of us who are building it using HTML as the foundation. Yes, we're having a lot of fun out there now, but it's critical to keep aware of the impact these technologies are bringing to our daily lives and even more important—the lives of our children.

My thoughts about HTML's future are a little less concerned with how the code will look, or what types of programs designers will use to generate Internet media. Instead, I challenge you to ask how can we, as Web designers, work to find the best possible technical solutions that work to enhance this powerful medium? I've talked a lot about consistency, cleanliness, and organization in this chapter. But what I haven't done is also talk about the value of thought and independent ideas.

As an educator, it is quite apparent to me that what's often missing in books on Web design is the *why*. Ideally, you learn *how* to do a task, but you don't necessarily learn why you are doing that task and what potential ramifications—good or bad—it can do to effect the future.

I recently received an e-mail from a high school sophomore that brought this lesson home:

```
I love the Internet and most of all I love Web and Web
Graphic Design. I am hoping to make a career out of it one
day and plan on having fun while doing it. I was just won-
dering if you had any information on classes, colleges, good
Web design books, or any other ideas that would better my
chance of making a real life career out of Internet Design.
```

Along with sending some recommendations on classes, design books, and online resources, I sent this student the following thoughts, which I pass along to you in hopes you will take them to heart:

```
. . . you can bank on the fact that the Internet is going to
look very different in six years—when you're out of college
and looking for a job. To ensure that you'll have the skills
necessary to compete you'll have to split your time between
studying HTML and Web programming, the Web as an art form,
and perhaps most importantly—online community. To guide the
future as well as be a part of it you'll need equal parts of
technical, design, and human interest savvy. Make sure you
take plenty of computer science classes, but also get expe-
rience in art and psychology.
Remember that no matter the future of Web design, you will
need to have integrated, interdisciplinary skills that will
plant your feet firmly in what has been separate worlds for
far too long—that of science, and that of art. You must
become a Renaissance man, but with your eyes planted firmly
on the future.
```

Independent thought is the vertical axis upon which tomorrow's horizon centers. As you proceed through the technical as well as theoretical issues throughout this book, I encourage you to remain focused on your unique experiences. Will it help your HTML code? I believe it will. I know it's helped mine—because I realize that what I put out there has got to be my very best.

chapter 3

THE ART OF INTERFACE

THE ART OF
INTERFACE

Dressing for success is a major part of professional achievement. Your smile, your demeanor, and your outward appearance play an enormous role in how you are perceived and thus able to move through the world.

A Web site, too, must be dressed for success. A site's interface is the first thing visitors will react to when they reach your Web address. In order to make the visitor's experience one that encourages him or her to explore your site fully you must make the best possible impression.

One aspect of interface is similar to outward appearance. Even though the true beauty or wealth of a person may lie within—by and large if they do not present themselves in an appropriate fashion, their beauty may be passed over. Interfaces must be visually appealing and follow logical, accepted presentations for people to be attracted and willing to interact. Much of this is gained through the quality of a Web site's graphic design.

But a pretty face isn't everything. Think about how you interact with others. You've probably heard that you can attract more flies with honey than with vinegar—and it's true! This is your personal interface. If you're a curmudgeon at work—unfriendly or moody—people are going to avoid you. If you're pleasant, easy to work with, and open to input from others, you'll find that you can win a lot more acceptance and work more efficiently.

In order to make your Web sites work you're going to have to pay attention to the outward appearance and the *personality* of your site. Enough time has been spent designing interfaces—whether it's computer software or multimedia presentations—that time-honored methods have been developed which can be employed to address both the structural appearance and inner personality of a Web site.

The Need to Know

Interface design has typically been the domain of people working in fields such as computer applications development or multimedia design. Those individuals learn about interface and how to make people as comfortable as possible with the material they are developing. They have the basic concepts down, but they may not know how to apply it to the Web.

Furthermore, some Web designers have training in interface concept, but many do not. Sadly, books written to help those designers interested in strengthening skills and knowledge miss the important information you'll find in this chapter.

Regardless of your background, pay special attention to the way interface has been broken down in this chapter, as well as the descriptions of new media theory in the context of interface (see "The Stuff Sites Are Made Of" section later in this chapter). You will also find a significant attention paid to navigation. Instead of leaving it in its safe nest *within* the description of interface, it has been pulled out and described in detail.

As Web designers, you need to know not only the basics of general interface design, but how these concepts interrelate and operate with the new media environment. An interface can be designed for an individual application, but new media environments demand a different kind of thinking. As you'll learn, the Web is not linear and it is not self-contained. You will have to think not only of your Web site design, but your site design as it relates to the rest of the Web. This is why so much emphasis is placed on navigation. Not only must people be able to navigate within your site easily, but they must also be able to navigate out to other sites as well. To not offer virtual doorways out onto the Web leaves the commercial designer at risk of limiting visitor's choices.

The Five Features of Interface Design

Interface design can be broken down into five essential areas to make it accessible to the broad range of people studying the Web:

- Metaphor
- Clarity
- Consistency
- Orientation
- Navigation

Each of these areas has both a theoretical reason for being and a set of practical methods that can be immediately applied to a site's design. Learning both will place you securely in the driver's seat. Theory serves you because you understand *why* you choose to employ a certain practice. Method shows you *how* to take this theory and realize it on the physical plane.

Metaphor

In design, a metaphor is the symbolic representation of the structure you're attempting to build. A metaphor acts as a familiar visual aid upon which you construct the entryway, interiors, doors, and windows of your environment.

When designing a Web site interface, you'll often select images that will symbolize areas of your site; these images are your metaphors for each area. Metaphors can be very specific, or they can be abstract.

Think about your computer's interface. Both the Macintosh and PC Windows 95 platforms use an office metaphor. Your workspace is a "desktop" and your files are kept in file folders. These are visually represented with icons, as shown in Figure 3.1.

FIGURE 3.1

File icons in Windows 95

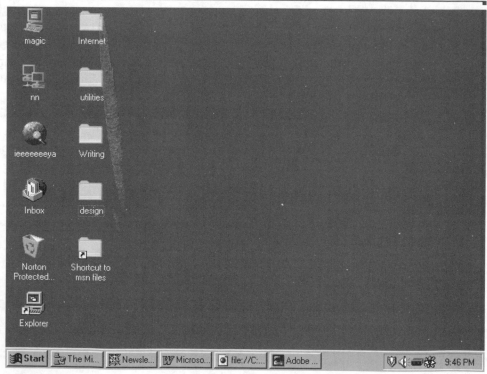

Metaphors are usually strongest when employing very concrete, familiar concepts. There are times when more abstract or conceptual ideas can be effective. More frequently, a combination of the two are intertwined to provide an engaging experience.

Figure 3.2 is the navigation bar of the *Tucson Weekly*'s Web site. Note how each section's option has a visual image to help represent that section's intent. This is how you can apply metaphor to a Web site.

FIGURE 3.2

*Navigation bar from
Tucson Weekly*

CURRENTS

CITY WEEK

MUSIC

REVIEW

BOOKS

CINEMA

BACK PAGE

FORUMS

SEARCH
ARCHIVES

Clarity

Every element on a page should have a reason for being there. Furthermore, that reason should be apparent to the visitor. Your selection of metaphors will help with this, but you can also do several things to support these visuals on your pages.

One of the ways to support your metaphor while ensuring accessibility is to use words in addition to images. If you look carefully at the upper-left button in Figure 3.3, the designer has used a sky to symbolically depict "background." Then, in order to help clarify the image's purpose, the designer added a "B" to relate the literal word to the metaphoric symbol. This helps round out metaphor by going past the feel of the button's function, and clarifying its purpose.

FIGURE 3.3

Metaphor and clarity

Other methods that are necessary to support clarity is ensuring that anything that appears on your page—image maps, buttons, links, spot art, Java applets—clearly performs the purpose for which it is intended. For example, an arrow button that links to a continuing page should point right and a button returning to the previous page should point left. A link to a mail option should be coded to pull up a mail reader, not a command for the newsreader to appear. Confusion and chaos are frustrating for all of us, particularly for the person trying to get to your offerings and being unable to do so because your directions are simply too hard to follow.

Consistency

You arrive at a Web site. The graphics are attractive, the layout is interesting, the navigation options immediately apparent and available. You think, "Wow, this is going to be a *great* site." So, you click a link. The terrain is unfamiliar, there's nothing you recognize. In fact, you think that you might have taken a wrong turn off of that cool site.

What happened to the inviting design? The good-looking graphics? The great layout and unique color scheme?

All too often on the Web, you'll find an attractive front door, but as you enter the site, the design is lost. If you decide to stay at an inconsistent site long enough, you're likely to see dramatically different background colors, inconsistent or cliché font styles, and irregular headers and navigation. In short, you can't tell from one page to the next where in the Web world you are.

This is due to a failure of *consistency*. Consistent design means carrying an interface's features through the entire site. Consistency is gained by:

- **Using the site's metaphor throughout the site**—The symbols you choose should remain intact as users move through the site, creating a sense of familiarity.

- **Keeping graphic elements compatible**—Graphics should be similar in style from one page to the next. In other words, if you create a header with a drop shadow, all of your headers should have that drop shadow.

- **Maintaining a consistent color palette**—While you can switch the colors around to some degree, you must work from a pre-determined palette in order to help keep a site consistent (see Chapter 15 and the color reference section in the center of this book).

- **Arranging navigation options uniformly**—If you've created graphical navigation that runs along the margin, and a text-based option along the bottom, keep those navigation elements the same throughout the site.

- **Working carefully with fonts**—Font styles, whether used in your headers, body text, or as decorative elements within your page, must be consistent in terms of face, color, and size. If you've designed a page using one font for headers and another for the body—don't switch that order on another page. Similarly, if you've made all of your headers purple and your body text black, continue that pattern. Size counts, too. Keep body text, header, and footer fonts the same point size throughout the site (see Chapter 19 for examples of font use).

Can you ever deviate from these rules? Yes, and some of the best designers do it all the time. There's an old saying that claims you've got to know the rules in order to break them, and that holds true with design. If you are working in familiar territory and have a strong understanding of what you are doing, deviation from the norm can be interesting and cutting-edge.

"Computing technology holds great promise for those challenged by conventional methods. The design of alternative user interfaces may provide those individuals with a new way to demonstrate their talent and skills."

WALLACE MURPHY, JR., Author, *Human-Computer Interface Design*

If you're relatively new to design, sticking to the rules will give you a much better chance of achieving professional results. This translates into having your visitors get the clearest and best possible experience from your site—because you've helped them feel at ease and kept them from confusion.

Orientation

A site visitor must know where he or she is within a given site every step of the way. It's your job to ensure that no one gets lost. By building upon the concepts of metaphor, clarity, and consistency, along with a few other tricks, you can ensure that you do the job of keeping your visitors well-oriented within a site.

You can ensure that your visitors are oriented within your site through these methods:

- **Each page within the site has a title**—Using the HTML `<title>` tag command, be sure to clearly mark each individual page with not only the name of the site, but the name of the page as well. This information appears in the title bar of the browser—not in the page design itself. It is, however, an essential method of ensuring orientation:

`<title>The Groovy Music Site: New Bands Page</title>`

- **Headers that define the page's identity are clearly available**—Whether you use an HTML-based text header (Figure 3.4), a graphics-based stylized header (Figure 3.5), or even if your header is a bit less than traditional (Figure 3.6) be sure that your page is identified within the design of the page itself.

- **Use footers**—Placing information such as the site's name and/or location, the copyright information, and an e-mail link within the footer area of a page, as shown in Figure 3.7, enables site visitors to get a *lot* of information about where they are and where they can get additional information about you or your company.

Orientation works in concert with the other aspects of interface design in creating a cohesive product. It's especially important to have this cohesion as sites grow—the potential for confusion rises exponentially to an increase in Web site pages. So, whether you have three pages or three thousand, orientation plays a strong role in keeping the pieces of a site's interface together.

FIGURE 3.4

*This page's header
is text-based.*

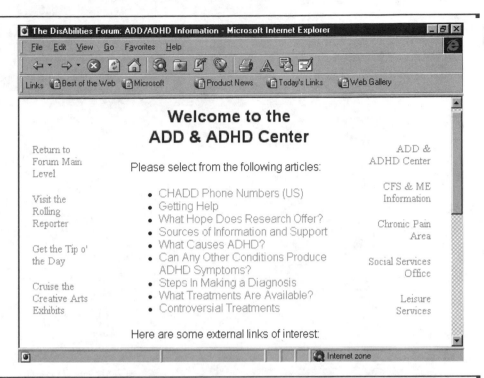

FIGURE 3.5

*This page uses a
graphic for its
header.*

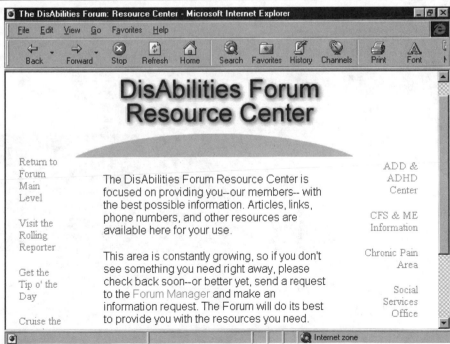

FIGURE 3.6

*An untraditional
graphic header*

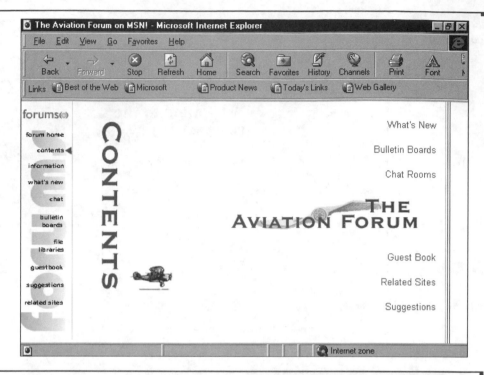

FIGURE 3.7

*The information
below the graphics
on this page helps
with orientation.*

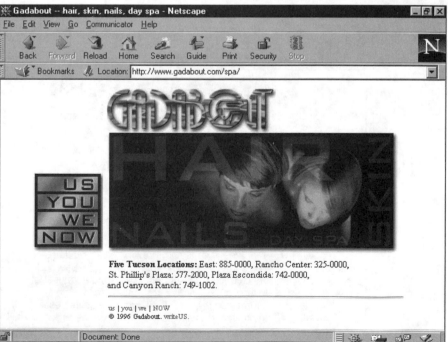

Navigation

Some designers think navigation is just a matter of offering up site section options and linking to those areas. While that's a primary purpose of navigation, there are several other issues involved with creating navigation, including:

- **Site structure**—The hypermedia environment of the Web is extremely powerful, offering a number of ways of constructing a site outside of the familiar linear approach of other mediums such as books and newspapers.

- **Navigation location**—Where on a site do you put navigation? Top, bottom, right, and left are the most common, but combinations are often used.

- **Navigation media**—As Web technology matures, so do the types of media available to the designer to deliver site information, including images that are enhanced with sound and animation using JavaScript, Shockwave, or Flash. For more information on multimedia and Web programming, see Part VII.

- **Management of growing data**—As sites age, they also amass information in leaps and bounds. How to maneuver through all of this information in a pleasing way is an aspect of good navigation.

Navigation is as much a part of interface design as any of the other concepts introduced here, although if any one is studied more than another, it's navigation. For this reason, we will focus more intently on navigation later in this chapter. A visit to that section offers up some technical as well as visual examples of how navigation is achieved and used.

The Stuff Sites Are Made Of

Sugar and spice and everything nice didn't cover what *I* was made of—I was also a bit of the tomboy, with worms and snails and puppy dog's tails added to the mix! Sites, like people, are diverse. And, like children, Web sites need structure and guidance to give them the best chance of thriving as they grow.

To that end, a strong dose of new media theory can help you, as a Web designer, gain a more focused idea of how new media works, and therefore, how you can tap into the power of the Web environment.

NOTE

New media is the convergence of more traditional types of media such as text, graphics, audio, video, and animation, within an interactive environment. A CD-ROM multimedia presentation is such an environment, as is the Web.

In this section, you'll get a healthy serving of new media theory as it applies to site structure. We'll then move on to the practical applications of that theory so you can put it to use in the work you do today.

Site Structure and Theory

What is a Web site? On the surface, it's an electronic presentation on a network that has a specific intent. Whether that intent is to share ideas, sell products, evangelize a point of view, or provide entertainment and information, a Web site's job is to *present* its intent via the digital environment in which it resides.

How that information is presented can occur in a number of ways. For instance, information can be *static*, which is simply text or graphical information that is posted on the Web that does not change or offer options beyond the most simplistic. Presentations of this nature are better suited to a brochure, because they don't tap into the Web's *interactive* power.

New media is not static. The Web is an important example of new media, which is active, choice-driven—not a passive media like television, which doesn't offer too many interactive options. Furthermore, the Web is a media that is connected to us personally, relating people to other people worldwide.

> *"This is a new medium. Though it has aspects similar to analog communication, it's one where we must constantly try to figure out what is constant and relevant. We're constantly trying to figure out new things to add value."*
>
> CLEMENT MOK, in an interview with Interactive Age Magazine, 1997

Consider the following scenario. A child is watching cartoons on TV. He laughs at the character's antics, he is involved with their personalities and activities emotionally, but he cannot touch them, he cannot alter their actions, and he cannot have a personal interaction with them.

Another child, sitting at a computer with an educational CD-ROM chooses her direction, interacts with characters, and makes decisions on how and when she wants to involve herself with a given subject.

The Web is best used for interactive presentations. Not only is a personal interaction with a Web site's information available, but so is interaction with other people—often living in other cities or on other continents. Interactivity in the Web environment is not only informational, it is cultural. Many new opportunities for global communication and information exchange are made available as a result.

Where does this interactivity come from? The starting point is the Web's technical structure. Originally, it was a hypertext environment, delivered through the *hypertext transfer protocol* (HTTP). The desire that HTTP's creators had was to allow for the publication of text-based documents that could be hyperlinked to references and resources *within* that document.

It didn't take long before hypertext became *hypermedia*. When graphical interfaces became available and began supporting non-text media such as photographs or art, that media in turn took advantage of the HTTP protocol. This meant that you could set a graphic up as the clickable link into the next document.

Today's Web designers have many, many options that allow them to embrace interactivity—both on the informational and community level. Forms (Figure 3.8), interactive games, multimedia events such as virtual reality or live cameras (Figure 3.9), community bulletin boards, and real-time chat rooms (Figure 3.10) are programmed using a variety of methods and placed upon the hypertext protocol.

FIGURE 3.8

A feedback form on the Ramada Inn site

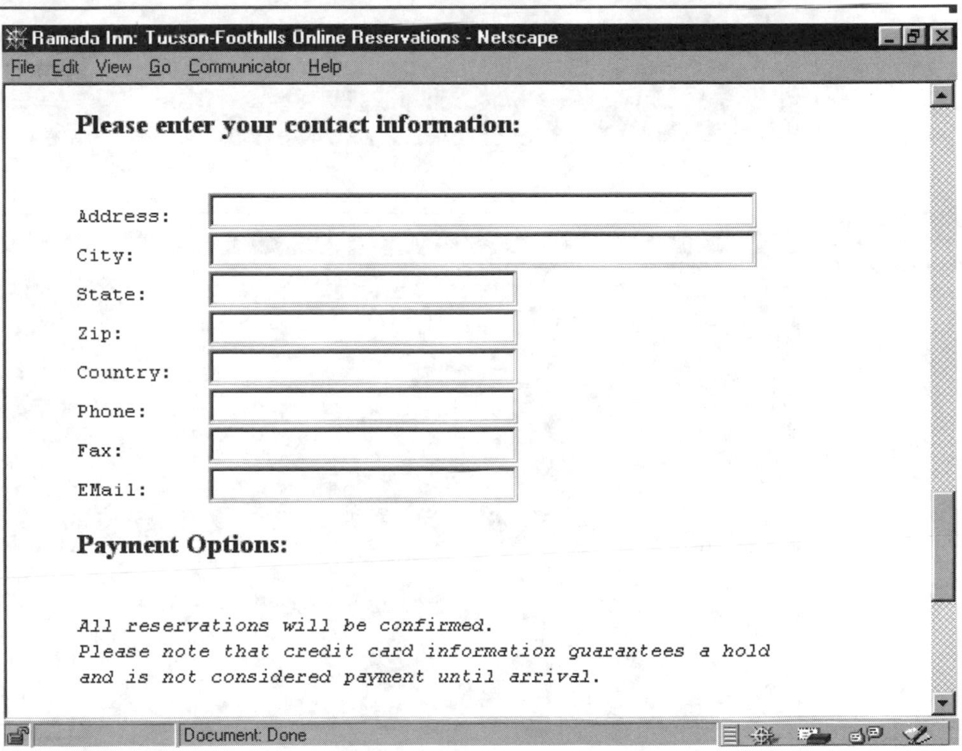

Ramada Inn: Tucson-Foothills Online Reservations - Netscape

File Edit View Go Communicator Help

Please enter your contact information:

Address:

City:

State:

Zip:

Country:

Phone:

Fax:

EMail:

Payment Options:

All reservations will be confirmed.
Please note that credit card information guarantees a hold
and is not considered payment until arrival.

Document: Done

FIGURE 3.9

Web Evangelist Justin Hall appearing live via a Web camera on the Club Congress site.

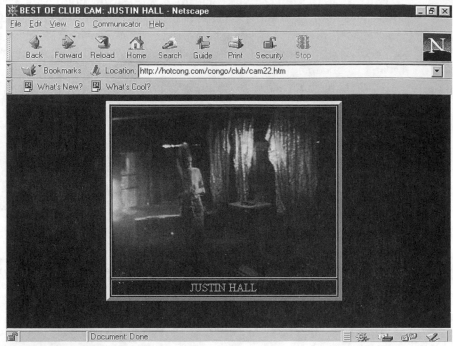

FIGURE 3.10

Real-time chat on Atomic Media

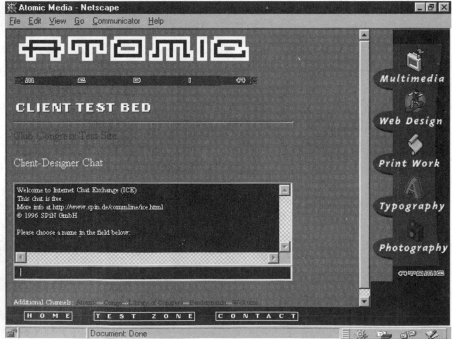

An evolutionary concept of the Web that stems from the hypermedia environment is its *non-linear* quality. Unlike a book, which is read page-by-page, Web sites can be constructed in a variety of ways. A hypertext or media link can take you from the middle of a sentence or a thought to another, ancillary thought.

In the western world, we've been taught to read left-to-right, receive information passively from a source such as television, and process it by organizing it on a timeline.

What happens when a person is interacting with a non-linear environment is that he or she can depart from this linear structure into one that allows for tangential and choice-driven information retrieval. This provides the opportunity to create new methods of organizational structures—beyond the timeline.

> *"The non-linear structure of hypertext encourages the reader to consider the information based on its context."*
>
> LEN HATFIELD, from the HyperTheory Web site, Virginia Polytechnic Institute

Interestingly, the human brain deals with information much like the Web does. The linear structures we've been exposed to in our educational process are an imposed structure.

Consider how the human memory works. My father is only a memory to me now, but when I think of him I can reconstruct his image in my mind. Yet I don't have a specific place in my brain that is labeled "father" that has all the data about him stored within it. In fact, studies on human memory teach us that not only are individual memories scattered around the brain, specific parts of memory are too. So the image of my father's eye might reside in one place, his nose in another, his smile in still another.

To reconstruct his face in my mind's eye, my brain has to send neural impulses throughout my brain, pick up the information from here and there, and shuttle it back to a central receiving area. Of course, this is a very rudimentary description of the process, but if it strikes you as a Web designer as being familiar, you're correct.

The Web browser is that central receiving area, and the HTML code works as the organizational structure behind which commands to "go here and retrieve this" or "go there and retrieve that" occur. The bits of information that make up an individual page are actually *separate and tangential* data that is organized and placed into a main container.

Deep stuff. But it's important for you to know—you can harness the power of interactivity and appropriate design when you understand the environment.

Practical Application of Linearity

Most people have, through education and enculturation, been given a linear structure upon which to interpret information. It is therefore very important to give enough linearity to a site for it to be comfortable and navigable. How much or how little linearity you, as the designer, decide to place within a site will often depend upon what you are presenting, and to whom.

For example, if you're offering a Web magazine, you're going to want to maintain some kind of linear navigation so people can relate the structure of that magazine to the page-by-page concept to which they are accustomed. A trendy nightclub's site can be more experimental because the target audience will be comfortable with that experimentation.

We're going to start with a linear site example, move into a hierarchical structure, and then we will learn how to add tangential, non-linear options to the site. This example will give you a formula upon which to standardize future designs—and a formula from which you can deviate when you are ready and feel it appropriate to do so.

A linear site would be akin to a book. Each page is placed to the conceptual right of the next. The maximum navigation would be a means to move one page forward, and a method of returning back one page. Figure 3.11 shows an example of this type of layout.

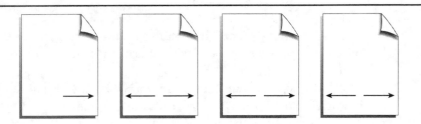

Since the linear site runs only along the horizontal, to make it hierarchical a vertical axis needs to be added. The sub-pages expand upon the main ideas of their parent pages. Figure 3.12 shows an example of a hierarchical page layout. Note that the navigation options in this phase are forward and back as well as up and down.

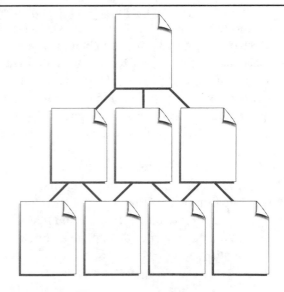

Now we'll add non-linear options to the site, including pages placed behind and in front of the existing up/down and side/side options (Figure 3.13).

FIGURE 3.13

Non-linear layout

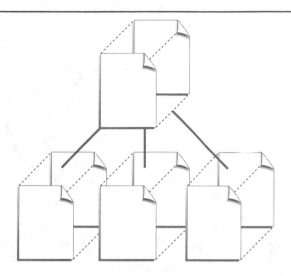

Links from any place within the site to another place within the site is known as internal linking (Figure 3.14).

FIGURE 3.14

Internal linking

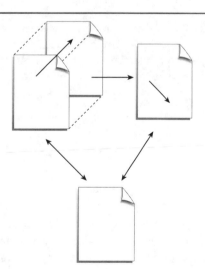

Links to information on sites outside your own would be external linking (Figure 3.15).

FIGURE 3.15

Links to external sites

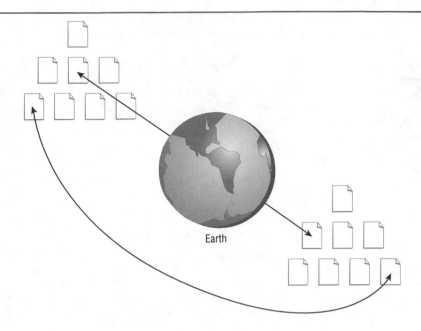

Earth

OFF line!

Think about other examples of non-linear environments including kiosks, Web-based virtual reality presentations, and interactive computer games. Write out the features that you think makes your selections non-linear. Are there linear aspects to these examples as well? Spend some time exploring how linearity works in your everyday world.

Site Structure and Practice

Now that you have an ample amount of theory, you can begin bringing the more esoteric notions you've learned into practice. An effective way of doing this is to take the structures discussed and assign actual purpose and events to them. This brings you back around to the *presentation* aspect of interface. The following sections detail various site components that put theory into action.

Home Page

The home page is the page with which you meet and greet site visitors. A home page is either a page with a logo or other identifying mark used as the greeting but containing limited navigation options—often referred to as a *splash page* (Figure 3.16)—or a working page with complete information and navigation options (Figure 3.17). Home pages usually reside at the root of a Web address using `index.htm`, `index.html`, `default.htm`, or `default.html` as its default page. For example, by typing `http://www.designstudio.net/`, you pull up the Design Studio's home page. So will `http://www.designstudio.net/index.html`. Depending upon the Web server or individual's taste, the page might have an address that differs from this type of convention, however.

FIGURE 3.16

*The BrainBug
splash page*

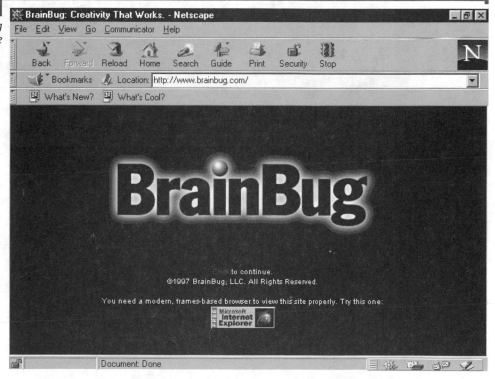

FIGURE 3.17

Working welcome page at The Weekly Wire

Home pages of either type must not deviate from interface concepts such as consistency and clarity. Continuity from a splash page can be achieved with palettes and fonts, even though the look of the page is somewhat different than the internal pages.

> *"Design strategies for home pages vary, based on the function and needs of typical users of the site, the aesthetic and design goals for the site, and on nature and complexity of the organization of the Web site as a whole."*
>
> PATRICK J. LYNCH AND SARAH HORTON, Authors, *Yale C/AIM Web Style Guide*

About Page

This page offers up information *about* the product, company, or project you are presenting to your audience. It's an important aspect of interface, because it helps round out issues of clarity. Beyond that, this page can be used to share important information that helps the visitor understand your intentions, such as important job openings or a site's newest feature. Figure 3.18 shows an effective about page for BrainBug.

FIGURE 3.18

*The about page on
BrainBug*

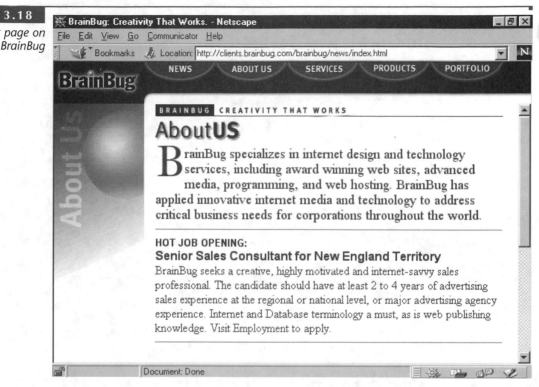

Content Pages

Content is king, so it is said. Content pages may range from a few pages of information to tens of thousands of pages of data. What matters is that content pages have an identity of their own within the bigger spectrum of a site.

If you have a few pages of content, this can be addressed simply by ensuring that each page is identified for its particular actions. On my Web site, I have broken content down into the various activities I do, such as books, articles and columns, poetry and music, and so forth. Each of these pages is clearly identified (Figure 3.19).

Larger sites have the challenge of breaking content into sections that support more content. An example of this is the *Tucson Weekly*. Newspapers typically have sections such as Arts, Music, and the like. The *Tucson Weekly* takes each of these content sections and then places articles that fit within those content sections in the appropriate place (see Figures 3.20 and 3.21).

FIGURE 3.19

The Articles and
Columns page on
molly.com

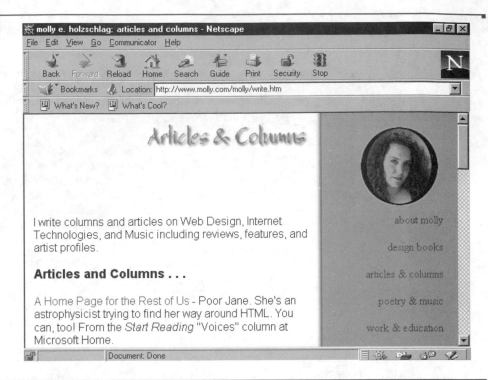

FIGURE 3.20

The Music section
on Tucson Weekly

FIGURE 3.21

*A music article on
Tucson Weekly*

Contact Page

I've never been so frustrated as the times I've wanted to write to a company for more information, or even just to express my feelings about their site, and couldn't find a way to get in touch. Contact is an essential part of interactivity and should be made very, very available throughout a site. Because you want to offer your potential customers a myriad of ways to get in touch with you, a contact page should hold the following information:

- **E-mail contact(s)**—Some sites only have one e-mail contact, and that's fine. However, if you are a large organization, you might want to offer e-mail addresses for various contacts including general information, a Webmaster, or specific members of the organization.

- **Postal "snail mail" address**—It's nice, but not necessary, to offer up a standard mailing address where people can write should they want more information.

- **Phone number(s)**—Depending upon the type of organization, phone numbers will either be very important or not that important to include. Commercial sites offering a product should provide a phone number—especially of the toll-free variety. If you want to buy a product, you want the option of taking your questions or concerns to a live person. However, if your site is more informational than customer service or commerce-driven, offering a phone number might not be a priority.

- **FAX number(s)**—FAX numbers are also helpful when you are providing goods and services.

It's important to remember that any personal information can be retrieved both by curious visitors with less-than-ethical intentions, or by Web and mail robots (known as "bots") that companies use develop e-mail lists to send junk mail. How do you avoid this? You can set up a forms-based contact method that doesn't show the address in the code, which will provide you with protection. I personally encourage as much contact information as possible, but designers should be aware of the issues that can arise out of the sharing of contact information.

Additional Content

Web sites are beginning to contain more activities as part of their expanding content. These include games, forums, feedback forms, chat rooms, and a variety of multimedia events. This content needs to be organized within the site's structure in a logical fashion. How you do this will often depend upon the importance of that content in the greater scheme of the site. For example, on the DisAbilities Forum site developed for the Microsoft Network, I've added numerous chat rooms and bulletin boards. Network members use these areas to exchange information, experiences, and support. Because these activities are central to the community around the Web site, I've made the chat and BBS content available as close at hand as possible.

Navigation

Navigation is as much a part of interface design as it is a unique entity in Web design. As sites become more sophisticated, having fixed, primary routes of navigation is advantageous to the Web designer. He or she can use these ideas as a given—and either choose to work with them because they are familiar, honored methods, or to deviate because the environment and nature of the design calls for it. Navigation also extends to secondary routes such as off-site linking, offering added choice, and interactivity.

*"Real-world navigation is a combination of knowing where you are,
where you're going, and how and when you'll get there."*

Ragan's Web Content Report

Navigation in terms of a site's interface design requires two areas of study: layout
and media.

Layout

The *place* in which primary route navigation appears is critical to the maintenance of
site structure, consistency, and clarity. There are four standard places for Web navigation: left, right, top, and bottom. Typically, more than one of these navigation options
are used within a site. For example, you might decide you want a left-based set of navigation buttons. But, for the sake of consistency and accessibility, you will also want
to place a bottom-based text navigation.

Left-Margin Navigation

Because Web sites usually scroll on the vertical, left- and right-margin navigation has
become extremely popular. To accomplish a left- or right-margin navigation scheme,
layout includes using tables or frames. The following simple examples will provide
some guidelines; more information can be found in Chapter 13.

 OTE

Bear in mind that the following examples are very simplistic for the purposes of understanding the *layout* of the interface rather than the graphic design of the page. In
more advanced design examples, you'll see these tables laid over background graphics or increased in complexity and media styles.

Tables   Tables allow you to lay out left- or right-margin navigation by dividing a
page into columns. Here's an example of the HTML used to create a left-margin table:

```
<html>

<head>
<title>A Simple Table for Left Margin Navigation</title>
</head>

<body>

<table>
<tr>
```

```
<td width="200">

Navigation links go here:
<p>

<a href="link1.htm">Link I</a>
<p>

<a href="link2.htm">Link II</a>
<p>

<a href="link3.htm">Link III</a>

</td>

<td width="375">
Content goes in this section. Duis autem vel eum iriure dolor in hendrerit
in vulputate velit esse molestie consequat, vel illum dolore eu feugiat
nulla facilisis at vero eros et accumsan et iusto odio dignissim qui blandit
praesent luptatum zzril delenit augue duis dolore te feugait nulla facilisi.
<p>

Nam liber tempor cum soluta nobis eleifend option congue nihil imperdiet
doming id quod mazim placerat facer possim assum. Accumsan et iusto odio
dignissim qui blandit praesent luptatum zzril delenit augue duis dolore te
feugait nulla facilisi.

</td>
</tr>
</table>

</body>
</html>
```

Figure 3.22 shows the results of the above HTML.

OTE

Looks like Greek to you? The gibberish you see in this table example is referred to as *greeking*, or dummy text. It simply takes up the space where standard body text will go so you can effectively lay out a page even if you don't have the content yet, or want to create a mock-up of the site.

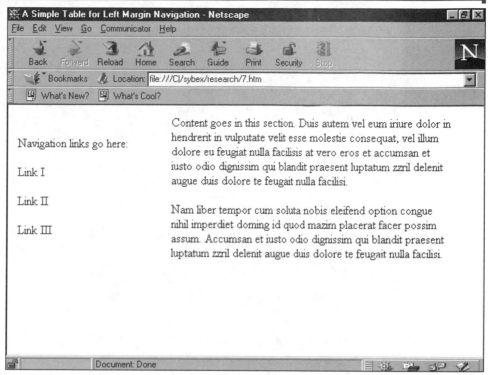

Frames   Frames provide a static section. In this case, the left section will be static, and the information will be loaded into the right area.

It takes a minimum of three unique HTML-coded documents to make up a single viewable page if you're using frames. Frames-based pages always require a *frameset*, and then each frame area requires a separate HTML document to call up the information in that area.

The frameset holds all of the information regarding how and where the frames will be drawn. For example, the columns (indicated with the cols= attribute) are set to allow for 200 pixels to the left, and 400 to the right. Load the frameset into the browser, and the correct frame configuration will appear.

In this case, there's a minimum amount of information, including the pixel width of the right frame, and defining which frame is the menu and which is the content page.

```
<html>
<frameset cols="200,400">
<frame src="menu.htm">
```

```
<frame src="right.htm">
</frameset>
</html>
```

The menu page is a standard HTML page with the navigation options:

```
<html>

<head>
<title>The Left Frame Navigation</title>
</head>

<body>

Navigation links go here:
<p>

<a href="link1.htm">Link I</a>
<p>

<a href="link2.htm">Link II</a>
<p>

<a href="link3.htm">Link III</a>
<p>

</body>
</html>
```

Then the content page, entitled `right.htm`, indicates that the information contained within that page falls into the right section:

```
<html>

<head>
<title>The Right Frame Content</title>
</head>

<body>

Duis autem vel eum iriure dolor in hendrerit in vulputate velit esse
molestie consequat, vel illum dolore eu feugiat nulla facilisis at vero eros
et accumsan et iusto odio dignissim qui blandit praesent luptatum zzril
delenit augue duis dolore te feugait nulla facilisi.
<p>
```

```
Nam liber tempor cum soluta nobis eleifend option congue nihil imperdiet
doming id quod mazim placerat facer possim assum. Accumsan et iusto odio
dignissim qui blandit praesent luptatum zzril delenit augue duis dolore te
feugait nulla facilisi.
<p>

</body>
</html>
```

Remember that everyone's HTML coding style will be different. My style tends to run toward a very sparse type of coding. For example, I'll use a <p> (paragraph) tag after a paragraph instead of using the other legal method of placing them before a paragraph and using a closing </p> tag. My technique is legal, but possibly less commonly seen since the proliferation of WYSIWYG software programs. Figure 3.23 shows the final results of the above HTML.

FIGURE 3.23

Left margin, frames-based navigation

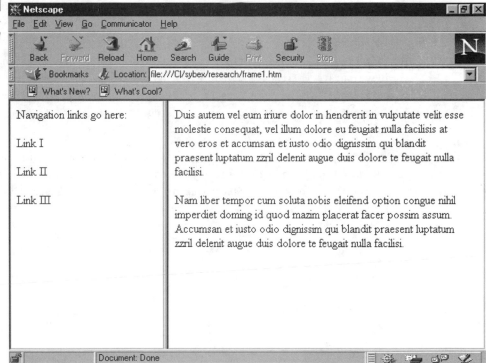

Right-Margin Navigation

Right-margin navigation is commonly used, but less so than left-based options. It makes an interesting choice for designers who wish to give a familiar navigation system to their audience, but want to stray away from the more commonly seen left-based systems.

Tables   To create a simple table with a right navigation column, all you need to do is reverse the concept introduced for left navigation. In other words, all of the information for the right navigation will appear *after* the content column:

```
<html>

<head>
<title>A Simple Table for Right Margin Navigation</title>
</head>

<body>

<table>
<tr>

<td width="375">
Content goes in this section. Duis autem vel eum iriure dolor in hendrerit
in vulputate velit esse molestie consequat, vel illum dolore eu feugiat
nulla facilisis at vero eros et accumsan et iusto odio dignissim qui blandit
praesent luptatum zzril delenit augue duis dolore te feugait nulla facilisi.
<p>

Nam liber tempor cum soluta nobis eleifend option congue nihil imperdiet
doming id quod mazim placerat facer possim assum. Accumsan et iusto odio
dignissim qui blandit praesent luptatum zzril delenit augue duis dolore te
feugait nulla facilisi.
<p>

</td>

<td width="200">

Navigation links go here:
<p>

<a href="link1.htm">Link I</a>
<p>

<a href="link2.htm">Link II</a>
<p>
```

```
<a href="link3.htm">Link III</a>

</td>

</tr>
</table>

</body>
</html>
```

Figure 3.24 shows the right-margin navigation column.

FIGURE 3.24

*Right-margin, table-
based navigation*

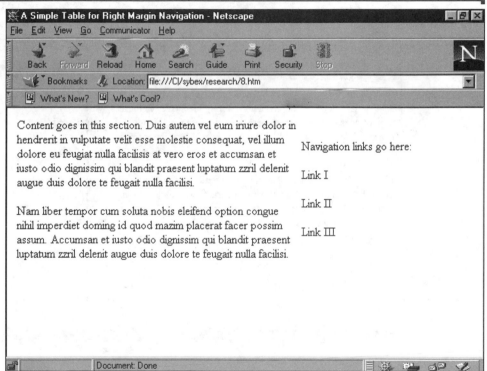

Frames

To place your navigation in the right frame, all you need to do is change the information in the frameset. For clarity's sake, rename the content from `right.htm` to `left.htm`
because it will appear in the left frame. That information should be placed first. Just
as with the table navigation, what appears in the left should always come before what
appears on the right.

```
<html>
<frameset cols="400,200">
<frame src="left.htm">
<frame src="menu.htm">
</frameset>
</html>
```

Figure 3.25 shows the results of the above HTML.

FIGURE 3.25

Right-margin, frames-based navigation

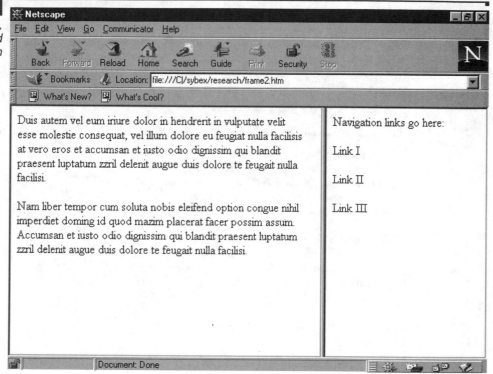

Top-Margin Navigation

To lay out navigation along the top of a page, you can once again use tables or frames. Top navigation is advantageous because it leaves plenty of room for design and content. But it should always be designed with care, because the top part of a page is one of the first places the eye will fall. If you have elements there that are more distracting than functional, you run the risk of confusing rather than enabling the site visitor.

Tables   Tables offer controlled, non-static placement of text or media. To create a simple top navigation using tables, you'll focus on table rows <tr> as well as columns:

```
<html>

<head>
<title>Simple Top Margin Table Layout</title>
</head>

<body>

<table>
<tr>

<td align="center">

[<a href="link1.htm">Link I</a>] [<a href="link2.htm">Link II</a>]
[<a href="link3.htm">Link III</a>]

</td>

</tr>

<tr>

<td>

Content goes in this section. Duis autem vel eum iriure dolor in hendrerit
in vulputate velit esse molestie consequat, vel illum dolore eu feugiat
nulla facilisis at vero eros et accumsan et iusto odio dignissim qui blandit
praesent luptatum zzril delenit augue duis dolore te feugait nulla facilisi.
<p>

Nam liber tempor cum soluta nobis eleifend option congue nihil imperdiet
doming id quod mazim placerat facer possim assum. Accumsan et iusto odio
dignissim qui blandit praesent luptatum zzril delenit augue duis dolore te
feugait nulla facilisi.
<p>

</td>
</tr>
</table>

</body>
</html>
```

In Figure 3.26, you can see how this code appears when viewed by a browser.

FIGURE 3.26

Top-margin, table-based navigation

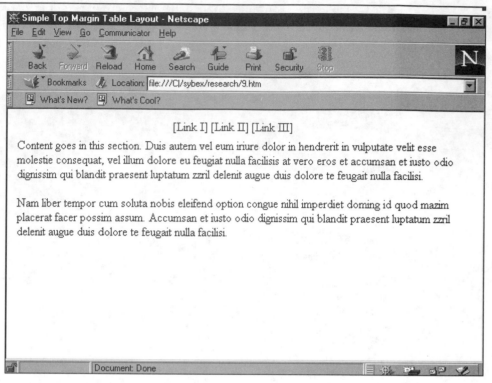

Frames Frames can also be used to achieve top-margin navigation. As with tables, there's a shift of focus from columns to rows. Within a frameset that is being used to create top-margin navigation, you'll use the rows attribute rather than the cols attribute. Furthermore, your HTML pages should be named to reflect the frame area, such as top.htm and main.htm instead of the right and left used in earlier examples.

```
<html>
<frameset rows="150,300">
<frame src="top.htm">
<frame src="main.htm">
</frameset>
</html>
```

The results of the above HTML appear in Figure 3.27.

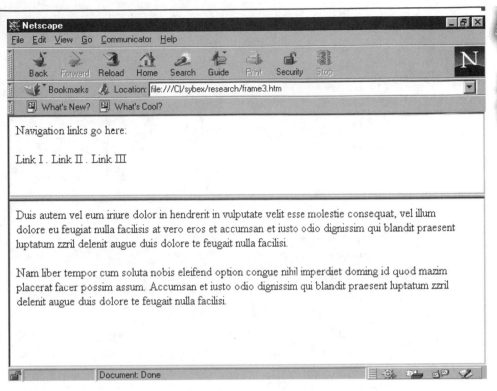

FIGURE 3.27

*Top-margin, frames-
based navigation*

Navigation links go here:

Link I . Link II . Link III

Duis autem vel eum iriure dolor in hendrerit in vulputate velit esse molestie consequat, vel illum dolore eu feugiat nulla facilisis at vero eros et accumsan et iusto odio dignissim qui blandit praesent luptatum zzril delenit augue duis dolore te feugait nulla facilisi.

Nam liber tempor cum soluta nobis eleifend option congue nihil imperdiet doming id quod mazim placerat facer possim assum. Accumsan et iusto odio dignissim qui blandit praesent luptatum zzril delenit augue duis dolore te feugait nulla facilisi.

Bottom-Margin Navigation

Perhaps the most standard type of navigation, bottom-margin navigation can be as simple as placing text links along the bottom of a page to more complex by using a table to control placement, or a frames-based layout to include a static navigation option.

Unless your right, left, or top-margin navigation options are text-based, it's a good idea to use a text-based navigation system along the bottom. The reason is that it addresses the accessibility issues that are so important. Furthermore, when a visitor is at the bottom of a page, he or she can simply use the text as an option instead of scrolling back to the first screen of the page to navigate the site.

Tables   To create a bottom-margin navigation with tables, simply reverse the order of the top-margin design:

```html
<html>

<head>
<title>Simple Bottom Margin Table Layout</title>
</head>

<body>

<table>
<tr>

<td>
Content goes in this section. Duis autem vel eum iriure dolor in hendrerit
in vulputate velit esse molestie consequat, vel illum dolore eu feugiat
nulla facilisis at vero eros et accumsan et iusto odio dignissim qui blandit
praesent luptatum zzril delenit augue duis dolore te feugait nulla facilisi.
<p>

Nam liber tempor cum soluta nobis eleifend option congue nihil imperdiet
doming id quod mazim placerat facer possim assum. Accumsan et iusto odio
dignissim qui blandit praesent luptatum zzril delenit augue duis dolore te
feugait nulla facilisi.
<p>

</td>

</tr>

<tr>

<td align="center">

[<a href="link1.htm">Link I</a>] [<a href="link2.htm">Link II</a>]
[<a href="link3.htm">Link III</a>]

</td>
</tr>
</table>

</body>
</html>
```

In Figure 3.28, you'll see how the navigation appears along the bottom.

What Every Web
Designer Must Know

FIGURE 3.28

*Bottom-margin,
table-based
navigation*

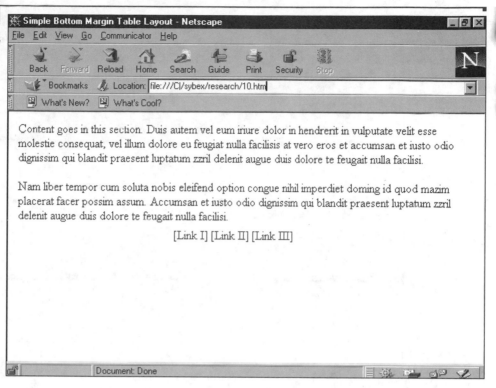

Frames By taking the top navigation frameset example and altering the row order as well as changing the file names to clarify, you'll create a static, bottom-margin navigation frame:

```
<html>
<frameset rows="300,150">
<frame src="main.htm">
<frame src="bottom.htm">
</frameset>
</html>
```

Figure 3.29 shows the results of the above HTML.

FIGURE 3.29

*Bottom-margin,
frames-based
navigation*

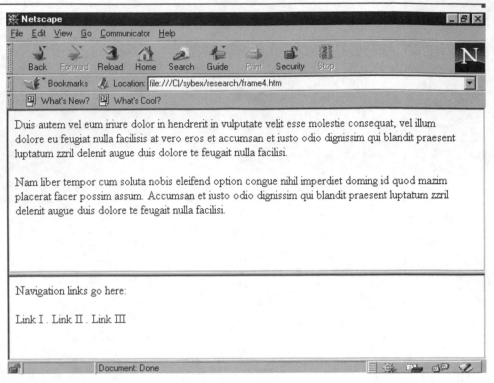

Combined and Ancillary Navigation

As mentioned earlier, one important navigation combination is adding text-based options to address site accessibility. But there are other combinations of navigation that are important. They include using media and text in any of the four standard margin options, or adding navigation in an unusual or unexpected place, as you can see on the Core Wave page shown in Figure 3.30.

Ancillary navigation includes additional intra-site linking and linking to related external sites. For example, in Figure 3.31, there are many pieces of media that are linked to other areas within the site, adding to the intrigue and unusual nature of the site. By adding ancillary options, you create a site that embraces interactivity more completely.

When linking to related, external sites, you support the material on your own site and provide the visitor with a complete experience. However, you must carefully plan when and where to place links because you don't want your site visitors leaving too soon.

FIGURE 3.30

*Center navigation
on Core Wave*

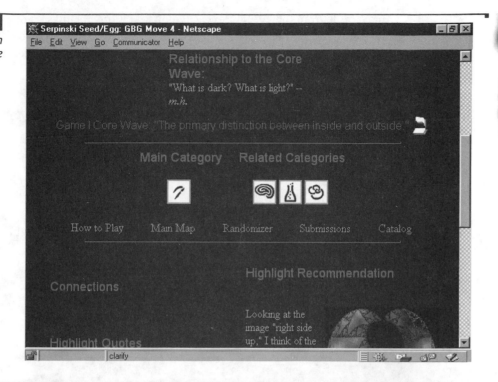

FIGURE 3.31

*The top-left circular
animation links to
another page within
the Core Wave site.*

An example from the *Tucson Weekly* demonstrates off-site links (Figure 3.32). While links are also provided within the articles, these links serve to enhance the reader's experience by providing information that is topically-related but tangentially-linked in the non-linear environment.

Navigation Media

The media you can use to enable navigation is fairly limited in scope. The following elements are considered standard options of navigation delivery:

- **Text**—This is the familiar HTML-based anchor that allows you to select a piece of text and hyperlink it to another HTML document:

```
<a href="about.htm">Go to the About Page</a>
```

- **Fixed graphics**—Whether appearing as graphical bullets, small metaphorical icons, or decorative buttons, individual graphics are hyperlinked by placing them within an HTML anchor. Note that the graphic code literally takes the place of the text shown in the text link example:

```
<a href="about.htm"><img src="images/about.gif"></a>
```

- **Image maps**—An image map is a single graphic with HTML code matched up to coordinates within the graphic's design. In other words, if you have a picture of a hand, each finger might be designated as a "hot" or linked section that, when clicked, leads to another area of the site.

Image maps are coded using two standard methods: server-sided, and client-sided. *Server-sided* maps rely on the server to interpret the code via a CGI program (see Chapter 24). This takes a bit of extra time to process. In recent years, browsers have been built that automatically interpret an image's coordinates if they are properly coded into the HTML. These are *client-sided* maps and are much faster and more elegant, as shown here:

home   about mark   products   events   contact

Here's the coordinate code example for a simple client-sided map:

```
<map name="marcmap">
<area shape="rect" coords="0,0,53,30" href="index.htm">
<area shape="rect" coords="53,0,162,30" href="about.htm">
<area shape="rect" coords="162,0,255,30" href="products.htm">
<area shape="rect" coords="255,0,327,30" href="events.htm">
<area shape="rect" coords="327,0,410,30" href="contact.htm">
<area shape="rect" coords="0,0,440,46" nohref>
</map>
```

- **Enhanced media**—Other methods of hyperlinking involve using a variety of media that perform the same function as text links or buttons but use enhancements such as animation or audio along with the link option. Media of this nature includes using Macromedia Flash or Shockwave (see Chapter 23) or JavaScript code (see Chapter 24).

Next Up

Metaphor, interactivity, new media, interface, navigation. All of these terms pack a heavy wallop for a single chapter's learning. If anything, that alone should impress upon you the true depth of what interface design is all about. You shouldn't feel overwhelmed, however, because as you work through this book, and reflect upon the sites you may have already designed, you will begin to see how these concepts fit together.

ON line!

Enjoy the Web sites from associated examples within this chapter:

- **BrainBug:** http://www.brainbug.com/
- **The Tucson Weekly:** http://www.tucsonweekly.com/tw/
- **Atomic Media:** http://www.hotcong.com/
- **Club Congress:** http://www.hotcong.com/congo/
- **Ramada Foothills:** http://www.desert.net/ramada/
- **Gadabout Salons:** http://www.gadabout.com/
- **Core Wave:** http://www.corewave.com/
- **The Weekly Wire:** http://www.weeklywire.com/

You will also see how you can begin to apply these interface design tenets when creating or redesigning sites, and how they will empower you. Interface design in its most simplistic definition is tying up the many parts of a Web site and wrapping it up into an attractive, useable package.

chapter 4

THE DESIGN STUDIO FRONT OFFICE

THE DESIGN STUDIO FRONT OFFICE

As the summary chapter for Part I of *Web by Design*, the Front Office is the place where preliminary information is gathered before moving into the vast and varied rooms of Web design. It is here that you pause for a bit, reading and reviewing the concepts and methods that make up the foundation of a good Web site. Each of the seven parts of *Web by Design* offers such a review, and each review has a corresponding section on the Design Studio Web site. The corresponding site for this chapter is called the Front Office.

You can reach the Design Studio at http://www.designstudio.net/.

This chapter pulls together the ideas and techniques you've studied in Chapters 1–3:

- What makes a Web site accessible
- HTML absolutes for designers
- The components of Web site interface

By using a combination of review, deconstruction, quizzes, and tasks, you'll refine and demonstrate the knowledge you've gained so far. Also, you can re-test your knowledge down the road, flesh out those weak spots, and pat yourself on the back for the things you've learned.

Accessibility: Review

Accessibility ideally means that the sites you build are useable by anyone regardless of geographical location, physical limitations, and technological restrictions. Whether you choose to make a site fully accessible depends upon:

- Your audience
- Your site's intent

For the Web designer, this choice is paramount. It's a serious decision that should be made because the designer is educated about the issues, understands the matrix in which he or she is designing, and seeks to make a well-thought-out choice regarding accessibility.

Main Concepts

There are primarily three influences and three issues that Web designers must understand and evaluate when designing accessible sites.

The Influences

The influences are generally considered to be technological issues that sway the methods of creating accessible design. They include:

- **Computer platform**—Platforms include the computer hardware and operating system; the three main types are the PC, the Macintosh, and UNIX.

- **Browsers**—Web browsers are the user interface software and components that allow individuals to interact with a Web site. We will focus on two graphical browsers: Microsoft's Internet Explorer and Netscape's Navigator. Lynx is the common text-based Web browser and will be frequently referred to throughout *Web by Design*. While most people access the Web, important populations such as the blind rely on text-based rather than graphic-based interfaces.

- **Design standards and conventions**—Whether a technique has been formalized as a standard or is so commonly used as to be a convention is less relevant than whether or not that technique is accessible. However, an understanding of standards and conventions can empower Web designers to make good decisions about very broad accessibility, such as reaching browsers other than the most popular ones.

The Issues

Accessibility issues are those concerns that must be addressed when designing accessible sites:

- **Readability**—In terms of access, readability is ensuring that no matter the what type of user interface (graphical or text-based), the information is available to the site visitor.

- **Context**—The purpose of a given piece of text or media must match up with the context in which the media exists. For example, an audio clip should be labeled so as to describe that its purpose is understood as being auditory rather than visual or computational.

- **Function**—Web sites often require input from a user. However, forms and other input methods are not always accessible. In order to provide accessible function, offering alternatives such as printable order forms or toll-free phone numbers can assist in making your site more accessible, and therefore more successful.

Page Deconstruction

In order to demonstrate the accessibility review highlights in action, we will look at the code from the Design Studio's Front Office page.

The following code sets up the page, with title and body information. The multi-column table used to lay out the page is included:

```
<html>

<head>
<title>The Design Studio by Molly: Front Office</title>
</head>

<body bgcolor="#FFFFFF" background="images/ds-bakr.gif" text="#000000"
link="#666633" vlink="663300" alink="#FFFFFF">

<table border="0" width="590" cellpadding="10" cellspacing="0">
<tr>

<!--begin left margin-->
```

In the following column, which is used primarily for visual design, you should include descriptive alt attributes within the image tags:

```
<td width="125">

<img src="images/dsh.jpg" width="112" height="102" border="0" alt="The Design
Studio by Molly Header ">
```

```
<img src="images/clear.gif" width="1" height="188" border="0" alt="spacer">

</td>
```

Another visually important space is added, with the `alt` attribute once again in use:

```
<td width="25">

<img src="images/clear.gif" width="25" height="1" border="0" alt="spacer">

</td>

<!--begin text area-->
```

NOTE

Using <font> tags fixes the size of a font, and doesn't allow for those with low vision to manually switch font sizes. However, browsers allow individuals to set default fonts to a larger size (Figure 4.1).

FIGURE 4.1

Default font size set to 22 points

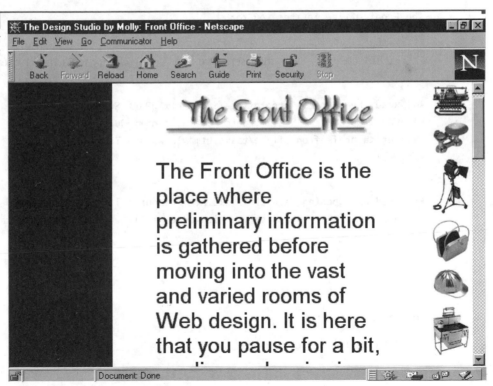

The third column, which includes readable text, is formatted using paragraphs.

```
<td width="320" bgcolor="#FFFFFF">
```

```
<img src="images/fo-hed.gif" width="300" height="100" border="0" alt="front
office header" align="right">
```

```
<br clear="all">
```

```
<font face="arial">
```

```
The Front Office is the place where preliminary information is gathered before
moving into the vast and varied rooms of Web design. It is here that you pause
for a bit, reading and reviewing the concepts and methods that make up the
foundation of a good Web site.
<p>
```

```
Primary concepts include what makes a Web site accessible, HTML absolutes for
designers, the components of Web site interface
<p>
```

```
The Front Office invites you to:
<p>
```

The link choices below are descriptive, explaining clearly what the link leads to:

```
<ul>
<li>Read the <a href="frontoffice/index.htm">Part Summary</a>
<li>Check out the <a href="frontoffice/quiz.htm">Quiz and Answers</a>
<li>Get <a href="frontoffice/tasks.htm">Tasks and Task Materials</a>
</ul>
<p>
```

```
Extended and updated <a href="links.htm">resource links and recommendations</a>
are also available to assist you with accessibility, HTML, and interface design.
```

```
</font>
<p>
```

```
<!--begin text navigation-->
```

```
<div align="center">
```

```
<font face="arial" size="1">
```

Text-based link options are made available in addition to the graphic navigation:

```
[ <a href="office.htm"> front office </a> ]
[ <a href="planning.htm">planning room</a> ]
[ <a href="color.htm">color lab</a> ]
<br>

[ <a href="space.htm">space place</a> ]
[ <a href="workshop.htm">workshop</a> ]
[ <a href="media.htm">multimedia center</a> ]
<br>

[ <a href="index1.htm">welcome</a> ]
[ <a href="contact.htm">contact</a> ]

</font>
</div>

<!--begin copyright and mailto-->

<div align="center">

<font size="1">

<i>Copyright &copy; <a href="mailto:molly@molly.com">Molly E. Holzschlag</a>,
1997, 1998</i>

</div>
</font>
</td>

<td width="25">

<img src="images/clear.gif" width="25" height="1" border="0" alt="spacer">

</td>

<!--begin navigation column-->
```

The navigation map not only includes an `alt` attribute description of the graphic itself, but also adds instructions to alert users there are text navigation options on the page:

```
<td valign="top" width="50">

<img src="images/navmapt.gif" width="50" height="362" border="0"
alt="navigational image map, text navigation available" usemap="#navmapt">

</td>
</tr>
</table>

<!--begin map data-->
```

Finally, each part of the image map offers `alt` attributes for descriptive purposes:

```
<map name="navmapt">
<area shape="rect" alt="go to front office" coords="0,1,49,47"href="office.htm">
<area shape="rect" alt="go to planning area"
coords="0,48,49,96"href="planning.htm">
<area shape="rect" alt="go to the color lab" coords="0,97,49,177"
href="color.htm">
<area shape="rect" alt="go to the space place" coords="0,178,49,243"
href="space.htm">
<area shape="rect" alt="go to the workshop"
coords="1,244,49,293"href="workshop.htm">
<area shape="rect" alt="go to the multimedia center"coords="0,294,49,361"
href="media.htm">
<area shape="default" nohref>
</map>

</body>
</html>
```

Figure 4.2 shows how the page looks in a standard graphical browser. In Figure 4.3, you can see that the text and links of the page are fully accessible in Lynx, a text-based browser.

FIGURE 4.2

The Front Office in Netscape 4.0

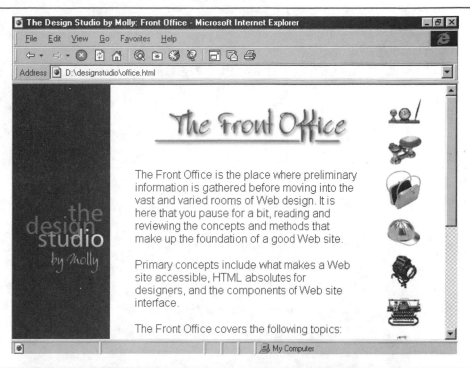

FIGURE 4.3

The Front Office in Lynx

Accessibility: Quiz

Please answer the following multiple choice questions.

1. Which of the following is *not* considered a computer platform:

   a. Macintosh

   b. UNIX

   c. PC

   d. HTTP

2. Web browsers are always:

   a. graphical

   b. cross-platform

   c. capable of reading standard HTML

   d. commercially sold for a specific price

3. A Web standard:

   a. remains consistent over HTML and Web products

   b. is a procedure that formalizes new product features

   c. is overseen by a committee such as the W3C

   d. all of the above

4. An HTML convention:

   a. is a feature that is not yet standardized

   b. helps keep HTML features from running amok

   c. is what allows a site to be accessible

   d. is what designers should always follow procedurally

5. Accessible readability is:

   a. the clarity of words on a page

   b. information that is available to all Web visitors regardless of interface

   c. a clear reference to a link or button's function

   d. a text-only page

Please answer true or false for the following statements.

6. The alt attribute can be used to help you describe a graphic.

7. The more links you have, the more accessible a page is.

8. Link descriptions should always say "click here" or offer some similar directive.

9. An accessible page has no multimedia such as RealAudio, or programming such as JavaScript.

10. If you're using an interactive form for product ordering, it's helpful to be sure that you have a printable order form as well.

Write out short answers to the following questions.

11. Name three groups of people that accessible design considers.

12. After having studied a bit about accessibility, what are your personal thoughts on the issue? How can you apply these thoughts and beliefs to your own site?

Answers to the quiz can be found on the Design Studio Web site at http://www.designstudio.net/frontoffice/ and at the end of this chapter.

Accessibility: Task

The task is to make a simple, accessible page with graphics and links. For this task you will need:

- A simple HTML page template
- Two graphics (a photograph and graphic header will do nicely)
- Two real-life URLs that you can link to on the page

You can find the ingredients for the task on the Design Studio site, in the Front Office section at http://www.designstudio.net/frontoffice/tasks.htm.

Follow these steps:

1. Open the template in your HTML text editor or editing environment (Figure 4.4).

2. Add the graphic header (Figure 4.5). Be sure to include a description within the alt attribute.

3. Write a paragraph and place two of the links within that paragraph, using descriptive, natural language.

4. Place the photograph on the page, again using an appropriate alt attribute description.

5. Add a "page next" and "page back" link option along the bottom for text navigation.

6. View the page in both a graphical and a text-based browser (Figure 4.6).

FIGURE 4.4

The template being edited in HomeSite

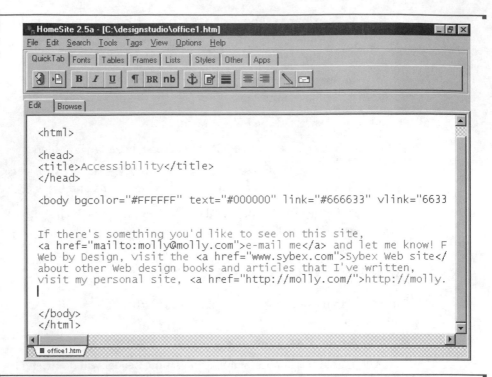

FIGURE 4.5

Adding the graphic header

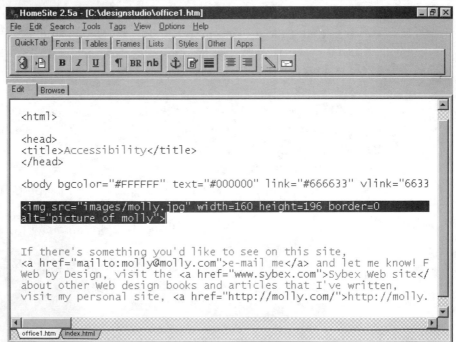

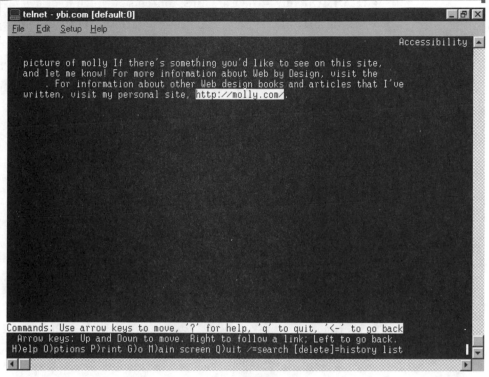

FIGURE 4.6

*The accessibility task
example in Lynx*

HTML Absolutes: Review

Chapter 2 is concerned with putting HTML practices that serve to enable Web designers into a concise and precise package. The following practices are highlighted:

- General HTML principles including tags, attributes, and structure
- HTML tools such as editors, converters, environments, and specialty programs
- Custom templates
- Future perspectives

Each of these practices and concepts help designers work faster, cleaner, and when combined, provide a matrix in which individual perspectives can grow.

Main Concepts

A synopsis of HTML absolutes includes:

- **Tags**—An HTML tag is what alerts the browser to a new type of information.
- **Attributes**—An attribute gives a tag a specific characteristic or set of characteristics.

- **HTML structure**—There are three concepts of which to be aware:

  1. Most HTML tags have an opening and closing tag component.

  2. Neatly organized pages enable you—and others—to navigate the code easily.

  3. Contained HTML makes it easier to write—when you enter a tag, also enter its companion tag (if it has one, of course).

- **HTML tools**—There are four types of HTML tools:

  1. Text editors. Text editors are native to the operating system of a computer and output pure text. An HTML coder must know the code in order to work within a text editor. Many coders prefer this method, feeling that they have more control over how the code is written.

  2. HTML editing environments. An HTML editing environment is software that has a text editor at its center, and adds power tools such as colors for tag identity, toolbars for common tags and attributes, table and frames wizards, and spell and syntax checkers.

  3. HTML converters. Converters take a technically prepared document from software such as a word processor or desktop publishing program and convert it into HTML.

  4. WYSIWYG editors. "What-You-See-Is-What-You-Get" editors are complete software packages. Using a graphic interface, you'll never have to touch the actual code. You place your text and graphics as you wish them to appear on the page, and the software processes the HTML for you.

- **HTML tag absolutes and page layout**—Chapter 2 points out the importance of certain HTML tags such as <html>, <head>, <title>, and <body> and their companion closing tags. Anchoring, text formatting, lists, and image tags are all discussed in detail.

- **Comment tagging**—Comment tags enable coders to work with long or involved documents with speed and accuracy. Comments help keep track of sections of HTML, such as header, body, and footer information.

- **Page identity, copyright, and contact**—By identifying individual pages, placing appropriate copyright symbols on a page, and ensuring that contact is easy for site visitors, designers add critical information for site visitors.

- **META tagging**—META tags provide a description and relevant keywords to pages with major databases.

- **Custom templates**—Creating site templates with information specific to a given site's design can enable numerous coders to work on a site with added ease. Custom templates also keep a site's design consistent because the main code information remains the same except where the designer chooses to deviate from that template.

- **Future considerations**—While the future is bound to bring many changes to the Web, and to HTML itself, one of the most important issues for Web designers is to understand is that they are defining a new medium. The work they do will have far-ranging impact on the future of both interactive media and global communications.

Page Deconstruction

Using the same Front Office page, you'll examine how hand-coded, structurally appropriate HTML looks. Notice the following:

- Tags are flushed right.
- Spaces are placed between certain groups of tags for readability and clarity.

```
<html>

<head>
<title>The Design Studio by Molly: Front Office</title>
</head>
00000000
<body bgcolor="#FFFFFF" background="images/ds-bakr.gif" text="#000000"
link="#666633" vlink="663300" alink="#FFFFFF">

<table border="0" width="590" cellpadding="10" cellspacing="0">
<tr>
```

Here's an example of comment tagging in action:

```
<!--begin left margin-->

<td width="125">

<img src="images/dsh.jpg" width="112" height="102" border="0" alt="The Design
Studio by Molly Header">
<img src="images/clear.gif" width="1" height="188" border="0" alt="spacer">

</td>

<td width="25">

<img src="images/clear.gif" width="25" height="1" border="0" alt="spacer">

</td>

<!--begin text area-->
```

```
<td width="320" bgcolor="#FFFFFF">

<img src="images/fo-hed.gif" width="300" height="100" border="0" alt="front
office header" align="right">

<br clear="all">

<font face="arial">
```

Standard paragraph structure:

```
The Front Office is the place where preliminary information is gathered before
moving into the vast and varied rooms of Web design. It is here that you pause
for a bit, reading and reviewing the concepts and methods that make up the
foundation of a good Web site.
<p>

Primary concepts include what makes a Web site accessible, HTML absolutes for
designers, the components of Web site interface
<p>

The Front Office invites you to:
<p>
```

An unordered, or bulleted, list:

```
<ul>
<li>Read the <a href="frontoffice/index.htm">Part Summary</a>
<li>Check out the <a href="frontoffice/quiz.htm">Quiz and Answers</a>
<li>Get <a href="frontoffice/tasks.htm">Tasks and Task Materials</a>
</ul>
<p>

Extended and updated <a href="links.htm">resource links and recommendations</a>
are also available to assist you with accessibility, HTML, and interface design.
<p>

</font>
```

Once again, a comment tag that helps to identify this section of HTML as the text navigation area:

```
<!--begin text navigation-->

<div align="center">

<font face="arial" size="1">
```

```
[ <a href="office.htm">front office</a> ]
[ <a href="planning.htm">planning room</a> ]
[ <a href="color.htm">color lab</a> ]
<br>

[ <a href="space.htm">space place</a> ]
[ <a href="workshop.htm">workshop</a> ]
[ <a href="media.htm">multimedia center</a> ]
<br>

[ <a href="index1.htm">welcome</a> ]
[ <a href="contact.htm">contact</a> ]

</font>
</div>
```

A comment tag to identify the copyright information:

```
<!--begin copyright and mailto-->

<div align="center">

<font size="1">

<i>Copyright &copy; <a href="mailto:molly@molly.com">Molly E. Holzschlag</a>,
1997, 1998</i>

</div>
</font>
</td>

<td width="25">

<img src="images/clear.gif" width="25" height="1" border="0" alt="spacer">

</td>
```

The graphical navigation is also identified using comment tags:

```
<!--begin navigation column-->

<td valign="top" width="50">

<img src="images/navmapt.gif" width="50" height="362" border="0"
alt="navigational image map, text navigation below" usemap="#navmapt">

</td>
</tr>
</table>
```

The map data is identified using comment tags as well:

```
<!--begin map data-->

<map name="navmapt">
<area shape="rect" alt="go to front office" coords="0,1,49,47"href="office.htm">
<area shape="rect" alt="go to planning area"
coords="0,48,49,96"href="planning.htm">
<area shape="rect" alt="go to the color lab" coords="0,97,49,177"
href="color.htm">
<area shape="rect" alt="go to the space place" coords="0,178,49,243"
href="space.htm">
<area shape="rect" alt="go to the workshop"
coords="1,244,49,293"href="workshop.htm">
<area shape="rect" alt="go to the multimedia center"coords="0,294,49,361"
href="media.htm">
<area shape="default" nohref>
</map>

</body>
</html>
```

Individual areas within this HTML are contained, keeping it neat and organized. Any coder could conceivably pick up where another has left off and know where to make updates and changes because the code is navigable, clear, neat, and clean.

HTML Absolutes: Quiz

Please answer the following multiple choice questions.

1. HTML was not originally designed to focus on:

   a. the text within a document

   b. the appearance of a document

   c. the functionality of a document

   d. the delivery of a document

2. Most HTML tags:

   a. are logical

   b. have opening and closing tags

   c. accept attributes

   d. all of the above

3. Which of the following software cannot be used to generate HTML:

   a. Allaire's HomeSite

   b. Microsoft FrontPage

   c. Microsoft Word

   d. none of the above

4. A relative link:

   a. links to a page within a site using the full address

   b. links to an external site using the full address

   c. links a point on a page to another point on that page

   d. links pages existing on the same server using an annotated address

5. Comment tags:

   a. use the <comment> tag to hide information from the browser

   b. don't use a special tag

   c. are helpful for navigating HTML code

   d. are necessary for all HTML coding—without them a page won't work

Please answer true or false for the following statements.

6. META tags enable a designer to set keywords.

7. Custom templates sometimes cause consistency problems.

8. Many coders prefer to code by hand rather than using a fancy software program.

9. HTML is a fixed language.

10. Web design is interdisciplinary.

Write out short answers to the following questions.

11. Is there a particular method of coding that you currently use? If so, what is it and why do you use it? If you're just starting out, which of the options in this chapter seem most appealing to you, and why?

12. Do you believe community issues are important for a Web designer? Why or why not?

HTML Absolutes: Task

In this task you will create a template using the code for the Front Office page. Follow these steps:

1. Copy the code by either typing what you see here in the book into your HTML editor, or by downloading it from the Front Office task page at `http://www` `.designstudio.net/frontoffice/tasks.htm`.

2. Remove the title.

3. Remove the header graphic.

4. Delete all of the paragraphs and lists, so that no readable text but all the code remains in the sample.

5. Add comment tags to guide the placement of title, header graphic, and text areas.

6. Save the file as `temp.htm`.

7. Re-open the file and follow your own comments and directives. If you knew what to do with the page, you did a good job.

Site Interface: Review

User interface is possibly one of the most overlooked issues in Web design, yet it is the point-of-contact between a site visitor and a Web site. This makes site interface a crucial part of design, and all aspiring as well as practicing Web designers should understand the main objectives of interface form. Chapter 3 covers the following interface concerns:

- The five features of interface design
- Web site structure in theory and practice
- Navigation methods and media

The learning involved when studying site interface is significant. This book addresses the issues in a concise method intended to put them on the desk of any Web designer, ready to be put to use.

Main Concepts

Here's a closer look at the concepts of interface design:

- **Metaphor**—Design metaphor is the visual representation of both the total and individual aspects of your site's components.

- **Clarity**—No element should exist on a page without a clear reason for being, whether it's technical or aesthetic. Clarity works to enforce metaphor by bringing any abstractions into the concrete world.

- **Consistency**—A user interface has familiar qualities despite the fact that the layout or presentation of individual pages might differ. Consistency is achieved by keeping metaphor strong throughout the site, ensuring that graphic elements are compatible, and adhering to fonts and color palettes uniformly throughout the site.

- **Orientation**—Where are you? If you're on a site and you get lost, chances are the designer forgot about some simple techniques that enable orientation. These include labeling pages via titles, headers, and footers.

- **Navigation**—How you get from here to there and back again is a critical part of how sites are designed. Navigation issues include the structure of a site, the location of navigation devices on a page, and what media is used to deliver navigation options.

Interfaces for new media involve:

- **Interactivity**—Web sites are ideally not passive. They demand action and choice from site visitors.

- **Non-linear environment**—The hypertext structure of the Web creates a non-linear environment. Web designers need to understand non-linearity in order to harness its power and really work with it to create interesting and unique, but still comprehensible, navigation options.

- **Site structure**—Individual pages that make up the structure of a site include the home page, the about page, content pages, the contact page, and pages for additional or specialized content such as multimedia, forms, and games.

Page Deconstruction

Once again you're going to use the same code you're becoming so familiar with, from the Design Studio's Front Office, this time examining it for site interface design issues.

```
<html>

<head>
```

The title is clearly labeled:

```
<title>The Design Studio by Molly: Front Office</title>
</head>

<body bgcolor="#FFFFFF" background="images/ds-bakr.gif" text="#000000"
link="#666633" vlink="663300" alink="#FFFFFF">
```

Using a table-based layout, we'll create a right-margin navigation system with left and top-margin headers:

```
<table border="0" width="590" cellpadding="10" cellspacing="0">
<tr>

<!--begin left margin-->

<td width="125">
```

The dsh.jpg header defines the site, and aids in orientation and clarity.

```
<img src="images/dsh.jpg" width="112" height="102" border="0" alt="The Design
Studio by Molly Header ">
<img src="images/clear.gif" width="1" height="188" border="0" alt="spacer">

</td>

<td width="25">

<img src="images/clear.gif" width="25" height="1" border="0" alt="spacer">

</td>

<!--begin text area-->

<td width="320" bgcolor="#FFFFFF">
```

The page header defines the page's purpose, giving it clarity and orientation.

```
<img src="images/fo-hed.gif" width="300" height="100" border="0" alt="front
office header" align="right">

<br clear="all">

<font face="arial">

The Front Office is the place where preliminary information is gathered before
moving into the vast and varied rooms of Web design. It is here that you pause
for a bit, reading and reviewing the concepts and methods that make up the
foundation of a good Web site.
<p>
```

Primary concepts include what makes a Web site accessible, HTML absolutes for designers, and the components of Web site interface.

```
<p>
```

The Front Office invites you to:

```
<p>

<ul>
<li>Read the <a href="frontoffice/index.htm">Part Summary</a>
<li>Check out the <a href="frontoffice/quiz.htm">Quiz and Answers</a>
<li>Get <a href="frontoffice/tasks.htm">Tasks and Task Materials</a>
</ul>
<p>
```

Extended and updated <a href="links.htm">resource links and recommendations</a> are also available to assist you with accessibility, HTML, and interface design.

```
<p>

</font>

<!--begin text navigation-->

<div align="center">

<font face="arial" size="1">
```

Bottom-margin text navigation not only speaks to accessibility, but the thematic concept of user choice.

```
[ <a href="office.htm">front office</a> ]
[ <a href="planning.htm">planning room</a> ]
[ <a href="color.htm">color lab</a> ]
<br>

[ <a href="space.htm">space place</a> ]
[ <a href="workshop.htm">workshop</a> ]
[ <a href="media.htm">multimedia center</a> ]
<br>

[ <a href="index1.htm">welcome</a> ]
[ <a href="contact.htm">contact</a> ]

</font>
</div>

<!--begin copyright and mailto-->

<div align="center">

<font size="1">
```

The copyright information and mailto command allow for clarity, consistency, and of course—contact.

```
<i>Copyright &copy; <a href="mailto:molly@molly.com">Molly E. Holzschlag</a>,
1997, 1998</i>

</div>
</font>
</td>

<td width="25">

<img src="images/clear.gif" width="25" height="1" border="0" alt="spacer">

</td>

<!--begin navigation column-->

<td valign="top" width="50">
```

The right-margin navigation makes use of an image map with client-sided data coded into the HTML.

```
<img src="images/navmapt.gif" width="50" height="362" border="0"
alt="navigational image map, text navigation below" usemap="#navmapt">

</td>
</tr>
</table>

<!--begin map data-->

<map name="navmapt">
<area shape="rect" alt="go to front office" coords="0,1,49,47"href="office.htm">
<area shape="rect" alt="go to planning area" coords="0,48,49,96"
href="planning.htm">
<area shape="rect" alt="go to the color lab" coords="0,97,49,177"
href="color.htm">
<area shape="rect" alt="go to the space place" coords="0,178,49,243"
href="space.htm">
<area shape="rect" alt="go to the workshop" coords="1,244,49,293"
href="workshop.htm">
<area shape="rect" alt="go to the multimedia center" coords="0,294,49,361"
href="media.htm">
<area shape="default" nohref>
```

```
</map>

</body>
</html>
```

Examine Figure 4.7, which is the primary navigation map for the Design Studio site.

FIGURE 4.7

*Design Studio
navigation*

The overall metaphor is a Design Studio, which has numerous rooms. The first is the Front Office, depicted by a pen set. This is a concrete metaphor, easily understood by most. The next section, the Planning Room, uses a scale as the metaphor. This is more abstract—the idea is that planning often means weighing issues.

The Space Place is represented with a purse. There's subtle humor there—at least for me—since I never have room in *my* purse, no matter how big it is! Humor is always a nice touch in metaphor. The Workshop is represented by a hard hat, which is also a ready metaphor. I've used a stagelight to represent the Color Lab. Without light, there is no color, so while also abstract, the metaphor is consistent. The Type Mill is represented by a typewriter, and the Multimedia Center is represented by an old, compartmentalized oven—again a humorous abstraction. The overall effect is clever, attractive, and clearly understandable and accessible with the text-only navigation available at the bottom of the page.

Site Interface: Quiz

Please answer the following multiple choice questions.

1. Design metaphor can be:

   a. a desktop with files

   b. concrete

   c. abstract

   d. all of the above

2. Which is not a method of ensuring consistency?

   a. Using metaphor throughout a site

   b. Ensuring font styles are consistent

   c. How navigation is arranged

   d. Ensuring that a mail option doesn't pull up a newsreader

3. Interactivity includes:

   a. user choice

   b. user passivity

   c. user activity

   d. answers a and c

4. Non-linear structures are:

   a. hierarchical

   b. experienced left-to-right, such as in a book

   c. tangential

   d. none of the above

5. Navigation should always appear

   a. on the top of a page

   b. on the bottom a page

   c. on the side of a page

   d. on one or all of the above

Please answer true or false for the following statements.

6. Tables and frames are common layout methods for navigation.

7. It's wise to offer text-based navigation along with graphical navigation.

8. A home page must always look the same as the rest of a site.

9. A book is considered non-linear.

10. Another example of interactive media is a computer game.

Write out short answers to the following questions.

11. Describe how non-linearity relates to the human brain.

12. Why is it important for some amount of linearity to be included in most Web sites?

Site Interface: Task

In this task you will create a series of three metaphoric symbols to represent an about page, a content page, and a contact page. You can select from the graphics found at `http://www.designstudio.net/frontoffice/tasks.htm`. However, you may prefer to draw or choose your own from other sources.

Follow these steps:

1. Choose one of the following site themes:

    a. My Home Page

    b. The Big Money Corporation

    c. Xeno's Skate n' Surf

2. Now select an appropriate set of symbols to represent each page within the context of your site.

3. Are the symbols concrete or abstract? Write a paragraph describing what you chose, and why you chose it.

Answer Key

The following key provides the correct answers to the quizzes in this chapter.

Accessibility

Multiple Choice

    1. The correct answer is D. HTTP is hypertext transfer protocol and is not considered a computer platform.

Continued

2. The correct answer is C. Web browsers are *always* capable of reading standard HTML but may not be graphical, cross-platform, or sold commercially.

3. The correct answer is D. A Web standard keeps consistency over HTML and Web products, is a procedure that formalizes new product features, and is overseen by committee.

4. The correct answer is D. An HTML convention is what designers follow procedurally. A convention might be standardized, but it can also be a problem in cross-platform design as it might *not* be standard. Conventions have nothing specific to do with accessibility.

5. The correct answer is B. Readability makes information available to all Web site visitors.

True or False

6. True. The `alt` attribute can be used to describe a graphic image.

7. False. Too many illogical links can confuse site visitors.

8. False. Avoid clichés and make link descriptions truly descriptive.

9. False. An accessible page can support technology, it's up to the designer to ensure that the technology is explained, or that the information contained within that technology is available via other avenues of distribution, such as a text document.

10. True. A printable form along with an interactive one keeps ordering options wide open.

Short Answers

Note that your answers may vary, but the main concepts described here should be touched upon.

11. Three groups requiring accessibility include international audiences, the blind, and the mobility impaired.

12. This question will relate to your personal experiences and opinions, there are no correct answers.

HTML Absolutes

Multiple Choice

1. The correct answer is B. HTML was originally designed to deal with text, functionality, and delivery of a document; the appearance of a document was not a primary concern of HTML.

2. The correct answer is D. Most HTML tags are logical, have opening and closing tags, and accept attributes.

Continued

3. The correct answer is D. Allaire's HomeSite, Microsoft FrontPage, and Microsoft Word can all be used to generate HTML.

4. The correct answer is D. A relative link uses annotated addresses.

5. The correct answer is C. Comment tags are helpful for navigating HTML code.

True or False

6. True. META tags can be used to set keywords.

7. False. Custom templates help eliminate consistency problems.

8. True. Many coders prefer to code by hand.

9. False. HTML is an evolving, changing language.

10. True. Web design is interdisciplinary.

Short Answers

11 and **12.** These questions will relate to your personal experiences and opinions, there are no correct answers.

Site Interface Quiz

Multiple Choice

1. The correct answer is D. Design metaphor can be a desktop with files, a concrete image, or an abstract one.

2. The correct answer is D. Using metaphor consistently, ensuring font styles are consistent, and the arrangement of navigation all relate to consistency in interface. A mail option should not pull up a newsreader, but this is a problem of clarity as opposed to consistency.

3. The correct answer is D. Interactivity includes user choice and user activity.

4. The correct answer is C. Non-linear structures are tangential.

5. The correct answer is D. Navigation can appear on the top, bottom, or side of a page, or in any combination.

True or False

6. True. Tables and frames are used frequently to lay out navigation.

7. True. Text-based alternatives assist with accessibility and clarity.

8. False. A home page can be different from internal pages, but the trick is pulling the design elements through the rest of the site.

Continued

9. False. Books are linear.

10. True. Computer games are interactive.

Short Answers

11. Non-linearity relates to the human brain in that memory is a non-linear process.

12. A certain amount of linearity is necessary in Web site design because most people have been exposed to linear processes and are therefore comfortable with them. Keeping some linearity in a site makes that site a more familiar experience for visitors.

Next Up

Now that you have a thorough understanding of accessibility, HTML style, and site interface design, it's time to move on to the site planning stage. The information you've learned in Part I of *Web by Design* gives you a greater ability to study how information is managed. Invariably, this will aid your planning—and ultimately the sites that come out of that planning—by providing you with insight into both the personal and global issues that go in to sophisticated Web design.

PART II

designing for success

chapter 5

PLANNING DESIGN

PLANNING DESIGN

If you build a house with no plan or design, your house doesn't stand much of a chance of long-term survival. This is even more true if you try to build that house in an unstable environment—the winds of change will rush in and knock your hard work down, leaving you exposed to the elements.

Careful planning and evaluation of your needs and the surrounding environment help guide you to construct a strong and safe home. Because the Web is a similarly unstable environment, the same level of care must be put into the planning stage of a site's development. The creation of a site plan—the blueprint of your Web site—means you have a much better shot at designing a site that will not only stand through the stormy weather, but survive and even thrive.

Your objective is to build a Web site that functions successfully today and looks toward the long-term future. One way to meet that objective is to make sure you've got a good plan. In this chapter, you will:

- Define your site.
- Find out just how your audience plays a large role in what—and how—you design.
- Prepare your long- and short-term site goals.
- Become familiar with and develop a site plan.

Site planning is as much a part of design as the foundational issues of accessibility, HTML style, and interface you've already explored. Before you can get into the nitty-gritty of literal design, it's wise to know what you're building, why you're building it, and for whom you are building it.

Defining Your Site

To continue with the house metaphor, defining your Web site is like deciding what kind of house you want—and where you want to build it.

The forms that Web sites take vary wildly. Some designers are working on corporate information centers, others are designing entertainment databases, newspapers and magazines, point-of-sales catalogs, artistic projects, and even online communities.

If you've been working as a designer for some time, chances are you have had the opportunity to design for any number of these, as well as other types of sites. You are well aware that knowing a site's type is imperative to design success. If you build a ranch house but your client wanted a Cape Cod style home, you're in trouble! So, the first step in defining your site is to determine what type of site you're designing, because each one is going to have unique challenges and issues.

The next question is where to put what you build. If the client bought an ocean-view plot but you felt it would be more fun to build the house in the middle of the woods, you're out of a job. Yes, I've stretched the metaphor a bit far—no one out there is going to be *that* confused or uncaring. But I want to stress the importance of why these issues need to be dealt with early on in a site's life. The issue of *where* will often be defined by your client; generally, it will be either on the Internet proper (a standard Web site), on an internal network (referred to as an *intranet*), or it may be in between—on an *extranet*.

ON line!

Here's some background on extranets:

- **whatis.com:** Check out this site for a good definition of an extranet, `http://whatis`
  `.com/extranet.htm`.
- **PCWeek Online:** This site has a great article on extranets, `http://www8.zdnet`
  `.com/pcweek/opinion/1111/11neteff.html`.

Types of Sites

Each type of site carries with it a unique set of challenges and considerations that you, as the Web designer, must address. Here's a look at site types and some of the apparent issues you'll need to think about.

Identity Sites for Corporations, Legal, and Financial Firms

Sites intended for corporate identity purposes tend to require the designer to be very specific in designing a look and feel that is consistent with the corporation's existing identity. This means working with trademarks, pre-designed logos, and following pre-determined color schemes (see Figure 5.1). Any developed Web site must work with pre-existing identities, yet have unique features that help the site to stand alone. The idea is to have the Web site enhance the corporate identity, make it easily available to any interested individual, and expand on activities in which the corporation is involved.

FIGURE 5.1

The MainStay Communications logo and identity must be preserved in the site's design.
`http://ybi.com/mainstay/`

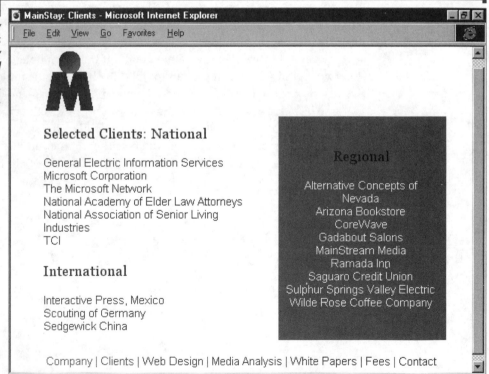

Entertainment Sites

Typically, entertainment sites such as those dedicated to film and games need to be a bit more cutting-edge than other corporate identities out on the Net. For the designer, this means being able to offer a range of multimedia, programming, and flexible design ideas. Figure 5.2 shows the Web site for Max Cannon's popular comic strip, Red Meat, a site that is as twisted yet as interesting as the strip itself. The designers use a variety of animation, unusual design metaphor, and JavaScript to appeal to Cannon's audience.

FIGURE 5.2

JavaScript, animations, and daring design on Red Meat at `http://www.redmeat.com/`

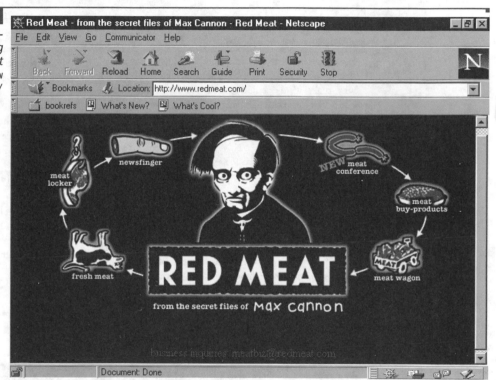

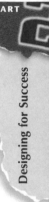

PART

2

Designing for Success

Newspapers and Magazines

Some of the Web's most popular sites are online publications such as newspapers and magazines. The big question when dealing with online publications is how to deal with the growing amount of data that begins to pile up. Designers have to prepare methods of archiving back issues and offering search options for the publications. Furthermore, speed is of the utmost importance here—so your tools are critical. In the case of the *Albuquerque Alibi*, archived articles can be accessed by selecting links under the Previously button (Figure 5.3). The paper is processed by a proprietary news processing program (Figure 5.4) developed by DesertNet Designs and Weekly Wire's CEO, Wil Gerken.

FIGURE 5.3

The Albuquerque Alibi keeps articles accessible.

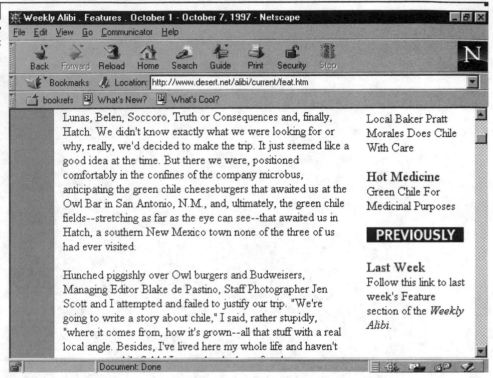

FIGURE 5.4

Time stamp on Alibi placed by proprietary processing software

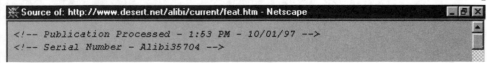

 ON line!

A descriptive list of helpful data management tools can be found at
http://www.gov.nb.ca/hotlist/wwwdbase.htm.

Point of Sales Sites

Providing a storefront on the Net brings up an important series of security questions such as how to keep credit card information safe, and ensure that transactions are private. Other issues include how to manage shopping carts and database-intensive activities. Shopping online often requires a visitor to be able to move from page-to-page, putting things in his or her virtual cart. The technology used on the Web site must keep this information straight. Plenty of footwork is required in terms of how sales-oriented sites are served to the public. Your designs will often be incumbent upon these issues. Figure 5.5 shows a storefront for the Wilde Rose Coffee Company on the Web.

FIGURE 5.5

Wilde Rose Coffee Company

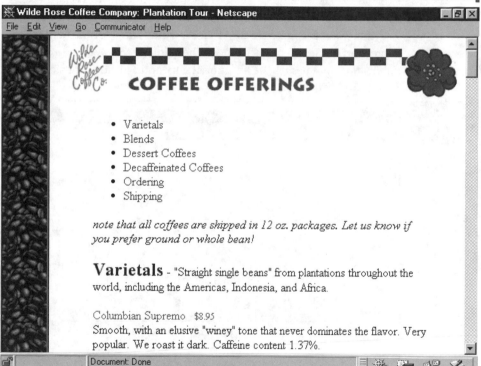

PART

Designing for Success

line!

To begin researching how to create effective commerce-oriented sites, visit ClickZ, an online advertising magazine with articles and resources on a wide range of Web commerce information, http://www.clickz.com/.

Artistic Projects

In many cases, art sites are challenged by issues of relating the meaning or intent behind a particular project to the audience. Oftentimes there are highly charged, extremely creative people involved in pulling off the more interesting art projects you find online, and it's important that you as a designer can communicate with the artist so as to be able to design a site that conveys the artistic meaning.

An especially exciting aspect of working on artistic Web projects is that you can often tap into cutting-edge uses of hypermedia. Remember the discussion about non-linearity in Chapter 3? Artistic sites are one of the best places in which you can be creative with the Web's environment. Joel Neelen, artistic director for Our House, an online artistic cooperative, has worked with other artists to combine online art with offline events, bringing the hypermedia and virtual world together into reality (Figure 5.6).

Other good examples are a Web zines, which allow for the written (and other media) expression of ideas. One such zine is The Brink (http://www.brink.com/), a controversial publication that pushes the limits of literary and artistic expression.

FIGURE 5.6

Our House brings the Web to the walls of a Belgian Coal Mine.

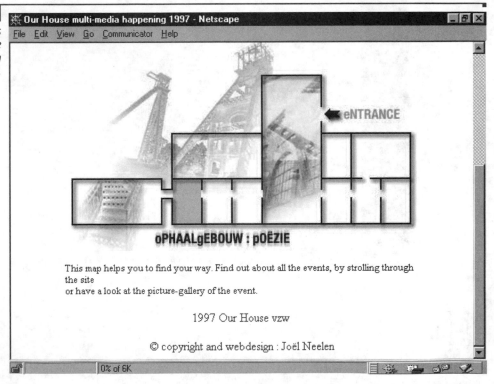

Community Sites

Building community is a growing issue on the Web. People are not only online looking for information, they want to connect with one another. One way Web sites are giving people with common interests, but diverse backgrounds and locations, a sense of place is through the creation of online communities. Designers are addressing this need by adding community-oriented features such as bulletin boards and chatrooms. A design challenge that arises is keeping the interface for the pages or gateways controlling these sites somewhat consistent. Talk Back on the *Tucson Weekly*, shown in Figures 5.7 and 5.8, is a good example of this consistency. While you can see from the screen shots that the interface design is unique, the integration of the BBS options into areas of the publication that contain items of interest aids in the ease of use. This, in turn, encourages Web visitors to enjoy these options with less of a learning curve. Furthermore, site designers can place such features in areas where controversial issues can drive the postings and subsequent responses.

PART 2

Designing for Success

FIGURE 5.7

Interactive community via Web-based BBSs on the Tucson Weekly

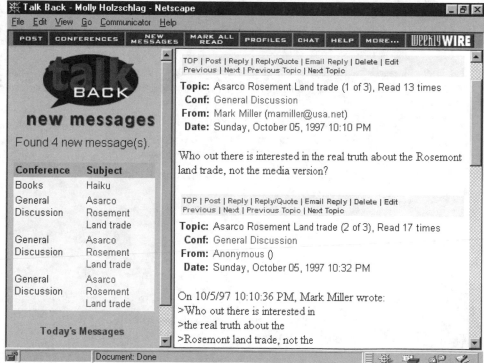

FIGURE 5.8

Java-based chat interface on the Tucson Weekly

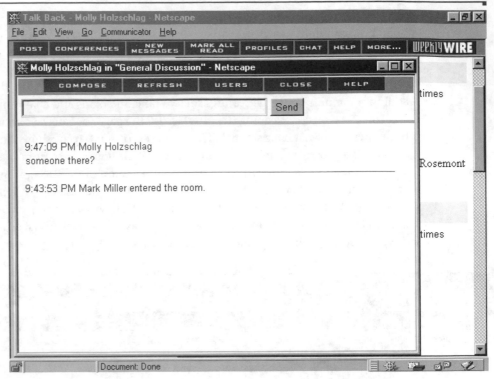

Another method that can help build online community is to use newsgroup or chat configurations that launch software right from the Web browser, such as Annex.Com provides (shown in Figures 5.9 and 5.10). BBSs and chats generally require the purchase and implementation *or* the creation of packages that will run interactive BBSs and chats online.

ON line!

The following companies offer chat or BBS software and demos.

- **Allaire:** Online conferencing from a respected developer of Web-based software. http://www.allaire.com/.
- **WebBoard:** From O'Reilly Software, http://webboard.oreilly.com/.
- **Focus:** This software comes from UK Web, known for its Web servers (such as Apache and Stronghold) and software, http://www.ukweb.com/focus/focus.html.

FIGURE 5.9

The Annex builds community using newsgroups.

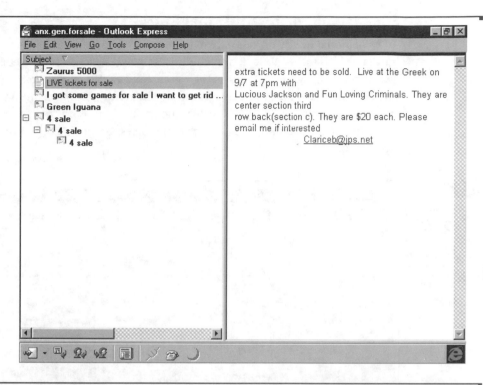

FIGURE 5.10

Chats on the Annex

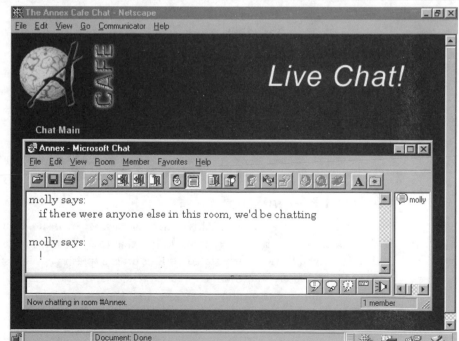

Educational or Institutional Sites

An educational or institutional site must be highly informational. For the designer, this translates into more subtle design choices. However, it does *not* translate into boring design choices. Figure 5.11 shows the New School for Social Research's Media Studies site. Designer Kayo Matsushita used a steady but gentle hand to create a site that is both attractive in design *and* very accessible. Such a site focuses on the content of the site rather than using flavor-of-the-month technologies. Graphics are well-thought out, and layout emphasizes important information.

FIGURE 5.11

Media Studies at New School

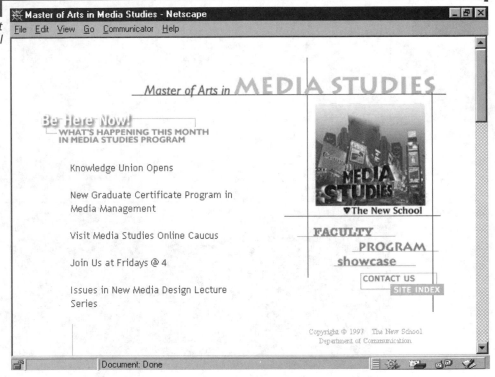

Personal Promotions

Some sites promote a person and his or her services. My own site, located at http://www.molly.com, is an example of just that (see my home page in Figure 5.12). I use a photograph and clearly stated options on the splash page, causing the viewer to know immediately that the site is related to a person. Photographs emphasize this point by continually reminding the viewer that the site points out the work of an individual.

FIGURE 5.12

Molly's home page

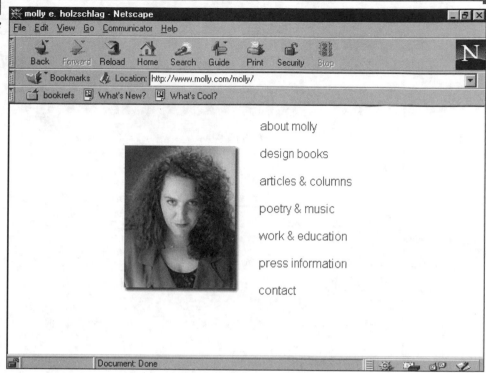

PART
2

Designing for Success

Search Engines and Databases

You're probably familiar with search engines. Large ones such as Yahoo, infoseek, and AltaVista help Web users to find information from distant locations on the Web. Smaller engines exist on regional or individual sites, allowing visitors to search that site for the information they're looking for. These powerful tools are often backed up by large databases of information. Databases are becoming increasingly more important on the Web, allowing for the storage of a wide range of information that can be made available to site visitors.

Desert Links is one such company which brings regional activities and resources to the desktops of Web visitors by categorizing the Web sites of regional businesses, organizations, news sources, and entertainment information. Individuals visiting Desert Links can search for specific information, or visit by area of interest. Figure 5.13 shows the search field on Desert Links, where visitors can type in their interest area and let the Web do the work of finding the information stored in the vast file structures that make up Desert Links.

FIGURE 5.13

Desert Links search field

Children's Sites

Sites designed for children are challenging because you must balance entertainment with education and reach the appropriate age group. The Web can offer a lot for kids, but it's important to keep in mind that there are Web sites that many parents will consider inappropriate for their children. How do you provide safe sites for kids? Visit http://www.rsaci.org/ and http://www.childsafe.org/ for more information on the special issues involved with safe sites.

Combination Sites

You will also notice combinations of the different types of sites described previously. For example, you might find a newspaper with community chatroom, or a corporate Web site where they are selling their products. There are even sites that combine community *and* point-of-sales, which can be extremely effective. One such example is Saturn Cars; you can visit their Web site at http://www.saturncars.com/. Their legendary marketing campaign builds on individual and community experiences surrounding the ownership of Saturn vehicles. The Web is a natural environment for such marketing strategies.

ON line!

Enjoy the following successful Web site examples divided up by type. You never know, you might work on these someday.

Identity:

- **Phoenix Home Life:** For an insurance company, this site is a *lot* of fun, `http://www.phl.com/`.
- **Buffalo Exchange:** Recycled clothing is not only fashionable, it's a culture, `http://www.desert.net/buffalo/`.

News and Magazines:

- **WORD:** One of my all-time favorite magazines, the articles are interesting and the site takes full advantage of the Web's hypermedia environment, `http://www.word.com/`.
- **Wired:** You can count on Wired to do the strange and absurd with design. Not everyone likes it, but all designers should go have a look, `http://www.wired.com/`.
- **Lumiere:** This is a fashion magazine, always worth a look for its bold design, `http://www.lumiere.com/`.

Entertainment:

- **MSN:** MSN provides a very personalized interface as well as a one-stop shop for entertainment, news, stock quotes, and custom hot links, `http://www.msn.com/`
- **Sundance Channel:** A beautiful Web site dedicated to an independent film cable channel, `http://www.sundance.com/`.

Artistic:

- **Arizona ArtNet:** This network of Southwestern galleries is a must-see for fans of Native American art, `http://www.azartnet.com/artnet/`.
- **Mythopoeia:** Breathtaking and cutting-edge photography by Suza Scalora offers fun use of the Internet for non-linear exploration, `http://www.myth.com/`.

Community:

- **The Well:** While most of the community activities are for members only, it's worth looking at the Web site. The Well is considered one of the founding parents of online communities, and has been in existence for more than twelve years, `http://www.well.com/`.
- **Planet Out/Out.com:** A global community for alternative lifestyles, `http://www.out.com/`.

Continued

PART **2**

Designing for Success

ON line! *(continued)*

Educational:

- **DIAL:** Education online via the New School for Social Research—one of the World's best universities, specializing in media, music, art, and culture, `http://www.dialnsa.edu/`.

- **Parsons School of Design:** Looking to become a serious student of design? Visit this impressive school's site, `http://www.parsons.edu/`.

Personal Promotions:

- **Mathew Cooper, Escape Artist:** One of the best personal sites I've ever seen, because it's really weird, `http://www.loop.com/~straitjacket/`.

Search Engines:

- **Infoseek:** This widely-used search engine is a favorite, with its simple interface, strong search engine, and news extras, `http://www.infoseek.com/`.

- **AltaVista:** Powerful beyond words, `http://www.altavista.digital.com/`.

Children's Sites:

- **The Yuckiest Site on the Internet:** Its physical home is New Jersey, but it offers some great fun for kids the world over, `http://www.nj.com/yucky/`.

- **Freezone:** This is a kid's community, `http://freezone.com/`.

You will probably work with a number of site types or combinations of types as a Web designer. The important thing to remember is that each site offers opportunities—and challenges. You will need to think carefully in the planning phases of each site so that you incorporate appropriate and interesting services to keep visitors coming back.

Site Categories

There are a three Web site categories with which you should become familiar, the Internet, intranets, and extranets. The Internet is where the most commonly found Web sites reside. Intranets contain Web-based sites that are closed to the population at large, used primarily by corporations. The newest breed of Web site is found on an extranet, a hybrid of public and private access. All of these site categories are accessed using a Web browser, and are built with HTML and other Internet-related technologies.

Internet Sites

Internet sites are those sites found on the free-ranges of the Net. An Internet Web site is defined by the following:

- It is publicly accessible.
- Its users can be anyone on the Internet.
- Its information comes from a variety of places—personal opinion, publications, and other resources.

The Internet-based site is the oldest and most venerable It comes in many forms, and can range in design quality from simplistic attempts (Figure 5.14) to sophisticated design (Figure 5.15). Internet Web sites are both frustrating and exciting because of the disparity in how they are designed, maintained, and navigated. The one thing certain about Internet Web sites is that there is no certainty! That's frustrating, because you can go from one site with great information that's poorly designed and managed, to a site that looks great but has no content. It's a mixed bag of tricks.

In the same breath, the free-range characteristic of the Internet is what gives it its potential, and its unique charm. The idea that anyone has a soap box, a place to express themselves publicly is an exciting part of our growing global culture.

Many of you reading this book are either currently responsible for the design and maintenance of Internet Web sites, or hope to be. While most of the following concepts are carried through to intranet and extranet design, they are especially important to consider when designing standard Internet Web sites:

- Internet Web sites should be available across computer platforms—in other words, *accessible*. No matter the platform you're using, you should be able to get to the information without any difficulty.
- Along with cross-platform compatibility, Web sites on the Internet should be viewable by at least the mainstream graphical Web browsers, such as Internet Explorer or Netscape Navigator.

NOTE

But what about all of those other people using Netscape version 1.0? For the designer, it's not just the browser type, but the version that matters as well. A good rule of thumb is to design mainstream sites for the version number one full number back from where you are currently. At this writing, Netscape and Internet Explorer are both at versions 4.0. Ideally, you'll design to support 3.0 browsers, although you'll vary this depending upon the site you're designing.

PART

2

Designing for Success

FIGURE 5.14

A simplistic but effective design

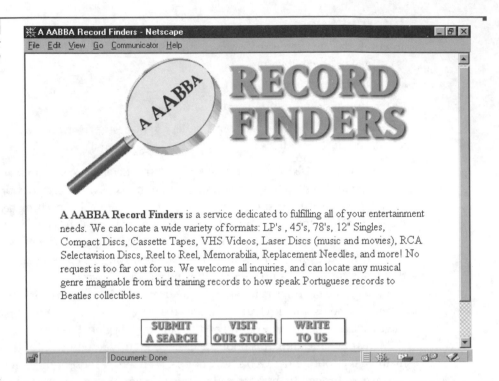

FIGURE 5.15

Sophisticated, contemporary Web design

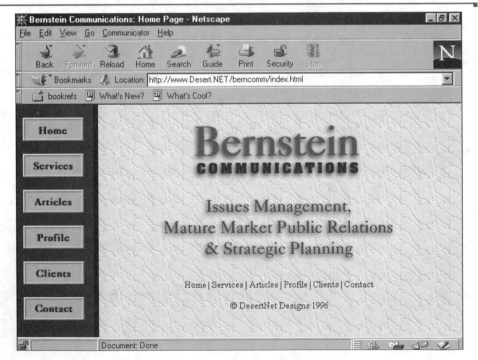

- Text accessibility should be available on all sites. It's not just a matter of making the information available to individuals who turn off their images. There are two groups of people who require text access—those without sophisticated equipment, such as might exist in underdeveloped, distant countries, and the blind. If you have concerns about how to do this, refer back to Chapter 1.

- Internet Web sites should be optimized for speed, meaning that the graphics and text should load quickly, as many people are still accessing sites with 14.4 modems. I know it's hard to believe, but it's true.

Intranet Sites

An intranet is a private, internal network used in businesses and industry and is proprietary in services and information. An intranet site uses Web technology, but access is controlled, unlike the publicly available Internet. Intranets may well be where the real money for Web designers is made these days—and they also may be why you're reading this book. Many individuals in a variety of positions within their companies are being handed the job of coordinating aspects of the company's intranet, and many Web designers are being called upon to do intranet sites large and small, such as the State of Connecticut's DAS Property Distribution Center, shown here in Figure 5.16.

Designing for Success

FIGURE 5.16

State of Connecticut intranet

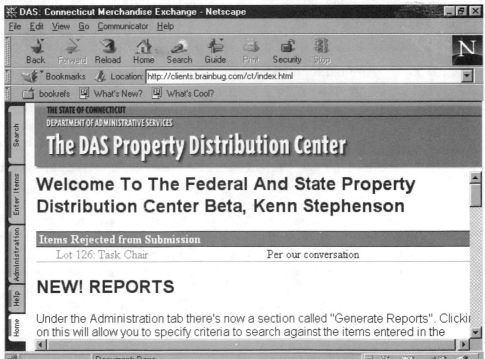

Whether you are a professional Web designer or a part of a company and have been given the job of working on an intranet site, you'll be aggregating content, creating documents in HTML, preparing graphics, and troubleshooting problems.

While a primary concern of intranet design is security, there is paradoxically more freedom for designers within the intranet environment. The reason for this is that most companies who are developing intranets have standardized hardware and software. In other words, everyone on your intranet is using the same stuff—which allows for greater design flexibility and accessibility.

 TIP

For more information on intranets and intranet security, see *Mastering Intranets* by Pat Coleman and Peter Dyson (Sybex, 1997).

Unlike design for Internet sites, intranet design allows the designer to:

- Make use of single-platform technologies. An example of this would be if your intranet uses Windows NT, you can freely employ native and third-party NT technologies such as advanced databases without worrying about cross-compatibility issues.

- Design to browser-centric specifications. If everyone is using Netscape Navigator, your job as a designer just got easier. You don't have to worry about cross-browser issues, and can employ Netscape tags and technologies without the fear that people won't be able to access the material.

- Design for higher speed connectivity. Local systems don't necessarily use modems. Very often, intranets operate at high speed, which gives you a distinct advantage in the design court. This doesn't mean that you'll throw what you learn in this book about graphic optimization out the window, but it does mean you can rest a little easier in terms of overall file size considerations.

One of the main challenges for the intranet designer is coming up with interfaces that can be used by anyone. People who have little experience with the Internet are motivated to be there because they want the entertainment, goods, and services available to them online. Intranets are different—some people in a company may otherwise have no interest in computers and technology, and are motivated because they have to learn how to use the tools their job requires them to use. You will be challenged to make the site very usable while still projecting a compelling design.

Extranet Sites

An extranet is the newest contender, and an interesting combination of the more common Internet and intranets. Extranets are:

- Semi-private
- Internal networks between closely-related companies
- Networks that contain information that is often proprietary and shared under non-disclosure or a spirit of trust

The "third wave" of Internet sites, extranet sites (an example of which is shown in Figure 5.17) pose a unique environment that essentially lies in between the free-range Internet and the privacy of an intranet. Extranets are basically the collaboration between industries and their related parties that have common interests and require the sharing of specific information.

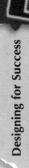

PART

Designing for Success

FIGURE 5.17

This password protected area is the entrance to an extranet.

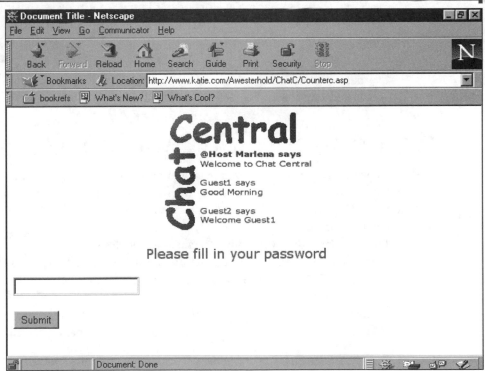

Let's say you own the world's largest manufacturer of Molly Hooks. Your hooks are used mostly in custom homes. You want to make information available to your corporate customers, as well as create forums where questions about Molly Hook products can be answered by tech support, suggestion boxes can be offered for customers to recommend improvements in the product, and customers can purchase hooks online.

What you specifically do not want is just anyone walking in and reading company data that is not meant for the general public. You also want to ensure that while your consumers get the best data, your competitors don't get their hands on information that lies within the company. Your primary concern is filling the needs of this very specific audience with Internet-based, accessible, interactive information.

> *"The extranet is a blend of the public Internet and the closed intranet . . . ."*
>
> JAKOB NIELSEN, Intranet vs. Internet Design

Extranets hold the following challenges for designers:

- While those accessing an extranet might be from the private corporate sector, they are not necessarily using the same computer platforms as the host company. Therefore, designers have to comply with standard cross-platform considerations.

- Similarly, an extranet developer can't know what browsers visitors are able to access. As a result, extranets have to be cross-browser compatible.

- Speed issues are once again in effect. While many variables are controlled with extranets, they typically aren't design variables. As a result, designers have to make sure their pages load swiftly and accurately over modems that might be slower than the higher technology of internal intranet circumstances.

Determining Your Audience

Understanding who it is that you're providing information for will guide *every* aspect of your Web site's presentation—from the way in which you design the information, to the voice you use when presenting that information, right on through to the visual design of your site.

But not every client that comes to you as a Web designer, or every project that crosses your desk, is going to clearly define the audience, much less look toward the ultimate goal of the site and how a Web site itself might alter the audience. Audience analysis is going to be your job.

Audiences vary, and this is important to bear in mind. Audiences for Web sites should first focus on a target or niche market, and then expand from that point.

> *"Don't fake it—know your audience, because they all have built-in BS detectors."*
>
> DAN HUFF, Editor, *Tucson Weekly*

For example, if the company you're doing a site for is interested in marketing a piece of software that is only available on the Windows 95 and NT platforms, you'll want to understand the needs of that audience in order to deliver the best information to them via your Web site. But say this company *has* plans to build for the Macintosh—you don't want to forget that these potential customers need to know about the upcoming product. Also, just because someone might be a primary Mac user doesn't mean that he or she won't want the software for a second PC, or a spouse's PC, or what have you.

The following three methods will help you define your audience:

1. **Begin by defining your main target market.** A main target market for a grunge rock music CD and cookie combo pack could be 20-25 year old white males in the U.S. and U.K.

2. **Expand out to include other potential markets.** Another target for the product might be women of the same age and status.

3. **Include other, peripheral markets that may in fact benefit from your goods and services.** Who else might enjoy a grunge rock music and cookies CD pack? Younger teens could make up the broad market, and possibly older individuals in their 30s and 40s.

However, using these methods is only the beginning. You will need to look at any relevant statistics or market research available and analyze them in the context of this method. If you've never done demographic research, and you really want to have the Web sites that you design achieve commercial viability, it's a good time to begin looking at quantitative statistics, as well as qualitative data that you, or an external marketing research firm, can provide.

PART

Designing for Success

ON line!

Here are several resources to help you do market and demographic research:

- **Facts on File:** You can find this vast resource at any good public or University library. It provides tons of information on everything from politics to medicine to human interest to trivia. For more information about Facts on File, check out their Web site at http://www.lib.ua.edu/facts.htm.

- **U.S. Census Bureau:** http://www.census.gov/

- **The Internet Advertising Resource Guide, Planning:** http://www.admedia.org/internet/planning.html

- **KnowX:** A free and/or low-cost public records search, http://www.knowx.com/.

- **Marketing tools and resources:** http://www.marketingpower.com/sources/default.htm

Let's examine a few case scenarios to bring you a little closer to understanding the job of determining your audience.

Let's pretend you have a magazine called the *Off-Beat Underground Music Review*, and your desire is to make your 'zine available to underground music lovers on the Net. Your audience is fairly defined, and when you consider it in terms of demographics, the people interested in such a site are typically young, single, and energetic. Even without much investigation, you know a bit about how you're going to design for this audience and even what colors and technologies you can use on the Web site: RealAudio for the latest music releases, video clips of interviews, and interactive games with celebrity guests.

Now let's say your friend Tom Tomaro, Ph.D., is interested in creating an academic, philosophical think tank where philosophers, spiritual leaders, and theologians from all around the globe join in to study problems of ethics and morality. While the individuals he is dealing with are probably mature and highly intelligent, they are bound to come from extremely diverse cultural backgrounds. How do you make these interesting but very different people comfortable in a shared environment? Obviously a more conservative approach will have to be used in terms of language, technology, and design.

The underground music site could be hip and sassy with lots of bright, flashy colors, wild fonts, and a variety of available Web technologies. Figure 5.18 shows a mock-up of this potential underground site. Dr. Tomaro's site, on the other hand, is going to be more sedate, as shown in Figure 5.19. This doesn't mean unattractive, but it does mean using more muted colors, less trendy language, and a standard of information delivery that will be available to the broader-based demographic.

Now, if you're not convinced yet as to the importance of audience, take a moment to visualize the underground music site with a conservative look and feel. Colors are muted, the emphasis is on text, and design styles such as fonts and art are not fancy or wild. Visitors will say "later!" And Dr. Tomaro's site with neon colors and trendy language? I think not.

> *"The web allows the audience to control the media. The flow of information is customized by each visitor, it is being tailored to his/her interest. Each visitor has a separate experience with your web site and in effect with your organization. No other type of media allows you to have this one on one relationship with potentially millions of visitors! What will your web site offer to visitors, how will you appeal to these visitors. Why should they seek out your organization on the web? Good web design answers these questions."*
>
> VbyDesign, http://vbydesign.com/

FIGURE 5.18

A mock-up of a flashy site in which frames, JavaScript, fonts, and animations abound.

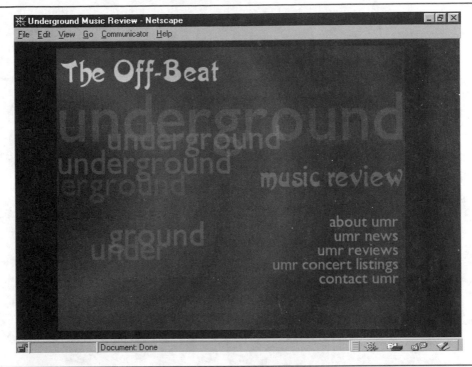

FIGURE 5.19

A more sedate look and feel

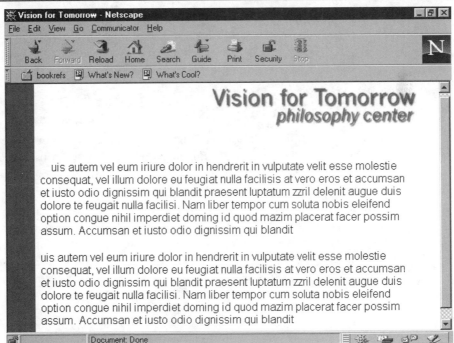

PART

2

Designing for Success

How to make Web sites *appropriate* will be answered by an analysis of your audience. Whether you use statistical data or informal methods, the bottom line is that you need to perform a thoughtful examination of that audience before jumping in to managing information and creating a design.

OFF line!

The following survey will help you get thinking about your audience and their needs:

1. Describe your current audience in detail. Include information such as:

   age

   gender

   financial status

   location

   marital status

2. Include other information that might be more specific to your produce, service, or information provision project.

3. If you're going to create a commercial Web site, what audience(s) do you see entering the picture that you might not have reached through your current methods? This is the peripheral audience we discussed earlier in this chapter.

4. If you're working on an intranet site, what would you describe as the current and future general user of the intranet?

Defining Short- and Long-Term Goals

My mother uses an old Yiddish saying that always rings loud and true throughout my life and work: "Man plans and God laughs." This is a humorous but succinct acknowledgment of the fact that although you can make plans, those plans are always going to be affected by the fickle and chaotic hands of fate.

But just as this must not prevent you from setting goals in your life, the knowledge that a Web site's goals may have to constantly adjust and re-adjust themselves should never get in the way of having those goals. Instability and change can actually be your best friends—readying you and your site to meet unstable demands with as stable, yet flexible, a structure as possible.

"Goals are more measurable than purpose, and will give you a clearer target . . . until you clearly know your destination, you can't develop a good road map, and you'll end up all over the place!"

DR. BARBARA STRAND, DocB's Web Design Clinic

Short-term goals are those that must be met immediately despite the long-term plans you might have in mind. Let's visit my friend Tripper for an example of such goals.

Tripper owns a skate and surfboard shop in Santa Monica, California. He has designed a very popular, unique type of skate wheel. His ultimate dream is to bring skate and surf fashions and gear to a worldwide audience. The long-term goal is to put a full catalog of his products on the Web, but the immediate need is to provide people with these skate-board wheels.

In this instance, Tripper's short-term goal is to provide one product, but the long-term goal is to provide a wide range of products for his audience.

Let's explore another more corporate scenario. Ms. Cosmo works for a company that makes a calibrating instrument for satellites. Her boss has just told her to find a number of top scientists interested in developing a better product for the company. The intent, or short-term goal, is to put up a public Web site describing the company, highlighting the specific project, and calling for resumes from qualified individuals. Ultimately, however, the company wants to foster a private forum for interested corporations and individuals worldwide that are developing new technologies for satellite calibration, creating a global and progressive resource. This would be their long-term plan.

As you can see by these examples, a short-term need is very often a piece of the long-term puzzle. The key is in understanding both, and then planning ways in which to meet them.

Because Tripper knows he will be adding an entire catalog around his primary product, he can create a tiered plan that first creates the pages introducing his company and his product, and a method of contact. As time goes on, the single product section can be extrapolated to include an entire catalog.

Similarly, Ms. Cosmo's public search for scientists can enable her end goal of creating a private community. From the submissions she receives via her Web site, a hand-selected group can be created, and a gated extranet created between the corporations associated with Ms. Cosmo's firm is involved with *and* the scientist group.

Some good and bad short- and long-term goals:

- A good short-term goal is to increase a company's visibility.

- A bad short-term goal is to make a million dollars overnight.

- A good short-term goal is to have a Web site to show competitive goals to clients immediately. If a competitor has a Web site, so should you or your client.

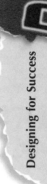

PART

Designing for Success

- A bad short-term goal is to rush a Web site *just* to keep up with the competition. Building an effective Web site should preclude just getting it out there as fast as you can.
- A good long-term goal is to increase profitability for your client or company.
- A bad long-term goal is to rely on a Web site for all of a company's profits.
- A good long-term goal is to better market and brand a product.
- A bad long-term goal is to expect that a Web site will fulfill all marketing needs.

As you can tell, balance is the name of the game here. Any goal that is too radical—such as make a million bucks overnight—isn't going to play. That doesn't mean it can't happen—hey, Arizona had a hurricane this summer! But odds are highly against risky thinking like that and it's also better not to put all Web marketing ideas into one basket. In short, all goals should be reasonable.

OFF line!

Make a checklist of your short and long-term goals. Goals should be realistic. The following points will help guide you through the process of putting together your own short and long-term planning:

1. What is the most immediate, pressing need that a Web site will fulfill for your project or company?
2. Do you have a particular product or idea that you wish to express to a public or corporate audience?
3. What do you envision for the future in terms of a Web site? A catalog of sales? Customer service? Private forums and information centers? A searchable database?

Developing a Site Plan

A primary objective of this chapter is to help you gather knowledge about any project and create a site plan. This plan will start you off by examining important issues such as audience and intent *before* you jump into project development and potentially create a hazardous site.

Here's a step-by-step look at a site plan. We'll use the underground music magazine as a theoretical example to help you through the process.

1. Define a specific site type (identity, personal, art) as well as category (Internet, intranet, or extranet) that you will develop a plan for, and prepare an introductory statement about the site.

Example:

The *Off-Beat Underground Music Review* Web site will be a standard Internet site. Its primary objective is to provide news and reviews about what's happening in the world of underground music.

2. Provide an analysis of your audience—current and anticipated.

Example:

Audience members include anyone on the Internet with an interest in underground music. Demographic studies show that this audience is dominated by Caucasian males in the English-speaking world (U.S., Canada, Great Britain) age 16-26 who are single and come from middle to upper-middle-class families. A secondary audience includes Caucasian men and women between the ages of 26-40 who are single, married, or in non-traditional relationships. These individuals are in the middle to upper-middle-class.

3. Is the site cross-platform compatible? Is it cross-browser compatible? Or will you be able to take advantage of platform-specific technologies?

Example:

The *Off-Beat Underground Music Review* will be cross-platform and cross-browser compatible from Netscape and IE versions 3.0 and above. It will not take advantage of platform or browser-specific technologies other than those conventionally used with these browsers, such as table-based layouts, GIF animations, JavaScript, and font styles.

4. Provide an overview of short- and long-term goals for the site.

Example:

The immediate, short-term goal of this project is to make the current and future issues of the publication available on the Web site.

PART

Designing for Success

Long-term goals include providing an online catalog, chat and BBS offerings to underground music fans, and eventually, live events via RealAudio and RealVideo.

By using these steps, you can get your feet on terra firma and get ready for the next step—dealing with the actual content.

Next Up

You know the type of site you're building and the considerations those types bring up. You've evaluated your audience and have a clear idea of where the site project is today, and where it needs to go. You've even got a plan. You're ready to start adding the details to your metaphoric house. Chapter 6 will help you build on the planning rendered here by focusing on how content is acquired, re-purposed, modified, and created for the Web.

chapter 6

INFORMATION MANAGEMENT

INFORMATION
MANAGEMENT

How you design and manage information is going to help determine the success of your Web site. Whether you're designing for the Web-at-large or for an intranet or extranet, the gathering, placement, and maintenance of the information you provide is one of the largest challenges you will face as a designer. Visitors to a site require your expertise to empower their experience by providing the information and services they are after in an efficient—and timely—manner.

Lack of organization in the foundational stages of a site's plan is precisely why so many Web sites are a confusing rather than pleasant experience for visitors. The Web is filled with poorly organized sites due to a lack of experience on the designer's part; no understanding of audience, intent, and the Web environment; and an inability to anticipate growth. All of these pitfalls can be avoided by learning logical skills that address the management issues that a Web site demands.

A good place to begin is to organize the information you need by preparing a format to fit the data you gather into. This forces you to look closely at your goals, your audience, and to try to understand how to fit your information into a hypermedia environment; remember you examined that in detail in Chapter 3.

This chapter will help you build a powerful foundation from which to manage information and look ahead to the design and implementation of your intended site. This includes learning why certain writing styles will enhance or detract from the intent of your site and how to put the information you've collected so far into a literal example using a storyboard or site map.

Key issues in this chapter include:

- Selecting content
- Re-purposing content for the Web
- Writing for the Web
- Preparing a storyboard or site map

Some might argue that this isn't Web design. You're looking for the meat-and-potatoes of design work: graphics, typography, layout. You'll get plenty of that later in this book, so think first before you feel compelled to rush through the planning and information management stages of a site's design.

> *"As important as the visual aspects, there's also the more abstract ones such as navigation, structuring of content, use of language, and other media in support of communicating ideas."*
>
> ALAN RICHMOND, The Web Developer's Virtual Library

Yes, great art can be made in a creative frenzy, but refined art takes a combination of practice, planning, skill, *and* creative insight.

Selecting Content

Content comes from two primary sources. It can be culled from current information that you have, such as brochures, catalogs, pamphlets, company reports, advertising, and marketing campaigns, or it can be created from scratch.

Selecting content is an important issue to consider when preparing to plan your site. The need for written content to be generated by you or your team is going to almost undoubtedly exist, whether it's to create entire pages of information or write introductory paragraphs and comments that help make the site flow better.

By analyzing what content you *do* have, you give yourself a viable starting point for the management of that content.

Survey of Current Content

Begin content selection by collecting (or having your client collect) the content that is available. At this stage of the game, more is better than less—you can throw things out later that aren't workable. Next, evaluate that content in terms of the goals and audience you defined in the previous lessons. What will be appropriate for the short term? The long term? What is current and accurate for your audience of today, and what might you have to alter or expand in order to reach other audiences that will be using your site?

Answer the following questions in order to prepare your content for the Web.

1. What is the primary intent of the Web site?

Possibilities:

To sell a specific product, to provide customer service, to allow company access to financial data, to provide a search center, to offer entertainment, to provide a news service

Example:

Quire's Classical Music Company's primary intent is to sell classical music CDs, tapes, and sheet music on the Web. The company has worked out of a warehouse in Hoboken, New Jersey, for 25 years, offering mail-order services only. The idea of a global, online market is attractive because it can exponentially expand Quire's point-of-sales activities.

2. Describe the current material you have, if any, in detail.

Possibilities:

Brochures, annual reports, press releases, past advertising, resumes, financial data

Example:

Quire's currently has a quarterly catalog available on newsprint. The catalog uses very few photographs or graphics, and is produced in black and white. The inventory from the catalog will be the primary content of the Web site. Ancillary materials include:

- Company overview
- Ordering methods
- Shipping information
- Special corporate deals
- Sales and contact information

3. Does your current material address that intent? If so, what do you have that fits well? What doesn't?

Example:

All of the current material can be used; however, most of the information is not graphical. There are some photographs available, and the company logo could stand being updated. So while the current material is fine for text resources, a good deal of work will have to go into creating a more visually-appropriate design for the Web.

4. What material already in existence is missing from what you have collected?

Possibilities:

All material that you'll need for the site's development should be re-checked to ensure that nothing has been overlooked that could be useful on the Web site.

Example:

Artist profiles and photographs are sent regularly to Quire's. Obtaining this information would be a terrific addition to the Web site.

By answering these questions thoroughly, you'll know what you have and what you need to throw away. Set the material you want to use aside as you focus on what you'll need to create.

Writing for the Web

Once you've decided what material you need to develop, it's important to take a close look at what goes in to the art of writing for the Web. There are several reasons why writing for the Web is different than standard expository.

- Attention span on the Web is short—therefore, your copy must get to the site's point, the intent, as fast as possible.
- Audiences tend to be diverse. From a readability standpoint, copy must be clear and concise.
- Visually, Web space is small and restrictive. Sentences, paragraphs, and pages should be kept short. In Figure 6.1, designer Mark Prince's Web Thing site shows how the use of bursts of text keep the reading load light but the message clear.
- Just as a graphic look and feel can attract or repel visitors, so can a site's voice. The right voice can make or break the success of a site.

FIGURE 6.1

Short bursts of text are easier to read.

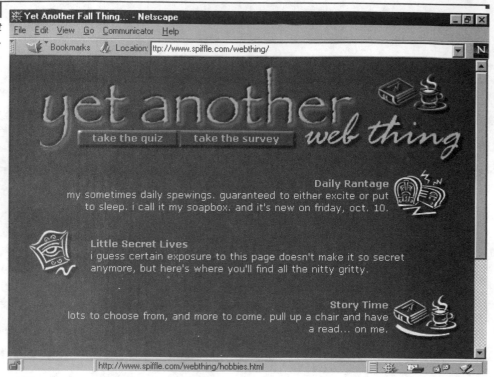

OFF line!

Here's a trick that well-known electronic journalist Brock Meeks (Wired Magazine, MSNBC) taught in an online journalism class:

If you want an example of the kind of writing that works well on the Web, buy a copy of USA Today and the New York Times. Find several articles on the same subject, and study the treatment. While the Times is invariably going to give you more depth, USA Today is going to bullet-point, caption, and pared-down information.

Guess which paper's style is more appropriate for the Web? USA Today. I know, it's a scary thought! But try it—the lesson was an extremely valuable and lasting one.

A site's value is likely to be found in its words. Therefore, it's imperative to recognize that words are as much a part of design as any other component—graphics, programming, or multimedia.

Intent

Imagine yourself as the audience for a moment, visiting our surfer friend Tripper's Web site from Chapter 5. You stumbled upon it because a Web magazine you were reading had a link advertising cool new skate wheels, and you followed it. Now you can't figure out where you are. You see lots of cool colors and you dig the unusual fonts, shapes, and surf music coming through your computer's speakers. But you start looking around the site and you can't find anything that explains what the site is about. You get frustrated, and you leave.

Poor Tripper has failed to express his site's intent—to sell you special skate wheels—and he's failed to get you to the information as fast as possible.

Knowing the intent of your site is the next step in developing specific site goals. Tripper *knew* the goal was to sell his special wheels. What he didn't do was take that to the next level and *tell* you in clear, concise terms that his site's intent is to do just that.

Know that intent, and let the audience know it too. Tripper would have saved himself a lot of trouble if he had done his homework and made his intent clear on the home page, as shown in Figure 6.2.

PART 2

Designing for Success

FIGURE 6.2

Tripper's intent is clear

Tripper would have kept you there, and probably sold you some wheels. Don't let your visitors skate off—express the intent clearly and right away.

Clarity

You'll remember clarity from your study of interface. Clarity plays a significant role in the issue of effective Web site writing. It's your job—not the audience's—to explain what your site is offering and herd visitors right to the meat of the matter.

Yes, you can have fun with language, but always be sure that your language makes sense—if not to the general public, at the very least to your audience!

Remember Ms. Cosmo? Her site is entitled: *The Planetary Consortium of Geo and Astrophysicists Satellite Calibration Procurement Center*. I might not know exactly what this means, but I'm sure the people it's intended for do! That's what counts.

Another site, entitled Quire's Classical Music, is set up like this:

Anyone who visits this site, and understands English, will have no trouble whatsoever knowing what the site is about, and where to go. The information is *clear*. The intent is *clear*. No muss, no fuss, just the nitty-gritty.

Precision

Web visitors don't want to wade through long paragraphs and endlessly scrolling pages—it's important to keep sentences, paragraphs, and pages short. Bulleted or numbered lists are helpful to isolate ideas as well as create plenty of visual space; they keep things very clean and simple. Figure 6.3 shows a page from Ms. Cosmo's Planetary Consortium page. Notice that resources are organized in an easy-to-read, bulleted list. Web visitors will appreciate being able to get to the information they need quickly and easily.

> *"Skimming instead of reading is a fact of the Web and has been confirmed by countless usability studies. Web writers have to acknowledge this fact . . ."*
>
> JAKOB NIELSEN, Alertbox, Writing for the Web

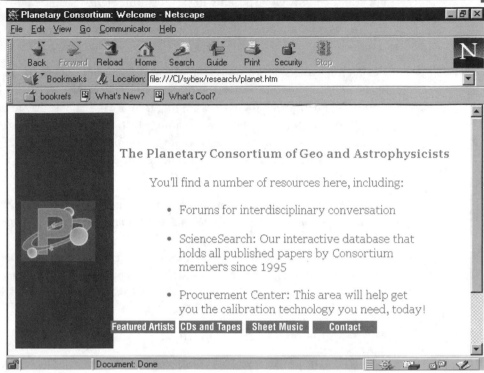

FIGURE 6.3

Bulleted lists help keep selections simple.

Voice

A Web site should not read like a brochure, a simple advertisement, or a printed catalog. With the exception of areas of sites that provide detailed information such as white papers, financial reports, employee data, and the like, the pages with which your site visitors interact will be presented quite differently.

> *" . . . the pages that seem to be the most successful are those that use a 'bursty' style. Short, factual, well-written, prose with interesting links seems to attract the biggest audience."*
>
> Guide to Web Style, Sun Microsystems, Inc.

Speak to your audience in a voice that they'll be comfortable with. Tripper's site can have a passage that reads:

Hey all you dudes and dudettes! Tripper's in town and he's got the best gear around. Ready to make some sparks? That's cool, surf n' click on over to Tripper's Gear o' Rama for all that's rad.

But could you imagine speaking to Consortium scientists this way?

Hey all you most excellent Astrophysicists! Nebula Calibration is havin' a Calibration Celebration. Jet on over to the Calibration Station for all that rocks in the universe.

Well, it might be good for a moment of comic relief, but I doubt too many are going to find it amusing for long. Besides, consider that the Consortium is a worldwide organization. Even if Tripper's audience is coming from Australia, it's okay to use slang with them—it's part of the ambience. But on a high-tech site that caters to scientists from around the globe, this sort of thing is bound to confuse.

I'm going to switch it around to make my point especially clear. Here's some copy for the Consortium:

Welcome to The Planetary Consortium of Geo and Astrophysicists. The Consortium is an interactive communications center for the global exchange of new and relevant information in the scientific community.

There are several new areas to be aware of, including the resumé newsgroup. Newcomers should take advantage of this area to upload their current resumés and any other current activities of interest to Consortium members. We also now offer an annotated help file, which can be reached by following the "help" link below.

And here's the same voice used for Tripper:

Welcome to Tripper's Skate and Surf. Skate and Surf's current objective is to promote Tripper- Wheels, a patented skate wheel for today's active skater. In due time Tripper's expects to add a full-service catalog offering the latest in skate and surf fashions and relevant equipment.

Please be sure to visit our new get-to-know-you area. Upload your current activities or any other items of interest to skate and surf enthusiasts. Tripper's has a new help area, available by following the link marked "help," found at the bottom of your computer screen.

Ho, hum! Skater and surf kids hanging around through that? Unlikely. It's clear, but it is *boring* to the faster audience that Tripper's is bound to draw.

Appropriate is the word to remember.

ON line!

One of my favorite examples of voice on the Web can be found at the M&Ms Web site at `http://www.m-ms.com/`.

Copyediting

This one is straightforward. There is nothing more ugly than an error-filled Web site. Even if people don't consciously notice the errors, a sense of unprofessional presentation slips through.

Some common errors:

- **Spelling**—Be sure that all words are spelled properly.
- **Contractions**—One mistake I see all the time that starts me frothing at the mouth is the misuse of "its" and "it's." Remember, "its" is the possessive, "it's" is the contraction of the two words "it" and "is." Be especially careful with this type of grammatical error—it really can shine an unflattering light on an otherwise well-thought-out Web site.
- **Punctuation**—Missing commas, periods, or inconsistent use of punctuation can be very disconcerting.
- **Grammar**—Check your work! Is it well written? Can you tell? As an author I can tell you from experience that even trained professional writers make a *lot* of mistakes. That's why we have editors.
- **Typographical errors**—Even if you are a good writer and you've worked hard to make your copy look good, it's possible you've made some typos here and there, or used spaces poorly.

> *"Make your text clear, concise, and to the point. Most Internet users are well educated. Misspelled words and incorrect usage can make you look like you don't care."*
>
> SONIA LYRIS AND DEVIN BEN-HUR, *Seven Rules for Highly Effective Web Pages*

If you have concerns about the quality of the writing, hire a professional writer. If you want to ensure that your copy is clean, hire a copyeditor. This is not something you can skimp on if you want your sites to be truly professional.

Re-Purposing Content

Whether your primary information is culled from existing material or created fresh, the bottom line is that it's going to have to be technically re-purposed for use on your Web site. Re-purposing, in the context of this discussion, is taking content from its native form and converting it into workable, digital formats.

Content will come in a variety of formats. Some common ones include:

- Print documents
- Word-processed documents

- Spreadsheets

- Quark or Pagemaker files (common in the news and publishing industry)

- EPS files (common in high-end graphics production)

- TIFF, PCX, BMP, or other bitmapped graphics not appropriate for Web use

Bear in mind that while electronic documents might *seem* to be a better method—re-purposing them for the Web can cause technical difficulties. One such difficulty relates to platform. Say you're working on a PC platform, but your client's data is all prepared on the Macintosh. While some electronic files are readable by your PC, that's only true if they are transferred electronically. Your PC won't read a Macintosh disk (although a Macintosh disk will read a PC).

You can get around this problem by clearly communicating your preferred electronic formats. If you can't find common ground, default to high-quality print outputs, which you can use to scan or type the information directly into the site.

Here are some basic suggestions to get around technical re-purposing of electronic documents:

- Have all graphics and text saved to separate documents.

- Ask that copy is presented in either plain text, or a format that you can work with on your platform. Again, default to print if you can't find common ground.

- If you're getting graphics in electronic format, try to get the highest quality files available. This means uncompressed files—you'll handle the size reduction and compression later on.

There's an acronym you've probably seen around—GIGO. It means *garbage in, garbage out*. Start with the best stuff, and end up with a higher quality product all around.

Storyboarding and Site Mapping

The next critical step is to create a representation of your site. There are two commonly used methods to do this, storyboarding and site mapping. *Storyboarding* is a method drawn from the production phases of other media, such as film, animation, and television. Storyboarding is the act of drawing out the literal plan of your site, page by page. It's especially applicable in terms of setting up a nice flow of information, much like the figures I demonstrated in Chapter 3, during the discussion of interactivity.

> *"If you have only a hazy idea of how one section of your site relates to other areas, if you have no comprehensive narrative or clear sense of organization, your readers will know it soon enough, and most of them will leave in pursuit of better organized material."*
>
> LYNCH AND HORTON, Authors, *Yale C/AIM Web Style Guide*

An increasingly popular method of organizing your site is by creating a *site map*. A site map looks much like a family tree, showing the levels and sub-levels of a site. A top-level would be the main content pages, such as the home page, and any other pages you determine should sit on that level. Some people place introductory content and contact pages on that level, others prefer to drop such pages down to the next level (a sub-level). All subsequent pages that break off from these pages are considered sub-levels. Site maps can be created in a number of ways, including using a shareware program such as CLEARWeb, shown in Figure 6.4, a proprietary program such as Visio, shown in Figure 6.5, creating an outline in Word or another word processor, or drawing the map by hand.

ON line!

For more information on site-mapping tools, visit:

- **Visio:** `http://www.visio.com/`
- **CLEARWeb:** `http://www.clearweb.com/`

PART 2

Designing for Success

FIGURE 6.4

Site mapping with CLEARWeb

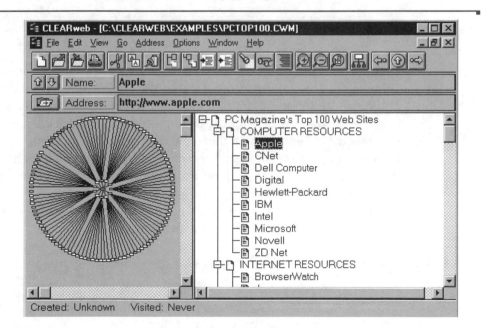

FIGURE 6.5

Visio's home page

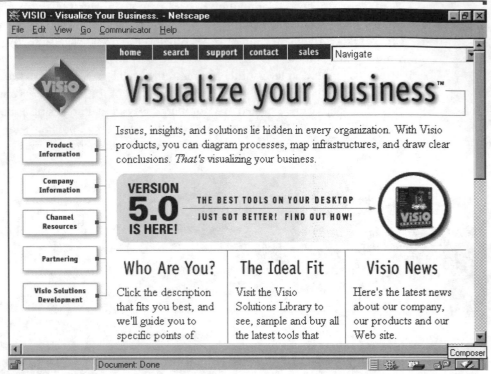

How you or your company choose to create the physical representation of the site is unimportant. In fact, when I worked at DesertNet, I got to watch history in the making. The *Tucson Weekly*'s multi-linear navigation is one of the best examples of effective interface design in the hypermedia environment. How did this interesting navigation come about? Wil Gerken, then the lead Web engineer of the company, used a large chalkboard to map out his ideas. Every day we could see the changes he was making—the additions and subtractions to what eventually became a very complex—and very successful—interface design.

The point, then, is to have a workable structure that complements the site plan. Together, you have created a powerful set of building tools for your site's design.

OTE

Whichever method you choose, express your site's structure first to yourself and then to others who will be examining and perhaps even using the map to work on the site. With that in mind, the objective is to be clear.

Here are three simple steps that will enable you to create a site map.

1. Define each page within the top level of your site. From the example discussed earlier, I've chosen the following for Tripper's site:

   - What UP!
   - About Tripper's Skate n' Surf
   - Skate n' Surf Topics
   - Surf Links
   - Help!

2. Now define the sub-levels of your site. You'll want to do this for all of the areas of your site, but in this example we'll break out the "Topics" section only:

   - Skate n' Surf Games
   - Skate n' Surf Chat Rooms
   - Skate n' Surf BBSs
   - Tripper's Catalog

3. Now you can add third-level tiers:

   - Tripper's Wheel of Fortune
   - Skater Chat
   - Surfer Chat
   - Skater BBS
   - Surfer BBS

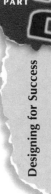

PART

Designing for Success

Pay specific attention to how the levels relate to one another. If the examples in number one represent the critical points of your site, you're going to want to be sure you link back to those pages from other levels within your site.

In fact, a good way to map this out is to sketch it out in hierarchical form first, with the top level pointing to the pages of the second, and so forth. Then, think about linking from bottom to top—thinking carefully if it's necessary to get from one place to another.

For example, getting from the Wheel of Fortune to the BBS is probably not necessary, but getting from the Wheel of Fortune to Skate n' Surf games is.

Finally, think about how to cross-link pages outside of the hierarchy. What if I wanted to get from the Surfer Chat to the Surfer BBS? What's the best way to get there without having to go through three clicks? In a case like that, a direct link might be in order.

Once you've worked through the various areas of your own site's example, it's time to begin figuring out ways to link the pages cleverly. It would be helpful to refer back to Chapter 3 and the discussion of interface. Think about the obvious links necessary, but then think about other ways that you can add to the interactive experience of the site by offering options to your audience.

This information can, again, be rendered in a storyboard fashion, or using a written outline form with comments.

Next Up

Managing information effectively is a potent way of ensuring that the sites you develop have a strong foundation. Management cannot be separated from Web design—it's impossible to create Web sites that are sturdy as well as flexible. Knowing what your material needs are, how to organize those needs, and how to work with those needs provides you with the ability to change those needs as it becomes necessary. You're on top of the project—you understand what it took to get there, and how to take it into the future.

Next up is a look at site logistics—how to address the somewhat cumbersome but important site success issues such as legal issues, domain name registration, site indexing, and site marketing.

chapter 7

WEB SITE
LOGISTICS

WEB SITE LOGISTICS

Many of the issues discussed in this chapter are important to focus on as you design your site—and at times, long after the site is in operation. As the chapter title claims, the discussion here will concentrate on logistics. As a Web designer, in order to compete professionally and qualify your sites as masterful, you need to be knowledgeable about the following:

- Legal issues
- Registering a domain
- Site indexing
- Marketing your Web site

By examining the logistics of a site, a designer prepares the site for its public life. The work in this phase of design can be thought of as the socialization of a site—how well it will be thought of by its visitors, how it will be protected from vulnerability, and how strongly prepared the site will be to move into the future.

Legal Considerations

Internet law is still a very gray area. There are new laws being created regularly to deal with the issues that the Internet is bringing to the forefront of the legal arena. Common mistakes regarding Internet law are made every day by Web developers—but as any good lawyer will tell you, ignorance of the law is no excuse.

Some common legal problems and considerations include:

- **Using copyrighted graphics or photos**—Be sure that the graphics and photos you have chosen for your Web site are legal for you to use—meaning you've created them yourself (as in Figure 7.1), or you've procured permission for them. If someone else holds a copyright on something that you are using, you are in danger of being sued for copyright infringement. If you want to use something that is copyrighted by another individual or company, then contact them and see if you can get that all-important permission in writing.

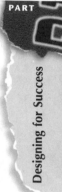

FIGURE 7.1

These headers are original designs for the Design Studio site.

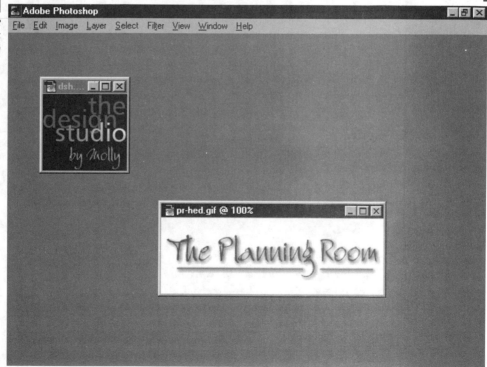

PART

Designing for Success

- **Placing copyrighted articles on your site**—Just because an article is out on the Net doesn't mean you can use it. Just as making copies of a print magazine article is an illegal act, so is reproducing an entire Web article that you have not first secured written permission from the owner to reproduce. When in doubt, choose a link to the article rather than reproducing that article on your site (see Figure 7.2).

FIGURE 7.2

If you don't hold the copyright on an article, you can link to it instead.

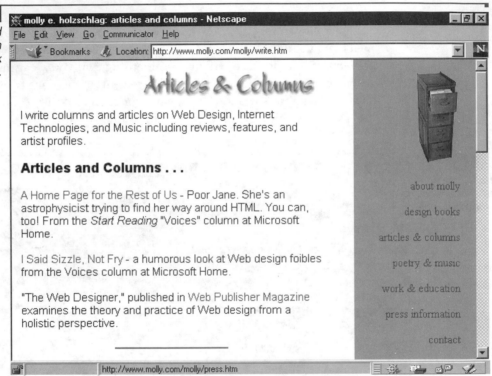

> *"Copyright protection subsists . . . in original works of authorship fixed in any tangible medium of expression, now known or later developed, from which they can be perceived, reproduced, or otherwise communicated, either directly or with the aid of a machine or device."*

Section 102(a) of the Copyright Act

- **Distributing software that doesn't belong to you**—If you have a download area on your site, and you take a program that is owned by someone else and make it available for download from your site, you are violating copyright. Be very careful when distributing software. Get permission in writing from the owner, link to the manufacturer's home page, or don't do it.

- **Making statements about other people that are unfounded or untrue**—If you publish a piece that criticizes an individual or make statements that can harm their professional reputation, you could be found guilty of libel. This is happening with increasing frequency on the Web, so be careful what you say.

- **Offering prizes, sweepstakes, gaming, or gambling online**—These acts are potentially very dangerous and should not be pursued unless you have consulted with an attorney who is schooled in online law and can advise you.

- **Distributing pornographic or adult-oriented material**—This is also a potentially dangerous area, and individuals interested in providing adult-oriented material should seek legal counsel before doing so, as well as research methods of protecting their site from the wandering eyes of children (Figure 7.3).

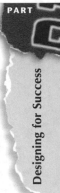

PART 2

Designing for Success

FIGURE 7.3

The ChildSafe home page

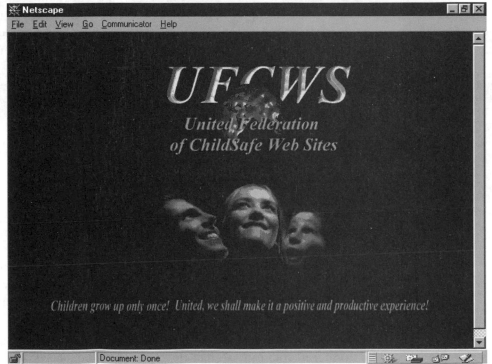

UF**CWS**

United Federation of ChildSafe Web Sites

Children grow up only once! United, we shall make it a positive and productive experience!

ON line!

Two really good sites that deal with child safety issues include:

- **ChildSafe:** http://www.childsafe.com/
- **RSACi:** http://www.rsac.org/

Both of these sites offer ideas and ratings systems for Web sites.

While it's impossible to stay on top of all of the issues within the Net's changing legal environment, there are some important considerations for which you should be prepared. These concerns hold true for all types of Internet sites.

- **Copyright of pages**—Naturally, much of the material that will be on your pages, whether they've been created for Internet, intranet, or extranet purposes, is going to be proprietary. You will need to follow standard copyrighting procedures including the placement of the copyright © symbol, copyright holder's name, and year of copyright on your site pages. Bear in mind that the Web is an international venue, so be sure to research your legal copyright needs and adhere to them strictly. An example of copyright information is shown in Figure 7.4.

FIGURE 7.4

Example of copyright on the Tucson Weekly

  © 1995-97 Tucson Weekly . Info Booth

"Copyright law is totally out of date. It is a Gutenberg artifact . . . it will probably have to break down completely before it is corrected..."

NICHOLAS NEGROPONTE, Being Digital

- **Trademark protection**—Similarly, you will probably have logos and other symbols and products that carry service marks. These should be clearly marked, and any important terms and conditions should be clearly spelled out somewhere on the site.

- **Proper use of images and text from other sources**—If you are using outside sources for art and materials that are to appear on your site, be absolutely certain that you have handled the legal issues involved with their use. For example, some stock photography isn't royalty-free, and you will have to pay fees and/or make proper attribution to the photographer or company. Similarly, if you bought art for your site, be sure you keep all contracts and files stored carefully.

- **Insurance**—If you are providing a source for anything that puts you at risk for a lawsuit, it's a good idea to get plenty of insurance to cover that risk. One example would be if you were providing a shareware software download site. If somehow a proprietary piece of software landed on that site, and you missed it, the owner of that software has grounds to sue you. By carrying the proper insurance (for Web sites, you want to have liability and errors and omissions insurance—very expensive but well worth it if you *do* run into a problem) you save yourself headaches and possibly a lot of money.

PART 2

Designing for Success

ON line!

Many people feel that the Web should not be regulated at all. This topic has been hotly debated since the Net has grown in popularity. Some sites that explore this idea include:

- **ACLU Cyberliberties:** American Civil Liberties Union perspectives on freedom on the Net, at `http://www.aclu.org/issues/cyber/hmcl.html`.
- **Citizens Internet Empowerment Coalition:** First Amendment rights and the Internet, at `http://www.ciec.org/`.
- **Electronic Frontier Foundation:** One of the first freedom-oriented organization on the Net. Recent news, activism, and information regarding freedom on the Net, at `http://www.eff.org/`.

OFF line!

What do you think about Net regulation? Explore the sites in the previous Online! sidebar and write out some of your thoughts on the issue. How do your opinions potentially effect your work as a Web designer?

Frequently Asked Legal Questions

Here are some common questions—and answers—about legal concerns on the Net:

What if I have a copyrighted image I want to use, but only want to use a portion of it. I'm going to crop it and retouch it in Photoshop so the original won't look the same. Is this legal?

No, it's not legal. Since the original material is copyrighted, you do not have the right to alter it in any way, and doing so can result in legal action against you.

What if I want to quote from another article, book, magazine—how much can I legally quote?

This relates to *fair use*. Typically, fair use is about up to one paragraph of material quoted and fully referenced—you must acknowledge the author and the source. However, it's still wise to run any reprint past an attorney to be sure you are within legal limits.

I thought if something was really old—like before 1940 or so—it's public domain and I can use it. Is this true?.

Not necessarily. The information could very well have been copyrighted by the estate that owns the material. You must look for the copyright notice, or find out from a legal professional if something is truly in the public domain or not before reproducing it.

There are many issues at hand, and it's impossible to cover all but the obvious within this lesson. For absolute safety—don't play around. Get a skilled attorney who understands the Net, copyright, and trademark issues, and find an insurance agent who has sold similar policies and can accurately provide you with guidance on necessary insurance.

ON line!

The following resource sites will help provide you with more information on legal and insurance issues:

- **The Internet Law and Policy Forum:** This site keeps up with various legal issues of concern to the Net community, and works to create " . . . a neutral venue in which to develop solutions to the challenging legal and policy questions of the Internet." See http://www.ilpf.org/.

- **The World Wide Web Consortium's Policy Page:** This site is a great jumping-off spot for a variety of up-to-date information on legal and policy issues such as intellectual property rights and how to protect youth from adult-oriented material. See http://www.w3.org/Policy/Overview.html.

Domain Registration

Domain names, for general purposes, are customized URLs (Web site addresses) that help identify your site (Figure 7.5).

http://www .designstudio .net/ helps identify the site associated with this book

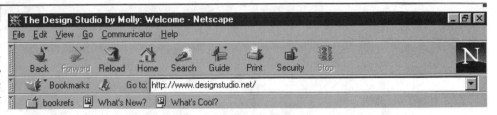

Registering a domain is imperative for public businesses on the Net. Domains help create or extend your company brand, making you more visible and therefore, easier to find.

> *"Domain names have become a vital component of corporate identity, as important as a trademark or brand name."*
>
> Net Profit, the Journal of Internet Business Strategy

Do a little experiment. Type in the name of a major company or well-known product into your Web browser's location field (or go to File/Open Location) with the standard http://www.FillInYourName.com/ addressing. For my experiment, I typed in http://www.kleenex.com/. I got to the parent company that makes Kleenex, Kimberly-Clark (shown in Figure 7.6). Note that domain registrations are finicky—this isn't an accurate way of checking to see if a domain is registered, but it does demonstrate how a domain can be helpful.

Just for fun I tried it again. I looked up one of my favorite department stores, Macy's. I eliminated the apostrophe, knowing that it's not a recognized symbol for URLs, and I typed in http://www.macys.com/ (Figure 7.7).

FIGURE 7.6

Typing in a domain name

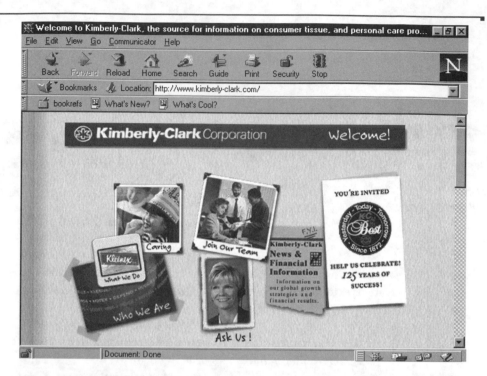

FIGURE 7.7

Typing in another domain—with success

Voila! There I was, ready to whip out my credit card and do some online shopping.

In these cases, branding had initially been done by the companies through traditional media, not on the Internet. However, there are examples of branding on the Web. Think about Yahoo, or infoseek, or HotWired. You know exactly where to go, don't you? This is what you're going to want for your business customers.

Now, if your efforts are to create a home page or other design that you don't want to promote in this fashion, you can forgo a domain name. If it isn't going to help you in some way, don't spend the money and the effort. Why, then, did I register my name as my domain, `http://www.molly.com/`? Well, my home page also serves as a point of contact for readers of my books and columns, so it has enough business thrust to make it important to have a domain name (Figure 7.8).

FIGURE 7.8

`http://www.molly.com/`

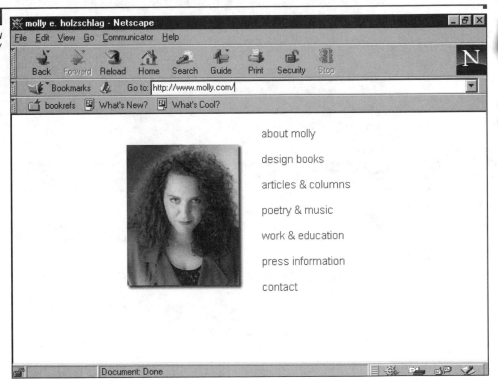

Domain names aren't free, and you have to be absolutely sure that no one has the name you want. It costs $100 to register a domain name for two years, and $50 per year after that to maintain it. A visit to the InterNIC—the organization that regulates, tracks, and offers domain name services—will provide more details: `http://www.internic.net/`.

PART

Designing for Success

For intranet and extranets, domains are handled differently since they aren't on the free ranges of the Internet. You'll want to consult with your systems administrator for information on how to handle registering non-Internet domains.

Searching for a Domain Name

You can search the availability of a domain name by following this procedure:

1. Make a list of possible domain names you'd like to use, following the rules at http://www.internic.net/.

2. Click the InterNIC's registration services search feature to see if that name is available by selecting Whois from the Registration Services menu.

3. In the search field, enter your target string. For example, when I wanted to see if designstudio.com was available, I typed in designstudio.com. and hit Enter.

4. The query will show you if the name is registered. As you can see, my original choice for this Web site was, in fact, already taken, and a form with all of the contact information popped up (see Figure 7.9). I tried the process again with designstudio.net and found that the name was not listed as being registered. I received a message saying "no match," and from there went on to actually register the domain (Figure 7.10).

FIGURE 7.9

http://www
.designstudio
.com/ was taken

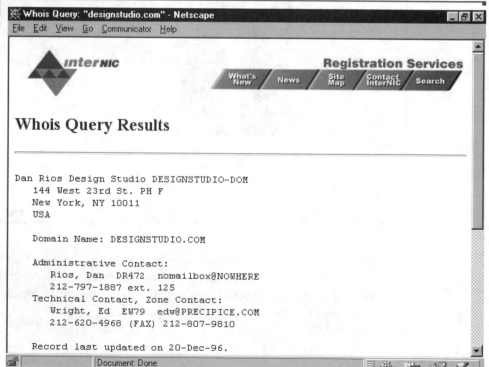

FIGURE 7.10

http://www.
designstudio.net
is now registered

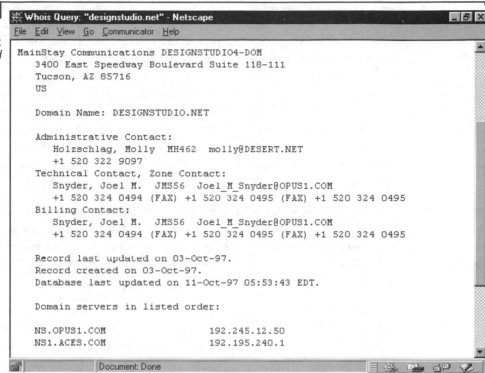

```
Whois Query: "designstudio.net" - Netscape                    _ 8 X
File  Edit  View  Go  Communicator  Help

MainStay Communications DESIGNSTUDIO4-DOM
    3400 East Speedway Boulevard Suite 118-111
    Tucson, AZ 85716
    US

    Domain Name: DESIGNSTUDIO.NET

    Administrative Contact:
        Holzschlag, Molly   MH462   molly@DESERT.NET
        +1 520 322 9097
    Technical Contact, Zone Contact:
        Snyder, Joel M.   JMS56   Joel_M_Snyder@OPUS1.COM
        +1 520 324 0494 (FAX) +1 520 324 0495 (FAX) +1 520 324 0495
    Billing Contact:
        Snyder, Joel M.   JMS56   Joel_M_Snyder@OPUS1.COM
        +1 520 324 0494 (FAX) +1 520 324 0495 (FAX) +1 520 324 0495

    Record last updated on 03-Oct-97.
    Record created on 03-Oct-97.
    Database last updated on 11-Oct-97 05:53:43 EDT.

    Domain servers in listed order:

    NS.OPUS1.COM                    192.245.12.50
    NS1.ACES.COM                    192.195.240.1

            Document: Done
```

OTE

Even if you've received a "no match" it's possible that someone has registered the
domain but the paperwork is incomplete. You'll have to proceed with the registration
process at that point in order to fully determine if the domain name is available.

Site Indexing

Site indexing is a process by which you ensure that people looking for your site are
going to have the maximum chance of finding it. This is an important step in commercial Web site post-production, and is also beneficial for the personal page enthu-
siast. The information in this lesson doesn't especially apply to intranet or extranet

concerns, although those of you who will be working on such sites can only benefit from learning about site indexing, especially if one day you find yourself responsible for creating or working on something out on the open Net. Furthermore, search products do exist for intranets, and very often intranet designers will be called upon to utilize indexing techniques.

Basically, you, or a company you designate to do the job, will register your site with a variety of online *search databases*. These search databases, or search engines as they are sometimes referred to, come in different forms. Some, like Yahoo, infoseek, and Excite, are broken down into categories and often offer a complete range of services such as entertainment, news, and site reviews. Sites like these rely primarily on the author (or a designated company hired by the author) of a page to register that page.

> *"Registering with search engines is one of the first things you should do once your site is complete. Not only is this the best way to assure that you will, eventually, come up in someone's search, but search engines often take time to register a site's existence. So the earlier you file your submissions, the better."*
>
> AMY COWEN, "Spotlight your Site," Ebusiness

Others, such as AltaVista and Webcrawler, are referred to as web worms or web crawlers. These sites have engines that burrow through the Web and find new Web sites, registering them as they come upon them. While many of the first type of search engines use this technique too, in this case, the primary purpose is to provide a search point and jumping-off place, not an advanced entertainment service.

Either way, you'll want to get on as many of the available engines as possible. There are several ways to do this.

Make sure all of your Web site pages are META tagged for search purposes (Figure 7.11). Refer back to Chapter 2 for directions on how to quickly and easily do this. The worms look for this information, and this gives you more control over the description and key words that will be available on that given engine.

Register your site on as many directories as you can, and follow up to ensure that those entries are recorded.

If you don't have the resources to do aggressive site indexing in-house, go ahead and hire a company that specializes in site indexing; `http://www.submit-it.com/` provides information on how to do this.

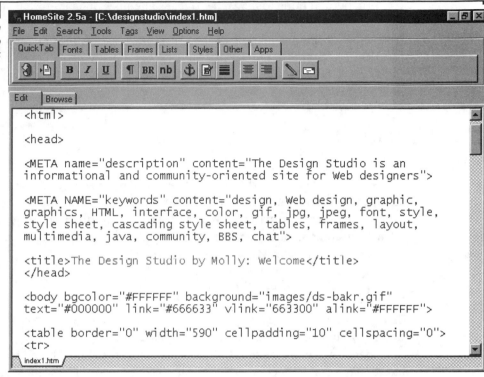

```
HomeSite 2.5a - [C:\designstudio\index1.htm]
File  Edit  Search  Tools  Tags  View  Options  Help

QuickTab | Fonts | Tables | Frames | Lists | Styles | Other | Apps

Edit  Browse

<html>

<head>

<META name="description" content="The Design Studio is an
informational and community-oriented site for Web designers">

<META NAME="keywords" content="design, Web design, graphic,
graphics, HTML, interface, color, gif, jpg, jpeg, font, style,
style sheet, cascading style sheet, tables, frames, layout,
multimedia, java, community, BBS, chat">

<title>The Design Studio by Molly: Welcome</title>
</head>

<body bgcolor="#FFFFFF" background="images/ds-bakr.gif"
text="#000000" link="#666633" vlink="663300" alink="#FFFFFF">

<table border="0" width="590" cellpadding="10" cellspacing="0">
<tr>

index1.htm
```

ON line!

The following sites are well-known search engines:

- **Yahoo:** http://www.yahoo.com
- **Lycos:** http://www.lycos.com
- **Alta Vista:** http://www.altavista.digital.com/
- **infoseek:** http://www.infoseek.com/
- **Excite:** http://www.excite.com/
- **Wired's HotBot:** http://www.hotbot.com/
- **Magellan Internet Guide:** http://www.mckinley.com/
- **WebCrawler:** http://www.webcrawler.com/

PART

Designing for Success

One important thing to remember is that sometimes no matter what you do, search engines will take a long time to get you listed. It pays to be persistent and follow-up. Getting names of individuals on the inside of indexing organizations and developing a relationship with them can be very helpful—especially if you plan on indexing many sites over a period of time. And, again, if you want to avoid the hassles, you can hire a professional indexing company.

Marketing

Web marketing is an extremely important issue for public, commercial Internet sites, yet it's often overlooked in the planning stages. However, designers are getting more and more savvy in regards to marketing, especially because the immense growth of the Web. In order to get past the layers and layers of information and get your sites to potential customers, intelligent marketing strategies are going to be a strong method of ensuring long-term success.

Getting the Word Out

There are two major marketing options that should be considered when planning the future of your Web site, *branding* and *online marketing*.

As mentioned in the section entitled "Domain Registration," branding is the familiarization of your product or service within the population. Think about Xerox or Coca Cola—any major product that has achieved such success with its presence has done a great job at branding. This is done in a variety of ways, including matching the product to a specific tag-line or jingle, color and design scheme, and trademarked logo.

Marketing done online helps get people to your site. This is done using several methods including:

- Ad banners
- Cross promotions and linking
- Seasonal promotions
- Offline marketing
- Other media

I'll take a more explicit look at online marketing techniques in the upcoming sections.

Ad Banners

For publicly accessible Web sites, advertising banners are an excellent way to get attention for your site, and give attention to others. Similarly, using a banner-style announcement on intranet or extranet pages can call attention to a variety of activities. While most of this lesson will focus on Internet ad banners, many of the ideas here can be applied to sites found on intranets and extranets.

The first question you need to answer with regard to banners is whether you truly need them. If you are looking to enhance your visibility, sell products, or if you have any other reason to use visually-oriented announcements, banners are a great idea. They particularly make sense when you are looking to increase revenue for your site. Popular companies such as DoubleClick (http://www.doubleclick.net/) can help set you up in an advertising pool. This method puts another company in charge of the ad banners that you design for your site, placing your banners in a common pool and promoting them on other sites all over the Net that match with your demographic target.

Here are some guidelines and questions to help you determine if banner advertising is right for you:

- You've branded yourself elsewhere—as within a domain name—and you are looking for further branding and exposure.

- You have an aggressive marketing budget—most banner programs work on a per-thousand block view basis, meaning you'll pay per block. On popular sites, this can cost hundreds of dollars or more a day.

- You've done good target market research, and understand your goals and directives.

"The banner is like the outer envelope of a direct mail piece. The Web site content compares to what is in the envelope. Like direct mail, on the banner ad you might offer a free premium, special value, or question that they want answered."

ROY SCHWEDELSON, CEO, WebConnect

Advertising banners on the Internet typically adhere to a specific dimension of 468 × 60 pixels (see Figure 7.12). The only time it's a good idea to deviate from this convention is when you are either advertising within your own public Internet site (Figure 7.13) with no intentions of running those ads anywhere else, or when you are using such banners for intranet or extranet use.

PART 2

Designing for Success

FIGURE 7.12

Standard-size ad banner, 480 × 60

More alternative news than you can stake a shick at...weekly WIRE

FIGURE 7.13

Non-standard-size ad banner, 375 × 50

buy sell trade Buffalo EXCHANGE

Banners should also follow some of these guidelines:

- Banners should be GIF or JPEG files. Some companies use other technologies as well, such as Java or Shockwave. Of course, if you are in an intranet environment, you have more control over what technologies are available to you.

- Banners should be fairly small in file size. 8KB is a good maximum for GIF or JPEGs.

- Animated GIFs are a popular method of getting inviting, active information into a banner and should be no more than 12KB. Images should not loop more than three times.

ON line!

For more information and guidelines regarding advertising, check out these two ad banner leaders:

- **Doubleclick:** http://www.doubleclick.net/
- **AdBot:** http://www.adbot.com/

Other Methods

There are a variety of other methods of online advertising with which you should be familiar.

- **Cross promotions and linking**—Do you do regular business with others who have a Web presence? What kinds of promotions can you put together that would benefit both of you? One example is linking—making sure your colleague's site is accessible from yours, and vice-versa.

  "The idea is to think of links as business assets . . . links could be the basis of joint marketing agreements . . . they could be a community-building effort."

  ROSS RUBIN, Jupiter Communications

- **Seasonal promotions**—Keep your Web site fresh with seasonal events, holiday specials, and the like. Be sure to follow up with your Web activities with appropriate marketing activities (Figure 7.14).

FIGURE 7.14

Halloween comes to the Buffalo Exchange

- **Other media**—Do you currently advertise for your company on radio or TV? How about in the newspaper? If you do, be sure your ads are current and point people to your Web site. You might even consider creating a special ad just for your Web site.

- **Company brochures, business cards, letterhead, promotional materials**— Any printed materials you have should incorporate your Web site URL and any information that will point your clients to your site, potentially increasing your traffic and the site's viability. Other promotional materials, such as pens, mugs, hats, t-shirts—even billboards—are great ways to promote your site offline as well.

Growth

Web sites that find themselves especially successful require constant updates, revisions, and expansion. Web designers do well to plan for the logistics of managing this kind of growth.

Open-ended design is a phrase I've coined to describe site design that have areas that allow for natural growth. The Buffalo Exchange site, `http://www.desert.net/buffalo/`, has added numerous areas since its original launch in 1995 (see Figure 7.15). By designing the "where" area with open-ended design in mind, the additions to the area are fairly simple: add a hot spot on the map for the new location, add a text link, and add a page based on the location page template. Using this technique, the designers at Buffalo Exchange have successfully added sites as the company has grown throughout the western United States.

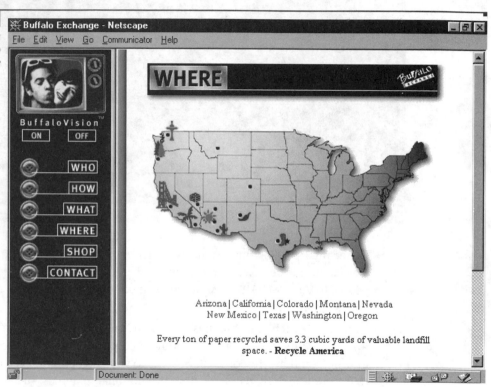

Another method of ensuring growth is by adding features such as specialty links to additional, and possibly unforeseen, areas (Figure 7.16). The Buffalo Exchange catalog, shown in Figure 7.17, came online this year and was never in the original site plan—it was unforeseen.

FIGURE 7.16

Specialty links to the catalog

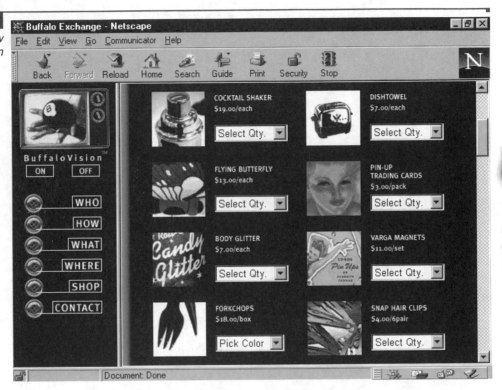

FIGURE 7.17

The catalog, a new addition

The fact that the site was planned so well in advance speaks to the ability of the designers; they can readily go in and make additions that don't detract from the overall appeal of the site. This is a take-home lesson for every Web designer. Planning, information management, and site logistics such as open-ended design are *imperative* design elements for the long-term.

Next Up

Next up is the review chapter for Part II. You'll go over the main ideas you've learned in the last three chapters, and have the opportunity to quiz yourself and practice some of the applicable topics found here.

THE DESIGN STUDIO
PLANNING ROOM

THE DESIGN STUDIO PLANNING ROOM

The Planning Room is metaphorically represented on the *Web by Design* site with a set of scales. When you plan for something, you must research and weigh the parts that will eventually make up the whole. Whether it's how you build your house, or how you construct a Web site—the individual parts have a significant impact on the results of the project. The planning stage is the best opportunity you will have to sketch your vision and make eraser marks *before* that vision is brought into reality.

This chapter synthesizes the ideas and techniques you've been exposed to in Part II:

- Planning a Web site
- Managing a site's information
- Preparing for the legal and social life of your Web site

You'll review, deconstruct, quiz yourself, and perform tasks in this chapter in order to deepen and polish the learning you've accumulated thus far.

Planning Design: Review

Planning design is the process by which you determine how your site will operate immediately, and how it will grow, change, expand, and succeed in times to come.

Meeting that objective is not difficult if you do the groundwork. There are four steps to follow:

- Define the site.
- Characterize your audience.
- Determine short- and long-term goals.
- Prepare a formal site plan.

How is this part of Web design? The answer is simple—by creating a sturdy foundation, you can build with greater strength and flexibility. The Web is a chaotic place. Tackle these issues first, and you've put a little order into that chaos—giving you a site built to withstand any storm.

Main Concepts

There are four main concepts in the planning stage that should be addressed *before* you begin designing. However, sometimes you'll have to apply them after the fact—particularly when you have a site that you want to improve.

- **Define the site**—There are types of sites and site categories. Types of sites are what the site's purpose is—to sell, entertain, communicate, support, promote, or educate. The site category is determined by *where* that site is delivered, and how. This includes the "free-range" of the Internet (a public site), the walled interior of an intranet (a private site), and the bridge in between—the extranet.

- **Determine the audience**—This critical step helps guide the way in which you design. First, you must define your primary target market using demographic techniques—age, sex, location, financial situation. Then, expand to include secondary markets—groups of people outside the primary market who will naturally have an interest in your product or service, or those that you would like to add to your current market. Finally, peripheral markets should be identified.

- **Set goals**—What do you want to achieve with your site right now? It's extremely helpful to know what the sponsoring company's immediate desired site results are. List these desires as short-term goals. Then, think about the future. Do you want to add services? Obviously you cannot pre-determine everything, but adding things that seem necessary and feasible over time is an important part of this process.

PART 2

Designing for Success

- **Create a site plan**—The site plan is the formal gathering of your research. It should be put together in a standard business plan format, describing your intent, goals, and demographics. The site plan gives you a reference point to return to time and again as you work through the detailed processes involved in site design.

Site Deconstruction

The Design Studio site plan helped determine the resulting look, feel, action, and interaction of this book's companion site. Following are some examples taken from that plan.

Site Overview

The Design Studio will be an informational and community-oriented Web site. It is both an adjunct tool for the book, *Web by Design: The Complete Guide*, and a stand-alone site that provides Web design activities and resources.

The site is both educational and community-based. It shares the goals of providing information on Web design to its visitors and creating an environment in which those visitors can interact with one another. It will be delivered via the Internet, and is considered a public Internet site.

The site is available to users of any computer platform. It supports text-only browsers, and graphical browsers that read HTML tables. Some of the information in specific areas of the site require software plug-ins, Java support, and other advanced technologies. These areas are for demonstration purposes and do not make up the bulk of the site.

Audience

The primary audience of this site includes men and women, ages 22-45, who are middle class, and located in first-world countries such as the United States and United Kingdom. They are single or married, with an interest in the profession of designing Web sites.

The secondary audience includes young men and women, ages 17-22, who are students interested in learning about the profession of Web site design.

Peripheral audiences include non-professionals interested in researching various aspects of Web design, or who are looking for communities discussing current Web design information and issues.

Site Goals

The immediate goal of the site is to provide support for the companion book, *Web by Design*. Community is of equal importance—for it brings the interactive element of the site to fruition. Therefore, the site will have both informational and community-oriented options upon launch.

Long-term goals involve expanding the site to include updated information regarding Web technologies such as HTML, Web graphic design, multimedia design, and Web programming. Other long-term goals include responding to the questions and concerns voiced by the community as it develops.

Planning Design: Quiz

Please answer the following multiple choice questions:

1. Which of the following is *not* considered a site category:

   a. intranet

   b. commercial

   c. identity

   d. promotional

2. A site can be which of the following types:

   a. public

   b. private

   c. educational

   d. all of the above

3. Online newspapers and magazines often:

   a. require planning to deal with large amounts of data

   b. have a similar look and feel

   c. are considered extranet sites

   d. all of the above

4. Designing children's sites can be challenging because:

   a. a balance of education and entertainment should be achieved

   b. child safety on the Net is difficult to ensure

   c. children don't know how to use the Web

   d. a and b

5. Internet sites:

   a. are public

   b. can be accessed by anyone on the Net

   c. gather information from a wide range of sources

   d. all of the above

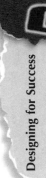

Please answer true or false for the following statements.

6. An intranet is proprietary in services and information.

7. Intranets require a designer to design for single platforms only.

8. Audience demographics can include a description of marital status.

9. A good long-term goal is to shift a company's profits entirely to the Web.

10. A bad long-term goal is to market and brand a product.

Write out short answers to the following questions.

11. Name three aspects of intranet design.

12. Do you think a site plan is an effective design tool? Why or why not?

Answers to the quiz can be found on the Design Studio Web site, `http://www.designstudio.net/planning/`, and at the end of this chapter.

Planning Design: Task

The task is to prepare a site plan.

For this task you will need:

- A text editor or word processor
- A real or imaginary site project example

You can find helpful ingredients including a site plan template for the task on the Design Studio site in the Planning section, `http://www.designstudio.net/planning/tasks.htm`.

Follow these steps:

1. Open the template provided on the site or a new file within your text editor or word processor (Figure 8.1).

2. Write a paragraph or more describing the site type, form, and intent (Figure 8.2).

3. Add a description of your site's primary, secondary, and peripheral audiences.

4. Complete a list of your site goals for the short- and long-term.

5. If you have a business plan that accompanies the project, add that to the file.

6. Save the file with a name such as siteplan or siteplan.doc.

FIGURE 8.1

The site plan template

The Design Studio: Web Site Plan

[enter company name]
[enter date]
prepared by: [enter your name]

Overview

[in this section, write an overview of your project, answering the following questions within your paragraphs:

What is the breadth and scope of your project?

What kind of Web site are you developing—commercial Internet, Intranet, or Extranet?

What are the strengths and limitations of this choice?

Is your site cross-platform, cross browser compatible?

Will you be able to take advantage of platform-specific technologies?

How will your site be built? Will you use an individual or a team? Why did you choose the model that you have?

List the three to five main purposes of your site]

FIGURE 8.2

The Web site overview

The Design Studio: Web Site Plan

September, 1997
Prepared by: Molly E. Holzschlag

Overview

The Design Studio will be an informational and community-oriented Web site. It is both an adjunct tool for the book, *Web by Design: The Complete Reference*, and a stand-alone site that provides Web design activities and resources.

The site is both educational and community-based. It shares the goals of providing information on Web design to its visitors and creating an environment in which those visitors can interact with one another. It will be delivered via the Internet, and is considered a public Internet site.

The site is available to users of any computer platform. It supports text-only browsers, and graphical browsers that read HTML tables. Some of the information in specific areas of the site require software plug-ins, Java support, and other advanced technologies. These areas are for demonstration purposes and do not make up the bulk of the site.

Audience

Information Management: Review

Information management guides what is considered royalty on the Web: content. Without it, you have no direction, no leadership, no substance. Dealing with information is one of the most difficult tasks you will face as a designer. Yes, graphics have to be great, but you don't need any graphics at all to have a site that people want to *use*. You need content.

Information management includes:

- Selecting content
- Writing for the Web
- Re-purposing content for the Web
- Preparing a storyboard or site map

Stepping through these routines will ensure that designers don't make mistakes with that all-critical data.

Main Concepts

Here is an overview of the main concepts in information management:

- **Surveying current content**—What is the intent of your Web site? By answering this question, you can begin to determine whether the current content you have addresses the meaning of the site. Also, plug it into the larger picture of the site plan. Toss out what doesn't work, and keep what does or what can be reworked to fit the site's goals. Is there anything missing? Go back over and see if there's something you or your client might have forgotten. List out what you have and what you'll need to create.

- **Writing for the Web**—Web writing is different from standard print writing in several ways. To appeal to the short attention span on the Web, you'll need to keep your copy to the point. The content must be concise and clear. Sentences, paragraphs, and pages must be kept short. Voice must be appropriate for the audience, and finally, work must be carefully edited for grammatical accuracy, spelling, and other possible errors.

- **Repurposing content**—In order for content to be Web-ready, it will have to be processed from existing print or computer-processed formats. Remember the acronym GIGO. Have the best content going *in* to the project, and you're less likely to have garbage coming out.

- **Storyboarding and site mapping**—Getting some kind of visual representation of your site is going to be extremely helpful in order for you to effectively place the content you collect and develop logically within your Web site. You can use software such as CLEARWeb or Visio to help you do this; you can create a text-based outline, a hand drawing, use a standard storyboard such as is found in film and animation, or even use a blackboard to sketch out your ideas.

Site Deconstruction

To create the content for the Design Studio, I followed these steps:

1. First, I determined what current content I had, and what content I was going to need. I found that much of the content would be taken or re-purposed from *Web by Design*. For example, the quizzes and tasks came from the book, but much of the ancillary documents had to be created. Other content had to be created. I worked with my research assistant, Lee Anne, to build resource lists and gather URLs that would fill in the resource areas.

2. Next, I had to create and re-purpose content. Any text that did not come from the book was created for the site. Much of the text had to be re-purposed both in terms of the technology (text to HTML) and the longer expository of book-writing to a shorter, more appropriate Web style.

3. Finally, I sketched the design of the site on a storyboard. I do storyboards when I can—I just take a whiteboard and fill it up. Figure 8.3 shows a mock-up of my storyboard that I did for the Design Studio site.

PART 2

Designing for Success

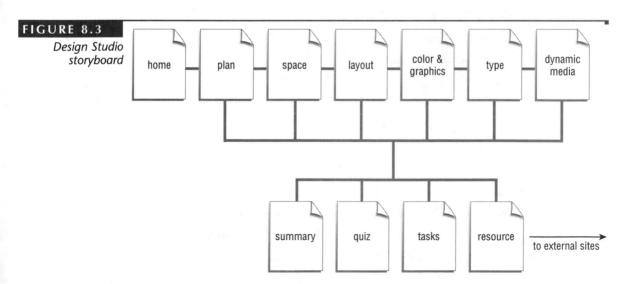

FIGURE 8.3

Design Studio storyboard

Information Management: Quiz

Please answer the following multiple choice questions.

1. Content comes from the following sources:

   a. brochures

   b. catalogs

   c. current advertising

   d. all of the above

2. Which is *not* an immediate part of information management:

   a. site intent

   b. graphic design

   c. re-purposing content

   d. none of the above

3. Which of the following is not overtly important to Web writing:

   a. attention span

   b. financial status of the visitor

   c. a and c

   d. none of the above

4. Which print newspaper best exemplifies Web writing?

   a. The New York Times

   b. The Wall Street Journal

   c. USA Today

   d. all of the above

5. Copyediting:

   a. is time consuming

   b. is not necessary

   c. is helpful

   d. is imperative

Please answer true or false for the following statements.

6. Information saved in electronic form never presents a problem for Web designers.

7. It is better to have text and graphics saved to a single, word-processed document such as Microsoft Word.

8. Storyboarding can be achieved using a sketch pad and pencil.

9. Site mapping must adhere to a hierarchy rather than a non-linear structure.

10. Site mapping is ideally performed after a site is built, giving you a good idea of what exists where.

Write out short answers to the following questions.

11. If you are a working Web designer and use other methods of information management, please describe them here. Are they effective? Why or why not? If you have not managed information, do you believe that information management techniques are going to help you in designing a good site? Why or why not?

12. Name another situation where thorough planning is helpful in ensuring better results.

Information Management: Task

In this task, you will create a site map of the site project you chose for the last task. You will need:

- Either a word processor, a sketch pad, a white or blackboard, or a copy of CLEARWeb or Visio. A link to a CLEARWeb demo is available at the Design Studio site, `http://www.designstudio.net/planning/tasks.htm`.

- Your site plan and the summary questions that you answered in the first task in this chapter.

- The guidelines found in Chapter 6, or on the Design Studio site at the URL listed above.

Draw or make an outline of your site. If you have a print output of the storyboard or map, add it to the site plan you've created. Now you have a powerful set of tools available when you begin to produce your site.

Site Logistics: Review

A Web site on the Internet holds enormous potential—potential for success due to interesting content, design, and savvy marketing; potential for vulnerability due to lawsuits, lack of insurance, and poor planning. The key concepts to remember from the chapter discussing site logistics include:

- Legal issues such as copyright, trademark, and insurance
- Searching for and registering a domain name

PART 2

Designing for Success

- Indexing your site with search engines and databases
- Marketing your Web site successfully
- Planning for the future of your site

The end results of being prepared enhance the potential for success, while diminishing the risk born of vulnerability. *Web by Design* speaks to these concerns by providing a basic understanding of them and resources for more information about them.

Main Concepts

Here's a closer look at the logistics of site development:

- **Legal considerations**—Copyright, trademark, software distribution, accuracy and originality of information, prizes and gaming online, and the distribution of adult-oriented material are all concerns that require consultation with a skilled attorney. Insurance is important to protect Web site developers—you'll do well to do research on errors and omissions and liability with a professional insurance agent who has some understanding of online legal issues.

- **Domain registration**—The importance of a domain is often debated. I believe that it is an important part of successfully branding a site—and the products and services available on the site as well. Registering for a domain registration isn't difficult and is currently priced very reasonably. A visit to the InterNIC (`http://www.internic.net`) will provide designers with all of the necessary tools to search and register domain names.

- **Site indexing**—Worms, crawlers, and engines, oh my! Getting your site listed on the many search mechanisms out there is an important step in the design process. By properly META tagging your site and doing the background research on site indexing—or hiring a firm such as the one shown in Figure 8.4 to do it for you—you increase your ability to be found on the ever-growing Net.

- **Marketing**—A Web site can be an advertisement, but you should always bear in mind that it must be advertised too. This is done through a variety of mechanisms, including advertising banners, seasonal promotions, offline marketing, and support through other media such as television, radio, and newspapers.

- **Navigation**—How you get from here to there and back again is a critical part of how sites are designed. Navigation issues include the structure of a site, the location of navigation devices on a page, and what media is used to deliver navigation options.

- **Open-ended design**—Preparing a site for future expansion, growth, and change is a logistical concern that is best addressed early on. You're not going to be able to predict all the things your site needs—or even what direction the Net is going to go in—but including whatever you *can* anticipate will empower you tremendously.

FIGURE 8.4

Submit It!

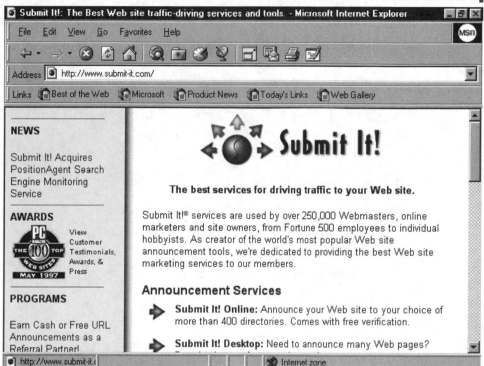

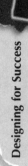

Site Deconstruction

The Design Studio is undergoing or preparing to undergo a variety of logistical issues as this chapter is being written. They include:

- **Legal concerns**—Consultation with a copyright and trademark attorney is underway. Pages are being reviewed for content accuracy, appropriate copyright and trademark paperwork is in the process of being submitted, and notices are being prepared. The site is owned by a private communications company, which holds an errors and omissions and liability policy to protect against any unforeseen problems.

- **Domain registration**—The domain `designstudio.net` has been registered with the InterNIC.

- **Site indexing**—META tag descriptions and keywords are being put into place, and the services of a professional indexing company will be secured to complete the site indexing process.

- **Web site marketing**—Ad banners will be created and used on selected sites. The site is co-marketed with this book and takes advantage of the book itself for extended marketing.

- **Open-ended design**—The long-term goals of this site include being able to respond to changes and growth in each specific technology addressed. Also, the community will undoubtedly drive the site by asking for things that we might not have anticipated. As a result, the structure is made as flexible as possible in order to expand as needed.

Site Logistics Quiz

Please answer the following multiple choice questions.

1. Which of the following holds the least legal risk:

    a. offering an online sweepstakes

    b. distributing adult material

    c. offering your own, original material

    d. all of the above

2. Is it legal to say whatever you want online?

    a. Freedom of speech is protected by the Constitution, so yes.

    b. If you're the press, you can say anything you want.

    c. Criticism that can harm a professional reputation might be viewed legally as libel, so no, it is not legal to say whatever you want online.

    d. a and b

3. A registered domain:

    a. is free

    b. is offered at a one-time fee

    c. requires a start-up and yearly renewal fee

    d. requires a yearly fee but no startup

4. You search for a domain using a tool called:

    a. registration services

    b. InterNIC

    c. Whois

    d. none of the above

5. Site indexing includes:

    a. crawlers

    b. worms

    c. engines

    d. all of the above

Answer true or false for the following statements.

6. Site indexing requires you to hire a professional firm.

7. Ad banners are an inexpensive way of advertising a site.

8. Linking isn't considered an aspect of site marketing.

9. Seasonal promotions are a good way to draw attention to your site.

10. Open-ended Web site design allows for natural and easy growth.

Write out short answers to the following questions.

11. Explain why something that is old may not be in the public domain.

12. What is your favorite search engine, and why?

Site Logistics Task

In this task you will create a list of marketing ideas for your Web site. All you need is a piece of paper and a pencil, or your favorite text or word-processing program.

Write several sentences to address the following:

1. Are you going to use an ad banner for your site? If so, why? If not, why not?

2. Make a list of sites that you feel will be good to link to. Think about common goals and complementary activities. Also, make a notation by the site name if you intend to ask for a reciprocal link.

3. What seasonal promotions are appropriate for your individual project? Think about the holidays and celebrations your primary target audience enjoys, and incorporate them into ways of promoting your site.

4. What other media do you want to include in your marketing? Write a list of where you'll print, announce, or otherwise advertise your Web site.

Answer Key

The following key provides the correct answers to the quizzes in this chapter.

Planning Design

Multiple Choice

1. The correct answer is A. An intranet is a category rather than a type of site.

2. The correct answer is D. Public, private, and educational are all types of sites.

3. The correct answer is A. Newspapers and magazine sites often require management of large amounts of data.

4. The correct answer is D. A balance of entertainment and education is a strong approach to a child's site, and child safety issues are a significant concern. Many children know how to use the Web and are often more adept at it than their parents!

5. The correct answer is D. Internet sites are public, can be accessed by anyone on the Net, and gather information from a wide range of sources.

True or False

6. True. An intranet is proprietary.

7. False. The problem with this statement is the word "only." Intranet designers will very often only need to design for a single platform, but this is not an absolute truth.

8. True. Marital status is frequently used in demographic studies.

9. True. A company can become completely Web-based, but it would be foolish to make this a short-term goal.

10. False. Marketing and branding are *always* a good goal.

Short Answers

Note that your answers may vary, but the main concepts described here should be touched upon.

11. Private, usually single-platform, and often corporate.

12. Your answer should describe the importance of planning a site.

Continued

Information Management

Multiple Choice

1. The correct answer is D. Content can come from brochures, catalogs, and current advertising.

2. The correct answer is B. Graphic design comes later in the Web design process.

3. The correct answer is B. Financial status of a visitor is not overtly important in writing for the Web.

4. The correct answer is C. USA Today offers an excellent look at the short, sharp style of writing that is best for the Web.

5. The correct answer is D. Copyediting is imperative!

True or False

6. False. Many electronic files are not cross-platform compatible.

7. False. Keep text and graphic files separate.

8. True. Many storyboards are created using pad and pencil.

9. False. Site mapping can be hierarchical or non-linear.

10. False. Map a site first.

Short Answers

11 and **12.** These questions will relate to your personal experiences and opinions; there are no correct answers.

Site Logistics

Multiple Choice

1. The correct answer is C. Offering original material bears less risk.

2. The correct answer is C. Criticism that can harm a professional reputation might be viewed as libel.

3. The correct answer is C. Domains require a start-up and yearly fee.

4. The correct answer is C. Search for domain names using a tool called Whois.

5. The correct answer is D. Crawlers, worms, and engines are all site indexing tools.

Continued

True or False

6. False. You can perform site indexing yourself.

7. False. Ad banners can run from mildly to extremely expensive.

8. False. Linking is an important part of site marketing.

9. True. Seasonal promotions are an excellent marketing method.

10. True. Open-ended design affords natural and easy growth.

Short Answers:

11. Copyrights can be carried through an estate. Just because something is old does *not* mean it is in the public domain.

12. I personally like infoseek. What's your favorite?

Next Up

It's time to put aside logistics and legalese, marketing, indexing, and registration. You have a solid understanding of these elements, and you're ready to roll up your sleeves and get down to the production part of design work.

The next part of *Web by Design* features working with Web graphic design technology, color, and shape. It is at this point that you move from the foundational elements of design into the practical applications of technology.

PART III

inner space: designing for the screen

chapter 9

GIVE ME MY
WEB SPACE

GIVE ME MY
WEB SPACE

You've undoubtedly heard someone—boyfriend, wife, child, or friend—proclaim, "I need my space!" Room to breathe, express, expand, and rest is a necessity in our increasingly stressful lives.

The Web is large, with room to grow. The only limitations are technological, and Web designers are a part of the very group that is working hard to push those limits. Whether it's the implementation of broader bandwidth so more information can pass quickly through the Net or advancements in computer hardware to protect and serve the Net's core of information, technology is proving to be only as limited as we are.

However, while the virtual rooms of the Net are potentially limitless, the way in which it is viewed is not. Limitations of computer processors, video cards, and monitors create a series of challenges for designers.

The first of these challenges is that when you view the Web, it is contained in a relatively small space. Most people only see the Web through 15- or 17-inch monitors, many at 640×480 resolution, others at 800×600 resolution, still others at higher resolutions. Some have larger monitors, some have smaller, but the majority of Web visitors fit right in the middle.

Which leads us to the second challenge—variation. The only way to design with some consistency is to know in advance that everyone is viewing the Web at different sizes and resolutions.

How to deal with this contained and varied space is the designer's third challenge. He or she must use HTML and graphic techniques in order to achieve balance and create readable and consistent pages.

In this chapter, you'll learn to:

- See the Web in a contained space
- Achieve efficient design within a small space
- Align text and media
- Relate text and media to one another

NOTE

The term "media" in this case refers to graphics, audio, video, animation—any non-text element that takes up space on a page. Text refers only to HTML-based text.

Learning how to work with space will be one of the most important things you will ever learn as a Web designer. No matter how skilled you are at HTML coding, Web programming, or Web graphic technology, if you don't develop spatial skills, you run the risk of having your designs end up looking amateur.

The Web as a Visual Container

When I describe the Web as being a contained space, I mean that all of the information you see on a Web site is placed within a vessel. In fact, there's more than one vessel holding a Web site's information. You not only have the confines of the physical monitor to deal with, but you also have the Web browser software surrounding your design.

Contained space is not unfamiliar to us. Look at the pictures on a wall. They are framed and matted. The frames are akin to the parameters of a computer monitor, the matting around the picture can be compared to the Web browser's toolbars, status bar, and sidebars. But here's the difference: You don't spend hours looking at a framed picture. You look for a few minutes, then you look away.

But the Web, for some, is where a considerable amount of time is spent. Even television and film, with which people engage for large amounts of time, don't have the internal matting of a browser with which to contend. Furthermore, TVs and movie screens tend to be pretty large.

As a designer, you will have to work to make your visitor comfortable in this contained space—where you want that person to stay for a while, and come back again and again.

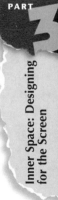

The Shape of Things

If anyone ever called me a square, I'd be insulted! I like to think I'm a free-minded person, with plenty of emotional capacity to allow and even celebrate variety.

Computer monitors are rectangular. Square. They don't offer a lot of flexibility or freedom for the information contained within their less-than-shapely parameters.

Web browsers are square, too. They fit into the monitor's shape, like a box within a box. So how do you, as a designer, take this restrictive, predominant shape and work to alter the square into something a little more flexible?

A big step in gaining visual interest and helping improve the quality of the limited space on the Web is to divert attention from all the squares with the use of other shapes. Rectangles seem to be pervasive on the Web, with big, chunky headers and square figures dominating design (as shown in Figure 9.1). Using shape and getting away from heavy blocks of information can instantly change the relationship the human eye has with the shape of the computer (Figure 9.2).

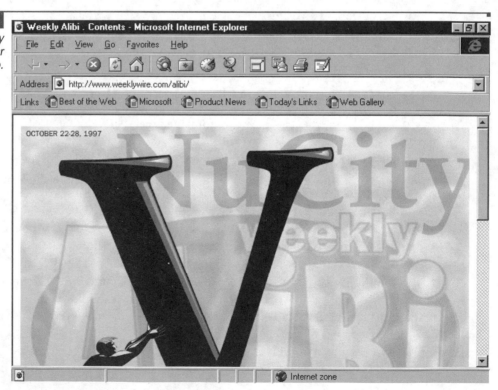

FIGURE 9.1

Rectangular, chunky designs are all over the Web.

Depart from the rectangle for a fresh perspective.

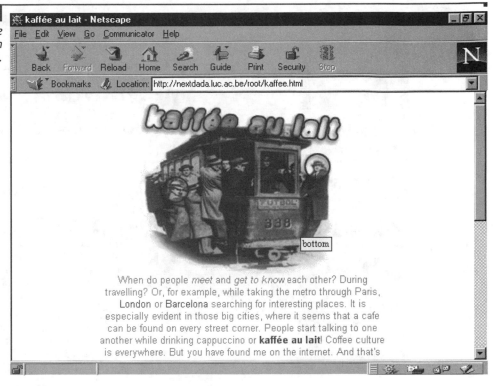

More about designing with shape can be found in Chapter 17. For the time being, keep in mind that shape plays an important role in altering the visual perception of space.

Computer Resolution

How much is your real estate worth? As mentioned earlier, computer monitors are measured both in terms of monitor size and the resolution that the actual hardware, such as the video card or amount of video RAM, can support.

Resolution is simply how many pixels appear on a line. It is generally thought that most people are viewing the Web at 640×480 or 800×600 resolution. This means their visual real estate worth is determined by how many pixels per line are being viewed.

640×480 resolution, an example of which is shown in Figure 9.3, allows for 640 pixels across a total of 480 lines of viewable screen space. 800×600 resolution (Figure 9.4) comes in at a higher value, with 800 pixels running along a total of 600 lines per screen. Many monitors have the capacity for a range of resolution values—my monitor supports the lower resolution of 640×480 as well as 1600×1200 resolution. But my hardware doesn't support the higher range because I need at least 8MB of video RAM.

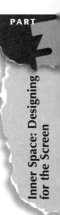

FIGURE 9.3

A Web page at 640 × 480 resolution

The higher the numeric value of a resolution, the crisper and clearer the images are that the monitor is going to output—assuming that all the hardware is functioning properly. Ideally, Web designers will have monitors that support a range of resolutions, so they can test the way sites appear at those various resolutions. As you will come to learn, resolution plays a large role in how a site is designed.

But before we get into the design solutions, let's talk about another challenge to Web space. You already know that the browser creates a visual constraint, but that's not all it does! Web browsers eat up spatial real estate. The toolbars (Figure 9.5) and the status bar (Figure 9.6) of a Web browser take up a certain amount of the vertical space. The sidebar (Figure 9.7) and scroll bar (Figure 9.8) consume horizontal space. You can somewhat customize the toolbars on a browser and gain space, as in Figure 9.9, but many Web visitors leave their browsers on the default, which sucks up the maximum space allowed (Figure 9.10).

FIGURE 9.4

The same page
at 800 × 600
resolution

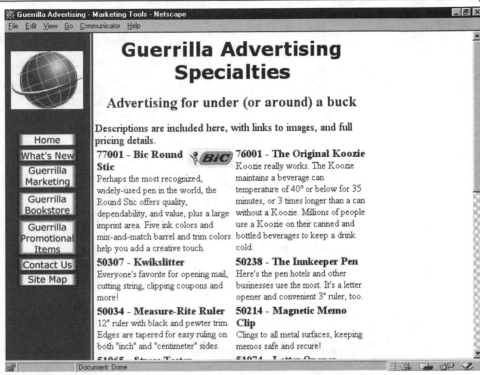

FIGURE 9.5

Netscape's full
toolbar set

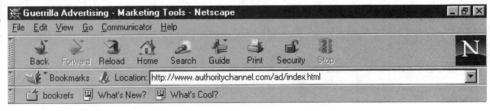

FIGURE 9.6

The Internet
Explorer status bar

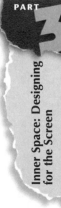

PART

3

Inner Space: Designing
for the Screen

FIGURE 9.7

Netscape's left sidebar

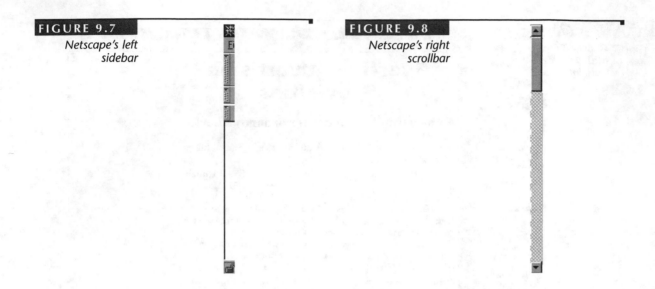

FIGURE 9.8

Netscape's right scrollbar

FIGURE 9.9

Maximum space in Internet Explorer

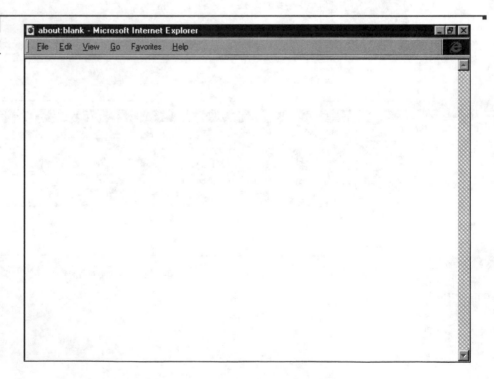

FIGURE 9.10

Minimum space in
Netscape

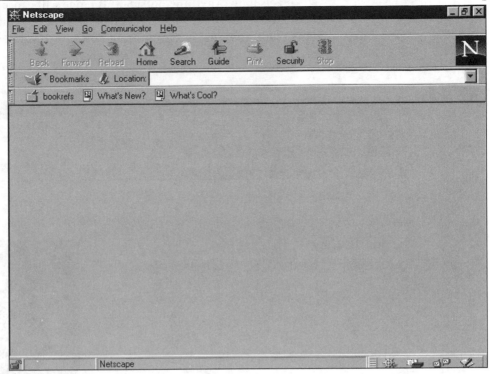

Different browser brands and versions take up different amounts of pixels. You can get a measurement by doing a screen shot of a browser in action, and then measuring the pixel areas in Photoshop.

Solutions for Designers

Solutions to the spatial constraints of shape, resolution, and browser differences do exist. They include:

- **Design to the lowest denominator**—Always design with the 640×480 screen resolution in mind. To do this, you'll need to work within the maximum available space per screen. Most designers feel that a safe screen area is 595 pixels

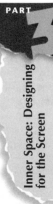

wide, by 295 pixels long. Anything outside this range will cause a horizontal scroll to appear, which looks very unprofessional (Figure 9.11). Furthermore, no graphic (other than the one exception noted below) should exceed either dimension, nor should a table or any other element.

FIGURE 9.11

Horizontal scroll bar

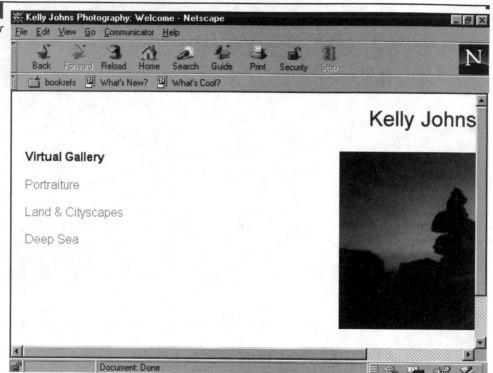

For a very cool downloadable ruler that designers can use to remind themselves of the graphic limitations, visit the Web Page Design for Designers Web site at `http://ds.dial.pipex.com/pixelp/wpdesign/wpdintro.shtml`.

ON line!

- **Keep higher resolution audiences in mind**—If you're using background graphics (see Chapter 16), they will tile in order to create the background image. For this reason, you will have to design margin-style background graphics with a higher resolution—you should pay particular attention to width. Furthermore, background graphics do not influence the browser in any way and will not cause a horizontal scroll despite their width (Figure 9.12). It is also possible that added space will appear at higher resolutions, but does not affect the design, which you can see in Figure 9.13.

FIGURE 9.12

A background graphic creates the colored margin in this example.

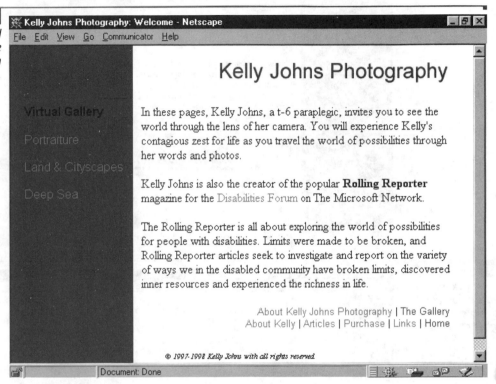

- **Test your pages**—This is *always* true, but important enough to bear repeating here. Pages should be tested on a variety of systems and with different browsers. Do they scroll horizontally? You may have a problem. Look at each page in a variety of resolutions—do they work or are they problematic, with repeating tiled backgrounds (as in Figure 9.14)? Testing your pages keeps your work looking its best from one computer to another.

"It's bad enough to have to scroll in one (vertical) direction; having to scroll in two directions is intolerable."

LYNCH AND HORTON, AUTHORS, *Yale C/AIM Web Style Guide*

Inner Space: Designing for the Screen

PART

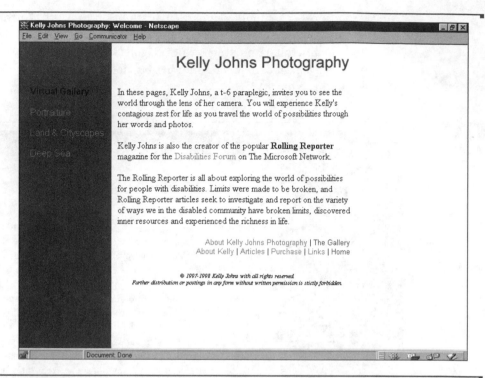

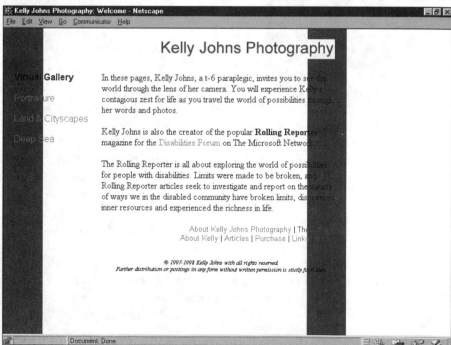

Working Efficiently in a Small Space

Design techniques drawn from methods used in visual and interior design can help designers work within the space of the Web. They include freeing up space by altering a visitor's visual perception of that space, and rearranging virtual furniture and knick-knacks so that a sense of balance between design elements can be achieved.

Constraints

Since the Web is already a constrained, constricted space, why constrain it more? Still, many people do, and it works in direct opposition to you if you're trying to achieve graceful design.

There's a phenomenon on the Web that I call the "box-it" problem. You've probably seen it—you may even be guilty of perpetrating it.

Go back to the picture-frame metaphor we looked at earlier. Now, think about photographs and graphics you've seen on the Web—some design amateurs, and even some professionals, seem to think that using a border or table around a photo or other graphic image makes it look good (Figure 9.15).

It doesn't.

FIGURE 9.15

Tables around an image look amateurish.

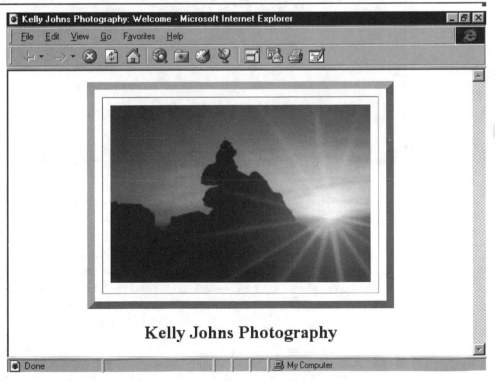

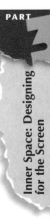

PART

Inner Space: Designing for the Screen

The reason is because there is yet *another* frame around that image. The computer is framing the browser, which is framing the Web page, which is framing the frame which frames the natural edge of the image.

The space is constrained to begin with—don't add more restrictions! Freeing up images gives visitors the perception that the space is broader, more open (Figure 9.16). While the *inclination* might be to frame the pretty picture—which works well for a picture on a wall where there is plenty of space—Web space in comparison is tiny.

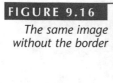

FIGURE 9.16

The same image without the border

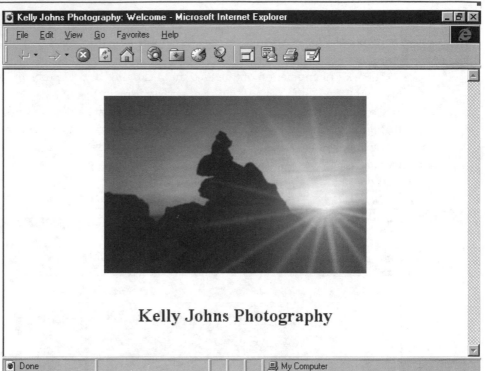

When working with images or tables, it's usually wise to use a value of "0" for the border attribute. Sometimes, tables with borders can be used to achieve a good-looking page that doesn't feel constrained. Check out Chapter 10 for more information on how to best use tables and frames for layout design.

You can always add special effects to images to make them attractive, such as the drop shadow in Figure 9.17, or you can keep a flat look, which can be just as attractive (Figure 9.18). More on graphic effects can be found in Chapter 16.

FIGURE 9.17

A drop shadow adds a dimensional effect.

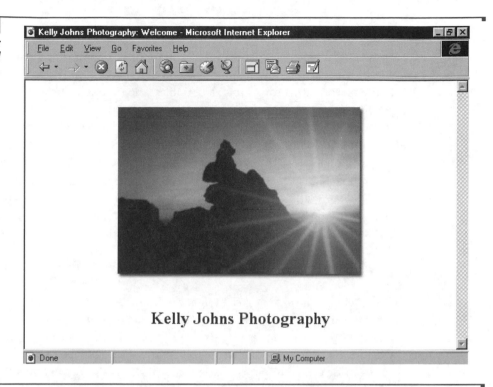

FIGURE 9.18

Flat images look fine, too.

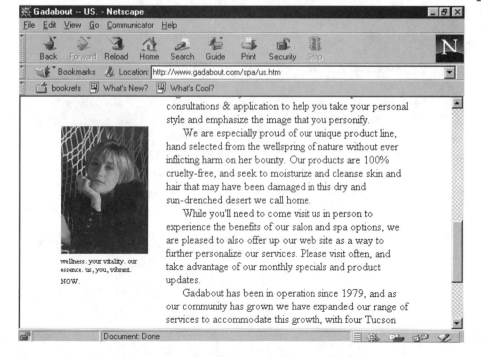

Clutter

I always like to tell the story about the New York apartments of my childhood. My aunts always had every piece of furniture brought over from the old country jammed into the place, and on top of that, lace doilies, and on top of those, knick-knacks and doo-dads and all kinds of stuff!

I always felt horribly tense in this environment. I couldn't move around; it seemed as though I would literally suffocate in the clutter. It wasn't that my aunts weren't clean, goodness knows they were immaculate; they just had so much jammed into an already small space.

If you have a tiny room with no windows, how do you make it look bigger? One thing you can do is paint it white, or at least a light color. You can also remove all the knick-knacks and doo-dads and furnish it sparsely, simply. Furthermore, there's the old mirror trick—adding a *sense* of space to the room.

I have a design rule. It's not original, but it's not much followed on the Web: Less is more.

Simplicity, in the case of Web design, can be a very potent technique. No, this doesn't mean you have to restrict yourself. The site in Figure 9.19 has plenty going on. But notice how everything is very specifically placed. That's the key to success with clutter on the Web. Your Web visitors won't run the risk of feeling tense and out of place in those cramped rooms. Instead, they'll want to sit down and stay a while.

Weight and Size

Weight is how heavy an image appears on a page. Images that are too heavy create a visual sluggishness, much like heavy furniture in a small room. You want to avoid very heavily weighted graphics, like the one shown in Figure 9.20, and go for smaller, crisper looks, as in Figure 9.21.

Another issue is *size*—how large should images appear to be on the page, how long should a page scroll. I believe images should never be larger than a single screen, and in most cases, they need to be much smaller. There are exceptions to this, but a designer has to know what he or she is doing in order to get away with it.

How long should a screen scroll? It's best to keep it no longer than three screens. Much more than that and you're making your audience work too hard. You don't want that.

Keep your weight down, and your size in balance, and you're well on your way to better looking sites.

FIGURE 9.19

This site has lots of stuff, but plenty of visual space.

FIGURE 9.20

This graphic is very heavy.

FIGURE 9.21

Less weight equals more space.

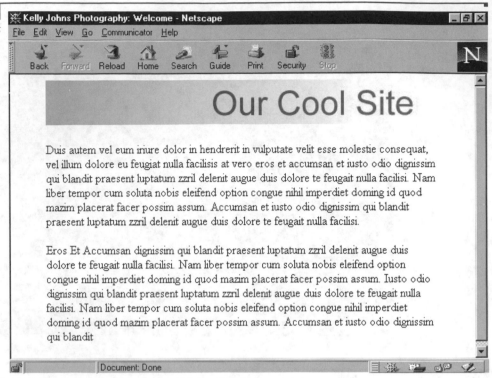

Relating Text and Media

The relationship between text and media is important to how space is perceived. If text is too close to a graphic, that cluttered, cramped sense can result. Similarly, if text is too far away from a graphic, it's going to cause a problem with balance.

In this section, you'll learn how to align text and media to achieve that balance. You'll learn how to do this with conventional HTML, style sheets, and tables—all common methods that designers use to achieve a steady look.

Alignment

Alignment refers to the where, and how, text and images are placed on a page. Text alignment is also termed *justification*, particularly in the world of print media.

The alignment of text is both about readability and visual appeal. English is typically left justified, which means it begins at the left margin of a page and has a ragged right edge. Left justification is, and should remain, the standard for body text.

However, there are times when you'll want to justify text differently. For example, shorter bursts of text can be very interesting when right-aligned, and centering comes in handy in certain instances. The centering of text is horribly overused, though, and this practice should be limited to specific instances which we'll discuss throughout the upcoming demonstrations.

The appearance of an image on a page, particularly in relation to text, also has much to do with how a page is perceived.

Conventional HTML

There are several alignment methods to be aware of in conventional HTML. They include aligning divisions and paragraphs, which can include images or other media; aligning images or media on the horizontal and vertical axis; and *floating*—a method used to align and balance text and images or other media.

Divisions and Paragraphs

<div> . . . </div>   This is the *division* tag and it's one of the most powerful methods of dividing and aligning blocks of information. Anything within a division will be aligned to the attribute for that division. The three attributes for division include:

center   This will center all the data within the division. Centering should usually be reserved for smaller bits of text. Copyright information at the bottom of a page is a good candidate (Figure 9.22).

```
<div align="center">

<font face="times, garamond" size="1">

<i>&copy; 1997-1998 Kelly Johns with all rights reserved.
<br>
Further distribution or postings in any form without
written permission is stictly forbidden. </i>
</font>

</div>
```

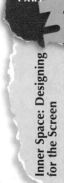

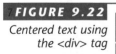

FIGURE 9.22

*Centered text using
the <div> tag*

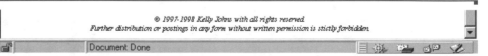

© 1997-1998 Kelly Johns with all rights reserved.
Further distribution or postings in any form without written permission is stictly forbidden.

Document: Done

NOTE

Many Web designers still use the <center>...</center> tag option for centering text. I advise against it—the <div align="center"> method is much more stable.

left This attribute makes all information left aligned. Since this is a page's normal default alignment, you'll rarely use it, unless you're working within a table cell or other area of a page that is aligned differently.

right This attribute will right-align your data. Notice how both the text, and the image, are aligned to the right of the page in Figure 9.23.

```
<div align="right">

<img src="images/kel.jpg" width="350" height="235" border="0" alt="Sunset Photograph">
<p>

Duis autem vel eum iriure dolor in <a href="dummy.htm">hendrerit in vulputate</a>
velit esse molestie consequat, vel illum dolore eu feugiat nulla facilisis at
vero eros et accumsan et iusto odio dignissim qui blandit praesent luptatum zzril
delenit augue duis dolore te feugait nulla facilisi.

</div>
```

<p>. . .</p> Using the paragraph tag with both the starting and ending tag, combined with the same attributes as found within the <div> tag, will create the exact same type of alignment.

```
center  All of the text in this example will be centered:
<p align="center">

Duis autem vel eum iriure dolor in hendrerit in vulputate velit esse molestie
consequat, vel illum dolore eu feugiat nulla facilisis at vero eros et accumsan
et iusto odio dignissim qui blandit praesent luptatum zzril delenit augue duis
dolore te feugait nulla facilisi.

</p>
```

left Once again, left is the standard default for paragraphs, so you will rarely, if ever, use this attribute with a paragraph tag.

right The following data will align right:

```
<p align="right">

Duis autem vel eum iriure dolor in hendrerit in vulputate velit esse molestie
consequat, vel illum dolore eu feugiat nulla facilisis at vero eros et accumsan
et iusto odio dignissim qui blandit praesent luptatum zzril delenit augue duis
dolore te feugait nulla facilisi.

</p>
```

FIGURE 9.23

Right alignment using the <div> tag

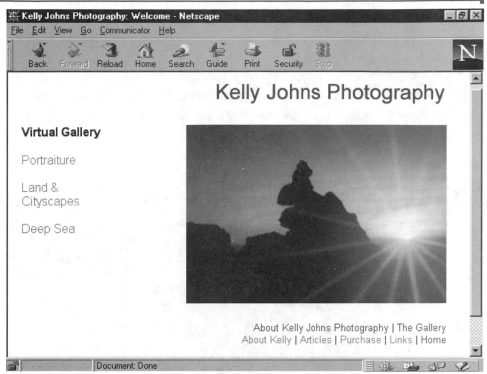

 TIP

As you can see from the previous code example, paragraph alignment requires an opening and closing tag at each section of data. Therefore, if you are attempting to align more than just one section on a page, it's quicker and neater to use the <div> option.

Alignment of Media

Images and other media can be aligned within their respective tags. They can be aligned on either the horizontal or vertical axis.

Horizontal alignment includes the left and right attributes. To align an image, use the `align=` attribute :

```
<img src="my-image.gif" align="left" border="0" width="200" height="200">
```

Other media, such as a Flash object, would follow similar syntax, but you'll note that the `object` tag itself contains the string within the opening tag, and requires a closing tag as well.

```
<object
classid="clsid:D27CDB6E-AE6D-11CF-96B8-444553540000"
codebase="fsplash.cab" align="right" border="0" width="451"
height="230">
</object>
```

To obtain more control over how the image or object appears with text, you can use the <br> tag with the following attributes:

<br clear="right">   Use this after a left-aligned image to force the body of text to the right (Figure 9.24).

FIGURE 9.24

Breaking to the right

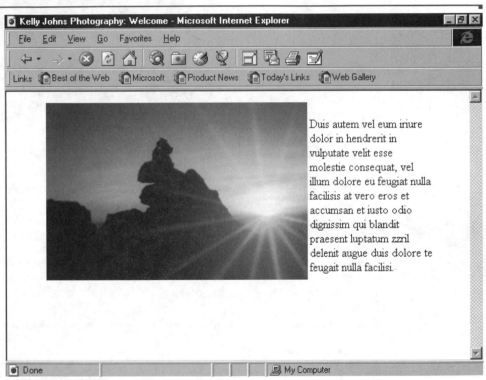

<br clear="left">   If you've right-aligned an image, this will argue the body of text to appear at the right of the image (Figure 9.25).

<br clear="all">   Use this to clear all information away from the image (Figure 9.26).

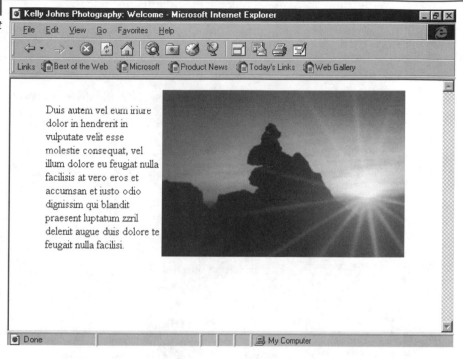

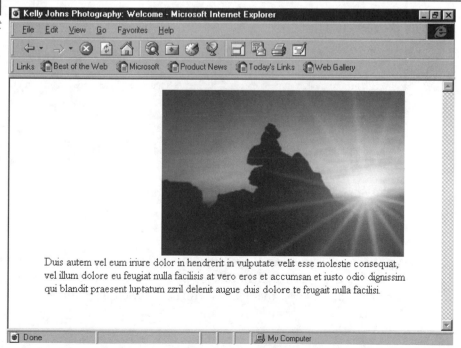

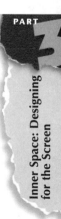

PART

Inner Space: Designing
for the Screen

Vertical alignment uses a number of attributes, including:

align="top" This will align the top of the image or media to the top of a given line.

align="middle" Middle alignment is to the middle of a line.

align="bottom" The bottom of an image will align with the bottom of the line.

Figure 9.27 shows an example of each of these alignment options.

FIGURE 9.27

Vertical alignment

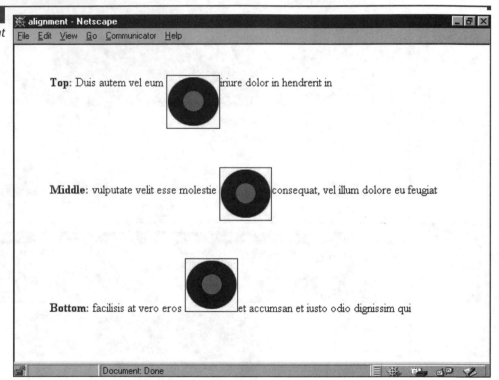

For other attributes specific to individual browsers or HTML versions, check out Appendix A and B.

Floating Images

Another important method available that allows you to align media is referred to as *floating*. This is a more dynamic alignment that relies on the relationship of blocks of text to an image *within* that text. Floating is a powerful technique, as it creates space on a page in a natural fashion.

Floating is created by eliminating any breaks after the image. For example, if you have an image and want to float it within a paragraph, you'll first place and align the image, and then add the paragraph, never using any break between the image and paragraph:

```
<img src="images/kel.jpg" width="350" height="235" border="0" alt="Sunset
Photograph">

Duis autem vel eum iriure dolor in hendrerit in vulputate velit esse
molestie consequat, vel illum dolore eu feugiat nulla facilisis at vero eros
et accumsan et iusto odio dignissim qui blandit praesent luptatum zzril
delenit augue duis dolore te feugait nulla facilisi.
<p>
```

Figure 9.28 shows the results. Note how the text wraps around the image. This is floating. But also notice that the text is flush against the image. In order to make the image and text look less cluttered, you can use attributes that control horizontal and vertical spacing.

FIGURE 9.28

Floating text

PART 3

Inner Space: Designing for the Screen

hspace   This is *horizontal space*. It controls how much white space is placed around the horizontal space (left and right sides) of the image.

vspace   *Vertical space* places white space to the vertical space to the top and bottom of the image.

Let's change the image code in our previous example to the following:

```
<img src="images/kel.jpg" width="350" height="235" border="0" hspace="10"
vspace="10" alt="Sunset Photograph">
```

You'll see in Figure 9.29 that a nice amount of space has been added between the image and the text.

Tables

Tables can control the placement of any image or object with a great deal of precision. Using table attributes, you can also add enough visual space to avoid clutter problems.

The following is a code example of an HTML page with a photograph, several text areas with alignment properties, and a graphic header.

```html
<html>
<head>
<title>Kelly Johns Photography: Welcome</title>
</head>

<body bgcolor="#FFFFFF" text="#000000" link="#999933" vlink="#993300"
alink="#FFFFFF">
```

The table's attribute, `cellpadding="10"`, is the command for 10 pixels to be placed between the text and the table border.

```html
<table border="0" width="595" cellpadding="10" cellspacing="0">
<tr>
```

All of the information in this cell is aligned to the right. Therefore, we don't code the image to align, because the cell alignment attribute and value right-aligns all of the information within that cell. The `valign` attribute (vertical alignment) is an attribute that aligns the table cell information to the top of the cell. This attribute is discussed in greater detail in Chapter 13.

```html
<td width="595" valign="top" colspan="2" align="right">
<img src="images/kel-hed.gif" width="400" height="35" border="0" alt="Kelly
Johns Photography (header image)">
</td>
</tr>

<tr>
```

The next cell uses no horizontal alignment, so the information within it defaults to the left:

```html
<td valign="top">

<font face="arial,helvetica">

<b>Virtual Gallery</b>
<p>

<a href="port.htm">Portraiture</a>
<p>
```

```
<a href="land.htm">Land & Cityscapes</a>
<p>
<a href="image.htm">Deep Sea</a>
<p>

</font>

</td>
```

The text in this section aligns naturally to the left default as it is not defined in the table cell:

```
<td valign="top" width="445">
```

```
In these pages, Kelly Johns, a t-6 paraplegic, invites you to see the world
through the lens of her camera. You will experience Kelly's contagious zest for
life as you travel the world of possibilities through her words and photos.
<p>
```

```
Kelly Johns is also the creator of the popular <b>Rolling Reporter</b>
magazine for the <a href="http://forums.msn.com/disabilities/">Disabilities
Forum</a> on The Microsoft Network.
<p>
```

```
The Rolling Reporter is all about exploring the world of possibilities for
people with disabilities. Limits were made to be broken, and Rolling
Reporter articles seek to investigate and report on the variety of ways we
in the disabled community have broken limits, discovered inner resources and
experienced the richness in life.
<p>
</tr>
```

```
<tr>
```

```
<td align="right" colspan="2">
```

```
<font size="2" face="arial,helvetica">
```

```
<a href="aboutk.htm">About Kelly Johns Photography</a> |
<a href="gallery.htm">The Gallery</a>
<br>
<a href="kelly.htm">About Kelly</a> |
<a href="articles.htm">Articles</a> |
```

```
<a href="purchase.htm">Purchase</a> |
<a href="links.htm">Links</a> |
<a href="index.htm">Home</a>

</td>
</tr>
</table>
<p>
```

Here the <div> tag centers the text. We could have also created another table row and aligned it to the center. Either approach is legitimate, it's just a matter of preference.

```
<div align="center">
<font face="times, garamond" size="1">
<i>&copy; 1997-1998 Kelly Johns with all rights reserved.
<br>
Further distribution or postings in any form without
written permission is stictly forbidden. </i>

</font>
</div>

</body>
</html>
```

Figure 9.30 shows the page as it is designed. To show how the tables control the placement of images, give the border attribute a value of "1." Figure 9.31 shows the control lines of the table.

Style Sheets

Style sheets are a powerful means to add layout and design information to an HTML page without disturbing the purity of the markup language. However, the practical application of this in commercial Web design is currently questionable. Style sheet compliant browsers are currently limited to Internet Explorer versions 3.0 and above and Netscape Navigator 4.0, and are not necessarily fully compliant with significant bugs remaining in these versions.

There are many arguments as to why style sheets should be adopted for style. One such argument is that HTML was never meant to be a design tool. But it has become just that, complete with tacked-on design tags. Whether designers will ever fully adopt style sheets for layout and design over those tags added to HTML is yet to be seen.

PART

3

Inner Space: Designing
for the Screen

FIGURE 9.30

Table-based alignment

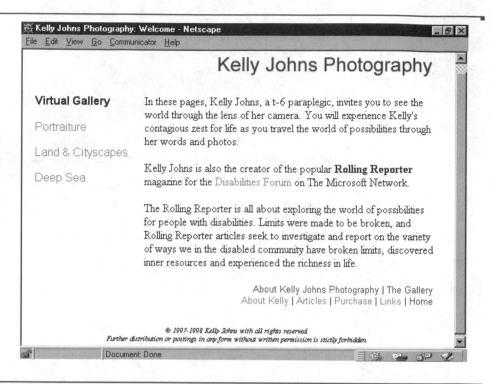

FIGURE 9.31

Borders set to "1" to see table-based layout

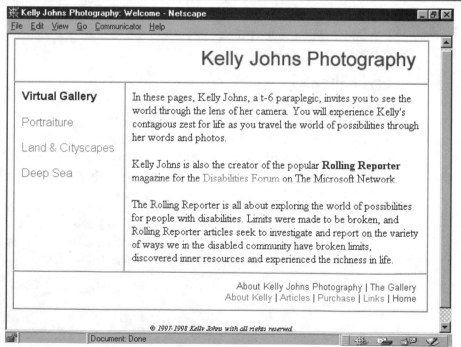

Style sheets can be inline, embedded, or linked. *Inline* style places the style element into an HTML tag within a given HTML page. An *embedded* style sheet is a combination of all of the style information for a page placed at the top of that page. A *linked*, or external, sheet is very similar in look to an embedded style sheet, but it's saved as a separate file, and can be linked to from numerous pages. Any page that links to it will adopt those styles. For more information on style sheets, you can visit the Design Studio Web site at http://www.designstudio.net/.

The application of style sheets is, at the time of this writing, not realistic for most Internet-based sites. The reason? Other than a few of the lesser-known browsers, only Internet 3.0 and above, and Netscape 4.0 and above can support cascading style sheets. Even then, that support is unstable. Practical Web design at this time must still embrace more conventional HTML practices. Still, there's nothing that prevents a designer from using both simultaneously, and there certainly is every reason for designers to become more familiar with style sheets.

ON line!

This chapter only provides a very rudimentary description of style sheets. For more information on their use, I highly recommend a visit to WebReference's style sheet links page at http://www.webreference.com/html/css.html.

For practical purposes, you'll be seeing style sheet examples as well as conventional HTML throughout this book. This gives you the ability to design using either or both.

Text alignment in style sheets can be accomplished using the text-align attribute. You can place this attribute in any HTML tag where it makes logical sense to do so. Common places to add the alignment attribute include the <div>, <p>, or <span> tags:

```
<div style="text-align: right">
All of the information in this division will be aligned to the right.
</div>

<p style="text-align: left">
This text will align left.
</p>

<span style="text-align: center">
This text appears centered.
</span>
```

Figure 9.32 shows how this text appears in a browser that supports style sheets.

FIGURE 9.32

*Style sheet
alignment*

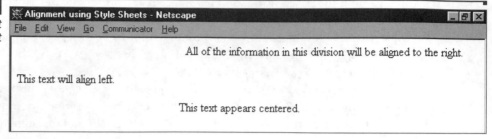

The text-align attribute can be added to embedded or linked style sheets as well:

```
P {font-family: times; font-size: 12pt; text-align: right}
```

This style will control all standard paragraphs by ensuring that they use a 12-point Times font that is right aligned.

Positioning of graphics and advanced style sheet issues can be studied further in *Mastering HTML 4.0* (Sybex, 1998).

Sizing Text and Images

To create a good-looking page that keeps text and media balanced involves not only how space is delegated, but also how much of it is used. A huge graphic next to a tiny bit of text is going to be unsightly. Similarly, an enormous header combined with a tiny graphic will look strange.

How you size text, images, and other media is going to play a big part in the way your page appears. You want to bring balance to the page through the use of graphics and text. Figure 9.33 shows a too-large graphic next to too-tiny text. Figure 9.34 shows too-large text combined with a miniscule graphic. A perfect example of why achieving balance is so important.

FIGURE 9.33

Big graphic, tiny text

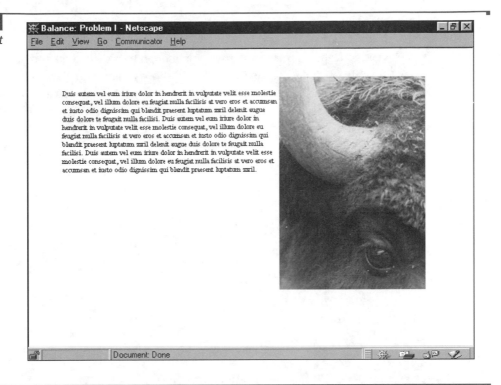

FIGURE 9.34

Big text, tiny graphic

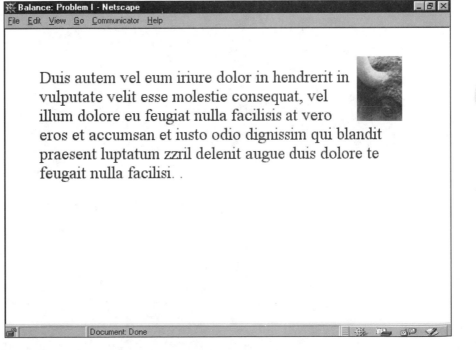

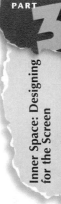

Next Up

As if the concepts in this chapter weren't enough to provide you and your site visitors with plenty of space, the next chapter will show you how to gain even *more* space, as well as providing guidelines to ensure that your sites are consistent from page to page.

chapter 10

EVEN MORE
WEB SPACE

EVEN MORE WEB SPACE

C an't this woman get enough space? I *know* that's what you're thinking at this point—there's an entire chapter devoted to the topic and I'm *still* rambling on about it!

The fact is, space is so critical to design, and particularly to Web design, that enough cannot be written about it. It is crucial that you not only learn how to work with space—but that you understand why these issues are so important.

In the last chapter, we examined what makes Web space challenging and how to address some of the constraints involved in the Web.

This time, we're going to take a look at what you don't see and to learn how to use these techniques to make a very visible difference in your design work.

In this chapter, we will discuss:

- Calculated design
- White space
- The use of margins
- Proximity
- How to achieve white space and proximity with standard HTML

- Table-based approaches to space
- Style sheet control

By making a habit of these techniques, you will ensure that space and spatial relationships become natural in your work. It will be a painless process for you—and add maximum comfort for your site visitors.

The Things You Don't See

One of the topics most covered when I was a Media Studies graduate student was how to look for what was *not there*. This may seem strange, but the power of omission is no error. When it comes to media, the most brilliant designers understand that what is left *out* of a design can be as important as what is put *in* to that design.

This relates both to the *content*—the literal elements included (or not included) on a given page—and to *spatial* awareness. The lack of an included object may in fact weigh the same, conceptually, as an object. This lack, or omission when anticipated, is referred to as *white space*.

Content

If you're doing a print advertisement that sells a vitamin complex to mature adults, it's going to be in your best interest to leave out anything that portrays or symbolizes weakness, sickness, lack, or want. The idea is to present an image of health, strength, abundance, and fulfillment. So, you might choose to picture a happy older couple on the golf course. The trees are tall and strong; the green is lush and fertile. The people are smiling; their hair is thick and lustrous; they are happy, trim, fit, and enjoying their time mightily.

Take the same picture, but place a walker near the husband. Add an oxygen tank next to the woman. How effective is this ad going to be at selling a vitamin that's supposed to make you healthy and strong? Not very!

Yes, this is an exaggerated example—the things you choose to leave out or put in to a design will be more subtle than this. But the metaphor clearly shows you why certain things must be left out, while other items bear the focus of the piece.

Sound calculated and cold? Advertising is extremely calculated, and anyone who thinks that successful advertisers get that way by being careless or by chance is making a grave mistake. Similarly, serious thought must be put into any presentation—particularly if your design is set up to advertise a given product.

PART

Inner Space: Designing for the Screen

Does this mean you have to be unethical? No. Calculated? Absolutely. Thinking about what isn't there is as critical to a site design as what is.

OFF line!

Open a copy of your favorite print magazine and select one advertisement. Write down what you see, and think about what you don't see. What has been omitted from this advertisement that makes it successful? In this case, look for subtleties. Are there people in the ad? Products? Think about the concept of the ad, and how its designers have delivered it. Analyze why the items left *out* of the ad can be just as persuasive as those that are *in* the ad.

White Space

What *isn't* there also relates to space. The absence of text, a graphic animation, or an object or action on a Web page means that there is space in its place. This absence of stuff is called white space. As a designer, you want white space desperately.

White space leads the eye. It rests the eye at intervals between activity. It balances and strengthens the impact of your message. It is what isn't there—but what in essence, is *totally* there.

> *"The presence of white space is a symbol of smart, of class, of simplicity, of the essence of refinement. The absence of white space is a symbol of vulgarity, of crassness, of schlock, of bad taste."*
>
> KEITH ROBERTSON, On White Space / When Less is More

It's important to remember that white space isn't necessarily white. It is whatever color or design the background space of the environment is. So, if your Web page is designed with a black background, as in Figure 10.1, white space is actually black space. Similarly, if you use a background graphic pattern, as in Figure 10.2, then the pattern is also white space.

FIGURE 10.1

White space can be black.

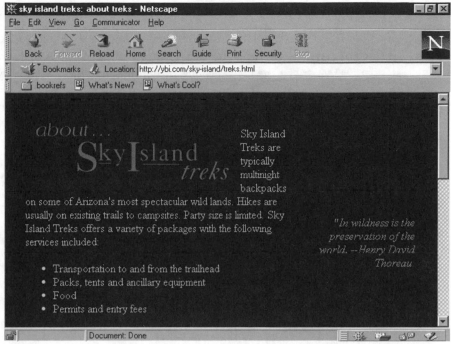

FIGURE 10.2

Background patterns are considered white space.

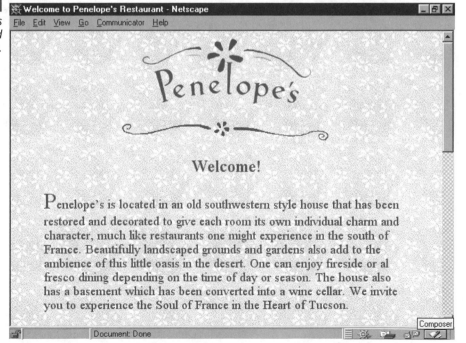

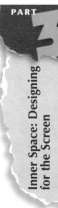

Margins Sweet Margins

One way to add space, enhance readability, and avoid a site that looks like a cliché is to be sure you have margins on your page. There are three methods to do this: by using a standard HTML trick called *blockquoting*; by defining margins in the body tag (this is a browser-specific method); and through the use of style sheets.

Blockquotes

The `<blockquote>` tag and its companion, `</blockquote>`, placed around page content, will instantly create margins and give you precious white space to the left and right of that content. Here's a sample of how to do that:

```
<html>
<head>
<title>Blockquoting = White Space!</title>
</head>

<body bgcolor="#FFFFFF" text="#000000" link="#FFCC99"
vlink="#9999CC" alink="#FFFFCC">

<blockquote>
Duis autem vel eum iriure dolor in hendrerit in vulputate velit esse moles-
tie consequat, vel illum dolore eu feugiat nulla facilisis at vero eros et
accumsan et iusto odio dignissim qui blandit praesent luptatum zzril delenit
augue duis dolore te feugait nulla facilisi.
<p>

Nam liber tempor cum soluta nobis eleifend option congue nihil imperdiet
doming id quod mazim placerat facer possim assum. Accumsan et iusto odio
dignissim qui blandit praesent luptatum zzril delenit augue duis dolore te
feugait nulla facilisi.
<p>

</blockquote>
</body>
</html>
```

Compare this page (Figure 10.3) to the same page with the blockquoting stripped from the code (Figure 10.4), and you will see a significant difference in the look of the page.

FIGURE 10.3

Blockquotes create white space along margins.

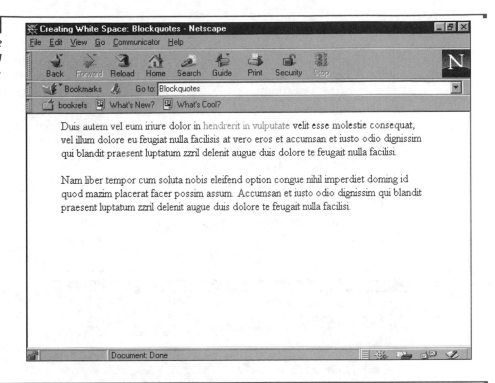

FIGURE 10.4

Remove the block-quotes and lose precious white space.

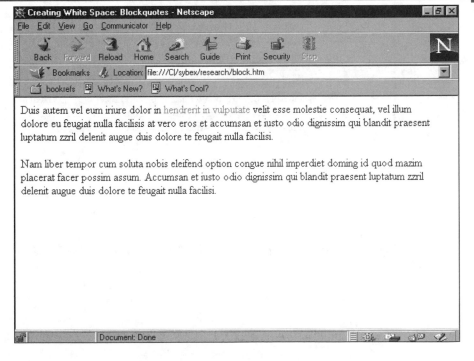

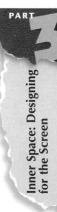

PART

Inner Space: Designing for the Screen

Body Tag Margins

Internet Explorer versions 3.0 and above support two <body> tag attributes that you can use when designing specifically for that browser. These are the leftmargin="x" and topmargin="x" attributes, providing control over the left and top margins of a page. For example, if you wanted to have about 120 pixels of white space to the left, and flush your page to the top of the browser's available page space, you would use the following syntax:

```
<body leftmargin="120" topmargin="0">
```

This page, shown in Figure 10.5 , has white space to the left, and reduces the top margin (space between the first line and the top of the viewing space) to "0." However, this code is not supported by Netscape. Figure 10.6 shows what the same code looks like in Netscape.

FIGURE 10.5

Left- and top-margin space

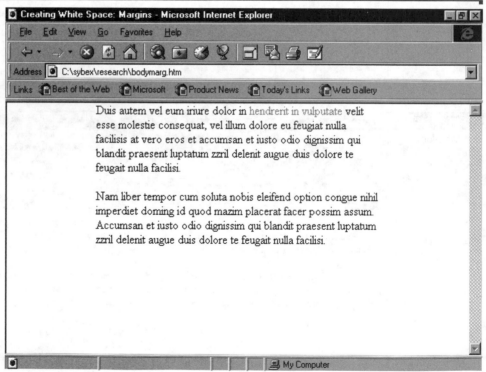

FIGURE 10.6

The same code is
ignored by
Netscape.

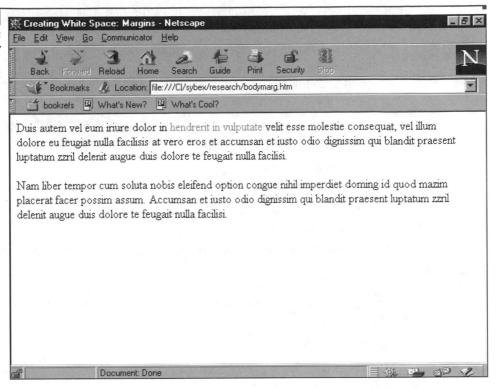

FIGURE 10.6

The same code is
ignored by
Netscape.

A "0" value for a top margin can be used to flush text or images to the top of the visible space. Interestingly, this can open space elsewhere on the page by maximizing the available space. If you visit http://www.microsoft.com/ with Internet Explorer, you'll see how the top navigation is flush top. Visit the site with Netscape, and you'll note that the entire spacing of the page is different.

Margins Using Style Sheets

Fourth-generation browsers (browsers with a 4.0 release or higher, such as Internet Explorer 4.0, or Netscape Navigator 4.0 or higher) that have cascading style sheet

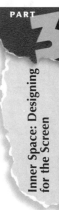

support allow for very specific margin control through style-based margin attributes. These attributes can control a page when set into the BODY style tag.

margin-left   To set a left margin using style sheets, select an amount of space in points, inches, centimeters, or pixels. The following code sets a left margin to $3/4$ of an inch:

```
{margin-left: .75in}
```

margin-right   Right margins can be created with the same spatial measurements. In this case, the example calls for 50 pixels of right-margin space:

```
{margin-right: 50px}
```

margin-top   The following code increases the space between the browser interface and the text by 20 points:

```
{margin-top: 20pt}
```

To flush information to the top of the page, use a margin-top value of 0 pixels:

```
{margin-top: 0px}
```

The following syntax shows an example of embedded style controlling a page's margins:

```
<html>

<head>
<title>Creating White Space: Style Sheet Margins</title>

<style type="text/css">
<!--

BODY {background: #FFFFFF;
      color: #000000;
      margin-left: 100px;
      margin-right: 100px;
      margin-top: 0px}
A {color: #999999}

-->
</style>

</head>

Duis autem vel eum iriure dolor in <a href="dummy.htm">hendrerit in
vulputate</a> velit esse molestie consequat, vel illum dolore eu feugiat
```

```
nulla facilisis at vero eros et accumsan et iusto odio dignissim qui blandit
praesent luptatum zzril delenit augue duis dolore te feugait nulla facilisi.
<p>

Nam liber tempor cum soluta nobis eleifend option congue nihil imperdiet
doming id quod mazim placerat facer possim assum. Accumsan et iusto odio
dignissim qui blandit praesent luptatum zzril delenit augue duis dolore te
feugait nulla facilisi.
<p>

</body>
</html>
```

In Figure 10.7, you can see the results of style as seen in Internet Explorer 4.0. Figure 10.8 shows the same page when tested with Netscape 4.0. Note that the style is ignored—despite the fact that Netscape is supposed to support style sheets. This is a frustrating but realistic example of browser incompatibilities.

FIGURE 10.7

Style in Internet Explorer 4.0

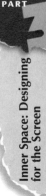

FIGURE 10.8

This style is ignored in Netscape 4.0.

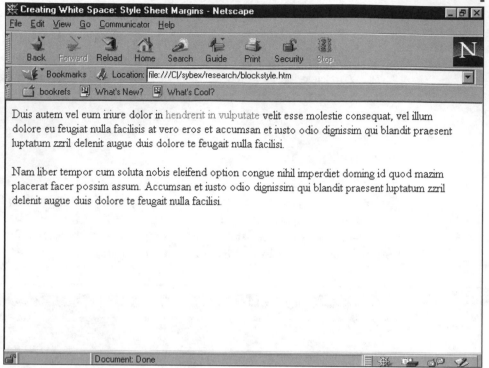

Duis autem vel eum iriure dolor in hendrerit in vulputate velit esse molestie consequat, vel illum dolore eu feugiat nulla facilisis at vero eros et accumsan et iusto odio dignissim qui blandit praesent luptatum zzril delenit augue duis dolore te feugait nulla facilisi.

Nam liber tempor cum soluta nobis eleifend option congue nihil imperdiet doming id quod mazim placerat facer possim assum. Accumsan et iusto odio dignissim qui blandit praesent luptatum zzril delenit augue duis dolore te feugait nulla facilisi.

Proximity

Proximity is how close—or how far—one object is to another object. In designing Web sites, you should try to place objects within a realistic distance from one another *and* from the boundaries of the browser interface and screen.

In Chapter 9, we looked at HTML alignment, tables, and style sheets as they control placement and alignment of objects. Now you'll get to take a closer look at controlling proximity with the same basic techniques.

Standard HTML

The spaces in between objects can be *horizontal* and *vertical*. Proximity in standard HTML is controlled with breaks, paragraphs, and pre-formatted text.

Breaks, <br>, place a single carriage return between objects or text areas. In this case, the break appears between the title "Give me a Break" and the paragraph beneath it (Figure 10.9).

```
<html>
<head>
<title>Break Example</title>
</head>
<body bgcolor="#FFFFFF" text="#000000" link="#999999"
vlink="#CCCCCC" alink="#FFFFCC">
<b>Give me a Break!</b>
<br>
Duis autem vel eum iriure dolor in <a href="dummy.htm">hendrerit in
vulputate</a> velit esse molestie consequat, vel illum dolore eu feugiat
nulla facilisis at vero eros et accumsan et iusto odio dignissim qui blandit
praesent luptatum zzril delenit augue duis dolore te feugait nulla facilisi.
</body>
</html>
```

FIGURE 10.9

Space gained with the break tag

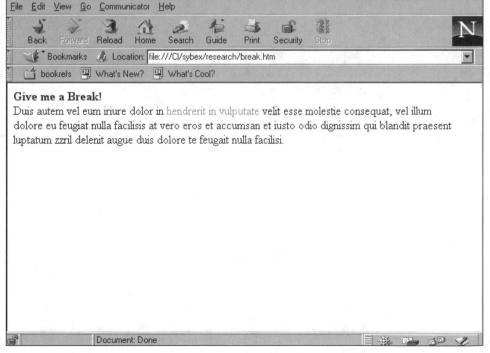

PART

3

Inner Space: Designing for the Screen

Paragraphs, <p>, place a single carriage return and single space between objects or text areas. You can see the difference between a <br> and a <p> if you compare Figure 10.10 with the previous Figure 10.9.

```
<html>

<head>
<title>Paragraph Break Example</title>
</head>

<body bgcolor="#FFFFFF" text="#000000" link="#999999"
vlink="#CCCCCC" alink="#FFFFCC">

<b>Give me a Paragraph Break!</b>

<p>
Duis autem vel eum iriure dolor in <a href="dummy.htm">hendrerit in
vulputate</a> velit esse molestie consequat, vel illum dolore eu feugiat
nulla facilisis at vero eros et accumsan et iusto odio dignissim qui blandit
praesent luptatum zzril delenit augue duis dolore te feugait nulla facilisi.

</body>
</html>
```

FIGURE 10.10

Space gained with the paragraph tag

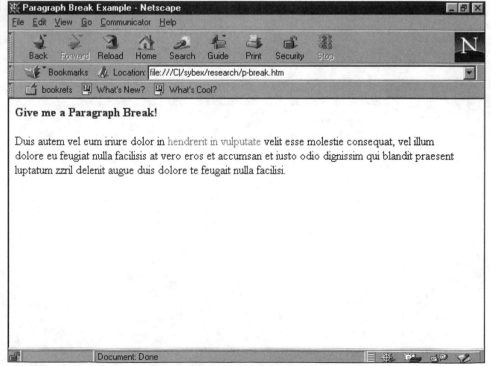

Pre-formatted text, <pre>, will add as many carriage returns as you add between the opening and closing tags:

```
<html>
<head>
<title>Pre-formatted Example</title>
</head>
<body bgcolor="#FFFFFF" text="#000000" link="#999999"
vlink="#CCCCCC" alink="#FFFFCC">
<b>Give me a Pre-formatted Break!</b>
<pre>

</pre>
Duis autem vel eum iriure dolor in <a href="dummy.htm">hendrerit in
vulputate</a> velit esse molestie consequat, vel illum dolore eu feugiat
nulla facilisis at vero eros et accumsan et iusto odio dignissim qui blandit
praesent luptatum zzril delenit augue duis dolore te feugait nulla facilisi.
</body>
</html>
```

The results can be seen in Figure 10.11.

FIGURE 10.11

Space gained with the pre-formatted text tag

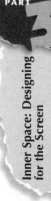

PART

Inner Space: Designing for the Screen

TIP

Common hacks to get space include stacking blockquotes or using list tags. These are marginally acceptable methods—it's better to use tables or style sheets instead, as they offer much more standardized control of proximity.

Vertical space between objects can be controlled with pre-formatted text as follows:

```
<html>

<head>
<title>Pre-formatted Text: Vertical Space</title>
</head>

<body bgcolor="#FFFFFF" text="#000000" link="#999999"
vlink="#CCCCCC" alink="#FFFFCC">

<b>Give me a Vertical Break!</b>
<p>

<pre>
Duis       autem      vel       eum
iriure     dolor      in        hendrerit
in         vulputate  vlit      esse
molestie   consequat  vel       illum
</pre>

</body>
</html>
```

Figure 10.12 shows the vertical space created by the pre-formatting tags.

The non-breaking space character   can be used to achieve vertical space. Each character creates one space, which can be seen in Figure 10.13.

```
<html>

<head>
<title>Non-Breaking Space</title>
</head>

<body bgcolor="#FFFFFF" text="#000000" link="#999999"
vlink="#CCCCCC" alink="#FFFFCC">
```

```
<b>Give me a Non-Breaking Space Break!</b>
<p>

Duis        autem
       vel    <br>
eum         iriure    
    dolor        <br>

</body>
</html>
```

Using visible characters to create space and a visual division between objects is a common technique, particularly in text-based navigation (Figure 10.14). You can use a period, a vertical bar, or square brackets for example. Be creative!

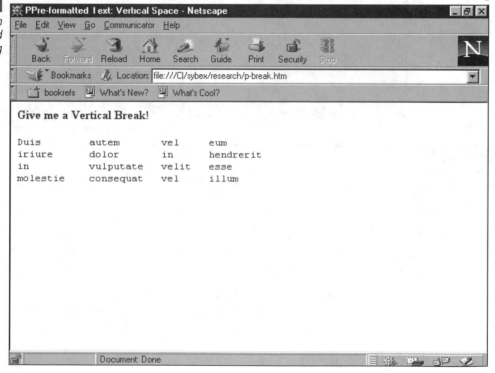

FIGURE 10.12

Vertical space with the pre-formatted text tag

FIGURE 10.13

Vertical space with
the non-breaking
space character

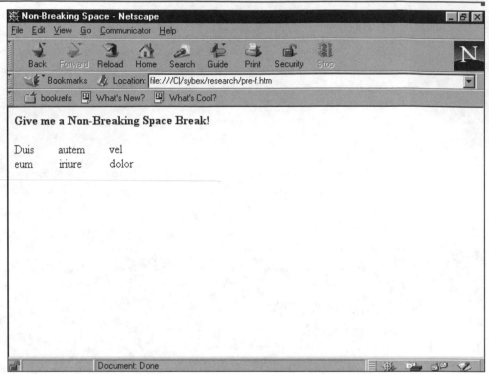

FIGURE 10.14

Visible characters,
such as a vertical
bar, help create a
division.

home | us | youSKIN | youHAIR | weDO | weTALK | NOW

Tables

Vertical and horizontal space can be controlled simultaneously using `cellpadding` and `cellspacing` attributes within the table tag. I touched on this in the previous chapter; here are some more explicit examples.

Cellpadding

The following code calls only for `cellpadding`, which controls the amount of space *between* what's in a cell and the cell wall. I've used a border of "1" here, so you can easily see the distance between the text and the cell's border (Figure 10.15).

```
<html>

<head>
<title>Space With Cellpadding</title>
</head>

<body bgcolor="#FFFFFF" text="#000000" link="#999999"
vlink="#CCCCCC" alink="#FFFFCC">

<table border="1" cellpadding="20">
<tr>

<td>
<img src="molfresc.jpg" width="143" height="150" border="0" alt="fresco
style painting">
</td>

<td>
Duis autem vel eum iriure dolor in <a href="dummy.htm">hendrerit in
vulputate</a> velit esse molestie consequat, vel illum dolore eu feugiat
nulla facilisis at vero eros et accumsan et iusto odio dignissim qui blandit
praesent luptatum zzril delenit augue duis dolore te feugait nulla facilisi.
Duis autem vel eum iriure dolor in <a href="dummy.htm">hendrerit in
vulputate</a> velit esse molestie consequat, vel illum dolore eu feugiat
nulla facilisis at vero eros et accumsan et iusto odio dignissim qui blandit
praesent luptatum zzril delenit augue duis dolore te feugait nulla facilisi.

</td>
</tr>
</table>

</body>
</html>
```

When the border is removed, we end up with plenty of white space cushioning the graphic and text, as shown in Figure 10.16.

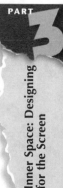

PART 3

Inner Space: Designing
for the Screen

FIGURE 10.15

The cellpadding *attribute inserts space between border and text areas.*

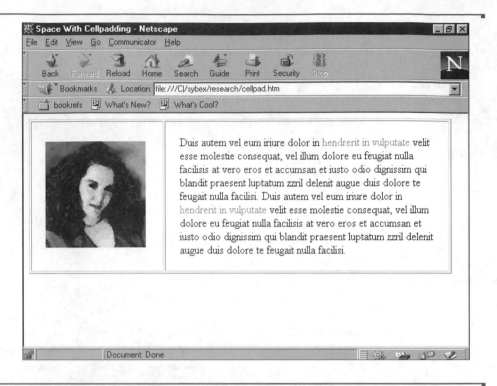

FIGURE 10.16

Remove the border for pure white space.

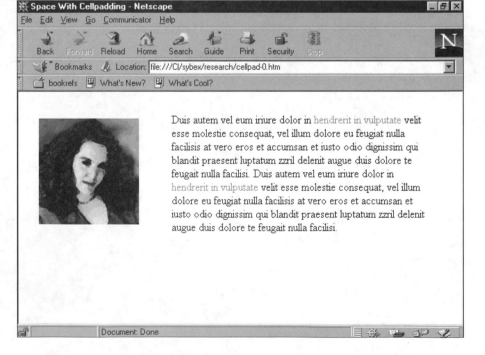

Cellspacing

Space can also be controlled with the `cellspacing` attribute. This controls the space between cells (Figure 10.17).

```html
<html>

<head>
<title>Space With Cellspacing</title>
</head>

<body bgcolor="#FFFFFF" text="#000000" link="#999999"
vlink="#CCCCCC" alink="#FFFFCC">

<table border="1" cellspacing="20">
<tr>

<td>
<img src="molfresc.jpg" width="143" height="150" border="0" alt="fresco
style painting">
</td>

<td>
Duis autem vel eum iriure dolor in <a href="dummy.htm">hendrerit in
vulputate</a> velit esse molestie consequat, vel illum dolore eu feugiat
nulla facilisis at vero eros et accumsan et iusto odio dignissim qui blandit
praesent luptatum zzril delenit augue duis dolore te feugait nulla facilisi.
Duis autem vel eum iriure dolor in <a href="dummy.htm">hendrerit in
vulputate</a> velit esse molestie consequat, vel illum dolore eu feugiat
nulla facilisis at vero eros et accumsan et iusto odio dignissim qui blandit
praesent luptatum zzril delenit augue duis dolore te feugait nulla facilisi.

</td>
</tr>
</table>

</body>
</html>
```

If we remove the table border, the results are indistinguishable, as shown in Figure 10.18. This demonstrates how the `cellspacing` and `cellpadding` attributes on their own can be used to control space very precisely.

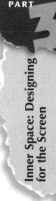

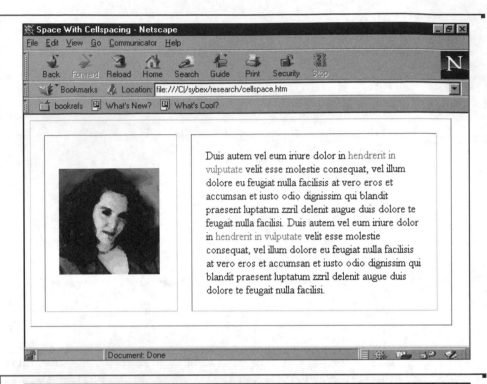

FIGURE 10.18

cellspacing *removes borders for space.*

"Each element on the page is important, but how it all fits together is what makes your site work or not."

CYNTHIA PENCHINA, Penchina Web Design

All Together Now

By using both attributes together, you can further control space. In the following example, both cellpadding and cellspacing have a numeric value of "20."

```
<html>

<head>
<title>Space With Cellspacing and Cellpadding</title>
</head>

<body bgcolor="#FFFFFF" text="#000000" link="#999999"
vlink="#CCCCCC" alink="#FFFFCC">

<table border="1" cellspacing="20" cellpadding="20">
<tr>

<td>
<img src="molfresc.jpg" width="143" height="150" border="0" alt="fresco
style painting">
</td>

<td>
Duis autem vel eum iriure dolor in <a href="dummy.htm">hendrerit in
vulputate</a> velit esse molestie consequat, vel illum dolore eu feugiat
nulla facilisis at vero eros et accumsan et iusto odio dignissim qui blandit
praesent luptatum zzril delenit augue duis dolore te feugait nulla facilisi.
Duis autem vel eum iriure dolor in <a href="dummy.htm">hendrerit in
vulputate</a> velit esse molestie consequat, vel illum dolore eu feugiat
nulla facilisis at vero eros et accumsan et iusto odio dignissim qui blandit
praesent luptatum zzril delenit augue duis dolore te feugait nulla facilisi.

</td>
</tr>
</table>

</body>
</html>
```

In Figure 10.19, you can see there is space between the elements *in* the individual table cells as well as between the cells themselves.

PART

3

Inner Space: Designing for the Screen

FIGURE 10.19

Cellspacing *and* cellpadding *create space around and in between objects.*

For variation, try different values between cellpadding and cellspacing.

```html
<html>

<head>
<title>Space With Cellspacing and Cellpadding: Variation</title>
</head>

<body bgcolor="#FFFFFF" text="#000000" link="#999999"
vlink="#CCCCCC" alink="#FFFFCC">

<table border="1" cellspacing="10" cellpadding="20">
<tr>

<td>
<img src="molfresc.jpg" width="143" height="150" border="0" alt="fresco
style painting">
</td>
```

```
<td>
Duis autem vel eum iriure dolor in <a href="dummy.htm">hendrerit in
vulputate</a> velit esse molestie consequat, vel illum dolore eu feugiat
nulla facilisis at vero eros et accumsan et iusto odio dignissim qui blandit
praesent luptatum zzril delenit augue duis dolore te feugait nulla facilisi.
Duis autem vel eum iriure dolor in <a href="dummy.htm">hendrerit in
vulputate</a> velit esse molestie consequat, vel illum dolore eu feugiat
nulla facilisis at vero eros et accumsan et iusto odio dignissim qui blandit
praesent luptatum zzril delenit augue duis dolore te feugait nulla facilisi.

</td>
</tr>
</table>

</body>
</html>
```

This table has more space between the cells, and more space between the cell
object and cell wall, as shown in Figure 10.20.

FIGURE 10.20

*Example of variation
in padding and
spacing values*

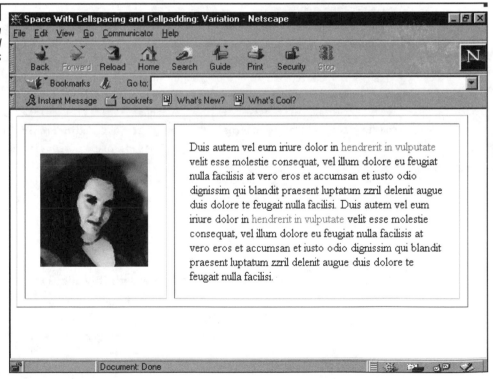

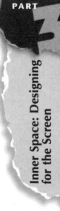

Alignment

Another variation would be to align elements within the cells after creating your table-based space.

```
<html>

<head>
<title>Space With Cellspacing and Cellpadding: Alignment</title>
</head>

<body bgcolor="#FFFFFF" text="#000000" link="#999999"
vlink="#CCCCCC" alink="#FFFFCC">

<table border="1" cellspacing="20" cellpadding="10">
<tr>

<td>
<img src="molfresc.jpg" width="143" height="150" border="0" alt="fresco
style painting">
</td>

<td valign="top">
Duis autem vel eum iriure dolor in <a href="dummy.htm">hendrerit in
vulputate</a> velit esse molestie consequat, vel illum dolore eu feugiat
nulla facilisis at vero eros et accumsan et iusto odio dignissim qui blandit
praesent luptatum zzril delenit augue duis dolore te feugait nulla facilisi.
Duis autem vel eum iriure dolor in <a href="dummy.htm">hendrerit in
vulputate</a> velit esse molestie consequat, vel illum dolore eu feugiat
nulla facilisis at vero eros et accumsan et iusto odio dignissim qui blandit
praesent luptatum zzril delenit augue duis dolore te feugait nulla facilisi.

</td>
</tr>
</table>

</body>
</html>
```

Note how the text in the right-hand cell now vertically aligns to the top (Figure 10.21).

FIGURE 10.21

Right cell content is vertically aligned to top.

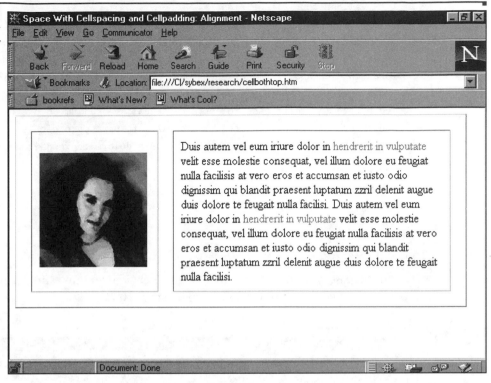

Yet another variation is to add horizontal alignment:

```
<html>

<head>
<title>Space With Cellspacing and Cellpadding: Alignment</title>
</head>

<body bgcolor="#FFFFFF" text="#000000" link="#999999"
vlink="#CCCCCC" alink="#FFFFCC">

<table border="0" cellspacing="20" cellpadding="10">
<tr>

<td align="right">
<img src="molfresc.jpg" width="143" height="150" border="0" alt="fresco
style painting">
</td>
```

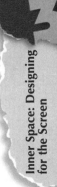

```
<td valign="top" align="right">
Duis autem vel eum iriure dolor in <a href="dummy.htm">hendrerit in
vulputate</a> velit esse molestie consequat, vel illum dolore eu feugiat
nulla facilisis at vero eros et accumsan et iusto odio dignissim qui blandit
praesent luptatum zzril delenit augue duis dolore te feugait nulla facilisi.
Duis autem vel eum iriure dolor in <a href="dummy.htm">hendrerit in
vulputate</a> velit esse molestie consequat, vel illum dolore eu feugiat
nulla facilisis at vero eros et accumsan et iusto odio dignissim qui blandit
praesent luptatum zzril delenit augue duis dolore te feugait nulla facilisi.

</td>
</tr>
</table>

</body>
</html>
```

In this case, you end up with right-aligned text and an interesting, jagged space between the graphic and text, as shown in Figure 10.22.

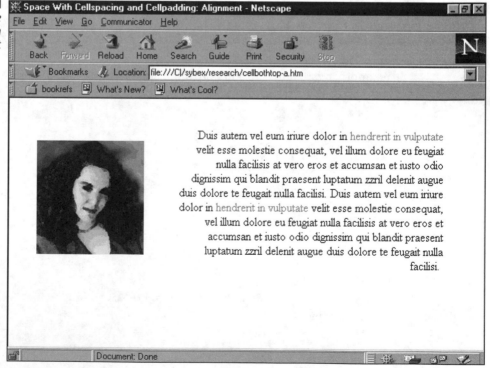

Cellpadding and cellspacing will control space between rows as well. This makes it easy to control longer sections of information.

```
<html>

<head>
<title>Space With Cellspacing and Cellpadding: Alignment</title>
</head>

<body bgcolor="#FFFFFF" text="#000000" link="#999999"
vlink="#CCCCCC" alink="#FFFFCC">

<table border="1" cellspacing="20" cellpadding="10">
<tr>

<td>
<img src="molfresc.jpg" width="143" height="150" border="0" alt="fresco
style painting">
</td>

<td>
Duis autem vel eum iriure dolor in <a href="dummy.htm">hendrerit in
vulputate</a> velit esse molestie consequat, vel illum dolore eu feugiat
nulla facilisis at vero eros et accumsan et iusto odio dignissim qui blandit
praesent luptatum zzril delenit augue duis dolore te feugait nulla facilisi.
Duis autem vel eum iriure dolor in <a href="dummy.htm">hendrerit in
vulputate</a> velit esse molestie consequat, vel illum dolore eu feugiat
nulla facilisis at vero eros et accumsan et iusto odio dignissim qui blandit
praesent luptatum zzril delenit augue duis dolore te feugait nulla facilisi.

</td>
</tr>

<tr>

<td>
Duis autem vel eum iriure dolor in <a href="dummy.htm">hendrerit in
vulputate</a> velit esse molestie consequat, vel illum dolore eu feugiat
nulla facilisis at vero eros et accumsan et iusto odio dignissim qui blandit
praesent luptatum zzril delenit augue duis dolore te feugait nulla facilisi.
Duis autem vel eum iriure dolor in <a href="dummy.htm">hendrerit in
vulputate</a> velit esse molestie consequat, vel illum dolore eu feugiat
nulla facilisis at vero eros et accumsan et iusto odio dignissim qui blandit
praesent luptatum zzril delenit augue duis dolore te feugait nulla facilisi.

</td>
```

PART 3

Inner Space: Designing for the Screen

```
<td>

Duis autem vel eum iriure dolor in <a href="dummy.htm">hendrerit in
vulputate</a> velit esse molestie consequat, vel illum dolore eu feugiat
nulla facilisis at vero eros et accumsan et iusto odio dignissim qui blandit
praesent luptatum zzril delenit augue duis dolore te feugait nulla facilisi.
Duis autem vel eum iriure dolor in <a href="dummy.htm">hendrerit in
vulputate</a> velit esse molestie consequat, vel illum dolore eu feugiat
nulla facilisis at vero eros et accumsan et iusto odio dignissim qui blandit
praesent luptatum zzril delenit augue duis dolore te feugait nulla facilisi.

</td>

</tr>

</table>

</body>
</html>
```

Figure 10.23 shows both vertical and horizontal space created with these techniques.

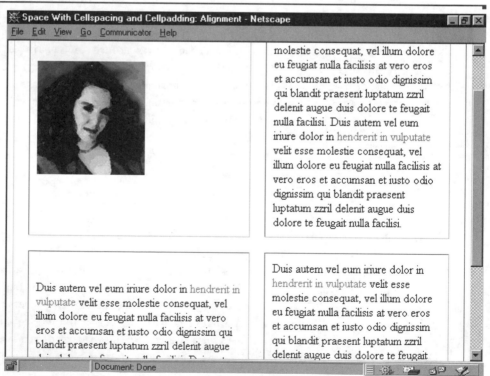

FIGURE 10.23

Vertical and horizontal space between rows.

TIP

A clever method to specifically control white space with tables is to create empty cells or rows, and fill them with a transparent graphic to fix the width. See the Space Place page deconstruction examples in Chapter 11 for examples of this technique.

Further refinements to the code add variation. In this case, you can use the colspan attribute to make the bottom table row span the full two columns. Figure 10.24 shows how the layout is controlled. If the border is turned off, you can see clearly how the space compliments the objects on the page (Figure 10.25).

FIGURE 10.24

*Column span
example*

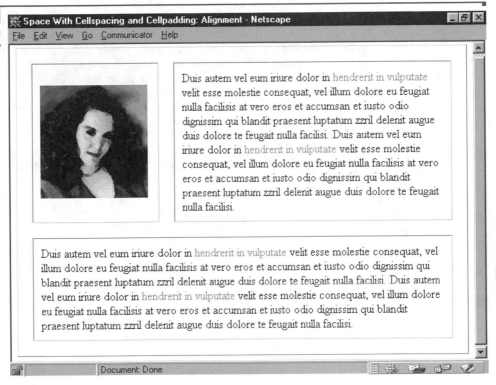

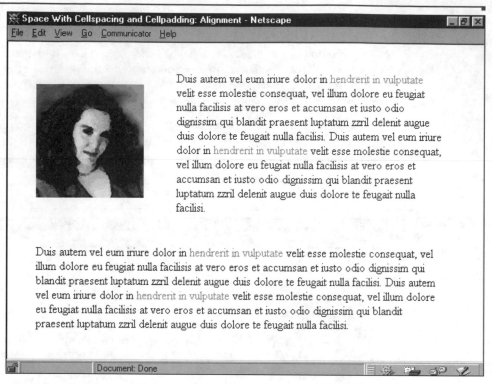

FIGURE 10.25

Space and objects can get along.

Better Control

Width controls can be added to tables and table cells to gain better control of the cell sizing.

```
<html>

<head>
<title>Space With Cellspacing and Cellpadding: Better Control</title>
</head>

<body bgcolor="#FFFFFF" text="#000000" link="#999999"
vlink="#CCCCCC" alink="#FFFFCC">

<table width="595" border="1" cellspacing="20" cellpadding="10">
<tr>
```

```
<td width="143">
<img src="molfresc.jpg" width="143" height="150" border="0" alt="fresco
style painting">
</td>

<td>
Duis autem vel eum iriure dolor in <a href="dummy.htm">hendrerit in
vulputate</a> velit esse molestie consequat, vel illum dolore eu feugiat
nulla facilisis at vero eros et accumsan et iusto odio dignissim qui blandit
praesent luptatum zzril delenit augue duis dolore te feugait nulla facilisi.
Duis autem vel eum iriure dolor in <a href="dummy.htm">hendrerit in
vulputate</a> velit esse molestie consequat, vel illum dolore eu feugiat
nulla facilisis at vero eros et accumsan et iusto odio dignissim qui blandit
praesent luptatum zzril delenit augue duis dolore te feugait nulla facilisi.

</td>
</tr>

<tr>

<td colspan="2">
Duis autem vel eum iriure dolor in <a href="dummy.htm">hendrerit in
vulputate</a> velit esse molestie consequat, vel illum dolore eu feugiat
nulla facilisis at vero eros et accumsan et iusto odio dignissim qui blandit
praesent luptatum zzril delenit augue duis dolore te feugait nulla facilisi.
Duis autem vel eum iriure dolor in <a href="dummy.htm">hendrerit in
vulputate</a> velit esse molestie consequat, vel illum dolore eu feugiat
nulla facilisis at vero eros et accumsan et iusto odio dignissim qui blandit
praesent luptatum zzril delenit augue duis dolore te feugait nulla facilisi.

</td>

</tr>

</table>

</body>
</html>
```

Figure 10.26 shows the layout with controls, and Figure 10.27 shows the borderless results.

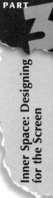

PART 3

Inner Space: Designing for the Screen

FIGURE 10.26

Gain better layout control using width values.

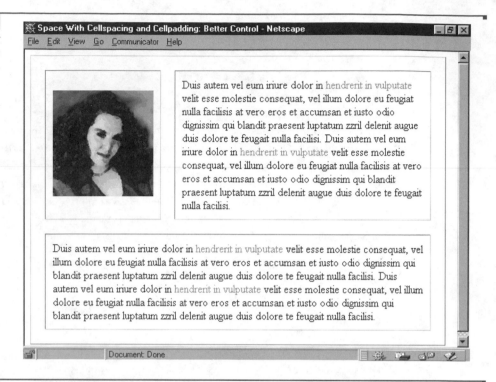

FIGURE 10.27

Space compliments objects

A variation on the row theme can be achieved by using two separate tables and then adding either paragraph, break, or pre-formatted text tags to control the amount of white space between them (Figure 10.28). This technique is known as *stacking*. In this example, pre-formatted text controls the space:

```
<html>

<head>
<title>Stacking Tables</title>
</head>

<body bgcolor="#FFFFFF" text="#000000" link="#999999"
vlink="#CCCCCC" alink="#FFFFCC">

<table border="1" cellspacing="20" cellpadding="20">
<tr>

<td>
<img src="molfresc.jpg" width="143" height="150" border="0" alt="fresco
style painting">
</td>

<td>
Duis autem vel eum iriure dolor in <a href="dummy.htm">hendrerit in
vulputate</a> velit esse molestie consequat, vel illum dolore eu feugiat
nulla facilisis at vero eros et accumsan et iusto odio dignissim qui blandit
praesent luptatum zzril delenit augue duis dolore te feugait nulla facilisi.
Duis autem vel eum iriure dolor in <a href="dummy.htm">hendrerit in
vulputate</a> velit esse molestie consequat, vel illum dolore eu feugiat
nulla facilisis at vero eros et accumsan et iusto odio dignissim qui blandit
praesent luptatum zzril delenit augue duis dolore te feugait nulla facilisi.

</td>
</tr>
</table>

<pre>

</pre>

<table border="1" cellspacing="20" cellpadding="20">
<tr>

<td>
<img src="molfresc.jpg" width="143" height="150" border="0" alt="fresco
style painting">
</td>
```

```
<td>

Duis autem vel eum iriure dolor in <a href="dummy.htm">hendrerit in
vulputate</a> velit esse molestie consequat, vel illum dolore eu feugiat
nulla facilisis at vero eros et accumsan et iusto odio dignissim qui blandit
praesent luptatum zzril delenit augue duis dolore te feugait nulla facilisi.
Duis autem vel eum iriure dolor in <a href="dummy.htm">hendrerit in
vulputate</a> velit esse molestie consequat, vel illum dolore eu feugiat
nulla facilisis at vero eros et accumsan et iusto odio dignissim qui blandit
praesent luptatum zzril delenit augue duis dolore te feugait nulla facilisi.

</td>
</tr>
</table>

</body>
</html>
```

FIGURE 10.28

Stacked tables

As you can see from these examples, the options and variations are fairly limitless. Experiment on your own to come up with interesting uses of space.

OTE

More information on layout controls can be found in Chapter 12 and Chapter 13.

Style Sheet Positioning

I love tables for layout, and it may be getting hard to teach this old dog new tricks. However, style sheets are involved in controlling space, and I encourage you to investigate style methods in further references, both online and in print. Check in the following Online! sidebar as well as in Chapter 9 for a list of good starting points.

Style sheets allow you to position elements, and add various attributes to them, such as borders, padding, and spacing. There are attributes for horizontal and vertical positioning, and because style sheets allow you to specifically define width and height, position can be precise.

Ideally, this control improves the concept of table-based layout. You can define almost any properties you want to apply to a page using style sheets. The following example shows the simple layout we looked at earlier, in Figure 10.18, using style sheet positioning:

```
<html>

<head>

<style type="text/css">

<!--
.img1 { position:          absolute;
     left:                 60;
     top:                  100;
     align:                center;
     padding-left:         20pt;
     padding-right:        20pt;
     padding-top:          20pt;
     padding-bottom:       20pt }
.sp1 { position:           absolute;
     width:                305;
     top:                  20pt;
     left:                 280;
     padding-left:         20pt;
     padding-right:        20pt;
     padding-top:          20pt;
     padding-bottom:       20pt }

-->
```

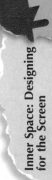

```
</style>
<title>Space with Style</title>
</head>

<body bgcolor="#FFFFFF" text="#000000" link="#999999" vlink="#CCCCCC"
alink="#FFFFCC">

<img class="img1" src="molfresc.jpg" width="200" height="150" border="0"
alt="fresco style
painting">

<span class="sp1">
Duis autem vel eum iriure dolor in <a href="dummy.htm">hendrerit in
vulputate</a> velit esse molestie consequat, vel illum dolore eu feugiat
nulla facilisis at vero eros et accumsan et iusto odio dignissim qui blandit
praesent luptatum zzril delenit augue duis dolore te feugait nulla facilisi.
Duis autem vel eum iriure dolor in <a href="dummy.htm">hendrerit in
vulputate</a> velit esse molestie consequat, vel illum dolore eu feugiat
nulla facilisis at vero eros et accumsan et iusto odio dignissim qui blandit
praesent luptatum zzril delenit augue duis dolore te feugait nulla facilisi.
</span>

</body>
</html>
```

Figure 10.29 shows the results.

But there's a big problem with positioning. First of all, it's one of the most complex uses of style sheets. Second, current browser support for style sheets is quite limited and unstable. So, once again you are faced with the fact that style sheets are, at least at the time of this writing, an option that is both available and restricted in use.

And, while the HTML 4.0 specifications emphasize the use of style sheets for page layout and spatial control *over* standard HTML and especially table-based control, this is not practical for the current Web designer. Most, if not all, of your sites have *not* been developed with style sheets but with HTML 3.2 specifications (or lower). Style sheets are not backward-compatible, nor are they at the ready for designers.

Does this mean you shouldn't explore positioning? It all depends upon your audience and your needs. The Online! sidebar offers some resources on style sheet positioning—check them out for an in-depth look at how to use style sheet positioning successfully.

FIGURE 10.29

Style sheet positioning example

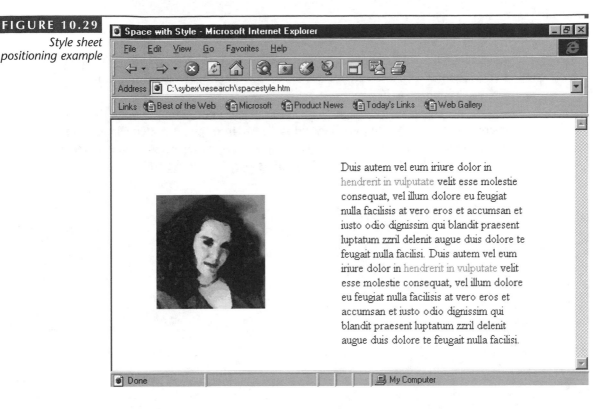

ONline!

- **World Wide Web Consortium, Positioning Draft:** Official CSS draft on positioning, http://www.w3.org/TR/WD-positioning.

- **Web Review: Web Coder, Absolute Positioning with CSS:** Excellent overview of using absolute positioning by Nick Heinle, http://webreview.com/97/06/27/coder/index.html.

- **SiteBuilder Network, Cascading Style Sheets in Internet Explorer 4.0:** See *Positioning Properties* for an overview of positioning, http://www.microsoft.com/workshop/author/css/css-ie4-f.htm.

In Print:

- *HTML Stylesheet Sourcebook* by Ian S. Graham, 1997. Published by John Wiley & Sons, this tutorial has some good resource information on style sheet positioning.

PART

Inner Space: Designing for the Screen

Next Up

If we haven't created enough space by now, there's little hope that we will *ever* do so! In this chapter, you not only learned why space is so important and how to get it, but what space means to design.

Chapter 11 will review the methods and concepts discussed in this and the previous chapter. Then, it's time to move beyond space and into the integrated relationship that exists between space and objects on a complete page—and within a complete site. This is layout, and you'll learn design foundations as well as conventional methods of achieving integration.

chapter 11

THE DESIGN
STUDIO
SPACE PLACE

THE DESIGN STUDIO SPACE PLACE

Space is the absence of any tangible piece of design. Yet, it is wholly design—and from its use, design either falters or succeeds.

Space is visually important. It guides the eye; it offers a cushion between harder edges; it allows a place for the mind to rest for a moment before absorbing more data.

But space has another place in design—a culturally determined one that speaks to why it is seen as so precious.

In a fascinating essay on white space called "On White Space/When Less is More," designer Keith Robertson gets to the crux of why space is so culturally important. "White space," he writes, "is extravagance. White space is the surface of the paper on which you are printing showing through and on which you are choosing *not* to print."

If economics are a concern, he goes on to point out, the designer will use as much space on a page as possible. But if prosperity reigns, it's a sign of the privileged to waste space. It's no accident that in poorer countries with less available food, people who have extra body fat are considered attractive. Where abundance prevails, thin (to the point of *dangerously* thin) people are prized.

How does this relate to a computer screen? It's simple—space on the computer is prized. If one is to follow Robertson's ideas about space, the low availability of visual real estate on the computer demands that refined, sophisticated, and privileged design will have plenty of space.

A good point for designers to ponder. Regardless of philosophy, the practical reality is that from a purely technical standpoint, space is imperative because it puts some needed breathing room into design. We need it to give our eyes that cushion, that greatly desired guidance, the moment to pause and absorb the information—and ideally the beauty—of what lies before us.

This chapter serves to help you consolidate space. It zeroes in on the type of space in which we as designers work, and the very real and practical methods used to deal with that space, including:

- Computer space
- Constraint, clutter, weight, and size
- Alignment and floating
- The importance of what you don't see
- Margins
- Proximity

Use the reviews, deconstructions, quizzes, and tasks in this chapter to extend your spatial design skills. The companion resource center on the Web is available at http://www .designstudio.net/space.htm.

Web Space: Review

I need my space, you know that. And you need yours. Understanding this creates the foundation for a terrific relationship.

Avoiding conflict is easy if you understand the following:

- The way the Web is contained
- How to work effectively in that contained space
- How to align text and media
- How to encourage positive relationships between text and media

Address these issues and both you and your site can take advantage of the inviting space that results.

Main Concepts

Get to the crux of space relations by first understanding the parameters involved.

- **The Web is a visual container**—Space on the Web is contained. It's important to first note that Web space is rectangular. Two things enforce this rule: the shape of your monitor, and the way a Web browser interface fits into the monitor.

PART 3

Inner Space: Designing for the Screen

- **Computer resolution affects space**—Monitors, computers, and video graphics cards all work in tandem. One of the results of this relationship is *resolution*. This is how many pixels are available per viewable screen. The most common resolution is 640 pixels in width, and 480 pixels in height. Other resolutions include the common 800×600, the less common 1024×768, right on up to very high resolutions such as 1600×1200.

- **Designers create solutions to deal with contained space**—The savvy designer knows how to free a design from the contained space of the Web. One way is to remove constraints such as borders and tables from around objects. Another is to avoid clutter, and balance the weight and size of page objects. Designers take this very limited environment and work their magic to create space.

- **Span the lowest and middle denominators**—Designers address the resolution differences by ensuring that they work within the lowest available space, which when the browser interface is taken into account, is safely 595 pixels wide by 295 pixels in length per screen. The exception to this rule is when creating vertical background tiles—you'll want to make those longer to accommodate higher resolutions (see Chapter 16).

Page Deconstruction

The Design Studio's Space Place section, located at `http://www.designstudio.net/space.html`, offers a number of code tricks to create white space. We'll walk through the Space Place's main page first, and look at how space is achieved.

```
<html>

<head>
<title>The Design Studio by Molly: Space Place</title>
</head>
```

The background graphic on this page is designed to be viewed appropriately at low and high resolutions. Figure 11.1 shows the background figure at 640×480 resolution. Figure 11.2 shows the same page at 800×600 resolution, demonstrating that while there's a visible difference, the basic design integrity is intact.

```
<body bgcolor="#FFFFFF" background="images/ds-bakr.gif" text="#000000"
link="#666633" vlink="663300" alink="#FFFFFF">
```

FIGURE 11.1

Space Place page at 640×480 resolution

The Design Studio by Molly: Space Place - Microsoft Internet Explorer

File   Edit   View   Go   Favorites   Help

The Space Place

Space is the absence of any tangible piece of design. Yet, it is wholly design--and from its use design either falters or succeeds. Space is visually important. It guides the eye, it offers a cushion between harder edges, it allows a place for the mind to rest for a moment before absorbing more data.

Space is imperative because it puts some needed breathing room into design. We need it to give our eyes that needed cushion, that greatly desired guidance, the moment to pause and absorb the information--and ideally the beauty--of what lies before us.

Select from the following:

- Part Summary
- Quiz and Answers
- Tasks and Task Materials

Extended and updated resource links and recommendations are also available to assist you with accessibility, HTML, and interface design.

Part Summary   Quiz & Answers   Tasks   Resources

[front office] [planning room] [space place]
[workshop] [color lab] [multimedia center]
[welcome] [contact]

Copyright © Molly E. Holzschlag, 1997

My Computer

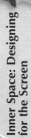

PART
3

Inner Space: Designing
for the Screen

FIGURE 11.2

*Space Place page
at 800×600
resolution*

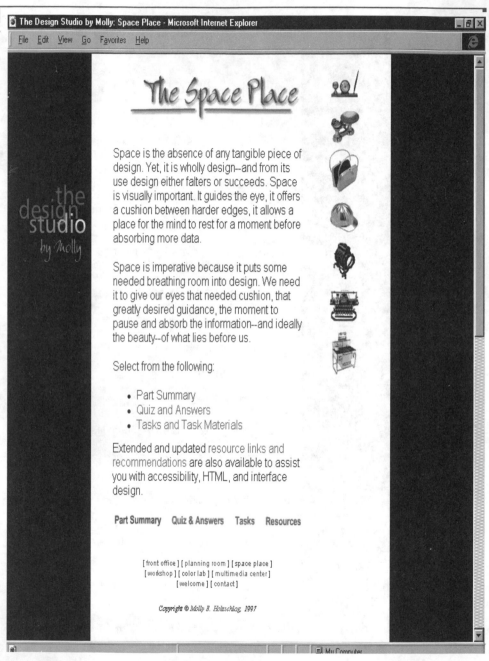

A table is used to help control space. By setting the table's total width to "580," we can ensure that computers with different resolutions will see the same basic design. Furthermore, the table border is set to "0" to remove any constraints.

```
<table border="0" width="580">
<tr>

<!--begin left margin-->
```

Vertical alignment of the table cell controls how the objects within it will be aligned. A long, clear spacer graphic firmly fixes the graphic 250 pixels from the top of the table.

```
<td width="125" valign="top">

<img src="images/clear.gif" width="1" height="250" border="0" alt="spacer">

<img src="images/dsh.jpg" width="112" height="102" border="0" alt="The
Design Studio by Molly Header ">

</td>
```

You can also use a clear graphic as well as a separate table cell to fix a 25-pixel width of space. This space is both horizontal *and* vertical, although the vertical size is not fixed and will dynamically adjust to the length of the information within the cell.

```
<td width="25">

<img src="images/clear.gif" width="25" height="1" border="0" alt="spacer">

</td>

<!--begin text area-->
```

The following cell is set to 320 pixels in width. Note the left alignment of the image, and the subsequent break and clearing. This aligns the header image as well as freeing up space to add the text.

```
<td width="320">

<img src="images/sp-hed.gif" width="300" height="100" border="0"
alt="The Space Place" align=right>
<br clear=all>

<font face="arial">
```

The text that follows has margins due to the fixed pixels and table cells to either side of the text area.

```
Space is the absence of any tangible piece of design. Yet, it is wholly
design--and from its use design either falters or succeeds.
Space is visually important. It guides the eye, it offers a cushion between
harder edges, it allows a place for the mind to rest for a moment before
absorbing more data.
<p>

Space is imperative because it puts some needed breathing room into design.
We need it to give our eyes that needed cushion, that greatly desired
guidance, the moment to pause and absorb the information--and ideally the
beauty--of what lies before us.
<p>

Select from the following:
<p>
```

More space is naturally created by the indentation caused by the unordered list tag.

```
<ul>
<li><a href="space/index.htm">Part Summary</a>
<li><a href="space/quiz.htm">Quiz and Answers</a>
<li><a href="space/tasks.htm">Tasks and Task Materials</a>
</ul>
<p>

Extended and updated <a href="links.htm">resource links and
recommendations</a> are also available to assist you with accessibility,
HTML, and interface design.
</font>
```

The following syntax uses the division tag to center align the Flash navigation bar and subsequent text navigation. It's important to remember that this centering takes place *within* the text table cell, so the information centers there rather than on the visible page.

```
<div align="center">

<!--begin ie flash navigation-->

<object classid="clsid:D27CDB6E-AE6D-11cf-96B8-444553540000"
codebase="http://active.macromedia.com/flash2/cabs/swflash.cab#version=2,0,0,0"
border="0" width="316" height="58">
```

```
<param name="Movie" value="../images/subnav.swf">
<param name="Loop" value="False">
<param name="Play" value="True">
<param name="BGColor" value="FFFFFF">
<param name="Quality" value="high">
<param name="Scale" value="Showall">

<!--begin netscape flash navigation-->

<embed src="../images/subnav.swf"
pluginspage="/shockwave/download/index.cgi?P1_Prod_Version=ShockwaveFlash"
type=application/futuresplash width="316" height="58" loop=false
quality=high play=true>

</object>
<br>

<!--begin text navigation-->

<font face="arial" size="1">
[ <a href="office.htm"> front office </a> ] [ <a href="planning.htm">planning
room</a> ] [ <a href="space.htm">space place</a> ]
<br>

[ <a href="workshop.htm">workshop</a> ] [ <a href="color.htm">color lab</a> ]
[ <a href="media.htm">multimedia center</a> ]
<br>

[ <a href="index1.htm">welcome</a> ]  [ <a href="contact.htm">contact</a> ]

</font>
</div>
<p>

<!--begin copyright and mailto-->

<div align="center">

<font size="1">

<i>Copyright &copy; <a href="mailto:molly@molly.com">Molly E.
Holzschlag</a>, 1997</i>

</div>
</font>
</td>
```

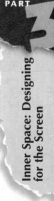

PART

3

Inner Space: Designing
for the Screen

Here again you see the fixed table cell that creates the right margin.

```
<td width="25">

<img src="images/clear.gif" width="25" height="1" border="0" alt="spacer">

</td>

<!--begin navigation column-->

<td valign="top" width="50">

<img src="images/navmap3.gif" width="50" height="395" border="0"
alt="navigational image map, text navigation below" usemap="#navmap3">

</td>
</tr>
</table>
<!--begin map data-->

<map name="navmap3">
<area shape="rect" coords="0,0,57,46" href="office.htm">
<area shape="rect" coords="0,48,57,98" href="planning.htm">
<area shape="rect" coords="0,100,57,160" href="space.htm">
<area shape="rect" coords="0,162,57,214" href="workshop.htm">
<area shape="rect" coords="0,216,57,275" href="color.htm">
<area shape="rect" coords="0,278,57,330" href="type.htm">
<area shape="rect" coords="0,332,58,393" href="media.htm">
<area shape="default" nohref>
</map>

</body>
</html>
```

Web Space: Quiz

Please answer the following multiple choice questions.

1. Which of the following is the lowest common computer monitor resolution:

    a. 640×480

    b. 800×600

    c. 1024×768

    d. 1600×1200

2. The higher the numeric value of a resolution:

   a. the lower the quality of the images

   b. the darker the images will be

   c. the crisper and cleaner the images will be

   d. none of the above

3. Maximum space for cross-platform compatibility is:

   a. 640×480 per screen

   b. 800×600 per screen

   c. 500×300 per screen

   d. 595×295 per screen

4. Common constraints that designers should avoid include:

   a. bordered tables around images and text

   b. bordered tables around images or objects

   c. special effects such as shadows or edges

   d. a and b

5. An average Web page should scroll a maximum of:

   a. five screens

   b. two screens

   c. three screens

   d. as many screens as the designer likes

Please answer true or false for the following statements.

6. The division tag `<div>` can be used to align blocks of information.

7. Floating images are created by eliminating any break between an image and surrounding text.

8. Tables are not a strong method of controlling alignment.

9. A designer should always use style sheets for alignment.

10. A good-looking page balances text, media, and space.

Write out short answers to the following questions.

11. Briefly describe the three types of style sheets.

12. What role do the `hspace` and `vspace` attributes play in the following code?

```
<img src="images/kel.jpg width="350" height="235" border="0" hspace="10"
vspace="10" alt="sunset photograph">
```

Answers to the quiz can be found on the Design Studio Web site, `http://www`
`.designstudio.net/space/`, and at the end of this chapter.

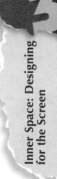

PART

3

Inner Space: Designing
for the Screen

Space and Alignment: Task

The task is to work with alignment using standard HTML.

For this task you will need:

- An HTML editor (not a WYSIWYG editor)

- An image

You can find helpful ingredients including an image from the Design Studio site at http://www.designstudio.net/space/tasks.htm.

Follow these steps:

1. Open the template provided on the site or a new file within your text editor or word processor (Figure 11.3).

2. To the image code, add the align= attribute.

3. Add a value of "right" (Figure 11.4).

4. Add a break <br clear="all"> after the image code (Figure 11.5).

FIGURE 11.3

HTML template for alignment task

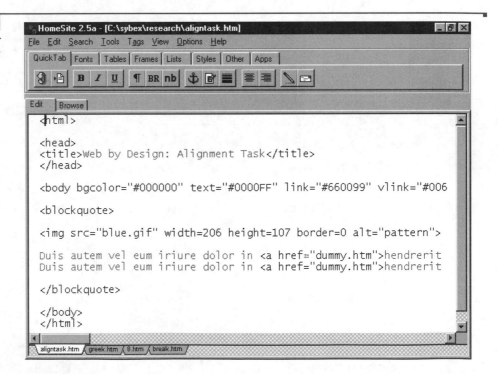

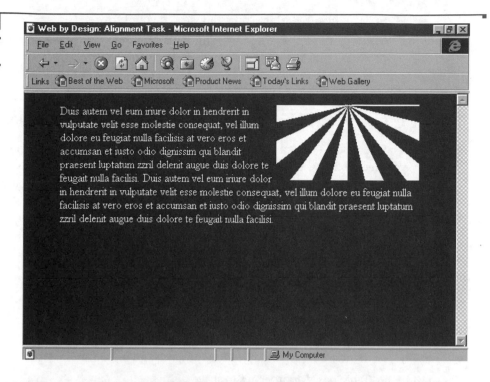

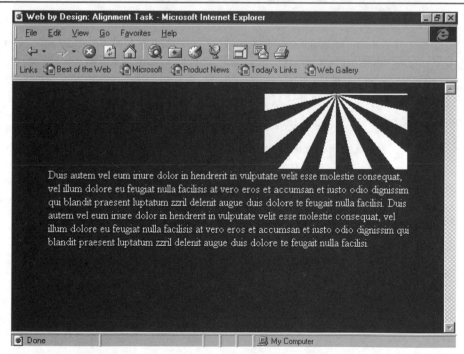

5. Save the file as `align1.htm` and view in your browser.

6. Go through the exercise again, replacing the `align` and `clear` attributes with other available attributes, and compare your results.

Even More Web Space: Review

As if we haven't conspired to create enough space—there are a number of techniques you need to know to create and control space with great precision. Beyond the technology is media theory—the *ideas* that help calculate what people should and should not see—subtly manipulating what people think and do by what you show them.

In the case of space, this manipulation occurs by controlling what does *not* appear on a page. This is referred to as *calculated design*. Combine this with advanced methods of control, and the impact can be dangerous.

These methods and concepts include:

- White space
- Margins
- Proximity
- Standard HTML-based control of space and proximity
- Table-based approaches to space
- Cascading style sheets

Familiarizing yourself with these techniques will certainly advance not only your skills, but result in more visually appealing and useful design.

Main Concepts

Let's take a closer look at the main concepts involved in creating more Web space:

- **Calculated content**—What's missing from the page? It might be something you *want* to leave out. Calculated content involves forethought on the designer's part. He or she takes a solid evaluation of what should visually be involved in a design. What's left out results not only in more space—but space that carries significant subliminal impact.

- **White space**—This is the absence of anything but the page's background color or design. Wherever content, text, or other media do not appear, white space does. In design, the goal is to use this space wisely—controlling how much or how little of it the site visitor gets to see.

- **Margins**—Vertical space around the body of a page creates a visual cushion and helps instill a freer, more relaxed visual environment. Margins can be created using standard HTML through the <blockquote> tag or, in Internet Explorer, the margin attributes in the <body> tag. HTML tables are commonly used for margin control, and cascading style sheets offer up the most powerful but least cross-browser compatible margin techniques.

- **Proximity**—Want to get close? Proximity is how close or how far visual pieces are from one another. By controlling the proximity of objects on the horizontal and vertical lines of a page, you can emphasize a specific object, point the eye over and toward another object, and create a general balance that is visually satisfying to the visitor. Proximity can be gained by using standard HTML tags, table-based layouts, and cascading style sheets.

Site Deconstruction

This time we'll look at the Part Summary for the Space Place on the Design Studio at
`http://www.designstudio.net/space/`.

```
<html>

<head>
<title>The Design Studio by Molly: Part III Summary</title>
</head>
```

As with the former example, this page also uses a background graphic that can be viewed at low resolution, as in Figure 11.6, as well as other resolutions, as in Figure 11.7.

```
<body bgcolor="#FFFFFF" background="../images/sp-bak.gif" text="#000000"
link="#666633" vlink="663300" alink="#FFFFFF">
```

PART

3

Inner Space: Designing
for the Screen

FIGURE 11.6

*The Space Place
Part Summary at
640×480*

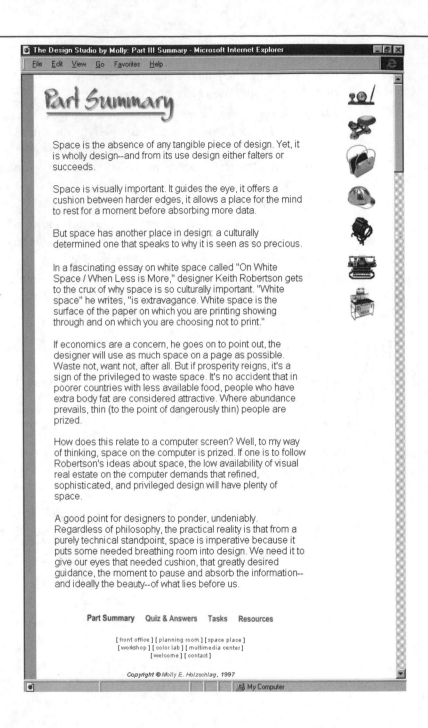

The Design Studio by Molly: Part III Summary - Microsoft Internet Explorer

File   Edit   View   Go   Favorites   Help

Part Summary

Space is the absence of any tangible piece of design. Yet, it is wholly design--and from its use design either falters or succeeds.

Space is visually important. It guides the eye, it offers a cushion between harder edges, it allows a place for the mind to rest for a moment before absorbing more data.

But space has another place in design: a culturally determined one that speaks to why it is seen as so precious.

In a fascinating essay on white space called "On White Space / When Less is More," designer Keith Robertson gets to the crux of why space is so culturally important. "White space" he writes, "is extravagance. White space is the surface of the paper on which you are printing showing through and on which you are choosing not to print."

If economics are a concern, he goes on to point out, the designer will use as much space on a page as possible. Waste not, want not, after all. But if prosperity reigns, it's a sign of the privileged to waste space. It's no accident that in poorer countries with less available food, people who have extra body fat are considered attractive. Where abundance prevails, thin (to the point of dangerously thin) people are prized.

How does this relate to a computer screen? Well, to my way of thinking, space on the computer is prized. If one is to follow Robertson's ideas about space, the low availability of visual real estate on the computer demands that refined, sophisticated, and privileged design will have plenty of space.

A good point for designers to ponder, undeniably. Regardless of philosophy, the practical reality is that from a purely technical standpoint, space is imperative because it puts some needed breathing room into design. We need it to give our eyes that needed cushion, that greatly desired guidance, the moment to pause and absorb the information-- and ideally the beauty--of what lies before us.

Part Summary   Quiz & Answers   Tasks   Resources

[front office] [planning room] [space place]
[workshop] [color lab] [multimedia center]
[welcome] [contact]

Copyright © Molly E. Holzschlag, 1997

My Computer

FIGURE 11.7

The same page at 800×600

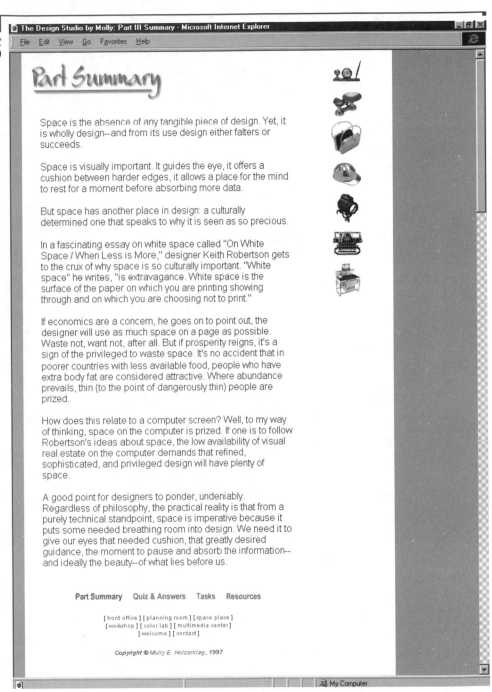

The Design Studio by Molly: Part III Summary - Microsoft Internet Explorer

File   Edit   View   Go   Favorites   Help

Part Summary

Space is the absence of any tangible piece of design. Yet, it is wholly design--and from its use design either falters or succeeds.

Space is visually important. It guides the eye, it offers a cushion between harder edges, it allows a place for the mind to rest for a moment before absorbing more data.

But space has another place in design: a culturally determined one that speaks to why it is seen as so precious.

In a fascinating essay on white space called "On White Space / When Less is More," designer Keith Robertson gets to the crux of why space is so culturally important. "White space" he writes, "is extravagance. White space is the surface of the paper on which you are printing showing through and on which you are choosing not to print."

If economics are a concern, he goes on to point out, the designer will use as much space on a page as possible. Waste not, want not, after all. But if prosperity reigns, it's a sign of the privileged to waste space. It's no accident that in poorer countries with less available food, people who have extra body fat are considered attractive. Where abundance prevails, thin (to the point of dangerously thin) people are prized.

How does this relate to a computer screen? Well, to my way of thinking, space on the computer is prized. If one is to follow Robertson's ideas about space, the low availability of visual real estate on the computer demands that refined, sophisticated, and privileged design will have plenty of space.

A good point for designers to ponder, undeniably. Regardless of philosophy, the practical reality is that from a purely technical standpoint, space is imperative because it puts some needed breathing room into design. We need it to give our eyes that needed cushion, that greatly desired guidance, the moment to pause and absorb the information-- and ideally the beauty--of what lies before us.

Part Summary   Quiz & Answers   Tasks   Resources

[front office] [planning room] [space place]
[workshop] [color lab] [multimedia center]
[welcome] [contact]

Copyright © Molly E. Holzschlag, 1997

My Computer

PART
3

Inner Space: Designing for the Screen

I've chosen a table-based layout again. While `cellpadding` or `cellspacing` could have been used to achieve white space, I chose to fix the width and use spacer graphics and table cells for positioning.

```
<table border="0" width="580">
<tr>

<!--begin text area-->

<td valign="top" width="500">

<img src="../images/clear.gif" width="15" height="1" border="0"
alt="spacer">

<img src="../images/sum-hed.gif" width="234" height="69" border="0"
alt="front office header">
<p>

<font face="arial">
```

Here we have a `<blockquote>`, which helps keep the text nice and tight, with plenty of margin space. In this case, the `<blockquote>` is used within a table cell. Paragraph tags add horizontal strips of space for ease of reading (Figure 11.8).

```
<blockquote>

Space is the absence of any tangible piece of design. Yet, it is wholly
design--and from its use design either falters or succeeds.
<p>

Space is visually important. It guides the eye, it offers a cushion between
harder edges, it allows a place for the mind to rest for a moment before
absorbing more data.
<p>

But space has another place in design: a culturally determined one that
speaks to why it is seen as so precious.
<p>

In a fascinating essay on white space called "On White Space / When Less is
More," designer Keith Robertson gets to the crux of why space is so
culturally important. "White space" he writes, "is extravagance. White space
is the surface of the paper on which you are printing showing through and on
which you are choosing not to print."
<p>
```

If economics are a concern, he goes on to point out, the designer will use as much space on a page as possible. Waste not, want not, after all. But if prosperity reigns, it's a sign of the privileged to waste space. It's no accident that in poorer countries with less available food, people who have extra body fat are considered attractive. Where abundance prevails, thin (to the point of dangerously thin) people are prized.
<p>

How does this relate to a computer screen? Well, to my way of thinking, space on the computer is prized. If one is to follow Robertson's ideas about space, the low availability of visual real estate on the computer demands that refined, sophisticated, and privileged design will have plenty of space.
<p>

A good point for designers to ponder, undeniably. Regardless of philosophy, the practical reality is that from a purely technical standpoint, space is imperative because it puts some needed breathing room into design. We need it to give our eyes that needed cushion, that greatly desired guidance, the moment to pause and absorb the information--and ideally the beauty--of what lies before us.

</blockquote>
<p>

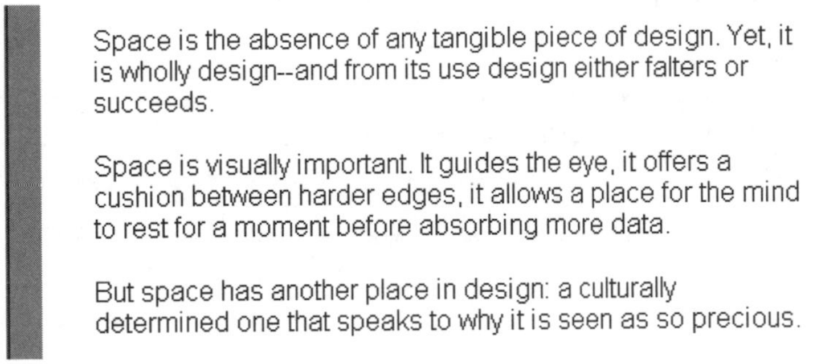

FIGURE 11.8

Text and margins are controlled with blockquote and paragraph tags.

Space is the absence of any tangible piece of design. Yet, it is wholly design--and from its use design either falters or succeeds.

Space is visually important. It guides the eye, it offers a cushion between harder edges, it allows a place for the mind to rest for a moment before absorbing more data.

But space has another place in design: a culturally determined one that speaks to why it is seen as so precious.

PART

Inner Space: Designing for the Screen

The Flash navigation system is controlled within the table cell by a division-based center alignment:

```
<div align="center">

<!--begin ie flash navigation-->
```

```
<object classid="clsid:D27CDB6E-AE6D-11cf-96B8-444553540000"
codebase="http://active.macromedia.com/flash2/cabs/swflash.cab#version=2,0,0,0"
border="0" width="316" height="58">

<param name="Movie" value="../images/subnav.swf">
<param name="Loop" value="False">
<param name="Play" value="True">
<param name="BGColor" value="FFFFFF">
<param name="Quality" value="high">
<param name="Scale" value="Showall">

<!--begin netscape flash navigation-->

<embed src="../images/subnav.swf"
pluginspage="/shockwave/download/index.cgi?P1_Prod_Version=ShockwaveFlash"
type=application/futuresplash width="316" height="58" loop=false
quality=high play=true>

</object>
<br>

<!--begin text navigation-->

<font face="arial" size="1">

[ <a href="office.htm"> front office </a> ] [ <a href="planning.htm">planning
room</a> ] [ <a href="space.htm">space place</a> ]
<br>

[ <a href="workshop.htm">workshop</a> ] [ <a href="color.htm">color lab</a> ]
[ <a href="media.htm">multimedia center</a> ]
<br>

[ <a href="index1.htm">welcome</a> ]  [ <a href="contact.htm">contact</a> ]
</font>

</div>
<p>

<!--begin copyright and mailto-->

<div align="center">

<font size="1">
```

```
<i>Copyright &copy; <a href="mailto:molly@molly.com">Molly E.
Holzschlag</a>, 1997</i>

</div>
</font>
</td>
```

A fixed table cell with a clear GIF creates space on the right—between the text and the navigation (Figure 11.9).

```
<td width="25">

<img src="../images/clear.gif" width="25" height="1" border="0"
alt="spacer">

</td>

<!--begin navigation column-->

<td valign="top" width="50">

<img src="../images/navmap3.gif" width="50" height="395" border="0"
alt="navigational image map, text navigation below" usemap="#navmap3">

</td>

</table>

<!--begin map data-->

<map name="navmap3">
<area shape="rect" coords="0,0,57,46" href="office.htm">
<area shape="rect" coords="0,48,57,98" href="planning.htm">
<area shape="rect" coords="0,100,57,160" href="space.htm">
<area shape="rect" coords="0,162,57,214" href="workshop.htm">
<area shape="rect" coords="0,216,57,275" href="color.htm">
<area shape="rect" coords="0,278,57,330" href="type.htm">
<area shape="rect" coords="0,332,58,393" href="media.htm">
<area shape="default" nohref>
</map>

</body>
</html>
```

PART

Inner Space: Designing
for the Screen

FIGURE 11.9

A fixed table cell and clear graphic create space between the text and the right navigation bar.

28-JAN-1998 11:19:40.80

News

The big news is that this site is somewhat live! Be sure to check with the info section in order to use this site to its fullest.

"Make your text clear, concise, and to the point. Most Internet users are well educated. Misspelled words and incorrect usage can make you look like you don't care." -- Sonia Lyris and Devin Ben-Hur

Want to submit a tip or quote? E-mail it along with the source and it will be entered into the Design Studio's database.

[welcome!] [front office] [planning room]
[space place] [workshop] [color lab] [type mill]

In Figure 11.10, the table border is set to a value of "1" so you can see the layout's structure.

FIGURE 11.10

The table border shows the layout.

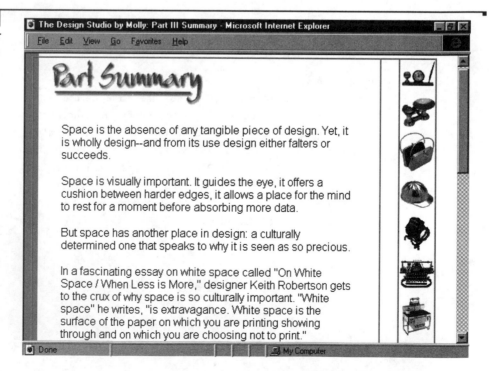

Even More Web Space: Quiz

Please answer the following multiple choice questions.

1. Calculating a site's content means:

    a. unethically manipulating an audience

    b. thinking carefully about what not to include in a design

    c. setting up the technical layout of a design

    d. using table-based controls to manage space

2. White space can be:

    a. blue

    b. a floral pattern

    c. pure white

    d. all of the above

3. The margin attribute is effective:

    a. always

    b. only in Netscape 2.0 or above

    c. only in Internet Explorer 3.0 or above

    d. only in Netscape and IE 4.0 or above

4. Cascading style sheets allow for:

    a. top-margin control

    b. left-margin control

    c. right-margin control

    d. all of the above

5. Which of the following techniques can specifically control proximity?

    a. blockquotes

    b. body tag attributes

    c. cellpadding

    d. none of the above

PART

Inner Space: Designing for the Screen

Please answer true or false for the following statements.

6. Cascading style sheets are an ideal cross-platform method of creating margins.

7. Blockquotes can't be seen by Internet Explorer 3.0 and above.

8. The `cellspacing` attribute can be used to create white space.

9. Cascading style sheet positioning requires little study.

10. HTML 4.0 recommends style sheets over tables for layout control, despite problems with browser compatibility.

Write out short answers to the following questions.

11. Provide an example of calculated design.

12. Give several reasons why space is so important.

Even More Web Space: Task

In this task, you will experiment with the Space Place Part Summary code to gain a better understanding of various spatial controls.

- Download the task file, which includes the code and graphics, from `http://www.designstudio.net/space/task.htm`.

- In the `<body>` tag, add margin values and check in Internet Explorer 3.0 or above (Figure 11.11).

- Add `cellpadding` and `cellspacing` to the `<table>` tag, with a value of your choice (Figure 11.12).

Follow the various space control methods described in Chapters 9 and 10. See how much you can mess up the page. Once it's complete chaos, try to put it back together without peeking at the original code.

Add a top margin value of "0" to the syntax.

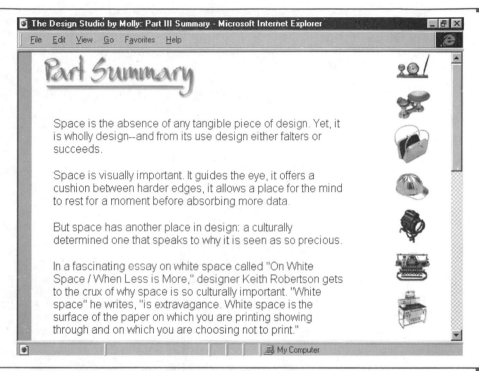

Look what happens when cellpadding and cellspacing values of "20" are added.

PART

3

Inner Space: Designing for the Screen

Answer Key

The following key provides the correct answers to the quizzes in this chapter.

Web Space

Multiple Choice

1. The correct answer is A. 640×480 is the lowest common computer monitor resolution.

2. The correct answer is C. The higher the numeric value of a screen's resolution, the crisper and cleaner the images will appear.

3. The correct answer is D. According to Yale C/AIM, a respected design guide, the maximum space for cross-platform compatibility is 595×295.

4. The correct answer is D. Avoid bordered tables around images, text, and objects.

5. The correct answer is C. Three screens is a good maximum scroll.

True or False

6. True. Use the `align` attribute with the `<div>` tag to achieve alignment.

7. True. To float an image, align it but do not follow the image with a break of any kind.

8. False. Tables are an excellent way to control alignment.

9. False. Style sheets pose cross-platform problems and therefore should be used only when the audience is clearly capable of supporting style sheets.

10. True. Balance is a credible and important aspect of creating good-looking pages.

Short Answers

Note that your answers may vary, but the main concepts described here should be touched upon.

11. Three types of style sheets include inline, embedded, and linked.

12. The `hspace` and `vspace` attributes control horizontal and vertical space around images or objects.

Even More Web Space

Multiple Choice

1. The correct answer is B. Calculated design means thinking about what to and what *not* to include in a Web site.

2. The correct answer is D. White space refers to the background space, no matter its color or pattern.

Continued

3. The correct answer is C. The `margin` attribute still has not been adopted by Netscape and is therefore only acceptable to use for Internet Explorer 3.0 and above.

4. The correct answer is D. You can control top, left, and right margins with style sheets.

5. The correct answer is C. Cellpadding can influence proximity.

True or False

6. False. The use of style sheets is limited to browsers that support them.

7. False. Blockquotes can most certainly be seen by Internet Explorer 3.0 and above.

8. True. Cellspacing can be used to create white space.

9. False. Style sheet positioning is complex and requires significant study.

10. True. HTML 4.0 does recommend the use of style sheets for layout control despite the cross-browser problems.

Short Answers

11 and **12.** These questions will relate to your personal experiences and opinions, there are no correct answers.

Next Up

Now that I've inundated, bombarded, and burdened you with the importance of space, it's time to move along to something else.

In the next four chapters of *Web by Design*, the study of layout will help you understand how to take all of this space and actually work with it to create design. You'll get a look at how graphic designers approach layout, and how Web designers create the code to control that layout. This combination of design concepts and Web techniques will help you gain a powerful grip on the delivery of solid, thoughtful pages that have lasting impact.

PART

3

Inner Space: Designing
for the Screen

PART IV

total control: web page layout

chapter 12

LAYOUT METHOD

LAYOUT
METHOD

S ome of the world's finest art began as a blank canvas. Then, the artist mixed the paint or gathered the pastels and very carefully stepped up to that canvas. In a frenzy of creativity, the artist began to literally splatter, smear, scribble, throw, rip, and swirl the media—and the emotions carried with it—onto the canvas. No plan, no precision, no measurement. Sheer enthusiasm and unbridled creativity.

This method could occasionally be a very interesting way to approach Web art. But for commercial design, a lack of planning, precision, and measurement is *not* going to help you win accolades, praise, and immortality.

The commercial designer must approach a subject with consideration and care. You might notice that I mention this time and again—with just cause. Web designers who have no formal training in design haven't been taught method. Your strengths lie elsewhere, and you've had to achieve method on your own. There will be many of you who do have exposure to design, and you are at a distinct advantage when it comes to working with the layout design of a page. Still others have little idea how to approach this.

This chapter will provide you with solid methodology that you can begin applying to your site layout. And while it is duly acknowledged that as a commercial designer you will *think* before you act, you are encouraged here to throw away the constraints of the Web and explore the blank canvas with passion. This combination of inspiration and control will lead you to new and clever design potential.

Issues covered in this chapter include:

- Page elements
- How to plan a page
- The meaning of shape
- Placing a header
- Accommodating text
- Working with media
- Combining techniques

Using these methods, you'll discover interesting and unusual ways of approaching your blank canvas as well as just plain having fun.

Page Elements

Every Web page has a standard set of elements that you'll be working with. There are so many options that it is impossible to cover them all here, but we can break down a page into its most simplistic pieces, and then look at several methods of approaching layout.

This will give you the opportunity to see layout techniques in action, and try them out on your own. I encourage you to develop your own techniques—invariably you will find ways of doing things that best suit your style. So, use the ideas in this chapter as a foundation—a jumping off point for your own layout ideas.

The elements we'll work with in this chapter include:

- **Page dimension**—This will be your workspace—the area in which you design.
- **Shape**—Shapes play an incredibly important role in design success—you'll learn here what shapes mean and a few ways of working with them.
- **Headers**—Most, if not all, pages will have at least one header. Whether these are graphical or HTML-based is almost irrelevant at this point. What you should focus on is *placement*.
- **Text**—Again, the emphasis on this chapter isn't the *how* or *what*. Set aside the "content is King" idea and think about text here as simply another element to place creatively on a page.
- **Media**—Whether it's a piece of art, an animation, a photograph, or streaming video, the importance here is *where* the media will fit into the bigger picture.

Page Dimension

As you learned in Chapter 9, the Web is made up of lots of rectangles. Instead of creating blocky, cliché looks, today's designer needs to take a fresh approach to Web design. One of the ways to do this is to understand a Web page's restrictions—and attempt to move beyond them.

First, you need to define the general dimensions of your page. Typically, a Web page will be vertical—but the length will vary from one to three (or occasionally more) screens.

While Web pages need to be designed both horizontally and vertically, what's seen screen-by-screen (remember, each screen in a cross-compatible design is 595 × 295 pixels) is a more realistic way to approach shaping your page (Figure 12.1). The reason is that this is how your audience will be viewing the page—in chunks where emphasis is horizontal rather than vertical. Of course, this doesn't mean that the vertical design is to be disregarded (Figure 12.2).

FIGURE 12.1

The initial screen of the Film Vault offers a singular chunk of design.

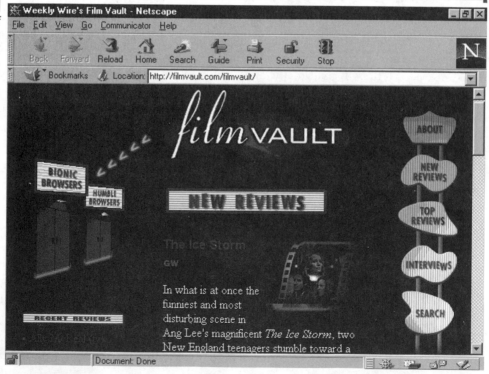

FIGURE 12.2

*The full page is
carefully laid out.*

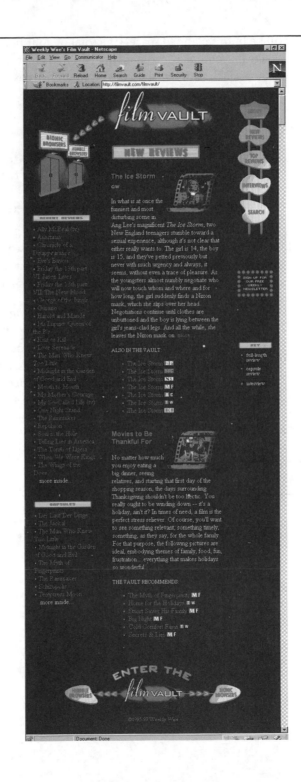

It will be in this planned space—the total of your horizontal and vertical design—that you create your page layout. Many designers first sketch out their pages, either by hand with a sketch pad, in a graphics program such as Photoshop, or with a desktop publishing program like QuarkXPress.

 I P

Instead of creating a Web design from the HTML code on up, create a design *independent* of the Web's constraints first. Then fit the HTML to the design. This can help you key in on new ideas.

Using sketching techniques helps you set up your page as well as gives you the freedom to be creative—planning what you want to see rather than what the constraints of the computer screen and Web environment force upon you. I personally use a sketch pad (Figure 12.3) before rendering a site's look (Figure 12.4).

> *"Never design with the limitations of technology in mind. This pushes the envelope of what's possible. Create a design, then figure out how to make it work. Often amazing breakthroughs happen when you are trying to find a workaround to 'standard' methods. Actually HTML should not even be tinkered with until the design has been laid out."*
>
> ERIC PICARD, President and Executive Producer, Waterworks Interactive

I like the fact that sketching by hand takes me away from the computer rather than keeping me within its confines. I can work out the considerations for the computer space *after* I've had my stroke of genius!

FIGURE 12.3

Sample sketch

FIGURE 12.4

Resulting design

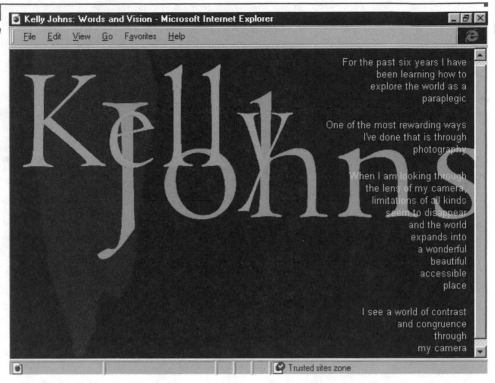

Kelly Johns: Words and Vision - Microsoft Internet Explorer

File   Edit   View   Go   Favorites   Help

For the past six years I have
been learning how to
explore the world as a
paraplegic

One of the most rewarding ways
I've done that is through
photography

When I am looking through
the lens of my camera,
limitations of all kinds
seem to disappear
and the world
expands into
a wonderful
beautiful
accessible
place

I see a world of contrast
and congruence
through
my camera

Trusted sites zone

Shape

Once you've got a clean environment with which to work, start thinking about shapes. Shape is powerful, and should be regarded as a pertinent element of layout design.

What many people aren't aware of is the subliminal power of shape. As we learned earlier with space issues and the way design is calculated, media artists study the significance of design elements.

Shapes hold unspoken meanings. It may feel like a stretch to think that shape can express to people that your industry is a corporate giant, or that a given product is effective and worth the high dollar value you've placed upon it. Designers address a site's intent and the needs of an audience by using shape, among other design techniques, to get the message across in a powerful way. Study the meanings of shape and use them mindfully and you will subtly yet effectively drive the intent home.

> *"Geometry is knowledge of the eternally existent."*
>
> PLATO

Some time ago, I read a book by author Michael S. Schneider, *A Beginner's Guide to Constructing the Universe*. Even though I had been aware of the importance of shape in design, this book deepened my respect and understanding of shape because it demonstrated the link between geometry (specifically shape and numbers), and nature.

OFF line!

Michael S. Schneider's intriguing book, *A Beginner's Guide to Constructing the Universe: The Mathematical Archetypes of Nature, Art, and Science,* is published by HarperPerennial, 1995.

This study can be of enormous value to Web designers as we struggle daily to accommodate the demands of a technical and artistic environment. If we remember that all shapes can be found in nature, it isn't difficult to step from the natural environment to see how strongly what we do as artists can affect the nature of humans.

Common Shapes

Here's an overview of common shapes and the ideas that they express.

- **The circle**—Circles express connection, community, wholeness, endurance, movement, and safety. If your goal is to convince a Web visitor that your company can deliver these things, use circles in your design. Circles also ascribe to the feminine: warmth, comfort, sensuality, and love (Figure 12.5).

FIGURE 12.5

Circles convey warmth, community, and wholeness.

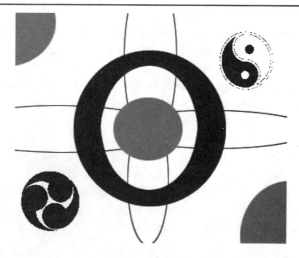

- **The rectangle**—Order, logic, containment (you'll remember our discussion of the computer's shape, no doubt), and security. Rectangles are excellent choices if you want to express an "in-it-for-the-long-haul" concept regarding a company's image.

  As Michael Schneider pointed out in his book, because a rectangle is the geometric result of adding a fourth point to shape, it is also the foundation for three-dimensional objects. This suggests mass, volume, and anything that is solid. Many major industries use rectangles in their logo design (Figure 12.6).

FIGURE 12.6

Rectangles suggest order, containment, and solidity.

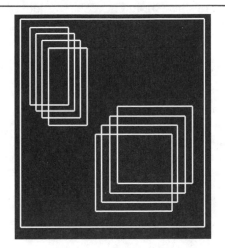

- **The triangle**—Triangles captivate and invigorate. Want to prevent your site visitors from falling asleep? Wake them up with the triangle, which also represents power, balance, law, science, and religion (the Scales of Justice and Star of David are excellent examples). Triangles are often compared to the masculine: strength, aggression, and dynamic movement (Figure 12.7).

FIGURE 12.7

Triangles represent power, balance, law, and religion.

"I'm finding it very difficult to 'escape the right angle.' I still find it a very crisp and uncluttered element of design. The circle is becoming a more important shape in my head, but I haven't translated that to any level of implementation just yet. I like circles not only because they're beautiful and symmetrical, but also because they can convey so many meanings if you open your mind to it."

AARON BERTRAND, Desktop Innovations

The use of shape should never be overlooked. Aside from a shape's persuasive powers, it can help bring a distinct look to your pages.

OFF line!

In order to see the incredible influence shape can have on design, take some standard construction paper and cut shapes out of the paper. Look through the shape at the world around you—walk around your house or office and see how the shape's parameters effect what you see. The results are sure to be inspirational.

The Header

A main header serves to define a page's intent and content. It can be plainly rendered, HTML-based text, or in most cases these days, a graphic. The advantage to graphic headers is that they can be specifically designed with color and type to match any existing branding the company or product in question might have.

Graphics are also easier to position on a page. Whether using table placement, frame-based layout, or cascading style sheet positioning, a graphic's placement can be specifically controlled.

In terms of layout, your main header will serve as the pivotal point of your design. Despite the fact that the header is critical to the content, for the purpose of layout design, you'll need to depart from the meaning and look at the header as a line or block (Figures 12.8 and 12.9).

FIGURE 12.8

Page header as line

FIGURE 12.9

Page header as block

Text

Text in layout is also seen as a line or block. Unlike headers, however, text can be broken into columns (Figure 12.10) or mixtures of columns and rows (Figure 12.11).

Text, as you'll learn later in the chapter, can also be shaped. This offers up interesting possibilities for combining techniques.

While you should think of sections of text as objects, you can't ever sacrifice readability for design. This is especially true of the Web, where the available space is at a minimum. The idea is to combine design *and* readability, giving your message greater impact.

> *" . . . your layout must not merely be an appendage to the words but a fundamental part of the communication process . . . the successful design will enhance or distill the message conveyed by the words and provide the visual environment in which that message can most effectively be conveyed."*
>
> G RAHAM D AVIS , Author, *Quick Solutions to Great Layouts*

FIGURE 12.10

Text in columnar form

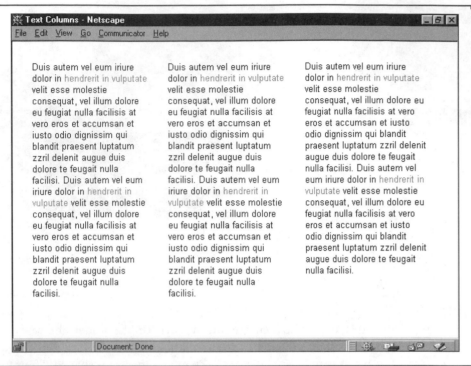

FIGURE 12.11

Columns and rows of text

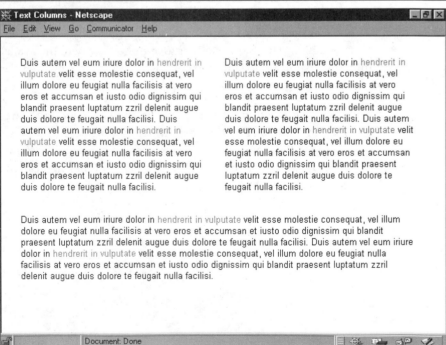

Media

Whether it's a logo, photograph, art, animation, or inline delivery of video, media is also considered an object when working with layout.

The most important issue with media is trying to keep a nice balance of information on the vertical and horizontal. You don't want to cut off a photograph on a screen, as in Figure 12.12. You *do* want to marry the individual screen space to the whole of the page, however. Figure 12.13 shows a long screen shot of the Weekly Wire page. There's a variety of media and text on this page, but the designer has taken specific care to find a balance with the horizontal and vertical space.

FIGURE 12.12

The photo on this page is cut off, disregarding the importance of the horizon line.

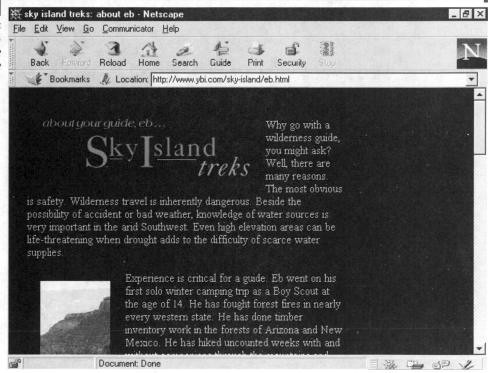

FIGURE 12.13

Another page from the same site pays better attention to the horizontal and vertical lines.

Grand Canyon Sky Island Treks - Netscape

File Edit View Go Communicator Help

Sky Island
treks

Sky Island treks is *the* answer for novice and first-time backpackers interested in the ultimate hiking experience. The idea is to create the most memorable experience for the treker, instilling and inspiring a love for the outdoors while teaching fundamental techniques for treading lightly on the earth.

With increasing pressure on public lands, newcomers to outdoor recreation are sure to benefit from Sky Island's no-trace ethic, which teaches respect for wildlife values, water conservation, other forest users, route selection, handling of biological and inert wastes, fire safety, and overall attituded and ambiance.

Owen's Valley from Near Mt. Whitney

I went to the woods because I wished to live deliberately, to front only the essential facts of life, and see if I could not learn what it had to teach, and not, when I came to die, discover that I had not lived. -- Henry David Thoreau

Sky Island's philosophy stems from guide Eb Eberlein's love of people and the vast beauty of Arizona's National Forests and Parks. In order to share his romance with Arizona's magnificent and varied appeal, Eb created Sky Island's personalized guide service options as outlined below.

Home · About Treks · About Eb · Treks Schedule, 1997

Home | About Treks | About Eb | Treks Schedule

Sky Island Treks: Call 520 - 792 - 1083 or email

© Sky Island Treks, 1997

Photo Credit: Cassius Eberlein

Document: Done

Layout Method: Step-by-Step

Now we get to the fun stuff! We're going to step through several layouts in order for you to get a feel for how elements work together.

Hopefully, these examples will inspire you to create layouts of your own design. In Chapter 14 you'll find tasks associated with the Design Studio's Web site (http://www .designstudio.net/) that involve layout. However, I cannot encourage you enough to work autonomously with the ideas expressed here. You'll enjoy the process, and what's more, you'll come up with unique design ideas.

Choosing a Shape

In the following examples, we'll look at how shape can initially be incorporated into a design. The focus is on the design—not on the technique. You'll get a closer look at the HTML process behind these designs in Chapter 13.

Example 1

In this real-world design example, the circular design was already a pre-determined part of the design. I was given a Microsoft Network standard navigation bar that *had* to reside on the left side of the page (Figure 12.14).

FIGURE 12.14

Pre-determined navigation design

Remember that circles express community and safety. I immediately saw that I could put the pre-determined shape to work to the advantage of the DisAbilities Forum design.

In order to do that, I started with the fixed page dimensions that I had to work with (one screen for the splash page) and made the sketch that you see in Figure 12.15.

FIGURE 12.15

Initial sketch for DisAbilities Forum splash page

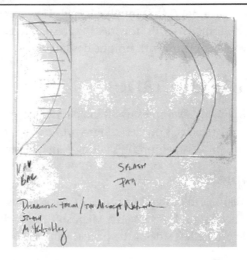

With one stroke of a pencil the foundation for a design was born. When you look at what this shape does, in detail, you can begin to see the impact of shape in design.

- With the arc image repeating, a reinforcement of community is expressed.

- The space *between* the two images creates a "safety" zone—a symbolic containment that seeks to protect.

- The arcs both point to the right, which is associated in most cultures as being the continuum, representing ongoing life and the future. The mind is subtly moved toward that future.

Community, safety, *and* progress. The impression of the shape in this design is far-reaching.

Example 2

Because there are so many rectangles on the Web, I tend to avoid their use. However, they are especially strong when relating to corporate and stable identities.

One client, Bernstein Communications, is very involved in crisis management and senior relations—particularly as they pertain to politics, management, and large corporate identities. The company wanted a very simple, definitive, orderly, and stable Web presence.

Of course, the rectangle was in order. Figure 12.16 shows a sketch of the rectangles used in the main page design.

FIGURE 12.16

*Rectangular sections
for Bernstein
Communications*

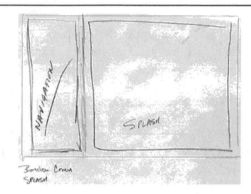

It's simple—easily understood by everyone—and conveys a weight and constancy that pleases the client and serves the audience.

Example 3

Next we come to the triangle. This shape is very prevalent but much less obvious than rectangles or circles. Figure 12.17 shows a sketch of the triangular shapes used for student Aidan Hoyal's splash page.

FIGURE 12.17

Triangular design

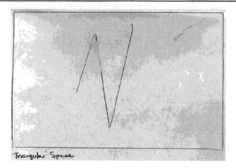

You'll notice that the angles create a sense of invigorating motion, logic, science, and order. The designer offers his approach to the page, saying:

"I envision the organization as one which deals mostly with numbers and statistics (tracking data) rather than with politics. Its audience, however, might include politicians and others interested in this type of information on endangered species (e.g., biologists, zoologists, and other research scientists)."

This real-life explanation shows another designer's approach to shape and how other designers achieve meaning in the work they do—making the experience for their audience paramount in their design.

Adding the Header

The next step is to add a primary header to the page, which will be sketched as either a line or a block, depending upon the style and weight you feel is appropriate for your design.

Example 1

I wanted to balance the weight of this page. On the left is the navigation bar, so in order to bring some weight to the right of the page without interfering with the forward movement created by the arc, I added the header to the upper-right corner. Figure 12.18 shows the results.

Header added to upper-left of splash

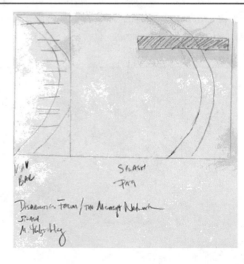

At this point, the sketch seems somewhat out of balance, but the addition of text and other media will address that issue.

Example 2

In keeping with the bold, secure feel of this rectangular design, the header is sketched in as a somewhat weighty, central piece, as shown in Figure 12.19.

FIGURE 12.19

Centrally placed, heavy block for header

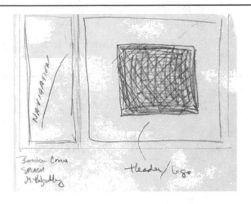

This layout now exhibits even greater stability with the addition of the header line.

Example 3

As with the first example, it makes sense to add a forward-moving directional piece to this design. The header line achieves that when placed in the upper-right corner of the layout (Figure 12.20).

FIGURE 12.20

Medium-weight header line at upper-right of layout

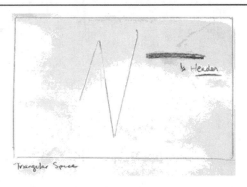

At this point, we're ready to balance the design by adding text.

Adding Text

Text will fill in the empty portions of layout—with the exception of necessary white space, of course. Whether it's a selection of a few paragraphs, or only a single extra word, the text serves to extend as well as balance the design.

Example 1

In this example, text will be used dynamically on the main splash page. A general look is sketched out in Figure 12.21.

I also sketched out a look for longer, internal pages, which you can see in Figure 12.22.

FIGURE 12.21

Text sketched into the layout

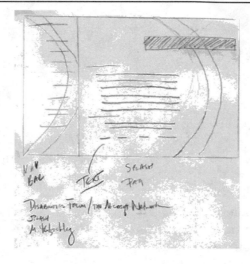

FIGURE 12.22

Text sketched into a longer page layout

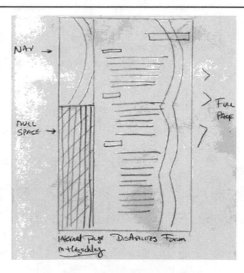

Preparing both of these sketches provided me with enough groundwork for the entire top-level of this site.

Example 2

As with Example 1, in Figure 12.23 you can see a sketch of the splash page text layout, with the main block broken out into separate headers. The text layout for a content page is shown in Figure 12.24.

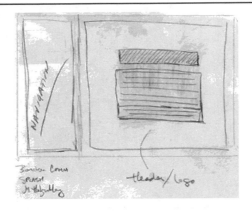

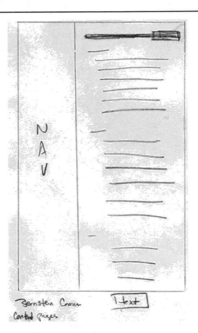

Note in this case that the header is less dense and not centered on the page, rather, it's brought to the top. The rectangular shape remains.

Example 3

In this case, text for the splash page is kept short. There is only one small selection (Figure 12.25).

For longer pages, the logo can be moved up toward the top of the page, and columns put in place for text layout (Figure 12.26).

FIGURE 12.25

Small text selection on splash

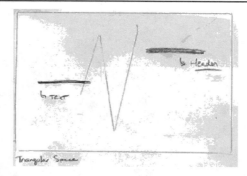

FIGURE 12.26

Columnar layout

Placing Additional Media

Whether you have photos, line art, animation, or inline media, you'll need to accommodate their placement on a page.

Example 1

I've chosen to use an animation as the main header on this splash page. You can kill two proverbial birds with one stone by using the same space for media and a header. However, I want to have an additional icon on the page, so I've incorporated a sketch for this (Figure 12.27). Figure 12.28 shows off the final, real-life results.

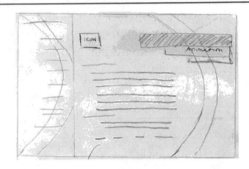

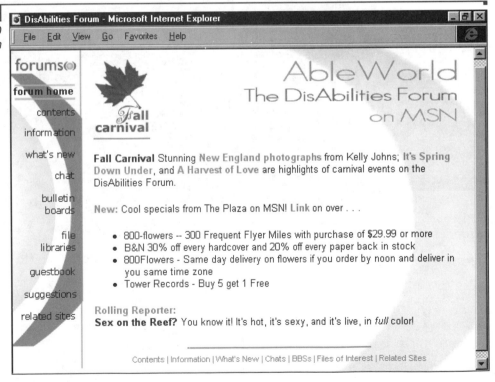

From shape, to header, to text, to media, this page has come a long way. A few simple strokes and the layout developed visually into a strong presentation.

Example 2

In this instance, the navigation buttons are the primary media of any consequence. They've been blocked out in a stack of squares, creating a rectangular image together, with rectangular sections in their unique form (Figure 12.29). Figure 12.30 shows the results of the splash page.

The client wanted one instance of a photograph on a linked page. The following sketch in Figure 12.31 demonstrates how it was accommodated. And Figure 12.32 shows the final page results.

FIGURE 12.29

Sketch of rectangular navigation buttons

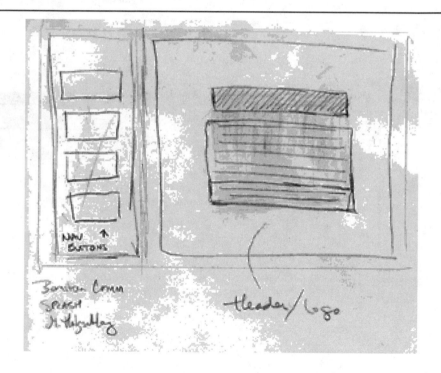

FIGURE 12.30

*Page at 640×480
resolution*

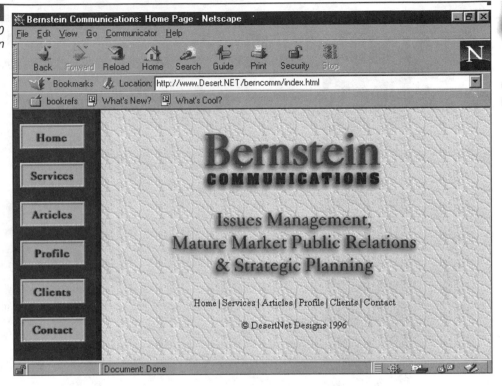

FIGURE 12.31

*Sketch including
photo*

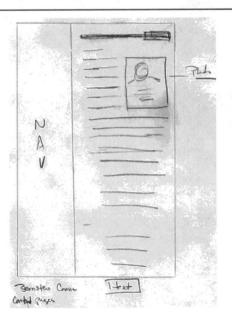

FIGURE 12.32

Actual page with photographic media

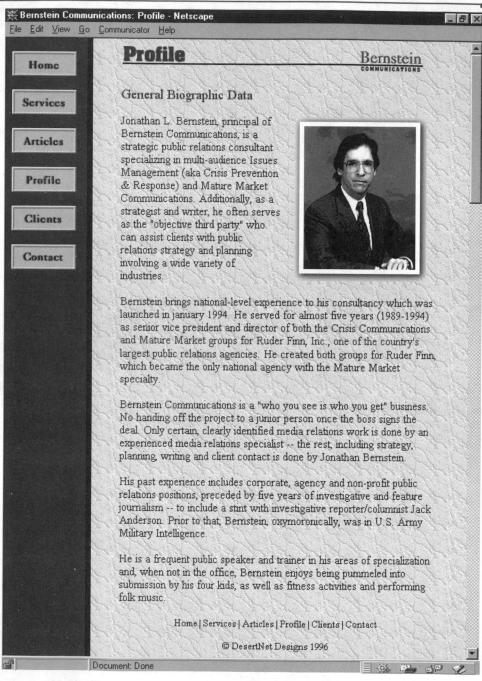

Bernstein Communications: Profile - Netscape

File Edit View Go Communicator Help

Profile

Bernstein
COMMUNICATIONS

Home

Services

Articles

Profile

Clients

Contact

General Biographic Data

Jonathan L. Bernstein, principal of Bernstein Communications, is a strategic public relations consultant specializing in multi-audience Issues Management (aka Crisis Prevention & Response) and Mature Market Communications. Additionally, as a strategist and writer, he often serves as the "objective third party" who can assist clients with public relations strategy and planning involving a wide variety of industries.

Bernstein brings national-level experience to his consultancy which was launched in january 1994. He served for almost five years (1989-1994) as senior vice president and director of both the Crisis Communications and Mature Market groups for Ruder Finn, Inc., one of the country's largest public relations agencies. He created both groups for Ruder Finn, which became the only national agency with the Mature Market specialty.

Bernstein Communications is a "who you see is who you get" business. No handing off the project to a junior person once the boss signs the deal. Only certain, clearly identified media relations work is done by an experienced media relations specialist -- the rest, including strategy, planning, writing and client contact is done by Jonathan Bernstein.

His past experience includes corporate, agency and non-profit public relations positions, preceded by five years of investigative and feature journalism -- to include a stint with investigative reporter/columnist Jack Anderson. Prior to that, Bernstein, oxymoronically, was in U.S. Army Military Intelligence.

He is a frequent public speaker and trainer in his areas of specialization and, when not in the office, Bernstein enjoys being pummeled into submission by his four kids, as well as fitness activities and performing folk music.

Home | Services | Articles | Profile | Clients | Contact

© DesertNet Designs 1996

Document: Done

Example 3

For this example, the splash page design is totally media, as the entire image (Figure 12.33) is hyperlinked to another, internal page.

Repeating the triangular image, Hoyal has also created a navigational map, with hot areas linking to other sections of his site (Figure 12.34).

In this instance, the angles serve to guide the eye as well as send a message of alert, persistent order.

FIGURE 12.33

*World monitor
splash graphic*

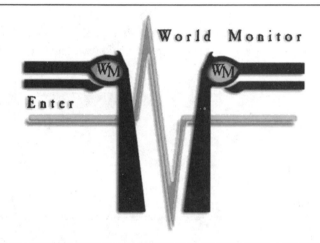

FIGURE 12.34

Image map

Another Approach

For those designers who prefer to do mock-ups on the computer rather than on a sketch pad, I recommend using a professional publishing package such as QuarkXPress, or doing the mock-ups graphically in Photoshop.

Designer Eric Picard of Waterworks Interactive shares his Photoshop method. Picard is regarded not only for his expert designs but for his digital media and Web design courses at the prestigious Main Photographic Workshops. Using Photoshop layers, Picard starts out with a transparent background. From there, he adds a header, text options, media, and finally background color. You can see this progression in the graphics below. He saves the file with layers so as to add, take away, and create different combinations of the elements on his page.

One advantage of this method is that all of the information is in graphic format—ready for conversion or export to appropriate file types. By using layers, Picard can substitute one look for another—if he wants to try the design out with a white versus blue background, he only needs to mask one layer and show another. Still another advantage of this method is that he can store the entire look and feel of the site in one Photoshop file. It is archived for later use should updates be needed.

Creating Fashionable Layout

Other approaches can be added to this simple layout method to enhance the visual experience and extend a layout's significance and flexibility. Two notable methods are the interplay you can achieve with shape and text, and the combination of shapes to create other shapes. In each case, you visually and psychologically increase the power of your design.

Text as Shape and Shape as Text

Sculpting text into shape can create compelling design. The one concern is readability—you should never sacrifice the site visitor's ability to read the content in order to stage a cool visual effect.

However, seeing text as shape will enhance your approach to layout. Consider Figure 12.35, in which a sentence is shaped in the form of a question mark. This kind of text as shape can be employed both functionally and artistically, depending upon what you are trying to achieve.

FIGURE 12.35

Text as shape

what i
want is
to
un
der
st
a
n

d

When approaching a layout, think about how text can be used symbolically, to guide the eye, or to create interesting visual texture.

Juxtapose the concept, and shape can be seen as text. This animated sequence from Aaron Bertrand's Desktop Innovations site demonstrates the visual impact that shape as text can convey. The following three screen shots show the letter "I" being dotted.

Shot 1   Shot 2   Shot 3

"When you see the circle come in and dot the 'I', you get the feeling there is a lot more behind the name than just a bunch of letters."

AARON BERTRAND, Desktop Innovations

Combining Shape

Using one shape to create another can build on the psychological impact that shapes convey. A powerful example of this can be seen in Luis Rocandio's logo development and Web design for Corporacion G6 Sistemas in Venezuela. Rocandio begins with a three-dimensional, oval shape.

He then combines the oval shapes to create a triangular shape for the logo.

Finally, the logo is encased in a mix of circular and rectangular combinations.

The strength of this logo is quite intense. It contains all of the psychological powers of the individual shapes. Combined with a simple but effective page layout, the final expression is one of great potency and security. It's especially interesting to examine how Rocandio has taken the logo's theme and repeated it in a tiled background.

Normally, I'm not a big fan of this technique, but in the case of this design, the background reinforces the logical and stable sentiments the company expresses, as you can see in the final results shown in Figure 12.36.

FIGURE 12.36

The resulting page is solid and powerful.

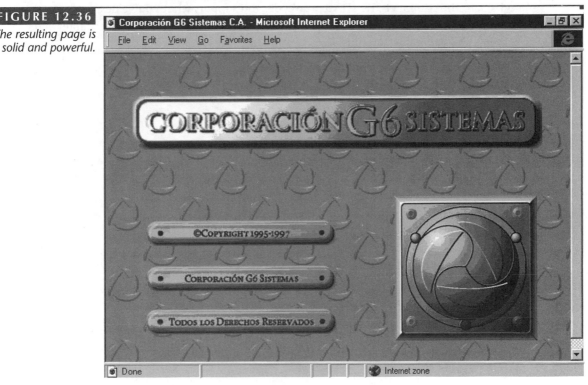

Next Up

Is this all there is to layout? No way. Entire books are written on this subject—and some designers focus so intently on layout that it becomes a specialty.

This chapter is meant to provide a starting place from which to further study layout design, and inspire you to work with a variety of tools in different circumstances. If anything, it will help you get away from your computer for a bit and spend time looking at the natural world. Then, come back to your computer, and design with ideas inspired by your unique perceptions and experiences. HTML is great, HTML is good, but it should serve you—not the other way around.

You've learned about space, you've been exposed to the elements of a page. The next step is to look at how to interpret your design into the working world of the Web. To go back to the computer, the HTML, the code, and support what you've designed. The next chapters do just this, taking a closer look at how the layouts in this chapter and beyond are literally constructed.

chapter 13

LAYOUT
TECHNOLOGY

LAYOUT
TECHNOLOGY

This chapter puts the knowledge of space and layout you've been exposed to thus far into the context of total layout control. We'll delve further into some familiar territory including the standard and tables-based technologies you've seen exemplified throughout the early passages of this book. We'll also look at how HTML syntax combines with the concepts of space, shape, and object placement to result in the blueprint of your Web site's layout design.

The basics of frames will also be covered. Frames relate to layout in contemporary design as they provide a delivery system for sections of a layout to be fixed. For example, if you want the navigation section of your interface to be static, you can create it with frames. Your layout design remains intact, but certain parts of the page become dynamic. Finally, we'll glance at style sheet positioning because of its growing importance in HTML-based layout design.

This chapter focuses on:

- Standard layout design using HTML
- Table-based design concepts
- Table syntax

- Frames-based design concepts
- Frames syntax
- Style sheet positioning

Certainly, one chapter devoted to the complex and emerging technologies of Web design layout is not going to be enough. Therefore, you'll see plenty of references, both here in the text and on the *Web by Design* companion Web site at http://www.designstudio.com/workshop/, that will help you master the areas of layout that interest you most.

We've examined the standards at several intervals throughout this book, particularly in the study of space, and must return to them again because space and layout are intrinsically linked. In these examples, however, think about the *whole* of a page's design rather than just the specific parts.

In the following section, we'll examine methods of text-based layout, graphic layout, and pull the ideas together in several real-world examples.

Standard HTML Formatting

Standard HTML formatting involves breaking up the page with balanced amounts of text, graphics and other media, and space. While your sketches can prepare the foundation for this, you'll need to get up-close and personal with HTML code in order to really manipulate blocks of text or media.

The first step in managing text with standard techniques is to determine *how much* you have for the entire site. This will help you break up text into realistically approachable pages. For individual pages within the site, a reasonable layout runs between one and three screens per page (Figure 13.1), possibly more if you don't go too overboard or if your work isn't *just* text. No one wants to scroll through page after page of text-only.

The following code shows about three screens worth of text before any text formatting has been added to the page. Pay attention to how this amount of text changes visually in the figure examples throughout the process.

```
<html>
<head>
<title>Text Example</title>
</head>

<body bgcolor="#FFFFFF" text="#000000" link="#999999"
vlink="#CCCCCC" alink="#FFFFCC">
```

Duis autem vel eum iriure dolor in hendrerit in vulputate velit esse molestie consequat, vel illum dolore eu feugiat nulla facilisis at vero eros et accumsan et iusto odio dignissim qui blandit praesent luptatum zzril delenit augue duis dolore te feugait nulla facilisi. Nam liber tempor cum soluta nobis eleifend option congue nihil imperdiet doming id quod mazim placerat facer possim assum.

Accumsan et iusto odio dignissim qui blandit praesent luptatum zzril delenit augue duis dolore te feugait nulla facilisi. Eros Et Accumsan dignissim qui blandit praesent luptatum zzril delenit augue duis dolore te feugait nulla facilisi. Nam liber tempor cum soluta nobis eleifend option congue nihil imperdiet doming id quod mazim placerat facer possim assum. Iusto odio dignissim qui blandit praesent luptatum zzril delenit augue duis dolore te feugait nulla facilisi.

Nam liber tempor cum soluta nobis eleifend option congue nihil imperdiet doming id quod mazim placerat facer possim assum. Accumsan et iusto odio dignissim qui blandit. Vendrerit In Vulputate Duis autem vel eum iriure dolor in hendrerit in vulputate velit esse molestie consequat, vel illum dolore eu feugiat nulla facilisis at vero eros et accumsan et iusto odio. Occumsan Aliquam dignissim qui blandit praesent luptatum zzril delenit augue duis dolore te feugait nulla facilisi. Nam liber tempor cum soluta nobis eleifend option congue nihil imperdiet doming id quod mazim placerat facer possim assum.

Eros Et Accumsan dignissim qui blandit praesent luptatum zzril delenit augue duis dolore te feugait nulla facilisi. Nam liber tempor cum soluta nobis eleifend option congue nihil imperdiet doming id quod mazim placerat facer possim assum. Iusto odio dignissim qui blandit.

Accumsan dignissim qui blandit praesent luptatum zzril delenit augue duis dolore te feugait nulla facilisi. Nam liber tempor cum soluta nobis eleifend option congue nihil imperdiet doming id quod mazim placerat facer possim assum. Iusto odio dignissim qui blandit praesent luptatum zzril delenit augue duis dolore te feugait nulla facilisi.

Nam liber tempor cum soluta nobis eleifend option congue nihil imperdiet doming id quod mazim placerat facer possim assum. Accumsan et iusto odio dignissim qui blandit. Duis autem vel eum iriure dolor in hendrerit in vulputate velit esse molestie consequat, vel illum dolore eu feugiat nulla facilisis at vero eros et accumsan et iusto odio.

```
</body>
</html>
```

FIGURE 13.1

Three screens of text before the addition of space and media

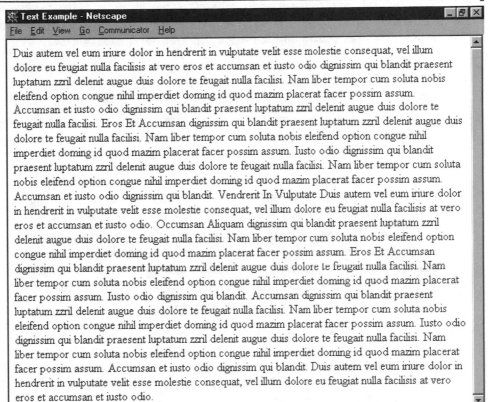

Now, add margins using the <blockquote> or <margin> tags (Figure 13.2). This is necessary to create that all-important white space. Here is the text with blockquotes added:

```
<html>
<head>
<title>Text Example</title>
</head>

<body bgcolor="#FFFFFF" text="#000000" link="#999999"
vlink="#CCCCCC" alink="#FFFFCC">

<blockquote>

Duis autem vel eum iriure dolor in hendrerit in vulputate velit esse molestie
consequat, vel illum dolore eu feugiat nulla facilisis at vero eros et accumsan et
```

iusto odio dignissim qui blandit praesent luptatum zzril delenit augue duis dolore te feugait nulla facilisi. Nam liber tempor cum soluta nobis eleifend option congue nihil imperdiet doming id quod mazim placerat facer possim assum.

Accumsan et iusto odio dignissim qui blandit praesent luptatum zzril delenit augue duis dolore te feugait nulla facilisi. Eros Et Accumsan dignissim qui blandit praesent luptatum zzril delenit augue duis dolore te feugait nulla facilisi. Nam liber tempor cum soluta nobis eleifend option congue nihil imperdiet doming id quod mazim placerat facer possim assum. Iusto odio dignissim qui blandit praesent luptatum zzril delenit augue duis dolore te feugait nulla facilisi.

Nam liber tempor cum soluta nobis eleifend option congue nihil imperdiet doming id quod mazim placerat facer possim assum. Accumsan et iusto odio dignissim qui blandit. Vendrerit In Vulputate Duis autem vel eum iriure dolor in hendrerit in vulputate velit esse molestie consequat, vel illum dolore eu feugiat nulla facilisis at vero eros et accumsan et iusto odio. Occumsan Aliquam dignissim qui blandit praesent luptatum zzril delenit augue duis dolore te feugait nulla facilisi. Nam liber tempor cum soluta nobis eleifend option congue nihil imperdiet doming id quod mazim placerat facer possim assum.

Eros Et Accumsan dignissim qui blandit praesent luptatum zzril delenit augue duis dolore te feugait nulla facilisi. Nam liber tempor cum soluta nobis eleifend option congue nihil imperdiet doming id quod mazim placerat facer possim assum. Iusto odio dignissim qui blandit.

Accumsan dignissim qui blandit praesent luptatum zzril delenit augue duis dolore te feugait nulla facilisi. Nam liber tempor cum soluta nobis eleifend option congue nihil imperdiet doming id quod mazim placerat facer possim assum. Iusto odio dignissim qui blandit praesent luptatum zzril delenit augue duis dolore te feugait nulla facilisi.

Nam liber tempor cum soluta nobis eleifend option congue nihil imperdiet doming id quod mazim placerat facer possim assum. Accumsan et iusto odio dignissim qui blandit. Duis autem vel eum iriure dolor in hendrerit in vulputate velit esse molestie consequat, vel illum dolore eu feugiat nulla facilisis at vero eros et accumsan et iusto odio.

```
</blockquote>
</body>
</html>
```

FIGURE 13.2

*Add blockquotes for
that all important
white space.*

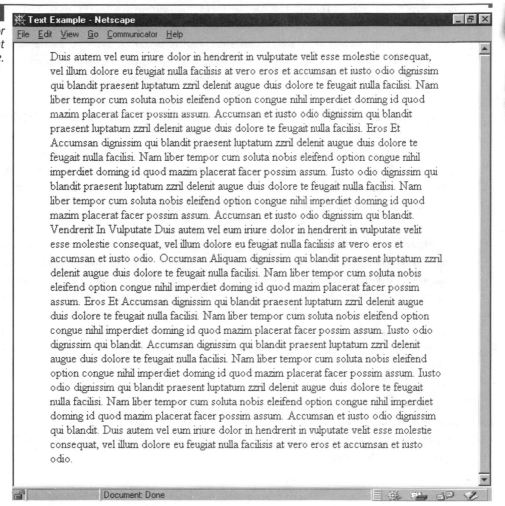

Attention span on the Web is short. It's in your best interest to serve your audience by ensuring that paragraphs are equally short. Therefore, after breaking up text into pages, break up your page into logical sections of short paragraphs (Figure 13.3). The syntax with paragraph tags added:

```
<html>
<head>
<title>Text Example</title>
</head>
<body bgcolor="#FFFFFF" text="#000000" link="#999999"
vlink="#CCCCCC" alink="#FFFFCC">
<blockquote>
```

Duis autem vel eum iriure dolor in hendrerit in vulputate velit esse molestie consequat, vel illum dolore eu feugiat nulla facilisis at vero eros et accumsan et iusto odio dignissim qui blandit praesent luptatum zzril delenit augue duis dolore te feugait nulla facilisi. Nam liber tempor cum soluta nobis eleifend option congue nihil imperdiet doming id quod mazim placerat facer possim assum.
<p>

Accumsan et iusto odio dignissim qui blandit praesent luptatum zzril delenit augue duis dolore te feugait nulla facilisi. Eros Et Accumsan dignissim qui blandit praesent luptatum zzril delenit augue duis dolore te feugait nulla facilisi. Nam liber tempor cum soluta nobis eleifend option congue nihil imperdiet doming id quod mazim placerat facer possim assum. Iusto odio dignissim qui blandit praesent luptatum zzril delenit augue duis dolore te feugait nulla facilisi.
<p>

Nam liber tempor cum soluta nobis eleifend option congue nihil imperdiet doming id quod mazim placerat facer possim assum. Accumsan et iusto odio dignissim qui blandit. Vendrerit In Vulputate Duis autem vel eum iriure dolor in hendrerit in vulputate velit esse molestie consequat, vel illum dolore eu feugiat nulla facilisis at vero eros et accumsan et iusto odio. Occumsan Aliquam dignissim qui blandit praesent luptatum zzril delenit augue duis dolore te feugait nulla facilisi. Nam liber tempor cum soluta nobis eleifend option congue nihil imperdiet doming id quod mazim placerat facer possim assum.
<p>

Eros Et Accumsan dignissim qui blandit praesent luptatum zzril delenit augue duis dolore te feugait nulla facilisi. Nam liber tempor cum soluta nobis eleifend option congue nihil imperdiet doming id quod mazim placerat facer possim assum. Iusto odio dignissim qui blandit.
<p>

Accumsan dignissim qui blandit praesent luptatum zzril delenit augue duis dolore te feugait nulla facilisi. Nam liber tempor cum soluta nobis eleifend option congue nihil imperdiet doming id quod mazim placerat facer possim assum. Iusto odio dignissim qui blandit praesent luptatum zzril delenit augue duis dolore te feugait nulla facilisi.
<p>

Nam liber tempor cum soluta nobis eleifend option congue nihil imperdiet doming id quod mazim placerat facer possim assum. Accumsan et iusto odio dignissim qui blandit. Duis autem vel eum iriure dolor in hendrerit in vulputate velit esse molestie consequat, vel illum dolore eu feugiat nulla facilisis at vero eros et accumsan et iusto odio.
<p>

</blockquote>
</body>
</html>

FIGURE 13.3

Paragraphs should be short and to the point.

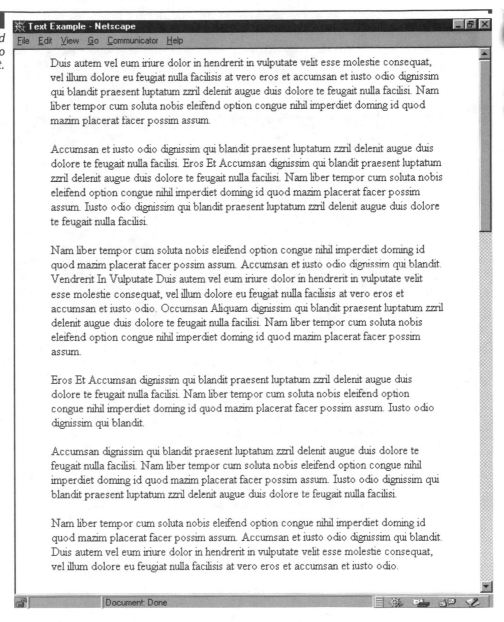

Some people choose to use the non-breaking space characters   to create indentation in paragraphs. The results are quite readable, as you can see in Figure 13.4. The following three non-breaking space characters before the paragraph show you how to achieve this technique:

```
      Duis autem vel eum iriure dolor in hendrerit in vulputate
velit esse molestie consequat, vel illum dolore eu feugiat nulla facilisis at vero
```

eros et accumsan et iusto odio dignissim qui blandit praesent luptatum zzril delenit augue duis dolore te feugait nulla facilisi. Nam liber tempor cum soluta nobis eleifend option congue nihil imperdiet doming id quod mazim placerat facer possim assum.

<p>

FIGURE 13.4

You can use non-breaking space characters to achieve paragraph indentation.

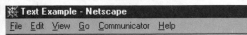

Duis autem vel eum iriure dolor in hendrerit in vulputate velit esse molestie consequat, vel illum dolore eu feugiat nulla facilisis at vero eros et accumsan et iusto odio dignissim qui blandit praesent luptatum zzril delenit augue duis dolore te feugait nulla facilisi. Nam liber tempor cum soluta nobis eleifend option congue nihil imperdiet doming id quod mazim placerat facer possim assum.

Accumsan et iusto odio dignissim qui blandit praesent luptatum zzril delenit augue duis dolore te feugait nulla facilisi. Eros Et Accumsan dignissim qui blandit praesent luptatum zzril delenit augue duis dolore te feugait nulla facilisi. Nam liber tempor cum soluta nobis eleifend option congue nihil imperdiet doming id quod mazim placerat facer possim assum. Iusto odio dignissim qui blandit praesent luptatum zzril delenit augue duis dolore te feugait nulla facilisi.

Nam liber tempor cum soluta nobis eleifend option congue nihil imperdiet doming id quod mazim placerat facer possim assum. Accumsan et iusto odio dignissim qui blandit. Vendrerit In Vulputate Duis autem vel eum iriure dolor in hendrerit in vulputate velit esse molestie consequat, vel illum dolore eu feugiat nulla facilisis at vero eros et accumsan et iusto odio. Occumsan Aliquam dignissim qui blandit praesent luptatum zzril delenit augue duis dolore te feugait nulla facilisi. Nam liber tempor cum soluta nobis eleifend option congue nihil imperdiet doming id quod mazim placerat facer possim assum.

Eros Et Accumsan dignissim qui blandit praesent luptatum zzril delenit augue duis dolore te feugait nulla facilisi. Nam liber tempor cum soluta nobis eleifend option congue nihil imperdiet doming id quod mazim placerat facer possim assum. Iusto odio dignissim qui blandit.

Accumsan dignissim qui blandit praesent luptatum zzril delenit augue duis dolore te feugait nulla facilisi. Nam liber tempor cum soluta nobis eleifend option congue nihil imperdiet doming id quod mazim placerat facer possim assum. Iusto odio dignissim qui blandit praesent luptatum zzril delenit augue duis dolore te feugait nulla facilisi.

Nam liber tempor cum soluta nobis eleifend option congue nihil imperdiet doming id quod mazim placerat facer possim assum. Accumsan et iusto odio dignissim qui blandit. Duis autem vel eum iriure dolor in hendrerit in vulputate velit esse molestie consequat, vel illum dolore eu feugiat nulla facilisis at vero eros et accumsan et iusto odio.

Document: Done

Remember that lists are also a good way to break up space and help shape a page's layout. You can add them wherever your design calls for them, or where they feel logical. Figure 13.5 shows the use of lists with the same text.

```
<html>
<head>
<title>Text Example</title>
</head>

<body bgcolor="#FFFFFF" text="#000000" link="#999999"
vlink="#CCCCCC" alink="#FFFFCC">

<blockquote>

      Duis autem vel eum iriure dolor in hendrerit in
vulputate velit esse molestie consequat, vel illum dolore eu feugiat nulla
facilisis at vero eros et accumsan et iusto odio dignissim qui blandit
praesent luptatum zzril delenit augue duis dolore te feugait nulla facilisi.
Nam liber tempor cum soluta nobis eleifend option congue nihil imperdiet
doming id quod mazim placerat facer possim assum.
<p>

      Accumsan et iusto odio dignissim qui blandit praesent
luptatum zzril delenit augue duis dolore te feugait nulla facilisi. Eros Et
Accumsan dignissim qui blandit praesent luptatum zzril delenit augue duis
dolore te feugait nulla facilisi. Nam liber tempor cum soluta nobis eleifend
option congue nihil imperdiet doming id quod mazim placerat facer possim
assum. Iusto odio dignissim qui blandit praesent luptatum zzril delenit
augue duis dolore te feugait nulla facilisi.
<p>

<ul>
<li>Nam liber tempor cum soluta nobis eleifend option congue nihil imperdiet
doming id quod mazim placerat facer possim assum. Accumsan et iusto odio
dignissim qui blandit.
```

```
<li>In Vulputate Duis autem vel eum iriure dolor in hendrerit in vulputate
velit esse molestie consequat, vel illum dolore eu feugiat nulla facilisis
at vero eros et accumsan et iusto odio.

<li>Occumsan Aliquam dignissim qui blandit praesent luptatum zzril delenit
augue duis dolore te feugait nulla facilisi. Nam liber tempor cum soluta
nobis eleifend option congue nihil imperdiet doming id quod mazim placerat
facer possim assum.
</ul>
<p>

      Eros Et Accumsan dignissim qui blandit praesent
luptatum zzril delenit augue duis dolore te feugait nulla facilisi. Nam
liber tempor cum soluta nobis eleifend option congue nihil imperdiet doming
id quod mazim placerat facer possim assum. Iusto odio dignissim qui blandit.
<p>

      Accumsan dignissim qui blandit praesent luptatum zzril
delenit augue duis dolore te feugait nulla facilisi. Nam liber tempor cum
soluta nobis eleifend option congue nihil imperdiet doming id quod mazim
placerat facer possim assum. Iusto odio dignissim qui blandit praesent
luptatum zzril delenit augue duis dolore te feugait nulla facilisi.
<p>

      Nam liber tempor cum soluta nobis eleifend option
congue nihil imperdiet doming id quod mazim placerat facer possim assum.
Accumsan et iusto odio dignissim qui blandit. Duis autem vel eum iriure
dolor in hendrerit in vulputate velit esse molestie consequat, vel illum
dolore eu feugiat nulla facilisis at vero eros et accumsan et iusto odio.

</blockquote>
</body>
</html>
```

FIGURE 13.5

*The page with a
list added.*

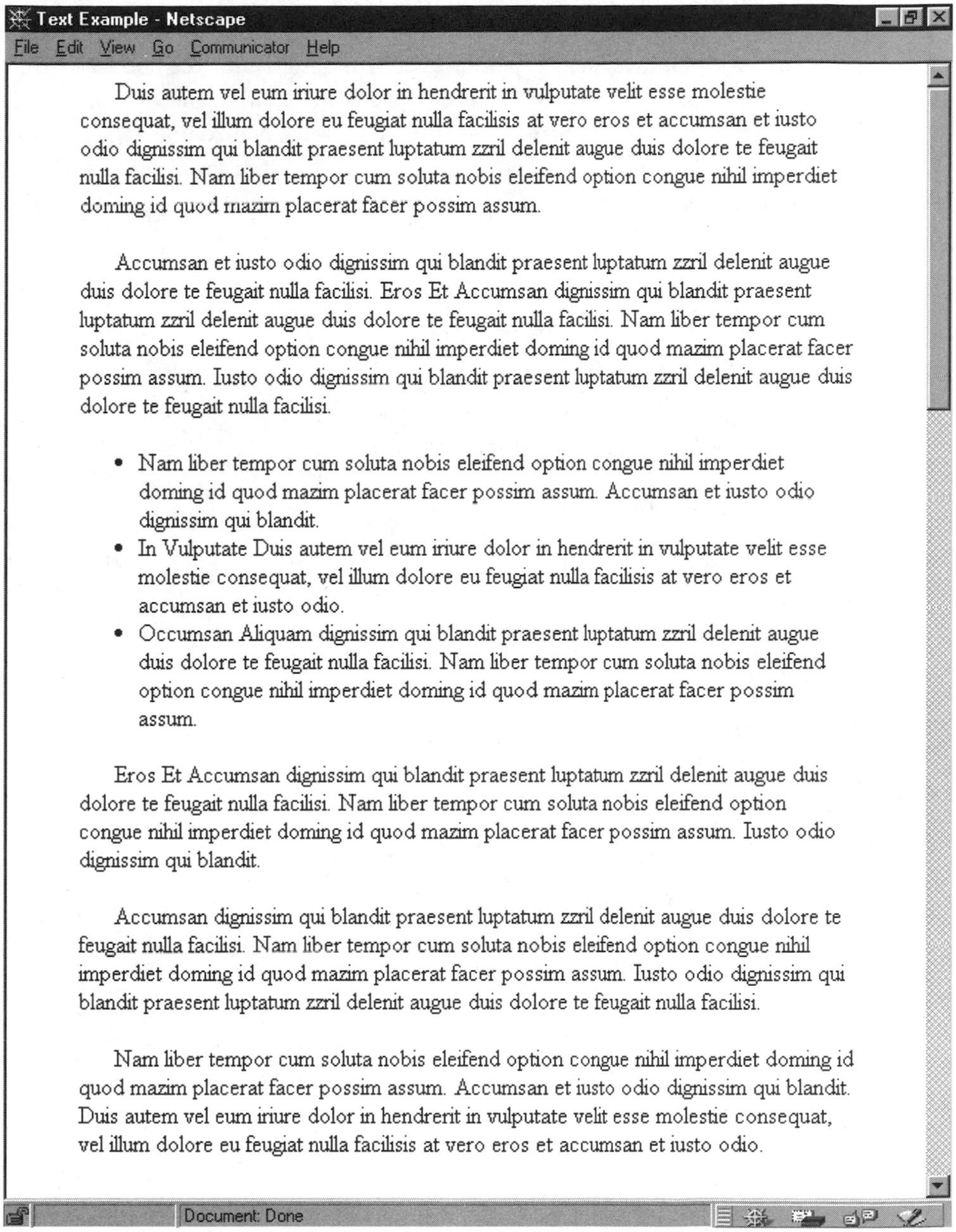

Text Example - Netscape

File   Edit   View   Go   Communicator   Help

Duis autem vel eum iriure dolor in hendrerit in vulputate velit esse molestie
consequat, vel illum dolore eu feugiat nulla facilisis at vero eros et accumsan et iusto
odio dignissim qui blandit praesent luptatum zzril delenit augue duis dolore te feugait
nulla facilisi. Nam liber tempor cum soluta nobis eleifend option congue nihil imperdiet
doming id quod mazim placerat facer possim assum.

Accumsan et iusto odio dignissim qui blandit praesent luptatum zzril delenit augue
duis dolore te feugait nulla facilisi. Eros Et Accumsan dignissim qui blandit praesent
luptatum zzril delenit augue duis dolore te feugait nulla facilisi. Nam liber tempor cum
soluta nobis eleifend option congue nihil imperdiet doming id quod mazim placerat facer
possim assum. Iusto odio dignissim qui blandit praesent luptatum zzril delenit augue duis
dolore te feugait nulla facilisi.

- Nam liber tempor cum soluta nobis eleifend option congue nihil imperdiet
  doming id quod mazim placerat facer possim assum. Accumsan et iusto odio
  dignissim qui blandit.
- In Vulputate Duis autem vel eum iriure dolor in hendrerit in vulputate velit esse
  molestie consequat, vel illum dolore eu feugiat nulla facilisis at vero eros et
  accumsan et iusto odio.
- Occumsan Aliquam dignissim qui blandit praesent luptatum zzril delenit augue
  duis dolore te feugait nulla facilisi. Nam liber tempor cum soluta nobis eleifend
  option congue nihil imperdiet doming id quod mazim placerat facer possim
  assum.

Eros Et Accumsan dignissim qui blandit praesent luptatum zzril delenit augue duis
dolore te feugait nulla facilisi. Nam liber tempor cum soluta nobis eleifend option
congue nihil imperdiet doming id quod mazim placerat facer possim assum. Iusto odio
dignissim qui blandit.

Accumsan dignissim qui blandit praesent luptatum zzril delenit augue duis dolore te
feugait nulla facilisi. Nam liber tempor cum soluta nobis eleifend option congue nihil
imperdiet doming id quod mazim placerat facer possim assum. Iusto odio dignissim qui
blandit praesent luptatum zzril delenit augue duis dolore te feugait nulla facilisi.

Nam liber tempor cum soluta nobis eleifend option congue nihil imperdiet doming id
quod mazim placerat facer possim assum. Accumsan et iusto odio dignissim qui blandit.
Duis autem vel eum iriure dolor in hendrerit in vulputate velit esse molestie consequat,
vel illum dolore eu feugiat nulla facilisis at vero eros et accumsan et iusto odio.

Document: Done

Finally, you want to use graphics or other media as functional aspects of your page, such as with linked graphics, navigation buttons, and with image maps. Or, you can include graphics, such as a photograph, as design enhancements (see Figure 13.6), artwork, or fully constructed parts of a page, such as in a main splash graphic. The code for the text example with an added graphic follows. Notice how the page is beginning to take on an attractive shape, and that with the addition of space and other layout techniques, the original jumbled text is formatted into three full screens of information.

```
<html>
<head>
<title>Text Example</title>
</head>

<body bgcolor="#FFFFFF" text="#000000" link="#999999"
vlink="#CCCCCC" alink="#FFFFCC">

<blockquote>

      Duis autem vel eum iriure dolor in hendrerit in
vulputate velit esse molestie consequat, vel illum dolore eu feugiat nulla
facilisis at vero eros et accumsan et iusto odio dignissim qui blandit
praesent luptatum zzril delenit augue duis dolore te feugait nulla facilisi.
Nam liber tempor cum soluta nobis eleifend option congue nihil imperdiet
doming id quod mazim placerat facer possim assum.
<p>

<img src="sydney.jpg" width="146" height="98" hspace="5" vspace="5"
border="0" align="right" alt="sydney opera house at night">

      Accumsan et iusto odio dignissim qui blandit praesent
luptatum zzril delenit augue duis dolore te eugait nulla facilisi. Eros Et
Accumsan dignissim qui blandit praesent luptatum zzril delenit augue duis
dolore te feugait nulla facilisi. Nam liber tempor cum soluta nobis eleifend
option congue nihil imperdiet doming id quod mazim placerat facer possim
assum. Iusto odio dignissim qui blandit praesent luptatum zzril delenit
augue duis dolore te feugait nulla facilisi.
<p>

<ul>
<li>Nam liber tempor cum soluta nobis eleifend option congue nihil imperdiet
doming id quod mazim placerat facer possim assum. Accumsan et iusto odio
dignissim qui blandit.
```

```
<li>In Vulputate Duis autem vel eum iriure dolor in hendrerit in vulputate
velit esse molestie consequat, vel illum dolore eu feugiat nulla facilisis
at vero eros et accumsan et iusto odio.

<li>Occumsan Aliquam dignissim qui blandit praesent luptatum zzril delenit
augue duis dolore te feugait nulla facilisi. Nam liber tempor cum soluta
nobis eleifend option congue nihil imperdiet doming id quod mazim placerat
facer possim assum.
</ul>
<p>

      Eros Et Accumsan dignissim qui blandit praesent
luptatum zzril delenit augue duis dolore te feugait nulla facilisi. Nam
liber tempor cum soluta nobis eleifend option congue nihil imperdiet doming
id quod mazim placerat facer possim assum. Iusto odio dignissim qui blandit.
<p>

      Accumsan dignissim qui blandit praesent luptatum zzril
delenit augue duis dolore te feugait nulla facilisi. Nam liber tempor cum
soluta nobis eleifend option congue nihil imperdiet doming id quod mazim
placerat facer possim assum. Iusto odio dignissim qui blandit praesent
luptatum zzril delenit augue duis dolore te feugait nulla facilisi.
<p>

      Nam liber tempor cum soluta nobis eleifend option
congue nihil imperdiet doming id quod mazim placerat facer possim assum.
Accumsan et iusto odio dignissim qui blandit. Duis autem vel eum iriure
dolor in hendrerit in vulputate velit esse molestie consequat, vel illum
dolore eu feugiat nulla facilisis at vero eros et accumsan et iusto odio.

</blockquote>
</body>
</html>
```

When graphics and media are being used as functional media, such as a link, place
them using the <img> or <object> tag and any alignment attribute you wish but avoid
using any kind of border, as it constrains the space.

Graphics and media used to enhance the page should be arranged in the fashion
you've determined with your layout sketches. Typically, standard HTML layouts will
apply to the most simple of pages, such as those with limited text and graphics, or splash
pages where a map or hyperlinked graphic is the main attraction.

FIGURE 13.6

A graphic added to the page

Duis autem vel eum iriure dolor in hendrerit in vulputate velit esse molestie consequat, vel illum dolore eu feugiat nulla facilisis at vero eros et accumsan et iusto odio dignissim qui blandit praesent luptatum zzril delenit augue duis dolore te feugait nulla facilisi. Nam liber tempor cum soluta nobis eleifend option congue nihil imperdiet doming id quod mazim placerat facer possim assum.

Accumsan et iusto odio dignissim qui blandit praesent luptatum zzril delenit augue duis dolore te eugait nulla facilisi. Eros Et Accumsan dignissim qui blandit praesent luptatum zzril delenit augue duis dolore te feugait nulla facilisi. Nam liber tempor cum soluta nobis eleifend option congue nihil imperdiet doming id quod mazim placerat facer possim assum. Iusto odio dignissim qui blandit praesent luptatum zzril delenit augue duis dolore te feugait nulla facilisi.

- Nam liber tempor cum soluta nobis eleifend option congue nihil imperdiet doming id quod mazim placerat facer possim assum. Accumsan et iusto odio dignissim qui blandit.
- In Vulputate Duis autem vel eum iriure dolor in hendrerit in vulputate velit esse molestie consequat, vel illum dolore eu feugiat nulla facilisis at vero eros et accumsan et iusto odio.
- Occumsan Aliquam dignissim qui blandit praesent luptatum zzril delenit augue duis dolore te feugait nulla facilisi. Nam liber tempor cum soluta nobis eleifend option congue nihil imperdiet doming id quod mazim placerat facer possim assum.

Eros Et Accumsan dignissim qui blandit praesent luptatum zzril delenit augue duis dolore te feugait nulla facilisi. Nam liber tempor cum soluta nobis eleifend option congue nihil imperdiet doming id quod mazim placerat facer possim assum. Iusto odio dignissim qui blandit.

Accumsan dignissim qui blandit praesent luptatum zzril delenit augue duis dolore te feugait nulla facilisi. Nam liber tempor cum soluta nobis eleifend option congue nihil imperdiet doming id quod mazim placerat facer possim assum. Iusto odio dignissim qui blandit praesent luptatum zzril delenit augue duis dolore te feugait nulla facilisi.

Nam liber tempor cum soluta nobis eleifend option congue nihil imperdiet doming id quod mazim placerat facer possim assum. Accumsan et iusto odio dignissim qui blandit. Duis autem vel eum iriure dolor in hendrerit in vulputate velit esse molestie consequat, vel illum dolore eu feugiat nulla facilisis at vero eros et accumsan et iusto odio.

Document: Done

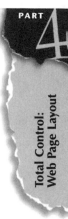

Example

In Chapter 12, we looked at several examples of layouts, including a plain splash page with a graphic as its main feature. Here's the standard HTML code for that page:

```html
<html>
<head>
<title>Splash Screen</title>
</head>
<body text="#000000" bgcolor="#FFFFFF" link="#FF0000" vlink="#800080"
alink="#0000FF">
<div align="center">
<a href="storyboard.htm"><img border="0" src="splash.gif" height="323"
width="432"></a>
</div>
</body>
</html>
```

No surprises here! It's a very straightforward page with the layout design relying heavily on the graphic, you can see the page in Figure 13.7.

FIGURE 13.7

The splash page as it appears in Netscape 4.0.

Tables

Even though you've already been exposed to numerous examples of tables in this book, let's go back and take a careful look at how those tables are constructed. Table tags are really very simple, but with the variety of attributes available to you, the application is somewhat complicated. Be sure to refer to Appendix A, where HTML tags and attributes are covered. In fact, I recommend that you refer to it regularly as you work, as the information there will appeal to your own knowledge level and learning style.

 I P

> Much of the information on tables and frames in this chapter is derived from another of my books, *The Laura Lemay Web Workshop Guide to Designing with Stylesheets, Tables, and Frames*, (Sams.net, 1997). In that book, the basic lessons learned in this chapter are applied to a broader spectrum of layout and interface design. Any designer interested in studying a wide variety of tables and frames-based layouts will enjoy the workbook style of that book. For more information, visit `http://www.molly.com/`.

There are only three tags that are absolutely necessary when designing with tables:

`<table>` This tag determines the beginning of a table within an HTML document. As with the majority of HTML tags, after all of the elements are placed within a table, the end of a table is denoted by the companion tag, `</table>`.

`<tr>` Table rows are identified with this tag, which literally determines a row—the left-to-right, horizontal space within a table. Table rows are closed with the `</tr>` tag.

`<td>` Individual table cells are defined by this tag, also referred to as the "table data" tag. The table cell tags are particularly critical, for a number of reasons which you'll see as we look at various applications of the tag. For this introduction, remember that the `<td>` tag and the information contained therein *determines the columnar structure* of a table. The `<td>` tag closes with the `</td>` tag.

Now that you've got the basics, let's look at the attributes you might wish to use along with these core tags. There are many, and their use begins the departure away from straightforward coding to the complicated job of using HTML as a serious layout technology.

`align="x"` Align tables on a page with this attribute. Options allow `"x"` to equal left or right. Because the latest browsers default alignment to the left, and it's commonplace to center tables using other tags, the only really effective use of this attribute is when you specifically want an entire table placed to the far right of the browser field, as in Figure 13.8.

color reference

An effective understanding of color can significantly empower the Web designer. *Web by Design*'s color reference includes:

▶ **The 216 colors of the Web safe palette.** The first four pages of the color reference show each Web safe palette color, along with the hexadecimal and RGB values you'll need when working with these colors.

▶ **A selection of pre-set color swatches and applied examples.** Use these for inspiration, and use your imagination and personal style to achieve custom, original color design.

▶ **The subtractive color wheel.** Subtractive color synthesis is the theory on which all natural color rests. Computer color, which works on additive theory, can be much more unstable and limited than subtractive color. Learn from the stability and flexibility of natural color before shifting your perspective to the constraints of Web color.

It's important to point out that print is often more vivid than the color attainable on the computer screen. Expect to see some variation between color appearing on these pages and what you'll see within your browser. Please also note that the color swatches in this reference are interpretive. You are encouraged to create your own combinations and applications!

Digital versions of the material found in this section can be found at http://www.designstudio.net/color/.

The Color Safe Palette

990033 R: 153 G: 000 B: 051	**FF3366** R: 255 G: 051 B: 102	**CC0033** R: 204 G: 000 B: 051	**FF0033** R: 255 G: 000 B: 051	**FF9999** R: 255 G: 153 B: 153	**CC3366** R: 204 G: 051 B: 102
FFCCFF R: 255 G: 204 B: 255	**CC6699** R: 204 G: 102 B: 153	**993366** R: 153 G: 051 B: 102	**660033** R: 102 G: 000 B: 051	**CC3399** R: 204 G: 051 B: 153	**FF99CC** R: 255 G: 153 B: 204
FF66CC R: 255 G: 102 B: 204	**FF99FF** R: 255 G: 153 B: 255	**FF6699** R: 255 G: 102 B: 153	**CC0066** R: 204 G: 000 B: 102	**FF0066** R: 255 G: 000 B: 102	**FF3399** R: 255 G: 051 B: 153
FF0099 R: 255 G: 000 B: 153	**FF33CC** R: 255 G: 051 B: 204	**FF00CC** R: 255 G: 000 B: 204	**FF66FF** R: 255 G: 102 B: 255	**FF33FF** R: 255 G: 051 B: 255	**FF00FF** R: 255 G: 000 B: 255
CC0099 R: 204 G: 000 B: 153	**990066** R: 153 G: 000 B: 102	**CC66CC** R: 204 G: 102 B: 204	**CC33CC** R: 204 G: 051 B: 204	**CC99FF** R: 204 G: 153 B: 255	**CC66FF** R: 204 G: 102 B: 255
CC33FF R: 204 G: 051 B: 255	**993399** R: 153 G: 051 B: 153	**CC00CC** R: 204 G: 000 B: 204	**CC00FF** R: 204 G: 000 B: 255	**9900CC** R: 153 G: 000 B: 204	**990099** R: 153 G: 000 B: 153
CC99CC R: 204 G: 153 B: 204	**996699** R: 153 G: 102 B: 153	**663366** R: 102 G: 051 B: 102	**660099** R: 102 G: 000 B: 153	**9933CC** R: 153 G: 051 B: 204	**660066** R: 102 G: 000 B: 102
9900FF R: 153 G: 000 B: 255	**9933FF** R: 153 G: 051 B: 255	**9966CC** R: 153 G: 102 B: 204	**330033** R: 051 G: 000 B: 051	**663399** R: 102 G: 051 B: 153	**6633CC** R: 102 G: 051 B: 204
6600CC R: 102 G: 000 B: 204	**9966FF** R: 153 G: 102 B: 255	**330066** R: 051 G: 000 B: 102	**6600FF** R: 102 G: 000 B: 255	**6633FF** R: 102 G: 051 B: 255	**CCCCFF** R: 204 G: 204 B: 255

The Color Safe Palette (continued)

33CC99 R: 051 G: 204 B: 153	**00CC99** R: 000 G: 204 B: 153	**66FFCC** R: 102 G: 255 B: 204	**99FFCC** R: 153 G: 255 B: 204	**00FF99** R: 000 G: 255 B: 153	**339966** R: 051 G: 153 B: 102
006633 R: 000 G: 102 B: 051	**336633** R: 051 G: 102 B: 051	**669966** R: 102 G: 153 B: 102	**66CC66** R: 102 G: 204 B: 102	**99FF99** R: 153 G: 255 B: 153	**66FF66** R: 102 G: 255 B: 102
339933 R: 051 G: 153 B: 051	**99CC99** R: 153 G: 204 B: 153	**66FF99** R: 102 G: 255 B: 153	**33FF99** R: 051 G: 255 B: 153	**33CC66** R: 051 G: 204 B: 102	**00CC66** R: 000 G: 204 B: 102
66CC99 R: 102 G: 204 B: 153	**009966** R: 000 G: 153 B: 102	**009933** R: 000 G: 153 B: 051	**33FF66** R: 051 G: 255 B: 102	**00FF66** R: 000 G: 255 B: 102	**CCFFCC** R: 204 G: 255 B: 204
CCFF99 R: 204 G: 255 B: 153	**99FF66** R: 153 G: 255 B: 102	**99FF33** R: 153 G: 255 B: 051	**00FF33** R: 000 G: 255 B: 051	**33FF33** R: 051 G: 255 B: 051	**00CC33** R: 000 G: 204 B: 051
33CC33 R: 051 G: 204 B: 051	**66FF33** R: 102 G: 255 B: 051	**00FF00** R: 000 G: 255 B: 000	**66CC33** R: 102 G: 204 B: 051	**006600** R: 000 G: 102 B: 000	**003300** R: 000 G: 051 B: 000
009900 R: 000 G: 153 B: 000	**33FF00** R: 051 G: 255 B: 000	**66FF00** R: 102 G: 255 B: 000	**99FF00** R: 153 G: 255 B: 000	**66CC00** R: 102 G: 204 B: 000	**00CC00** R: 000 G: 204 B: 000
33CC00 R: 051 G: 204 B: 000	**339900** R: 051 G: 153 B: 000	**99CC66** R: 153 G: 204 B: 102	**669933** R: 102 G: 153 B: 051	**99CC33** R: 153 G: 204 B: 051	**336600** R: 051 G: 102 B: 000
669900 R: 102 G: 153 B: 000	**99CC00** R: 153 G: 204 B: 000	**CCFF66** R: 204 G: 255 B: 102	**CCFF33** R: 204 G: 255 B: 051	**CCFF00** R: 204 G: 255 B: 000	**999900** R: 153 G: 153 B: 000

Color Swatches

1. Primaries

Primary colors evoke a childish, playful sentiment. Use color sparingly for maximum impact.

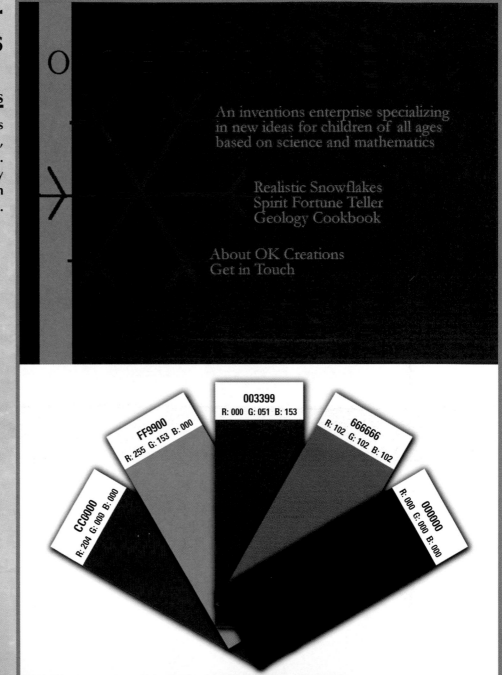

An inventions enterprise specializing in new ideas for children of all ages based on science and mathematics

Realistic Snowflakes
Spirit Fortune Teller
Geology Cookbook

About OK Creations
Get in Touch

CC0000 R: 204 G: 000 B: 000

FF9900 R: 255 G: 153 B: 000

003399 R: 000 G: 051 B: 153

666666 R: 102 G: 102 B: 102

000000 R: 000 G: 000 B: 000

EDUCATION   EXPERIENCE   COMMITTEES   ORGANIZATIONS   CONTACT

CURRENTS

Linus Kafka currently serves as law clerk for the honorable John M. Quigley, presiding Domestic Relations Judge of the Arizona Superior Court for Pima County.

ABOUT LINUS KAFKA

With interests in family law matters as
well as general civil litigation,
Kafka is a member of the American Trial
Lawyers Association,
the American Bar Association,
the Phi Delta Phi Legal Fraternity,
and sits on a number of Arizona State
Bar committees.

He has also served as a law clerk at the
Department of Justice in Washington, D.C.,
and for the Office of the Pima County Attorney.

(c) 1998, Linus Kafka, Esq.

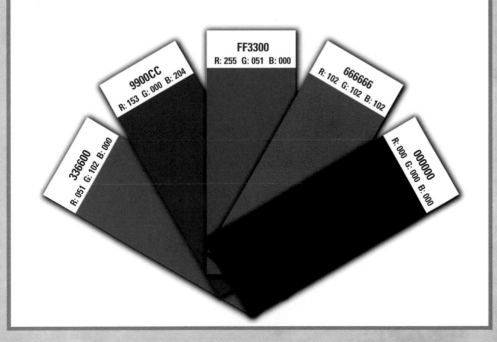

9900CC
R: 153 G: 000 B: 204

FF3300
R: 255 G: 051 B: 000

666666
R: 102 G: 102 B: 102

336600
R: 051 G: 102 B: 000

000000
R: 000 G: 000 B: 000

3. Professional (Red)

Use red minimally for impact and a serious tone.

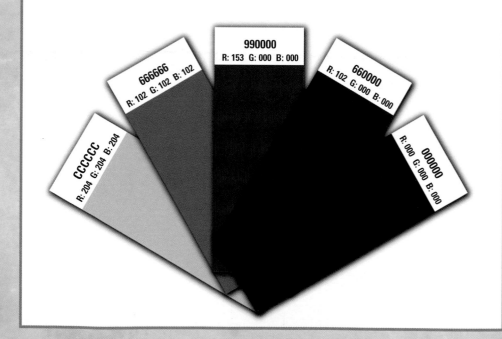

Education
Employment
Courses
Books
Essays
Reviews
Presentations
Poetry
Organizations
Contact

Dr. Phillipa Kafka
Professor of English &
Director of Women's Studies

Kean University
Union, New Jersey

What's New:

Kafka's most recent book, (Un)Doing the Missionary Position: Gender Asymmetry in Contemporary Asian American Women's Writing is now available. Contact <u>Greenwood Press</u> for detailed information and ordering options.

Please visit the <u>Kean University catalog</u> for a current listing of available courses.

CCCCCC
R: 204 G: 204 B: 204

666666
R: 102 G: 102 B: 102

990000
R: 153 G: 000 B: 000

660000
R: 102 G: 000 B: 000

000000
R: 000 G: 000 B: 000

4. Professional (Blue)

Send a corporate message with this sedate and serious combination.

Linus Kafka, Esq.

Education

Committees

Organizations

Contact

Linus Kafka currently serves as law clerk for the
Honorable John M. Quigley,
Presiding Domestic Relations Judge
of the Arizona Superior Court for Pima County.

With interests in family law matters,
as well as general civil litigation,
Kafka is a member of the
American Trial Lawyers Association,
the American Bar Association,
the Phi Delta Phi Legal Fraternity
and sits on a number of Arizona State Bar
committees.

He has also served as a law clerk at the
Department of Justice in Washington, D.C.
and for the Office of the Pima County Attorney.

education | Committees | Organizations | Contact

(c) 1998, Linus Kafka, Esq.

5. Warm

The warm color palette exudes a friendly, happy mood.

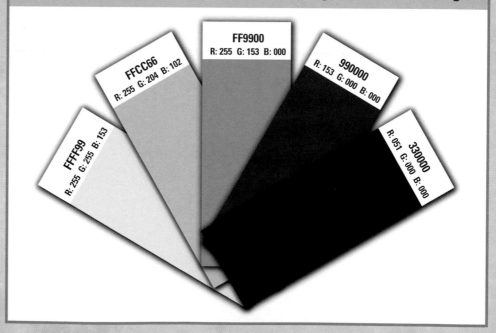

Courage

Sisters

about cs | events | CDs
lyrics | press | contact

From the earth-and-plains honesty of the midwest, Patty brings her love for the land and people into music with highly melodic soprano vocals and gentle guitar.

The harder streets of New Jersey gave Molly her cynical edge, rougher vocal stylings and haunting guitar licks.

The combination creates a whole.

Sisters of different lands coming together to paint stories of the world in poetry, sing their truth with complex harmonies, provoke thought and inspire hope through their evocative blends.

Rise with them above unique challenges and extraordinary realities into a place of Courage.

FFFF99
R: 255 G: 255 B: 153

FFCC66
R: 255 G: 204 B: 102

FF9900
R: 255 G: 153 B: 000

990000
R: 153 G: 000 B: 000

330000
R: 051 G: 000 B: 000

Dr. Phillipa Kafka
Professor of English &
Director of Women's Studies

Kean University
Union, New Jersey

Education
Employment
Courses
Books
Essays
Reviews
Presentations
Poetry
Organizations
Contact

What's New:

Kafka's most recent book, (Un)Doing the Missionary Position: Gender Asymmetry in Contemporary Asian American Women's Writing is now available. Contact Greenwood Press for detailed information and ordering options.

Please visit the Kean University catalog for a current listing of available courses.

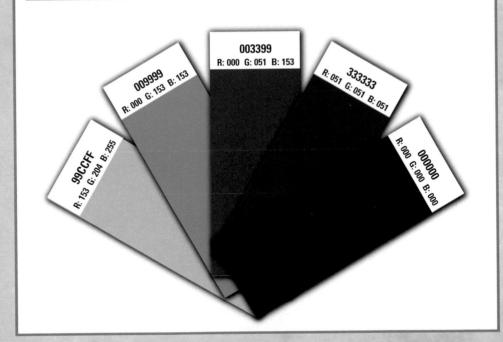

003399
R: 000 G: 051 B: 153

009999
R: 000 G: 153 B: 153

333333
R: 051 G: 051 B: 051

99CCFF
R: 153 G: 204 B: 255

000000
R: 000 G: 000 B: 000

6. Cool

The cool palette is cultured and aloof.

7. Rich

Combine the rich jewel-tones with black for an elegant, powerful site.

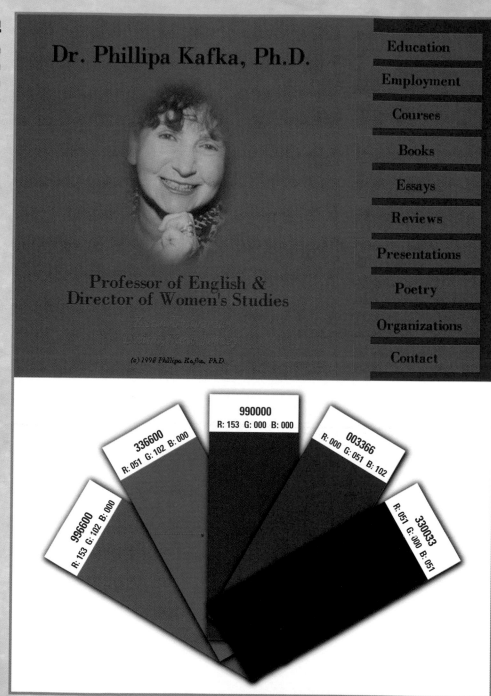

Dr. Phillipa Kafka, Ph.D.

Professor of English &
Director of Women's Studies

(c) 1998 Phillipa Kafka, Ph.D.

Education

Employment

Courses

Books

Essays

Reviews

Presentations

Poetry

Organizations

Contact

996600
R: 153 G: 102 B: 000

336600
R: 051 G: 102 B: 000

990000
R: 153 G: 000 B: 000

003366
R: 000 G: 051 B: 102

330033
R: 051 G: 000 B: 051

Rentorations, Limited

Meeker Street House, South Orange, New Jersey

We specialize in refurbishing
distinctive historic buildings
as unique apartments
while preserving
their architectural integrity.

We evaluate, plan and execute
careful and economical renovations
which make older buildings safe,
up to code and comfortable
without compromising them.

Historical Interiors ~ Antique Cabinetry ~ Architectural Re-Creations
~ Tour of Homes ~
About Rentorations ~ Get in Touch

Copyright 1998, Rentorations Limited

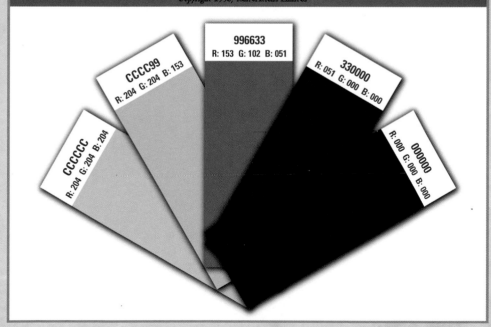

CCCCCC
R: 204 G: 204 B: 204

CCCC99
R: 204 G: 204 B: 153

996633
R: 153 G: 102 B: 051

330000
R: 051 G: 000 B: 000

000000
R: 000 G: 000 B: 000

9. Clashing

Use red and blue against one another for dramatic results. Balance with gray and black.

ok creations

Inventions
Catalog
History
Resources
Contact

An inventions enterprise specializing
in new ideas for children of all ages
based on science and mathematics

For kids of all ages

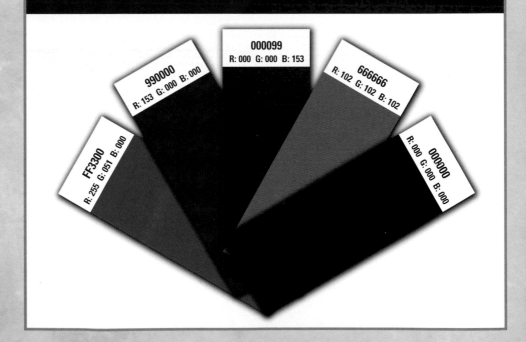

990000
R: 153 G: 000 B: 000

000099
R: 000 G: 000 B: 153

666666
R: 102 G: 102 B: 102

FF3300
R: 255 G: 051 B: 000

000000
R: 000 G: 000 B: 000

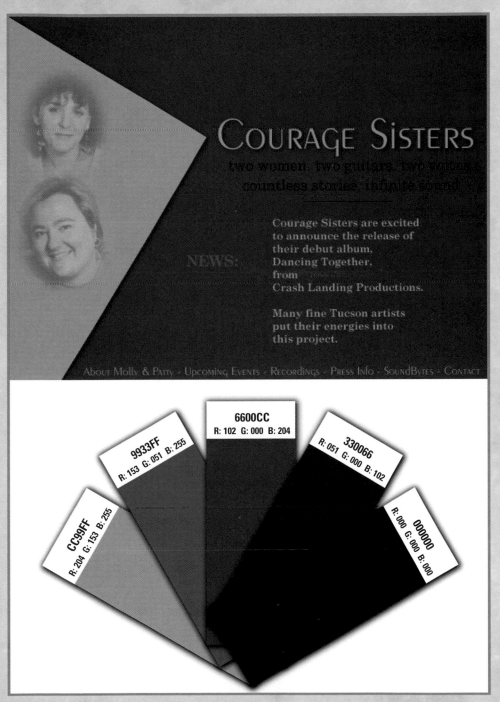

10. Monochromatic

This subtle palette provides a range of values. Experiment with monochromatic palettes in different hues.

11. Natural

This palette provides a down-to-earth tone.

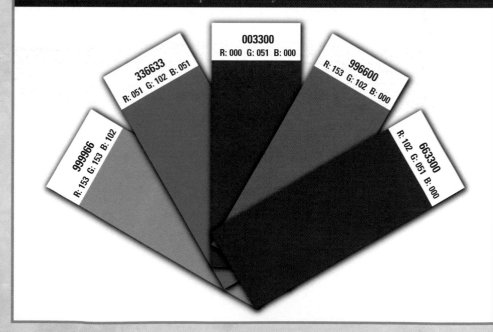

Rentorations, LTD.

We specialize in refurbishing distinctive historic buildings as unique apartments while preserving their architectural integrity.

We evaluate, plan and execute careful and economical renovations which make older buildings safe, up to code and comfortable without compromising them.

Meeker Street House, 1800s

Recreation of Original Architectural Elements
Historical Interiors ~ Antique Cabinetry ~ About Rentorations ~ Contact

003300
R: 000 G: 051 B: 000

336633
R: 051 G: 102 B: 051

996600
R: 153 G: 102 B: 000

999966
R: 153 G: 153 B: 102

663300
R: 102 G: 051 B: 000

Linus Kafka, Esq.

Linus Kafka currently serves as law clerk for the Honorable John M. Quigley, Presiding Domestic Relations Judge of the Arizona Superior Court for Pima County.

With interests in family law matters, as well as general civil litigation, Kafka is a member of the American Trial Lawyers Association, the American Bar Association, the Phi Delta Phi Legal Fraternity and sits on a number of Arizona State Bar committees.

He has also served as a law clerk at the Department of Justice in Washington, D.C. and for the Office of the Pima County Attorney.

education | Committees | Organizations | Contact

(c) 1998, Linus Kafka, Esq.

Education

Committees

Organizations

Contact

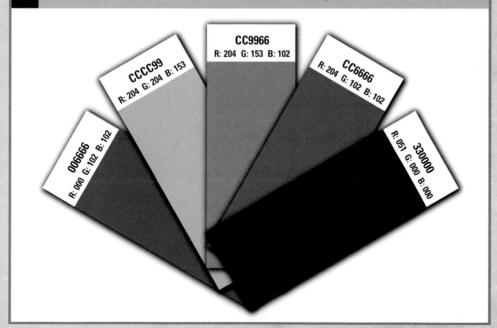

CC9966
R: 204 G: 153 B: 102

CCCC99
R: 204 G: 204 B: 153

CC6666
R: 204 G: 102 B: 102

006666
R: 000 G: 102 B: 102

330000
R: 051 G: 000 B: 000

13. Retro

Use brighter colors in small areas for maximum impact.

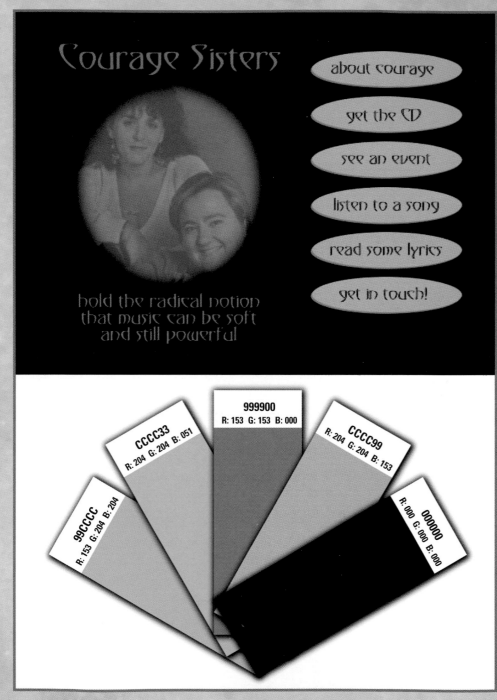

14. Shocking

These colors are effective at setting a mood, but use bright colors sparingly.

Historical Interiors

Antique Cabinetry

Architectual Recreations

Mechanical Upgrades

Tour of Homes

About Rentorations

Contact

Rentorations

Specializing in refurbishing
distinctive historic buildings
as unique apartments while
preserving their architectural integrity.

Historical Interiors | Antique Cabinetry | Architectural Recreations

Mechanical Upgrades | Tour of Homes | About Rentorations

Contact

(c) Copyright 1998 Rentorations LTD.

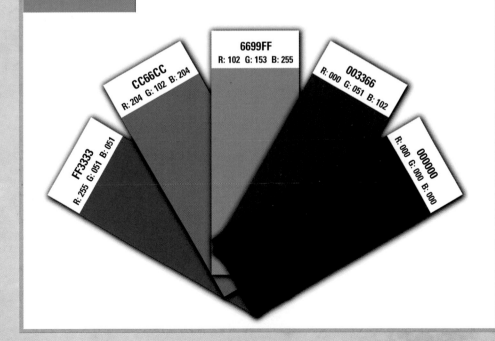

FF3333
R: 255 G: 051 B: 051

CC66CC
R: 204 G: 102 B: 204

6699FF
R: 102 G: 153 B: 255

003366
R: 000 G: 051 B: 102

000000
R: 000 G: 000 B: 000

Linus Kafka, Esq.

An attorney in Tucson, Arizona, Kafka currently serves as law clerk for the Honorable John M. Quigley, Presiding Domestic Relations Judge of the Arizona Superior Court for Pima County.

With interests in family law matters, as well as general civil litigation, Kafka is a member of the <u>American Trial Lawyers Association</u>, the <u>American Bar Association</u>, the Phi Delta Phi Legal Fraternity and sits on a number of Arizona State Bar committees.

He has also served as a law clerk at the Department of Justice in Washington, D.C. and for the Office of the Pima County Attorney.

Kafka received his law degree from the <u>University of Arizona</u> and holds a Bachelors degree from <u>Rutgers College</u> and a Masters degree from <u>New York University</u>.

He became licensed to practice law in the state of Arizona in 1996 and in the Federal District Court for Arizona in 1997.

Education | Experience | Organizations | Committees | Contact

(c) Copyright 1998, Linus Kafka, Esq.

Education

Experience

Organizations

Committees

Contact

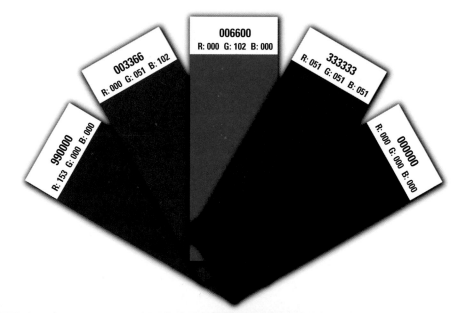

003366
R: 000 G: 051 B: 102

006600
R: 000 G: 102 B: 000

333333
R: 051 G: 051 B: 051

990000
R: 153 G: 000 B: 000

000000
R: 000 G: 000 B: 000

ok creations

An inventions enterprise specializing in
new ideas for children of all ages
based on science and mathematics

Some of our creations include:

Realistic Snowflakes
Spirit Fortune Teller
Geology Cookbook:
featuring Volcano Cake

Catalog | Samples | Online Experiments
About OK Creations | Consulting Services
Cool Inventions on the Net | Contact

16. Sporty

**Youthful and
energetic, use
brighter colors
sparingly as they
can be hard on
the eyes.**

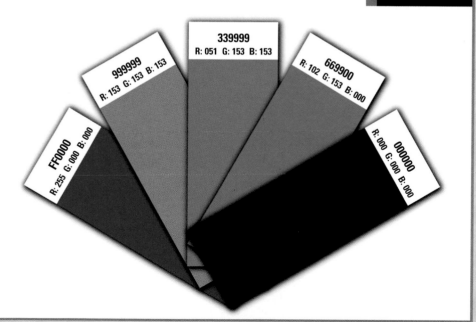

FF0000
R: 255 G: 000 B: 000

999999
R: 153 G: 153 B: 153

339999
R: 051 G: 153 B: 153

669900
R: 102 G: 153 B: 000

000000
R: 000 G: 000 B: 000

17. Tranquil

This soft color palette is soothing.

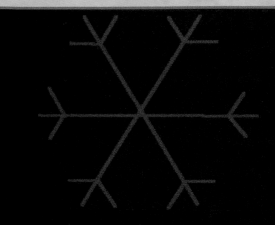

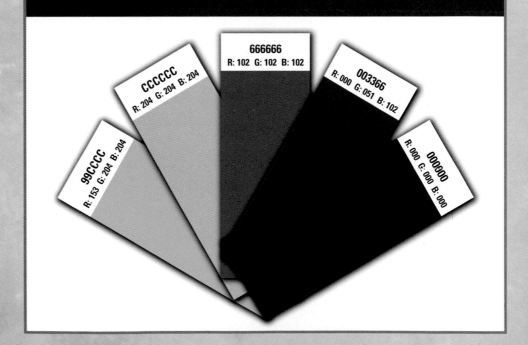

OK CREATIONS

An inventions enterprise
specializing in new ideas
for children of all ages
based on science and mathematics

REALISTIC SNOWFLAKES * SPIRIT FORTUNE TELLER * GEOLOGY COOKBOOK

666666
R: 102 G: 102 B: 102

CCCCCC
R: 204 G: 204 B: 204

003366
R: 000 G: 051 B: 102

99CCCC
R: 153 G: 204 B: 204

000000
R: 000 G: 000 B: 000

Courage Sisters

Sisters of different lands
come together
to paint stories of the world
in poetry,
sing their truth
with complex harmonies,
provoke thought and
inspire hope
through their
evocative blends.

About Patty & Molly
Upcoming Events
CD's & Tapes
Soundbytes
Contact

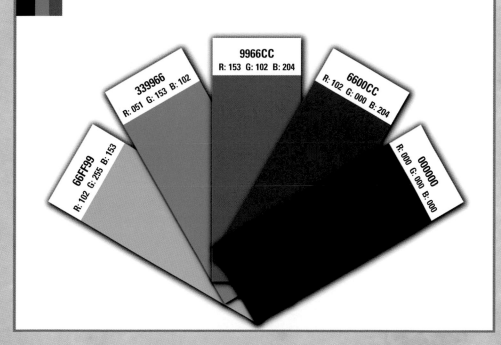

66FF99
R: 102 G: 255 B: 153

339966
R: 051 G: 153 B: 102

9966CC
R: 153 G: 102 B: 204

6600CC
R: 102 G: 000 B: 204

000000
R: 000 G: 000 B: 000

19. Vibrant

The contrast of red and blue give this palette power and zip.

ok creations

An inventions enterprise specializing in new ideas for children of all ages based on science and mathematics

Some of our creations include:

Realistic Snowflakes
Spirit Fortune Teller
Geology Cookbook:
featuring Volcano Cake

Catalog | Samples | Online Experiments
About OK Creations | Consulting Services
Cool Inventions on the Net | Contact

Copyright 1998, OK Creations

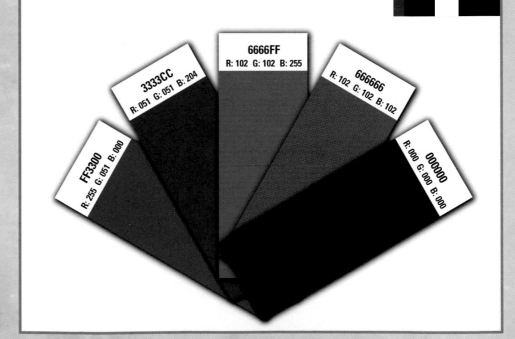

FF3300
R: 255 G: 051 B: 000

3333CC
R: 051 G: 051 B: 204

6666FF
R: 102 G: 102 B: 255

666666
R: 102 G: 102 B: 102

000000
R: 000 G: 000 B: 000

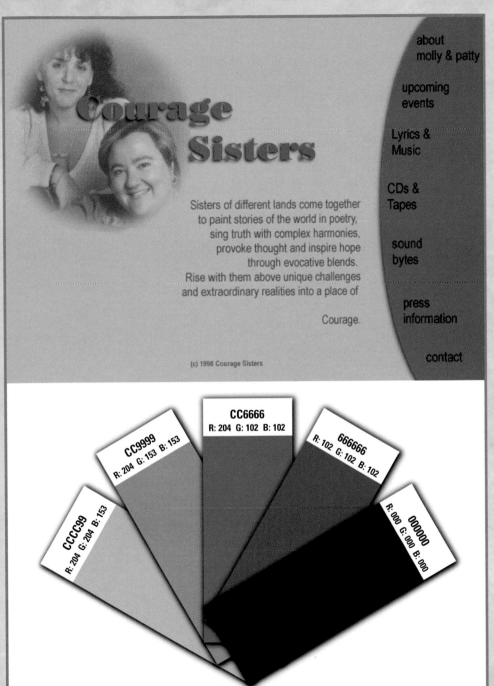

Courage Sisters

Sisters of different lands come together
to paint stories of the world in poetry,
sing truth with complex harmonies,
provoke thought and inspire hope
through evocative blends.
Rise with them above unique challenges
and extraordinary realities into a place of

Courage.

(c) 1998 Courage Sisters

about
molly & patty

upcoming
events

Lyrics &
Music

CDs &
Tapes

sound
bytes

press
information

contact

CCCC99
R: 204 G: 204 B: 153

CC9999
R: 204 G: 153 B: 153

CC6666
R: 204 G: 102 B: 102

666666
R: 102 G: 102 B: 102

000000
R: 000 G: 000 B: 000

20. Soft

This palette conveys a femininity.

21. Bright

These colors enhance one another. Use sparingly so as not to overwhelm. Balance is achieved with black.

About Rentorations ~ Get in Touch ~ Resources

Ren**t**orations

We specialize in refurbishing distinctive historic buildings as unique apartments while preserving their architectural integrity.

Historical Interiors

Antique Cabinetry

Architectual Recreations

Tour of Homes

FF9900
R: 255 G: 153 B: 000

FF3333
R: 255 G: 051 B: 051

336600
R: 051 G: 102 B: 000

006666
R: 000 G: 102 B: 102

000000
R: 000 G: 000 B: 000

22. Metallic

To achieve metallic effects, use gradations from one color to another. Gradations should be used in small areas online to avoid banding and large file sizes.

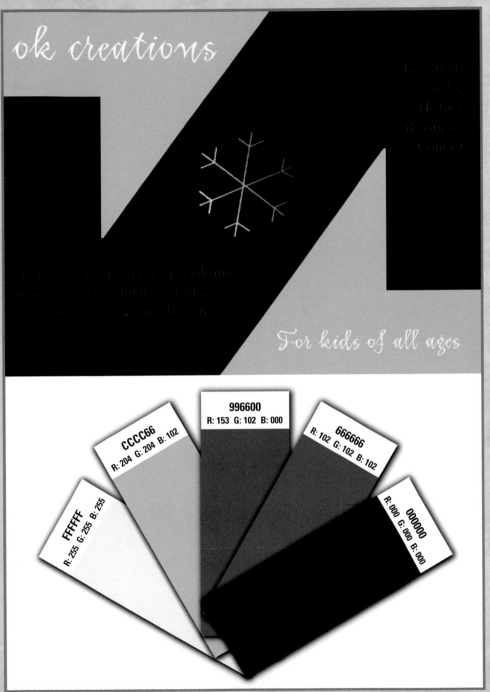

ok creations

A nonprofit organization specializing in art education for children of all ages based on science and mathematics.

For kids of all ages

CCCC66
R: 204 G: 204 B: 102

996600
R: 153 G: 102 B: 000

666666
R: 102 G: 102 B: 102

FFFFFF
R: 255 G: 255 B: 255

000000
R: 000 G: 000 B: 000

23. Sophisticated

Convey a modern look with this color palette.

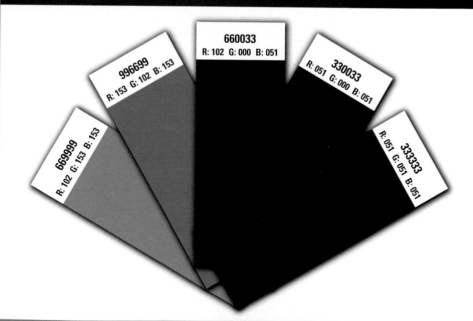

Rentorations, ltd.

We specialize in refurbishing distinctive historic buildings as unique apartments while preserving their architectural integrity.

We evaluate, plan and execute careful and economical renovations which make older buildings safe, up to code and comfortable without compromising them.

Historical Interiors

Antique Cabinetry

Recreation of Original Architectural Elements

About Rentorations

Contact

669999 R: 102 G: 153 B: 153

996699 R: 153 G: 102 B: 153

660033 R: 102 G: 000 B: 051

330033 R: 051 G: 000 B: 051

333333 R: 051 G: 051 B: 051

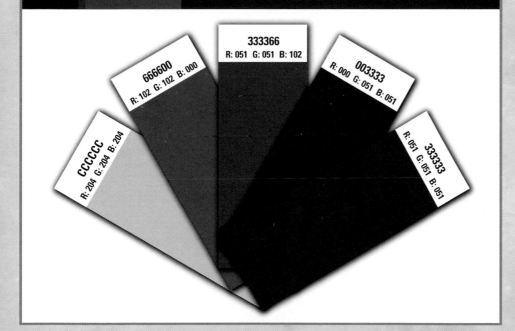

✳ ok creations

An inventions enterprise
specializing in new ideas
for children of all ages
based on
science and mathematics.

Some of our creations include:
Realistic Snowflakes
Spirit Fortune Teller
Geology Cookbook:
featuring the famous
Volcano Cake.

Inventions

Catalog

History

Resources

Contact

CCCCCC
R: 204 G: 204 B: 204

666600
R: 102 G: 102 B: 000

333366
R: 051 G: 051 B: 102

003333
R: 000 G: 051 B: 051

333333
R: 051 G: 051 B: 051

24. Muted

This palette is a bit
more subtle and
masculine than a
strict sophisticated
palette.

The Color Wheel

The subtractive color wheel interprets colors found in nature. Becoming familiar with the primary, secondary, and tertiary colors within subtractive synthesis (see Chapter 17) helps give Web designers a strong foundation from which to study the more volatile, inconsistent colors found in the technical world.

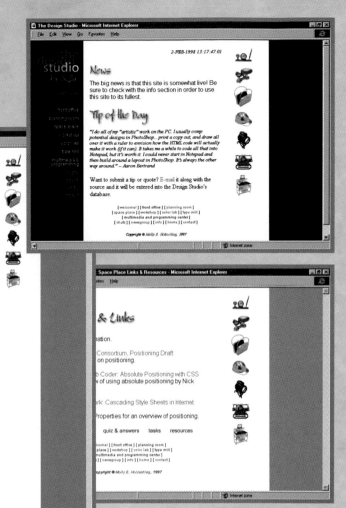

The Design Studio Site

Shown here is a collage of various pages from the companion Web site. You can see it in its entirety at `http://www.designstudio.net/`.

The Design Studio - Microsoft Internet Explorer
File Edit View Go Favorites Help

2-FEB-1998 13:17:47.01

News

The big news is that this site is somewhat live! Be sure to check with the info section in order to use this site to its fullest.

Tip of the Day

"I do all of my "artistic" work on the PC. I usually comp potential designs in PhotoShop... print a copy out, and draw all over it with a ruler to envision how the HTML code will actually make it work (if it can). It takes me a while to code all that into Notepad, but it's worth it. I could never start in Notepad and then build around a layout in PhotoShop. It's always the other way around." -- Aaron Bertrand

Want to submit a tip or quote? E-mail it along with the source and it will be entered into the Design Studio's database.

[welcome!] [front office] [planning room]
[space place] [workshop] [color lab] [type mill]
[multimedia and programming center]
[chats] [newsgroup] [info] [home] [contact]

Copyright © Molly E. Holzschlag, 1997

🌐 Internet zone

The Design Studio by Molly: Front Office Part Summary - Microsoft Internet Explorer
File Edit View Go Favorites Help

Part Summary: Front Office

The Front Office is the place where preliminary information is gathered before moving into the vast and varied rooms of Web design. It is here that you pause for a bit, reading and reviewing the concepts and methods that make up the foundation of a good Web site. This section pulls together the ideas and techniques that make up the preliminary bed upon which to rest your designs.

Web Site Accessibility

Accessibility ideally means that the sites you build are approachable by anyone regardless of geographical location, physical limitations, and technological restrictions. Whether you choose to make a site fully accessible depends upon:

- Your audience
- Your site's intent

HTML Absolutes

HTML Absolutes is concerned with getting HTML practices that serve to enable Web designers across in a concise and precise package. General HTML principles including tags, attributes, and structure play a major role in the HTML show. HTML tools such as editors, converters, environments, and specialty programs will determine efficiency and style. Custom templates can serve you and your company well by setting up a specific method for all to follow.

Each of these practices and concepts help designers work faster, cleaner, and when combined, provide a matrix in which individual perspectives can grow.

User Interface

User interface is possibly one of the most overlooked issues in Web design, yet it is the point-of-contact between a site visitor and a Web site. This makes site interface a crucial part of design, and all aspiring as well as practicing Web designers should understand the main objectives of interface form. Web by Design covers the following interface concerns:

- The five features of interface design
- Web site structure in theory and practice
- Navigation methods and media

The learning involved when studying site interface is significant. This book addresses the issues in a concise method intended to put them on the desk of any Web designer, ready to be put to use.

part summary   quiz & answers   tasks   resources

[welcome!] [front office] [planning room]
[space place] [workshop] [color lab] [type mill]
[multimedia and programming center]
[chats] [newsgroup] [info] [home] [contact]

Copyright © Molly E. Holzschlag, 1997

Space Place Links & Resources - Microsoft Internet Explorer
...tes Help

& Links

...nation.

...Consortium, Positioning Draft
...on positioning.

...b Coder: Absolute Positioning with CSS
...v of using absolute positioning by Nick

...ork: Cascading Style Sheets in Internet

...Properties for an overview of positioning.

quiz & answers   tasks   resources

...come!] [front office] [planning room]
...place] [workshop] [color lab] [type mill]
...multimedia and programming center]
...] [newsgroup] [info] [home] [contact]

...opyright © Molly E. Holzschlag, 1997

🌐 Internet zone

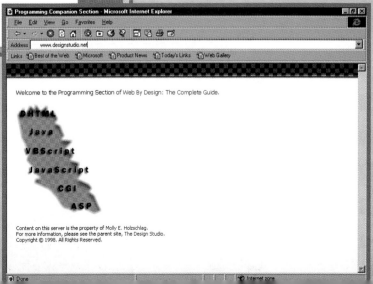

Programming Companion Section - Microsoft Internet Explorer
File Edit View Go Favorites Help

Address www.designstudio.net

Links Best of the Web   Microsoft   Product News   Today's Links   Web Gallery

Welcome to the Programming Section of Web By Design: The Complete Guide.

DHTML
java
VBScript
JavaScript
CGI
ASP

Content on this server is the property of Molly E. Holzschlag.
For more information, please see the parent site, The Design Studio.
Copyright © 1998. All Rights Reserved.

Done   🌐 Internet zone

our knives and forks af

...er, not
we'll be the
drowned out by the
most obvious is
ngful evaluation the
1996 abolished next is
What comes now be
which are just now
of new reform plan—and
elfare-reform for cutti
tention

AFD
the firs
forming
the c
suc

com/herman/mi
on and for
Finally
the world of mo
ife design. Charl
ng the gods. The
d chairs have be
rs by Herman Mi
nes' chairs, sof
site (offered a
y, the name
ely, the site h
re in short
correct o

LER
5 LINKS 1

FIGURE 13.8

*A right-aligned
table*

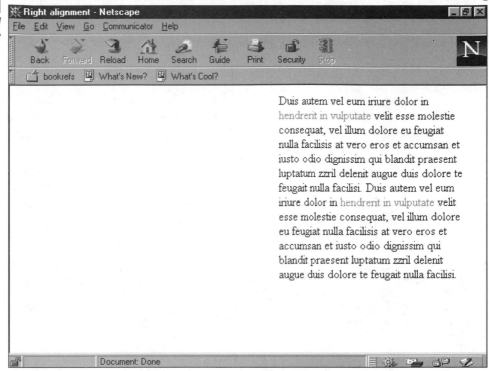

Duis autem vel eum iriure dolor in
hendrerit in vulputate velit esse molestie
consequat, vel illum dolore eu feugiat
nulla facilisis at vero eros et accumsan et
iusto odio dignissim qui blandit praesent
luptatum zzril delenit augue duis dolore te
feugait nulla facilisi. Duis autem vel eum
iriure dolor in hendrerit in vulputate velit
esse molestie consequat, vel illum dolore
eu feugiat nulla facilisis at vero eros et
accumsan et iusto odio dignissim qui
blandit praesent luptatum zzril delenit
augue duis dolore te feugait nulla facilisi.

 I P

Want to center your table on the page? There are several legal ways to do so. The
two most simple include placing the table between the <center> tag, and its closing
tag, </center>, or using the <div> tag. Division tags are much more stable in cross-
platform environments. In this case, you'll place the tag and
attribute before your table, and after you've closed the table, close the division with
.

border="x"   The "x" is replaced with a value from "0" on up. This value
defines the width of the visual border around the table.

cellspacing="x"   Cellspacing defines the amount of space between each individual table cell; in other words, between visual columns. The "x" requires a
value from "0" on up.

`cellpadding="x"` This attribute calls for the space around the edges of each cell within the table—literally, its "padding."

`width="x%"` *or* `width="x"` To define the width of a table, you can choose to use a number that relates to the percentage of browser space you wish to span, or a specific numeral which will be translated into pixel widths.

When given the option of defining a table by percentage or pixel width, it's generally better to use pixels. The reason is that then you can count each used pixel in a space. For example, if you have a table that is 595 pixels wide, you must be sure that all of the elements within that table *do not exceed* 600 pixels. Percentages are less accurate, yet they can be handy when your desire is to use a visual portion of a space that is not dependent on literal pixel count. An example of this would be to create a table that is 75 percent of the browser area—this section will remain proportionately the same no matter what screen resolution with which you're viewing the page.

line!

Not every browser supports or handles attributes, pixels, or percentages in the same fashion. For browser-specific descriptions, visit the browser company's home page.

The two most important browsers for Web designers are:

- **Internet Explorer:** Information about this browser is provided at its home on Microsoft at http://www.microsoft.com/ie/.
- **Netscape Navigator:** The home page for this company is located at http://home .netscape.com/.

T I P

Be sure to read the latest release notes applicable to your version of the browser for specific and timely information regarding that browser's technology. Ultimately, you must test your work in different browsers to see the results first-hand.

With the `<table>`, `<tr>`, and `<td>` tags, you've got the foundation for all table-based layout design in hand. It seems simple, and in many ways, it is. But knowing when to use a row or a column can sometimes be very challenging.

Web browsers are essential to the way HTML is deciphered. Tables are fairly well supported in most browser versions 2.0 and above. As you already know, computer platform, monitor size and type, and screen resolution all may influence the way an HTML page looks. It's always wise to test your work with a variety of browsers and where possible, try and view your work on different platforms.

Rows and Columns

I learned how to understand the application of tables through the wise guidance of Wil Gerken, CEO of DesertNet and Weekly Wire. I, like many other people with limited natural spatial abilities, was having a very difficult time interpreting how to relate table syntax to the concept of layout.

Working on the original design of the Film Vault, Wil made me take the layout and try to work *from* the design *to* the HTML. I had to take the image and figure out how cells and rows would configure most simply to create the layout.

After making several erroneous attempts with the sketches, I became so frustrated that I gave up for a while. It took some time for the exercise to sink in (Figure 13.9), but once it did, the understanding was total and has remained with me—enough for me to venture out on my own, designing interesting table-based layouts.

FIGURE 13.9

The Film Vault's table header configuration with columns and spanning

The upshot is that while some of you will already have either natural spatial abilities or well-developed ones, those that do not will need a little practice.

Approach tables first from the columnar layout. What can you control vertically? The vertical is where you'll find some of the greatest flexibility in terms of control by first spatially placing items and then confirming their placement with cell attributes allowed in the <td>, or table cell (column) tag.

Keep in mind that graphics can be stacked and placed in tables, too, so don't get stumped by graphics that run vertically, as these two in Figure 13.10, which are in the same table cell. Remember also that graphics are used in tables as backgrounds, such as the black left panel and white main section of the Design Studio site (Figure 13.11) and as unseen holders to fix space on both the horizontal and vertical lines in a design (Figure 13.12).

FIGURE 13.10

This vertical graphic is actually two sections placed together by the table.

FIGURE 13.11

*A page from the
Design Studio—the
black and white sec-
tions are created by
a graphic with a
table laid on top.*

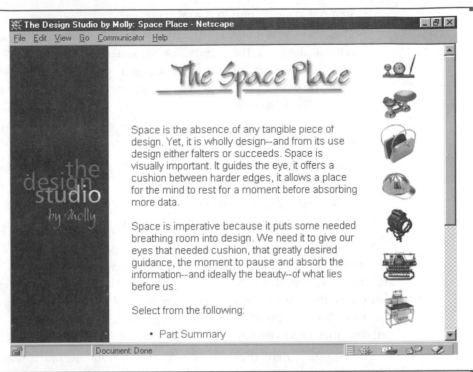

FIGURE 13.12

*Arrows indicate
where spacer GIFs
have been used to
fix positioning.*

Attributes that are helpful in the table cell are:

align="x"   When you use this attribute within a table cell, the data inside the cell will align with the literal value you assign to the attribute. In other words, a left value will left-justify the text or graphic you place within the cell, the middle value will center the information, and a value of right will justify the information to the right of the cell.

colspan="x"   This attribute refers to the number of columns the cell you are working with will span.

rowspan="x"   As with colspan, rowspan refers to the span of the cell; in this case, how many rows the cell will stretch.

valign="x"   The vertical alignment of a table cell will place the information therein to the top, middle, or bottom of the cell.

Now that we've looked at some of the specific table cell attributes, let's move on to the table row. The two notable attributes for use in rows include align, which controls the row's spatial alignment, and valign, which determines the vertical placement of all the data within a row. It's rare to see table row attributes used. It seems that most designers prefer the surrounding HTML, <table> attributes, and <td> table cell data attributes to determine the attributes applied to table layouts.

align="x"   Here, the values for "x" are not numeric, rather they are literal and include left, right, and center.

valign="x"   Again, the values for vertical alignment are not numeric. Vertical alignment can be top, middle, bottom, or baseline.

You will need to think very carefully about rowspan and colspan. The introduction of these attributes critically changes the way tables can be used. With these attributes, you can have one cell spanning multiple columns or rows as in the code below and in Figure 13.13, or many cells using a variety of span attributes to create a wide selection of visual field options.

```
<html>

<head>
<title>colspan and rowspan</title>
</head>

<body bgcolor="#FFFFFF" text="#000000" link="#999999"
vlink="#CCCCCC" alink="#FFFFCC">

<table border="1" cellspacing="20" cellpadding="10">
<tr>
```

```
<td rowspan="2">
Rowspan with value of two
</td>

<td>
column (no span)
</td>

<td>
column (no span)
</td>
</tr>

<tr>

<td colspan="2">
second row with column span: value of "2"
</td>

</tr>

</tr>

</table>

</body>
</html>
```

FIGURE 13.13

An example of colspan *and* rowspan

| Rowspan with value of two | column (no span) | column (no span) |
| | second row with column span: value of "2" | |

line!

Visit any Web site that uses tables and attempt to reconstruct it by drawing out what you think the table cell and row structure is. Build a table using this configuration and see if it works. Only *after* doing this should you peek at the source code for that page.

Example

In Chapter 12's layout method examples, we looked at the site for Bernstein Communications. This site uses a straightforward table-based design. Below is the code from a content page in its entirety. Take a close look at the table's structure and identify how the various attributes control the layout.

```html
<!-- site by desertnet designs: sales@desert.net -->
<!-- design director: molly holzschlag -->
<!-- graphic design:  amy burnham -->
<!-- online editor: molly holzschlag -->
<!-- content provided by bernstein communications -->

<!-- begin header -->

<html>

<head>
<title>Bernstein Communications: Profile</title>
<meta name="keywords" content="business, communications, bernstein,
jonathan, del webb, mature, market, planning, crisis, management, nasli,
mature market, desert, desertnet, desert net">
<meta name="description" content="expert issues management, mature market
public relations, and strategic planning">
<meta name="author" content="molly e. holzschlag, amy burnham, jonathan
bernstein">
</head>

<body bgcolor="#FFFFFF" text="#000000" link="#0000FF" vlink="#0000CC"
alink="#FFFFFF" background="brn_bkgd.gif">

<!-- end header -->

<table border="0" cellspacing="0" cellpadding="0" width="600">
<tr>

<!-- begin menu column -->

<td valign="top" align="left" width="97">

<img src="brn_nav.gif" alt="Navigation (text at bottom)" width="87"
height="298" border="0" usemap="#brn_nav">
<p>

<!-- begin spacer -->
```

```
<td width="55">
<img src="spacer.gif" width="55" height="1">
<br>
</td>

<!-- end spacer -->

<td valign="top">
<p>

<img src="brn_h3.gif" alt="Profile Header" width="406" height="35"
border="0">
<p>

<font size="+1" color="990000">General Biographic Data</font>
<p>

<img src="brn_ph1.gif" alt="Jonathan Bernstein" width="179" height="219"
hspace="15" border="0" align="right">
```

Jonathan L. Bernstein, principal of Bernstein Communications, is a
strategic public relations consultant specializing in multi-audience
Issues Management (aka Crisis Prevention & Response) and Mature Market
Communications. Additionally, as a strategist and writer, he often
serves as the "objective third party" who can assist clients with public
relations strategy and planning involving a wide variety of industries.
```
<p>
```

Bernstein brings national-level experience to his consultancy which was
launched in january 1994. He served for almost five years (1989-1994) as
senior vice president and director of both the Crisis Communications and
Mature Market groups for Ruder Finn, Inc., one of the country's largest
public relations agencies. He created both groups for Ruder Finn, which
became the only national agency with the Mature Market specialty.
```
<p>
```

Bernstein Communications is a "who you see is who you get" business. No
handing off the project to a junior person once the boss signs the
deal. Only certain, clearly identified media relations work is done by
an experienced media relations specialist -- the rest, including
strategy, planning, writing and client contact is done by Jonathan
Bernstein.
```
<p>
```

His past experience includes corporate, agency and non-profit public
relations positions, preceded by five years of investigative and feature
journalism -- to include a stint with investigative reporter/columnist Jack
Anderson. Prior to that, Bernstein, oxymoronically, was in U.S.Army Military
Intelligence.
<p>

He is a frequent public speaker and trainer in his areas of
specialization and, when not in the office, Bernstein enjoys being
pummeled into submission by his four kids, as well as fitness activities and
performing folk music.
<p>

```
<font size="2">
<center>
<a href="index.html">Home</a> |
<a href="services.html">Services </a>|
<a href="articles.html">Articles</a> |
<a href="profile.html">Profile </a>|
<a href="clients.html">Clients</a> |
<a href="contact.html">Contact</a>
<p>

<font size="2">
<a href="http://desert.net/designs/">&#169; DesertNet Designs 1996</a>
</font>

</center>

</td>

<!-- begin spacer -->

<td width="30" rowspan="2">
<img src="spacer.gif" width="30" height="1">
<br>
</td>

<!-- end spacer -->

</tr>
</table>
```

```
<map name="brn_nav">
<area shape="rect" coords="0,10,86,41" href="index.html">
<area shape="rect" coords="0,60,86,92" href="services.html">
<area shape="rect" coords="0,113,86,143" href="articles.html">
<area shape="rect" coords="0,162,85,194" href="profile.html">
<area shape="rect" coords="0,213,85,246" href="clients.html">
<area shape="rect" coords="1,267,85,296" href="contact.html">
<area shape="default" nohref>
</map>

</body>
</html>
```

If you paid close attention to this code, you should have noticed the use of graphics as background and placeholders within this layout. If you're still unsure of how this works, visit the Bernstein Communications site at http://www.desert.net/berncomm/, take the code by choosing View ➤ Source, and copy and paste it into your HTML editor. You can save the graphics to your own hard drive, and reconstruct the page. Exercises of this nature can be very helpful in assisting you with gaining an intimate knowledge of how powerful and useful tables are in laying out design.

Frames

Frames have been rather controversial in Web history. Some designers and visitors love them, others have strong, personal dislike for them. Not only is there the literal and technical division of browser space that frames create, but a philosophical division as well. Fortunately, all this dispute has not stopped the progress and development of frame-based layout design. Most Web designers are beginning to agree that the survival of frames is a fortunate twist of fate, for frame technology now has moved to the forefront as a very powerful page-formatting device.

The argument, which has held fast on either extreme since Netscape released frames technology, has a certain logic to it. The reason surrounds the curse and blessing of what frames do—the breaking up of space. Your in-depth study of space in this book will immediately assist you in seeing the problem. For the common computer owner with a 15- to 17-inch average screen size, and an available resolution of either 640×480 pixels or 800×600 pixels, visual real estate is on the medium to low end of the spectrum.

Take this space and add to it the pixels that a Web browser's interface takes up, from about 5 to 15 on either vertical margin, anywhere from 25 to 150 on the top margin, and about 25 on the bottom margin. At best, on a 640×480 resolution screen, the total used pixels reduces your viewing space to 630×430, at worst, 595×295 pixels.

Now add a bordered, frame-based design to the mix, as seen in Figure 13.14, and you can quickly see why some individuals have gotten upset. Frames literally take what is a small, contained space and break that space up into smaller, even more contained spaces. Until borderless frames became available, only the most technologically adept and design savvy could use frames as part of design well, and even then at the risk of upsetting visitors to the pages they built. It is still good protocol to provide "no frame" options for Web browsers that do not support them, and for Web visitors that maintain a passionate dislike for frames.

FIGURE 13.14

The Loft Cinema uses bordered frames.

Borderless frames have bridged the churning waters, however. When Microsoft's Internet Explorer Web browser introduced the <frameborder=x> attribute and Netscape Navigator 3.0 introduced a similar feature quickly thereafter, the face of frames changed. In fact, the face of frames can now disappear altogether, if a designer so desires. Setting the frame border to a value of "0" makes the three-dimensional frame borders go away, offering seamless integration between frame divisions.

This moved frames from its position as an organizational tool to one of layout control. With borderless frames, as with borderless tables, individual sections of a page can be defined and controlled. But where tables can only be used on a page-by-page basis, frame technology introduces *static* and *targeted* aspects, allowing portions of the visible screen to remain static while others can be targeted, or changed, with the simple click of a link.

With the control that borders allow, you can now make better choices about how to employ frames. Whether you use dimensional borders for a controlled-space interface, or to create pages with frames as the silent blueprint for a complex and dynamic design, you are ultimately empowered by the new and ongoing additions to frame technology.

Frame Structure

Before the practical aspects of how to design a framed page are introduced, I'd like to demonstrate a fundamental aspect of frame design. Much like tables, frames are built in columns and rows. Tables, as mentioned earlier in this chapter, get a bit complex with the ways columns and rows are spanned, creating a technological blur between horizontal and vertical reference points. Frames approach the issue in a much more straightforward fashion—a column is an overtly vertical control, a row a horizontal one.

Frame syntax is very clear. Rows are referred to as rows, columns as cols. Both columns and rows can be defined in terms of pixels or percentages. For example, cols="240,*" calls for a left column with a *width* of 240 pixels, and the right column, called by the asterisk, will take up the remainder of the available viewing space—whatever that remainder is. This means that with frames, your layout can expand or contract to a variety of resolutions.

To add more columns, you simply define each one in turn. If you wanted to create four columns of equal percent, the syntax would read cols=25%,25%,25%,25%. In Figure 13.15 you can see a bordered frame design with four such columns.

Rows work the same way. If you wanted to create rows rather than columns, you would simply change the syntax to rows="240,*" and the results would be a top row with a *height* of 240 pixels. To create four individual rows of equal percent, you would call for rows=25%,25%,25%,25%, as shown in Figure 13.16.

FIGURE 13.15

Four framed columns

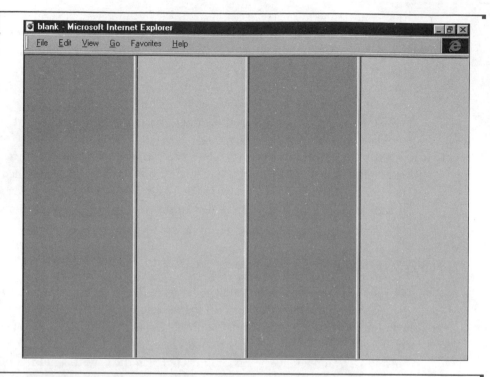

FIGURE 13.16

Four framed rows

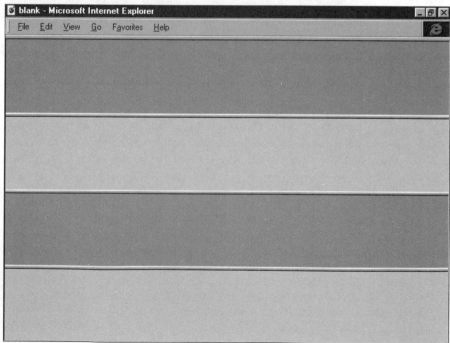

To create combinations of columns and rows, the values are simply stacked into the appropriate tags and pages of the framed site, as with the code for the Loft Cinema:

```
<html>
<head>
<title>Welcome to the Loft Cinema</title>
</head>

<frameset cols="210,*">
<frameset rows="175,*">
<frame src="flick1.htm" scrolling="no" marginwidth="1" marginheight="5"
name="flick" noresize>
<frame src="menu.htm" scrolling="auto" marginwidth="5" marginheight="25"
name="menu" noresize>
</frameset>

<frame src="welcome.htm" scrolling="auto" marginwidth="25" name="right"
noresize>
</frameset>
```

The attributes seen here are explained in further detail in the following section.

Elements of Framed Pages

As with tables, there are three elements absolutely necessary to build a framed page. And, as you advance through various aspects of working with frames, you will see that they can get a bit complicated—depending upon the ways you wish to employ them. But at the most basic level, all framed sites begin with the factors introduced here.

ON line!

A well laid out frame-based site offering up-to-date HTML information, including beginning to advanced level frames data is Sizzling HTML Jalfrezi. Point your browser to http://www.woodhill.co.uk/html/html.htm for all the HTML tags fit to print.

Remember this equation: One page of HTML code *plus* the total number of each frame desired equals the amount of HTML pages necessary to create one visible frame-based Web page.

The reason for this is that frame layouts require a controlling HTML document that gives the instructions on how the framed page is to be set up. This control is called the *frameset*. The frameset defines an HTML page for each individual frame in the layout's design.

The Frameset

Consider the frameset as the control page of your framed site. In it, you'll argue primarily for the rows and columns you wish to create, as well as the individual HTML pages that will fill those rows or columns. This is done using two major tags, as follows:

<frameset>   This tag for the frame and its basic arguments define rows and columns. The frameset information is closed with a corresponding </frameset> tag.

<frame>   The frame tag argues individual frames within the frameset. This includes the location of the HTML document required to fill the frame, utilizing the src="x" where "x" is equal to the relative or absolute URL to the location of the HTML page. A variety of other <frame> attributes will be covered later in this chapter.

Remember that a framed page requires one HTML page for each individually defined area *plus* one HTML page for the control, or frameset, page.

Frameset attributes include the following:

cols="x"   As we learned earlier, this attribute creates columns. An "x" value is given for each column in the framed page, and will be either a pixel value, a percentage value, or a combination of one of those plus the *, which creates a *dynamic* or *relative size* frame—the remainder of the framed space.

rows="x"   This attribute is used to create rows in the same fashion that the column attribute is used.

border="x"   The border attribute is used by Netscape Navigator 3.0 and above to control border width. Value is set in pixel width.

frameborder="x"   Frameborder is used by the Internet Explorer browser to control border width in pixels. Netscape Navigator 3.0 and above uses the attribute with a yes or no value.

framespacing="x"   Used by Internet Explorer, this attribute controls border width.

Use these tag attributes for individual frame control:

frameborder="x"   Use this attribute to control frameborders around individual frames. Netscape Navigator requires a yes or no value, whereas Internet Explorer will look for a numeric pixel width value.

marginheight="x"   This attribute argues a value in pixels to control the height of the frame's margin.

marginwidth="x"   This attribute argues for a frame's margin width in pixels.

name="x"   This critical attribute allows the designer to name an individual frame. Naming frames permits *targeting* by links within other HTML pages. Names must begin with a standard letter or numeral.

noresize   Simply place this handy tag in your string if you don't want to allow resizing of a frame. This fixes the frame into the position.

scrolling="x"   By arguing yes, no, or auto, you can control the appearance of a scrollbar. A yes value automatically places a scrollbar in the frame, a no value ensures that no scrollbar ever appears. The auto argument turns the power over to the browser, which will automatically place a scrollbar in a frame *should it be required.*

src="x"   The "x" value is replaced with the relative or absolute URL of the HTML page you wish to place within the frame at hand.

The Noframe Tag Option

There is an additional tag that you can use in the frameset. This tag supplies a much-needed option to allow for non-frame browsers and text-only browsers to access information within a frame-based site. Keeping to the current trends *and* incorporating no-frame and text access addresses cross-browser issues by enabling not only those who *require* text access, but those who prefer it as well.

The way to achieve this in a framed site is by employing the <noframe> tag. This is placed in the frameset page after the necessary frame syntax. Within the <noframe> tags you can place the syntax for an entire page that links to non-framed pages within the site, allowing for complete access to your information. Or, you can choose to simply say that the site in question is not available to browsers that do not support frames. Here's an example of the Loft Cinema's frameset with the <noframe> syntax in place:

```
<!-- site by desertnet designs:  sales@desert.net-->
<!-- web engineer:  molly holzschlag-->
<!-- design director: matt straznitskas  -->
<!-- online editor:  molly holzschlag -->
<!-- content provided by the loft cinema and desertnet designs -->

<html>
<head>
<title>Welcome to the Loft Cinema</title>
</head>
```

```
<frameset cols="210,*">
<frameset rows="175,*">
<frame src="flick1.htm" scrolling="no" marginwidth="1" marginheight="5"
name="flick" noresize>
<frame src="menu.htm" scrolling="auto" marginwidth="5" marginheight="25"
name="menu" noresize>
</frameset>

<frame src="welcome.htm" scrolling="auto" marginwidth="25" name="right"
noresize>
</frameset>

<noframe>

<body bgcolor="#000000" text="#FFFFFF" link="#97D7C9" vlink="#A2B3E9"
alink="#FFFFFF">

<center>
<img src="frames/99.jpg" width="180" height="125" border="0" alt="The Loft
Cinema"><p>
<img src="graphics/welcome.jpg" width="360" height="72" border="0"
alt="Welcome"><p>
<h3><i>Tucson's Premier Art Theater</i></h3>
</center>

<blockquote>
```

The Loft Cinema has been bringing art and specialty films to appreciative
Tucson audiences for nearly 25 years; and as long as there are producers,
directors, and distributors willing to make the kind of films we like to
show, we may be around for another 25 years. `<p>`

We have won the Tucson Weekly's `<b>`Best Movie Theater Award`</b>` each year
for too many years to remember, an award of considerable achievement since
we have the savvyest customers around. After many years on the University of
Arizona campus in our original single-screen location we moved in 1991 to
our current two-screen location on busy Speedway Boulevard. In our big house
we still present films on the large screen format that has disappeared in
the multiplexes.`<p>`

As a locally-owned business the Loft has had to rely upon the devotion and
expertise of many Tucsonans, including Nancy Sher, Bob Campbell, Jacqui

```
Tully, Shirley Pasternack, Anita Royal and Cliff Altfeld, and many others,
as well as a long line of film-loving staff members. We continue to show the
Rocky Horror Picture Show as we have since 1978.<p>

We are currently exploring the possibility of showing American and foreign
classics on our big screen at 1:00 pm on Saturday and Sunday. If you think
it's a good idea and want to suggest some films for us to bring in
<a href="mailto:nuloft@aol.com">E-mail us!</a>

The Loft is located at 3233 E. Speedway Blvd. in the heart of Tucson. Our
telephone number is (520) 795-7777.  When in Albuquerque visit the Loft's
sister theater, The Guild Cinema at 3405 Central Ave NE, (505) 255-1848.<p>

</blockquote>

<center>
<h3>Thanks for supporting The Loft!</h3>
</center>

<center>
<font size="2">
<a href="welcome.htm">Welcome</a> |
<a href="showing.htm">Now Showing</a> |
<a href="coming.htm">Coming Attractions</a> |
<a href="neighbor.htm">In the Neighborhood</a>
<p>
</font>

<font size="1">&#169; 1996 The Loft Cinema</font>
</center>

</body>

</noframe>

</html>
```

Figure 13.17 shows the page as it would appear without frames.

Between the various ways individual browsers work, and the variety of attributes common to contemporary browsers, it's easy to see why frames confuse many designers. If you start simple, however, and move on from there, you'll find interesting ways of employing frames in your layout design.

FIGURE 13.17

The Loft Cinema's home page as viewed without frames.

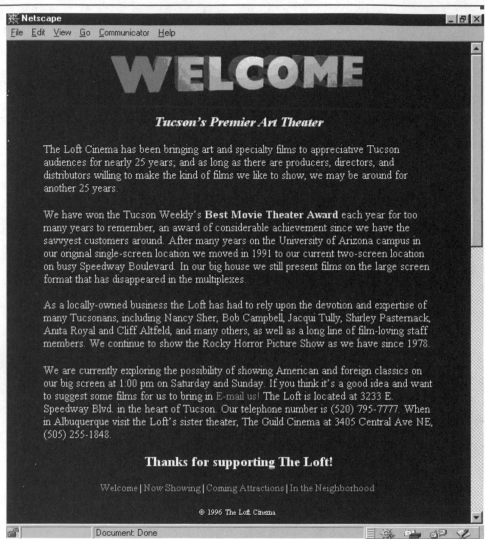

Example

The DisAbilities Forum layout design studied in Chapter 12 provides an excellent, easy-to-understand example of a frames-based layout. This is a borderless example, with a total of—you guessed it—three pages of code to make up the one main page layout.

Here's the frameset code:

```
<head>

<title>DisAbilities Forum</title>
```

```
</head>

<frameset cols="95,20%" framespacing="0" frameborder="0">
  <frame src="sidebar.htm" name="forum_sidebar" scrolling="no">
  <frame src="welcome.htm" name="ForumMain" noresize>
</frameset>

</html>
```

ARNING

Notice how there is *no* <body> tag used in a frameset. This is of critical importance. A <body> tag in a frameset will cause some browsers, including Internet Explorer 4.0, to ignore the entire frameset syntax, resulting in a blank page delivered to your screen.

OTE

The only exception to the "no <body> tag in a frameset" rule is when you are using the <noframe> tags for browsers that do not support frames. It's okay to use a <body> tag *inside* the noframe syntax, but never outside.

The DisAbilities Forum code that you see here has been designed to sit on the proprietary side of the Microsoft Network. Therefore, there isn't much need to include access for no-frames browsers, as the only browsers capable of accessing the pages in the first place are Internet Explorer 3.0 and above, and the MSN Program Viewer, which is based on Internet Explorer code and supports frame syntax.

Let's assume for a moment that the DisAbilities Forum is accessible without a membership. If you needed to be sure you could make it available to everyone who visits, you would want to include, at the very least, a <noframe> option with a comment letting people know the site was frame-based. An example of this would be:

```
<head>

<title>DisAbilities Forum</title>

</head>

<frameset cols="95,20%" framespacing="0" frameborder="0">
  <frame src="sidebar.htm" name="forum_sidebar" scrolling="no">
  <frame src="welcome.htm" name="ForumMain" noresize>
</frameset>

<noframe>

Attention! This site must be accessed with a browser that supports frames.
```

```
Thank you,
The DisAbilities Forum Management

</noframe>
</html>
```

This option is courteous, and can also be expanded to include links to frameless portions of the site, or to other resources that might assist visitors.

Now let's look at the page code for the main page of the DisAbilities Forum. First, there's the menu page to the left of the frame. Here's the syntax for that page, which includes the <object> tags to make the Flash navigation work properly:

```
<html>

<head>

<!-- This page holds the navbar -->

<title> The DisAbilities Forum </title>

<script language="vbscript">

sub navbar_fscommand(byval command, byval args)
    select case command
        case "show_all" parent.location.href="http://forums.msn.com"
        case "home" parent.forummain.location.href = "welcome.htm"
        case "contents" parent.forummain.location.href = "contents.htm"
        case "info" parent.forummain.location.href = "info.htm"
        case "new" parent.forummain.location.href = "whatsnew.htm"
        case "chat" parent.forummain.location.href = "chatmain.htm"
        case "bbs" parent.forummain.location.href = "bbsmain.htm"
        case "file" parent.forummain.location.href = "libmain.htm"
        case "guestbook" parent.forummain.location.href =
            "news://msnnews.msn.com/msn.forums.disabilities.guestbook"
        case "suggestions" parent.forummain.location.href =
            "news://msnnews.msn.com/msn.forums.disabilities.suggestbox"
        case "sites" parent.forummain.location.href = "linksmain.htm"
    end select
end sub

</script>

</head>

<body bgcolor="#c0c0c0" leftmargin="0" topmargin="0">
```

```
<object
  id="navbar"
  classid="clsid:d27cdb6e-ae6d-11cf-96b8-444553540000"
  width="100%" height="100%">
  <param name="movie" value="images/navbar.spl">
  <param name="quality" value="high">
  <param name="loop" value="false">
  <param name="play" value="false">
  <param name="scale" value="showall">
  <param name="devicefont" value="true">
  <param name="salign" value="tl">
  <param name="menu" value="false">
</object>

</body>
</html>
```

As you can see, the syntax here is for a functional Web page (Figure 13.18). This page is loaded, because of the frameset's command, into the left frame. In this case, the page includes the navigation.

FIGURE 13.18

The visible content for the left frame

The right frame also holds the syntax for a fully viewable Web page, as follows. Note that the right frame will always load the body pages of the site in this design.

```
<html>

<head>
<title> Welcome Page - AbleWorld: The DisAbilities Forum on MSN. </title>
</head>

<style>

BODY {background: url(images/bak2.jpg) FFFFFF; color: 000000}
H3 {font: 14pt arial; color: 60099}
.1 {font: 11pt arial; color: 000000; text-align: right}
.2 {font: 12pt arial; color: 000000; text-align: left}
.3 {font: 10pt arial; color: 000000; text-align: left}
.4 {font: 11pt arial; color: 9966FF; text-align: right}
.5 {font: 8pt arial; color: FF9933; text-align: center}
A {color: 9999CC; text-decoration: none}

</style>

<body bgcolor="#FFFFFF" text="#FFFFCC" link="#FFCC99" vlink="#9999CC"
alink="#FFFFCC" background="images/bak2.jpg">

<table border="0" width="505" cellpadding="5" cellspacing="0">
<tr>

<td class="3" width="200">

<a href="http://forums.msn.com/needlearts/carnival/default.htm"
target="_top"><img src="images/fall_w.gif" width="75" height="100"
border="0" alt="To Fall Carnival"></a>

<hr color="#FF9933" width="75" noshade>
</td>

<td class="1" valign="top" width="300">

<img src="images/dis-ani1.gif" width="300" height="100" border="0" alt=" ">

</td>
</tr>

<tr>
<td class="3" width="500" colspan="2">
```

```
<b>Fall Carnival</b>
Stunning <a href="http://forums.msn.com/disabilities/ne1.htm"><b>New England
photographs</b></a> from Kelly Johns;
<a href="http://forums.msn.com/disabilities/spring.htm"><b>It's Spring Down
Under</b></a>,
and <a href="http://forums.msn.com/disabilities/harvest.htm"><b>A Harvest of
Love</b></a> are highlights of carnival events on the DisAbilities Forum.
<p>

<a href="whatsnew.htm"><b>New:</b></a>

Cool specials from The Plaza on MSN!
<a href="links.htm"><b>Link</b></a> on over . . .
<p>

<ul>

<li>800-flowers -- 300 Frequent Flyer Miles with purchase of $29.99 or more
<li>B&N 30% off every hardcover and 20% off every paper back in stock
<li>800Flowers -- Same day delivery on flowers if you order by noon and
deliver in you same time zone
<li>Tower Records -- Buy 5 get 1 Free

</ul>

<a href="http://forums.msn.com/disabilities/rr/default.htm"
target="_top"><b>Rolling Reporter:</b></a>
<br>
<b>Sex on the Reef?</b> You know it! It's hot, it's sexy, and it's live, in
<i>full</i> color!
<p>

<div class=5>

<hr color="#FF9933" width="50%" noshade>

<a href="contents.htm">Contents</a> |
<a href="info.htm">Information</a> |
<a href="whatsnew.htm">What's New</a> |
<a href="chatmain.htm">Chats</a> |
<a href="bbsmain.htm">BBSs</a> |
<a href="libmain.htm">Files of Interest</a> |
<a href="linksmain.htm">Related Sites</a>
```

```
        </div>
      </td>
    </tr>
  </table>

</body>
</html>
```

Not only is the code just examined filled with standard HTML links, but it's laid out using tables. You can see what the page looks like in Figure 13.19. Indeed, this is a common practice—using frames to control interface aspects of the layout, and tables to control layout within individual pages.

OTE

If you're wondering why the navigation is forced right in the figure, it's due to the fact that I'm viewing *without* the frameset. Without frames to control the layout, the positioning deteriorates.

All in all, a powerful combination that can ensure ultimate control of any Web page design.

FIGURE 13.19

This page is forced right when placed in the context of the frameset.

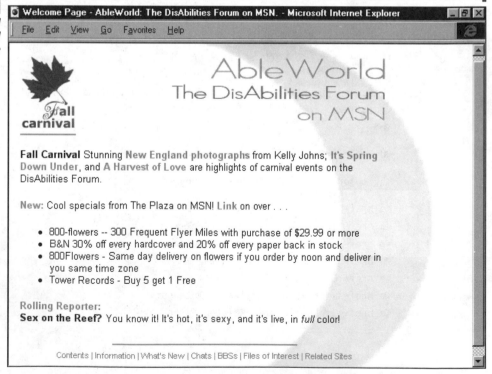

Style Sheet Positioning

HTML 4.0 calls for the use of cascading style sheet positioning over the use of tables and frames for layout control.

There are two primary problems with this. First, the majority of existing Web pages use standard, table-based, or frame-based methods of layout. That's an awful lot of Web pages! Furthermore, while style sheets will be a powerful method of layout control, positioning with style sheets is complicated enough to confuse even advanced designers. Until we have truly compatible browsers—even current 4.0 level browsers are preciously limited when it comes to the ultimate power of style sheets—style sheets will be limited in their use as positioning and layout controls. More common uses, as you will see in Chapter 20, revolve around typographic control.

These limitations are why I've opted to leave out anything but a brief "heads-up" regarding style sheet positioning. Until they become a realistic approach to contemporary Web design, it's almost confusing to add them to what is already a complicated soup.

With that in mind, use the references I've included throughout this book to explore style sheet positioning on your own. One sure-fire way of getting updated information on style sheets is with a visit to the World Wide Web Consortium, `http://www.w3.org/`. Also, be sure to check with the references provided on the Design Studio site, `http://www.designstudio.net/` as they will be updated with news as time goes by.

Next Up

With layout method and layout technology concepts tucked snugly under your belt, it's time to look at some of the applications of the technology as they exist in contemporary Web design. Chapter 14 looks at a number of working sites or site styles that are popular, and deconstructs them so you can see how they are built.

This deconstruction not only shows you how a lot sites are technically laid out, but also offers up a number of options for you to use the same code as templates for effective and contemporary site design. The advantage of this is obvious—you get to spend less time worrying about the technology and more time designing. The disadvantage is that without studying the technology, you don't provide yourself with the opportunity to explore wholly unique and creative layout possibilities.

This book should leave you with the best of both worlds—the methodology and the technological overview you can study over time, as well as at-the-ready layout styles that you can put to use right away.

chapter 14

APPLICATIONS OF LAYOUT TECHNOLOGY

APPLICATIONS OF LAYOUT TECHNOLOGY

When I was a kid I loved to take things apart and put them back together again. Unfortunately, my mother was not too fond of finding headless Barbie dolls around. I was also fascinated by the way things worked. Whether animate or inanimate, how this part went into that part, how something moved—my curiosity was cat-like in its intensity and remains, to this day, insatiable. As a child, the earthworm farm I kept in my closet captivated me. It went unnoticed for some time, but eventually my mother opened the closet door for something and found a big cardboard box filled with what was then nutrient-rich New Jersey soil and countless big, fat earthworms.

One of the reasons I love Web design is because it gives me the opportunity to put many aspects of life—science, technology, and most especially people—under the microscopic view of my computer screen. Whether it's researching information, creating new color schemes, e-mailing friends across the world, or figuring out how a Web page's parts fit together, the Web keeps me in touch with my not-so-inner child.

In this chapter, we'll take apart several Web pages and put them together again in the form of a usable template. The idea is to get you familiar with the way code works—from the most simple to the complex—you'll look at code *as it applies* to a page's layout.

This chapter will also show you layouts from a variety of working, real-time Web pages that you can put to use right away by simply adding the text and graphics of your choice.

In this chapter, we'll take apart and put together:

- Standard HTML Web pages
- A standard HTML template
- Table-based Web pages
- Table-based templates
- Frame-based Web pages
- Frame-based templates

I hope you'll have fun digging around in the virtual mud with me! Use the information here not only as a quick-start means of working with different layouts, but to inspire and develop your own.

Standard HTML Sites

The following pages are taken from Web sites that use standard HTML. No tables or frames, no fancy-schmancy coding. Straight-up, easy, workable designs are offered here for you to study in depth.

Penelope's Restaurant

I've used this site in a number of books because it's so darned pretty (see Figure 14.1). The design is so absolutely appropriate to the subject matter because it *works* as a conceptual design—despite the fact that there aren't any hoops, bells, and whistles.

Here's the code that makes the home page, which you can visit at http://www.desert .net/penelopes/.

```
<!-- site by mainstay communications and desertnet designs:
molly@desert.net-->
<!-- web engineer:  molly holzschlag -->
<!-- design director: Laura Valentino / Laura Valentino Designs -->
<!-- online editor: doug floyd -->
<!-- content provided by Penelope's Restaurant
and DesertNet Designs -->
```

```html
<html>
<head>
<title>Welcome to Penelope's Restaurant</title>
</head>

<body bgcolor="#FFFFcc" text="#cc0066" link="#3366cc" vlink="#999966"
alink="#ffff99" background="yellback.gif">

<div align="center">

<img  src="penelope.gif" alt="Penelope's" width="249" height="101"
border="0">
<p>

<img  src="blueline.gif" alt="blue line" width="300" height="28" border="0">

<blockquote>

<h2>Welcome!</h2>

</div>

<font size="+3">P</font><font size="+1">enelope's is located in an old
southwestern style house that has been restored and decorated to give each
room its own individual charm and character, much like restaurants one might
experience in the south of France. Beautifully landscaped grounds and
gardens also add to the ambience of this little oasis in the desert.  One
can enjoy fireside or al fresco dining depending on the time of day or
season.  The house also has a basement which has been converted into a wine
cellar.  We invite you to experience the Soul of France in the Heart of
Tucson.
</font>
<p>

<font size="+3">O</font><font size="+1">ur cuisine, featuring both
traditional, classical and provincial dishes while catering to the requests
for lighter sauces, relies on the freshest possible ingredients and may
occasionally provide hints of the ingredients from our southwestern locale.
Escargot, French onion soup, filet mignon, rack of lamb and a variety of
fresh fish and veal dishes are regular menu offerings.
</font>
<p>
```

```
<font size="+3">"C</font><font size="+1">onveniently located on North Swan
Road in Tucson, Arizona, it is easily accessible from all the major resorts
nestled in the foothills of the Santa Catalina Mountains. </font>
<p>

</blockquote>

<div align="center">

<img  src="blueline.gif" alt="blue line" width="300" height="28" border="0">
<p>

<a href="menus.htm"><img  src="menus.gif" alt="go to menus" width="124"
height="173" border="0"></a>
<a href="catering.htm"><img  src="catering.gif" alt="go to catering"
width="124" height="173" border="0"></a>
<a href="seating.htm"><img  src="seating.gif" alt="go to seating"
width="124" height="180" border="0"></a>
<p>

<img  src="blueline.gif" alt="blue line" width="300" height="28" border="0">
<p>

For Reservations or information call 520.325.5080
<p>
<font size="2">
<a href="http://desert.net/designs/">Site Design by DesertNet
Designs</a><br>
&#169; 1997 Penelope's Restaurant
</font>

</div>
</body>
</html>
```

The beauty of Penelope's lies not only in its oh-so-French visual art, but in the
simplicity of its code. As you see from this example, there is very little HTML and the
HTML that is used is as basic as it gets. The one minor exception to this is the use of
the <font> tag to create a drop cap and size the text.

FIGURE 14.1

*Penelope's
Restaurant Web site*

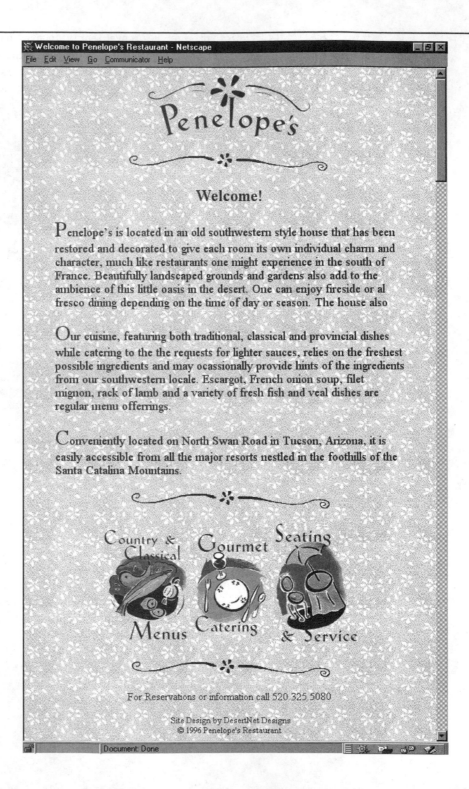

Flagstaff Festival of the Arts

Another site that is astonishingly simple yet very attractive is the one developed for
the 1996 Flagstaff Festival of the Arts in Flagstaff, Arizona (see Figure 14.2). This site is
laid out very much like the Penelope's site, but maintains its own unique look and feel.

```
<!-- site by desertnet designs:  sales@desert.net -->
<!-- design director:  molly holzschlag -->
<!-- graphic design:  jason steed and molly holzschlag -->
<!-- director of web engineering: wil gerken -->
<!-- online editor: molly holzschlag -->
<!-- content provided by jeff biggers, the flagstaff festival of the arts -->
<!-- Begin Header -->

<html>

<head>

<title>Bank One's Flagstaff Festival of the Arts</title>

</head>

<body bgcolor="#FFFFFF" text="#000066" link="#CC99CC" vlink="#333366"
alink="FFFFFF">

<center>

<img src="wch-sm4.gif" alt="water color header" width="400" height="135">

<br>

<img src="wc-ban.gif" alt="bank one banner" width="400" height="81">

</center>

<blockquote>

<!-- end header -->

In 1965 a group of citizens interested in the cultural development of
Flagstaff started a small summer music festival.  The objectives were
simple:  create an event to make wonderful music available to the community,
and enhance the Northern Arizona University music camp experience for
students.

<p>

These objectives were quickly reached.  The Flagstaff Festival of the Arts
grew into the premier summer music event in the state of Arizona.  The first
orchestra was comprised solely of faculty from the music camp.  Today, the
professional orchestra brings a wide array of world class soloists,
conductors, instrumentalists, and entertainers to the northland.

<p>
```

During the thirty-one year history of the Festival, thousands of volunteers and supporters have made it possible to present more than 900 events to over 388,000 people. More than 30,000 young musicians, coming from reservations, towns, and metropolitan areas, have had an opportunity to experience a professional orchestra.
<p>

With continued support from the business and cultural communities, Flagstaff's summer musical treasure will not only continue, but will grow from a state and regional favorite into a national event. We have returned to the simple objective of our beginnings—to make wonderful music available in our community.

```
<pre>

</pre>

<!-- Begin Footer -->

</blockquote>

<center>

<a href="head.htm"><img src="bass1.gif" alt="bass icon go to headliners"
width="105" height="125" border="0"></a>
<a href="sched.htm"><img src="bongo1.gif" alt="bongo icon go to schedule"
width="105" height="125" border="0"></a>
<a href="tickets.htm"><img src="clarine1.gif" alt="clarinet icon go to
tickets" width="105" height="125" border="0"></a>
<a href="lodge.htm"><img src="piano1.gif" alt="piano icon go to lodging"
width="105" height="125" border="0"></a>
<a href="links.htm"><img src="sax1.gif" alt="saxaphone icon go to links"
width="105" height="125" border="0"></a>
<p>

<font size="2">
<a href="index.htm">Home</a> | <a href="head.htm">Headliners</a> |
<a href="sched.htm">Schedule</a> | <a href="tickets.htm">Tickets</a> |
<a href="lodge.htm">Lodging</a> | <a href="links.htm">Links</a>
<p>

<a href="http://desert.net/designs/">Site Design by DesertNet Designs</a><br>
&#169; 1996, 1997 Flagstaff Festival of the Arts
</font>

</center>

<!-- End Footer -->

</body>
</html>
```

FIGURE 14.2

*Flagstaff Festival of
the Arts home page*

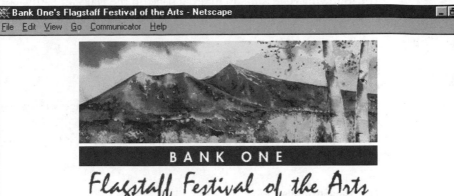

BANK ONE
Flagstaff Festival of the Arts

In 1965 a group of citizens interested in the cultural development of Flagstaff started a small summer music festival. The objectives were simple: create an event to make wonderful music available to the community, and enhance the Northern Arizona University music camp experience for students.

These objectives were quickly reached. The Flagstaff Festival of the Arts grew into the premier summer music event in the state of Arizona. The first orchestra was comprised solely of faculty from the music camp. Today, the professional orchestra brings a wide array of world class soloists, conductors, instrumentalists, and entertainers to the northland.

During the thirty-one year history of the Festival, thousands of volunteers and supporters have made it possible to present more than 900 events to over 388,000 people. More than 30,000 young musicians, coming from reservations, towns, and metropolitan areas, have had an opportunity to experience a professional orchestra.

With continued support from the business and cultural communities, Flagstaff's summer musical treasure will not only continue, but will grow from a state and regional favorite into a national event. We have returned to the simple objective of our beginnings--to make wonderful music available in our community.

Headliners   Schedule   Tickets   Lodging   Links

 Home | Headliners | Schedule | Tickets | Lodging | Links

 Site Design by DesertNet Designs
© 1996 Flagstaff Festival of the Arts

The following code is for an internal page on the Flagstaff Festival of the Arts site. The page is shown in Figure 14.3. Pay close attention to the alignment of the photos.

```html
<!-- site by desertnet designs:  sales@desert.net -->
<!-- design director:  molly holzschlag -->
<!-- graphic design:   jason steed -->
<!-- director of web engineering:  molly holzschlag, wil gerken -->
<!-- online editor: molly holzschlag -->
<!-- content provided by  jeff biggers, the flagstaff festival of the
arts -->

<!-- begin header -->

<html>

<head>
<title>Bank One's Flagstaff Festival of the Arts:  Headliners</title>
</head>

<body bgcolor="#FFFFFF" text="#000066" link="#CC99CC" vlink="#333366"
alink="FFFFFF">

<center>
<img src="hed-hed.gif" alt="Headliners Header" width="400" height="81"
border="0">
</center>

<blockquote>

<!-- end header -->

<center>

<font color="#66CC99" size="3">
Mark O'Connor . . . Jubilant Sykes . . . Turtle Island String Quartet
</font>

</center>
<p>
```

```
<img src="oconnor.jpg" alt="Picture of Mark O'Connor with Violin"
width="189" height="201" hspace="15" border="0" align="right">
<br clear="left">
<p>
```

The 1996 Festival opens Friday, July 5th, with fiddle virtuoso Mark O'Connor, who is hailed as the world's greatest fiddler. O'Connor won the International Fiddle Festival at age 13, and has recorded with artists as diverse as YoYo Ma and Willie Nelson. O'Connor's Concerto for Fiddle is an exciting and moving composition. O'Connor will also perform fiddle standards with the Orchestra.

```
<p>
```

```
<img src="sykes.jpg" alt="Picture of Jubilant Sykes" width="181"
height="218" hspace="15" border="0" align="left">
<br clear="right">
<p>
```

One of America's most powerful and joyful baritones, Jubilant Sykes performs with the Festival Orchestra on Sunday, July 14. Sony Records recently released Sykes' recording with the Royal Philharmonic. Recently completing a tour with the Boston Pops Orchestra, you won't forget his name, or his incredible performance. Sykes features songs from Copland as well as traditional Gospel Standards.

```
<p>
```

```
<img src="turtle.jpg" alt="Turtle Island Quartet" width="218" height="137"
hspace="15" border="0" align="right">
<br clear="left">
<p>
```

Considered one of the most innovative Quartets around, Turtle Island String Quartet from San Francisco will end the Festival season with a unique and exciting performance. Joining in is the Festival Orchestra. Breaking new ground, Turtle Island String Quartet is widely recognized as the premiere Jazz String Group in the United States.

```
<pre>
```

```
</pre>

<!-- begin footer -->

</blockquote>

<center>

<a href="head.htm"><img src="bass1.gif" alt="bass icon go to headliners"
width="105" height="125" border="0"></a>
<a href="sched.htm"><img src="bongo1.gif" alt="bongo icon go to schedule"
width="105" height="125" border="0"></a>
<a href="tickets.htm"><img src="clarine1.gif" alt="clarinet icon go to
tickets" width="105" height="125" border="0"></a>
<a href="lodge.htm"><img src="piano1.gif" alt="piano icon go to lodging"
width="105" height="125" border="0"></a>
<a href="links.htm"><img src="sax1.gif" alt="saxaphone icon go to links"
width="105" height="125" border="0"></a>
<p>

<font size="2">
<a href="index.htm">Home</a> | <a href="head.htm">Headliners</a> |
<a href="sched.htm">Schedule</a> | <a href="tickets.htm">Tickets</a> |
<a href="lodge.htm">Lodging</a> | <a href="links.htm">Links</a>
<p>

<a href="http://desert.net/designs/">Site Design by DesertNet
Designs</a><br>
&#169; 1996, 1997 Flagstaff Festival of the Arts
</font>

</center>

<!-- end footer -->

</body>
</html>
```

Another notable use of code in this example is the creation of space with pre-
formatted <pre> tags.

FIGURE 14.3

*Internal page for
Flagstaff Festival of
the Arts*

🔆 Bank One's Flagstaff Festival of the Arts: Headliners - Netscape

File   Edit   View   Go   Communicator   Help

HEADLINERS

Flagstaff Festival of the Arts

Mark O'Connor . . . Jubilant Sykes . . . Turtle Island String Quartet

The 1996 Festival opens Friday, July 5th, with
fiddle virtuoso Mark O'Connor, who is hailed as
the world's greatest fiddler. O'Connor won the
International Fiddle Festival at age 13, and has
recorded with artists as diverse as YoYo Ma and
Willie Nelson. O'Connor's Concerto for Fiddle is
an exciting and moving composition. O'Connor
will also perform fiddle standards with the
Orchestra.

One of America's most powerful and joyful
baritones, Jubilant Sykes performs with the Festival
Orchestra on Sunday, July 14. Sony Records
recently released Sykes' recording with the Royal
Philharmonic. Recently completing a tour with the
Boston Pops Orchestra, you won't forget his name,
or his incredible performance. Sykes features songs
from Copland as well as traditional Gospel
Standards.

Considered one of the most innovative
Quartets around, Turtle Island String Quartet
from San Francisco will end the Festival
season with a unique and exciting
performance. Joining in is the Festival
Orchestra. Breaking new ground, Turtle
Island String Quartet is widely recognized as
the premiere Jazz String Group in the United States.

Headliners   Schedule   Tickets   Lodging   Links

Home | **Headliners** | Schedule | Tickets | Lodging | Links

Site Design by DesertNet Designs
© 1996 Flagstaff Festival of the Arts

Document: Done

Dispatch

As a Web publishing software solution, Dispatch has evolved into the intelligence behind some of today's most popular—and much more complex—alternative news Web sites. The Dispatch method is a proprietary processing system for large amounts of text, links, and graphical data and is especially applicable to publications such as weekly newspapers.

What I like most about Dispatch's Web site beyond its straightforward design is the fact that the primary navigation is linear. You can page through the site using the forward and back buttons shown here.

Page Back   **Page Forward**

There is non-linear navigation introduced through linking, but for the most part, the site is read like a book.

The idea behind the Dispatch site was to mimic a newspaper. The results worked—while the Dispatch site design and layout itself is a bit conservative (Figure 14.4), the online newspapers Dispatch has gone on to process are not. These include the *Austin Chronicle*, *Boston Phoenix*, *Chicago NewCityNet*, *The Salt Lake City Weekly*, and the *Tucson Weekly*, among others.

Here's the Dispatch home page code:

```
<!-- Site by DesertNet Designs . sales@desert.net -->

<!-- Web Engineer . Wil Gerken -->
<!-- Design Director . Matt Straznitskas -->
<!-- Online Editor . Molly Holzschlag -->

<html>

<head>
<title>Dispatch: The Web Publishing Solution</title>
</head>

<body bgcolor="#ffffff" text="#000000" link="#108C42" alink="#000000"
vlink="#214A94">

<div align="center">
```

```
<img src="logo.jpg" alt="Dispatch - The Web Publishing Solution" width="436"
height="164">
<p>

</div>

<blockquote>

Your publication. The World Wide Web. An audience of thousands.
How do you make it happen fast, cheap and painlessly? <b>With Dispatch, of
course!</b>  Translate your pre-press files into a fully linked, ready-to-
surf publication with a complete navigation system, links and graphics
optimized for style, speed and efficiency.
<p>

<div align="center">
<h2>Hassle-free.  Little expense.  Hundreds of options.</h2>
</div>

<b>Dispatch</b> puts you on top of the Web revolution.  With proprietary
software tools, award-winning design and software engineering techniques,
<b>Dispatch</b> can make your paper one of the most attractive and
interactive online.
<p>

<div align="center">
<h2>Our experience.  Your brilliance.  Painless success.</h2>
</div>

</blockquote>

<div align="center">
<a href="layout.htm"><img src="pforward.gif" alt="Page Forward" border="0"
width="75" height="75"></a>
<p>
<font size="2"><a href="http://desert.net/designs/">Site Design by DesertNet
Designs</a><br>&#169; 1996, 1997 DesertNet</font>
</div>

</body>
</html>
```

Like Penelope's and the Flagstaff Festival of the Arts, Dispatch's layout was designed in early 1996. Despite the advancements made in both HTML and layout technologies, these sites stand as a testament to the fact that less is sometimes more. The logical layouts combined with well-designed graphics, easy-to-use navigation, and interesting, well-written content create sites that are timeless because of their design integrity.

FIGURE 14.4

Dispatch home page

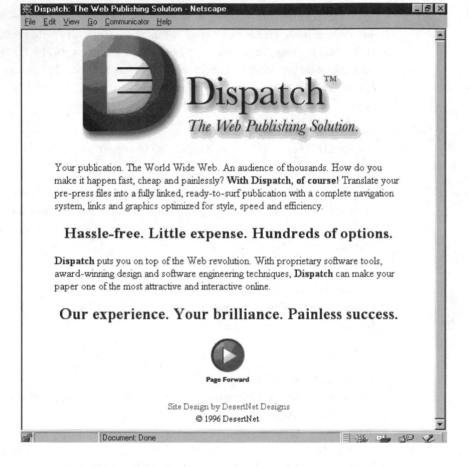

A Standard HTML Template

You might have noticed that the previous examples all have a specific visual layout order in common. First, there's a header, then the content, then the navigation. Beneath the navigation is contact and copyright information (remember the lessons we learned about interface in Chapter 3).

The following code template includes comment tags but otherwise achieves the layout as simply as possible. If you recall from our discussion in Chapter 2, templates can help expedite HTML coding as well as making sites appear more consistent. Anything in italics should be replaced with your own information.

```
<!-- Site by your name here . your e-mail address here -->

<!-- additional comments here -->

<html>

<head>
<title>Your site's title and page name here</title>
</head>

<body bgcolor="#your background color choice" text="#your text color"
link="#your link color" alink="#your active link color" vlink="#your visited
link color">

<!-- Begin Header -->

<div align="your alignment">(choose from center or right, eliminate division
tag for left aligned header)

<img src="logo.jpg" alt="your logo header here" width="image width here"
height="image height here" border="0">
<p>

</div>

<!-- Begin Content -->

<blockquote>

your first paragraph here
<p>

<img src="yourimagehere" alt="your description here" width="image width
here" height="image height here" border="0" hspace="your desired horizontal
space here" vspace="your desired vertical space here" align="your desired
alignment here">
<br clear="your desired break here">

your following paragraph here
<p>

another paragraph here
```

```
<p>

</blockquote>

<!-- Begin Graphic Navigation -->

<div align="center">

<a href="yourlink1.htm"><img src="yourbutton1.gif" alt="your button
description" width="your button width" height="your button height"
border="0"></a>

<a href="yourlink2.htm"><img src="yourbutton2.gif" alt="your button
description" width="your button width" height="your button height"
border="0"></a>

<a href="yourlink3.htm"><img src="yourbutton3.gif" alt="your button
description" width="your button width" height="your button height"
border="0"></a>
<p>

<!-- Begin Text Navigation -->

<font size="2">
<a href="index.htm">Home</a> |
<a href="anotherpage.htm">navigation link</a> |
<a href="anotherpage.htm">navigation link</a> |
<p>

<!-- Copyright and Contact -->

&#169; add year  add copyright holder's title
<p>
<a href="mailto:contact's e-mail address here">Contact Name Here</a>

</font>

</center>

<!-- end footer -->

</body>
</html>
```

From our earliest lessons on accessibility, you'll appreciate the text-based navigation options. Sites designed with this type of template are the most easily accessed by text-based browsers.

Be as flexible as you like with the template, of course. But all the basics are here—ready for you to use.

Table Layouts

Tables add a level of sophistication to a site. This doesn't mean that simple layouts such as those we just looked at are less useful or appealing, but tables are currently the definitive method for more advanced layout design. The following sites will show you some interesting—and entertaining—examples of table-based layout design.

Wilde Rose Coffee Company

The home page for the Wilde Rose Coffee Company is absolutely caffeinated, with dancing coffee cups galore. You'll have to check out http://www.desert.net/wilderose/ to see the animation for yourself, but Figure 14.5 gives you a look at the design.

FIGURE 14.5

Wilde Rose home page

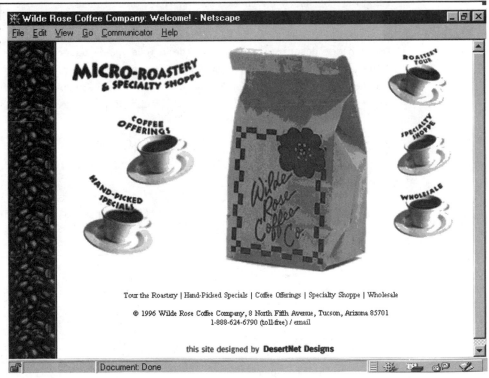

Here's the splash page code, which gives a nice example of how to lay out multiple graphics to create a seamless look:

```
<!-- site by desertnet designs:  sales@desert.net -->
<!-- design director: molly holzschlag -->
<!-- graphic design:   amy burnham -->
<!-- online editor: molly holzschlag -->
<!-- content provided by Wilde Rose Coffee Co. -->

<!-- Begin Header -->

<html>

<head>
<title>Wilde Rose Coffee Company:  Welcome!</title>

<meta name="keywords" content="coffee, java, micro, roastery, desserts,
roasting, beans, brew, brewing, ron rose, micki rose, amy rose, tucson,
arizona, southwest, desert, desertnet, tucson weekly, desert net, sonora">

<meta name="description" content="delicious hand-roasted coffees from one of
America's finest roasters, Ron Rose.  Woman owned, family-operated business
located in downtown Tucson in the Historic Hotel Congress, and found on the
palettes of the most sophisticated coffee fans world over.">

<meta name="author" content="molly e. holzschlag, amy burnham, the Wilde
Roses">

</head>

<body background="tile.gif" bgcolor="#ffffff" link="#55380d" vlink="#264230"
alink="#000000" text="#000000">

<!-- End Header -->

<table border="0" width="600" cellspacing="0" cellpadding="0">
<tr>

<!-- Begin Spacer -->

<td width="52" rowspan="2">
```

```html
<img src="spacer.gif" width="52" height="1" alt="">
<br>
</td>

<!-- End Spacer -->

<td align="center" valign="top" width=184>
<img src="text.gif" alt="header animation" width="184" height="66">
<p>

<img src="2cups.gif" alt="2cups animation" width="170" height="194"
border="0" usemap="#2cups">
</td>

<td align="center" valign="top" width="199">
<img src="bag.jpg" alt="bag" width="199" height="299">
</td>

<td align="center" valign="top">
<img src="3cups.gif" alt="3cups animation" width="91" height="260"
border="0" usemap="#3cups">
</td>

</tr>

<tr>
<td colspan="3" align="center" valign="top">

<p><br>
<font size="1">
<a href="tour-r.html">Tour the Roastery</a> |
<a href="monthly.html">Hand-Picked Specials</a> |
<a href="offerings.html">Coffee Offerings</a> |
<a href="shop.html">Specialty Shoppe</a> |
<a href="whole.html">Wholesale</a>
<p>

&#169; 1996 Wilde Rose Coffee Company, 8 North Fifth Avenue, Tucson, Arizona
85701
<br>
```

```
1-888-624-6790 (toll-free) / <a
href="mailto:wilderose@theriver.com">email</a>
</font>
<p>

<a href="http://desert.net/designs/"><img
src="http://desert.net/designs/dnd_w.gif" border="0" width="213" height="20"
alt="DesertNet Designs"></a>
</font>
</td>
</tr>

</table>

<!-- Begin Maps -->

<map name="3cups">
<area shape="rect" coords="1,3,87,78" href="tour-r.html">
<area shape="rect" coords="0,79,88,161" href="shop.html">
<area shape="rect" coords="0,164,88,256" href="whole.html">
<area shape="default" nohref>
</map>

<map name="2cups">
<area shape="rect" coords="2,4,166,96" href="offerings.html">
<area shape="rect" coords="2,98,168,193" href="monthly.html">
<area shape="default" nohref>
</map>

<!-- End Maps -->

</body>
</html>
```

Figure 14.6 shows the page with the table borders turned on, so you can get a feel for the way the layout influences the placement of the elements on the page.

FIGURE 14.6

Wilde Rose home page with table borders to show layout

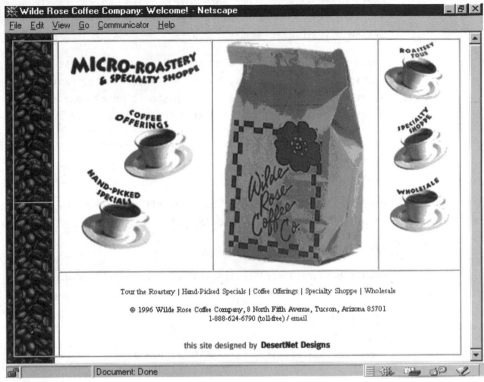

An internal page on the Wilde Rose Web site has tables being used for page layout with background graphics, photographic media, navigational media, and spacing.

```
<!-- site by desertnet designs:  sales@desert.net -->
<!-- design director: molly holzschlag -->
<!-- graphic design:   amy burnham -->
<!-- online editor: molly holzschlag -->
<!-- content provided by Wilde Rose Coffee Co. -->

<!-- Begin Header -->

<html>

<head>
<title>Wilde Rose Coffee Company:  Roastery Tour</title>
```

```
<meta name="keywords" content="coffee, java, micro, roastery, desserts,
roasting, beans, brew, brewing, ron rose, micki rose, amy rose, tucson,
arizona, southwest, desert, desertnet, tucson weekly, desert net, sonora">

<meta name="description" content="delicious hand-roasted coffees from one of
America's finest roasters, Ron Rose.  Woman owned, family-operated business
located in downtown Tucson in the Historic Hotel Congress, and found on the
palettes of the most sophisticated coffee fans world over.">

<meta name="author" content="molly e. holzschlag, amy burnham, the Wilde
Roses">
</head>

<body background="tile.gif" bgcolor="#ffffff" link="#55380d" vlink="#264230"
alink="#000000" text="#000000">

<!-- End Header -->

<table border="0" cellspacing="0" cellpadding="0" width="600">
<tr>

<!-- Begin Spacer -->
<td width="75">
<img src="spacer.gif" width="75" height="1" alt="">
<br>
</td>
<!-- End Spacer -->

<!-- Begin Text Column -->

<td align="left" valign="top">

<center>

<a href="index.html"><img src="roast.gif" alt="Tour the Roastery Header"
width="529" height="73" border="0"></a>
<p>

<center>

<table border="0">

<tr>
<td width="450" align="left" valign="top">
```

At the Wilde Rose Roastery we have a secret! We'll give you a hint--it has to do with great coffee. Okay, Okay--we can't keep a secret that's this good. Come a little closer, and we'll let the secret out of its burlap bag.<p>

<img src="ph1.jpg" alt="photo of Ron Rose" width="222" height="170" border="0" align="left">

Wilde Rose Roastery roasts every bean "Full City," French, or darker. So what's so special about that?
<p>

Well, most roasters roast their beans as light as they can. Roasting light produces less than memorable coffee, light in body, and light in taste. Dark roasted coffee is heavy in body, flavorful, and has lower caffeine and acidity. Dark roasted coffee should never be bitter--the skill of the roaster is your primary safeguard.
<p>

Our coffee is roasted in an antique Diedrich Roster in small batches. Automation is kept to a minimum--we rely on the craftsmanship of our roaster.
<p>

Our roastery is one of the few owned by a woman, Micki Rose, and has always been a family business.
<p>

<img src="wife.jpg" alt="Micki Rose" width="212" height="173" border="0" align="right">

Feel free to look at the varietals, blends, and dessert coffees we offer by looking at our "<a href="offerings.html">coffee offerings</a>", and each month, we offer you "<a href="monthly.html">hand-picked</a>" coffee specials. There is a <a href="wholsale.html">wholesale</a> section for restaurants, coffee houses, or retail stores interested in our high quality roasted beans.
<p>
<br clear=all>

<img src="ph2.jpg" alt="photo of Roastmaster Ron Rose" width="189" height="218" border="0" align="left">

It's a fact that wonderful coffee begins with high-quality "Arabica" green beans. The skill of the Roastmaster and the style of the roasting are nuances that make the difference between ordinary and extraordinary gourmet coffee beans.
<p>

Coffees do vary from country to country, region to region, climate to climate-- even harvest to harvest. Your palate will determine your preferences. Some prefer the brilliant clarity of beans from South American plantations, others, the heavy, "winey" flavor of African or Indonesian coffees. At Wilde Rose, we recommend experimenting, cupping a variety of coffees in much the same way we do when we select the beans offered to you.
<p>

<img src="ph3.jpg" alt="Roastmaster Ron at the Antique Diedrich Roaster" width="179" height="227" hspace="10" vspace="10" border="0" align="right">

No tour would be complete without a visit to view our gleaming copper and brass 50's vintage Diedrich roaster. The roasting chamber still retains the patina of coffee that has collected over thousands of roasts. We wouldn't swap it for the high-volume, full bag roasters in use today--we think that would take all the fun out of it!
<p>

A few words about our roastmaster--that's Ron! When you roast beans as dark as we do, seconds in the roaster measure the difference between glistening full-flavored beans and charcoal. This is the reason, along with consistency, that Ron roasts all of the beans himself. You can always tour our roastery in real-time, any time you're visiting Tucson, Arizona. Call in advance for a private roasting session, 1-888-624-6790.
<p>

Go to the <a href="offerings.html">Coffee Offerings</a> section for a complete list of the coffees we have available.
<p>

</td>
</tr>
</table>
</center>

```
<!-- Begin Footer -->

<center>

<nobr>
<font size="1">
<img src="nav1e.jpg" alt="roastery tour" width="101" height="106"
border="0">
<a href="offerings.html"><img src="nav2f.jpg" alt=" Coffee Offerings "
width="101" height="106" border="0"></a>
<a href="monthly.html"><img src="nav3f.jpg" alt=" Hand-Picked Specials "
width="104" height="106" border="0"></a>
<a href="shop.html"><img src="nav4f.jpg" alt=" Specialty Shoppe "
width="103" height="106" border="0"></a>
<a href="whole.html"><img src="nav5f.jpg" alt=" Wholesale " width="105"
height="106" border="0"></a>
</nobr>
<p>

&#169; 1996 Wilde Rose Coffee Company, 8 North Fifth Avenue, Tucson, Arizona
85701
<br>
1-888-624-6790 (toll-free) / <a
href="mailto:wilderose@theriver.com">email</a>
</font>
<p>

<a href="http://desert.net/designs/"><img
src="http://desert.net/designs/dnd_w.gif" border="0" width="213" height="20"
alt="DesertNet Designs"></a>

</center>

</td>
</tr>
</table>

</body>
</html>
```

Pay attention to the use of META tags as well as the way images use standard alignment *within* the table itself in this example. Figure 14.7 shows the page's layout in its entirety; it has the table borders turned on for you to see the way the layout is controlled.

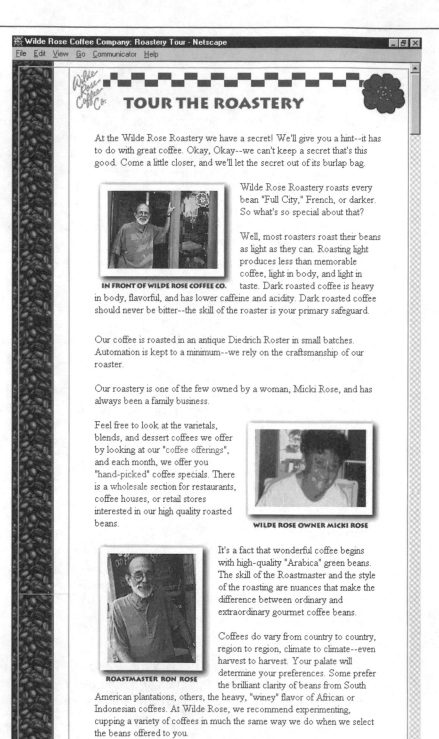

FIGURE 14.7

Continued

*Internal page for
Wilde Rose Web site*

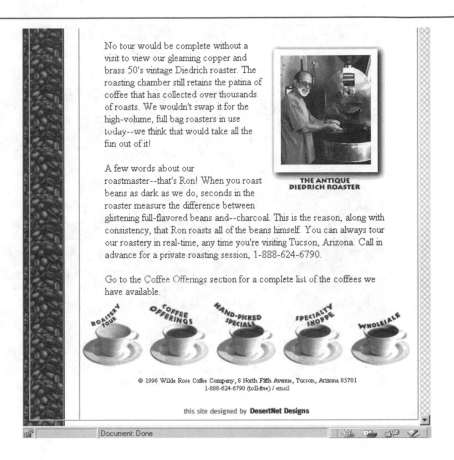

Max Cannon's Red Meat

Some of you might be familiar with the fresh (if you'll pardon the pun) and rather twisted Red Meat comic, which appears nationwide in alternative newspapers. If you're not yet familiar with Max Cannon's work, you soon will be—Cannon's syndication is growing and now includes the Village Voice. He's even got avid fans in the Czech Republic, where an "unofficial" fan Web site exists.

The official Red Meat site includes a nice spread of goodies from the weekly comic to newsworthy items, tasty promotional offerings, and even a popular bulletin board. Visit this virtual buffet in its live incarnation at `http://www.redmeat.com/`.

As with the Wilde Rose site, the splash page for Red Meat offers up a juicy method of laying out graphics (Figure 14.8).

FIGURE 14.8

The weird and wacky Red Meat home page

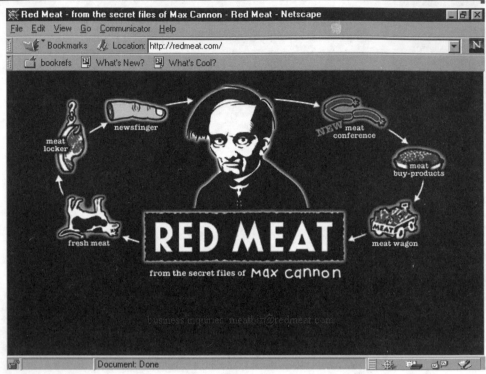

```
<html>

<head>
<title>Red Meat - from the secret files of Max Cannon - Red Meat</title>

<meta name="keywords" content="red, meat, red meat, Max, Cannon, Max Cannon,
Earl, Milkman Dan, Comic, strip, cartoon, humor, comedy, sick, twisted,
bizarre, migraine boy, dilbert, onion, alternative, hate, eightball, bagge,
clones, zippy, lost world, batman, robin">

<meta name="description" content="The most tasteless and twisted comic strip
in the world. From the secret files of Max Cannon.">

</head>

<body bgcolor="#000000" text="#ff0000" link="#ff0000" alink="#ff0000"
vlink="#ff0000">
```

```html
<center>

<table border="0" cellpadding="0" cellspacing="0">
<tr>

<td rowspan="2" align="right" valign="top"><img src="images/rm_s1.gif"
border="0" alt="" usemap="#rm_s1" width="186" height="271"></td>
<td valign="top"><a href="fresh.html"><img src="images/rm_an1.gif"
border="0" alt="" width="191" height="172"></a></td>
<td rowspan="2" align="left" valign="top"><img src="images/rm_s3.gif"
border="0" alt="" usemap="#rm_s3" width="183" height="271"></td>
</tr>

<tr>
<td valign="abstop"><a href="fresh.html"><img src="images/rm_s2.gif"
border="0" alt=" Fresh Meat " width="191" height="99"></a></td>
</tr>
</table>
<p><br>

<center>business inquiries: <a
href="mailto:meatbiz@redmeat.com">meatbiz@redmeat.com</a><center>
</center>

<map name="rm_s1">
<area shape="polygon" alt=" Meat Locker "
coords="27,73,40,54,41,27,48,19,65,19,74,32,74,56,81,71,81,103,67,114,63,133,
48,133,42,138,29,138,15,100,13,78" href="locker.html">
<area shape="polygon" alt=" Prime Cuts "
coords="90,57,100,74,180,75,183,55,183,33,152,14,116,17" href="prime.html">
<area shape="polygon" alt=" Fresh Meat "
coords="40,152,36,171,37,183,25,206,32,220,46,227,126,227,137,203,126,176,115,
175,106,167,109,146,90,142,78,148" href="fresh.html">
<area shape="rect" coords="146,170,185,270" href="fresh.html">
<area shape="default" nohref>
</map>

<map name="rm_s3">
<area shape="polygon" alt=" Smoky Links "
coords="6,50,14,72,102,72,113,51,71,29,55,10,4,24,1,38"
href="http://bbs.desert.net/~2/">
```

```
<area shape="polygon" alt=" Meat Buy-Products "
coords="102,99,125,76,151,84,179,93,181,105,177,133,105,133"
href="buy.html">
<area shape="polygon" alt=" Fun with Meat "
coords="68,225,155,225,146,208,148,174,152,160,135,148,104,156,82,160,67,176
,58,201" href="fun.html">
<area shape="rect" coords="0,169,45,270" href="fresh.html">
<area shape="default" nohref>
</map>

</body>
</html>
```

Plenty of active media on this page! Figure 14.9 shows the table layout. Be sure to pay attention to the way the graphics are broken up.

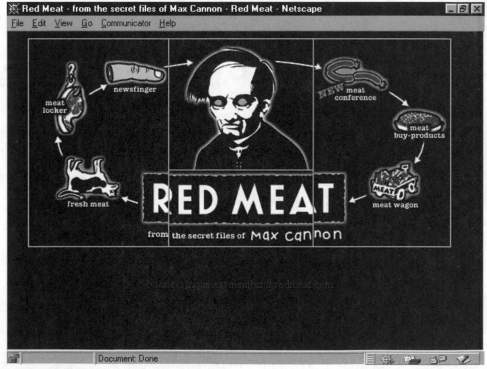

An internal page for the Red Meat site uses tables to accommodate advertising as well as text and graphic content. Notice the use of JavaScript in this code and the hilarious albeit extensive text.

```html
<html>

<head>
<title>RED MEAT - Meat Wagon</title>

<meta name="keywords" content="red, meat, red meat, Max, Cannon, Max Cannon,
Earl, Milkman Dan, Comic, strip, cartoon, humor, comedy, sick, twisted,
bizarre, migraine boy, dilbert, onion, alternative, hate, eightball, bagge,
clones, zippy, lost world, batman, robin">

<meta name="description" content="The most tasteless and twisted comic strip
in the world. From the secret files of Max Cannon.">

<script language="JavaScript">
<!-- JavaScript (c) 1996-97 DesertNet . http://desert.net/ -->
<!-- Author: Wil Gerken . wil@desert.net -->
<!-- Note: You are welcome to use this code, but we require that -->
<!-- you keep the copyright and author lines intact and that you  -->
<!-- email us so we can view your site also. Thanks. -->

// Define Browser Version (c) 1996-97 DesertNet
ver = "";
bName = navigator.appName;
bVer = parseInt(navigator.appVersion);
if (bName == "Netscape" && bVer >= 3) ver = "n3";

function imgToggle(imgObjectName, imgObjectState) {
  if (ver == "n3") {
    imgObject = new Object();
    imgObject = imgObjectName;
    imgObject.src = imgObjectState;
  }
}

function imgPreLoad(i, img) {
  if (ver == "n3") {
    cacheImg[i] = new Image();
    cacheImg[i].src = img;
  }
}
```

```
// Declare and Load Images
fresh = "images/rm_nav1b.gif";
locker = "images/rm_nav2b.gif";
prime = "images/rm_nav3b.gif";
smokey = "images/rm_nav4b.gif";
buy = "images/rm_nav5b.gif";
fun = "images/rm_nav6b.gif";
cacheImg = new Array();
imgPreLoad(0,fresh);
imgPreLoad(1,locker);
imgPreLoad(2,prime);
imgPreLoad(3,smokey);
imgPreLoad(4,buy);
imgPreLoad(5,fun);

// End Script -->
</script> </head>

<body bgcolor="#ffffff" link="#d60017" vlink="#29295a" alink="#000000"
text="#000000">

<center>

<table border="0" cellpading="0" cellspacing="0" width="600">
<tr>
<td align="center"><img src="images/ad_wagon.gif" align="left" alt=""
width="122" height="62"><br></td>
<td align="center"><a
href="http://commonwealth.riddler.com/Commonwealth/bin/statthru?257516"
target="_top"><img
src="http://commonwealth.riddler.com/Commonwealth/bin/statdeploy?257516"
height="60" width="460" alt=""></a>
<br></td>
</tr>

<tr>
<td colspan=2>
<br><br>

<img src="images/surrender.gif" width="600" height="87" alt="Surrender to the
mind-numbing effects of normalcy?  I don't think so...NOT WHEN THERE'S MEAT
TO BE HAD!Frivolity, excursions into the bizarre and generalized mirth.">
```

```
<br><br><br>
<p>

<img src="images/Lemonhead_Game.gif" alt="" width="600" height="216"><br>
<br><br><br><br><br><p>
<center>
<img src="images/fun_with_meat.gif" width="400" height="63" alt="meat
wagon">
</center>
<br><br><br><p>
<b>JELLIED BEEF MOLD RECIPE</b>
<font size="-1">- Submitted by Amy Burnham, Tucson AZ</font>
<p>

<img src="images/rm_ph1.jpg" align="right" alt="" width="248" height="205">

Meat set in gelatin and waiting in the refrigerator brings peaceof mind when
company's coming.
<p>
1-1/2 pounds boneless chuck beef
<br>
1 cup hot water
<br>
1 envelope unflavored gelatin
<br>
1/3 cup chopped celery
<br>
1/4 cup chopped onion
<br>
1/4 cup cubed dill pickles
<br>
10-1/2 ounce can condensed beef consomm&eacute;
<br>
```

NOTE

Wonder what the é stands for? It's a special character code that creates the accent mark on the word consommé. For more information on code characters, visit Appendix B.

1/2 teaspoon salt

1/8 teaspoon pepper

12 pimiento-stuffed olives

Strips of pimiento

Parsley

Olives
<p>
Simmer beef in water until tender. Remove meat; put through food chopped
using coarse blade. (There should be 2 c. ground beef.)

Cool broth; soften gelatin in 2 tablespoons broth.

Cook celery and onion in remainder of broth until tender, but still slightly
firm, about 10 minutes. Drain, save broth. Mix celery, onion and pickles
with meat.

Add enough broth to consomm&eacute; to make 2 cups; heat. Add softened
gelatin; stir to dissolve. Pour thin layer of gelatin into 1-1/2 quart loaf
pan; chill. To remainder of gelatin mixture add salt, pepper and beef.

Arrange olive slices and pimiento strips in design over gelatin in pan.

Spoon in beef mixture; chill.

To serve, unmold on platter. Garnish with parsley and stuffed
olives. Makes 8 servings.
<p>
Double the recipe for a crowd.
<p>
<b>FRENCH-FRIED WIENERS</b>
<font size="-1">– Submitted by Amy Burnham, Tucson AZ</font>
<p>

<img src="images/rm_ph2.jpg" align=right alt="" width="230" height="231">

A wondrous, whirling world of wieners awaits your family and funtime guests.
```
<p>

1 cup enriched flour
<br>
2 tablespoons sugar
<br>
1-1/2 teaspoons baking powder
<br>
1 teaspoon salt
<br>
2/3 cup yellow cornmeal
<br>
2 tablespoons shortening
<br>
1 slightly beaten egg
<br>
3/4 cup milk
<br>
1 pound (8 to 10) frankfurters
<p>
```
Mix together flour, sugar, baking powder, and salt. Stir in cornmeal. Cut in shortening till mixture resembles fine crumbs. Combine egg and milk; add to cornmeal mixture, stirring till well blended.
```
<br>
```
Insert wooden skewer into end of each frankfurter. Spread frankfurters evenly with batter. Fry in deep, hot fat (375°F) until brown,4 to 5 minutes.
```
<br>
```
For garnish, insert ends of skewers into a head of cabbage and serve with catsup and mustard. Makes 4 to 5 servings.
```
</td>
</tr>
</table>
</center>
<p><br>

<center>
<nobr>
```

```
<a href="fresh.html" onMouseover="imgToggle(fresh,'images/rm_nav1b.gif')"
onMouseOut="imgToggle(fresh,'images/rm_nav1a.gif')"><img
src="images/rm_nav1a.gif" name="fresh" border="0" width="84" height="94"
hspace="2" alt="fresh meat"></a>
<a href="locker.html" onMouseover="imgToggle(locker,'images/rm_nav2b.gif')"
onMouseOut="imgToggle(locker,'images/rm_nav2a.gif')"><img
src="images/rm_nav2a.gif" name="locker" border="0" width="51" height="94"
hspace="2" alt="meat locker"></a>
<a href="prime.html" onMouseover="imgToggle(prime,'images/rm_nav3b.gif')"
onMouseOut="imgToggle(prime,'images/rm_nav3a.gif')"><img
src="images/rm_nav3a.gif" name="prime" border="0" width="74" height="94"
hspace="2" alt="newsfinger"></a>
<a href="http://bbs.desert.net/~2/"
onMouseover="imgToggle(smokey,'images/rm_nav4b.gif')"
onMouseOut="imgToggle(smokey,'images/rm_nav4a.gif')"><img
src="images/rm_nav4a.gif" name="smokey" border="0" width="86" height="94"
hspace="2" alt="meat conference"></a>
<a href="buy.html" onMouseover="imgToggle(buy,'images/rm_nav5b.gif')"
onMouseOut="imgToggle(buy,'images/rm_nav5a.gif')"><img
src="images/rm_nav5a.gif" name="buy" border="0" width="81" height="94"
hspace="2" alt="meat-buy products"></a>
<img src="images/rm_nav6c.gif" name="fun" border="0" width="78" height="94"
hspace="2" alt="meat wagon">
<a href="http://weeklywire.com/htbin/pop.pl?p=ww"><img
src="images/rm_wwlogo.gif" border="0" width="64" height="94" hspace="2"
alt="Weekly Wire"></a>
</nobr>
<p>

<a href="http://www.redmeat.com/"><img src="images/copyright.gif" alt="(c)
1997 Max Cannon" width="91" height="16" border="0"></a>
</center>

</body>
</html>
```

Figure 14.10 shows these meaty recipes in their visually unappetizing form. We've left the table borders on so that you can see the page in its layout sections. When we first looked at the old cookbooks that inspired the content for this page we made a tangential observation: The American diet has improved considerably since the 1950s!

FIGURE 14.10

Red Meat internal page with borders on for layout view

SOLITAIRE
CLICK HERE TO PLAY

Surrender to the mind-numbing effects of normalcy?
NOT WHEN THERE'S MEAT TO BE HAD!!
FRIVOLITY, EXCURSIONS INTO THE BIZARRE & GENERALIZED MIRTH...

Johnny Lemonhead! I haven't seen you around since we boiled your Dachshund.

THE JOHNNY LEMONHEAD GAME

Hours of fun, and it doesn't cost a penny! The players take the role of Ted by saying "Johnny Lemonhead! I haven't seen you around since..." and fill in the rest with whatever comes to mind.

For example: "Johnny Lemonhead! I haven't seen you around since we filled your air conditioning unit with salmon."

— Submitted by Chuck Dolce (with Tom & Lori)

FUN WITH MEAT
CULINARY ABOMINATIONS FOR THE INTREPID

JELLIED BEEF MOLD RECIPE -- Submitted by Amy Burnham, Tucson AZ

Meat set in gelatin and waiting in the refrigerator brings peace of mind when company's coming.

1-1/2 pounds boneless chuck beef
1 cup hot water
1 envelope unflavored gelatin
1/3 cup chopped celery
1/4 cup chopped onion
1/4 cup cubed dill pickles
10-1/2 ounce can condensed beef consommé
1/2 teaspoon salt
1/8 teaspoon pepper
12 pimiento-stuffed olives
Strips of pimiento
Parsley
Olives

FIGURE 14.10

Continued

Red Meat internal page with borders on for layout view

Simmer beef in water until tender. Remove meat; put through food chopped using coarse blade. (There should be 2 c. ground beef.)

Cool broth; soften gelatin in 2 tablespoons broth.

Cook celery and onion in remainder of broth until tender, but still slightly firm, about 10 minutes. Drain, save broth. Mix celery, onion and pickles with meat.

Add enough broth to consommé to make 2 cups; heat. Add softened gelatin; stir to dissolve. Pour thin layer of gelatin into 1-1/2 quart loaf pan; chill. To remainder of gelatin mixture add salt, pepper and beef.

Arrange olive slices and pimiento strips in design over gelatin in pan.

Spoon in beef mixture; chill.

To serve, unmold on platter. Garnish with parsley and stuffed olives. Makes 8 servings.

Double the recipe for a crowd.

FRENCH-FRIED WIENERS -- Submitted by Amy Burnham, Tucson AZ

A wondrous, whirling world of wieners awaits your family and funtime guests.

1 cup enriched flour
2 tablespoons sugar
1-1/2 teaspoons baking powder
1 teaspoon salt
2/3 cup yellow cornmeal
2 tablespoons shortening
1 slightly beaten egg
3/4 cup milk
1 pound (8 to 10) frankfurters

Mix together flour, sugar, baking powder, and salt. Stir in cornmeal. Cut in shortening till mixture resembles fine crumbs. Combine egg and milk; add to cornmeal mixture, stirring till well blended. Insert wooden skewer into end of each frankfurter. Spread frankfurters evenly with batter. Fry in deep, hot fat (375°F) until brown, 4 to 5 minutes.

For garnish, insert ends of skewers into a head of cabbage and serve with catsup and mustard. Makes 4 to 5 servings.

fresh meat   meat locker   newsfinger   meat conference   meat buy-products   meat wagon   weekly WIRE

©1997 MAX CANNON

Document: Done

The Weekly Alibi

From quirky Albuquerque, NM comes this upbeat newspaper. The front page is laid out with a basic table design.

```
<!-- Site by DesertNet Designs / Weekly Alibi . sales@desert.net -->

<!-- Web Engineers . Wil Gerken . Nathan Hendler -->
<!-- Art Director . Missy Neal . Amy Burnham -->

<html>
<head>
<title>Weekly Alibi . Contents . <!-- DateStub --></title>
</head>

<body bgcolor="#ffffff" link="#d60017" vlink="#29295a" alink="#000000">

<!-- Begin Top -->

<table width="600" border="0" cellpadding="0" cellspacing="0">
<tr>
<td width="100%" valign="bottom" align="right">
<div align="left">
<img src="http://weeklywire.com/images/spacer.gif" width="20" height="0"
alt="">
<!-- DateStub -->
</div><br>
<img src="../images/cover-tagline.gif" alt="Albuquerque's News &
Entertainment Supersource " width="417" height="37"></td>

<td valign="bottom" align="left">
<img src="../images/cover-logo.gif" width="174" height="85" alt=" Weekly
Alibi"></td>
</tr>
</table>

<!-- End Top -->

<br><p>

<!-- Begin Middle -->
```

```
<table width="600" border="0" cellpadding="0" cellspacing="0">
<tr>
<td valign="top">
<a href="feat1.htm"><img src="cover.gif" alt="" width="177" height="215"
border="0"></a><p><br><p>
<a href="verypers.htm"><img src="../images/cover-personals.gif"
alt="Personals" width="177" height="41" border="0"></a><p>
<a href="http://www.desert.net/alibi/staff/index.htm"><img
src="../images/cover-staffpages.gif" alt="Staff Pages" width="177"
height="47" border="0"></a>
</td>

<td width="25">
<img src="http://weeklywire.com/images/spacer.gif" width="25" height="1">
</td>

<td width="100%" valign="top">

<img src="http://desert.net/alibi/images/cover-feature.gif" alt=""
width="131" height="37"><br>
<blockquote><b><a href="feat1.htm">The Hitchhiker's Guide to Monty
Python</a></b><br>
An interview with the writer of &#34;Hitchhiker's Guide to the Galaxy&#34;
and the director of &#34;The Life of Brian&#34; about their newest
collaboration.<br>
<tt><font size="-1">b y  D e v i n   D .   O '
L e a r y</tt></font></blockquote><br><p>

<img src="http://desert.net/alibi/images/cover-webextra.gif" alt=""
width="131" height="37"><br>
<blockquote><b><a href="webxc.htm">Stargazing in Cyberspace</a></b><br>
Surfing the Web with a guy who can't swim.<br>
<tt><font size="-1">b y  D e v i n   D .   O '
L e a r y</tt></font></blockquote><br><p>

<img src="http://desert.net/alibi/images/cover-film.gif" alt="" width="131"
height="37"><br>
<blockquote><b><a href="film1.htm">The Name Says It All</a></b><br>
```

```
Robin Williams makes a mess in Disney's latest.<br>
<tt><font size="-1">b y  D e v i n   D .   O '
L e a r y</tt></font></blockquote><br><p>

<blockquote>
<a href="feat1.htm">feature</a> | <a href="news.htm">news</a>
| <a href="film.htm">film</a> | <a href="music.htm">music</a> |
<a href="art.htm">art</a> | <a href="food.htm">food</a> |
<a href="comics.htm">comics</a>
</blockquote>

</td>
</tr>
</table>

<!-- End Middle -->

<p>

<!-- Begin Footer -->

<img src="http://weeklywire.com/images/spacer.gif" alt="" width="10"
height="10">
<a href="http://weeklywire.com/htbin/pop.pl?p=ww"><img
src="http://weeklywire.com/ww/images/logo_small.gif" width="50" height="58"
alt="Weekly Wire" border="0"></a><font size=1>   <a
href="http://weeklywire.com/htbin/pop.pl?p=alibi&t=c">&copy; 1996-97 Weekly
Alibi</a> . <a href="http://weeklywire.com/info/">Info Booth</a><br></font>

<!-- End Footer -->

</body>
</html>
```

In Figure 14.11 you can see the layout of the page along with the table structure.
Visit http://www.desert.net/alibi/ for the real-time version!

FIGURE 14.11

*Table layout of
the Weekly Alibi
home page*

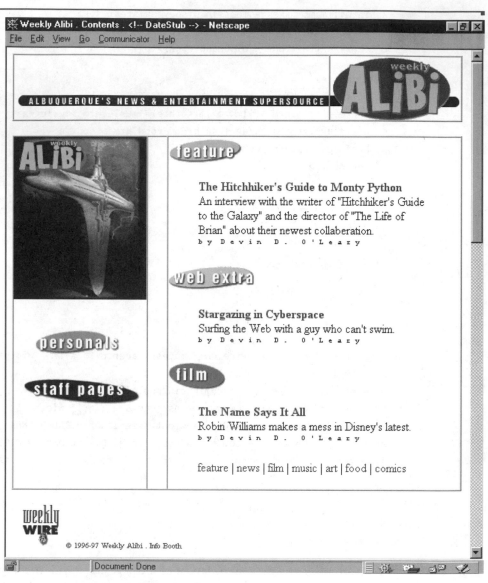

Internal pages for the *Albuquerque Alibi* site use a simple and colorful design, laid out with simple tables that accommodate background graphic, spacing, artwork, navigation media, and advertising. An example of an internal page is shown in Figure 14.12. Again, the borders are on so you can glimpse backstage at the music section's table-based layout.

```
<!-- Publication Processed - 10:58 AM - 11/29/97 -->
<!-- Serial Number - Alibi35763 -->
```

```
<!-- Site by DesertNet Designs / Weekly Alibi . sales@desert.net -->

<!-- Web Engineers . Wil Gerken . Nathan Hendler -->
<!-- Art Director . Missy Neal . Amy Burnham -->

<html>

<head>
<title>Weekly Alibi . Music . November 26 - December 2, 1997</title>
<meta name="keywords" content="Music, Tunes, Local, Live, Garage Band, Punk,
Alternative, Rock, Country, Blues, Acoustic, Solo, Folk, Jazz, Club, Venue,
Stage, Disco, Performance, Show, Concert, Song, Beer, Liquor, Smoke, Michael
Henningsen, Review, Burque, Albuquerque, New Mexico, Southwest, Alibi,
Newsweekly, desert, desertnet, desert net">
<meta name="author" content="wil gerken, nathan hendler, missy neal, amy
burnham">
</head>

<body background="../images/musbak.gif" bgcolor="#ffffff" link="#d60017"
vlink="#29295a" alink="#000000" text="#000000">

<table border="0" cellspacing="0" cellpadding="0" width="600">
<tr>

<td valign="top" align="left" width="65" rowspan="2">
<img src="../images/musv.gif" width="40" height="260" alt="Alibi Music"><br>
<img src="../images/spacer.gif" width="63" height="1">
</td>

<td valign="top" align="left" width="535" colspan="3">
<img src="../images/ad.gif" width="468" height="10"
alt="Advertisement:"><br>
<a href="http://commonwealth.riddler.com/Commonwealth/bin/statthru?246651"
target="_top"><img
src="http://commonwealth.riddler.com/Commonwealth/bin/statdeploy?246651"
height="60" width="460" alt=""></a>
<a href="blue.htm"><img src="../images/tforward.gif" width="58" height="60"
border="0" alt=" Page Forward "></a>
<br>
<img src="../images/spacer.gif" width="1" height="20">
</td>
</tr>

<tr>
```

```
<td valign="top" align="left">
<img src="../images/music.gif" width="150" height="95" hspace="5"
align="right" alt="News">

<font size="6">Week's Worth</font>
<p>
By <i>Michael Henningsen</i><p>
<!-- Begin Story -->
```

First Annual Duke City Songwriters' Showcase: OK, so technically,
nothing can be "first annual." But regardless of simple
semantics, the Dingo Bar is beginning what is intended to become
a regular event on Wednesday, Dec. 3-the Duke City Songwriters'
Showcase. Kimo, Naomi's Ben Hathorne, Jason Riggs and Roger
Jameson will be the featured performers for the debut event, bringing
original style and original music to the stage. My only hope is
that the good intentions behind this event include making it far
more frequent than annual. Like how about weekly, folks?
```
<p>
```

Special Guests: The New Mexico Jazz Workshop is pleased to announce
that season tickets are now available for their 1998 Guest Artist
Series. The concert series, as always, spans the many styles of
jazz and includes performances by many of the top names in the
genre today. Three season ticket packages provide you with the
opportunity to see any combination of artists. Season tickets
are available in limited quantity, and this is your only chance
to select prime seats before the series sells out. Call the New
Mexico Jazz Workshop at 255-9798 for more information, and don't
forget Yule Struttin' Saturday, Dec. 6 at the Albuquerque
Museum featuring Stan Hirsch, Lisa Polisar & Jack Manno and
Encantado.
```
<p>
```

Wouldn't it be Nice?: <i>Musician</i> magazine is currently accepting
entries for its 1998 Best Unsigned Band Competition. The contest
is open to unsigned bands and artists of every genre, and finalists
will be judged by Ani DiFranco, Joe Perry (Aerosmith), Moby, Art
Alexakis (Everclear), Keb' Mo' and Eric Johnson. Twelve winning
bands will be chosen and will be featured in <i>Musician</i> magazine
and appear on the publication's <i>Best Unsigned Band</i> compilation

CD. The grand prize-winning artist or band will also receive a
slew of gear from Yamaha and Fostex valued at more than $10,000.
<p>

Interested parties can obtain more information and an official
entry form by calling (toll free) (888)-SONGS98 or by accessing the
<i>Musician</i> magazine Web site (<a href="http://www.musicianmag.com/bub">
http://www.musicianmag.com/bub</a>).
Entries must be postmarked by Dec. 31, 1997.
<p>

<b>Come All Ye Faithful: </b>89.9 KUNM, for the second consecutive
year, is calling for local bands to record their favorite holiday
tunes (traditional or original) for a compilation to be aired
Sunday, Dec. 21 at 4 p.m. Bands are encouraged to sign up for
a one-hour recording slot at KUNM's studio on Dec. 1, 2 and 3.
Slots are on the hour, from 6:30 to 9:30 each day. Interested
parties may sign up at Wavy Brain. Call Brad Beshaw at 256-3686
for reservations and information.

<!-- End Story -->

<a href="../staff/index.htm"><img src="../images/hat.gif" align="top"
width="30" height="19" border="0" alt="Staff" hspace="5"></a>
<p>

<img src="../images/spacer.gif" width="375" height="1">
</td>

<td valign="top" align="left" width="25">
<img src="../images/spacer.gif" width="23" height="1">
</td>

<td valign="top" align="left" width="135">
<img src="../images/musthis.gif" width="130" height="20" alt="This
Week">

<center>
<font size="1">
November 26 - December 2, 1997
</font>
</center>
<p>

```
<!-- Begin Contents -->
<b><a href="showoff.htm">Showoff</a></b><br>
The Itals at El Rey Theater; Tsunami at the Launchpad; Stereolab at the
Launchpad.<p>

<b><a href="bark.htm">Giving It Their All/ The Joy of Cooking</a></b><br>
Local band reviews.<p>

<b><a href="music.htm">Week's Worth</a></b><br>
Albuquerque music news.<p>

<b><a href="tunes.htm">Tiny Tunes</a></b><br>
Mini-reviews of the freshest disks featuring the patented &#34;Alibi Rating
Scale&#34;.<p>

<b><a href="clublist.htm">Club Calendar</a></b><br>
The definitive list of koolest gigs for the week of <!- IssueDateStub ->.<p>

<b><a href="blue.htm">She's Got It!</a></b><br>
Burque has got the blues.<p>

<!-- End Contents -->
<!-- End Contents -->

<img src="../images/spacer.gif" alt="" width="125" height="1">
</td>
</tr>
</table>

<!-- Begin Menu -->

<center>

<table border="0" cellspacing="0" cellpadding="0">
<tr>

<td valign="top" align="left" width="55" rowspan="2">
<img src="../images/spacer.gif" alt="" width="55" height="1">
</td>

<td valign="bottom" align="center">
<a href="http://desert.net/htbin/mapimage.exe/alibi/11-26-97/nav.map"><img
src="../images/nav.gif" width="263" height="94" border="0" alt="Menu Image
Map" ismap usemap="#Menu"></a>
```

```
<p>

<map name="Menu">
<area shape="rect" coords="0,0,47,47" href="feat1.htm">
<area shape="rect" coords="48,0,97,47" href="news.htm">
<area shape="rect" coords="98,0,144,47" href="film.htm">
<area shape="rect" coords="145,0,192,47" href="music.htm">
<area shape="rect" coords="14,48,58,93" href="art.htm">
<area shape="rect" coords="59,48,109,93" href="food.htm">
<area shape="rect" coords="110,48,156,93" href="comics.htm">
<area shape="rect" coords="193,0,235,93" href="index.htm">
<area shape="rect" coords="157,48,192,93" href="index.htm">
</map>
</td>

<td valign="bottom" align="left">
<!-- NextWeekStub -->
<a href="../11-19-97/music.htm"><img src="../images/lastweek2.gif"
width="48" height="49" border="0" alt=" Last Week "></a><a
href="blue.htm"><img src="../images/pforward.gif" width="47" height="49"
border="0" alt=" Page Forward "></a>
<p>
</td>
</tr>
</table>

</center>

<!-- Begin Footer -->
<img src="../images/spacer.gif" width="55" height="1"><a
href="http://weeklywire.com/htbin/pop.pl?p=ww"><img
src="http://weeklywire.com/ww/images/logo_small.gif" width="50" height="58"
alt="Weekly Wire" border="0"></a><font size="1">   <a
href="http://weeklywire.com/htbin/pop.pl?p=alibi&t=c">&copy; 1996-97 Weekly
Alibi</a><br></font>
<!-- End Footer -->

</body>
</html>
```

FIGURE 14.12

Layout structure of an internal page from the Weekly Alibi

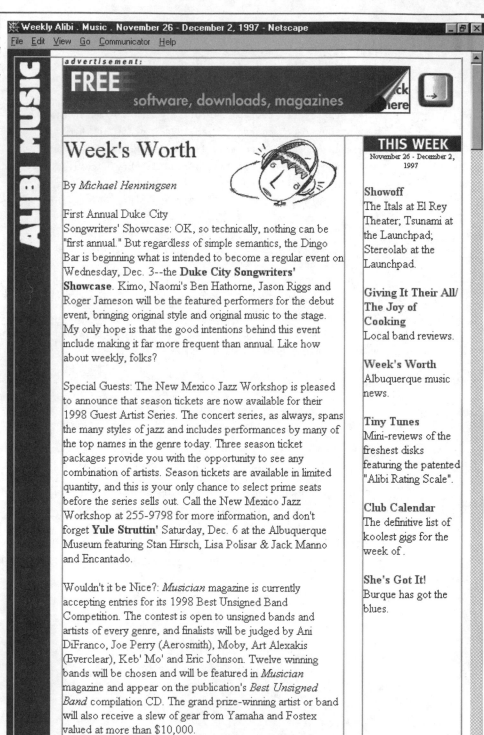

Weekly Alibi . Music . November 26 - December 2, 1997 - Netscape

File   Edit   View   Go   Communicator   Help

Week's Worth

By *Michael Henningsen*

First Annual Duke City Songwriters' Showcase: OK, so technically, nothing can be "first annual." But regardless of simple semantics, the Dingo Bar is beginning what is intended to become a regular event on Wednesday, Dec. 3--the **Duke City Songwriters' Showcase**. Kimo, Naomi's Ben Hathorne, Jason Riggs and Roger Jameson will be the featured performers for the debut event, bringing original style and original music to the stage. My only hope is that the good intentions behind this event include making it far more frequent than annual. Like how about weekly, folks?

Special Guests: The New Mexico Jazz Workshop is pleased to announce that season tickets are now available for their 1998 Guest Artist Series. The concert series, as always, spans the many styles of jazz and includes performances by many of the top names in the genre today. Three season ticket packages provide you with the opportunity to see any combination of artists. Season tickets are available in limited quantity, and this is your only chance to select prime seats before the series sells out. Call the New Mexico Jazz Workshop at 255-9798 for more information, and don't forget **Yule Struttin'** Saturday, Dec. 6 at the Albuquerque Museum featuring Stan Hirsch, Lisa Polisar & Jack Manno and Encantado.

Wouldn't it be Nice?: *Musician* magazine is currently accepting entries for its 1998 Best Unsigned Band Competition. The contest is open to unsigned bands and artists of every genre, and finalists will be judged by Ani DiFranco, Joe Perry (Aerosmith), Moby, Art Alexakis (Everclear), Keb' Mo' and Eric Johnson. Twelve winning bands will be chosen and will be featured in *Musician* magazine and appear on the publication's *Best Unsigned Band* compilation CD. The grand prize-winning artist or band will also receive a slew of gear from Yamaha and Fostex valued at more than $10,000.

THIS WEEK
November 26 - December 2, 1997

Showoff
The Itals at El Rey Theater; Tsunami at the Launchpad; Stereolab at the Launchpad.

Giving It Their All/ The Joy of Cooking
Local band reviews.

Week's Worth
Albuquerque music news.

Tiny Tunes
Mini-reviews of the freshest disks featuring the patented "Alibi Rating Scale".

Club Calendar
The definitive list of koolest gigs for the week of .

She's Got It!
Burque has got the blues.

FIGURE 14.12

Continued

*Layout structure of
an internal page
from The Alibi*

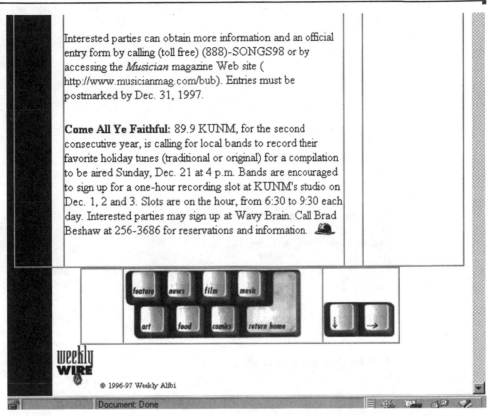

Interested parties can obtain more information and an official entry form by calling (toll free) (888)-SONGS98 or by accessing the *Musician* magazine Web site (http://www.musicianmag.com/bub). Entries must be postmarked by Dec. 31, 1997.

Come All Ye Faithful: 89.9 KUNM, for the second consecutive year, is calling for local bands to record their favorite holiday tunes (traditional or original) for a compilation to be aired Sunday, Dec. 21 at 4 p.m. Bands are encouraged to sign up for a one-hour recording slot at KUNM's studio on Dec. 1, 2 and 3. Slots are on the hour, from 6:30 to 9:30 each day. Interested parties may sign up at Wavy Brain. Call Brad Beshaw at 256-3686 for reservations and information.

© 1996-97 Weekly Alibi

Document: Done

Table Template

Here's a table-based template using a background graphic, content, spacer, and bottom-based navigation. The table template can assist you in creating sites with consistent, strong layouts that can be put to work quickly and with ease.

```
<!-- add your name and e-mail here -->

<html>

<head>
<title>add your site title and page here</title>
</head>

<body add your body colors and background graphic here>
```

```
<table border="0" width="580" cellpadding="10" cellspacing="0">
<tr>

<!--begin left margin-->

<td width="125">

</td>

<td width="25">

<img src="images/clear.gif" width="25" height="1" border="0 alt="spacer">

</td>

<!--begin text area-->

<td valign="top" width="340">

<img src="add your header here" width="x" height="x" border="0" alt="x">
<p>

Add paragraph here
<p>

Add another paragraph here
<p>

Add another paragraph here
<p>

<div align="center">

<!--begin navigation-->

<a href="yourlink1.htm"><img src="yourbutton1.gif" alt="your button
description" width="your button width" height="your button height"
border="0"></a>

<a href="yourlink2.htm"><img src="yourbutton2.gif" alt="your button
description" width="your button width" height="your button height"
border="0"></a>

<a href="yourlink3.htm"><img src="yourbutton3.gif" alt="your button
description" width="your button width" height="your button height"
border="0"></a>
<p>
```

```
<!--begin text navigation-->

<div align="center">
<a href="yourlink1.htm"><img src="yourbutton1.gif" alt="your button
description" width="your button width" height="your button height"
border="0"></a>

<a href="yourlink2.htm"><img src="yourbutton2.gif" alt="your button
description" width="your button width" height="your button height"
border="0"></a>

<a href="yourlink3.htm"><img src="yourbutton3.gif" alt="your button
description" width="your button width" height="your button height"
border="0"></a>
<p>

</div>

<!--begin copyright and mailto-->

<div align="center">

<font size="1">

<i>Copyright &copy; <a href="mailto:youre-mail here">Contact name here</a>,
1997</i>

</div>
</font>
</td>

</tr>
</td>

</table>
</body>
</html>
```

Want to use the left margin for navigation? Simply create buttons or text-based links in the first table cell (Figure 14.13). Or, switch the first cell and the third cell and create a background graphic with a border on the right for a right-based design, as shown in Figure 14.14. As you become more knowledgeable with JavaScript, navigation maps, and other media, you'll have the opportunity to really flex your layout and design muscles.

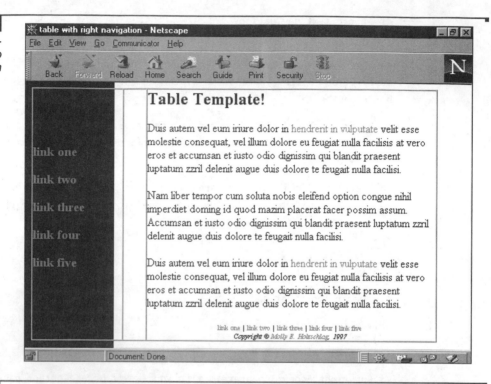

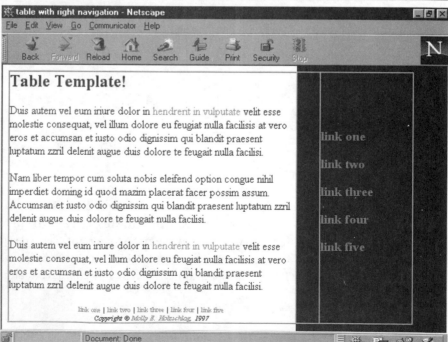

Frame Layouts

Frame-based layouts are especially handy when you want to have a certain part of your interface remain static, and other sections dynamic. Frames, as you learned in Chapter 13, can be bordered or borderless. Examples of each are shown in the following examples.

The Buffalo Exchange

You've seen the Buffalo Exchange site mentioned before, and it's one of the few framed sites that really works well with bordered frames. The site remains fresh and has grown considerably since I first worked on its design in 1996. Buffalo Exchange has done an admirable job of keeping up with seasonal marketing and other advertising techniques, so its site never gets boring (Figure 14.15).

The internal, framed pages of the Buffalo Exchange site are made up of three files. You know this because you see two framed sections, and you know that a framed site requires a unique file for each of the visible frames, plus the control file, known as the frameset.

FIGURE 14.15

The Buffalo Exchange splash page

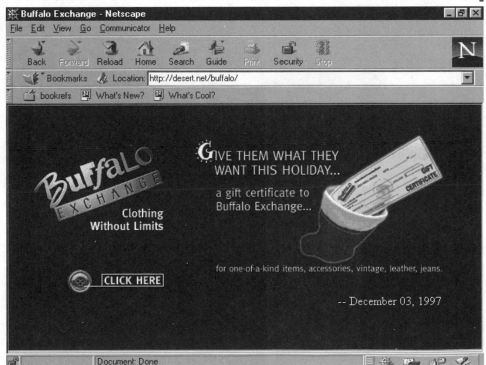

Here's the frameset code:

```
<!-- site by desertnet designs:  sales@desert.net -->
<!-- web engineer: wil gerken, doug floyd -->
<!-- art director:  amy burnham -->
<!-- content provided by Buffalo Exchange -->

<html>

<head>
<title>Buffalo Exchange</title>
<meta  name="description" content="Buffalo Exchange is a pioneering 17-store
resale clothing recycling business which operates directly with the public,
buying, trading, consigning, and, of course, selling good, fashionable
clothing and accessories at fair prices.">
<meta  name="keywords" content="resale, apparel, Levi, jeans, thrift, store,
clothing, consignment, disco, retro, designer, wear, career, casual, shoes,
footwear, environment, ecology, garment, gothic, vintage, fashion, clubwear,
styles, recycling, bargain, trade, cash, buy-sell-trade, accessories,
second-hand, overalls, shopping, re-use, 70s, 60s, 50s, leather, outfits,
rockabilly, dresses, boots, trends, textile, used, costume, buffalo">
</head>

<frameset cols="140, *">

<noframe>

<body background="images/bg.gif" bgcolor="#ffffff" text="#000000"
link="#5d3d2d" vlink="#38251b" alink="#000000">

<blockquote>

<h2>Sorry, your browser doesn't support frames!</h2>

You may view our <a href="what.htm">no frames version</a> or
<a href="http://home.mcom.com/comprod/mirror/index.html">download Netscape
2.0 now</a>.
<p>

<p><br clear="all">
<a href="catalog/index.html"><img src="images/bottombanner.gif" width="389"
height="35" alt="Click here to check out our Off the Beaten Path online
catalog..." border="0"></a>
<p>
```

```
<a href="http://desert.net/htbin/mapimage.exe/buffalo/menubar.map"><img
src="images/menubar.gif" width="401" height="27" border="0" ismap
usemap="#MenuBar"></a>
<p>

<map name="MenuBar">
<area shape="rect" coords="0,0,129,16" href="index.htmlx" target="_parent">
<area shape="rect" coords="130,0,169,16" href="who.htm">
<area shape="rect" coords="170,0,204,16" href="how.htm">
<area shape="rect" coords="205,0,242,16" href="what.htm">
<area shape="rect" coords="243,0,289,16" href="where.htm">
<area shape="rect" coords="290,0,324,16" href="catalog/index.html">
<area shape="rect" coords="325,0,387,16" href="contact.htm">
</map>

<font size="2">
<a href="http://desert.net/designs/" target="_parent">Site by DesertNet
Designs</a><br>
&#169; 1996-1997 Buffalo Exchange<p>
</font>
</center>

<!-- End Footer -->

</body>
</noframe>

<frame src="menu.htm" scrolling="no" marginwidth="0" marginheight="0"
name="menu">
<frame src="how.htm" scrolling="auto" marginwidth="0" marginheight="0"
name="right" noresize>
</frameset>

</html>
```

Of particular interest in the preceding code is the use of the <noframe> tag option, which offers up alternative site viewing opportunities. This is a fine example of accessible, cross-platform design because the design is contemporary but avenues of access are kept open to diverse site visitors.

Here's a look at the left-frame menu code:

```
<!-- site by desertnet designs:  sales@desert.net -->
<!-- web engineer: wil gerken, doug floyd -->
<!-- art director:  amy burnham -->
<!-- content provided by Buffalo Exchange -->

<html>

<body bgcolor="#000000" text="#ffffff">

<center>
<img src="images/spacer.gif" alt="" width="100" height="5"><br>

<a href="menuplay.htm"><img src="images/tv.gif" border="0" width="120"
height="79" alt="TV Slide Show!"></a><br>

<img src="images/buffvis.jpg" alt="Buffalo VIsion" width="118"
height="21"><br>

<a href="menuplay.htm"><img src="images/on.jpg" width="47" height="16"
border="0" alt="Start"></a>
<a href="menustop.htm"><img src="images/off.jpg" width="47" height="16"
border="0" alt="Off"></a>
<p>

<img src="images/menu.gif" border="0" usemap="#Menu" width="118"
height="168" alt="">
</center>

<map name="Menu">
<area shape="rect" coords="0,0,117,23" href="who.htm" target="right">
<area shape="rect" coords="0,24,117,52" href="how.htm" target="right">
<area shape="rect" coords="0,53,117,80" href="what.htm" target="right">
<area shape="rect" coords="0,81,117,109" href="where.htm" target="right">
<area shape="rect" coords="0,110,117,139" href="catalog/index.html"
target="right">
<area shape="rect" coords="0,140,117,167" href="contact.htm" target="right">
</map>

</body>
</html>
```

The menu, when viewed without the frameset, appears centered on the page (see Figure 14.16).

FIGURE 14.16

The menu without the control of the frameset

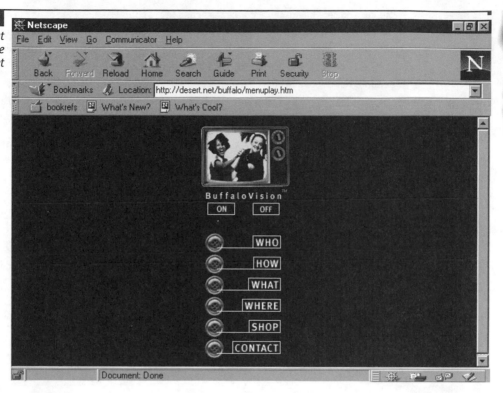

And here's the code for a content page:

```
<!-- site by desertnet designs:  sales@desert.net -->
<!-- web engineer: wil gerken, doug floyd -->
<!-- art director:  amy burnham -->
<!-- content provided by Buffalo Exchange -->

<!-- Begin Header -->

<html>

<head>
<title>Buffalo Exchange</title>
<meta  name="description" content="Buffalo Exchange is a pioneering 17-store
resale clothing recycling business which operates directly with the public,
buying, trading, consigning, and, of course, selling good, fashionable
clothing and accessories at fair prices.">
```

```
<meta   name="keywords" content="resale, apparel, Levi, jeans, thrift, store,
clothing, consignment, disco, retro, designer, wear, career, casual, shoes,
footwear, environment, ecology, garment, gothic, vintage, fashion, clubwear,
styles, recycling, bargain, trade, cash, buy-sell-trade, accessories,
second-hand, overalls, shopping, re-use, 70s, 60s, 50s, leather, outfits,
rockabilly, dresses, boots, trends, textile, used, costume, buffalo">
</head>

<body background="images/bg.gif" bgcolor="#ffffff" text="#000000"
link="#5d3d2d" vlink="#38251b" alink="#000000">

<blockquote>

<!-- End Header -->

<br>
<img src="images/how.gif" alt="How" width="401" height="54" border="0"
usemap="#Header">
<br>

<map name="Header">
<area shape="rect" coords="329,0,386,33" href="index.htmlx"
target="_parent">
</map>

<a href="giftcert.htm"><img src="images/giftcert_ad_holiday.gif" width="379"
height="45" alt="Holiday Gift Certificates Available" border="0"></a>

<p>
<h2><u>How It Works</u></h2>

At Buffalo Exchange we buy all of our used merchandise from customers
who bring it in. We buy all day, and select our inventory from
the best fashions, styles, sizes, fabrics, condition, and function.
<p>

<img src="images/globe_new.jpg" alt="Trade" hspace="10" width="151"
height="199" align="right">

We usually stick to our theme of natural fabrics, but sometimes
we do buy polyester, acetate, lycra, etc. when current style calls.
 We buy our clothing in good condition, without tears or stains.
<p>
```

When we buy outright, we inform the seller of the price at which we will sell the item. For each item purchased, the seller receives a set percentage of our selling price in cash or a larger percentage of our selling price in trade for other items in the store. Percentages can vary from store to store and region to region. There is no waiting for the items to sell before cash or trade is given.
<p>

For those customers who like to savor their trade, we have coupons which can be used at any of our stores at any time. Coupons are written up based on trade, and can not be turned back into cash.
<p>

<img src="images/nightclub.jpg" alt="Trade" hspace="10" width="138" height="216" align="left">

We buy all kinds of clothes -- Levi's, current sportswear, designer items, couture, vintage dresses, jackets, cowboy boots, bowling shirts, jeans, motorcycle jackets, women's suits and career separates, and all kinds of accessories. We buy such a wide range of styles that we don't specialize in any one item. This keeps our prices low, our inventory eclectic, and our customers coming back.
<p>

Our stores attract a loyal following of fashion hounds and bargain hunters because shopping at Buffalo Exchange is not like going into a thrift store and buying somebody's used clothing. Our selection changes hourly and is aimed at fashion-conscious people who appreciate good quality, style, and economy.
<p>

<h2><u>Commonly Asked Questions</u></h2>

Q: "What do you buy?" or sometimes put another way: "Why don't you take any of my stuff?"
<p>

<img src="images/how_retro.jpg" alt="" width="146" height="204" border="0" align="right" hspace="15">

```
<b>A:</b> (We try to train our folks to be tactful and not say things
like, &quot;Because it's out of fashion, ugly, and a terrible color,&quot;
etc.) But the real reason we don't take something is very simple: we don't
think it will sell. This, of course, will vary from location to location,
from season to season, from year to year, and on and on. Buying is not an
exact science. Some buyers will buy something that another buyer will not.
But, in general, there are certain things that we know will sell and others
that we know will not sell.
<p>

<b>Q: When do you buy?</b>
<p>

<b>A:</b> Whenever we are open, we buy. We are a service oriented business.
We are here for our customers, not for our convenience.
<p>
<br>

<h2><u>Choose To Re-Use</u></h2>
<p>

By buying -- selling -- trading clothing at Buffalo Exchange,
you are helping to reduce waste in our landfills.  Although re-use
will not change consumption patterns overnight, individuals are
beginning to realize the devastating impact of garbage.
<p>

<img src="images/recy.gif" alt="buffalo recycled logo" width="130"
height="134" border="0" align="left">

Over 250 million Americans are responsible for close
to 200 million tons of municipal solid waste generated
every year 3 1/2 lbs. of trash per person per day.
<p>

In this Age of Abundance, the idea of re-use is making a
comeback for a better tomorrow.
<p>

Together, by supporting re-use, recycling, and the reduction
of waste, we can protect our environment and the biodiversity that is
essential to our well being &amp; life on earth.
<p>

<!-- Begin Footer -->
```

```
<center>

<font size="2">
Paper manufactured from recycled pulp creates 75% less air pollution than
paper made from whole trees. - <b>Recycle America</b>
<p>
</font>

</blockquote>

<p><br clear="all">
<a href="catalog/index.html"><img src="images/bottombanner.gif" width="389"
height="35" alt="Click here to check out our Off the Beaten Path online
catalog..." border="0"></a>
<p>

<a href="http://desert.net/htbin/mapimage.exe/buffalo/menubar.map"><img
src="images/menubar.gif" width="401" height="27" border="0" ismap
usemap="#MenuBar"></a>
<p>

<map name="MenuBar">
<area shape="rect" coords="0,0,129,16" href="index.htmlx" target="_parent">
<area shape="rect" coords="130,0,169,16" href="who.htm">
<area shape="rect" coords="170,0,204,16" href="how.htm">
<area shape="rect" coords="205,0,242,16" href="what.htm">
<area shape="rect" coords="243,0,289,16" href="where.htm">
<area shape="rect" coords="290,0,324,16" href="catalog/index.html">
<area shape="rect" coords="325,0,387,16" href="contact.htm">
</map>

<font size="2">
<a href="http://desert.net/designs/" target="_parent">Site by DesertNet
Designs</a><br>
&#169; 1996-1997 Buffalo Exchange<p>
</font>
</center>

<!-- End Footer -->

</body>
</html>
```

Figure 14.17 shows the content page without the frame. In Figure 14.18, you can see
the final results when the frameset is controlling the individual pieces of the puzzle.

FIGURE 14.17

Buffalo Exchange content page without the frameset

How It Works

At Buffalo Exchange we buy all of our used merchandise from customers who bring it in. We buy all day, and select our inventory from the best fashions, styles, sizes, fabrics, condition, and function.

We usually stick to our theme of natural fabrics, but sometimes we do buy polyester, acetate, lycra, etc. when current style calls. We buy our clothing in good condition, without tears or stains.

When we buy outright, we inform the seller of the price at which we will sell the item. For each item purchased, the seller receives a set percentage of our selling price in cash or a larger percentage of our selling price in trade for other items in the store. Percentages can vary from store to store and region to region. There is no waiting for the items to sell before cash or trade is given.

Choosing to re-use can mean the world... save money and the planet at Buffalo Exchange

For those customers who like to savor their trade, we have coupons which can be used at any of our stores at any time. Coupons are written up based on trade, and can not be turned back into cash.

We buy all kinds of clothes -- Levi's, current sportswear, designer items, couture, vintage dresses, jackets, cowboy boots, bowling shirts, jeans, motorcycle jackets, women's suits and career separates, and all kinds of accessories. We buy such a wide range of styles that we don't specialize in any one item. This keeps our prices low, our inventory eclectic, and our customers coming back.

Where recycling is always in style

Our stores attract a loyal following of fashion hounds and bargain hunters because shopping at Buffalo Exchange is not like going into a thrift store and buying somebody's used clothing. Our selection changes hourly and is aimed at fashion-conscious people who appreciate good quality, style, and economy.

Commonly Asked Questions

Q: "What do you buy?" or sometimes put another way: "Why don't you take any of my stuff?"

A: (We try to train our folks to be tactful and not say things like, "Because it's out of fashion, ugly, and a terrible color," etc.) But the real reason we don't take something is very simple: we don't think it will sell. This, of course, will vary from location to location, from season to season, from year to year, and on an on. Buying is not an exact science. Some buyers will buy something that another buyer will not. But, in general, there are certain things that we know will sell and others that we know will not sell.

Q: When do you buy?

A: Whenever we are open, we buy. We are a service oriented business. We are here for our customers, not for our convenience.

Choose To Re-Use

By buying - selling - trading clothing at Buffalo Exchange, you are helping to reduce waste in our landfills. Although re-use will not change consumption patterns overnight, individuals are beginning to realize the devastating impact of garbage.

Over 250 million Americans are responsible for close to 200 million tons of municipal solid waste generated every year 3 1/2 lbs. of trash per person per day.

In this Age of Abundance, the idea of re-use is making a comeback for a better tomorrow.

Together, by supporting re-use, recycling, and the reduction of waste, we can protect our environment and the biodiversity that is essential to our well being & life on earth.

At any street corner the feeling of absurdity can strike any man in the face. - **Albert Camus** (1913-60), French-Algerian philosopher, author. *The Myth of Sisyphus,* ch. 1, "Absurd Walls" (1942; tr. 1955).

To check out our "Off the Beaten Path" online catalog ▶ CLICK HERE

BUFFALO EXCHANGE   WHO HOW WHAT WHERE SHOP CONTACT

Site by DesertNet Designs
© 1996-1997 Buffalo Exchange

Document: Done

FIGURE 14.18

*Buffalo Exchange
content page and
menu pages as
viewed through
the frameset*

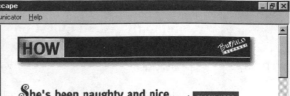

She's been naughty and nice... ▶ [CLICK HERE]
give her a gift certificate from Buffalo Exchange

How It Works

At Buffalo Exchange we buy all of our used merchandise from
customers who bring it in. We buy all day, and select our
inventory from the best fashions, styles, sizes, fabrics, condition,
and function.

We usually stick to our theme of
natural fabrics, but sometimes we do
buy polyester, acetate, lycra, etc.
when current style calls. We buy our
clothing in good condition, without
tears or stains.

When we buy outright, we inform the
seller of the price at which we will
sell the item. For each item
purchased, the seller receives a set
percentage of our selling price in cash or a larger percentage of
our selling price in trade for other items in the store. Percentages
can vary from store to store and region to region. There is no
waiting for the items to sell before cash or trade is given.

**Choosing to re-use
can mean the world...
save money and the planet
at Buffalo Exchange**

For those customers who like to savor their trade, we have
coupons which can be used at any of our stores at any time.
Coupons are written up based on trade, and can not be turned
back into cash.

We buy all kinds of clothes -- Levi's,
current sportswear, designer items,
couture, vintage dresses, jackets,
cowboy boots, bowling shirts, jeans,
motorcycle jackets, women's suits and
career separates, and all kinds of
accessories. We buy such a wide
range of styles that we don't specialize
in any one item. This keeps our prices
low, our inventory eclectic, and our
customers coming back.

**Where recycling
is always in style**

Our stores attract a loyal following of fashion hounds and bargain
hunters because shopping at Buffalo Exchange is not like going
into a thrift store and buying somebody's used clothing. Our
selection changes hourly and is aimed at fashion-conscious
people who appreciate good quality, style, and economy.

FIGURE 14.18

Continued

*Buffalo Exchange
content page and
menu pages as
viewed through
the frameset*

Commonly Asked Questions

Q: "What do you buy?" or sometimes put another way:
"Why don't you take any of my stuff?"

A: (We try to train our folks to be
tactful and not say things like,
"Because it's out of fashion, ugly,
and a terrible color," etc.) But the
real reason we don't take something
is very simple: we don't think it will
sell. This, of course, will vary from
location to location, from season to
season, from year to year, and on
an on. Buying is not an exact
science. Some buyers will buy
something that another buyer will not. But, in general, there are
certain things that we know will sell and others that we know will
not sell.

Q: When do you buy?

A: Whenever we are open, we buy. We are a service oriented
business. We are here for our customers, not for our
convenience.

Choose To Re-Use

By buying - selling - trading clothing at Buffalo Exchange, you are
helping to reduce waste in our landfills. Although re-use will not
change consumption patterns overnight, individuals are beginning
to realize the devastating impact of garbage.

Over 250 million Americans are
responsible for close to 200 million tons of
municipal solid waste generated every year
3 1/2 lbs. of trash per person per day.

In this Age of Abundance, the idea of
re-use is making a comeback for a better
tomorrow.

Together, by supporting re-use, recycling, and the reduction of
waste, we can protect our environment and the biodiversity that is
essential to our well being & life on earth.

The inherent vice of capitalism is the unequal sharing of blessings: the
inherent virtue of socialism is the equal sharing of miseries. - **Winston
Churchill,** 1874-1965.

To check out our "Off the Beaten Path" online catalog CLICK HERE

BUFFALO EXCHANGE   WHO HOW WHAT WHERE SHOP CONTACT

Site by DesertNet Designs
© 1996-1997 Buffalo Exchange

BrainBug

You may have noticed Matt Straznitskas' name on several of the designs in this chapter and elsewhere in *Web by Design*. His early Web acumen led him straight to big-time success with his very own Web design company, cleverly known as BrainBug.

BrainBug's site shows off what can be done with borderless frames in a very sophisticated fashion. Sites such as this one prove that frames have a very important place in layout technology, particularly in their borderless form. The results are seamless design but with advanced interface features. For example, the top-navigation frame is static throughout the site.

Here's a look at the borderless frameset. Look at all the zeroes in the attributes! Also, note the use of the <noframe> option here.

```
<html>
<head>
<!-- Site by BrainBug -->
<!-- http://www.brainbug.com -->
<!-- brainbug@brainbug.com -->
<!-- (860) 278-2200 -->

<!-- Copyright 1997, BrainBug -->

<title>BrainBug: Creativity That Works.</title>

<META name="description" content="BrainBug is a provider of digital media
communications for business.">

<META name="keywords" content="graphic, design, world, wide, web, internet,
advanced, media, digital,
communications, cdrom, print, connectivity, BrainBug, intranet, audio,
marketing, registration, online,
animation, sites">
</head>

<frameset frameborder="0" border="0" framespacing="0" rows="57,*">
<frame src="menu.html" scrolling="no" marginwidth="0" marginheight="0"
name="menu" noresize>
<frame src="index2.html" scrolling="auto" marginwidth="0" marginheight="0"
name="index2" noresize>

</frameset>
```

```
<noframe>
<body bgcolor="#FFFFFF">
<br>
<br>
<br>
<br>
<center><h1>Sorry!</h1>
<h2>You need a frames enabled browser to view this web site properly.<br>
Download one from <a href="http://www.microsoft.com">Microsoft</a> or <a
href="http://www.netscape.com">Netscape</a>.</h2>
</center>
</body>

</noframe>

</html>
```

Here's the top navigation menu:

```
<html>
<head>
<!-- Site by BrainBug -->
<!-- http://www.brainbug.com -->
<!-- brainbug@brainbug.com -->
<!-- (860) 278-2200 -->

<!-- Copyright 1997, BrainBug -->

<title>BrainBug, LLC</title>

<META name="description" content="BrainBug is a provider of digital media
communications for business.">

<META name="keywords" content="graphic, design, world, wide, web, internet,
advanced, media, digital,
communications, cdrom, print, connectivity, BrainBug, intranet, audio,
marketing, registration, online,
animation, sites">
</head>

<body bgcolor="#000000" background="../graphics/menu.jpg" link="#330099"
vlink="#666666">
```

```
<table cellspacing="0" cellpadding="0" border="0" width="600">
<tr>
<td valign="top" width="115">
<a href="../index.html" target="_top"><img src="../graphics/spacer.gif"
border="0" height="47" width="115" alt="BrainBug"></a>
</td>
<td valign="top" width="5">
</td>
<td valign="top" width="90">
<a href="../news/index2.html" target="index2"><img
src="../graphics/spacer.gif" border="0" height="22" width="89"
alt="News"></a>
</td>
<td valign="top" width="5">
</td>
<td valign="top" width="90">
<a href="../aboutus/index2.html" target="index2"><img
src="../graphics/spacer.gif" border="0" height="22" width="89" alt="About
Us"></a>
</td>
<td valign="top" width="5">
</td>
<td valign="top" width="90">
<a href="../services/index2.html" target="index2"><img
src="../graphics/spacer.gif" border="0" height="22" width="89"
alt="Services"></a>
</td>
<td valign="top" width="5">
</td>
<td valign="top" width="90">
<a href="../products/index2.html" target="index2"><img
src="../graphics/spacer.gif" border="0" height="22" width="89"
alt="Products"></a>
</td>
<td valign="top" width="5">
</td>
<td valign="top" width="90">
```

PART

4

Total Control:
Web Page Layout

```
<a href="../portfolio/index2.html" target="index2"><img
src="../graphics/spacer.gif" border="0" height="22" width="89"
alt="Portfolio"></a>
</td>
</tr>
</table>

</body>
</html>
```

Figure 14.19 shows the truth behind the navigation: it's actually a tiled background when viewed outside the frameset.

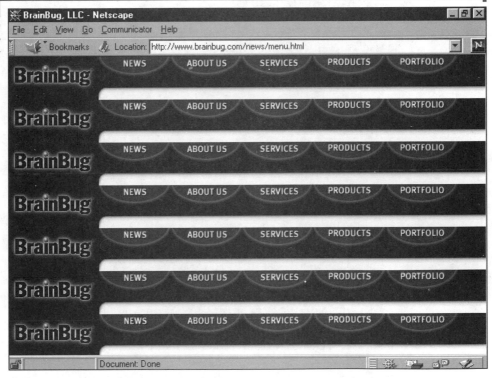

And a content page:

```
<html>
<head>
<!-- Site by BrainBug -->
<!-- http://www.brainbug.com -->
<!-- brainbug@brainbug.com -->
<!-- (860) 278-2200 -->

<!-- Copyright 1997, BrainBug -->

<title>BrainBug: News</title>

<META name="description" content="BrainBug is a provider of digital media
communications for business.">

<META name="keywords" content="graphic, design, world, wide, web, internet,
advanced, media, digital, communications, cdrom, print, connectivity,
BrainBug, intranet, audio, marketing, registration, online, animation,
sites">
</head>

<body bgcolor="#FFFFFF" link="#330099" vlink="#666666">

<table cellspacing="0" cellpadding="0" border="0" width="465">
<tr>
<td width="465" colspan="3" valign="top">

<a href="../index.html" target="_top"><img src="../graphics/sh-bb.gif"
border="0" height="16" width="79" alt="BrainBug"></a><a href="./index2.html"
target="index2"><img src="../graphics/sh-creativity.gif" border="0"
height="16" width="386" alt="Creativity That Works"></a><br>

<a href="./index2.html" target="index2"><img src="../graphics/h-news.gif"
border="0" height="39" width="350" alt="About Us"></a><br>
<font size="4" face="times, serif" color="#330099">
<img src="../graphics/b.gif" height="40" width="33" border="0" alt="B"
align="left">
rainBug is leading the digital revolution with the development of advanced
internet business solutions.
To learn more about BrainBug, read the latest news below and check out the
<a href="../aboutus/index2.html" target="index2">About Us</a>,
<a href="../services/index2.html" target="index2">Services</a>,
```

```html
<a href="../products/index2.html" target="index2">Products</a>, and
<a href="../portfolio/index2.html" target="index2">Portfolio</a> sections of
this web site.</font><br>

</td></tr>

<tr><td valign="top" width="300">
 <br>
<img src="../graphics/spacer.gif" height="1" width="300" border="0"><br>
<img src="../graphics/news.gif" border="0" height="15" width="300"
alt="Latest News"><p>

<a href="../aboutus/employment.html" target="content"><font face="helvetica,
arial" size="3">

<b>BrainBug Seeks A Senior Sales Consultant</b></font></a><br>

<p>BrainBug seeks a creative, highly motivated and internet-savvy sales
professional.  The candidate should have at least 2 to 4 years of
advertising sales experience at the regional or national level, or major
advertising agency sales experience. A strong understanding of Internet
terminology and market research is a must.

<p>Contact Barry Morrow, V.P. Client Services at 860.278.2200, or email <a
href="mailto:barry@brainbug.com">Barry@brainbug.com</a>.

<p><a href="./pr-medspan.html"><font face="helvetica, arial" size="3">
<b>MedSpan Appoints BrainBug and Salius Communications to Develop Its Web
Site</b></font></a><br>

Salius Communications and its technological partner, BrainBug, have been
chosen by
<a href"http://www.medspan.com">
MedSpan, Inc.</a> to provide
strategic planning, copywriting, design and implementation of the managed
care company's Web site.
The Web site will provide a resource for users to find up-to-date
information about
MedSpan and to get other helpful
health-related information.  <br>
```

```
<p>
 <a href="./pr-host.html"><font face="helvetica, arial" size="3">
<b>BrainBug Launches Web Hosting Services</b></font></a><br>

In August, BrainBug, LLC announced it has added Web hosting to
its roster of interactive services. Developed based on expressed client
needs, the service
is built on Windows NT 4.0 and will provide several advantages over
traditional UNIX-based
Web hosting services including the ability to dynamically capture Web page
information into a database.
<p>

<font face="helvetica, arial" size="3"><b>BrainBug's President
to speak at the
<a href="http://www.dci.com/explorer" target="_top">Microsoft Technology &
Business Conference and Exposition.</a></font></b><br>
Matt will be speaking on the advantages of using Dynamic HTML, as well as
demonstrating the basics on cascading style sheets and DHTML on December
3rd, 1997 at the Hynes Convention Center in Boston, MA.  BrainBug will
announce more details in the coming months.
 <p>
<a href="./pressreleases.html"><font size="3" face="helvetica,
arial"><b>More News</b></font></a>
</td>

<td width="25" valign="top">
<img src="../graphics/spacer.gif" height="1" width="25" border="0"><br>
</td>

<td width="140" valign="top">
 <br>

<img src="../graphics/techarticles.gif" border="0" height="43" width="140"
alt="tech">
<font size="2" face="helvetica, arial"><b>CURRENT ARTICLE:</b></font><br>
<a href="./hbj-auction.html"><font size="3" face="helvetica, arial">
<b>Going Once, Going Twice....</b></font></a><br>
Auction sites make their bid for online marketshare.
```

```
<P><a href="./articles.html"><font size="3" face="helvetica,
arial"><b>Article Library</b></a></font><p>

<a href="./books.html" target="content"><img src="../graphics/books.gif"
border="0" height="160" width="140" alt="Books"></a><p>
BrainBug has been widely featured in a number of <a href="./books.html"
target="content">best
selling internet books</a>.</font>
</td>

</tr>
<tr><td width="465" colspan="3">

<hr size="1" noshade>
<a href="http://www.microsoft.com/sitebuilder/" target="_top">
<img src="../graphics/sbn3small.gif" border="0" height="25" width="44"
align="right"></a>
<font size="1" face="helvetica, arial">
<a href="../index.html" target="_top">Home</a> |
<a href="../news/index2.html" target="index2">News</a> |
<a href="../aboutus/index2.html" target="index2">About Us</a> |
<a href="../services/index2.html" target="index2">Services</a> |
<a href="../products/index2.html" target="index2">Products</a> |
<a href="../portfolio/index2.html" target="index2">Portfolio</a> |
<a href="mailto:brainbug@brainbug.com">Email</a> </font><br>
<font size="1" face="times, serif">
&copy;1997 BrainBug, LLC. All Rights Reserved.
</font>

</td>
</tr>

</table>
</body>
</html>
```

Figure 14.20 shows the content page without the frameset. Add the menu page and view it through the frameset, and there you have it—a beautiful layout and design from one of the Web's most talented masters (Figure 14.21).

FIGURE 14.20

BrainBug content page without the frameset

NEWS

BrainBug is leading the digital revolution with the development of advanced internet business solutions. To learn more about BrainBug, read the latest news below and check out the About Us, Services, Products, and Portfolio sections of this web site.

LATEST NEWS

BrainBug Seeks A Senior Sales Consultant

BrainBug seeks a creative, highly motivated and internet-savvy sales professional. The candidate should have at least 2 to 4 years of advertising sales experience at the regional or national level, or major advertising agency sales experience. A strong understanding of Internet terminology and market research is a must.

Contact Barry Morrow, V.P. Client Services at 860.278.2200, or email Barry@brainbug.com.

MedSpan Appoints BrainBug and Salius Communications to Develop Its Web Site

Salius Communications and its technological partner, BrainBug, have been chosen by MedSpan, Inc. to provide strategic planning, copywriting, design and implementation of the managed care company's Web site. The Web site will provide a resource for users to find up-to-date information about MedSpan and to get other helpful health-related information.

BrainBug Launches Web Hosting Services

In August, BrainBug, LLC announced it has added Web hosting to its roster of interactive services. Developed based on expressed client needs, the service is built on Windows NT 4.0 and will provide several advantages over traditional UNIX-based Web hosting services including the ability to dynamically capture Web page information into a database.

BrainBug's President to speak at the Microsoft Technology & Business Conference and Exposition.

Matt will be speaking on the advantages of using Dynamic HTML, as well as demostrating the basics of cascading style sheets and DHTML on December 4th, 1997 at the Hynes Convention Center in Boston, MA.

More News

TECHNOLOGY ARTICLES

CURRENT ARTICLE:
Going Once, Going Twice....
Auction sites make their bid for online marketshare.

Article Library

BOOKS

BrainBug has been widely featured in a number of best selling internet books.

FIGURE 14.21

Add the frameset for a stunning layout

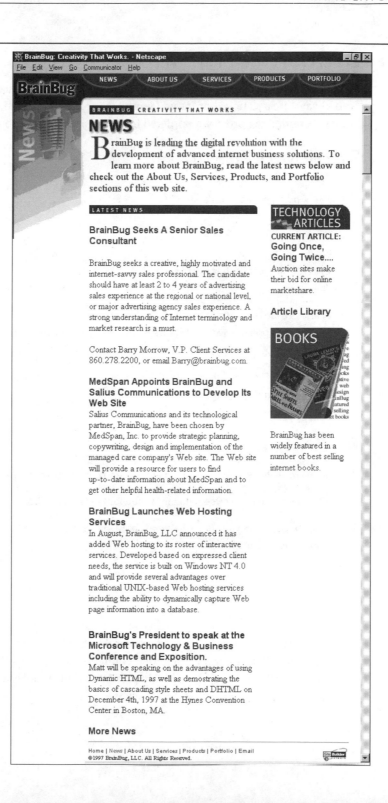

Frameset Template

You now have enough information on how to build the individual pages of a frame; you can always use a standard or framed template for the pages. The next step is to look at frameset templates: one for a bordered frameset, and another for a borderless frameset.

A Bordered Frameset

```
<!-- your comment here -->

<html>

<head>
<title>your title here</title>
</head>

<frameset cols="140, *">
<frame src="menu.htm" scrolling="no" marginwidth="0" marginheight="0"
name="menu">

<frame src="content.htm" scrolling="auto" marginwidth="0" marginheight="0"
name="content" noresize>

</frameset>

<noframe>

<body your body text, links, and graphic information here>

<h2>Sorry, your browser doesn't support frames!</h2>

Add any content you like here—a complete HTML page if you wish, to be viewed
by non-frames browsers

</body>
</noframe>

</html>
```

This frameset gives you two areas: a menu to the left and a content page to the right. If you switch the frame tag order, you'll end up with a right-based menu area. Be sure to check syntax options in Chapter 13 to add columns or rows, or to use attributes to suit individual taste and needs.

A Borderless Frameset

```
<!-- your comment here -->

<html>

<head>
<title>your title here</title>
</head>

<frameset frameborder="0" border="0" framespacing="0" rows="100,*">
<frame src="menu.html" scrolling="no" marginwidth="0" marginheight="0"
name="menu" noresize>
<frame src="content.html" scrolling="auto" marginwidth="0" marginheight="0"
name="content" noresize>

</frameset>

<noframe>

<body your body text, links, and graphic information here>

<h2>Sorry, your browser doesn't support frames!</h2>

Add any content you like here-a complete HTML page if you wish, to be viewed
by non-frames browsers

</body>
</noframe>

</html>
```

As you can see, the major difference in this template is the syntax that gets rid of the border. I really like the noresize and auto scrolling options. Once again, be sure to refer to the frame tag and attribute descriptions in Chapter 13. Also, Appendix A offers an extensive look at HTML tags and attributes. This helpful appendix can be used for quick reference whenever you're working on a site and don't want to search in the chapters.

Next Up

Remember your lessons from Chapters 1 and 2, in which we examined accessibility and HTML as it pertains to the designer? You may have noticed the many comment tags, META tags, and accessibility components that exist in the examples used in this chapter.

I'll be honest and tell you that I have a distinct bias toward the type of code you've seen up to this point. All of the primary designers involved in the sites we've looked at in this chapter come from the same school of thought: We prefer HTML editors over WYSIWYG software, we have specific ideas as to how layout should be approached, and we've all grown up together as Web designers, influencing one another in our work and manner of thinking.

The advantage of getting a glimpse into a distinct style and method is that you get to see how professionals do the job. Also, the design groups and companies governed by the ideas expressed here are each highly successful and well-known for their significant contributions to the field, so that professional knowledge comes with true experience.

But this doesn't mean that what you have learned about layout and technology is the *only* way, nor is it necessarily the *right* way. You will and should define your own road—that's part of what is so exciting and open about the field.

Chapter 15 offers a rigorous overview of layout design. In the next section we'll move on to one of my favorite aspects of Web design—Web graphic technology.

chapter 15

THE DESIGN
STUDIO
WORKSHOP

THE DESIGN STUDIO WORKSHOP

L ayout is the precise placement of elements into a specified area. This area is determined by the medium in which the designer works. In our case, the area is Web space.

In Chapters 9 through 11, we determined that Web space is a commodity and must be used with care. In order to make the experience aesthetically pleasing for visitors as well as technologically logical, you must be able to establish what elements are placed on the page and in what order.

Building on what you've learned in Part IV, in this chapter you'll be testing your mastery with quiz questions culled from the method, technology, and applications of design layout. You'll also have the opportunity to pick up your tools and create a blueprint, choose a technology, and construct layout design in a hands-on fashion.

It's time to examine your knowledge and skills by putting together a comprehensive layout and quizzing your accumulated knowledge.

You'll be testing and assembling:

- Layout planning and the layout sketch

- Layout strategies using standard, tables, and frames-based technology

- Building of a page using ready-made templates

The combination of review, deconstruction, quizzes, and tasks will help you move from apprentice to master of layout applications.

Layout Method: Review

Layout method is the creation of a blueprint for your site's pages. Whether you choose to sketch this blueprint by hand, use a drawing program such as Photoshop, or a desktop publishing application like QuarkXPress, the bottom line is to put the pieces of your page together *before* applying Web technology.

The following layout elements are common to most Web pages:

- Page dimension
- Shape
- Headers
- Text
- Media

Each of these elements has an important role in the design of a Web page which are critical because they build upon one another. Without first knowing something about a given page's dimensions, it's impossible to appropriately apply shape, place headers, design text layout, and integrate media into the overall design.

> *"Good Web page layout is one that enhances the content without over-powering, cluttering, or ignoring it."*
>
> CYNTHIA PENCHINA, Penchina Web Design

Main Concepts

The layout elements are sequentially applied when building a Web site. We'll look at each element and then review methods of sketching the elements.

The Elements

The following are the primary elements necessary to lay out a Web page using the method expressed in this book.

- **Page dimension**—This is the area in which you build your design. It is determined both by the spatial limitations of the Web (see Chapter 11 for space review specifics), and by your own aesthetic sensibilities.

- **Shape**—Beginning with a shape, or shapes, on the empty page enables the designer to deviate from the purely rectangular environment of the Web. This enables you to create interesting layout concepts that are less hindered by space constraints. Furthermore, shapes have powerful psychological significance and can be used to convey specific but subtle messages to site visitors.

- **Headers**—A header creates a linear point of reference on the page. It is from this point that you can further structure the design.
- **Text**—While readability is always an issue, how you lay out text on a page can add to its visual intrigue.
- **Media**—Graphics, inline audio and video, animations, and multimedia applications must be factored into the overall balance of a page's layout.

The Method

Using a sketch pad, Photoshop, or QuarkXPress, first determine your page dimension, and then sequentially add the elements. A full page layout is deconstructed in the next section in order to review the method in detail.

Page Deconstruction

The Workshop's Part Summary page on the Design Studio Web site (*http://www .designstudio.net/workshop/*) was constructed in sequence.

First, I determined that my page would run about two to three screens in length. I've followed a width and height approximation of 595×295 pixels in order to accommodate a 640×480 resolution.

My next step was to shape the page (see Figure 15.1). Straight-forward communication, stability, constancy, and strength were the expressions I wanted to use for this site. And, despite my general observation that rectangles are everywhere on the Web, rectangles express these issues. They are a familiar design easily approached by design novices as well as advanced designers.

FIGURE 15.1

*Shape on the
Design Studio
is defined.*

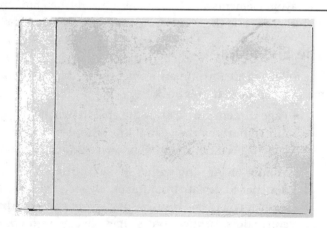

Figure 15.2 shows the sketch of the main header placement for this page; the one selected is a very traditional, familiar header placement in both print and Web-based designs.

> *"I rough out all web pages, including their relationships to one another, in a sketch book first. If I need a unique graphic element, I do rough sketches on paper and then build the images in my software."*
>
> DOUG DAULTON, Web Designer

FIGURE 15.2

Placement of summary header is sketched.

Text is laid out in simple paragraphs, with sub-headers, text navigation, and copyright information where necessary, which you can see sketched out in Figure 15.3.

FIGURE 15.3

Text placement is sketched.

Finally, media is placed, including a right navigation map, and a bottom-based, Flash sub-map (Figure 15.4).

FIGURE 15.4

Media is added to the sketch

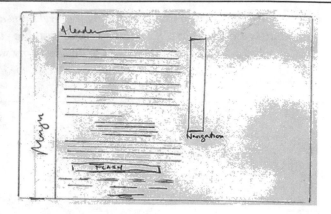

The result is a fairly basic design. No surprises and easy to get to the information—exactly what I desired in this layout.

Layout Method: Quiz

Please answer the following multiple choice questions.

1. Page dimension is:

    a. the dimension of your computer screen

    b. the area in which you design your page

    c. fixed at 640×480 pixels

    d. fixed at 595×295 pixels

2. Shape's role in design:

    a. is logical and emotional

    b. was first demonstrated by Plato

    c. requires the use of all primary shapes, rectangles, circles, and triangles, on a page

    d. requires the precise use of only one shape on a page

3. The triangle expresses:

    a. warmth, community, and wholeness

    b. stability, constancy, and containment

   c. balance, energy, and dynamic movement

   d. all of the above

4. A rectangle can be used to convey a sense of:

   a. warmth, community, and wholeness

   b. stability, constancy, and containment

   c. balance, energy, and dynamic movement

   d. all of the above

5. Circles communicate:

   a. warmth, community, and wholeness

   b. stability, constancy, and containment

   c. balance, energy, and dynamic movement

   d. all of the above

Please answer true or false for the following statements.

6. QuarkXPress can be used to lay out a Web page's design.

7. Readability is second to aesthetics when laying out text.

8. Inclusion of media is considered a step in the *Web by Design* method of layout.

9. Some people use Photoshop to lay out pages, but it isn't a very effective method.

10. Layout is ideally aesthetic as well as practical.

Write out short answers to the following questions.

11. You are designing a site for a major car corporation whose primary market is middle-class, older individuals who are shopping for reliability rather than flash. Which shape would you choose as a dominant one for this company and why?

12. Consider layout method options such as hand-rendering, Photoshop, or a desktop publishing program such as QuarkXPress. Which do you think you would prefer to use? What are some of the advantages and disadvantages to each in terms of your unique working habits?

Answers to the quiz can be found at the end of this chapter and on the Design Studio Web site, `http://www.designstudio.net/workshop/`.

Layout Method: Task

The task is to hand sketch layouts to a variety of concepts.

For this task you will need:

- A pencil
- A sketchpad

Read each scenario and sketch a single page to accommodate the given circumstances. Be adventurous!

OTE

I am going to refrain from providing screen shots or other visual examples in the next few scenarios so as to not impede your creativity.

Scene 1

Your client is a local attorney who wants to expand her personal injury services to the community. Prior advertising campaigns using her voice and face have left her questioning whether a more sophisticated, corporate presence would be a good direction for her Web site.

Determine a general shape, header placement, text layout, and layout of any additional material for her home page. When you are finished, write a short synopsis on your sketch and the rationale behind it.

Scene 2

A national children's toy company has hired you to do a commercial Web site that serves to advertise and sell their toys. Due to a past safety problem with one of their toys, they have embraced a "safety first" message in all of their advertising and communications media.

Sketch out a content page that invokes a sense of community and safety, as well as providing plenty of opportunities for photographic media and descriptions of various toys.

Write a short summary of your choices, and why you made them.

Scene 3

Your design company has been hired by a manufacturer of large-scale weapons, including a variety of warheads. The company wants you to create an extranet that will serve to open communications between the company and its international clientele. Sensitive information including blueprints of certain weapon systems will be included within the extranet content.

The design emphasis is on ease of use, with a sense of stability, reliability, and longevity to express confidence in buyers despite the volatile nature of such weaponry.

Your task is to sketch out an appropriate design. Once you've done this, summarize your approach and design rationale.

 OTE

Some issues challenge designers on a personal or political level. In most cases, the nature of employment is such that you will be required to carry out the task. Challenges of this nature can disturb a designer's ability to look at a given situation as objectively as possible. The idea is to use your skills with as much objectivity as you can despite the nature of a given task.

Layout Technology: Review

With a hands-on understanding of layout methods learned by working through the tasks in the prior section, you are ready to determine what technology is most appropriate to the layout you've designed. These technologies might draw from:

- Standard HTML
- Table-based design concepts
- HTML frames

In some cases, such as a controlled intranet environment, you will want to explore the use of cascading style sheet positioning as a layout approach.

Each of these technologies will serve your needs in terms of the literal application of your layout design.

Main Concepts

The four areas covered in Chapter 13 are conceptually reviewed in this section, including standard layout techniques, table-based applications, frame design, and style sheet positioning. If you have additional concerns, Appendix A or B are excellent references for HTML-related questions or problems.

Standard Layout Techniques

Standard HTML allows you to lay out pages in a simplistic but straightforward manner. Text is balanced and broken into logical sections of text and space. Headers can be text-based or placed in a variety of sensible places such as at the left, center, or right-hand top of a page, with sub-headers added where necessary. Lists assist in drawing out specific concepts and adding additional space to the page.

Media is handled through alignment techniques. Media can be left or right-justified or centered. Text can be forced to either side of a given piece of media, or wrapped around it by using the "floating" technique.

The advantage to standard HTML formatting is its ease of use. It is most appropriately applied to academic-style papers and wherever simplicity is a must. Standard HTML layouts are also extremely accessible to a wide range of browsers.

The disadvantages to standard HTML formatting lie primarily in the limitations. While such layouts can be very effective, they also run the risk of being boring; more complex designs are difficult to achieve without table, frame, or style sheet syntax.

> *"Often amazing breakthroughs happen when you are trying to find a workaround to 'standard' methods. Actually, HTML should not even be tinkered with until the design has been laid out. Sometimes I start with paper. Other times I just jump into Photoshop and start creating concepts."*
>
> ERIC PICARD, Waterworks Interactive

Table-Based Layout

Tables offer the most accessible and flexible formatting options for layout design. The reason is due mostly to the fact that individual table cells and rows offer fixed, specific placement of information. Furthermore, table cells and rows can work together with span, spacing, padding, alignment, and background to come up with a vast number of layout solutions.

Perfect? No. But the advantages are many. Graphics, text, and media can be laid out in simple as well as complex designs, and most common graphical browsers these days support tables.

Tables do have some disadvantages. The precision is better than any common approach to layout control with HTML. Style sheet positioning improves the precision, but they are limited in terms of access. Tables, when poorly written, can confuse designers as well as create problems with text-browser access to a given page.

Frames-Based Layout

Frames, despite their controversial history, have become a very acceptable method of laying out certain sites. The advantage is primarily in creating static sections of interface. If you'd like your navigation to stay fixed throughout the site, for example, frames can be used to do that.

The availability now of borderless frames has made using them more attractive for many designers. They achieve the static option, which is useful in interface design, and they do so without interference to the overall look and feel of the page. Some designers still enjoy the use of visible frames. As you've seen, some very nice sites can be created with them, particularly when the designer understands what he or she is doing.

The major disadvantage to frames is that they make a lot of extra work for the coder, which actually leads to another issue—accessibility. While the <noframe> option does exist, to use it and make the site fully accessible to non-frame browsers takes a significant amount of extra time due to the amount of code and content that must be generated.

Cascading Style Sheet Positioning

HTML 4.0 suggests that designers fully embrace style sheets as a method for adding design elements including layout to their pages. This is a great idea in theory, but in practice it is almost impossible at this point in the Web's history. This is largely due to browser incompatibilities and immature support for the type of style sheet needs that the technology is suggesting. This is especially true with current versions of Netscape 4.0, where style sheet implementation is less than stable. Even Internet Explorer, which supported style sheets as early as its 3.0 release, is unstable when it comes to accurate positioning with style sheets.

However, style sheet positioning is a sensible development and important for designers to follow up with. I heartily recommend you stay on top of this important technology as it will become increasingly important in your day-to-day work.

Page Deconstruction

Here's a look at the code used on the Workshop Part Summary page found on the Design Studio site. Notice that tables and related techniques make up the main layout technology behind the design. You'll also see the placement of media, and the use of standard HTML formatting such as blockquotes to gain margins for the text areas within a long table column.

```
<!-- Site by Molly E. Holzschlag molly@molly.com-->

<html>

<head>
<title>The Design Studio by Molly: Part III Summary</title>
```

```
</head>

<body topmargin="0" bgcolor="#FFFFFF" background="../images/work-bak.gif"
text="#000000" link="#666633" vlink="663300" alink="#FFFFFF">

<table border="0" width="580" cellpadding="0" cellspacing="0">
<tr>
••
<!--begin text area-->

<td valign="top" width="500">

<img src="../images/clear.gif" width="15" height="1" border="0"
alt="spacer">

<img src="../images/sum-hed.gif" width="234" height="69" border="0"
alt="front office header">
<p>

<font face="arial">

<blockquote>

There are three layout chapters in <u>Web by Design</u>, each covering an
aspect of layout theory, technique, and application, as follows:
<p>

<b>Layout Method</b>
<br>

Layout method is the creation of a blueprint for your site's pages. Whether
you choose to sketch this blueprint by hand, use a drawing program such as
Photoshop, or a desktop publishing application like QuarkXPress, the bottom
line is to put the pieces of your page puzzle together before applying Web
technology.
<p>

The following layout elements are common to most Web pages: Page dimension,
shape, headers, text, and media. Each of these elements has an important
role in the design of a Web page. The layout elements are sequentially
applied. Using a sketch pad, Photoshop, or QuarkXPress, you'll first
determine your page dimension, and then sequentially add the elements.
<p>
```

```
<b>Layout Technology</b>
<br>

With a hands-on understanding of layout concepts learned by working through
the tasks in the prior section, you are ready to determine what technology
is most appropriate to the layout you've designed. These technologies might
draw from:
<p>

<ul>

<li>standard HTML
<li>table-based design concepts
<li>HTML frames

</ul>
<p>

In some very exclusive cases such as a controlled intranet environment, you
will want to explore the use of cascading style sheet positioning as a
layout approach.

<b>Application of Layout Design</b>
<br>

The primary concern with application is to understand the way the technology
fits into the method. The deconstruction of Web sites is a great way to gain
a strong understanding of this process. In the task section of the Workshop
you will find a deconstruction exercise. In the resource section of the
Workshop, I've included links to sites that will provide you with many
opportunities to deconstruct--and reconstruct--a range of Web site layouts.

</blockquote>
<p>

<div align="center">

<!--begin ie flash navigation-->

<object classid="clsid:D27CDB6E-AE6D-11cf-96B8-444553540000"
codebase="http://active.macromedia.com/flash2/cabs/swflash.cab#version=2,0,0,0"
border="0" width="316" height="58">

<param name="Movie" value="../images/subnav.swf">
```

```
<param name="Loop" value="False">
<param name="Play" value="True">
<param name="BGColor" value="FFFFFF">
<param name="Quality" value="high">
<param name="Scale" value="Showall">

<!--begin netscape flash navigation-->

<embed src="../images/subnav.swf"
pluginspage="/shockwave/download/index.cgi?P1_Prod_Version=ShockwaveFlash"
type=application/futuresplash width="316" height="58" loop=false
quality=high play=true>

</object>
<br>

<!--begin text navigation-->

<font face="arial" size="1">

[ <a href="../office.htm">front office</a> ]
[ <a href="../planning.htm">planning room</a> ]
[ <a href="../space.htm">space place</a> ]
<br>

[ <a href="../workshop.htm">workshop</a> ]
[ <a href="../color.htm">color lab</a> ]
[ <a href="../media.htm">multimedia center</a> ]
<br>

[ <a href="../index.htm">welcome</a> ]
[ <a href="../contact.htm">contact</a> ]
</font>

</div>
<p>

<!--begin copyright and mailto-->

<div align="center">

<font size="1">

<i>Copyright &copy; <a href="mailto:molly@molly.com">Molly E.
Holzschlag</a>, 1997</i>
```

```
</div>
</font>
</td>

<td width="25">

<img src="../images/clear.gif" width="25" height="1" border="0"
alt="spacer">

</td>

<!--begin navigation column-->

<td valign="top" width="50">

<img src="../images/navmap3.gif" width="50" height="395" border="0"
alt="navigational image map, text navigation below" usemap="#navmap3">

</td>
</tr>
</table>

<!--begin map data-->

<map name="navmap3">
<area shape="rect" coords="0,0,57,46" href="office.htm">
<area shape="rect" coords="0,48,57,98" href="planning.htm">
<area shape="rect" coords="0,100,57,160" href="space.htm">
<area shape="rect" coords="0,162,57,214" href="workshop.htm">
<area shape="rect" coords="0,216,57,275" href="color.htm">
<area shape="rect" coords="0,278,57,330" href="type.htm">
<area shape="rect" coords="0,332,58,393" href="media.htm">
<area shape="default" nohref>
</map>

</body>
</html>
```

Figure 15.5 shows the Workshop Part Summary page as it appears currently; Figure 15.6 turns the table borders on so you can see the underlying table layout.

FIGURE 15.5

*The Workshop Part
Summary page*

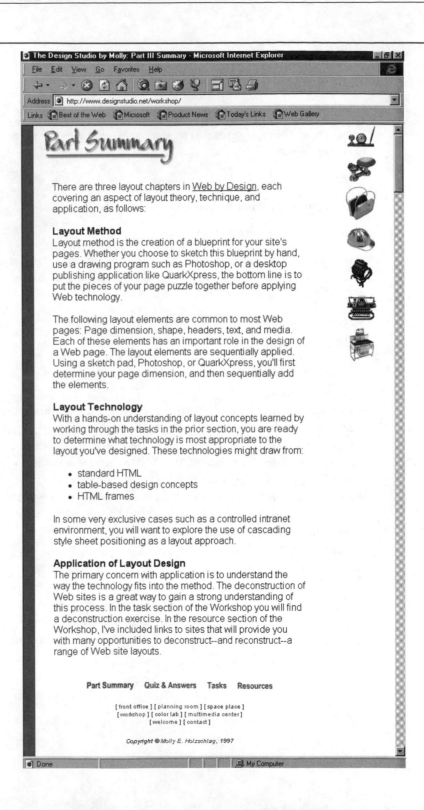

The Design Studio by Molly: Part III Summary - Microsoft Internet Explorer

File   Edit   View   Go   Favorites   Help

Address   http://www.designstudio.net/workshop/

Links   Best of the Web   Microsoft   Product News   Today's Links   Web Gallery

Part Summary

There are three layout chapters in Web by Design, each covering an aspect of layout theory, technique, and application, as follows:

Layout Method
Layout method is the creation of a blueprint for your site's pages. Whether you choose to sketch this blueprint by hand, use a drawing program such as Photoshop, or a desktop publishing application like QuarkXpress, the bottom line is to put the pieces of your page puzzle together before applying Web technology.

The following layout elements are common to most Web pages: Page dimension, shape, headers, text, and media. Each of these elements has an important role in the design of a Web page. The layout elements are sequentially applied. Using a sketch pad, Photoshop, or QuarkXpress, you'll first determine your page dimension, and then sequentially add the elements.

Layout Technology
With a hands-on understanding of layout concepts learned by working through the tasks in the prior section, you are ready to determine what technology is most appropriate to the layout you've designed. These technologies might draw from:

- standard HTML
- table-based design concepts
- HTML frames

In some very exclusive cases such as a controlled intranet environment, you will want to explore the use of cascading style sheet positioning as a layout approach.

Application of Layout Design
The primary concern with application is to understand the way the technology fits into the method. The deconstruction of Web sites is a great way to gain a strong understanding of this process. In the task section of the Workshop you will find a deconstruction exercise. In the resource section of the Workshop, I've included links to sites that will provide you with many opportunities to deconstruct--and reconstruct--a range of Web site layouts.

Part Summary   Quiz & Answers   Tasks   Resources

[front office] [planning room] [space place]
[workshop] [color lab] [multimedia center]
[welcome] [contact]

Copyright © Molly E. Holzschlag, 1997

Done   My Computer

FIGURE 15.6

*The Workshop Part
Summary page with
table borders on*

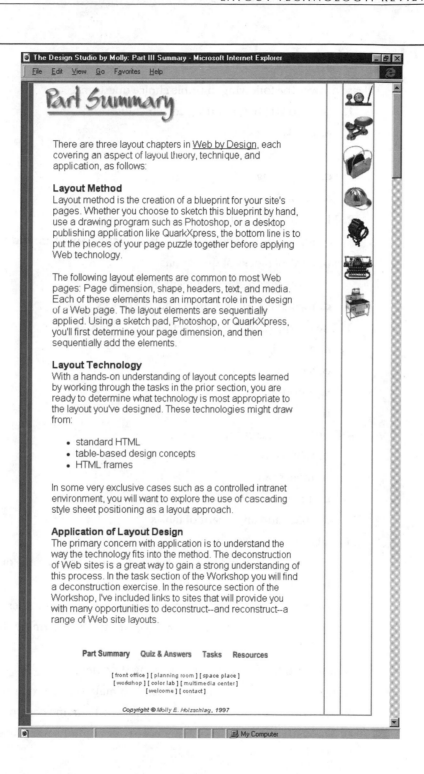

The Design Studio by Molly: Part III Summary - Microsoft Internet Explorer

File   Edit   View   Go   Favorites   Help

Part Summary

There are three layout chapters in <u>Web by Design</u>, each covering an aspect of layout theory, technique, and application, as follows:

Layout Method
Layout method is the creation of a blueprint for your site's pages. Whether you choose to sketch this blueprint by hand, use a drawing program such as Photoshop, or a desktop publishing application like QuarkXpress, the bottom line is to put the pieces of your page puzzle together before applying Web technology.

The following layout elements are common to most Web pages: Page dimension, shape, headers, text, and media. Each of these elements has an important role in the design of a Web page. The layout elements are sequentially applied. Using a sketch pad, Photoshop, or QuarkXpress, you'll first determine your page dimension, and then sequentially add the elements.

Layout Technology
With a hands-on understanding of layout concepts learned by working through the tasks in the prior section, you are ready to determine what technology is most appropriate to the layout you've designed. These technologies might draw from:

- standard HTML
- table-based design concepts
- HTML frames

In some very exclusive cases such as a controlled intranet environment, you will want to explore the use of cascading style sheet positioning as a layout approach.

Application of Layout Design
The primary concern with application is to understand the way the technology fits into the method. The deconstruction of Web sites is a great way to gain a strong understanding of this process. In the task section of the Workshop you will find a deconstruction exercise. In the resource section of the Workshop, I've included links to sites that will provide you with many opportunities to deconstruct--and reconstruct--a range of Web site layouts.

Part Summary   Quiz & Answers   Tasks   Resources

[front office] [planning room] [space place]
[workshop] [color lab] [multimedia center]
[welcome] [contact]

Copyright © Molly E. Holzschlag, 1997

My Computer

Layout Technology: Quiz

Please answer the following multiple choice questions.

1. Standard HTML formatting code includes:

    a. blockquotes

    b. the <br> tag

    c. the <p> tag

    d. all of the above

2. Blockquotes are helpful because they:

    a. format paragraphs with plenty of margin space around them

    b. control blocks of quotations

    c. allow for precise placement of images

    d. format HTML code into readable blocks

3. The   character is known as:

    a. a spacer

    b. a control character

    c. a non-breaking space

    d. an ampersand

4. The <tr> tag controls:

    a. table cells

    b. table rows

    c. all table attributes

    d. space and alignment of tables

5. Colspan and rowspan:

    a. make a series of text span the same width as any table on a page

    b. are HTML tags, not attributes

    c. create spanning from a given cell or row across another cell or row

    d. are attributes used in the blockquote tag to determine the width of the text block

Please answer true or false for the following statements.

6. It takes at least three pages of code to make a page with two or more frames.

7. The control file for a frame's layout is called a frame control.

8. The <noframe> tag allows designers to offer options to browsers that do not support frames.

9. Borderless frames allow for a seamless look.

10. You can set a frame to automatically scroll.

Write out a short answer to the following question.

11. What are your personal feelings on frames? Do you like to use them, or do you find them cumbersome? How do you feel about bordered frames versus borderless frames?

Layout Technology: Task

The task for this section is based on the work you did for the Layout Method task earlier in this chapter.

For each case study that you mocked up, come up with the technology or combination of technologies you would use to design the site.

Then, write a description of why you chose that technology. Could you have selected another? If yes, which one, and describe why that selection would work as an acceptable technology for the study.

Layout Application: Review

Applying layout is joining technology to the design you've created using layout method. After you've studied enough deconstruction of Web sites, as well as the *construction* of them on your own, you'll become quite adept at understanding how to apply layout technologies to your designs.

> *"I do all of my 'artistic' work on the PC. I usually comp potential designs in PhotoShop... print a copy out, and draw all over it with a ruler to envision how the HTML code will actually make it work (if it can). It takes me a while to code all that into Notepad, but it's worth it. I could never start in Notepad and then build around a layout in PhotoShop. It's always the other way around."*
>
> AARON BERTRAND, Desktop Innovations

Let's look again at some of the sites studied in Chapter 14, and some of the highlights from the deconstruction activities.

Main Concepts

The main concepts learned from site deconstruction include:

- **Simplicity can be visually effective and appealing**—Sites such as Penelope's Restaurant, Flagstaff Festival of the Arts, and Dispatch offer a clear sense that simple code and layout can work well for certain types of projects. Despite the similarities in construction, these sites each have an individual look and feel.

- **Table layouts are contemporary in style and offer advanced control options**—A visit to the Wilde Rose Coffee Co. shows the designer that layouts can be playful, yet maintain a semblance of HTML logic. Max Cannon's Red Meat home page is a fine example of using tables to cut through the sinew of graphic layout and make a design visually appetizing (despite the subject matter, of course . . .). Finally, the *Weekly Alibi* demonstrates another contemporary look and feel that uses space with energy and idealism.

- **Frames can be a sophisticated interface design system**—Through both the bordered example of Buffalo Exchange, and the borderless example of BrainBug, we've seen how frames can be used to create tasteful, navigable sites. The lasting impression is that designers can use either the bordered or borderless frame designs without sacrificing design usability and quality.

Page Deconstruction

Yeah, I think it would be overkill to have you deconstruct yet *another* site. But let me encourage you to get online and visit the Design Studio Workshop at `http://www.designstudio.net/workshop/` for links to interesting page layouts. Study these, as well as those that you come across in your daily world. What technologies are used to deliver the layout? Try to guess before looking at the source code.

Layout Application: Quiz

Please answer the following multiple choice questions.

1. Standard HTML applications:

   a. should not be used in today's Web design

   b. can be used effectively for simple, straightforward sites

   c. should only be used when accessibility is a concern

   d. are flexible enough to create advanced design

2. Table layout applications:

   a. are extremely flexible

   b. allow designers to lay out graphics, text, and media with greater precision than standard HTML

   c. are used for the Design Studio site

   d. all of the above

3. Bordered frames:

   a. are cumbersome and should not be used

   b. can be used effectively by a savvy designer

   c. use less total pages of code than borderless frames

   d. none of the above

4. Penelope's home page (`http://www.desert.net/penelopes/`) uses:

   a. standard HTML layout

   b. table-based layout

   c. frame-based layout

   d. none of the above

5. Red Meat's (`http://www.redmeat.com/`) content pages use:

   a. standard HTML layout

   b. table-based layout

   c. frame-based layout

   d. none of the above

Please answer true or false for the following statements.

6. Style sheet positioning is the most precise of layout applications.

7. Most contemporary layouts on the Web use tables because of the flexibility and accessibility of the application.

8. Borderless frames are the hardest application method for designers because of their complexity.

9. Standard layouts are good for academic-style papers published on the Web.

10. Combining layout applications is an accepted practice.

Write out a short answer to the following question.

11. Of the sites deconstructed in Chapter 14, which was your favorite, and why?

Layout Application: Task

To practice the application of layout, take the templates created in Chapter 14 and apply them to the case study design solutions you've worked with in this chapter. You should end up with three (or more, if you decide to try different applications or modifications of the design) layouts based on your own, unique approach.

"I have fallen in love with a whiteboard. I have a whiteboard that can print out what you draw, so you can keep a record of your scribbling. The next step is paper to scale and then a single image of what the site will look like. After that, move to templates and then create to your heart's content."

MATTHEW HALPIN, Designer

Answer Key

The following key provides the correct answers to the quizzes in this chapter.

Layout Method

Multiple Choice

1. The correct answer is B. Page dimension is the area in which you design your page.

2. The correct answer is A. The use of shape in design is both logical and emotional.

3. The correct answer is C. The triangle expresses balance, energy, and dynamic movement.

4. The correct answer is B. Stability, constancy, and containment is expressed through the rectangle.

5. The correct answer is A. Circles convey warmth, community, and wholeness.

True or False

6. True. You can use QuarkXPress to mock up Web page layouts.

7. False. Readability is considered to be of primary importance.

8. True. Inclusion of media is a step in layout method.

9. False. Photoshop can be an extremely effective way of laying out pages.

10. True. Ideally, a layout will be aesthetic as well as practical.

Short Answers

11. Using rectangles in this instance makes a lot of sense as you want to convey stability.

12. This answer is wholly personal, there is no right or wrong answer.

Layout Technology

Multiple Choice

1. The correct answer is D. All of the above are standard HTML formatting codes.

2. The correct answer is A. Blockquotes format paragraphs with margin space.

Continued

3. The correct answer is C. This character is a non-breaking space.

4. The correct answer is B. Table rows are correct.

5. The correct answer is C. Span given cells or rows across other cells or rows.

True or False

6. True. At least three pages of code are required to create a visible framed page.

7. False. The control file for a frame's layout is called a frameset.

8. True. Use the `<noframe>` tag to supply information to browsers that do not support frames.

9. True. Borderless frames create a seamless look.

10. True. You can control whether a frame scrolls or not.

Short Answers

11. This answer is wholly personal, there is no right or wrong answer.

Layout Application

Multiple Choice

1. The correct answer is B. Standard HTML can be used very effectively for straightforward sites.

2. The correct answer is D. Tables are flexible, allow for precision, and are used on the Design Studio site.

3. The correct answer is B. Bordered frames can be used effectively by savvy designers.

4. The correct answer is A. Penelope's uses standard HTML for layout.

5. The correct answer is B. The Red Meat site uses table-based layout.

True or False

6. True. Conceptually, style sheet positioning offers the most precise layout opportunities. However, the lack of browser support prohibits widespread use.

7. True. Tables are the layout method of choice for most designers.

8. False. Borderless frames are not the most difficult application method, style sheets are.

9. True. Most text-heavy documents are best laid out using standard HTML.

10. True. Using a combination of methods to lay out pages is a very accepted practice.

Short Answers

11. This answer is wholly personal, there is no right or wrong answer.

Next Up

Now that you know how to use space and lay out a page, it's time to work with the stuff you'll be using to fill in those spaces—color and graphics.

As with most Web concepts and practices you've learned so far, the Web is a limited place. Yet this limitation can act to serve and refine your skills, because you are challenged to be the best you can be *despite* those limitations. It's a wonderful lesson in many ways—intimidating to some, invigorating for others.

I personally embrace the challenge, as I've found that limitations on the Web as well as in my day-to-day life have helped me to become a more interesting person. In turn, I'm a more interesting designer!

PART V

bright sites: designing with color and graphics

chapter 16

ACHIEVING HIGH-END COLOR

ACHIEVING HIGH-END COLOR

ur very lives depend on light—it nourishes the fruits and vegetables that we eat, our physical bodies, and more. Light goes far beyond human sensory perception. But it is our own sensory perception that takes light and interprets it as color; color is dependent upon light.

This cycle is important because while color in and of itself is not a necessity for survival, it is an important part of our biological, social, and aesthetic worlds. Color is so integrated into our lives that its power goes unnoticed yet is tapped into everyday.

> *" . . . in reality, the objects around us would have no color were it not for light. For without light there is no color."*
>
> PHYLLIS RAE, Color in the Graphic Arts

Visual artists have to understand the subtle power of color in order to harness it and create art with impact. Web designers are no exception, and should take special care to study the lessons that color has to teach us.

This chapter covers a number of color issues that will help Web designers tap into that power, combine it with Web technologies, and use color to design successful Web sites with impact. Some of the topics featured include:

- The subtractive color wheel
- Color principles including hue, value, and intensity
- The sociological and psychological importance of color
- Computers and color

- Additive color
- Web color and safe palettes
- Creating individual site palettes
- Working with HTML to gain color for sites *before* employing graphics

The color reference section in the middle of this book is an important source for the color issues discussed in this chapter. Look over the color reference section now, and then come back to this chapter. You can then refer to it as necessary throughout your reading. The same references are available on the Design Studio Web site, where you can download various materials in graphic format and use them on your own. This will help you visualize the concepts here, and gain an understanding as to the why and how of color techniques.

Color Theory

Color has been studied for centuries, and there are many fine resources describing this evolution. Some of those resources can be found in the objects that make up fine art. Artists must relate to light and color to express their art, and so must you.

OFF line!

After reading the sections on color theory, visit a local art museum or gallery exhibit. Look at the art therein—whether it be painting, sculpture, photography, or mixed-media—and experience how the artist uses color. What kinds of color does the artist use? What do you feel when looking at the piece? Do you notice that your emotional response to the artwork is related to the way color is used? This exercise could (and should) be repeated as often as you like.

Color theory begins with the color wheel and proceeds into a breakdown of how variations of primary colors come into being. The computer environment is somewhat limited in its ability to properly exhibit color, but that is a limitation of technology and not of your ability to work within that technology once you have a good understanding of color theory.

Subtractive Color: Red, Yellow, Blue

The information in this section is based on the study of *Subtractive Color Synthesis*. Subtractive color absorbs, reflects, and transmits light. The synthesis is the process of this color in the natural world. Subtractive color begins with primary colors: red, yellow, and blue. The *subtractive color wheel* (see color wheel in color reference) is made up of a sampling of colors, including the three primary colors, as well as secondary, intermediate, and tertiary colors.

- **Primaries**—All colors are the result of some combination of three colors: red, yellow, and blue. These colors are referred to as *primary*, because they are the first colors to technically exist. Without them, no other color is possible.

- **Secondaries**—The next step is to mix pairs of the primaries together. For example, if you mix red and yellow, you come up with orange. Blue and yellow create green, and purple is created by mixing red with blue. Orange, green, and purple are the *secondary* colors found on the color wheel.

- **Intermediates**—When two primaries are mixed together in a ratio of 2:1, the results are referred to as *intermediate color*. These colors are gradations that lie between the primary and secondary colors.

- **Tertiaries**—Tertiary colors are combinations of primary colors in any other ratio than previously described.

"All colored objects contain pigments. Pigments are chemical or organic substances that possess different sensitivities to light. These sensitivities have the ability to absorb only portions of white light while reflecting others."

PHYLLIS RAE, Color in the Graphic Arts

Remember that this color wheel is based on the tactile world rather than the digital—it's the kind of color wheel you might be familiar with from childhood. It's important for you to gain a sense of how color is created and perceived off of the computer screen before you are introduced to the way it is created on the screen.

OFF line!

Want to get intimate with color? Visit your local art store, and pick up a flat acrylic paint and appropriate paper. If you're not sure what to buy, ask a salesperson for advice—they will know what you're trying to do if you tell them you're learning how to mix color. Buy three small tubes of pure red, yellow, and blue respectively. Add to that a tube each of black and white, and you're good to go! Following the ratio recommendations above, experiment on your own and see what you come up with.

If you have young children, this is an especially fun exercise to get them involved with—and to start them off with a rich appreciation for the colors in their world.

From your basic subtractive color wheel (see the color reference), a range of color components can emerge. The following relate directly to the color wheel.

- **Tints and shades**—Along with primary, secondary, tertiary, and intermediate colors, you can get *tints* by mixing colors with white to lighten, and *shades*, by adding black to a given color to darken it.

- **Similarity, complementary, and contrasts**—Colors that are adjacent to one another on the wheel, such as blue and purple, are considered to be *similar*. *Complementary* colors are those that are opposite on the wheel, such as orange and blue. Finally, *contrast* results from colors that are at least three (depending upon the color wheel you're looking at) colors removed from one another, such as red and green.

Other color components include properties, relationships, and effects.

Properties of Color

I'll admit it—I'm a shopaholic! I love clothing and shoes, and I especially love the color and textures of fabric. I often unwind by going on a shopping spree. I also enjoy looking through fashion catalogs, and one of my most relaxing times (until the credit card comes due, of course) is to sit back with a good catalog and a cup of hot Darjeeling tea.

Wine, chocolate, and peacock are only some of the colors that are in fashion this season. Where do these colors fit into the spectrum? What determines the difference between a navy blue and a peacock blue? What defines cinnamon versus cocoa?

Colors have properties, including hue, value, and saturation (also referred to as *intensity*). These properties are derived from the amount of color and how much light is used in that color.

- **Hue**—Hue is simply the visible difference of one color from another. For example, red is different than green, and purple is different than brown. Whether a color is primary, secondary, intermediate, or tertiary isn't important with regard to hue. Hues can be described as warm or cool.

    - **Warmth**—Hues found in the yellow-to-red range are considered to be *warm*. They emit a sense of heat.

    - **Coolness**—*Cool* colors are those ranging from green to blue. Think of ice blue, or the cool sense of a forest a deep green can inspire.

- **Value**—Chocolate brown is darker than tan, and sky blue is lighter than navy. A color's *value* is defined by the amount of light or dark in that color.

- **Saturation**—Also referred to as *intensity*, you can think of *saturation* as being the brightness of a color. Peacock blue is very bright, whereas navy is rather dull. Similarly, those popular neon lime greens reminiscent of the 1960s are much more intense than a forest green.

OTE

And what about black and white? As many people have heard described, black is all colors combined, and white is lack of color. Similarly, black can be described as absence of light, and white as *being* light. A more technical way to think about black and white is to refer to the properties of hue and saturation—which neither black nor white possess! Why then, are there "shades" of gray? The reason is found in *value*. The amount of light or dark in white or black determines the resulting value of gray (Figure 16.1).

FIGURE 16.1

Black, white, and gray values

Each hue can contain a different value and saturation. When you think of all the variations that are potentially held within each of these properties, you can begin to see that color is much more than meets the eye.

Color Relationships

I'm in a red rage! I'm green with envy over my ex-boyfriend's purple passion for that peaches n' cream blonde beauty he started dating. I'm so blue, in fact, that I've thought about whiting out his name from all of my little black books.

Colors, like people, have relationships with one another. Some, like a good marriage, are harmonious. Others, like the unhappy example in the former paragraph, are discordant. *Harmonious* colors are those that, when combined, foster a sense of peace and relaxation—a light shade of peach, a shade of light green, and a shade of dark green create a harmonious mix. *Discordant* colors are those that cause you to do a double-take—bright yellow and black can be considered discordant.

Color Effects

Beyond properties and relationships, there are special color effects. Silk and satin shine, the inside of a seashell has a multi-colored radiance, and religious imagery seems to be of an almost unworldly light. These effects can be created by artists and designers and can quickly add appeal to a given design.

Color effects include:

- **Luster**—Silk and satin are *lustrous*; they have a shining quality about them. This quality is the visual perception of small areas of light combined with black contrast. While this is achieved naturally with a given fabric's relationship to light, artists can create it by relying on black contrast between the lustrous areas and the background, as in the picture below.

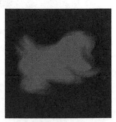

- **Iridescence**—I have a clamshell sitting on my desk. I found it on a New Jersey beach when I was a child. I was undoubtedly fascinated by the many colors inside that changed like a sparkling rainbow as I held it to the light. This is *iridescence* or *opalescence*. A designer can achieve an iridescent effect by using gray in the same areas of luster's black contrast.

- **Luminosity**—This effect is an interesting one—it relies on contrast just like its companions, luster and iridescence. However, *luminosity* is more about delicate light differences. Objects appear luminous when the contrast is very subtle.

PART 5

Bright Sites: Designing with Color and Graphics

- **Transparency**—Plastic wrap is *transparent*—it is clear. Transparent effects cause the eye to perceive the image as being see-through.

- **Chroma**—What happens when colored light hits a colored object? When the winter's white and streaming sun comes through my window and lands on the Saltillo tile on my sun porch, the areas where patches of sun land are lighter than the patches that are shaded. This effect is *chromatic* (chroma means color).

Today's sophisticated graphic programs, such as Photoshop, offer digital methods to achieve a wide range of effects. A Web designer can use Photoshop to create graphics (see Chapter 17) and can apply these effects as appropriate to his or her work.

What Colors Mean

Fast food restaurants often use yellow, red, and orange for their design motifs. Hotel rooms frequently use colors such as brown, tan, or shades of blue or green. A judge's chamber might have rich mahogany wood, green marble, deep maroon leather. Clothing, as I've already noted, can be any color.

The way we use color in our everyday lives—whether we are consciously aware of it or not—is very specific. It's no accident that a person who wishes to remain inconspicuous will choose neutral colors rather than shocking pink, or that a magazine's cover is bright.

Colors have potent psychological impact. This has been proven in many studies. That impact may also be different depending upon an individual's social upbringing. Purple, in the English-speaking western world, is associated with royalty, but in the Islamic world, it is associated with prostitutes! Similarly, black is the color of mourning for most people in the Western world, whereas white denotes mourning in many Eastern cultures.

> *"Color plays a vitally important role in the world in which we live. Color can sway thinking, change actions, and cause reactions."*
>
> J.L. MORGAN, Color Matters

Designers need to be familiar with the general meanings of color, and would do well to check with a client if that client has a specific audience. For example, if you were creating an Islamic online newspaper, knowing about that culture's color associations might keep you out of an unfortunate or embarrassing situation.

The following chart defines the meanings of prominently-used colors—bearing in mind that most readers of this book are from Western, Judeo-Christian cultures.

Color	Significance
Red	Love, passion, heat, flame, feminine power
Green	Fertility, peace, nature, earth
Blue	Truth, clarity, dignity, power
Yellow	Energy, joy, lightness of being
Purple	Royalty, wealth, sophistication
Brown	Masculinity, stability, weight
Black	Death, rebellion, darkness, elegance
White	Light, purity, cleanliness, emptiness

ON line!

Interested in taking a global color survey? Color Matters, an all-about-color Web site, has been cataloging global responses to the psychological responses to color for several years. Visit http://www.lavanet.com/~colorcom/ to participate.

Web Color Technology

Digital delivery of color information is rather different from the way the eye delivers color to the brain, and the way the brain deals with the perception of that color. Computers, in a sense, are finite in their ability to deliver color to the screen, because technology simply cannot achieve the more powerful abilities of tangible nature.

Computer Color: Additive Synthesis

Computers can do a pretty darn good job of dealing with color, but they must approach it from a different mathematical method than in the "real" world. The essence of color technology as defined by the computer is reliant upon three elements: the quality of

PART

5

Bright Sites: Designing
with Color and Graphics

the computer, the computer card, and the computer monitor. If one is substandard, computer color will be substandard.

It's also important to note that computer platforms handle color differently, as you will soon see. Also, what you are looking at color *through* is going to determine the quality of that color. In the case of Web design, it is the browser that limits color significantly; the designer must be well aware of this in order to deftly move through the digital world with strength and consistency.

Additive Color: Red, Green, Blue

But wait, Molly, you just taught me that red, blue, and *yellow* are necessary to create other colors. While this is true in the tactile world, in the digital world, the three primary colors are red, green, and blue referred to as RGB for short.

> *"Additive Color Synthesis is the method of creating color by mixing various proportions of two or three distinct stimulus colors of light."*
>
> JIM SCRUGGS, Author, *Color Theory*

How did this happen? Computer monitors and televisions cannot take paint, like you can, and mix it together to get other colors. They must *add* color based on the RGB system. Additive color is unlike the tangible world's subtractive color. In the RGB world, adding red to green creates yellow! If you did this with paint, pigment, or dye, you'd end up with a dark brown.

RGB values are derived from a method that numerically determines how much red, green, and blue make up the color in question. Each color contains a percentage of red, green, and blue. In Photoshop, you can use the color picker tool and get RGB values immediately (see Figure 16.2).

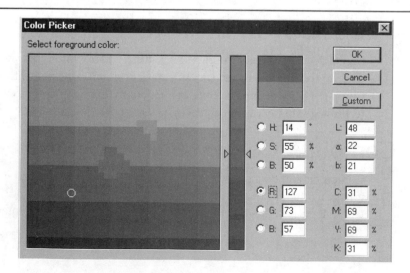

FIGURE 16.2

RGB options in Photoshop

If you turn to the center color reference section you will notice in the four-page safe color palette that each color contains values for red, green, and blue that are listed below the color.

NOTE

What about other color methods, like CMY color? Cyan-magenta-yellow color is used in print, which has specific requirements not immediately necessary for this Web design discussion. Print designers must be familiar with this color method in order to work with computer-to-print color.

Gamma

Of great significance to digital color, and specifically to Web color, is *Gamma*. Gamma is a complex mathematical system that, very simply described, influences the way the information on the computer screen is displayed. In order to display that information with the most accurate color, Gamma must often be corrected to the appropriate numerical value.

Different computer platforms offer different methods of dealing with Gamma correction. Macintosh and SGI machines come with the necessary equipment to perform Gamma correction—so unless your monitor is very old, or there is some malfunction with the system, Macs and SGI machines present color as accurately as possible. This is one reason why designers have preferred Macs, and why SGI machines are frequently used in video and animation production.

The PC, however, offers very little, if any, Gamma correction. Windows 3.1 is the worst perpetrator of the problem due to limitations of color and Gamma information in its code. Windows 95 offers some Gamma correction. PC video cards and monitors can solve the problem *if* they are top-of-the-line products. The better the video card and monitor (and the newer the product is), the better chance at Gamma correction.

To see how effective your computer set up is at dealing with Gamma, you can use a Gamma Measurement Image, as seen in Figure 16.3, which was created by Robert W. Berger of Carnegie Mellon University. You can pull this image up on your screen by visiting the Design Studio Web site.

PART 5

Bright Sites: Designing with Color and Graphics

FIGURE 16.3

Gamma Measurement Image

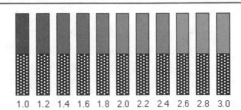

1.0 1.2 1.4 1.6 1.8 2.0 2.2 2.4 2.6 2.8 3.0

When a computer offers little or no Gamma correction, images will appear darker—so much so that a lot of the color that the viewer *should* see goes by misperceived, or completely unseen. This, in turn, means that your beautiful color schemes may not appear beautiful to a significant portion of your audience.

What can you do about this? Some experts claim that you should always work in higher contrasts in order to allow for the best chance of having your color seen. This isn't always realistic, so my recommendation is that you maintain a strong awareness of the problem, and design with high contrast *when you know the audience will require it.*

> *"If the issue is visibility, the answer is contrast. Recent legislation in the United States (the Americans with Disabilities Act), requires high contrasts between light and dark colors on all signage so that the visually disabled can see this information. All computers can deliver high contrasts between light and darks."*
>
> J.L. MORTON, Color Matters

To return to the very first chapter's lessons on accessibility—determine the importance of your viewing audience's need to see the information. If many of your visitors are older, or have known visual problems, a higher contrast design might be in your best interest. Also, for information-rich sites, you may always offer a downloadable or online text version of the site, being sure to use white and black (strong contrast) as the delivery mechanism for that information.

Safe Palettes

A safe palette is a palette containing 216 RGB colors that are going to remain as stable from one browser to another, between platforms, and at different monitor color capacities and resolutions as possible—taking into consideration the effects that problems with Gamma might create.

If colors outside the safe palette are used, many potential Web site visitors will experience *dithering*. This is the process by which the computer puts the color it has available into the color you've called for. Yes, that's right, if you've asked for a soft, pale yellow outside the safe palette, you might end up having visitors who see that color as bright neon!

So why only 216 colors, when many computers can display 256 colors, and most sold today display *millions* of colors?

The answer is "blame it on Microsoft."

When developing the Windows 3.1 Operating System for the PC, Microsoft reserved 40 colors from the original 256 to use as system colors. Since so many visitors to the Web use PCs, the problems stemming from this limitation have been far-reaching.

The second answer is "blame it on Netscape."

Once you're done blaming the problem on Microsoft, you can extend the blame to include Netscape—who developed a 216-color palette *into* the browser!

After you're done enjoying a few minutes sputtering mean words to software developers who have further complicated your life as a Web designer, you can thank several people for figuring out ways of providing solutions to the color problem. The *safe palette* is the result—a color palette that provides the 216 non-dithering colors. You can select from this palette to create your graphics and browser-based color. The color reference in the middle of this book includes a four-page safe color palette.

One such person who helped find a solution to the color issue is Victor S. Engel, who has provided thoughtful insight and useful tools for thousands of designers via his non-dithering Netscape color cube.

ON line!

The cube is viewable at the Design Studio Web site, http://www.design-studio.net/colorlab/ or at Engel's site, http://the-light.com/netcol.html.

Another individual who has done significant work organizing and distributing safe palette tools is Lynda Weinman. Weinman is a designer and author whose contributions to Web graphic design technology are vast and important.

ON line!

Visit Lynda Weinman at her Web site, http://www.lynda.com/. You'll find information on many aspects of Web graphic design, including a great deal of color information.

Photoshop 4.0 users are in luck—a safe palette is built right into the program. Those with other versions of Photoshop can transfer a safe palette and install it right into the program using a color lookup table (CLUT) provided by Weinman. You can find the CLUT and other color resources on the Design Studio site, http://designstudio.net/colorlab/.

RGB to Hexadecimal

In order to translate RGB color values into a system that HTML understands, you will have to convert the RGB value to *hexadecimal*.

Hexadecimal is the base sixteen number system, which consists of the numerals 0-15 and the letters A-F. A byte (8 bits) can be represented using two hexadecimal characters, which make any combination of binary information less cumbersome to understand. In relation to Web color, hexadecimal values *always* appear with six characters. For example, a hexadecimal value will look like this: "FFCCFF."

You can find the hexadecimal value of any color on your own by using a scientific calculator. Those individuals using Windows can access the scientific calculator right on their computer, as shown in Figure 16.4. Scientific calculators are those with more extended applications, such as offering binary and hexadecimal numeric systems within them. In Windows, simply select Accessories ➤ Calculator. Under View, you'll find the Scientific option. Other readers might have a scientific calculator on their desk, or one can be purchased inexpensively at any office supply store.

FIGURE 16.4

Using the scientific calculator in Windows 95

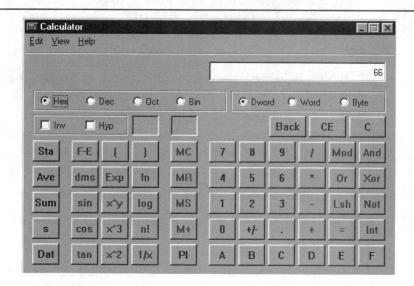

To find this value, you must first know the RGB values for a color. You can find out these values in a program like Photoshop. Pass your cursor over any color in any image you have open in Photoshop. If you select Window ➤ Show Info, the Info box will display the individual red, green, and blue values of the color in the form of numbers.

Figure 16.5 shows you this Info box as it appears in Photoshop. Simply enter each of the RGB values into the scientific calculator—one color at a time (red value first, and so forth). On the calculator, switch to "Hex." The calculator will then give you an alphanumeric or numeric combination for the corresponding color value.

FIGURE 16.5

RGB information in Photoshop

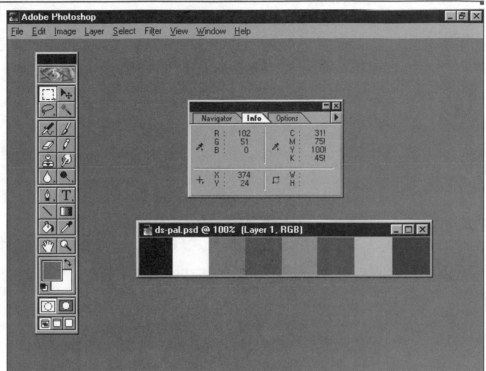

Say you have a palette including a mid-gray. The red value is 153, as are the green and blue values. The RGB value is then 153 153 153. Enter these into the calculator and the result of the RGB-to-hexadecimal conversion for the mid-gray color is: "999999." You should always end up with a total of six characters. Different colors will get different combinations, some with all the same numeric values, others in pairs, such as "CC9900."

NOTE

A "0" for a red, green, or blue value is going to be written as "00."

ONline!

Want to get RGB-to-hex values online? There are some fun and informative sites that offer this service, and here are a few for you to visit.

- **Beach RaT:** http://www.novalink.com/hex/
- **Russ's RGB to Hex Converter:** http://www.ecn.bgu.edu/cgi/users/mureg3/ tutorial/rgb-hex.scgi
- **Color Center:** http://www.hidaho.com/colorcenter/cc.html

Bear in mind that you still must understand the safe palette issue in order to use most online converters. They are paying attention to a broad-spectrum palette, not necessarily a safe one.

You'll use hexadecimal values in the next section, as you learn how to code HTML to achieve browser-based color.

Browser-Based Color Techniques

Fast load time without sacrificing aesthetic appeal should be every Web designer's goal. When you understand how color in the Web medium works, you can apply HTML to control those colors. Your creations will be rich and colorful, achieving energy and a vibrant look *before* a graphic is ever used. *Browser-based color* takes advantage of all of the color information residing on the client-side and never requires the browser to query the server.

Designers should rely on browser-based colors as much as possible. This can be done using the simple techniques to create background and link colors in the following discussions. The primary idea is to help you move color away from graphic images that take time to download.

This is not to say that graphics won't play a role in your design—of course they will. But with proper planning and an understanding of when and how to use safe color, you'll be able to add graphics to your already attractive sites with less concern about load times. Movement toward browser-based colors will free you to use your allotment of downloadable files for truly necessary, higher-quality graphics. This is a very effective way of adding a sense of professional style to your work.

Individual Palettes

When planning your site's visual appearance you'll want to begin by selecting an individual color palette for that site. You will then choose HTML-based background colors, text colors, link colors—as well as the colors you'll use within graphics. Your color selections for a specific site should be drawn from your knowledge of the audience, the subject matter, and the client's desires. Remember from the earlier discussion that color communicates emotion, so build your palette with this issue in mind.

A corporate Web site is going to have a distinctly different individual color palette than an entertainment-oriented site. Going back to the earlier lesson on color, a corporate site is going to look for a harmonious scheme, with pleasing, calming colors. An entertainment site might enjoy bolder use of color, including subtractive primaries—yellow, blue, and red.

The Design Studio Web site uses the contrast of black and white with a calming influence created by the palettes tertiary colors. I created the Design Studio's individual palette in Photoshop, and saved it as a Photoshop file in order to maintain the integrity of the palette. Also, I made certain I cataloged the RGB and hexadecimal values for each of my colors.

Design Studio Individual Palette Reference:

PART 5 — Bright Sites: Designing with Color and Graphics

Color	RGB Value	Hexadecimal Value
Black	000	000000
White	255, 255, 255	FFFFFF
Medium Olive	153, 153, 102	999966
Rust	153, 102, 0	996600
Peach	204, 153, 102	CC9966
Dark Olive	102, 102, 51	999933
Light Olive	204, 204, 153	CCCC99
Brick	102, 51, 0	993300

This information comes in very handy when I need to make updates or changes. Web designers should create a cataloging system as it will help to keep site information in order, and available for future reference.

Individual palette examples can be found in the color reference section at the center of this book. Use these palettes for inspiration in your own design work, or as jumping-off places to create your own unique palettes based on the safe, 216 non-dithering colors.

HTML and Browser-Based Color

In order to achieve browser-based color, use your individual palette as a guide. You'll be selecting these colors to prepare your site. It is in the HTML code that you can get maximum color control, as the browser interprets the hexadecimal information quickly and efficiently.

OTE

> Designers typically use standard HTML to achieve color effects. The HTML 4.0 standard, however, considers the <body> tag attributes—where much of browser-based color begins—to be deprecated in favor of cascading style sheets. For this reason, I'm including style sheet examples as well as standards that fit the HTML 3.2 publication.

You'll want to use hexadecimal values to design creative color combinations with backgrounds, links, and text. The most basic, and immediate application for designers is found within the HTML <body> tag, or the cascading style sheet BODY: element, where you can define backgrounds, text, and link styles. You can also use color in table cell backgrounds and, using style sheets, you can put color in almost any logical place, such as behind text, or as a backdrop for a given paragraph.

HTML 3.2 Methods

The <body> tag allows for the following color attributes:

bgcolor="x"   This value in hex argues the background color of the entire page.

text="x"   The text argument creates the color for all standard, non-linked text on the page.

link="x"   The color entered here will appear wherever you have linked text.

vlink="x"   A visited link will appear in this color

alink="x"   An *active* link—one that is in the process of being clicked, will appear in the color you argue for here.

A <body> tag with these attributes appears as follows. Simply place the hexadecimal value into the quote field. Begin each individual attribute with the "#" sign:

```
<body bgcolor="#000000" text="#FFFFFF" link="#CCCCCC" vlink="#999999"
alink="#666666">
```

Figure 16.6 shows the results.

FIGURE 16.6

HTML and hex colors create this gray-scale page

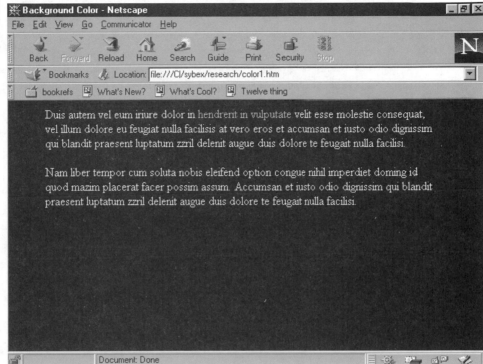

 line!

An excellent article on color by Dmitry Kirsanov can be found at http://www.webreference.com/dlab/15704/.

 I P

You may decide to use a background graphic on your page, in which case you will use the background="url" argument within the above string. This alerts the browser to load the graphic from the location specified. If you're using a background graphic, I highly recommend including a background color argument as well. This way your background color will load instantly, and your graphic will then load over that color. The end product is less jarring and creates a cohesive visual effect. For more information on creating background graphics, visit Chapter 17.

PART
5

Bright Sites: Designing with Color and Graphics

In this example, I've used the same color selections, added a background graphic, and set up a table to control the layout:

```
<html>

<head>
<title>Background Color w/ Graphic</title>
</head>

<body bgcolor="#FFFFFF" text="#000000" link="#CCCCCC" vlink="#666666"
alink="#999999" background="bak.jpg">

<table border="0" cellpadding="10" cellspacing="0" width="595">
<tr>

<td valign="middle" width="200">

<a href="about.htm">about us</a>
<p>

<a href="catalog.htm">catalog</a>
<p>

<a href="contact.htm">contact</a>

</td>

<td width="385">

<h2>Duis!</h2>
Duis autem vel eum iriure dolor in <a href="dummy.htm">hendrerit in
vulputate</a> velit esse molestie consequat, vel illum dolore eu feugiat
nulla facilisis at vero eros et accumsan et iusto odio dignissim qui blandit
praesent luptatum zzril delenit augue duis dolore te feugait nulla facilisi.
<p>

Nam liber tempor <b>cum soluta nobis</b> eleifend option congue nihil
imperdiet doming id quod mazim placerat facer possim assum. Accumsan et
iusto odio dignissim qui blandit praesent luptatum zzril delenit augue duis
dolore te feugait nulla facilisi.
<p>

Duis autem vel eum iriure dolor in hendrerit in vulputate velit esse
molestie consequat, vel <a href="dummy.htm">illum dolore eu feugiat</a>
nulla facilisis at vero eros et accumsan et iusto odio dignissim qui
<i>blandit praesent</i> luptatum zzril delenit augue duis dolore te feugait
nulla facilisi.
```

```
</td>
</tr>
</table>

</body>
</html>
```

The results of this effect can be seen in Figure 16.7.

FIGURE 16.7

*A background
graphic has been
added in this
example*

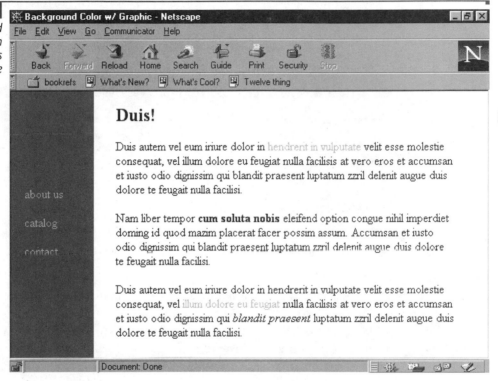

OTE

Some of you might have seen HTML color attributes that use the name of the color
rather than the hex value: `<body bgcolor="red" text="white" link="yellow" vlink=
"green">`. This method was introduced by Microsoft's Internet Explorer browser and is
compatible with some versions of other browsers. I suggest avoiding this technique. It's
not a standard or stable method of ensuring as accurate color as possible across platforms and browsers. It's also limited, and if you want to use colors from the complete
216 color safe palette, you'll end up having combinations of color names and hexadecimal values. In the end, this looks inconsistent and therefore unprofessional.

In this example, the graphic has been removed, and background color has been added to the left table cell:

```
<html>

<head>
<title>Background with Table Cell Color</title>
</head>

<body bgcolor="#FFFFFF" text="#000000" link="#CCCCCC" vlink="#666666"
alink="#999999">

<table border="0" cellpadding="10" cellspacing="10" width="595">
<tr>

<td valign="middle" width="200" bgcolor="#999999">

<a href="about.htm">about us</a>
<p>

<a href="catalog.htm">catalog</a>
<p>

<a href="contact.htm">contact</a>
</td>

<td width="385">

<h2>Duis!</h2>
Duis autem vel eum iriure dolor in <a href="dummy.htm">hendrerit in
vulputate</a> velit esse molestie consequat, vel illum dolore eu feugiat
nulla facilisis at vero eros et accumsan et iusto odio dignissim qui blandit
praesent luptatum zzril delenit augue duis dolore te feugait nulla facilisi.
<p>

Nam liber tempor <b>cum soluta nobis</b> eleifend option congue nihil
imperdiet doming id quod mazim placerat facer possim assum. Accumsan et
iusto odio dignissim qui blandit praesent luptatum zzril delenit augue duis
dolore te feugait nulla facilisi.
<p>

Duis autem vel eum iriure dolor in hendrerit in vulputate velit esse
molestie consequat, vel <a href="dummy.htm">illum dolore eu feugiat</a>
nulla facilisis at vero eros et accumsan et iusto odio dignissim qui
<i>blandit praesent</i> luptatum zzril delenit augue duis dolore te feugait
nulla facilisi.
```

```
</td>
</tr>
</table>

</body>
</html>
```

Figure 16.8 shows the grayscale design resulting from this syntax.

FIGURE 16.8

Table background color

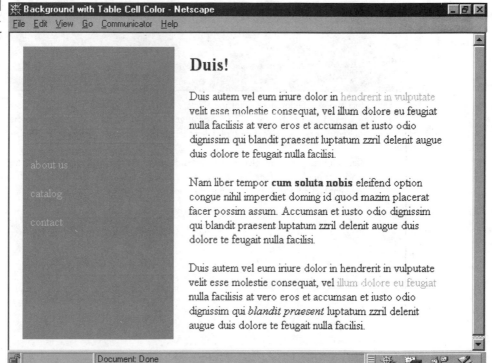

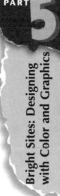

HTML 4.0 Method: Style Sheets

As introduced in Chapter 9, cascading style sheets are one way to control layout and design on the Web. In this case, style sheets can be used to control body background color, text color, and link colors.

To create the syntax mimicking the HTML 3.2 standard above with style sheets, use the following simplified syntax:

```
<style>
BODY {background: #FFFFFF; color: #000000}
A {color: #CCCCCC}
</style>
```

Figure 16.9 shows an HTML page with the style above applied.

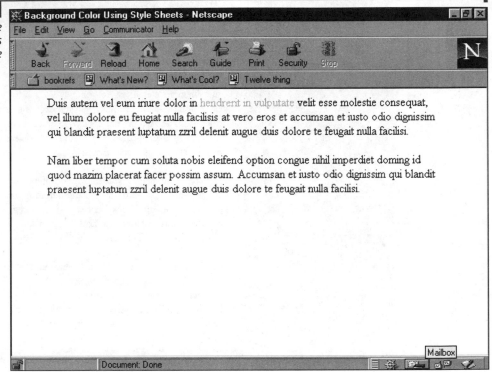

FIGURE 16.9

Style sheets create the color in this example

 OTE

There aren't style sheet standard methods for calling on visited or active links. *Pseudo-classes* appear in the style sheet literature to achieve this, but you should test them before use: A.link, A.visited, A.active.

To add the background graphic, place the URL into the background element string:

```
BODY {background: #FFFFFF url="images/bak.gif"; color: #000000}
```

Style can be used to enhance individual pieces of text, which you can see in Figure 16.10.

```
<span style="color: #CCCCCC; background: #FFFFFF">Colorful Me!</span>
```

Using the span tag, I've added style to a small block of text.

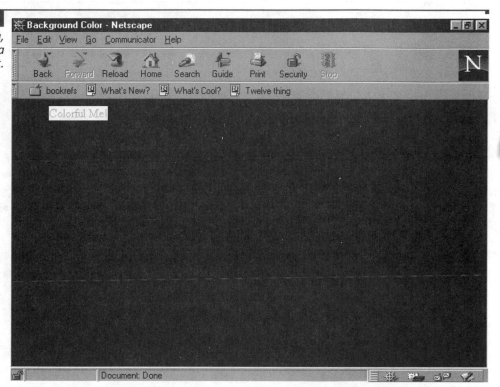

You can also use style as a backdrop for a complete paragraph, which is shown in Figure 16.11.

```
<p style="background: #666666">
Duis autem vel eum iriure dolor in <a href="dummy.htm">hendrerit in
vulputate</a> velit esse molestie consequat, vel illum dolore eu feugiat
nulla facilis at vero eros et accumsan et iusto odio dignissim qui blandit
praesent luptatum zzril delenit augue duis dolore te feugait nulla facilisi.
</p>

<p>
```

```
Nam liber tempor <b>cum soluta nobis</b> eleifend option congue nihil
imperdiet doming id quod mazim placerat facer possim assum. Accumsan et
iusto odio dignissim qui blandit praesent luptatum zzril delenit augue duis
dolore te feugait nulla facilisi.
</p>
```

FIGURE 16.11

Inline style can be used to highlight a complete paragraph

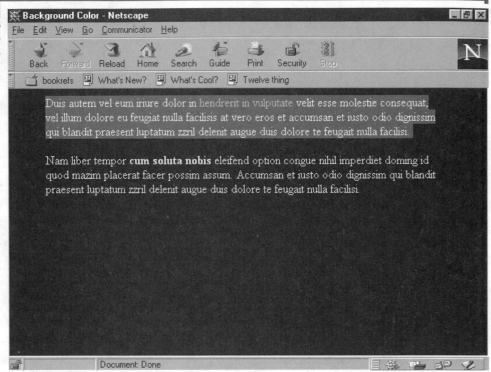

With these examples, you can get a glimpse at how style sheets can be very power-ful design tools—a great deal of information can be packed into them, easing up on the HTML. However, as mentioned countless times throughout this book, their use is limited by browser technology and distribution issues.

Using Unsafe Color

There are times when a designer will want to stray outside the safe palette. While I recommend using the safe palette whenever possible, it is restrictive because it has so few colors available. Designers might naturally become frustrated and instances in which you can deviate from the safe palette do exist.

- **You have a good idea that your audience is sophisticated in terms of their end-user technology.** A good example of this might be with intranet applications. When you know the type of computers, browsers, and monitors the majority of your audience uses, you have much more flexibility in terms of color choice. If most people are accessing your pages with high-end browsers and monitors, by all means use color as you see fit!

- **If you're less certain about your audience, but still interested in using unsafe color, test the colors for dithering at lower resolutions.** To do this, set your monitor resolution to 256 colors. If the color dithers (moves to the closest color within the system palette) you may find your soft yellow becomes glowing neon. This is not going to make you—or your client—too happy. Ideally, you'll also want to test your work on several other computers at a variety of resolutions with different browsers. If your results are stable enough to suit your tastes, you can feel somewhat confident that the colors will look good.

Next Up

Now that you're all colorful and bright, you're ready to think about adding graphics to your pages. You have developed strong concepts regarding spatial relationships and layout design, and you have been introduced to color theory and practice. It's time to study graphic technology and technique. Combined with the ideas learned in this, and previous chapters, you're well on your way to creating well-polished designs.

PART 5

Bright Sites: Designing with Color and Graphics

chapter 17

WEB GRAPHIC
TECHNOLOGY

WEB GRAPHIC TECHNOLOGY

C onfounding to some, challenging to others, Web graphics demand a precise and knowing hand. Plenty of myths surround the issue, and poor practices keep the Web looking less than slick.

Whether you come from a design background or are just learning how to create Web graphics, there is no reason not to demand the best from your Web site's look.

The goal is to create aesthetically pleasing, content-rich sites that load with speed. But how do you deliver this given the diversity of *bandwidth* that exists? Bandwidth refers to the amount of literal space available to transmit data. Connections can range in speed from the slower 14.4 modems to T1 lines common on many corporate desktops, to the broad-band cable modems that are cropping up around the world for relatively affordable prices.

The reason speed influences Web graphics is because the browser must have a short conversation, known as a *query*, with the Web server where the graphics reside. This query is essentially your HTML page saying "Yo, server! I need a graphic called `molly.jpg` from the images and I need you to send it now." The server looks for the file, delivers it, and your HTML code determines where and how to place it within your layout.

Web designers are typically forced to conserve bandwidth for those on a slower Net connection by keeping file sizes to a minimum. Unfortunately, many designers are not aware that there are techniques that can spare the loss of quality resulting from their efforts to meet low bandwidth demands. This sacrifice is due more to a lack of careful selection, optimization, and proper sizing and layout than the true limitations of Web graphic technology.

In Chapter 16, you became familiar with color, and how you can use it on the Web. Using browser-based color in your designs will greatly increase your ability to design pages with colorful features without compromising speed as the browser queries the server for graphic files.

This chapter will offer a close look at the myths surrounding Web graphics, help you define your Web graphic skill level, introduce you to Web graphic tools, and proceed to discuss the technology and techniques available to you, including techniques that will help you meet the demand of diverse bandwidth without ever compromising quality.

You'll examine:

- Your graphic skills
- Web graphic myths
- Web graphic tools
- Image preparation
- File formats
- Graphic techniques

This chapter will leave you with a wealth of skills that can help you become a better producer of Web graphics—and capable of either applying those skills immediately or overseeing the project management of those who can.

Myth Shmyth

Before we get started with the nitty-gritty, let's address a variety of Web graphic myths that exist. It's important to help eradicate misunderstandings about Web graphics from the start.

1. A fast loading site is more important than a good-looking site.

This is totally false. You can have a good-looking site that loads fast, too. Just look at the Weekly Wire XTRA page. It looks great and loads quickly (see Figure 17.1).

2. A graphic has to be tiny both dimensionally and in terms of kilobytes in order to be good.

Wrong again. A graphic should be visually appropriate in terms of dimension. It's what you do with the graphic that makes the difference in kilobytes, not how big or small it visually appears.

PART 5

Bright Sites: Designing with Color and Graphics

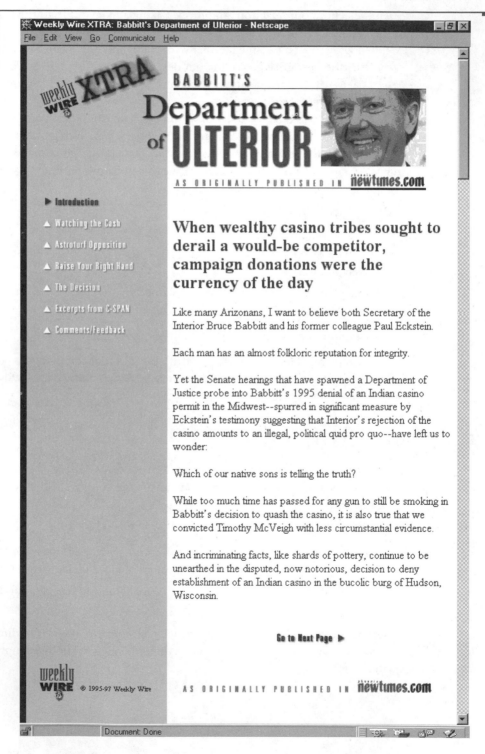

3. It's okay to have unclear and messy-looking graphics. Everyone knows that this is a limitation of the Web.

Bad-looking graphics come from limitations on the part of the Web designer. If you carefully plan what graphics a page requires, scan and process those images wisely, and then optimize them well, you'll have good looking images that serve to enhance rather than detract from your site.

4. Graphics are the primary way of getting design into a site.

Web site design is a combination of techniques, with graphics being only one part of that technique. By taking the advice of earlier chapters and relying on safe palettes, browser-based color techniques, and defined and consistent custom palettes for a site, you can have plenty of color and splash without *ever* using a graphic. Figure 17.2 shows a page from the Core Wave site; to see a color version, visit it at `http://www` `.corewave.com/`. It then stands to reason that you can use graphics to enhance what you've already created.

FIGURE 17.2

Core Wave demonstrates extraordinary use of browser-based color with precision graphics to create an unusual look and feel.

Myth shmyth! By following good Web graphic practices, you'll actually end up with a greater facility to choose graphics for your pages. When properly chosen, scanned, and optimized, these graphics will allow you to meet the needs of those with limited bandwidth, giving you clean, crisp images that load quickly and look terrific.

Graphic Skills Evaluation

There are typically two groups of individuals who are attempting to work with Web graphics. The first group is made up of professional graphic designers who have skills in print and computer-based design, but aren't particularly familiar with designing for the Web environment. The other group is made up of individuals who have little or no formal design background but come to the Web with an enthusiasm and desire to learn how to manage or work as members of Web graphic design projects.

> *"I am one of those web designers who came to this business with no education in terms of graphic design. I suppose the biggest challenge is finding out what it is that I don't know. Then, when you've figured out what it is you need to learn, you find out that many of the principles can't be applied to Web design. You go through this process of learning traditional design and then modifying it to fit the medium. I spend a lot of time learning from other Web designers who are going through the same process and have already come to some kind of understanding. "*
>
> CYNTHIA PENCHINA, Penchina Web Design

Both groups approach the task with a set of skills and challenges. This evaluation will describe those and help you position yourself to be ready for getting the most out of this chapter by providing tips, tricks, and words of wisdom from professionals in the field.

The Graphic Designer

Those of you with a graphic design background obviously have the edge in that you have practical as well as aesthetic skills, such as knowing how to use Photoshop or using graphics to enhance the look of a printed page. You are also more likely to keep up with available materials and resources, and understand how to use other software programs that are applicable for Web graphic design.

The challenge for a traditional graphic artist is to readjust your thinking to the Web's low-resolution environment. No high resolution work here, you're working at 72 DPI and only hundreds of pixels rather than thousands. If you can manage to reorganize your approach, you're almost guaranteed success. The expertise, judgement, and personal touch you've worked long and hard to develop can be expressed in this medium.

> *"The hardest thing for me was losing control. All the details you become accustomed to controlling are now almost completely out of your hands. Graphic designers are (hopefully) very detail oriented, and it can be very frustrating and frightening to lose so much control over your design."*
>
> AMY BURNHAM, Art Director, DesertNet Designs/Weekly Wire

If you don't learn to shift your thinking you run the risk of ending up in a situation where you mimic what you've done in the print arena. Your graphics will be too large in dimension and kilobyte size. Your design might not fit the constraints of the small realm of the computer screen. Worst of all, your personal frustration could persuade you to abandon Web graphics, which could result in the Web—which needs every great graphic designer it can get—losing the benefit of your unique talents.

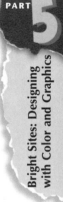

> *"The single hardest thing about moving from print to the Web is recognizing that with the Web, the designer does not control the delivery medium. In print, the designer specifies paper stock, inks, and finishes.*
>
> *The second hardest adjustment to make with the Web is that the delivery mechanisms are a work in progress, whereas print standards have been developing for many years. Everything about the Web is changing under our feet, as we design.*
>
> *The third hardest adjustment is that there are no Web equivalents to Quark, Pagemaker, or Illustrator. Despite the news of different Web layout and design tools, a Web designer still has to know how to manually mark up Web pages for best results. It is similar to having to take an Illustrator file and edit the PostScript by hand."*
>
> MATT STRAZNITSKAS, BrainBug

Graphic designers new to this environment need to remember these things:

- Keep an open mind.
- Read as much as you can.
- Practice the techniques.
- Study the work of other talented Web graphic artists.

Yes, you will have to face some unhappy truths. You'll sacrifice high-resolution design, broad-spectrum palettes, reasonable control of colors, and any vertical design worthy of mention. On the other hand, you'll end up challenging your design skills.

> *"Read as much as you can, try to stay current, explore what others in the industry are doing. Graphic designers are inherently well-suited to Web design because of our experience in organizing and repackaging large amounts of content. Concentrate on the design work, not the programming. Technology can be taught —its your ability to design and think creatively that most employers want."*
>
> AMY BURNHAM, Art Director, DesertNet Designs/Weekly Wire

Limitations are very often the catalyst that forces innovative solutions to problems. Use those limitations to grow. There will always be a need for good print designers, and there's nothing that says you can't do both. Get Web-savvy and you not only improve the aesthetics of the Web, but your marketability as well.

> *"Hold onto 50% of what you've learned in doing print design, and take the other 50% that you've learned and throw it out the window. What 50% do you keep? The knowledge of how to use type, grids, and color to create effective designs that are conceptually sound. What 50% do you discard? Anything having to do with paper stock, Pantone colors, and any sense of control over how your work is presented. Now use that empty space in your brain to absorb as many nuances about Web design as possible. Read every book, magazine article, and Web site that you can find. Learn about the 216 colors that you can use on the Web. Learn about how many pixels most people can see on a monitor without scrolling. Finally, learn to see the Web as an elastic space where creating flexible design is just as important as creating eye-catching design."*
>
> MATT STRAZNITSKAS, BrainBug

The Graphic Design Novice

It's possible that you are interested in the field of Web design and are exploring what skills you'll need to enter into the profession. Perhaps you are already working in Web design as a technologist, but don't have a graphic design background. For you, the formidable task is learning the methods and simultaneously gaining art skills—no easy quest! Fortunately, many excellent resources exist for you, and with a good dose of motivation and an open mind, you will definitely be able to live up to the challenge.

> *"The extent of my formal art education consists of an art class in high school that featured bullwhip and knife making in addition to drawing and pottery. Technology isn't all that different from traditional forms of art if you look at it the right way. I've seen large relational databases that have been created with such time and skill that I can see them as a work of art. My wife, a civil drafter, has commented on the design of roads and even sewer lines in the same manner. There are parallels in all things including technology and art."*
>
> CLAY NIFMANN, Armadillo Consulting & Graphics

There will be some individuals who are totally frustrated or simply not interested in the graphic elements of Web design. If you're one of these individuals and are responsible for the implementation of Web sites, you can hire graphic designers, photographers, and illustrators by the hour or in a permanent position to assist you in your goals.

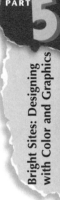

While I obviously want to encourage you to learn the concepts and methods involved with Web graphic design, I also am very concerned that the quality of work you do is the best it can be. If you're one of those people who believes firmly that you don't have an artistic bone in your body and you are unwilling to challenge that belief, that's okay. Web graphic designers can be hired to assist you. That's still no reason to not approach this chapter with enthusiasm, learning what you can to empower you in your goals.

PART 5

Bright Sites: Designing with Color and Graphics

ON line!

For a look at who in the Web world is offering high-quality graphic design services, check out http://www.portfolios.com/graphic_designers/.

Web Graphic Tools

Once you've evaluated where you stand in the realm of Web graphic design you should look at the tools you'll need. Whether you'll use them or simply have them for others on your team does not matter—there are some very specific tools you *must* have if you wish to address Web graphic concerns.

OTE

I'll be writing under the assumption that you have a decent computer (Mac, PowerPC, or PC—it doesn't matter the type just as long as it has plenty of disk space, RAM, and a 24-bit color card and monitor) and a flatbed scanner. These are the minimum of hardware requirements necessary to perform Web graphic technology tasks.

You'll need tools to sketch ideas, create designs, work with typography, enhance photos and art, scan images, and optimize graphics. This section will give you an overview of what these tools are, where to find more information about them, and give you an idea of their cost.

Photoshop: It's All That

In order to create and manage your graphics, several important tools will be necessary to have. The most important one, hands-down, is a program called Photoshop.

There are many designers working out there who like using other paint and photographic programs, and there are certainly a number of those programs that you'll use *in addition* to Photoshop. But make no mistake—the industry standard is Photoshop, and Photoshop is the standard to which you should hold yourself as a Web graphics professional.

Web design newsgroups and e-mail lists are loaded with flame wars on this topic, and I must admit I've participated in a few myself. I've heard arguments that CorelDraw is a perfectly acceptable, or Paint Shop Pro is an inexpensive alternative to the more costly Photoshop, but I don't buy the arguments.

Photoshop is powerful, sophisticated tool that enables you to take a Web graphic from concept to optimization without ever having to engage another piece of software. The strongest argument of them all is that if you want to be *marketable* as a Web designer, Photoshop skills are going to be an essential. Figure 17.3 shows you what the Photoshop interface looks like.

This doesn't mean you're not going to want other software. Professional graphic designers know that having additional tools such as an illustration program, 3-D graphics program, plug-in tools, and multimedia packages such as Director are going to further enhance the ability to create a variety of graphic and multimedia designs. But for now, Photoshop is your most important graphic design purchase.

FIGURE 17.3

The Photoshop
interface

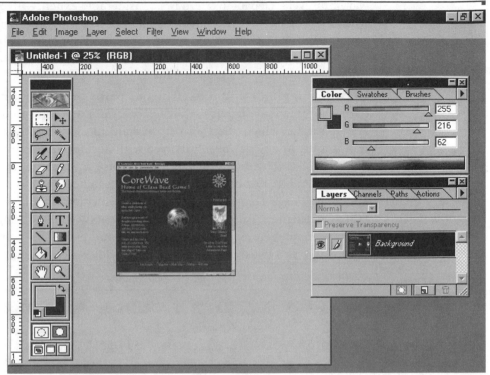

PART 5

Bright Sites: Designing
with Color and Graphics

Graphic Support Software

Other types of graphic software that you'll want to know about and consider for purchase include:

- **An animated GIF program**—Animated GIFs are an easy and popular way to get animations onto your page without resorting to alternatives that will cost more money and not be as cross-platform and cross-browser compatible. More on animated GIFs and related software can be found in Chapter 23.

- **Debabelizer Pro**—You can take tedious guesswork out of optimization with this powerful program that processes and optimizes graphics. Optimization is the process by which you gain control of as much data in a given graphic as you can during the compression process. While you can do everything that Debabelizer does to a graphic by hand in Photoshop, Debabelizer has the added advantage of batch processing files as well as offering up file type and size comparisons. Be wary however—Debabelizer Pro is a considerable expense. I've only used it when working for design companies requiring large quantities of graphic production. For smaller clients and specific applications I prefer to use Photoshop and do my optimization by hand. You'll need to evaluate your circumstances to come up with the most sensible approach.

- **Drawing programs and miscellaneous paint programs**—In addition to Photoshop, many designers use the full spectrum of Adobe products, particularly Illustrator, which offers a variety of drawing and typesetting options worthy of note. Adobe has been involved with desktop publishing and design software for so long their products have become the industry standard. There are also a number of other programs that designers find useful, including Microsoft's Image Composer (Figure 17.4) which enjoys a lot of popularity with PC-based designers. Paint Shop Pro comes in handy when looking for an inexpensive route before jumping in to the more serious commitment of Photoshop, and Ulead Technologies has a wide range of graphic programs.

FIGURE 17.4

Microsoft's Image Composer

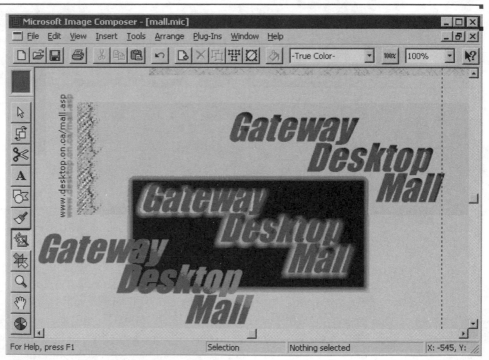

- **Graphic enhancement programs and plug-ins**—The way you present a graphic is as important as the graphic's quality itself. Look at the difference between the photograph in Figure 17.5 and the one in Figure 17.6. While either is acceptable, Figure 17.6 has the added intrigue of a photo treatment. This kind of enhancement adds a level of sophistication to your work. In this example, Photographic Edges from a company called Auto F/X have been used. Another very popular plug-in is Kai's Power Tools. Ulead also makes impressive, inexpensive, and popular graphics utilities, the company Web site is located at `http://www.ulead.com/`.

PART 5

Bright Sites: Designing with Color and Graphics

FIGURE 17.5

An unadorned photograph

FIGURE 17.6

The photograph with an edge effect applied

- **Graphic source material**—You'll want to have sources for icons, patterns, stock photos, and fonts. These can be acquired on CD-ROM and used royalty-free. Check the following Online! sidebar for online resources for graphic source materials.

NOTE

I have students and readers who complain about the high price and formidable learning curves of Web graphic tools. If you're just starting out, several thousand dollars for software does seem somewhat daunting, as does the expense and time spent learning the software, but the dollars and precious time you're going to shell out for software and education is very low compared to the high-quality results you're going to need in order to be competitive in the Web design industry.

For those of you starting out, visit the Internet Baglady at `http://www.dumpsterdive.com/`. This colorful and witty site has many free or low-cost resources as well as a rich library of links to related sites.

For professional projects, make sure you have stock photography, clip art, and fonts. Visit Image Club (listed in the Online! sidebar) for excellent lines on quality stock materials. Also, a visit to the Photodisc will provide you with a shopping source for plenty of stock photos, backgrounds and links to other sites of interest.

ON line!

The following resources will help you find prices and purchasing information on a range of products applicable to Web graphic design production.

- **Adobe Photoshop:** Product details, prices, and links to add-ons and plug-ins, `http://www.adobe.com/`.
- **Debabelizer:** Product information, pricing, and links, `http://www.debabelizer.com/`.
- **GIF Animation:** Royal Frazier has an excellent tutorial and products link site. Mirrors can be found all over the world—start at this site, `http://members.aol.com/royalef/`.
- **Photodisc:** Stock photography at its finest. An excellent selection of articles to help the Web graphic designer can be found here, `http://www.photodisc.com/`.
- **Image Club Graphics:** The best catalog source for all things related to graphic design, with plenty of Web graphic materials, `http://www.imageclub.com/`.
- **MetaTools:** A great source for filters and plug-ins, `http://www.metatools.com/`.

TIP

Stock art can get costly, too. But the results are worth it. Think smart. If you're doing a specific project, write the cost of the specialty goods you need for that project into the specs. This way you get the materials paid for *and* have them available for future work.

Another issue to consider is original source material. Many designers advocate using professional illustrators and photographers to provide the source material for your graphics. This is an ideal situation, but it's not realistic in every case. When you can afford professional, original work, by all means go for it. It supports other design professionals and brings a fresh, original look to the sites in question. When you can't choose this option, the software resources in this section should help you find a range of options from semi-professional to very high-quality stock materials.

The Five S's of Image Production

You've evaluated yourself, and assessed the tool situation. Now you're ready to move into the nitty-gritty of Web graphic production. I'm going to start you out with my five-fold philosophy.

Many of you will be familiar with the acronym GIGO. It stands for "garbage in, garbage out." The idea is that if you start with poor quality stock or resources, there's very little chance you will improve that quality without having to use every trick in the book and then some.

With that as a foundation, you can then move on to scan, size, select attractive treatments, and save your files in the appropriate format. The final step is perhaps the most complicated of all. As a result, it demands its own study, which we'll address later in the "File Formats" section.

Here's my five-fold philosophy, aptly termed the Five S's of Image Production.

1. Start with quality.

2. Scan the image.

3. Size images appropriately.

4. Select attractive treatments such as matting, filters, borders, and edge effects.

5. Save files in the proper format for the type of graphic image you're working with.

Now let's take an in-depth look at the steps in this process.

Starting with Quality

Whether you are using stock images or hiring an illustrator or photographer to provide them for you, it is vitally important that you use quality material. I say this only to fully impress upon you that if you take only one lesson away from this chapter, it's that *quality counts*. If you begin with good materials, you have the advantage of ending up with better results in less time. Remember, in order to get file sizes down, quality is often lost. Start with quality, and you can be much more confident that aggressively optimizing your graphics for speed won't result in terrible images.

Figure 17.7 is an example of good photographic material. Note how the image is clean and crisp. On the other hand, a messy source (Figure 17.8) will require much more time and effort to work with, and who knows what kind of results you'll achieve in that time.

PART 5

Bright Sites: Designing with Color and Graphics

FIGURE 17.7

A clean, crisp photo

FIGURE 17.8

A crumpled photo-copy will not suffice as source material.

Scanning Techniques

There are two principal issues that must be dealt with when scanning graphics for use on the Web:

1. Source material
2. Scanning resolution

How you deal with each of these issues can make a difference in the quality of the scan.

Source Material

Source material refers to *what* it is you're attempting to scan. Photos should be clear, clean, and of the highest quality possible. Hand-drawn or printed materials should also be very clean—look carefully for speckles or dust. Use a professional quality dusting gas to clean your source materials, and follow your scanner manufacturer's recommendations for cleaning your scanner's surface. Anything that you can clean up *before* you scan will greatly improve the quality of the scan.

Many graphic artists like to scan real objects. This is part of *organic design*—utilizing literal artifacts from the real-time world and using them to inspire computer-based graphics.

For Figure 17.9, I took a few things off of my desk and scanned them. Be creative with this technique. Again, the main concern is that the object and your scanning surface are both clear of dust and debris.

Scanning Resolution

While your scanner might offer a range of scanning resolutions, the end result of any image scanned for the Web is going to be 72 DPI. While some designers find that scanning at a higher resolution such as 300 DPI and *then* reducing to 72 DPI renders better results, the verdict is still out on whether that is true.

FIGURE 17.9
*Organic art objects
from my desk*

Whether you choose to scan at 72 DPI or scan at a higher resolution, like 300 DPI and reduce, is really a personal call. It's sometimes possible to get better end results by scanning at 300 DPI and then reducing to 72 DPI later on. On other occasions, that doesn't hold true. The difference in quality is often very slight—the type of difference that normally won't be seen when a figure is optimized for the Web. Find out what works best for your type of scanner and appeals to your sensibilities. Either way, the end result is going to be 72 DPI.

Yes, I hear the cries of print graphic artists as I write about 72 DPI. It's the lowest resolution on the totem pole. I have to remind you, though, that these images aren't going to be printed. In this environment, you don't *need* high resolution in order to make an image appear clear and attractive in the computer graphic environment.

Sizing Images

The issue of sizing images is proportion. I'm not referring to the kilobyte size of the image, but, the width and height of the image. You'll want to be sure that the literal dimensions of your graphics are proportionately appropriate for the Web environment. This does not include background graphics, which we'll cover in detail later in this chapter. The concern here is spot graphics and detail pieces such as buttons and rules.

After having thoroughly bombarded you with the resolution and constrained space issues involved in Web design, you needn't be reminded that you are working for standard computer screens, with a common resolution of 640×480 pixels. This means that in order to keep your designs within the dimensions of that resolution, the actual parts have to be smaller—particularly where width is concerned. Remember that there is actually *less* visible space than the 640×480 resolution because your Web browser's interface takes up some of that space as well.

Horizontal designs are rarely considered wise, unless you are really thoughtful about the design or have a significant reason to design that way. Figure 17.10 shows the home page of Circle of Friends, a group dedicated to raising awareness about spinal chord injuries. The horizontal design is appropriate as it communicates how many victims of such injuries view the world. Unless you have a such a provocative reason to design horizontally, it's usually wise to avoid it.

FIGURE 17.10

Horizontal design is a Web rarity. Check it out at www.circleoffriends.org

Images should always be less than an *absolute* maximum of 600 pixels in width, with 595 pixels being the recommended maximum.

The length of graphics will be determined by the overall layout of your individual page. It's wise to keep the length of your images approximate to each individual screen length. In other words, you should be able to see the entirety of an image without having to scroll down to see it. We studied this concept in the layout chapters of this book. Yale's HTML style guide recommends a screen length to run *no longer* than 295 pixels per screen.

Of paramount importance is the proportion of one element to other elements on the page. If you've done your layout preparation, you've got a jump start on this. Even so, keeping proportion and proximity (how close objects are to one another) in the forefront of your design mind is critical. The desire is to achieve a logical balance between the text, other images or media, and the image in question. Certainly there's room for variation in size, just be sure that the ultimate look isn't out of balance. Compare Figure 17.11, which shows a graphic photo that is out of balance with other elements on the page, to Figure 17.12. In that figure, the proportion is logical and therefore easy to look at.

FIGURE 17.11

*This page is out of
balance.*

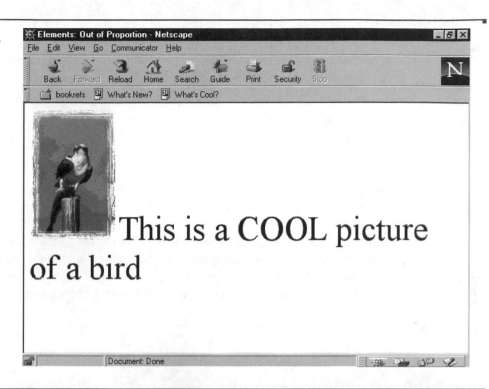

FIGURE 17.12

*The elements on
this page are logi-
cally proportioned.*

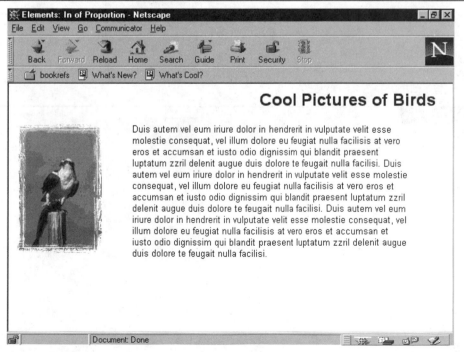

Selecting Graphic Enhancements

Graphic enhancements are added to your graphics using native Photoshop filters, plug-ins, or miscellaneous software. Some examples of enhancements include:

- Adding a light source
- Creating a drop shadow
- Adding an edge effect
- Using a special effect

These, and other enhancement techniques can bring life and dimension to your graphics. Adding effects helps make your site look more interesting, and therefore more professional.

Figure 17.13 is a photograph before a light source has been added. In Figure 17.14, a light source has been applied along with a drop shadow to add dimension to the photograph. Figure 17.15 shows the same photograph with an edge effect applied. Finally, Figure 17.6 shows the original photograph with a special ripple effect added to it.

FIGURE 17.13

A source photo

FIGURE 17.14

A drop shadow is added

FIGURE 17.15

An edge effect is applied

FIGURE 17.16

The source photo with a ripple effect

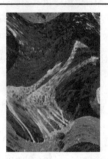

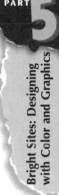

These techniques are truly the tip of the iceberg when it comes to Web graphic design. I highly recommend getting a good book on Photoshop production and working with the advanced techniques described.

Saving Files in Proper Format

You've heard me use the word *optimization* but may not know exactly to what it refers. In a nutshell, optimization is achieved by selecting a file format for the appropriate file of an image you are working on, and then using that format's native options to reduce the file's size in kilobytes while maintaining the highest quality image available.

So, saving files in proper format is not just the fifth step of good image production, it's the first step in optimization.

File Formats

There are two dominant and useful file formats used on the Web, the GIF and the JPEG (also known as JPG). Understanding the difference in how these file formats compress data is key to ensuring that the end product is speedy *and* attractive.

There are special considerations regarding each format. For example GIFs can be transparent, interlaced, or used to create animations. JPEGs can be progressively rendered, and enjoy the distinction of using a compression method that does not reduce the number of colors in an image.

OTE

Are there other file formats that can be used on the Web? The answer is yes, but they are either limited because they require a plug-in to view with the browser, or only a few browsers support them inline. One such file, the PNG, has received some attention in recent months. But PNG is not ready for primetime. For more information on PNG, visit *http://www.pcwebopedia.com/PNG.htm*.

How and when to use each of these types of files is critical to optimization, as you will soon see.

GIF

You'll hear this one pronounced with a hard "G." It makes sense to say it that way because the acronym stands for *Graphic Interchange Format*. However, the proper pronunciation is "jiff."

GIFs hold the distinction of being the longest supported graphic file format in Web design.

Technology

The GIF was created by Compuserve. Bear in mind that compression for any file type is based on mathematical algorithms that make little sense to most of us. We don't really need to understand that information in order to use graphics well, although the math-heads among you might enjoy researching the compression algorithms for the file formats discussed here. You have my blessing, and an express command to go forth and have fun.

Me? I'll stick to what I can understand (a math genius I am not). The type of compression used by GIFs is called *lossless*. In simple terms, this means that the information is saved by figuring out how much of an image uses the same information, and saving those sections with a specific numeric pattern. Therefore, flat images with little color stand to compress well—because they will have lots of sections of the same patterns.

A GIF palette is limited to 256 colors total. So, if you have 10 shades of yellow, that's 10 different numeric patterns. If you end up with too many patterns, the compression method has to figure out how to fit into the palette limitations. Often, what we see as one color is really many—yellow is made up of various pigments, or in the case of digitized colors, pixels of individual color.

GIF compression will throw out some of the repetitive information and select from the information it has. This means the pale yellow in your image might suddenly become a neon yellow.

Technique

In order to work well with GIFs, you need to know what kind of files are best served by lossless compression methods. GIFs tend to do very well with any image that has few colors, such as simple line art or images with flat color. This suggests that any images with many different colors, variations of color, light sources, gradients, and the like are *not* good candidates for GIF compression as they contain too much information!

Remember this equation: A good candidate for GIF compression equals an image that is simple and has few colors.

Figure 17.17 and Figure 17.18 are both good examples of GIF candidates. They are flat color line-drawings with no color gradations or complicated information.

This image is a good candidate for GIF optimization

Another example of a good GIF candidate

JPEG

Pronounce this one "jay-peg." You'll also see it spelled as JPG. The acronym stands for *Joint Photographic Experts Group*. A group of photographic experts got together to create the JPEG standard.

Technology

The math behind the JPEG is a bit more complex than the GIF. To describe the technology in understandable terms, consider JPEG a *lossy* compression method. Instead of hanging on to areas of important data, JPEG technology tosses out data that is deemed unimportant. Of course, it has to do this with some kind of logic, so the JPEG compression divides the image into square sections before it begins to apply the really advanced math.

This translates into JPEG compression offering you the decision as to how much compression you want. You can choose to keep lots of data intact, or lose a lot of data, depending upon the ratio you wish to employ. The result of losing too much data, however, might be the appearance of *artifacts*. These are weird ghost shapes or blocks of illogical color, which you can see in the photograph in Figure 17.19.

FIGURE 17.19

If JPEGs are compressed too much, artifacts appear.

Technique

Because lossy compression allows the designer to keep a lot of visual information, this means that unlike the GIF format, anything with a lot of color or gradients will translate well into the JPEG file format.

Good candidates for JPEGs include photographs—especially where there's lots of color resulting from light such as in skies, sunsets, and the like—and graphics using gradient fills.

Figure 17.20 shows a photograph saved as a JPEG. The gradation in the sky appears smooth and natural. There are subtle light changes in the image, which remain intact in the JPEG format but would most certainly be lost if a GIF were to be used.

FIGURE 17.20

The sky looks natural in this JPEG.

Optimization

As mentioned earlier, optimization is the process by which an image is reduced to its smallest file size while retaining its best quality.

The first step in optimization is to determine which file format is appropriate for the file. The general rule, as we've determined in our previous discussion, is as follows:

- The GIF file format is best used for line art and images with few colors.

- The JPEG file format is the best format for photographs and art with lots of colors and gradations of color.

There is sometimes a gray area between the use of GIFs versus JPEGs. One example is a black and white photograph with little gradation. In this particular instance, a GIF *might* be a better choice. It's difficult to tell unless you put the image through optimization with both. This is where Debabelizer Pro comes in handy, as it can make these comparisons for you. Another program that achieves this at a fraction of the cost is Photo Impact from Ulead Systems (`http://www.ulead.com/`).Very occasionally a graphic designer will *want* to exploit the dithering that occurs with GIFs in order to induce a specific effect. In this case, the designer will have to work with the graphic in a trial-and-error fashion until the desired look is achieved.

After determining the file type, the next step is to work with that file type's innate technology in order to get the lowest file size while retaining the best quality. The next sections will explain how this is done, and take you through a step-by-step example for optimizing both a GIF and a JPEG.

Working with GIFs

Using Photoshop 4.0, I'm going to show you how to reduce a file to its lowest attractive size. There are several terms you'll need to know. They are:

- **Indexing**—A software program such as Photoshop will take an image file and count its colors. If there are more than 256 colors in an image, indexing will reduce the palette to 256 colors. At that point, you have the freedom to determine if further reduction in colors is appropriate.

- **Palette type**—There are several types of indexed color palettes. The one that is most important to you is going to be the *adaptive* color palette. This palette allows you to determine the various aspects of the palette, such as color depth and dithering. Another important palette is the *exact* palette. You'll see this appear when an image already has less than 256 colors.

- **Color depth**—This is also referred to as *bit* depth. This is basically the amount of data that will be saved with your image. Optimization of GIFs largely depends upon your ability to reduce bit depth.

- **Number of colors**—This is the total number of colors in the image, which can be as low as 8 and as high as 256. Limiting colors is helpful in terms of reducing total file size. Typically, you'll only need to worry about managing your color depth, and the number of colors will reduce appropriately.

- **Dithering**—Dithering is the process of allowing the computer to make decisions as to what colors to put into an image. For example, if you have three yellows next to one another, the computer may select the yellow that is in its own palette. This means that your pastel could end up as a neon. You can control how much your colors dither in Photoshop, but ideally, you will not want any dithering at all.

GIF Optimization: Step-by-Step

Figure 17.21 shows a cartoon figure with few colors, that is line drawn and flat with no dimension. A perfect choice for a GIF.

When saved as a Photoshop file, the total kilobyte count of this file is 27KB. In order to reduce that file size, the first step is to *index* the colors. Select Image ➤ Mode ➤ Indexed Color as shown in Figure 17.22.

The Indexed Color dialog box will pop up. In this case, the image has very few colors, only 12. At this point you can choose to save it to the exact palette, but let's see how far we can go in terms of reducing this file's size.

From the Palette box, select "Adaptive", and make sure Dither is set to "None." In the Color Depth box, select "3 bits/pixel" which will give you a total of 8 colors (Figure 17.23). Click OK.

FIGURE 17.22

Selecting Indexed Color in Photoshop

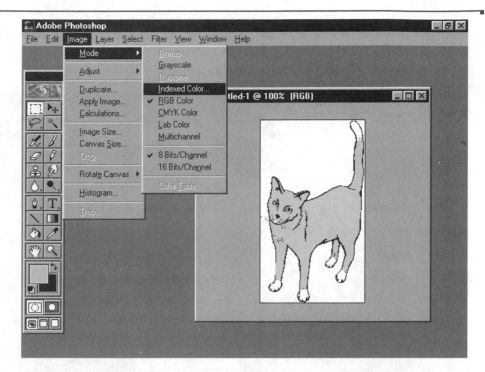

FIGURE 17.23

Working with the adaptive palette

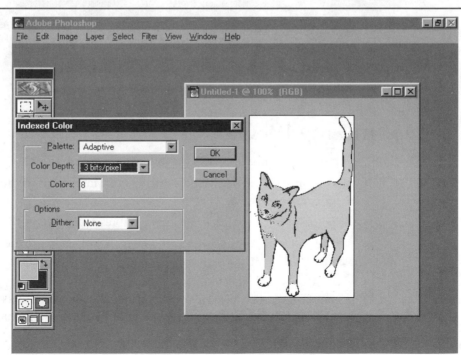

Finally, export the file as a GIF. Select File ➤ Export ➤ GIF89a (Figure 17.24), and you end up with a 4KB file. This is an extremely small file, but as you can see, the image is clean and crisp, and very worthy of the Web.

FIGURE 17.24

The GIF export interface in Photoshop

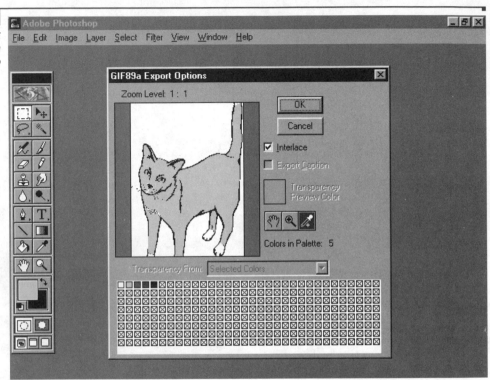

Optimizing JPEGs

JPEG compression in Photoshop has the following settings:

- **Maximum**—This is the highest setting, and maintains as much of the file's integrity as possible.
- **High**—Still a good choice, some lossy compression occurs at this level.
- **Medium**—Lossy compression really goes to work here, reducing the file size even more—but often at a noticeable degradation to the image's integrity.
- **Low**—At this level, most JPEGs are unacceptable as the appearance of artifacts becomes very noticeable. This setting should be avoided unless you are able to maintain the image's strength without encountering serious problems with clarity.

JPEG Optimization: Step-by-Step

Optimizing JPEGs is relatively simple. Begin with the stock or scan of material you want to make into a JPEG—in this case I've chosen a photo I took of a scene by the ocean at Waikiki. This is a perfect candidate for JPEG optimization, because it has lots of gradation in the sky area.

After scanning and sizing the image, select File ➤ Save A Copy. When you choose JPEG, a dialog box pops up, allowing you to determine which setting to choose. Select "Maximum" and save the file (Figure 17.25).

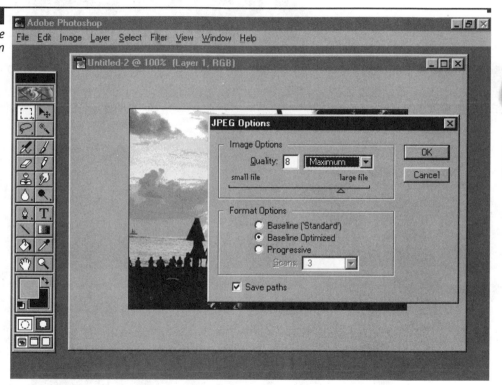

FIGURE 17.25

The Waikiki image saved at maximum

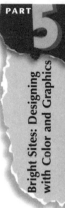

Go through this process for each selection: high (Figure 17.26), medium (Figure 17.27), and low (Figure 17.28). You can see the visual differences in the figures and the resulting quality and size. Note how the maximum and medium are very similar in quality, but not so similar in size—a difference of 6KB. Medium is less acceptable—if you look closely at the clouds, you can see the lossy compression taking its toll. The results seem as though someone took Vaseline and smeared it over the picture. Finally, the lowest setting, while offering up a small file size—only 8KB—degrades noticeably. Artifacts such as bands, smears, and blotches appear over the image.

FIGURE 17.26

The same image saved at high

FIGURE 17.27

At a medium setting, you can see subtle problems with the image.

FIGURE 17.28

At the low setting, the JPEG is degraded considerably.

Given this information, the high setting at 13KB would be the most logical choice. It's not as small as the lower settings, but the image's integrity is fairly intact. It's better to have a slightly higher file size at the cost of download time than poor looking images, which makes you look unprofessional.

 TIP

If you're still concerned about load-times, consider that an excellent total for a page is 45KB, and a very fair total is 65KB. Most pages are significantly higher than that. If you work to optimize your graphics carefully, and are very selective in which graphics you choose for your page, you'll end up with great looking pages that load evenly.

Unfair Play

Just for fun, I'm going to show you what happens when I try to optimize the line drawing as a JPEG and the photo as a GIF—demonstrating why careful selection of file type is a major aspect of optimization.

In Figure 17.29, I have taken the line drawing that we saved earlier as a 6-bit GIF (see Figure 17.21) and saved it as a JPEG at a high setting. There appears to be no difference in quality. But the file sizes? 25KB for the JPEG, and 4KB for the GIF—a 21KB difference! I then went ahead and saved the file as a low JPEG; the quality remains the same but the file size weighs in at 18KB—still too high.

FIGURE 17.29

The line drawing saved as a JPEG— looking good, but file size is inflated

Figure 17.30 shows the Waikiki photo saved as a 5-bit GIF. The degradation of the picture is obvious, and turnabout is unfair—the GIF is 25KB compared to the very attractive JPEG at 13KB.

FIGURE 17.30

As a GIF, this photo's quality degrades and the file size inflates.

As you begin to test out optimization techniques, you might find yourself frustrated at how time-consuming the process is. It will get faster and easier as you become more skilled. You will gain a sense of which file type to use, and then a feel of how to drop bit depth or select settings. It takes a little time at first, but the results are very satisfying.

Debabelizer Pro and Photo Impact can process files in batches and make your life a lot easier. Still, there's nothing like first knowing how to make good choices and what happens when you don't—you're better poised to use the software to its maximum power, as well as turning out pages that look terrific.

Additional Graphic Techniques

Three additional graphic techniques you'll want to be familiar with include:

- Progressive rendering
- Transparency
- GIF animation

Progressive rendering is the progressive appearance of graphics—a very handy technique that helps keep people's visual attention while graphics are loading. A site visitor will see the entire graphic appear in a fuzzy fashion, and then become progressively more clear.

This can be done in two ways on the Web. The most popular and effective is the use of *interlaced GIFs*. Figure 17.31 shows an interlaced GIF in the midst of rendering; Figure 17.32 shows the final form. This technique can be applied to any GIF. Photoshop supports interlacing, as do many plug-in tools.

FIGURE 17.31

An interlaced GIF in the process of rendering

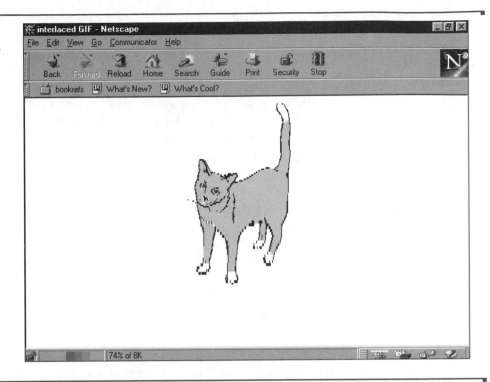

FIGURE 17.32

The GIF in its fully rendered form

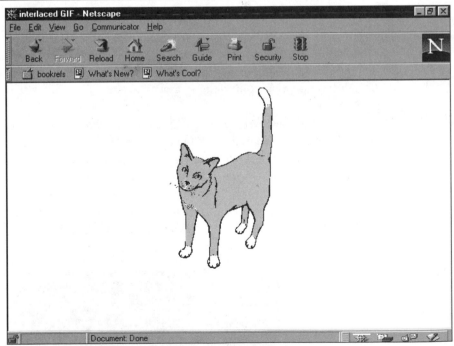

Progressive JPEGs are the JPEG answer to interlacing. You cannot interlace a JPEG, but there are programs, including Photoshop, that create what is known as a progressive JPEG. I'm personally not too fond of them, as I believe the technology is somewhat preliminary, not well-supported by browsers, and the quality is fairly inconsistent.

Without progressive rendering, JPEGs will scroll rather than render progressively, but if you've done your optimization, layout, and coding in a sensible fashion, it's not an obvious problem—particularly because the results are so attractive.

Transparency is the technique that allows you to create textured or multi-colored backgrounds and "tape" a graphic over them without disrupting the background design. It involves making certain colors transparent in the graphic, and having those transparent colors disappear when placed on a textured page. This technique takes a little bit of patience and time to learn, but can be done successfully in Photoshop.

Finally, *animated GIFs* take advantage of a looping element in the GIF format. They are an extremely popular way to add active media to your pages. More information about animated GIFs appears in Chapter 23.

Graphic Applications

Now that you know how to work with graphics we're going to look at the methods Web designers employ to come up with a variety of graphics used on a Web page.

Headers

Using graphical headers is a nice departure from rigid, HTML-based text. You can add logographic material, control your choice of fonts (see Chapters 19 and 20 for more information on typographic design), as well as add color, play with dimension, and add shadows.

Figure 17.33 shows a flat header with a typeface known as Whimsy. Already we've departed from the limitations of HTML-based text, and while you only see it in grayscale, the type uses a nice maroon color.

In Figure 17.34, more design has been added to the header. As a result, it is now more interesting, but there's still more you can do with it. In Figure 17.35 a lens flare is added, making the image a little fun. Compare the results here to a plain header as shown in Figure 17.36, and you can quickly see why graphic headers are so attractive to designers.

FIGURE 17.33

Flat header with Whimsy typeface

Fun with Fonts!

FIGURE 17.34

A design adds personality to the look

FIGURE 17.35

A lens flare adds some fun

FIGURE 17.36

A plain text header—Can you say "boring?"

Image Maps

An image map is a single image that is broken down into sections. These sections are made "hot." In other words, they are each linked to a separate Web page.

When creating image maps, first select an image that lends itself to mapping. Ideally, this means something that has very specific sections to it, as shown in Figure 17.37. Image maps can also be text with a design, as in Figure 17.38.

FIGURE 17.37

This image has specific areas that make it a good choice for mapping.

FIGURE 17.38

Maps are often text-based

Home · About Treks · About Eb · Treks Schedule, 1997

In either case, the individual areas must be noted by coordinates. There are two methods of processing these coordinates. One method is *server-sided*, which means that the information for the image map sits on the server and the browser must query the server to deliver the information. This method is more time-consuming and largely considered obsolete, so I'll only make mention of it here.

The method you'll want to use for maps is called *client-sided mapping*. This puts the coordinates right into your HTML, and the browser decodes them, rather than the server.

How do you get these coordinates? Mapping tools come in handy to do this for you. On the PC, you can use MapEdit. Figure 17.39 shows an image in the mapping interface.

FIGURE 17.39

Image mapping in MapEdit

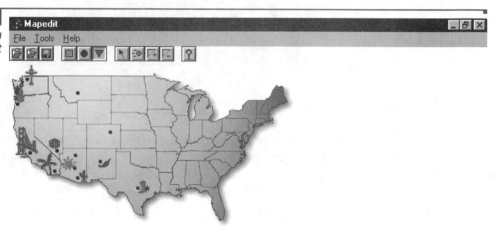

Here's a look at the syntax:

```
<map name="Map">
<area shape="polygon"
coords="17,9,51,9,51,34,35,34,26,37,18,37,9,31,3,14,16,18,15,10" href="wa.htm">
<area shape="polygon"
coords="7,66,34,66,34,91,66,120,71,129,67,133,69,140,51,141,45,132,29,124,29
,122,6,80,7,68" href="ca.htm">
<area shape="polygon"
coords="68,114,74,130,71,132,70,142,94,151,102,151,102,107,73,107,71,113,68,
113" href="az.htm">
<area shape="polygon"
coords="105,107,105,151,108,151,108,147,140,147,142,106,105,106" href="nm
.htm">
```

```
<area shape="polygon"
coords="36,66,70,66,70,104,68,108,65,112,65,114,35,89,36,68" href="nv.htm">
<area shape="polygon"
coords="145,110,161,110,161,125,185,131,198,133,199,144,202,153,201,162,178,
179,180,193,168,190,153,163,145,163,141,170,132,162,122,149,144,150,144,110"
href="tx.htm">
<area shape="polygon" coords="52,36,53,63,6,63,10,33,19,41,50,36" href="or
.htm">
<area shape="rect" coords="104,75,147,105" href="co.htm">
<area shape="polygon"
coords="59,15,135,15,135,46,92,48,90,52,79,53,73,43,68,42,70,35,59,25"
href="mt.htm">
</map>
```

In this case, each area that links to a page has its coordinates provided. Note that the polygon shape requires a lot of coordinates.

Background Graphics

Using graphics to create backgrounds is a great way to add style to your pages. However, be careful how you use them. The Web is filled with graphic backgrounds that are cliché, or that clash with the design. Background graphics should serve the design, not detract from it.

Backgrounds can be either GIF or JPEG formats. This will depend upon what kind of image you're using for your background. Be sure to try out your optimization skills when designing background images. With careful optimization, you can create very complex background designs that take up little memory.

Tiles

By using small tiles with a pattern, you can create a wallpaper effect. Essentially, the tiles are repeated both on the horizontal and vertical axis until they fill the available background.

Some of the issues you should be aware of when working with background tiles include:

- **File size**—A background tile should be appropriate in both dimensional size and kilobytes. Remember that the larger the file, the longer the load time—and the fewer available kilobytes for other graphics occur.

- **Seamed tiles**—If you have a visible border around your tile (Figure 17.40), you will end up showing the world the fact that background tiles are repeated (Figure 17.41). This effect may be desirous to your design, but be aware that seams show.

FIGURE 17.40

Tile with seams

FIGURE 17.41

*Seamed tiles show
the repeat pattern*

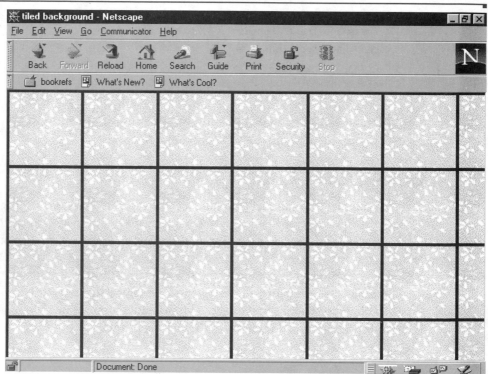

- **Seamless tiles**—These are harder to create and involve a fine hand. The objective is to make the tiles appear without any seam at all. You must anticipate how the tiles will fit together, and use advanced drawing techniques to ensure that a tile appears seamless. Figure 17.42 shows a seamless background tile, and Figure 17.43 shows the wallpaper-style results.

FIGURE 17.42

A seamless tile

FIGURE 17.43

*Seamless tile creates
a true wallpaper
effect.*

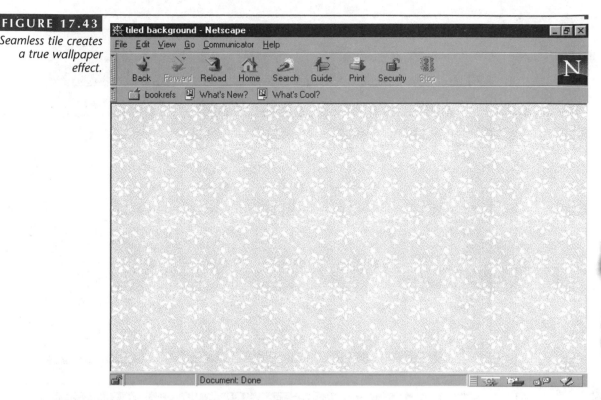

Another important concern is readability. Your background design should *never* interfere with a visitor's ability to read the text that will be placed on top of it. Be sure to fully test your design with the chosen text and link colors in order to ensure that both the aesthetic look of the tile and the clarity of any text remain intact.

Margin Backgrounds

This is an extremely popular way of designing backgrounds for the Web. You can create a right, left, or top margin to use with tables (as you've seen in Chapters 12 through 15). Some designers like to employ both a left and right margin, which can be a welcome departure from the standard left or right.

Margin backgrounds can be made up of flat color (Figure 17.44) or with a texture or design (Figure 17.45) in the margin field. The text field can be a flat color (Figure 17.46) or a texture (Figure 17.47). These combinations add a lot of visual interest to a site. Again, be careful that the backgrounds do not interfere with readability.

FIGURE 17.44

Flat color for a left-margin background graphic

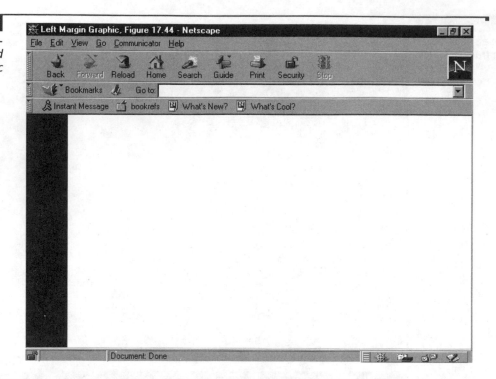

FIGURE 17.45

This background graphic has a design in the right margin.

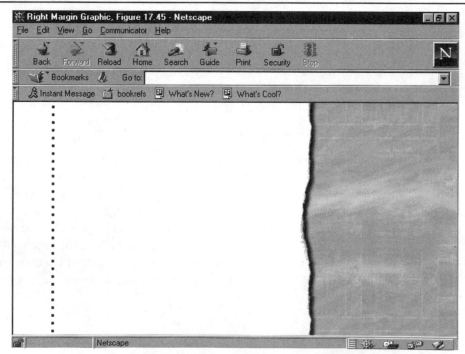

FIGURE 17.46

*Note the flat color
text field*

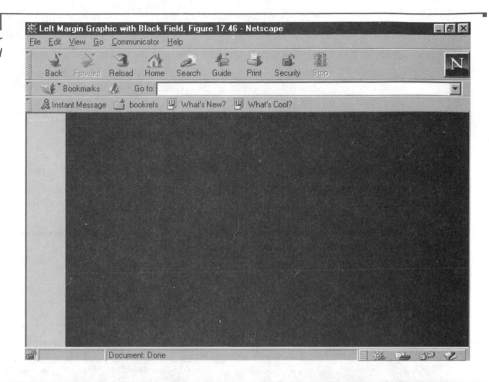

FIGURE 17.47

*In this case, the text
field is a texture.*

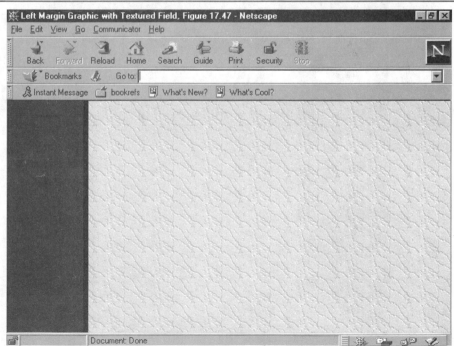

The major concern with margin backgrounds is size. Because all backgrounds are a repeated pattern, you'll have to understand how this pattern affects the design you're creating. The vertical repetition works to our advantage because we can keep the tile thin and use the vertical repeat to create our pattern. If a margin background's width is too short, however, it will repeat at inconvenient points along the horizontal axis in your design. Furthermore, this repetition causes problems at a variety of resolutions.

OTE

> Background graphics tile into the browser's available space. They do not affect width and height concerns. This means that you can have a very long background graphic. When used in the background, no horizontal scroll bar will be forced. However, the same graphic placed in the foreground will force a scroll bar.

If you create a tile that is 640 pixels in width, and you're viewing on a screen that has a 640×480 resolution, you'll see the background that you created without running the risk of repeating on the horizontal axis. But what happens when you view the same page at 800×600 resolution or higher? The tile repeats (Figure 17.48).

FIGURE 17.48

A background that's too short risks repeating at higher resolution.

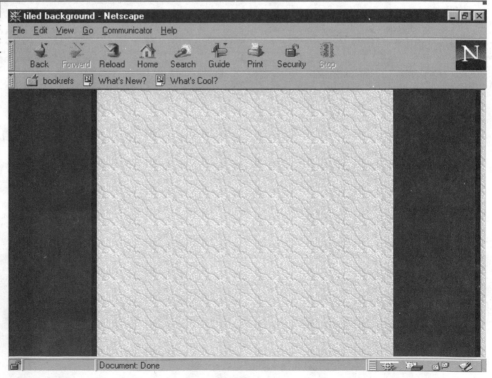

Designers remedy this by designing vertical tiles at an average of 1024 pixels in width. This covers a range of resolutions without running into a problem.

Top margin designs work in a similar fashion, but the repeat axis problem occurs in reverse. If you don't make the tile long enough to fit the page, the top margin will repeat (Figure 17.49) on the horizon. Therefore, top margin backgrounds should be long—as long as you need for a given page. The width can be kept short, however, as the tiling mechanism will fill the page appropriately (Figure 17.50).

FIGURE 17.49

Vertical tile repeating on the horizontal axis

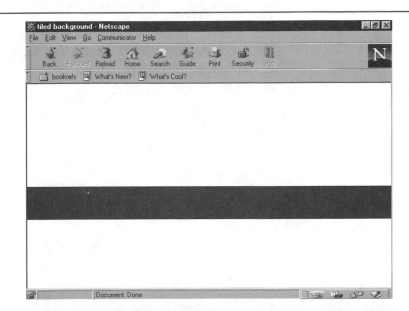

FIGURE 17.50

The full effect of a top-margin tile

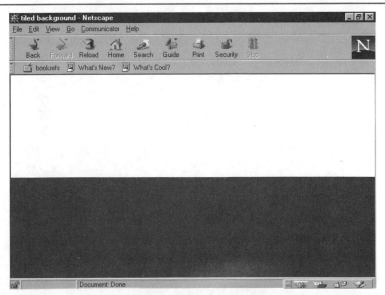

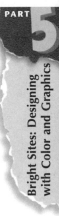

PART 5

Bright Sites: Designing with Color and Graphics

Full Background Design

There will be occasions where you'll want to use full images as a background. In these instances, you'll have to determine how to handle repetition. Another concern with full backgrounds is file size. Logically, the larger the file's dimensions, the bigger the file will be in terms of dimension.

This is where optimization comes in handy. If you design and optimize your background properly, the file sizes will be very small. The effects can be beautiful and interesting, as you can see in Figure 17.51 and Figure 17.52.

FIGURE 17.51

This full-page background repeats, but does so in an interesting fashion.

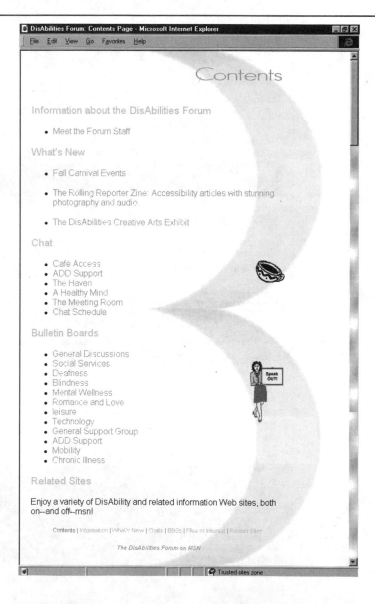

FIGURE 17.52

This full-page background is highly artistic and the repeat factor doesn't negatively affect the design.

Photos and Illustrations

Photos and illustrations can help illustrate a Web page. The trick with these kinds of images is to enhance the overall design rather than detract from it.

In Figure 17.53, you can see a photograph that is integrated with and relevant to the text on the page. Figure 17.54 shows a piece of clip art that performs a similar role.

Processing photos and illustrations should be done with precise optimization techniques in place. You already know that you don't want to have excessive amounts of graphics on a page. When you add up backgrounds, headers, and any image maps, you start running into higher numbers in the memory department.

FIGURE 17.53

The photograph is complimentary to the text and vice-versa.

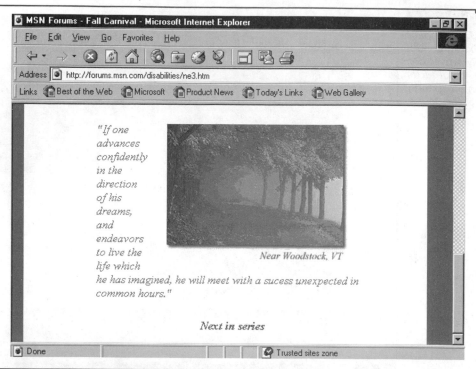

Next Up

I'd like to pause for a moment to help you gain insight into what this chapter has taught you. First, it helped you to define your skills as a Web graphic designer as they stand today. Then, it introduced and demystified several of the falsehoods surrounding the issue of Web graphics.

The method in this chapter has focused mostly on general graphic techniques and applications, with a strong emphasis on optimization. Some step-by-step instruction has been provided, but you'll need to do a lot more work with graphics in order to become completely adept with them. To that end, I'd like to recommend you visit the Design Studio Web site, `http://www.designstudio.net/color/` to access more resources and how-to's than can realistically be provided here.

My main piece of advice is that if you are not familiar with it, you must learn to work with Photoshop. It's a complex program, undeniably, but it will help you learn how to develop the vast skills necessary to really make the summary ideas in this chapter make long-lasting sense.

Up next is a review of color and graphics, complete with additional tasks and quizzes to help expand and confirm your learning thus far.

PART

5

Bright Sites: Designing with Color and Graphics

THE DESIGN STUDIO COLOR AND GRAPHICS LAB

THE DESIGN STUDIO COLOR AND GRAPHICS LAB

Light is necessary for color, and color is necessary for most Web graphic design. It's a rare Web site that's successfully done in black and white. The need for designers to understand color theory, computer color, Web color, and the combination of these with advanced graphic techniques is paramount.

If you envision the Web as a complex structure of intersecting roads with a range of legal speed limits for those roads, you end up with a very realistic Web metaphor. The information superhighway only has several legal speed limits. I tend to be a little heavier on the gas peddle than some, while others access the roadway at slower speeds. Then there are speed demons—people who go as fast as they possibly can go.

Now let's take the metaphor one step further. If you're designing a billboard that will sit alongside the road, you want to be sure that people get the message the billboard intends. You have to use color and images that will leave a lasting impact on the passerby, whether they zoom past at top speed, or slowly pass with more time to notice the details.

Web designers have to grab the attention of Web visitors, and they have to do it fast. Otherwise, the content of their site, be it an in-depth message or a slick advertisement, will be lost. In today's highly trafficked areas, Web designers have to catch attention and make the experience easy on the visitor.

Some are of the notion that catching this attention is best done through the use of cool-sounding noisemakers and virtual cartwheels. I'm of the school that requires a grounded foundation of design; more specifically, an interesting but readable layout, color palettes that are both inviting as well as thematically appropriate, and attractive, well-optimized graphics that serve to enhance rather than detract from the content of the page.

Does this mean there isn't a place for cool visuals and added noise? Of course not. But those things must also serve a Web site's purpose. And never, ever, can the use of those bells and whistles stand alone. They, too, require terra-firma.

How do you get grounded? In the past two chapters, the emphasis has been on understanding and using Web color and graphics. In this chapter, we'll review those issues and emphasize learning through a series of tasks and graphic deconstructions.

We'll highlight:

- Color theory
- Color principles
- Psychological impact of color
- Computer color
- Web color
- Web palettes

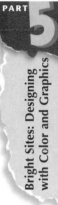

If there seems like a lot to Web color and graphics, you're right. There's so much that these chapters only can provide a jumping-off point. You'll have to explore avenues of formal design, aesthetic studies, imaging software, graphics applications, and design techniques on your own—far, far beyond the confines and comfort of this book.

For additional references and resources, please visit the Color Lab at the Design Studio, http://www.designstudio.net/color/. A hands-on experience with color can be enjoyed with a visit to the color reference in the center of the book.

Color: Review

For those individuals who have no visual limitations, color is a potent elemental and psychological factor in our lives. Even for the blind, color is an influence both socially and emotionally. I have found myself engaged in conversation with blind friends, referring to color despite the fact that I know they cannot see. But some have told me they totally relate to the *concept* of color, even if they do not know what it is. Red is passion, green is envy, blue is calm.

Color is used by designers as a visual method of expression. As individuals, we tend to gravitate toward certain colors, and stray away from others. The impact of color on our lives is profound.

What's *your* favorite color?

I can't say that I have one. I do know that I enjoy most colors, but it's always a matter of context. For example, I love the soft yellow blossoms on the cactus in the patch of desert behind my house. I adore the bright yellow flowers of the Cat Claw vines on my trellis. I'd wouldn't be caught dead *wearing* vibrant yellow; I'd feel jumpy and uncomfortable in it.

OFF line!

How do you relate to color? Think about your clothing or your home decor. Do you have certain themes running through your life? Now that you know what the impact of color is on your life, you can assess how you use it as a designer. You can think while acting— and strengthen your design acumen in the process.

The following issues are important to designers working with color:

- Subtractive color
- Color principles
- Psychological impact of color
- Additive color
- Web color

Color's impact is obviously vast. It is our role as designers to take that vast power and harness it, with clear intent and forethought, and to create designs that communicate effectively and with grace.

> *"Forget the high resolution stuff, enormous large files, and CMYK color, we're talking 'bout RGB here. The designer has to appropriate control of every tool necessary in order to create a Web page."*
>
> JOEL NEELEN, Graphic Designer / NextDada, Belgium

Main Concepts

The foundation of color is in color theory, which enables you to become familiar with how color is made. The next step is to work that theory into the world of the Web—a very different world, where color is created digitally rather than by the more intimate mixing of paint or dye.

Whether your fingers are in the paint or on the keyboard, your job is to make art: functional, appropriate, and hopefully, aesthetic.

Color Theory

The basis for all familiar color in the natural world is theorized by a process known as *Subtractive Color Synthesis*. The base of this process lies in the primary colors of red, yellow, and blue.

Primary colors are then broken down into secondary, intermediate, and tertiary color. All of these colors are referred to as subtractive because they absorb light in order to reflect back as color.

Other combinations of color result in tint and shade. Add white, get a tint. Add black, and you end up with a shade. How much or how little color and light go into a given color result in a number of properties. These properties include:

- **Hue**—This differentiates one color from another. For example, red is different than green.

- **Value**—A color's value is related to the amount of light that has been added to it. Add light to navy, and you end up with sky blue.

- **Saturation**—Also known as *intensity*, this is essentially how bright a color is. My peacock blue sweater is bright, and my navy pea coat is dull. They have different saturations.

- **Warmth**—Colors from yellow to red emit heat, and are referred to as warm colors.

- **Coolness**—Any color in the range of green to blue is considered to be a cool color.

Colors also have *relationships* with one another. Harmony can be inspired with soft colors. Discordance results when colors create visual tension. Color theory demonstrates *effects*, which are what make a given paint type appear glossy, or silk and satin shimmer and shine.

Psycho-Sociological Aspects of Color

As mentioned previously, color can have profound effects on an individual. Color serves to energize, calm and soothe, elicit sorrow, or express elegance. When colors are combined, they can signify a range of emotions. Additionally, color has definite social implications. Different societies attribute different reactions to color, and designers working with audiences from specific cultures would do well to study up on the meanings given to color by that group.

Computer Color Technology

Color in the natural world and computer-based color are distinctly different. Rather than *subtractive* color of the tactile world, computer color uses *additive* synthesis.

Additive Color Synthesis results in a red, green, blue (RGB) set of colors from which all other colors on the computer screen are created. This is distinctly different than subtractive color. Mix red and green in the natural world, and a dark brown results. But a computer adds red to green and ends up with yellow.

Another notable issue to remember is Gamma. This is a system that enables computers to display color. Web designers need to remember that Gamma is different on almost every platform, as well as between individual machines within those platforms. Be aware that Gamma problems will especially affect the way contrast and brightness are seen. If you know that a large portion of your audience is vision impaired, you might want to consider a higher contrast design.

Web Color

Because of foibles in the design and implementation of computer operating systems (notably Windows) and Web browsers, a palette of only 216 colors is deemed to be *safe*. This means that if you select from one of these colors, you have a much better chance of having your color appear more or less the same from computer to computer, platform to platform. You may elect to use colors outside of this palette, but if you do, it is highly recommended that you do some testing on a variety of platforms and machines to ensure that the color is somewhat stable.

The values in the 216 color safe palette are derived from RGB combinations. If you take the RGB values and individually convert them to the hexadecimal (Base 16) numeric system, you end up with a series of six total alphanumeric combinations per color. This combination is what is used by HTML to tell the browser which colors you'd like it to deliver.

The fact that safe palette color information is stored by the browser makes access to those colors very fast; so fast that it is in the designer's best interest to lean heavily on browser color in a design. Using safe-palette color in your designs can create expressive, artistic pages *before* a graphic ever enters into the situation.

Knowing this, you can create an *individual site palette*, which gives you a visual base for all the color you will use in your design. Examples of possible color combinations and applications can be found in the color reference section in the middle of this book.

> *"A difficult adjustment to make with the Web is that the delivery mechanisms are a work in progress, whereas print standards have been developing for many years. Everything about the Web is changing under our feet, as we design."*
>
> MATT STRAZNITSKAS, BrainBug

Page Deconstruction

Let's take a look at the Design Studio's use of color. An example of the safe color palette can be found in the color reference section in this book and on the Design Studio site, at http://www.designstudio.net/color/.

The Design Studio uses a palette of eight total safe colors, including black and white. These colors are all from the safe palette, and I've used their hexadecimal counterparts.

Here's the browser code from the main page, demonstrating the browser-based body, text, and link color attributes. The body background is white, the text is black, links are rust, visited links are olive, and the active link is white.

```
<body bgcolor="#FFFFFF" background="images/ds-bakr.gif" text="#000000"
link="#666633" vlink="663300" alink="#FFFFFF">
```

I chose to use eight total colors because I wanted to color-code the various subject areas as well as give myself plenty of flexibility while keeping the theme intact. Not every designer will want to use this many colors in a palette; some will choose to use more.

With the exception of black and white, the Design Studio colors are all secondary or intermediate. There are three shades of green (dark olive, olive, light olive) and three of red (maroon, rust, and peach). The colors are harmonious, in that the overall experience when viewing them is calming.

Black was chosen for elegance and white for practicality and to create higher contrast for reading areas. The other colors express a warmth, inviting you to relax and stay awhile. As you'll see, the larger sections of black on the site's main level are delivered with a background graphic.

Color: Quiz

Please answer the following multiple choice questions.

1. Color in the natural world is expressed theoretically as:

    a. Additive Color Synthesis

    b. Subtractive Color Synthesis

    c. tactile synthesis

    d. a primary color wheel

2. Saturation refers to:

    a. the hue of a color

    b. a color's luminosity

    c. a color's value

    d. the brightness of a color

3. The combination of black and yellow is:

    a. secondary

    b. harmonious

    c. warm

    d. discordant

4. The inside of a clam shell is:

    a. transparent

    b. iridescent

    c. saturated

    d. discordant

5. In most Western cultures, the color brown conveys:

    a. love and passion

    b. truth and clarity

    c. stability

    d. royalty and wealth

Please answer true or false for the following statements.

6. Computer color is based on Additive Color Synthesis.

7. Hexadecimal is the mathematical pattern upon which computer color is based.

8. Gamma strongly relates to the brightness and contrast on a video monitor.

9. A safe color palette is made up of 256 colors.

10. An individual palette must be three colors only.

Write out short answers to the following questions:

11. What colors do you personally find harmonious? Discordant? Is there a certain color that you love to wear and one that you cannot stand to wear? Why do you think this is?

Answers to the quiz can be found at the end of this chapter and on the Design Studio Web site at http://www.designstudio.net/workshop/.

Color: Task

The tasks here are to create color palettes first based on concept, and then literally in Photoshop, selecting from the safe palette provided on the Design Studio Web site.

For this task you will need:

- Pencil and paper
- A copy of this book
- Photoshop
- The color palette or Photoshop safe-palette color lookup table (CLUT, provided courtesy of Lynda Weinman) from the Design Studio Web site

Read through each option and then write out your color palette plan according to the color palette in the color reference section of this book. You may also choose to use any one of the pre-designed color palettes, as long as it fits your concept. Once you have that, follow these steps:

1. Open Photoshop.
2. Open the color palette file or CLUT file you've retrieved from the Design Studio site.

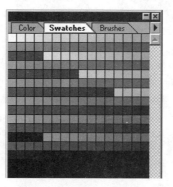

3. Create an RGB file, assuming a 50×50 pixel color square in which to place each individual color you've selected for the palette.

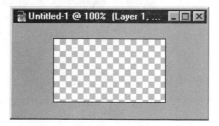

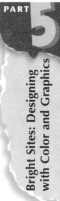

4. Using the color picker, select the first color in your palette.

5. Using the marquee tool, create your first color square (Figure 18.1).

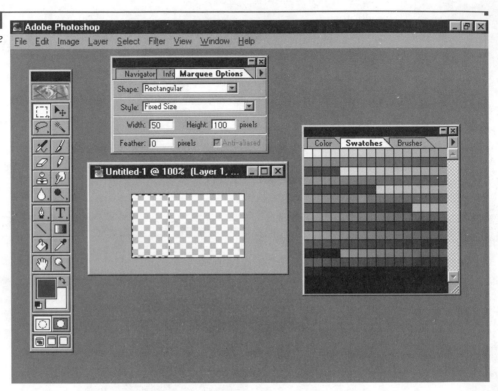

6. Select Edit ➤ Fill, and choose to fill the area with your selected color.

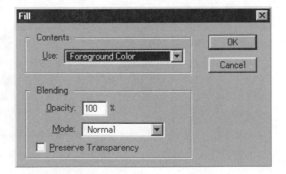

Be sure that the transparency checkbox is *not* checked or the color won't fill the square.

7. Continue this process until you've created your individual palette.

You should complete the process for each of the following scenes. This will give you some practice in creating palettes, get you comfortable working intentionally with color as an expressive modality, and create familiarity with the safe palette.

Scene 1

Your client is a very conservative corporation that owns a multi-billion-dollar national (U.S.) chain of discount retail stories. Their desire is to create an online presence complete with shopping, customer service, and an ongoing marketing presence including seasonal promotions.

They have made it very clear they want to promote a patriotic look that expresses traditional values. Your job is to come up with a color scheme that addresses this company's concern.

Scene 2

An alternative rock band has hired you to create their Web presence. Their music is loud, funky, and fun. They have an energetic and positive message to convey, and they are particularly concerned that despite their alternative style of music, they promote a healthy lifestyle to their youthful audience.

Your goal is to come up with a bright, energetic look and feel that balances the alternative aspect of their music with the positive sense of their music.

Scene 3

You've been asked to create an online classroom for a local community college. The student body is made up mostly of adults in their late 20s and early 30s. The design demands that you combine colors that keep students alert, but do not interfere with the focus necessary for a learning environment.

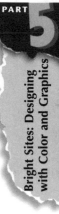

Web Graphic Technology: Review

A strong foundation in color theory and Web-based color application is of paramount importance before creating and implementing Web graphics. With that foundation in place, however, it's time to go to work adding graphics to enhance and enliven your Web site.

Issues for review are:

- Web graphic tools
- Image production techniques
- File formats
- Web graphic optimization
- Transparency, progressive rendering, and animated GIFs
- Web graphic applications

This review will serve to highlight the most critical areas of Web graphic production, but be sure to refer back to Chapter 17 for detailed information on these subjects, as well as supportive information related to Web graphic design.

> *"When I first studied graphic design, we used pencils and paint, scissors and paper, pens and knives. We drew logos and fonts on paper. We designed posters by making a collage. Graphic design was a hand craft.*
>
> *Near to my graduation, the academy bought their first Apple Macintosh computer. I hardly saw or used the machine before I left school. What was its contribution to our profession besides typing text in different fonts and sizes? I was there when they invented desktop publishing, even if I didn't know exactly what it meant then.*
>
> *Nowadays we can't imagine the graphic industry without these advanced computers. We can't imagine the World Wide Web without them. The Web environment fails without a computer. It is both the delivery mechanism and the most indispensable tool for web design. "*
>
> JOEL NEELEN, NextDada, Belgian Web Designer and self-proclaimed
> "Persona Non Graphica"

Main Concepts

Web graphic design is a vast area of study, with foundations in fine art and graphic design. Do you require a background in either of these areas in order to render great graphics? The answer isn't a clear yes or no. Rather, you must assess your own skills and desires in the greater spectrum of your Web design work. This will greatly influence how you approach the learning curve inherent to the subject.

Regardless of how serious a Web graphic designer you are or want to become, understanding the language, concepts, and methods will assist you—no matter what your goals might be.

Tools

I could simplify this review with one word: Photoshop.

> *"I love Photoshop. I started using it from 1996. I found it very easy to work, since I had previous experience working on a similar software but on a workstation (Getris Images). I use no Plug-ins or filters."*
>
> KISAN BHAT, Freelance Web Designer, India

I would also make a lot of people angry at me. First, because I've already soapboxed on the issue. Second, because many of you might disagree. In fact, see Tim Verpoorten's comments regarding his preference of software. But I remain fixed on the Photoshop issue. My bias is born of experience, and if you truly want to be marketable in the Web graphics field, you cannot do without this tool.

> *"I have been doing web design work for about three years and have no formal artistic training and have no artistic talent at all. To overcome this major deficit in my background I have had to use many pre-designed images and mold them together or have taken parts of them to use in my web sites. I have found that Jasc's Paint Shop Pro is at the level that I feel comfortable with using. It does not over-kill me with a large number of filters or effects that will slow me down, but allows me to manipulate the available public graphics to suit my needs. When I have to create an original Web site graphic, PSP gives me the freedom to design without a large amount of artistic training."*
>
> TIM VERPOORTEN, Computer House Reviews

PART 5

Bright Sites: Designing with Color and Graphics

Of course, other programs will play a significant role in your design. If I were asked to determine the least common denominator in terms of design tools necessary to achieve great results on the Web, I'd recommend Photoshop, a good GIF animation program, and a flexible but sophisticated stock art package.

Image Production Techniques

This area can be summed up with the Five S's of Image Production:

1. Start with quality.

2. Scan the image.

3. Size images appropriately.

4. Select attractive treatments.

5. Save files in the correct, optimized format.

Should you have any questions about any of these techniques in detail, refer back to Chapter 17. You might find it handy to copy this and tack it up somewhere near your work area, so that you can refer to it as necessary.

File Formats

While the technology behind file compression formats is complicated, it's easy to remember what file types are best for the Web, and how to use them.

1. There are two types of files that are widely available and accessible for inline Web viewing: the GIF and the JPEG (also written JPG).

2. GIFs are almost always the best format in which to save line art and flat-color graphics.

3. For photographs and files in which you must maintain the integrity of light sources and color gradations, the JPEG format is the way to go.

Optimization

Optimization is the practice of creating the smallest file size while retaining the highest visual quality possible. The first step in optimization is making good decisions in terms of file type. The next step is working with the technology innate to that file's type.

GIF images index the colors in the image, and you can reduce the amount of colors in a GIF to achieve lower file sizes. You'll want to walk through the process described in Chapter 17 to gain a strong sense of how this is done.

JPEGs work differently, offering maximum to low options. Maximum, high, medium, and low refer not to the amount of compression applied, but rather to the quality. Therefore, a JPEG saved at maximum setting will have the most information and therefore, the highest quality.

Sometimes a fine hand and well-trained eye is necessary to achieve the best optimization when working in Photoshop. Programs such as Debabelizer Pro offer comparative analysis and batch processing. If you're going to be processing large quantities of Web graphics, it might be in your best interest to give such a program a test drive.

Special File Considerations

There are three important file techniques with which to familiarize yourself. They are:

- **Transparency**—Only available for GIFs, this is the act of creating areas of the GIF that are clear and to allow background designs show through.

- **Progressive rendering**—This is the progressive appearance of graphics while a Web page loads. The advantage to progressive rendering is that it can keep the visitor interested in the image, convincing them to stay until the page loads. GIFs use a progressive rendering process referred to as interlacing. JPEGs have a similar option, referred to as progressive JPEG.

- **GIF animation**—GIFs can be animated, which adds a lot of potential to a site by offering a stable, well-supported format that adds active media to a page. More about GIF animations is available in Chapter 23.

Web Graphic Applications

Whether you're looking to design headers, image maps, background graphics, or add spot art such as illustrations or photographs to a page, you'll need to review the methods involved in creating Web graphic applications.

For some, optimization of Web graphics is the real trick. For others, coming up with fun and unique graphics that enhance a page is the real challenge. This area takes a lot of practice and time to learn well. The best review you can get with regards to Web graphics is one that gets you working hands-on with the medium. You'll find several such opportunities below, in the tasks section of this chapter.

Page Deconstruction

The Design Studio Color and Graphics Part Summary page uses only three graphics and one piece of multimedia. The graphics are a background graphic (Figure 18.2), a header graphic (Figure 18.3), and an image map (Figure 18.4).

PART

5

Bright Sites: Designing with Color and Graphics

FIGURE 18.2

Design Studio Color Lab background graphic

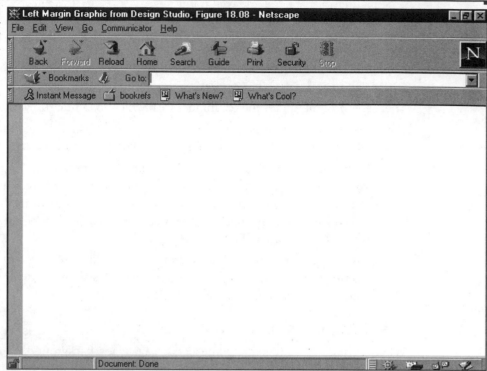

FIGURE 18.3

The Part Summary header.

The background graphic is 1020×6 pixels, and has been optimized as a GIF. It weighs in at only 1KB! The header graphic is 234× 69 pixels, and has also been saved as a GIF. It's size in kilobytes is only 5KB. The navigation map is a GIF too, measuring 50 pixels by 395 pixels. It is the largest graphic on the page, with a total weight of 10KB. The Flash graphic, which is considered a multimedia element, weighs in at 4KB.

The total weight of the graphics on this page is *only* 20KB. Yet it is simple to use, colorful, inviting, and easy to read.

This page exemplifies a popular philosophy that I've embraced when it comes to Web design: Very frequently, less is more.

> *"High-caliber gotcha-design is a matter of using the best and most promising of what technology is available to us to put together a useful, yet interesting, site."*
>
> ROY AUBRY, List Intern, Waterworks Interactive

FIGURE 18.4

The Design Studio main image map

Graphic Technology: Quiz

Please answer the following multiple choice questions.

1. I believe the most important graphics tool to be:

    a. Debabelizer Pro

    b. Paint Shop Pro

    c. Photoshop

    d. Microsoft Image Composer

2. Plug-ins are often used to:

    a. enhance graphic images

    b. provide a source of stock material

    c. layout graphics on a page

    d. help a designer determine which graphics are important to include on the page

3. Which of the following is *not* one of the Five S's of Image Production?

    a. saving

    b. scanning

    c. sorting

    d. sizing

4. What does the acronym GIGO stand for?

    a. get in, get out

    b. giggly indigo girls only

    c. garbage in, garbage on

    d. garbage in, garbage out

5. In scanning, source material refers to:

    a. the output graphic

    b. the input material

    c. the cleaning solution used to ensure that your scans come out clear

    d. none of the above

Please answer true or false for the following statements.

6. The proper scanning DPI for the Web is 600.

7. A photograph of a Waikiki sunset is probably best saved as a JPEG.

8. JPEGs should be made transparent when being used on a textured or patterned background.

9. Interlaced GIFs shouldn't be used because many browsers don't support them.

10. Background graphics can add color and personality to a site.

Write out short answers to the following questions.

11. Are graphics the primary way of getting design into a site? Why or why not?

12. Are you a technologist with no artistic background? A graphic designer interested in Web design? Describe your personal interest in Web graphic design.

Web Graphic Technology: Task

In this section, you will create a header graphic using Photoshop.

OTE

Advanced designers will find this task below their capabilities. Challenge yourselves to create a header in a style you've never attempted before, such as a vertical header, or a design using a lot of images. Then challenge yourself to fully optimize the graphic you've created.

You will need Photoshop and the safe palette or CLUT used earlier in this chapter for this task.

1. Open Photoshop.

2. Open the safe palette or CLUT.

3. Select File ➤ New.

4. Create a 300×100 file (be sure RGB is selected, and you have a transparent background).

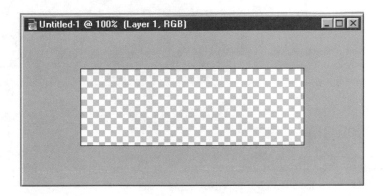

5. Using the color picker, select a dark color such as green or blue (Figure 18.5).

PART **5**

Bright Sites: Designing with Color and Graphics

FIGURE 18.5

A dark color using the color picker

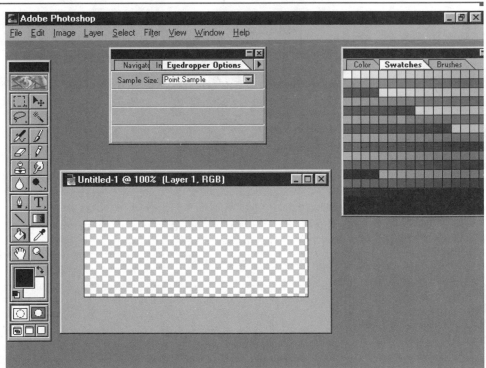

6. Select Edit ➤ Fill

7. Fill the file with the color you've selected.

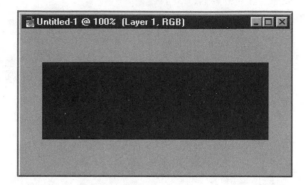

8. Choose another color with the color picker, this time a light color, such as yellow, peach, or white.

9. Select the type tool, and choose a font (I recommend using Times, at 18 points).

10. Type in the words **My Header**.

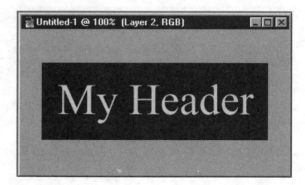

11. Since this file has only two colors, it's a perfect candidate for a GIF. To create this file as a GIF, select Image ➤ Mode ➤ Indexed Color, as in Figure 18.6. If Photoshop asks you to flatten layers, click Yes.

FIGURE 18.6

Selecting the Mode

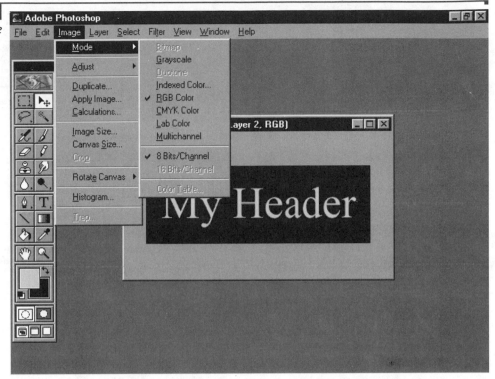

PART 5

Bright Sites: Designing with Color and Graphics

12. Select the Adaptive Palette.

13. Drop the Color Depth down to a value of "3 bits/pixel" (make sure no dither is selected) and click OK.

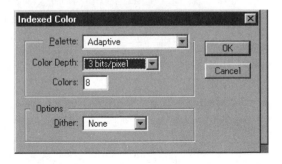

14. Go to File ➤ Export.

15. Choose GIF89a.

16. Make sure the Interlace option is clicked (Figure 18.7).

FIGURE 18.7

Interlacing the GIF

17. Click OK.

18. Select a file name and save the file.

Congratulations! You created an optimized graphic header.

At this point, you have all the information necessary to head out on your own and create background graphics and process images. Your next task is to continue practicing to your skill level.

Answer Key

The following key provides the correct answers to the quizzes in this chapter.

Color

Multiple Choice

1. The correct answer is B. Color in the natural world is expressed theoretically as subtractive.
2. The correct answer is D. Saturation refers to the brightness of a color.
3. The correct answer is D. The combination of black and yellow is considered discordant.
4. The correct answer is B. The inside of a clam shell is iridescent.
5. The correct answer is C. The color brown typically relates to stability.

True or False

6. True. Computer color is based on Additive Synthesis.
7. False. RGB is the pattern used by computers.
8. True. Gamma influences brightness and contrast.
9. False. A safe palette is made up of 216 colors.
10. False. You can make an individual palette with as many colors as you like.

Short Answers

11. This answer is wholly personal, there is no right or wrong answer.

Web Graphic Technology

Multiple Choice

1. The correct answer is C. Photoshop, Photoshop, Photoshop.
2. The correct answer is A. Plug-ins are often used to enhance graphic images.
3. The correct answer is C. Sorting is not one of the Five S's of Image Production.
4. The correct answer is D. Garbage in, garbage out.
5. The correct answer is B. Source material is the input material.

Continued

PART 5

Bright Sites: Designing with Color and Graphics

True or False

6. True. This is a trick question. While Web graphics should always end up at 72 DPI, the scanning DPI is up to your own personal discretion.

7. True. Photographs, particularly where there are lots of gradient colors, are best saved as JPEGs.

8. False. Another trick! While you should use transparent images over a textured or patterned background, JPEGs do not allow for transparency.

9. False. Interlaced GIFs are widely supported.

10. True. Background graphics can add color and personality to a site.

Short Answers

11. Graphics are *not* ideally considered a primary way of designing a site, but should be used along with other techniques in the quest for design.

12. This answer will depend upon your personal experience.

Next Up

Before we move on, think about the amount you've learned about design so far. The lessons have been formidable. You understand a great deal about Web concepts and practices such as accessibility, interface design, space, layout, color, and graphics.

Now we come to one of my favorite areas, typography. All Web technologies are evolving, and typography is no exception. There have been significant limitations to the use of type on the Web, and this causes designers a great deal of frustration, because typography is one of the most beautiful elements of design.

The next chapter will teach you some basic typographic principles, and then we'll go on to see how they are applied.

PART VI

the fine art
of fonts:
web typography

chapter 19

TYPOGRAPHIC
DESIGN

TYPOGRAPHIC DESIGN

You've already learned that color, shape, and space carry individual significance as well as greater meaning when they are combined. As designers, the objective is to learn how to use such elements together to create designs that have lasting impact.

Type is an aspect of design that, like color, shape, and space, carries its own significance. Type is made up of letters, which are the symbolic representation of a complex communication system—the complexity of which is thought to separate us from all other known living beings.

As is true to humanity, our manifestation of thought is often expressed through complicated and beautiful entities. What is represented symbolically is filled with the emotion of its creators, and in turn, evokes emotion from those that are exposed to the symbol. Type is no exception; as an extension of this intimate, evolutionary dynamic known as language, it, too, is complicated, emotional, and frequently beautiful.

". . . primitive man enhanced his environment with personal, symbolic, and pictorial decoration. This inherent desire to ornament continues to play a significant part in our lives. Witness the spray-can graffiti seen everywhere in our cities and the embellished typographic slogans and messages in a variety of media . . ."

MAGGIE GORDON AND EUGENE DODD, AUTHORS,
How to Create and Use Decorative Type

It isn't too difficult to understand, then, why typography is fascinating for many, so much so that some designers have spent their entire lives studying, creating, and admiring type. Philosophers have argued whether type is an extension of language, or if individual characters (known as *letterforms*) within an alphabet carry no significance on their own. Designers debate issues regarding design and readability. Conservative type designers insist that nothing should ever interfere with readability, while other, more adventuresome type designers suggest that type has in and of itself become an art form.

Despite the ongoing discussions regarding what type means to humankind and design, and regardless of the fact that some designers insist on legibility above all versus the new possibilities of using type as form, all are likely to agree that type impacts us personally and emotionally as well as within the world of graphic art.

Essential to humanity and profoundly important to design, the complexity of type is easy to misunderstand and, as a result, misuse. Web designers who have no formal training in typography are at a distinct disadvantage because they do not know that adding type to a design is as essential as adding elements of color, shape, and space.

This chapter attempts to give those of you who need an overview of basic typography an opportunity to learn a bit about type. Even graphic designers with experience in this area will appreciate the review.

Issues covered include:

- Type families and faces
- Type form
- Typographic considerations
- Color and type
- Combining type
- Typographic relationships

Web designers are quite restricted in terms of what can be done with type. Designers wishing to use typographic style must typically rely heavily on graphics to deliver that style, and the impact of emotion they carry. Fortunately, these restrictions are beginning to change, with the introduction of cascading style sheets and other Web-based type technologies. Chapter 20 will take the typographic basics learned here and translate them into practical application. Here, however, you will learn to think about type without limitation, providing a broad entry into the world of type design.

> *"Letter shapes and letter sizes are reasonably limited. But beyond that we rely primarily on emotion."*
>
> GERARD UNGER, from "Legible?"

PART

The Fine Art of Fonts: Web Typography

Families and Faces

These terms are surely no accident. My face contains within it characteristics and attributes of my family. I look a great deal like my father did; my face is structured with his cheekbones and jawline; my eyes are similar to the color of his eyes. I have a brother who also looks very much as my father looked, but while my brother and I share common traits, we don't look that much alike. Another brother shares facial characteristics with our mother, yet doesn't really look like her. These similarities are what demonstrate our familial origins, our differences, and our individuality.

Type is created and classified the same way. *Families* share similar qualities and attributes, but individual *faces* are just that—individual. A type family might have many individual faces within it, some with great variation, but there are certain common qualities that make the individual faces part of the greater whole.

The more in-depth you go in order to study typography, the more you see that there are a lot of variations within individual faces, too—which is one reason why the study of typography is such a serious and complex one.

 NOTE

Faces are also known as typefaces. A typeface is often referred to as a font. These terms are all interchangeable.

Technically speaking, typefaces add visual interest, identity, and style to a page. They are often a significant element in the emotional relationship a designer creates by combining type with other design elements.

> *"Choosing (and then using) typefaces is not a necessary evil: it is an act of creation, and/or helping another to create. It is an assist to communication which consists of far more than mere words."*
>
> DON DEWSNAP, AUTHOR, *Easy Type Guide: The 150 Most Important Typefaces*

There are many families of type, and we will look at a number of those along with a variety of faces.

It's important to remember that two dominant families of type exist. These are the *serif* and *sans serif* families. These families have the largest number of typefaces. It might surprise you to know that in total, there are thousands of typefaces in existence. Furthermore, within each given family are variations based on weight and style that make certain families especially large.

Other type families, including decorative, script, and monospaced, are introduced in the following sections to help give you a feel for how type families and faces work together.

OFF line!

These books will be especially helpful to you as you study typography:

- *The Mac is not a Typewriter* or *The PC is not a Typewriter*, by Robin Williams (Peachpit Press)
- *Desktop Publisher's Easy Type Guide*, by Don Dewsnap (Rockport Publishing)
- *Alphabet: The History, Evolution, and Design of the Letters We Use Today*, by Allan Haley (Watson Guptill Publishing)
- *Type and Layout*, by Colin Wheildon (Strathmore Press)

Serif

Serif type is considered to be about 500 years old. Serif characters are readily identified by the strokes that appear on individual letters. They are often elegant, and generally believed to be good for body text due to readability issues.

It is possible that the serif strokes create a line for the eye to follow, thereby acting as a visual guide (which you can see in Figure 19.1). No one really knows why readability tests have shown serif fonts to be superior for body fonts. What's more, those tests were made *before* the Web was around. While serif fonts are typically a browser's default body font, you'll find that there's a growing interest in the use of sans serif type for body text on the Web these days.

PART

6

The Fine Art of Fonts:
Web Typography

FIGURE 19.1

Serif typefaces create a line along the bottom and top of each row of text. This is thought to enhance readability.

If thou dost love, pronounce it faithfully:
Or if thou think'st I am too quickly won,
I'll frown and be perverse an say thee nay,
So thou wilt woo; but else, not for the world.

There are three main sub-sets of typefaces under the heading of serif. They include *oldstyle, modern,* and *slab serif.*

Oldstyle

It is believed that this group of serif fonts was derived from the pen-and-ink hand lettering of ancient scribes. The angled serif stroke of oldstyle typefaces is thought to have resulted from the scribe's hand lifting from the paper before moving on to the next letter section. Two common oldstyle typefaces include Times (Figure 19.2) and Garamond (Figure 19.3).

Times typeface close-up and as body text

If thou dost love, pronounce it faithfully:
Or if thou think'st I am too quickly won,
I'll frown and be perverse an say thee nay,
So thou wilt woo; but else, not for the world.

Garamond has an elegant and readable look.

The Garamond Type Face:
An Oldstyle serif type with an elegant look.

Times is perhaps the most recognizable of all typefaces. Most faces in this sub-category are referred to as *invisible* faces due to the fact that the reader is so used to seeing this typeface that the relationship to it is an invisible one. Oldstyle serifs are considered to be the most readable typefaces.

Modern

Typefaces in this sub-category all have serifs, but there's been a general flattening of the serif itself. Instead of emulating the natural slant of a scribe's careful handiwork, modern typefaces emulate the industrial age. They are angular, linear, and evoke a sense of order. Common to this style are the well-known and often-used Bodoni typeface (seen in Figure 19.4) and the Walbaum typeface (Figure 19.5).

Bodoni is considered a modern typeface.

Bodoni. A modern serif. Well known, oft-used.

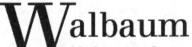

Walbaum
Modern typefaces make great headers, but deteriorate somewhat when used as body text. Note the smudges and lack of clarity.

It's fun to use modern faces in headers, because they tend to look impressive when set larger than common body type. As a general rule, these are not the most readable of the serif faces and should be chosen with care for body text application.

Slab Serif

As the name infers, these serif fonts have slab-like serifs, very thick and meaty. The actual letters are less slab-like, which creates a contrast. This contrast is said to influence the readability factor, making slab serifs good choices for large sections of body text.

A good example of a slab serif typeface is the popular New Century Schoolbook (Figure 19.6).

Century Schoolbook
Slab serifs are good for headers and body text.

Sans Serif

The sans serif family of typefaces doesn't have the strokes; in fact, sans serif letters are rounded and smooth. They are easy on the eye, and have been traditionally useful for headers rather than body text. Their use as body text in the Web environment is causing a shift in this tradition.

One reason for this trend might be that the rules of reading on a computer screen are different from that of reading in print. First, readers probably don't stay as long at the computer screen as they would reading a book, since a computer screen is harder to read from due to physical comfort issues (you can sit, stand, or even lie down with a book). Reading on a computer is also sure to tire one's eyes faster. Light and heat dry out the eyes fast, and people reading on a computer tend to blink less overall than those reading books or magazines.

PART

6

The Fine Art of Fonts: Web Typography

" . . . the Internet is still closer to print than broadcasting, and there is nothing more frustrating than meaningless or overused graphics. The solution lies in the right typeface . . ."

ROGER BLACK, AUTHOR, *Web Sites that Work*

Sans serif styles tend to be readable in terms of shorter sections of text. Paragraphs on the Web *should* be shorter than those in print, and this, too, may have some bearing on why sans serifs can be effective for body text on the Web.

OFF line!

Take a book, any book, off of a nearby bookshelf. Look at the body text. Is it serif or sans serif? How about the headers? Can you identify the type family for headers and body text in this random example?

How about this book? What kind of typeface is being used for body text, and what is being used for headers? If you can see the differences between serifs and sans serifs, you're already becoming familiar with type.

Common sans serif fonts include Arial and Helvetica, both extremely popular on the Web because they are supported by Microsoft products. Another sans serif font used on the Web with regularity is Verdana, a rather new typeface.

Compare Arial, shown in Figure 19.7, with Verdana, shown in Figure 19.8. Note the differences in appearance, including width of letters, height of letters, and of course, the shape of the letters. Here is a perfect example of members of the same family having similar features but very different looks.

FIGURE 19.7

Arial is a popular sans serif font.

> The Arial Typeface: A popular sans-serif.

FIGURE 19.8

Note the differences between Verdana and its familial cousin Arial.

> Verdana is noticeably
> different than its cousin Arial

Decorative

Decorative fonts have added features such as unusual strokes, calligraphic influences, variations in dimension, and unique shapes. Decorative type tends to be used best just as the name expresses, for decoration and enhancement. They rarely, if ever, make good body text.

> *"Decorative typography . . . is concerned with releasing calligraphy, lettering, type, text, and ornament from the strait jacket of traditional forms."*
>
> MAGGIE GORDON AND EUGENE DODD, AUTHORS,
> *How to Create and Use Decorative Type*

Decorative fonts can make good headers, particularly if they are readable or the header information is short. They are also very popular fonts to use on advertisements, such as banner ads.

Whimsy (Figure 19.9), Hollyweird (Figure 19.10), Arriba! (Figure 19.11), and Party (Figure 19.12) are all examples of decorative type. The typeface used for headers on the Design Studio site is also a decorative font, called Bergell (Figure 19.13). Compare these typefaces, noting the unusual features each contains that classify it as a decorative type. Notice that of these choices, Bergell is the most readable, which is why it can more safely be used as a header face.

FIGURE 19.9

Whimsy is a fun and decorative font.

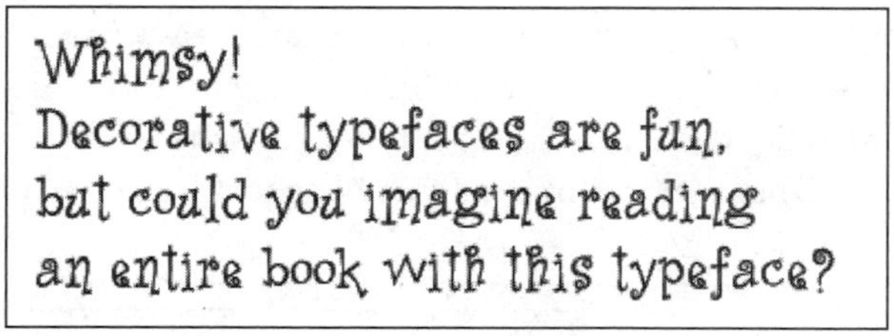

Whimsy!
Decorative typefaces are fun.
but could you imagine reading
an entire book with this typeface?

FIGURE 19.10

Hollyweird is a font with attitude.

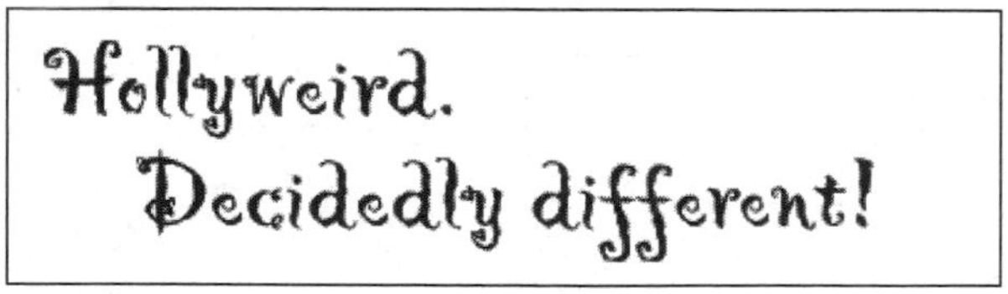

Hollyweird.
Decidedly different!

FIGURE 19.11

The Arriba! font is festive and uplifting.

Arriba! Arriba!

FIGURE 19.12

Party is a decorative font that expresses its intent clearly.

This typeface says "Let's Party!"

FIGURE 19.13

The Design Studio uses the Bergell font, an elegant and stylish typeface.

Bergell is stylishly elegant.

"Decorative fonts are easy to identify—if the thought of reading an entire book in that font makes you wanna throw up, you can probably put it in the decorative pot."

ROBIN WILLIAMS, AUTHOR, *The Non-Designer's Design Book*

Script

Script resembles script-style handwriting and calligraphic hand lettering. There are many, many script faces, each with characteristics that can easily create sub-categories from the sub-category in which they reside.

Script faces are poor choices for body text, but as with decorative faces, can make wonderful enhancements to headers and areas where text is used as a design element.

Gando (Figure 19.14) and Embassy (Figure 19.15) are examples of script. Note the readability differences in these typefaces—there's no problem when used as a larger header, but you can imagine that body text would be quite difficult to read.

FIGURE 19.14

Gando is a voluptuous hand-written font.

Gando is voluptuous.

FIGURE 19.15

Embassy is an elegant, expressive font.

Embassy. Expressively Elegant.

Monospaced Faces

The typefaces we've discussed so far can be categorized as *proportional* fonts. This means that each letter takes up the amount of space necessary for that letter. An "I" and an "M" will take up distinctly different amounts of space.

> *"When choosing the typeface or faces for your design, you will need to assess carefully the image you wish to convey. "*
>
> ALAN SWANN, Design and Layout

Monospaced fonts are those type faces where each individual character takes up the exact same amount of space as another character. An "M" is different than an "I" in width, but in a monospaced font, width is adjusted to be equal for every character in that font. Monospaced faces are used for both body and header text.

A common monospaced font is Courier (Figure 19.16).

FIGURE 19.16

Monospaced fonts are good for headers and body text.

```
Courier.
monospaced fonts
are good for headers
and body text
```

Recent trends in typeface design show take-offs on monospaced faces with decorative elements. One such font, called Schmutz, mimics type. Schmutz Clogged actually looks as though it were typed on a dirty typewriter (Figure 19.17).

FIGURE 19.17

Schmutz Clogged is casual and funny.

Schmutz clogged

OFF line!

Open your word processor and see what fonts you have. On a blank page, type a line from your favorite song or poem in a variety of different type faces from your list. After you're done, try to identify what family the face belongs to.

PART

6

The Fine Art of Fonts:
Web Typography

Type Form

Typefaces can have *form*. Form includes weight, width, and posture. Form specifically relates to the shape and direction in which a given typeface is presented.

Type Weight

As with human families and individuals within those families, some typefaces appear dark and heavy; others seem light and slender. Still others are normal, appearing to have an overall average weight and appearance. Type *weight* influences the way a given face will appear.

- **Roman**—If you belonged to an average weight class and you were a typeface, you'd be described as *Roman*. Roman type tends to be unadorned and simplistic (Figure 19.18).

Times Roman, unadorned.

- **Bold**—Typically used to emphasize information within body text, *bold* text should be used with a light hand. The more bold you use, the bolder the personality of your work. There are times where you'll want a page to shout to the world, but most of the time you'll want to be a bit more diplomatic. Figure 19.19 shows the Walbaum typeface in all bold on the right, and used sparingly on the left.

When you're using bold type, it's better **to use for emphasis** rather than the other way around.

When you're using bold type, it's better to use for emphasis **rather than the other way around.**

- **Light**—Slender, delicate type is referred to as *light*. Light typefaces carry less power than Roman or bold forms, but they can be perfect when a subtle, elegant touch is required. Figure 19.20 shows the Roman form of the sans serif font Arial, and Figure 19.21 shows the light version. Note the difference in presentation and emotion between the two forms. Roman appears to be more stable, and Arial light more gentle. Figure 19.22 shows a bold example to demonstrate the differences between the common weights of this typeface.

This is the Roman form of the Arial typeface

This is the light form of Arial

Arial Bold. Added weight, added presence.

Type Width

Typefaces can have a variety of widths, which refers to the actual space the face takes up along the horizontal axis.

- **Condensed**—Also referred to as *compressed*, a condensed form is one where the typeface is *smaller* in width than its Roman counterpart (Figure 19.23).

Trendex condensed. The letterforms are thinner.

- **Expanded**—Some refer to this width property as *extended*. It is the converse of condensed. Instead of less horizontal width on the face than a Roman counterpart, the typeface is wider, or expanded (Figure 19.24).

PART

6

The Fine Art of Fonts:
Web Typography

Minima expanded.
Note the width of the letterforms.

Type Posture

My mother used to tell me to "sit up straight." I never did, I *liked* to slouch. I'd hear this later in life, first from my piano teachers, then my guitar instructors. Did I listen? No. Today I pay a pretty price in chiropractic bills for not paying attention to what these mentors were trying to tell me about posture. Similar to this physical meaning, *type posture* is the angle at which a given typeface is set. There are two different types of postures, italic and oblique.

- **Italic**—Perhaps the most familiar of postures, *italics*, like bold forms, serve to emphasize text on a page. Italics have their historic roots in handwriting. Remember trying to get that exact right slant in your script? Italics work to get that slant (Figure 19.25).

Times Roman in italics looks like a handwritten style.

- **Oblique**—I like the word *oblique*. It sounds mysterious and intriguing. In fact, it's interesting to note that oblique type forms evolved after electronic methods. Because of this, there is a certain amount of rigidity to oblique forms, rather than a bend and a flex where necessary. This causes them to be less readable and sometimes rather awkward when compared to the more elegant italic form. Oblique typefaces are predominantly found in the sans serif category (Figure 19.26).

oblique is rigid

> When you were practicing handwriting in the first grade, there was probably some-one in class who kept slanting his or her letters to the left. In fact, it might have been you! This phenomenon is called *backslanting* and while it looks cool in some cases, most type designers frown upon it since it can be particularly difficult to read.

Other Typographic Considerations

Other considerations regarding type includes the size and proportion of type in rela-tion to other type and to an entire page; the direction of type along the horizontal and vertical axis; the horizontal space between letters (known as *kerning*); and the vertical space between lines of type (known as *leading*).

Size and Proportion

When working with typefaces it is important to consider their size and proportion to one another—and to other elements on a page.

Type is measured in a variety of ways, including *points* or *pixels*. Point measurement is based on print measurement, whereas pixel measurement uses a computer's pixel-based technology to interpret point size. Generally speaking, it's wisest to stick to the point system when setting type.

The most readable and suitable for body text is thought to be 12 point type. Smaller type can be used for footer and ancillary information, and larger type can be used in headers.

The size and proportion of a typeface is important to style and design. Size can help indicate what role the typeface is playing on the page—larger type is used for headers, medium sizes for body text, small sizes for notes and less-emphasized information such as copyright notices (Figure 19.27).

Varying type size on a page is important, but just as important is keeping that vari-ation consistent. You're looking for the visual interest and practical results that having different sizes of fonts on a page provide—however, you don't want to overwhelm your visitor with too much contrast or complete chaos.

PART

6

The Fine Art of Fonts:
Web Typography

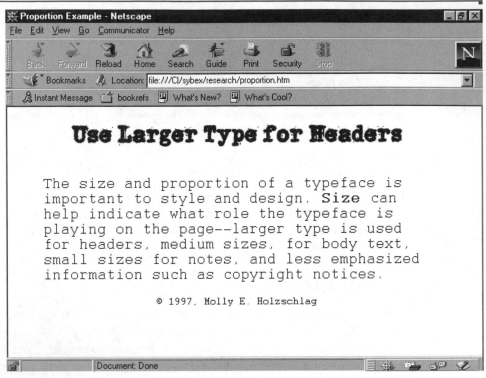

FIGURE 19.27

This page shows variations in size and proportion of the type used.

Direction

Up, down, left, right—the direction in which your typeface runs will have a significant impact on how it is perceived. Figure 19.28 shows a vertical header running along the left of the page. Note that a sense of motion is achieved with this look, which is appropriate for the subject matter, Aviation.

On the same page you can see the topic header, placed at the middle right of the design. Horizontal type is more stable, less full of motion. In this case, the header acts as an anchor to the sense of motion occurring on the rest of the page.

FIGURE 19.28

A vertical direction creates a sense of motion.

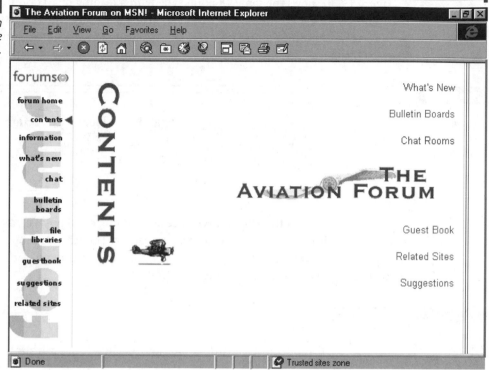

Leading

Typography also concerns itself with the space between lines, which is called *leading* (pronounced "led-ing"), also referred to as *line height*. How close or how far a line is from another influences readability tremendously.

Figure 19.29 shows 18 point type with a leading of 18 points. You'll see that for this typeface (which is Century Schoolbook), the space between the lines appears natural and easy to read.

FIGURE 19.29

18 point Century Schoolbook set with a leading of 18 points

Come, gentle night, come, loving, black-brow'd night,
Give me my Romeo; and, when he shall die,
Take him and cut him out in little stars,
And he will make the face of heaven so fine
That all the world will be in love with night
And pay no worship to the garish sun.

PART

6

The Fine Art of Fonts:
Web Typography

Figure 19.30 shows the same 18 point type with a leading of 10 points. Obviously, this is unreadable text, although occasionally using a leading which is less than the type size can create interesting visual effects—just don't sacrifice readability for intrigue.

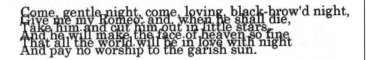

Come, gentle night, come, loving, black-brow'd night,
Give me my Romeo; and, when he shall die,
Take him and cut him out in little stars,
And he will make the face of heaven so fine
That all the world will be in love with night
And pay no worship to the garish sun.

Figure 19.31 shows the 18 point typeface at a leading of 30 points; you can see what occurs with readability at wider vertical spacing. The effect is interesting, and can be used for shorter bursts of text. However, for body text, avoid leading like this— it causes a strain on the eye, affecting readability.

Come, gentle night, come, loving, black-brow'd night,

Give me my Romeo; and, when he shall die,

Take him and cut him out in little stars,

And he will make the face of heaven so fine

That all the world will be in love with night

And pay no worship to the garish sun.

As a general rule, leading set close to the type's own point size will be suitable for body text. Any other value should be considered ornamental, and should be used sparingly.

Kerning and Spacing

Kerning is the space between individual letters within a font. In normal setting, you'll notice that letters touch one another and this can sometimes interfere with readability. This occurs frequently with serif fonts, although it can affect any font.

Kerning allows a typesetter to adjust this space. Doing so requires accessing information contained within the font. This information is contained in what is referred to as a kerning table. Kerning tables contain mathematical information related to the units of each letterform within the font.

Spacing is the horizontal space between letters *outside* the font. In other words, you don't have to access the kerning table to set a letter farther from or closer to another over the entire word.

Figure 19.32 shows an example of a 12 point Arial font with normal spacing. In Figure 19.33, the font has been spaced with a numeric space value of 2.

FIGURE 19.32

12 point Arial with normal spacing

> 12 point Arial with normal spacing

FIGURE 19.33

12 point Arial with a numeric space value of 2

> 12 point Arial with spacing set at 2

Like leading, spacing effects the readability of a passage. While the use of spacing can add visual interest to a page, unusual space values should be restricted to decorative or short bursts of text. Body text requires normal spacing to be attractive and comfortable to the reader.

Font Color

Adding color to fonts can help give a page distinction. As with size and face, a light touch is important—you don't want to overwhelm your site visitors with ten different colors on a page. In fact, sticking to two static colors—one for headers and auxiliary text, and one for body text—is a very safe way to get a bit of color into your design.

Color is also important to type design because the use of different colors will influence the way a word is perceived in relation to another.

Contrast is the name of the game when it comes to color design and type. Remember the lessons learned in Chapter 16? We discussed colors in terms of *warmth* and *coolness*. According to most designers, contrasting warm and cool colors can bring attention to certain words, while detracting emphasis from others.

PART

6

The Fine Art of Fonts: Web Typography

" . . . keep in mind that warm colors (reds, oranges) come forward and command our attention. Our eyes are very attracted to warm colors, so it takes very little red to create a contrast. Cool colors (blues, greens), on the other hand, recede from our eyes. You can get away with larger areas of a cool color; in fact you need more of a cool color to create an effective contrast."

ROBIN WILLIAMS, AUTHOR, *The Non-Designer's Design Book*

On the Web, you can use color for text, text-based headers, links, visited links, and active links. This gives you a lot of opportunity to apply color to text, but again, be subtle. Chapter 20 provides more information on how to use HTML and other, non-graphic technology to work with text.

Even when you are limited to black and white, you can use contrast to gain a sense of color. As mentioned earlier in the discussion of type forms, bold, italic, and oblique can be used to create emphasis within a page. Light type is softer and warmer than **bold** type, which literally jumps off the page.

Anti-Aliasing and Font Smoothing

Fonts are normally bitmapped, which means that they are made up of *squares* of information. What happens on the computer when you want to mimic the smooth, rounded letters of a favorite typeface? Jagged, ragged edges and sloppy-looking type.

In order to address this issue, designers use a technique known as *anti-aliasing*. This is the smoothing of those jagged edges by blurring and lightening certain pixels to make the results appear even.

Without anti-aliasing, type can appear jagged. Figure 19.34 shows a typeface before anti-aliasing is applied. Note the edges.

FIGURE 19.34

Without anti-aliasing, fonts appear jagged

Jagged Little Font

Now if the type is set with anti-aliasing, the results are much smoother (Figure 19.35).

FIGURE 19.35

Anti-aliasing smooths the jagged edges

Smooth Little Font

This technique works well for the Web wherever graphic-based type is used. But what of HTML-based type? The answer is in *font smoothing*, a capability built into the Windows 95 OS that smoothes screen fonts automatically.

OTE

Windows 95 users can download the font smoother from `http://www.microsoft` `.com/typography/grayscal/smoother.htm`.

Figure 19.36 shows an HTML-based header without font smoothing turned on. Compare these jagged edges with the smooth edges in Figure 19.37.

FIGURE 19.36

HTML-based header without font smoothing

PART

6

The Fine Art of Fonts: Web Typography

FIGURE 19.37

HTML-based header with font smoothing

ON line!

- **DesktopPublishing.Com:** An excellent all-around graphic design and typography resource, located at http://www.desktoppublishing.com/.
- **Microsoft's Typography on the Web:** Excellent resource for all that's happening in Web typography, located at http://www.microsoft.com/typography/web/default.htm.
- **Web Typography:** A moderated digest, located at http://www.acdcon.com/webtyp.htm.

Combining Type

Mixing font faces can not only make interesting and professional looking sites, but it's also fun! The problem is that many beginning designers try too hard—not realizing that less is often more when mixing fonts. I've seen some pages where a page designer has used five different fonts or more without ever considering what they were doing, or why.

Typefaces, like families, have relationships with one another. You can have a *harmonious*, long-term relationship or a *discordant*, disruptive relationship. You can also find a nice balance between the peaceful and the passionate, creating a *contrasting* relationship.

In type, harmonious relationships are built on similarities. My uncle likes to say that while opposites might attract, it's the analogous that endure. Use one type family and you're going to stay safe. Of course, you do run the risk of having a rather mundane life (Figure 19.38).

PART

6

The Fine Art of Fonts:
Web Typography

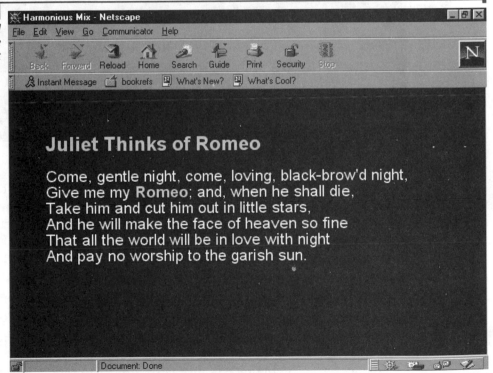

FIGURE 19.38

Arial header and Arial body font are harmonious but possibly boring.

Juliet Thinks of Romeo

Come, gentle night, come, loving, black-brow'd night,
Give me my **Romeo**; and, when he shall die,
Take him and cut him out in little stars,
And he will make the face of heaven so fine
That all the world will be in love with night
And pay no worship to the garish sun.

Discordant relationships are built on conflict. In type, this discord results when fonts that are too similar are mixed together. This creates a disturbing and problematic design, and it's a good idea to avoid relationships of this type (Figure 19.39).

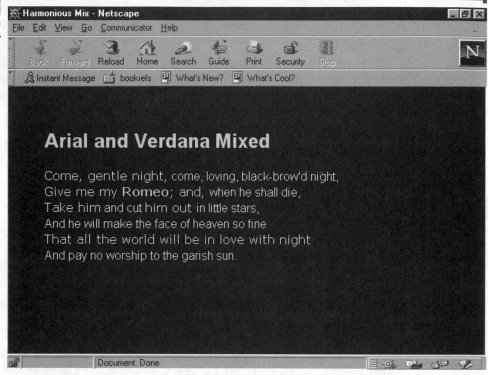

Contrasting relationships are often the most interesting, because you can choose types that are quite different from one another. If I use Whimsy for my header and Times for my body text, I have considerable differences between the typefaces and an interesting look results (Figure 19.40).

If you're not a skilled graphic designer with a typographic background, be careful when combining type. The following tips should help you begin mixing fonts.

- **Avoid mixing fonts from the same family.** For example, don't mix Garamond and Times as they are both serif fonts. Fonts from the same family are often too similar to create contrast—which you want—and too dissimilar to allow for continuity and legibility—which is necessary.

- **One way of combining type on a page without running into problems is to choose one sans serif and one serif face.** Use the sans serif for headers, and the serif for the body text, as in Figure 19.41. You can also switch this around and see if the results are acceptable (Figure 19.42).

FIGURE 19.40

Contrast works with Whimsy as a header and Times for text.

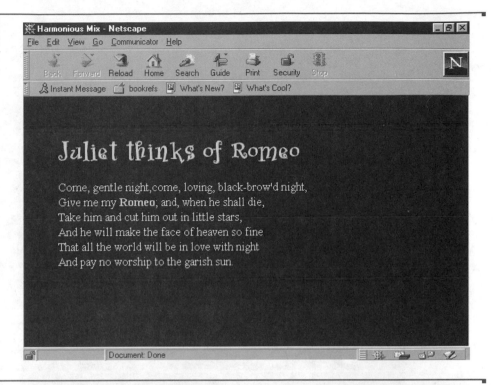

FIGURE 19.41

A page using sans-serif headers and serif body

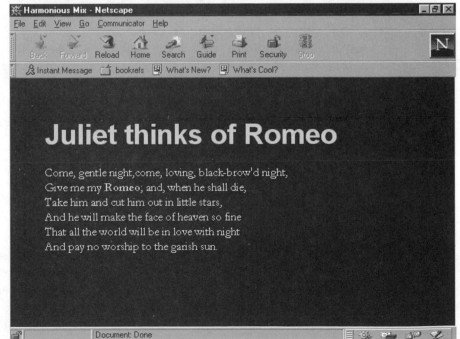

PART

6

The Fine Art of Fonts: Web Typography

FIGURE 19.42

Serif headers with sans serif body works on this page.

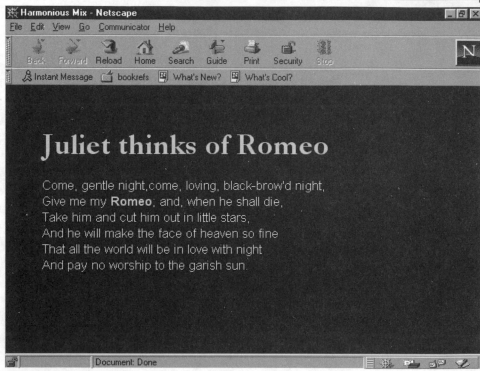

- **When in doubt, leave it out!** If you *think* it looks cool but aren't sure, avoid it until you have more experience. This is especially true if you are creating a commercial page—don't tread on uncharted territory without knowing where you want to end up. Success starts with a sense of confidence, and the chances are if you're unsure, your end design will reflect that lack of confidence.

"We shouldn't confuse legibility with communication."

DAVID CARSON, AUTHOR, *The End of Print*

Next Up

Now that you have a good foundation for typographic design, the challenge is to apply it. That's no easy task—the Web is a difficult environment at best for type. However, it's not impossible, and the good news is that with certain technologies, type on the Web is improving slowly but surely.

Chapter 20 looks at current and up-and-coming technologies that will assist you in applying what you've learned here about typography.

I didn't realize the importance and attraction of type until I worked closely with a graphic designer who had an avid appreciation of the field. As I began to work with type in the context of design, I not only developed a high regard for type, but an awe for the vast and diverse type families and faces that exist.

The lines and curves of type combined with the emotional impact of words affect me deeply. As a Web designer, I look forward to a day where type on the Web is as sophisticated as it is in print. Until then, I hope you'll learn as much about type as you can—preparing for that day and being fully ready to embrace the opportunities born of typographic communication.

PART

6

The Fine Art of Fonts:
Web Typography

chapter 20

WEB
TYPOGRAPHY

WEB TYPOGRAPHY

Web typography challenges the best of designers, no matter how skilled at type. The reason is simple: support for type is truly limited. There are only three basic alternatives that designers have when designing for type on the Web. These include using graphics to handle desired typographic elements, coding type with the HTML *<font>* tag, or using cascading style sheets.

Three options doesn't sound limited, but here's the catch: With HTML and style sheets, if a specific typeface doesn't exist on the machine used by your Web site visitor, that visitor *will not see* your beautiful type.

A further headache is the often-referred-to browser problem. Microsoft's Internet Explorer 3.0 and above have good style sheet support. Netscape introduced support for style sheets with the 4.0 version. Font tags were introduced in many 2.0 browser versions, but sometimes cause problems with compatibility—check Appendix B for a comparison list of fonts and style sheet support between browser types and versions.

OTE

One advantage if you're using the above-listed browsers is that the style sheet interpretation for typographic elements is pretty good, as compared to the less stable style sheet positioning. It is for this reason alone that I go into such detail with style sheets in this chapter.

The future holds great hope, however. With Microsoft's embedded fonts and the OpenType initiative, there are new technologies on the horizon that will make type within easy reach to designers.

Embedded fonts allow the designer to embed the font information for a specific page into the code of that page. The necessary fonts are then silently downloaded by the visitor's browser, allowing the fonts on that page to be seen. Interestingly, embedded fonts strip out any characters and letters in a font that are not used on that page. This means the embedded information can transfer with relative speed.

The OpenType initiative is a cooperative effort between Microsoft and Adobe, companies that have been at odds historically. But, in order to solve some of the typographic problems born of the Web environment, the two companies have put aside their differences and are working on fonts that will be instantly accessible to Web visitors. Recently, Adobe developed 12 original typefaces just for the Web. These typefaces include two serifs, a sans serif, a script, and two decorative faces.

ON line!

- **Microsoft Typography:** For up-to-date news on typographic technology, visit this site, `http://www.microsoft.com/typography/`.
- **Adobe:** This company site has terrific information on general and Web type as well as typographic tools for PC and Macintosh platforms, located at `http://www.adobe.com/`.

Despite the push-me, pull-you feel of the state of Web typography, you can begin working with the technologies that do exist. This chapter will help you do just that. You'll examine:

- Designing type with graphics
- HTML-based type techniques
- Using cascading style sheets to achieve greater typographic control

"In a printed piece, or on the Web, attractive, well-executed typography adds elegance and improves communication. Poor typographic execution can seriously degrade otherwise inspired design."

PAUL BAKER, PBTWeb

The most important thing to remember about typography on the Web is that advances are made at regular intervals. Keep up with the technology and you'll stay ahead of the pack when it comes to typographic applications in Web design.

PART

6

The Fine Art of Fonts: Web Typography

Approaching Web Typography

Whether you're looking to use type in the conservative fashion as a method to deliver your Web-based, written content, or you'd like to be adventurous and use type as artistic design, the more methods you can use to approach Web typography, the better equipped you are to achieve your typographic goals.

> *"Typography is becoming tribal, an initiation rite."*
>
> JOE CLARK, writings from Typo Expo 1996

I personally believe that type should do both—serve its function *and* be used artistically. The Web is a perfect opportunity to experiment. Obviously, when your client and audience want you to manage text you're going to be somewhat reigned in by convention. But there are times when you will have the opportunity or want to create more cutting edge designs.

Type can help you do this.

Again, Web typography can currently be approached with some stability through three vehicles: graphics, HTML, and cascading style sheets.

Graphics and Type

In many ways, putting type on a Web site as a graphic is currently the most stable method of ensuring your type design will be seen. Visitors don't have to have the font installed—they are seeing the font as part of a graphic. This gives you lots of control because not only can you select from any typeface you own, but you can color it to your tastes and add special effects, too.

Of course, the downside is the time that graphics take to download. Where you use graphics to handle the majority of your type, you'll need to take care to balance the typographic elements with the graphics necessary for your individual pages.

Here are a few tips to help you when working with type as a graphic:

- Select flat colors from the browser-safe palette (see the color reference in the middle of this book) to ensure the smallest file size even if you're using large type.

- Save flat-color, simple, graphic-based, typeset files as GIFs.

- If you add special effects such as shadows, gradient fills, metallic color, or if you use 3-D type, you should try saving your files as GIFs and JPEGs in order to compare the results. You might find that in certain instances, JPEGs will serve you better, whereas in other cases, you will get smaller files and a terrific look from GIFs.

- Remember our discussion in Chapter 19 regarding anti-aliasing? In most cases, you will want to anti-alias your fonts as you set the type on the graphic (see

Figure 20.1). However, anti-aliasing can become problematic when you want to set small type. It's especially wise to avoid anti-aliasing on any type that is less than 12 points, although you should experiment with both in order to get the best look (Figure 20.2).

Type that is 12 or more points should typically be anti-aliased.

It's helpful to anti-alias type that is 12 points or larger.

Small type that is not anti-aliased looks fine.

Smaller type often looks better without anti-aliasing.

Treat type-based graphics as you would any other graphic when coding. This means to be sure to use the appropriate tag and attributes, including width, height, alt, and any relevant alignment tags:

```
<img src="welcome.gif" width="300" height="100" alt="Welcome to Our House"
align="right">
```

Wherever possible, it's also a good idea to combine graphic-based type with type you create on the page. This way you lean less on the graphics to get your typographic point across.

HTML and Type

Aside from browser and individual user's font library support issues, the main problem with HTML type is that you can only use it along the horizontal. Also, you can't set it in specific points—you must rely on really poor sizing techniques. But you can do some interesting things with HTML type.

HTML type is delivered primarily through the <font> tag. The only exception to this is the header tags <h1> . . . </h1> through <h6> . . . </h6> which use a bold Times font to create a variety of headers ranging in size from large (size 1) to small (size 6). You'll want to use them now and then, but with so many other options, you might find them limiting as you work with different typefaces and sizes.

PART

6

The Fine Art of Fonts: Web Typography

The Font Tag

The <font> tag has numerous considerations in terms of widespread compatibility, but does help designers address type techniques through HTML. The <font> tag allows for a number of attributes, including face, size, and color.

The <font> tag follows standard HTML conventions, with an opening and closing tag enclosing the division of information you are applying the font attributes to:

```
<font>
Love is a smoke raised with the fume of sighs;
Being purged, a fire sparkling in lovers' eyes;
Being vex'd a sea nourish'd with lovers' tears:
What is it else? a madness most discreet,
A choking gall and a preserving sweet.
</font>
```

Of course, nothing happens until you add relevant attributes, which I'll show you as we look at the use of typefaces, forms, and color further on in the chapter.

Random Cheats

Getting other typefaces to appear using HTML is a trick many designers use. The most popular of these is the pre-formatted text tag <pre>, which will force a monospaced (usually Courier) typeface:

```
<pre>
Love is a smoke raised with the fume of sighs;
Being purged, a fire sparkling in lovers' eyes;
Being vex'd a sea nourish'd with lovers' tears:
What is it else? a madness most discreet,
A choking gall and a preserving sweet.
</pre>
```

Figure 20.3 shows the results.

You can also use the <tt> tag for a monospaced font:

```
<tt>
Love is a smoke raised with the fume of sighs;
Being purged, a fire sparkling in lovers' eyes;
Being vex'd a sea nourish'd with lovers' tears:
What is it else? a madness most discreet,
A choking gall and a preserving sweet.
</tt>
```

The results will be the same as shown in Figure 20.3.

FIGURE 20.3

*Using the <pre>
tag will force a
monospaced font.*

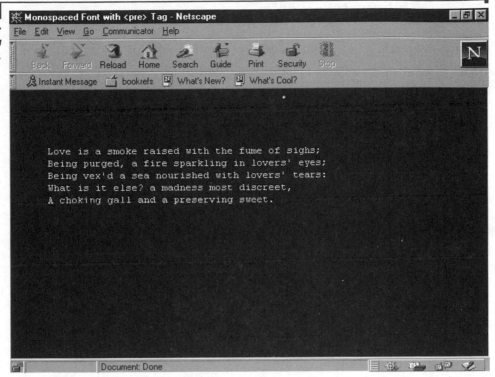

Monospaced Font with <pre> Tag - Netscape

File Edit View Go Communicator Help

Back Forward Reload Home Search Guide Print Security Stop

Instant Message bookrefs What's New? What's Cool?

```
Love is a smoke raised with the fume of sighs;
Being purged, a fire sparkling in lovers' eyes;
Being vex'd a sea nourished with lovers' tears:
What is it else? a madness most discreet,
A choking gall and a preserving sweet.
```

Document: Done

Style Sheets and Type

In Chapter 9 we went over some elementary ideas regarding style sheets. We're going to again review the main concepts here, as they pertain directly to how you will work with style sheet code to apply typography in the Web environment.

NOTE

To view style sheet information, you'll need a compatible browser. Individuals using Internet Explorer 3.0 and above or Netscape 4.0 or higher will be able to see style sheets. Of course, if a particular typeface is called for and doesn't exist on your visitor's own machine, the type will not be seen in that face.

There are three primary ways to use style sheets. They are the *inline* method, the individual page or *embedded* method, and the *linked* or external style sheet.

PART

6

The Fine Art of Fonts:
Web Typography

Inline Style Sheets

This approach exploits existing HTML tags within a standard HTML document and adds a specific style to the information controlled by that tag. An example would be controlling the indentation of a single paragraph using the `style="x"` attribute within the `<p>` tag. Another method of achieving this is with the `<span>` tag and the `style="x"` attribute combined.

An inline style example would be:

```
<span style="font: 14pt garamond">
Love is a smoke raised with the fume of sighs;
Being purged, a fire sparkling in lovers' eyes;
Being vex'd a sea nourish'd with lovers' tears:
What is it else? a madness most discreet,
A choking gall and a preserving sweet.

</span>
```

You could do the same thing with the paragraph tag:

```
<p style="font: 14pt garamond">
Love is a smoke raised with the fume of sighs;
Being purged, a fire sparkling in lovers' eyes;
Being vex'd a sea nourish'd with lovers' tears:
What is it else? a madness most discreet,
A choking gall and a preserving sweet.
</p>
```

Embedded Style Sheets

This method allows for the control of individual pages. It uses the `<style>` tag, along with its companion tag, `</style>`. This information is placed between the `<html>` tag and the `<body>` tag, with the style attributes inserted within the full `<style>` container. A short example follows:

```
<style>
P { font-family: arial, helvetica, sans-serif; }
</style
```

Linked Style Sheets

All that is required with linked style sheets is to create a style sheet file with the master styles you would like to express—using the same syntax you would with embedded style as follows:

```
<style>
P { font-family: arial, helvetica, sans-serif; }
</style
```

Save the file using the `.css` extension, for example, the file `paragraph.css`. Then, simply be sure that all of the HTML documents that will require those controls are *linked* to that document.

Within the `<head>` tag of any document you'd like to have adopt the style you've just created, insert the following syntax (keep in mind that the reference will have your own location and file name):

```
<link rel="stylesheet" href="paragraph.css" type="text/css">
```

Style Sheet Syntax

With embedded and linked style sheets, the attribute syntax is somewhat different than standard HTML syntax. First, attributes are placed within curly brackets; second, where HTML would place an equal (=) sign, a colon (:) is used; and third, individual, stacked arguments are separated by a semi-colon rather than a comma. Also, several attributes are hyphenated, such as `"font-style"`, or `"line-height."` A simple style sheet line looks like this:

```
{ font-style: arial, helvetica; }
```

As with HTML, style sheets tend to be quite logical and easy to understand.

 I P

The `<div>` (division) tag can be used like the `<span>` tag for inline control. The `<div>` tag is especially helpful for longer blocks of text, whereas `<span>` is most effective for adding style to smaller stretches of information, such as sentences, several words, or even individual letters within a word.

In a sense, the inline method of style sheet control defeats the ultimate purpose of cascading style sheets. The main point of the technology is to seek style control of entire pages or even entire sets of pages. The inline method should only be used where touches of style are required.

Families and Faces

Being able to use type families and faces can totally empower Web designers, because they can use those faces to fully express the emotion within the design being created. Limitations aside, we'll look at how typefaces and families can be used with graphics, HTML, and cascading style sheets.

Typefaces and Graphics

The most important thing to remember is selecting the typefaces you want to use for your body and header text *before* sitting down to set your type. Once you've determined what typefaces you'll be using, and you know the literal content of the graphic to be designed, the issue boils down to the tool you're going to use to set the type.

Most designers agree that to work with type, the ideal combination is Illustrator and Photoshop. Illustrator allows for a lot of control over the type you're setting, including kerning, which isn't available in Photoshop. Once you've set your type in Illustrator, you can then add your effects in Photoshop. The process is a bit time-consuming, however, and many Web designers have learned to be very creative using Photoshop alone.

Many designers who use Photoshop alone to set type are perfectly happy doing so. With the exception of kerning, most say they can achieve what they are after with what is available in Photoshop.

In Figure 20.4, you can see the Photoshop type tool is open and text is about to be set at 16 point, 16 line-spacing, anti-aliased, Oz Handicraft typeface. Figure 20.5 shows the results.

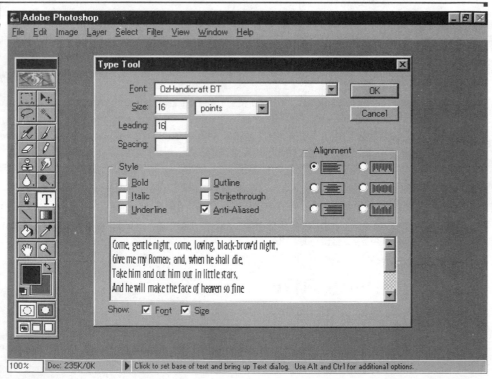

FIGURE 20.5

The type is set.

> Come, gentle night, come, loving, black-brow'd night,
> Give me my Romeo; and, when he shall die,
> Take him and cut him out in little stars,
> And he will make the face of heaven so fine
> That all the world will be in love with night
> And pay no worship to the garish sun.

Typefaces, Families, and the Font Tag

With the HTML <font> tag you can select any typeface that you like and use it in the face attribute. Again, the limitation is that you will run into a problem with who has what on any given machine.

There are really only a total of three type families and specific related typefaces that you can be almost absolutely sure will show up across platforms and on individual machines.

On the PC, the forms are serif, sans serif, and monospaced. The specific faces are Times New Roman, Courier New, and Arial, respectively.

Macintosh offers the same three forms, with Times, Courier, and Helvetica replacing Arial.

What does this mean to you as a designer? It's simple. The <font> tag has one rather intelligent aspect of its face attribute: you can stack any number of typefaces with a type family and hopefully end up covering your bases.

After tagging the section of text you'd like to apply font styles to, you add the face attribute, and then define the font names. The browser will look for the first font name called for, and if it doesn't find it, will move on to the next named font:

```
<font face="arial,helvetica">This text will appear as Arial or Helvetica,
depending upon which font is available</font>
```

If you'd like to add some stability to this syntax, you can add the family name at the end of the stack:

```
<font face="arial,helvetica,sans-serif">This text will appear as Arial or
Helvetica or the default sans-serif font, depending upon which font is
available</font>
```

It's important to remember that if a font face isn't available on a given machine, the default face will appear. Default is almost always a serif font such as Times, unless the user has selected another font for his or her default. So if you're mixing fonts, bear in mind that your sans serifs might appear as serifs, and vice-versa.

This lack of control can seem maddening! You can always forgo using type, but then you run the risk of having your pages appear ho-hum. Go for fonts, but do so thoughtfully, and wherever possible, stack the fonts along with a family name.

Style Sheets

Using a typeface family as a default is an excellent idea all around, as it covers the designer's font choices as completely as possible. Even if a specific font face is unavailable on a given computer, it's likely that a similar one in that font's family is available. An aware designer will place the first choice first, second choice second, and so forth, with the family name at the end.

You can approach fonts in style sheets using the font-family string. Style sheets will accept these in all three types of style sheet: inline, embedded, and linked.

An inline example (Figure 20.6) would be:

```
<span style="font-family:garamond,times,serif">
Love is a smoke raised with the fume of sighs;
Being purged, a fire sparkling in lovers' eyes;
Being vex'd a sea nourish'd with lovers' tears:
What is it else? a madness most discreet,
A choking gall and a preserving sweet.
</span>
```

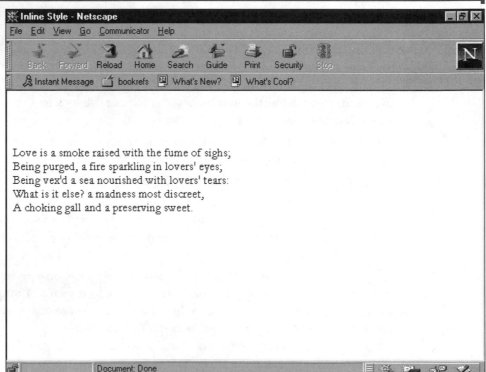

FIGURE 20.6

The results of an inline application of style

Since inline style can be used with any reasonable HTML tag, you could also do this:

```
<blockquote style="font-family:garamond,times,serif">
Love is a smoke raised with the fume of sighs;
Being purged, a fire sparkling in lovers' eyes;
Being vex'd a sea nourish'd with lovers' tears:
What is it else? a madness most discreet,
A choking gall and a preserving sweet.
</blockquote>
```

The results are that the browser not only picks up the style sheet information, but the HTML blockquote format as well (Figure 20.7).

FIGURE 20.7

Using inline style with the block-quote tag

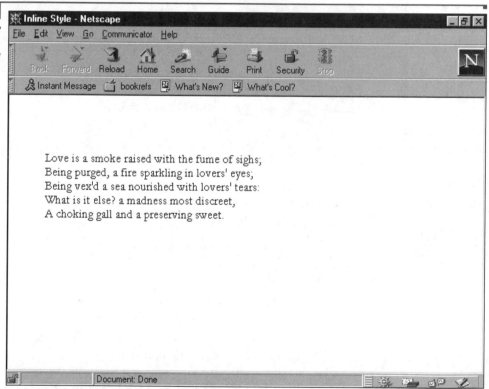

Here's an embedded (linked style will also look like this) example of the same concept. Let's say you wanted to apply a series of typefaces and family to an entire paragraph. The syntax would be:

```
P { font-family: arial, helvetica, sans-serif; }
```

In Figure 20.8, you can see that Garamond appears in all the paragraphs on the page.

PART

6

The Fine Art of Fonts:
Web Typography

FIGURE 20.8

Garamond is applied to all the paragraphs.

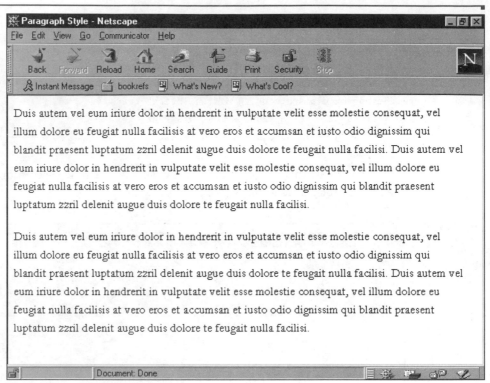

You can apply this style to the blockquote as well:

```
blockquote { font-family: arial, helvetica, sans-serif; }
```

Figure 20.9 shows the blockquoted section.

Font Family Support

There are specific families supported by style sheets, as follows.

- **Serif**—As you'll remember from Chapter 19, serif typefaces are usually the best choice for body text. A popular serif typeface other than Times or Garamond is Century Schoolbook. Let's say you want to have that appear first, but if someone doesn't have that font on their machine, you'd rather it search for Garamond than moving right away to Times. You can see the syntax below. The results can be seen in Figure 20.10.

```
{ font-family: century schoolbook, garamond, times, serif; }
```

FIGURE 20.9

In this instance, the embedded style controls the appearance of all the block-quoted material.

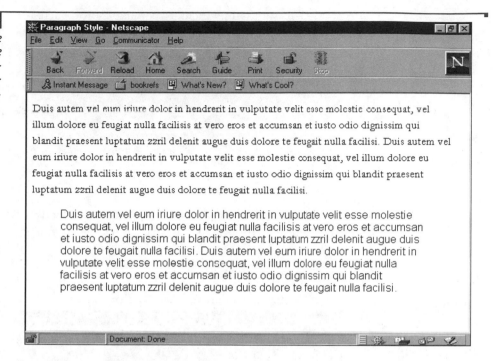

FIGURE 20.10

My browser shows the Century Schoolbook type-face, because I have that font.

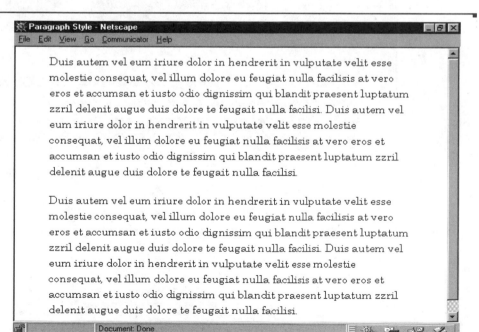

- **Sans serif**—This font family includes popular choices such as Arial, Helvetica, and Avante Garde. The same concept applies here, of course:

```
{ font-family: arial, helvetica, avante garde, sans-serif; }
```

OFF line!

Try this one on your own with a style sheet–compatible browser. What are your results? Do you see Arial, Helvetica, Avante Garde, or a default sans serif font?

- **Cursive**—Use this in place of *script*. These are the same as script typefaces—fonts that appear as though they have been handwritten. Figure 20.11 shows the results.

```
{ font-family: embassy, cursive; }
```

FIGURE 20.11

This typeface results from embedded style.

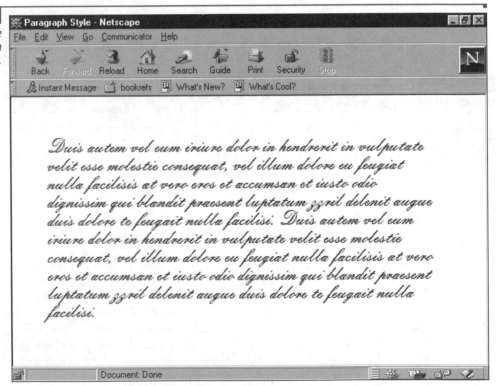

- **Fantasy**—Fantasy fonts are the same as the *decorative* typeface you learned about in Chapter 19. They are useful for stylish, fun headings and titles. They are not practical for body text. You can see the Whimsy typeface in Figure 20.12.

```
{ font-family: whimsy icg, fantasy; }
```

FIGURE 20.12

Here you see the Whimsy typeface.

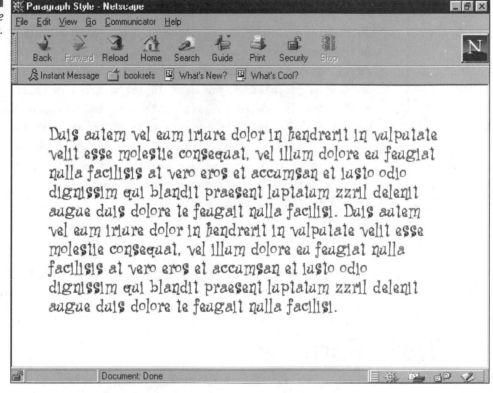

- **Monospace**—Like serif and sans serif options, you're familiar with the mono-spaced font. Figure 20.13 looks like the text was typed onto a page.

```
{ font-family: courier, monospace; }
```

Does anyone *still* use typewriters?

PART

6

The Fine Art of Fonts:
Web Typography

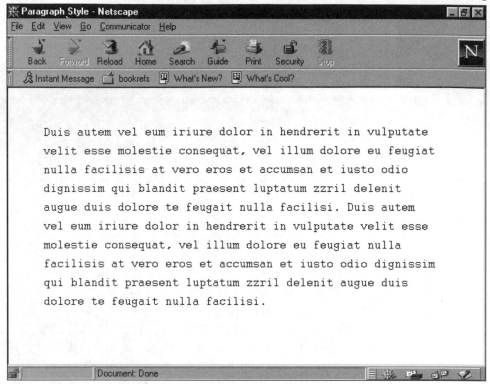

Type Form

Remember from our study of typographic design that form refers to such typographic concerns as weight and posture.

Type Form and Graphics

With graphics, you can address weight by choosing the exact typeface and weight you desire for your graphic. Figure 20.14 shows Arial Narrow.

FIGURE 20.14

Arial Narrow is set on a graphic.

Come, gentle night, come, loving, black-brow'd night,
Give me my Romeo; and, when he shall die,
Take him and cut him out in little stars,
And he will make the face of heaven so fine
That all the world will be in love with night
And pay no worship to the garish sun.

Posture is also dealt with when choosing the typeface. If you select the italic or oblique form of the typeface, you end up with that typeface. Figure 20.15 shows Century Schoolbook italicized. I love the look of this font in italics, it's very evocative of handwriting. In Figure 20.16, a bold weight Bodoni typeface is shown.

Century Schoolbook italicized

Come, gentle night, come, loving, black-brow'd night,
Give me my Romeo; and, when he shall die,
Take him and cut him out in little stars,
And he will make the face of heaven so fine
That all the world will be in love with night
And pay no worship to the garish sun.

Bold Bodoni

Come, gentle night, come, loving, black-brow'd night,
Give me my Romeo; and, when he shall die,
Take him and cut him out in little stars,
And he will make the face of heaven so fine
That all the world will be in love with night
And pay no worship to the garish sun.

Type Form and HTML

Standard HTML is more difficult when it comes to weight because you are dependent upon the end-user's library of fonts. If that user does not have the light, narrow, bold, demi-bold, or other weight you specify in the face attribute of the <font> tag, you're going to be out of luck. One thing you can do is stack the typeface's weight that you'd prefer with the typeface itself, and in some cases your font will be seen (Figure 20.17).

```
<font face="arial narrow, arial, helvetica, sans-serif">
Love is a smoke raised with the fume of sighs;
Being purged, a fire sparkling in lovers' eyes;
Being vex'd a sea nourish'd with lovers' tears:
What is it else? a madness most discreet,
A choking gall and a preserving sweet.
</font>
```

PART

6

The Fine Art of Fonts:
Web Typography

FIGURE 20.17

Using the font tag to achieve Arial Narrow

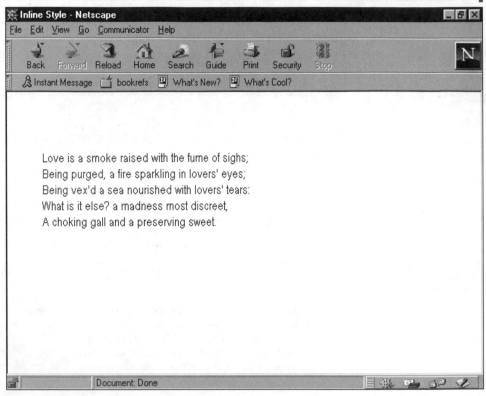

Italics are easily created with the italic tag <i> . . . </i>. Any text between a <font face> tag and an italic will appear in the italic version of that typeface, should the individual have the means of viewing the italic version.

```
<font face="arial narrow, arial, helvetica, sans-serif">
Love is a smoke raised with the fume of sighs;
Being purged, a fire sparkling in lovers' eyes;
Being vex'd a sea nourish'd with lovers' tears:
What is it else? a <i>madness</i> most discreet,
A choking gall and a preserving sweet.
</font>
```

Similarly, bold can be created with the bold tag <b> . . . </b>.

```
<font face="arial narrow, arial, helvetica, sans-serif">
Love is a smoke raised with the fume of sighs;
Being purged, a fire sparkling in lovers' eyes;
Being vex'd a sea nourish'd with lovers' tears:
What is it else? a <b>madness</b> most discreet,
A choking gall and a preserving sweet.
</font>
```

Hopefully, Shakespeare will forgive me for forcing emphasis on Romeo's already impassioned speech!

There is no tag for oblique postures.

Type Form and Style Sheets

As with font faces, font weights in style sheets rely on the existence of the corresponding font and weight on an individual's machine. A range of attributes are available in style sheets, including extra-light, demi-light, light, medium, extra-bold, demi-bold, and bold.

You'll notice that these selections are a bit more extrapolated than those introduced in Chapter 19. Follow the basic tips in that chapter with regard to use of weight, but also be aware that before assigning font weights, the typeface you are applying the weight to must have that weight available within the face. Many people are likely to have the Roman, light, or bold versions of a typeface, but are much less likely to have extra-lights or demi-bolds unless they have an extensive font collection on their computer.

An example of assigning a light weight to the Arial font can be found in Figure 20.18, and a bold weight to the Walbaum font in Figure 20.19.

FIGURE 20.18

Arial Narrow is achieved with style.

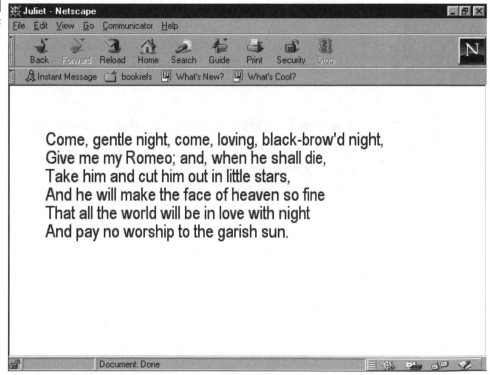

PART

6

The Fine Art of Fonts:
Web Typography

FIGURE 20.19

Bold gives weight to Walbaum.

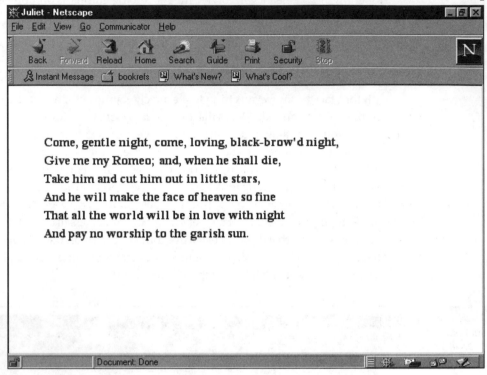

To achieve posture, there are three methods you'll have to rely on:

- `font-style` attribute
- `text-decoration` attribute
- standard HTML with bold or italic tags

Italics can be achieved using the `font-style` attribute or the `text-decoration` attribute. The `font-style` attribute typically dictates the style of text, such as placing it in italics. The appropriate syntax to do this would be:

```
{ font-style: italic; }
```

The `text-decoration` attribute:

```
{ text-decoration: italic; }
```

It seems obvious that bold should be considered a font style too, but there is no style sheet attribute supported by Internet Explorer 3.0 to achieve this. Therefore you'll have to revert to the use of standard HTML bold tags.

`<b>This text will appear in bold,</b> whereas this text will not.`

Dislike underlined links? With cascading style sheets, designers can now use the {text-decoration: none} attribute and argue to globally shut off underlined links. In embedded and linked style sheet formats, the syntax would follow the "A" value: A {text-decoration: none}. For inline style, simply place the value within the link you wish to control: `<a style="text-decoration: none" href="my.html">this link has no underline!</a>`.

Other Typographic Considerations

Other typographic considerations include size, proportion, leading, and kerning. Size and proportion can be addressed with HTML and cascading style sheets, leading is somewhat addressed by cascading style sheets, and kerning can currently be dealt with only by setting the type on a graphic.

Using Graphics

Because you can address almost any kind of typographic issue by using Illustrator, whose interface is shown in Figure 20.20, and Photoshop to set the type onto a graphic, graphics give the most flexibility when attempting typographic concerns that cannot be dealt with using HTML or style sheets.

Size and proportion will all depend on your own design and aesthetic. You can set type as small or large as you want, using points. Direction can also be managed; Figure 20.21 shows a vertical header. Leading is addressed within the programs, as is letterspacing and kerning (Figure 20.22).

Kerning can currently be achieved on the Web by first setting the type in a program such as Illustrator, and then saving it as a Web graphic using Photoshop. There is no HTML or style-sheet-based method to deal with kerning.

PART

6

The Fine Art of Fonts: Web Typography

FIGURE 20.20

Brainbug's Michelle Carrier sets her type in Illustrator.

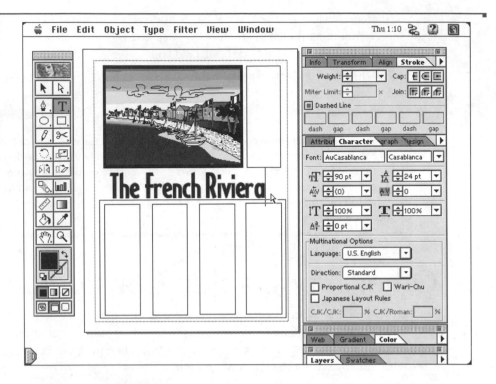

FIGURE 20.21

Setting a vertical header

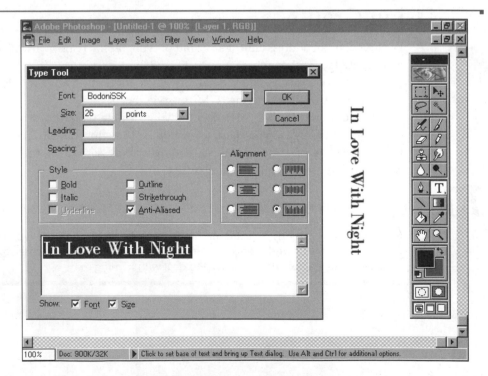

FIGURE 20.22
Using Illustrator for kerning

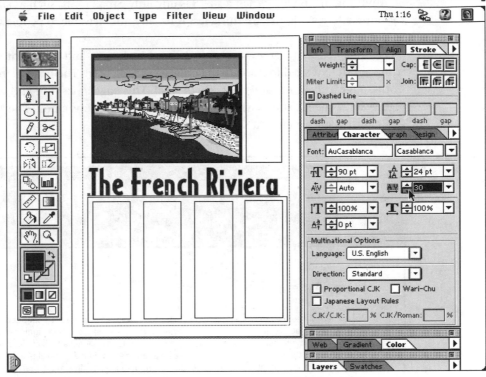

Type Size and HTML

The size attribute of the <font> tag allows you to set type based on a numeric system. Unfortunately, this system does not allow a designer to control type size using points. Furthermore, direction, leading, spacing, or kerning cannot be controlled with standard HTML.

Using the Size Attribute

Font sizing in HTML is pretty rudimentary, with whole-number values determining the size of the font. Default, standard size is "3"; anything higher is going to be larger, and anything lower will be smaller. You can also use negative numbers, such as "-1", to get a very small type size. Here's an example of a header using font face and size:

```
<font face="times,garamond,serif" size="5">
```

Anything much bigger than a size 5 is ungainly. Small fonts, such as size 1, are good for notes and copyrights. Anything less is usually not viewable to people with average-to-poor eyesight.

Figure 20.23 shows an example of a header, body text, and copyright notice, each using a different sized font. Note the typefaces being used. The header and copyright notice appear in Times, and the body in Arial. This page looks nice and neat, unlike Figure 20.24, which shows what happens when a coder runs amok. The "wave" effect came into vogue when font sizing first became available.

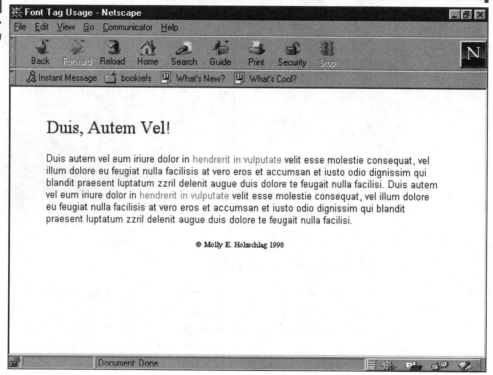

FIGURE 20.23

Using the <font> tag for page design

Some designers will argue that Figure 20.24 looks more interesting. They're right—it does, and I certainly don't want to discourage creativity. This particular effect was fun, but it quickly became cliché. I encourage you to study typography a little more closely and come up with original typographic applications.

FIGURE 20.24

The "wave" effect

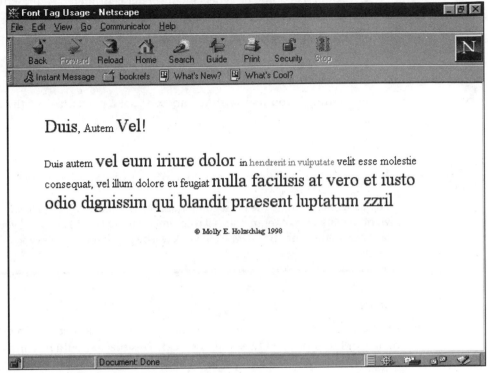

Style Sheets

Style sheets to the rescue! Size (with choice in measurement units) and leading can be applied using style sheets. Kerning is not an option in Web typography unless you set the type as a graphic.

Size

Sizing in style sheets offers the designer to size his or her fonts using five size options:

- **Points**—To set a font in point size, use the abbreviation pt immediately next to the numeric size:

  `{font-size: 12pt}`

- **Inches**—If you'd rather set your fonts in inches, simply place the abbreviation in next to the numeral size, in inches, of the font size you require:

  `{font-size: 1in}`

PART

6

The Fine Art of Fonts: Web Typography

- **Centimeters**—Some designers might prefer centimeters, represented by `cm` and used in the same fashion as points and inches:

  `{font-size: 5cm}`

- **Pixels**—Pixels are argued with the `px` abbreviation:

  `{font-size: 24px}`

- **Percentage**—You may wish to choose to set a percentage of the default point size:

  `{font-size: 50%}`

OTE

Point size is likely to be the most comfortable choice for designers, although some will want to work with other methods. I recommend using point size, but if you do choose another method, be *consistent*. Your work will be much more professional-looking as a result.

Leading

Leading is addressed in cascading style sheets with `line-height`. This refers to the amount of line spacing between lines of text. This space should be consistent, or the result is uneven, unattractive spacing. The `line-height` attribute allows designers to set the distance between the baseline, or bottom, of a line of text.

To set the leading of a paragraph, use the `line-height` attribute in points, inches, centimeters, pixels, or percentages in the same fashion you would when describing sizing attributes:

```
P { line-height: 14pt; }
```

Color and Type

Color adds interest to type. You can use contrasting colors to gain a variety of effects. You can emphasize certain passages or parts of a word, as in Figure 20.25, or use colored type to separate headers from body text.

FIGURE 20.25

Emphasizing type with color

COLOR MY WORLD

Creating Colored Type with Graphics

Again, graphics are your best bet when you really want to address color effects.

A helpful tip is to select your colors from the safe palette and be sure to always optimize your graphics appropriately (see Chapter 17). This will give you the best chances of having smaller file sizes and better color-matches between HTML and graphic colors.

HTML-Based Type and Color

The color attribute allows you to set any hexadecimal value you'd like to use when using the <font> tag. As ever, stick to safe-palette values, which you can find in the color reference of this book. An example of the <font> tag with the color attribute added looks like this:

```
<font face="times,garamond,serif" size="5" color="#003300">
```

Use hexadecimal code to select a color; the one that you see listed here is forest green. Some people and certain HTML editing programs will use the literal name of standard colors, such as blue, green, red, and the like. The hexadecimal codes, however, are much more stable in cross-browser, cross-platform environments.

ON line!

Hexadecimal color references:

- A chart of RGB and hexadecimal values can be found at `http://sdc.htrigg.smu.edu/HTMLPages/RGBchart.html`.

- Download the `nvalue.gif` or `nhue.gif` from the Design Studio at `http://www.designstudio.net/color/`. These charts have been provided courtesy of Lynda Weinman. You may also visit her Web site at `http://www.lynda.com/`.

These charts put color selection and hexadecimal values right at your fingertips!

Style Sheets and Color

Style sheets allow for a great deal of flexibility when it comes to the addition of color. Using hexadecimal codes, color can be added to actual attributes including other HTML tags used in the inline style sheet method.

```
<p style="color: #003300">
All of the text in this paragraph will appear in forest green.
</p>
```

PART

6

The Fine Art of Fonts:
Web Typography

With embedded and linked style sheets, you can add the color attribute to generalized rather than specific sections. In the following example, all level 2 headers appear in red. Note that other attributes have been added here, including typeface, size, and style.

```
<style>
H2 {font-family: arial, helvetica; sans-serif;
font-size: 14pt;
font-style: italic;
color: #FF0033;}
</style>
```

All Together Now

So far you've gotten a look at fragmented pieces of graphics, fonts, and styles. Here are full examples of each, in text and code.

Graphic Example

In this case, we'll use another quote from Romeo and Juliet, and set it using 20 point Trebuchet (a font available from Microsoft at http://www.microsoft.com/typography/) with a 20-point leading. The type is colored white, and applied to a flat black background. Then, a star motif is added to the background, and the file saved as a 5-bit GIF suitable for use as a background graphic.

Here's the simple HTML code to create the page:

```
<html>

<head>
<title>Juliet Speaks</title>
</head>

<body bgcolor="#000000" text="#FFFFFF" link="#00FF00" vlink="#FF0000"
background="juliet2.gif">
<pre>

</pre>
<div align="center">
<a href="next.htm"><i>next</i></a>
</div>
</body>
</html>
```

NOTE

There are 20 carriage returns between the <pre> tags, forcing the link to the bottom of the page.

In Figure 20.26 you can see the results. While a background graphic was used in this example, remember that you can set type on a graphic to be used anywhere on the page. You can place a graphic as a header, as body text, as part of body text and fix placement using tables (or style sheet positioning).

FIGURE 20.26

Graphic-based type design

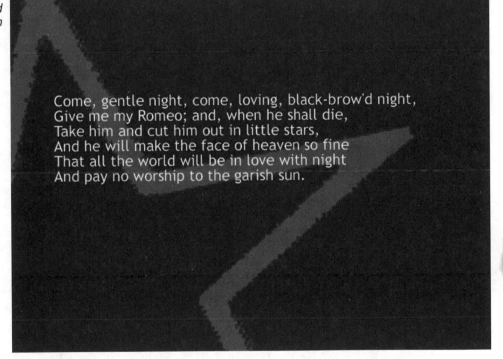

Come, gentle night, come, loving, black-brow'd night,
Give me my Romeo; and, when he shall die,
Take him and cut him out in little stars,
And he will make the face of heaven so fine
That all the world will be in love with night
And pay no worship to the garish sun.

Figure 20.27 is a screen shot of NextDada (`http://nextdada.luc.ac.be/`), one of Belgian graphic designer Joel Neelen's Web sites. In this shot, he has stacked a series of graphics on top of one another to achieve the typographic design on this page. Add to that some clever JavaScript, and the page is alive with visual intrigue founded on the graphic-based typographic elements.

PART
6

The Fine Art of Fonts:
Web Typography

FIGURE 20.27

Graphic-based typography in action on the NextDada site

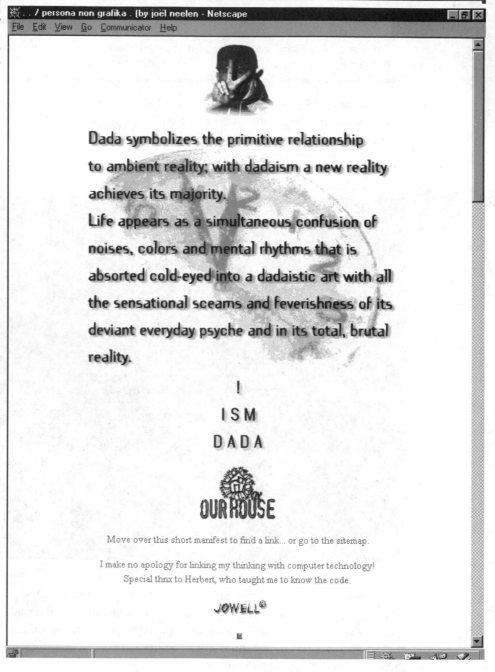

Dada symbolizes the primitive relationship to ambient reality; with dadaism a new reality achieves its majority.

Life appears as a simultaneous confusion of noises, colors and mental rhythms that is absorted cold-eyed into a dadaistic art with all the sensational sceams and feverishness of its deviant everyday psyche and in its total, brutal reality.

I

ISM

DADA

OUR HOUSE

Move over this short manifest to find a link... or go to the sitemap.

I make no apology for linking my thinking with computer technology!
Special thnx to Herbert, who taught me to know the code.

JOWELL©

Here's a look at Neelen's code.

```html
<html>
<head>
        <!-- Author: Joel Neelen -->
        <!-- e-mail: jneelen@luc.ac.be -->
<title>. . / persona non grafika . (by jo&euml;l neelen</title>
<meta name="description" content="The cyberplatform of Joel Neelen aka
{captain verruckt}">
<meta name="keywords" content="dada, nextdada, joel, neelen, travel,
travelling, kite, kiting, cerf-volant, art, graphics, jemen, yemen, jordan,
jordanie">
<meta name="author" content="Joel Neelen : jneelen@luc.ac.be">

<script language="JavaScript">

<!-- if the browser is not capable to JavaScript1.1 he will use this and do
nothing
function init()
{
  dummy=0;
}
function imgreplace(i,s,text)
{
  window.status = text;
  return true;
}
// end do nothing -->

</script>
<script language="JavaScript1.1">

<!-- to hide script contents from old browsers
function init()
{ // set the 7 images to be non-highlighted
document.sexstacy.src = "/picture/dada/dada1_1.gif"
document.castle.src = "/picture/dada/dada2_1.gif"
document.old.src = "/picture/dada/dada4_1.gif"
document.travel.src = "/picture/dada/dada5_1.gif"
document.art.src = "/picture/dada/dada6_1.gif"
document.kites.src = "/picture/dada/dada7_1.gif"
document.cinema.src = "/picture/dada/dada8_1.gif"
}
function imgreplace( imagename, source, text )
```

```
{
  eval( 'document.' + imagename + '.src = "/picture/dada/" + source' );
  setTimeout( 'window.status = "'+text+'"', 500 );
  return true;
}
// end hide contents from old browsers -->

</script>

</head>
<body onload="init();" bgcolor="#FFFFFF" text="#7297FF" link="#7297FF"
vlink="#F77307" alink="#F77307">

<center>
<table height="100%" width="420" cellspacing="0" cellpadding="2" border="0">
<tr align="center">
<td align="center">
<a href="root/kaffee.html" onmouseover="self.status='Something about the man
behind this web site.' ; return true">
<img src="picture/dada/dada0.gif" width="107" height="100" border="0"
alt="Joel"></a>
</td>
</tr>

<tr align="center">
<td align="center">
<a href="root/sex/sexstacy.html" onmouseover="return
imgreplace('sexstacy','dada1_2.gif','Monogamy is the message!');"
onmouseout="return imgreplace('sexstacy','dada1_1.gif','');return
true;"><img lowsrc="picture/dada/dada1_0.gif" src="picture/dada/dada1_2.gif"
width="420" height="36" border="0" name="sexstacy" alt="sexstacy"></a>
<br>

<a href="root/castle.html" onmouseover="return imgreplace('castle','dada2_2
.gif','The purpose could be to create a virtual community where people can
have fun and learn things.');" onmouseout="return
imgreplace('castle','dada2_1.gif','');return true;"><img lowsrc="picture/
dada/dada2_0.gif" src="picture/dada/dada2_2.gif" width="420" height="36"
border="0" name="castle" alt="castle"></a>
<br>

<img lowsrc="picture/dada/dada3_0.gif" src="picture/dada/dada3_1.gif"
width="420" height="36" border="0" alt="nothing">
<br>
```

```
<a href="root/index.html" onmouseover="return imgreplace('old','dada4_2
.gif','This link will bring you to my old homepage.');" onmouseout="return
imgreplace('old','dada4_1.gif','');return true;"><img lowsrc="picture/dada/
dada4_0.gif" src="picture/dada/dada4_2.gif" width="420" height="36" border="0"
name="old" alt="old homepage"></a>
<br>

<a href="root/travel/travel.html" onmouseover="return
imgreplace('travel','dada5_2.gif','Explore different cultural lifestyles and
backgrounds...');" onmouseout="return imgreplace('travel','dada5_1
.gif','');return true;"><img lowsrc="picture/dada/dada5_0.gif" src="picture/
dada/dada5_2.gif" width="420" height="36" border="0" name="travel"
alt="travel"></a>
<br>

<a href="root/art/artefact.html" onmouseover="return
 imgreplace('art','dada6_2.gif','Dadaism, for one thing, no longer stands
aside from life as an aesthetic manner...');" onmouseout="return
imgreplace('art','dada6_1.gif','');return true;"><img lowsrc="picture/dada/
dada6_0.gif" src="picture/dada/dada6_2.gif" width="420" height="36"
 border="0" name="art" alt="art"></a>
<br>

<a href="root/kites.html" onmouseover="return imgreplace('kites','dada7_2
.gif','A kite is a thing on the end of a string!');" onmouseout="return
imgreplace('kites','dada7_1.gif','');return true;"><img lowsrc="picture/
dada/dada7_0.gif" src="picture/dada/dada7_2.gif" width="420" height="36"
border="0" name="kites" alt="kites"></a>
<br>

<a href="root/cinema.cgi" onmouseover="return imgreplace('cinema','dada8_2
.gif','I felt an icy hand of fear grabbing me.');" onmouseout="return
imgreplace('cinema','dada8_1.gif','');return true;"><img lowsrc="picture/
dada/dada8_0.gif" src="picture/dada/dada8_2.gif" width="420" height="72"
border="0" name="cinema" alt="cinema"></a>

</td>
</tr>

<tr>
<td align=center>
            <!-- On reload this image will automatically change -->

<img src="picture/dada/dada3.gif" width=107 height=100 border=0 alt="D A D A">

            <!-- End on reload -->
```

PART **6**

The Fine Art of Fonts:
Web Typography

```
<br>
                    <!-- Start link to OUR HOUSE 1997 -->

<a href="http://www.ourhouse.be/" onmouseover="self.status='Get a glimpse of
the multi-happening Our House that took place in September1997' ; return
true" target="_blank"><img src="picture/dada/ourhouse.gif" width="107"
height="100" border="0" alt="Our House 1997"></a>

                    <!-- End link -->
<br>
<font size="-1">Move over this short manifest to find a link... or go to the
<a href="root/sitemap.html" onmouseover="self.status='SiteMap.' ; return
true">sitemap</a>.
<p>
I make no apology for linking my thinking with computer technology!</font>
<br>

<font size="-1" color="#789DB9">Special thnx to Herbert, who taught me to
know the code.</font>
<p>

<a href="root/mail.html" onmouseover="self.status='You can send me an e-
mail.' ; return true"><img lowsrc="picture/dada/jowell_0.gif" src="picture/
dada/jowell_1.gif" width=80 height=21 border=0 alt="JOWELL"></a>
<p>

<a href="http://www.nedstat.nl/cgi-bin/viewstat?name=nextcount"
target="_blank"><img src="http://www.nedstat.nl/cgi-bin/nedstat
.gif?name=nextcount" border="0" alt="" width="8" height="8"></a>

</td>
</tr>
</table>

</center>
</body>
</html>
```

Note the use of META tags, comment tags, table layout, and alt attributes. Neelen, like many Web designers concerned about the thoroughness of their work, takes special care not only with his typographic design, but the underlying code elements that make a site accessible, stable, and professional.

HTML Example

This example demonstrates the use of the font tag and its attributes. I want you to first look at the page, in Figure 20.28.

FIGURE 20.28

The Poetry and Music page from molly.com

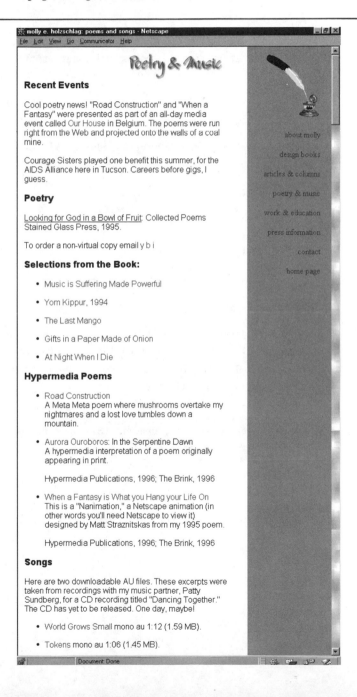

Then, predetermine all of the different fonts (graphics and HTML included) on the page *just by looking*. Make a list of those fonts.

Now, study the following code:

```
<!-- molly e. holzschlag: molly@molly.com -->

<html>
<head>
<title>molly e. holzschlag: poems and songs</title>
</head>

<body bgcolor="#000000" text="#000000" link="#993300" vlink="#993300"
background="images/mol-bak.gif">

<table border="0" width="600" cellpadding="5" cellspacing="0">
<tr>

<td valign="top" width="400">

<img src="images/pm-hed.gif" alt="poetry" width="300" height="50"
align="right">
<br clear="all">

<font face="arial,helvetica,sans-serif">

<h3>Recent Events</h3>

Cool poetry news! "Road Construction" and "When a Fantasy" were presented as
part of an all-day media event called <a href="http://www.ourhouse.be/">Our
House</a> in Belgium. The poems were run right from the Web and projected
onto the walls of a coal mine.
<p>

Courage Sisters played one benefit this summer, for the AIDS Alliance here
in Tucson. Careers before gigs, I guess.
<p>

<h3>Poetry</h3>

<u>Looking for God in a Bowl of Fruit</u>: Collected Poems
<br>

Stained Glass Press, 1995.
<p>
```

To order a non-virtual copy email <a href="mailto:ybi@ybi.com">y b i</a>
<p>

<h3>Selections from the Book:</h3>

<ul>

<li><a href="p-1.htm">Music is Suffering Made Powerful</a>
<p>

<li><a href="p-2.htm">Yom Kippur, 1994 </a>
<p>

<li><a href="p-3.htm">The Last Mango</a>
<p>

<li><a href="p-4.htm">Gifts in a Paper Made of Onion</a>
<p>

<li><a href="p-5.htm">At Night When I Die</a>

</ul>
<p>

<h3>Hypermedia Poems</h3>

<ul>

<li><a href="http://ybi.com/molly/rc/">Road Construction</a>

A Meta Meta poem where mushrooms overtake my nightmares and a lost love
tumbles down a mountain.
<p>

<li><a href="http://ybi.com/aurora/">Aurora Ouroboros</a>: In the Serpentine
Dawn

A hypermedia interpretation of a poem originally appearing in print.
<p>

Hypermedia Publications, 1996; The Brink, 1996
<p>

<li><a href="http://ybi.com/poetry/fant.html">When a Fantasy is What you
Hang your Life On</a>

This is a "Nanimation," a Netscape animation (in other words you'll need
Netscape to view it) designed by Matt Straznitskas from my 1995 poem.
<p>

Hypermedia Publications, 1996; The Brink, 1996

</ul>
<p>

<h3>Songs</h3>

Here are two downloadable AU files. These excerpts were taken from
recordings with my music partner, Patty Sundberg, for a CD recording titled
"Dancing Together." The CD has yet to be released. One day, maybe!
<p>

<ul>

<li><a href="images/wrldgrow.au">World Grows Small</a> mono au 1:12 (1.59
MB).
<p>

<li><a href="images/tokens.au">Tokens</a> mono au 1:06 (1.45 MB).

</ul>

</font>

</td>

<td valign="top" align="right" width="200">

<img src="images/poetry.gif" width="108" height="125" border="0" alt="pen
and ink">
<p>

<a href="molly.htm">about molly</a>
<p>

<a href="books.htm">design books</a>
<p>

<a href="write.htm">articles & columns</a>
<p>

```
<a href="poems.htm">poetry & music</a>
<p>

<a href="work.htm">work & education</a>
<p>

<a href="press.htm">press information</a>
<p>

<a href="contact.htm">contact</a>
<p>

<a href="index.html">home page</a>

</td>
</tr>
</table>

</body>
</html>
```

If you guessed three for the total amount of fonts being used on this page, you're correct. First, there's the header graphic, which uses the Bergell typeface. Then, there's the body text, which will appear as Arial, Helvetica, or whatever sans serif font you have available if those are not.

Finally, there's the type I've used in the right margin menu. Sharp readers will have noticed that *there is no font tag or attributes* used to create this font. Why?

Think about it for a second.

Can you identify the typeface?

It's a serif.

Specifically, it's Times.

Remember now? Serifs are the *default* font. Therefore, I didn't have to code for it.

 line!

Have some fun with this code! Change type using the font tag as often as you like, trying out different combinations, colors, sizes, and styles.

PART

6

The Fine Art of Fonts:
Web Typography

Style Sheet Example

Here, typeface, form, leading, and color have been assigned to this page using style sheets.

```html
<html>

<head>
<title>Style Sheet Example</title>

<style>

H1 { font-family: arial, helvetica, san-serif ;
font-size: 22pt;
color: #FFFF00; }

P { font-family: times, serif;
font-size: 18pt;
color: #FFFFFF;
line-height: 18pt; }

A { text-decoration: none;
font-weight: bold;
color: #CCFFCC; }

</style>

</head>

<body bgcolor="#000000">

<blockquote>

<h1>Juliet Thinks of Romeo</h1>

<p>
Come, gentle night, come, loving, black-brow'd night,<br>
Give me my <a href="romeo.htm">Romeo</a>; and, when he shall die,<br>
Take him and cut him out in little stars,<br>
And he will make the face of heaven so fine<br>
That all the world will be in love with night<br>
And pay no worship to the garish sun.
</p>
```

```
</blockquote>

</body>
</html>
```

Figure 20.29 shows the results.

FIGURE 20.29

Style applied to a page

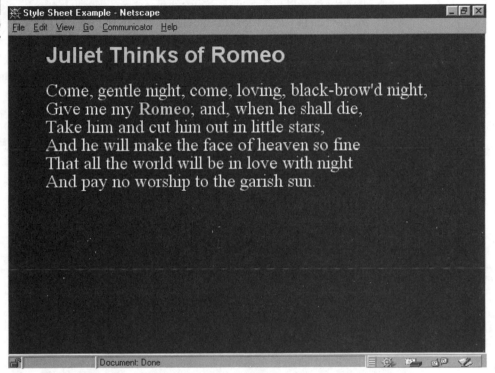

Obviously, these examples are just the very tip of the iceberg when it comes to the use of style sheets. Many options and more powerful applications are available, and I highly recommend you study more about style sheets as you learn more about typography. They will no doubt be a major player in how type on the Web is delivered with increasing sophistication.

PART

6

The Fine Art of Fonts:
Web Typography

Next Up

Chapter 21 will review the lessons learned about typographic design and Web typography, and get you working on tasks so you can begin working hands-on with type.

While type on the Web is still limited, there's a lot to come. Getting excited by and interested in typography now, you'll be ahead of the pack because you'll have a lot of great ideas that you'll be ready to apply with each new available technology.

It's interesting to think that what's happening on the Web might *seem* behind the times in terms of long-term graphic design techniques, but the environment is so provocative that anything can happen. What seems rudimentary can actually challenge us to learn new ways of working, and, in the end, might in fact end up influencing the print world from which the original inspiration came.

"Print will look to the interactive environment for inspiration."

JEFFEREY KEEDY, Emigre

chapter 21

THE DESIGN STUDIO TYPE MILL

THE DESIGN STUDIO TYPE MILL

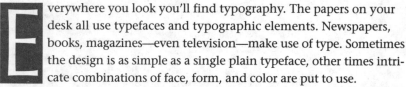

Everywhere you look you'll find typography. The papers on your desk all use typefaces and typographic elements. Newspapers, books, magazines—even television—make use of type. Sometimes the design is as simple as a single plain typeface, other times intricate combinations of face, form, and color are put to use.

Whether you use type to communicate specific words, as an art form in and of itself, or combine the communication and the art to create compelling designs, knowing a bit about how type is used will help you express your ideas to the people who come into contact with your work.

We know one thing: Web typography is young. It has many limitations, the primary one being that the type library on my computer is bound to be different from that on yours.

But as with all aspects of Web design, it is the challenges that make us the early pioneers of a new medium, responsible for working within as well as testing the limits of our work environment.

How conservative or experimental you can be will most certainly depend upon what job you're doing, who the audience is, and what your client might like or dislike. Where you can, I encourage you to experiment, but where you cannot, learn from the lessons in this book to keep your type design as interesting and as appropriate as possible.

This chapter synthesizes concepts and techniques that relate to:

- Typefaces and families
- Type form
- Size, proportion, and direction
- Leading, kerning, and spacing
- Type and color
- Combining type

Examples from the Design Studio Web site (`http://www.designstudio.net/type/`), quizzes, and general review will assist in expanding your typographic knowledge and technique.

Type Design: Review

This section will cover type topics as they relate to design. The idea here is to gain an understanding of typographic theory *in general* as opposed to immediately jumping into Web methods of typography.

This theory-oriented foundation will assist you as you move towards applying Web-based typographic techniques because you'll have a much more refined idea of the look you are after.

Main Concepts

The following sections detail the specific concepts you'll need to know about typographic design.

Type Families and Faces

Families of type share similar traits. Serif type all have serifs, or strokes, on the letterforms. Sans serif type tends to be more rounded, and have no strokes. Script mimics handwriting or calligraphy, and decorative type is fun, funky, and sometimes downright weird. Monospaced type looks like the letters that come from a typewriter. Each letterform in a monospaced font takes up the same width as any other. You can see each of these type families in Figure 21.1.

PART

6

The Fine Art of Fonts:
Web Typography

FIGURE 21.1

A view of each of the type families

Serifs have strokes

San Serifs have no strokes and tend to be rounded

Script typefaces look like handwriting

Decorative type is fun, funky, & even weird!

`Monospaced type is reminiscent of a typewriter.`

NOTE

There are other categories of families, sub-categories, and naming conventions used in typography. This book looks at the most common and widely seen families.

Faces within families are vast, and many different faces exist. Look through your type library and find out what faces you have. Can you identify their family of origin?

Type Form, Width, and Posture

Type form relates to the weight of a typeface. Some typefaces are light, others are bold, some have weights in-between those extremes such as demi-bolds or demi-lights. Width refers to the width of a typeface, which can appear as condensed (the letters appear compressed) or expanded, where the letters appear to have been extended.

Type posture refers to the way a type leans. There are two specific postures, italic and oblique. Italic can make a font look as though it is handwritten. Oblique is a less natural, technically forced lean of a typeface and tends to be less readable. Italics and obliques are used for emphasis.

Type Size, Proportion, and Direction

Type size is usually measured in points, but other measurement forms such as pixels do exist. You are encouraged to work with points for the purposes of Web design unless you are an accomplished type designer and have an understanding of how to work with size in other measurement units.

Proportion is how one piece of type relates to another. Sometimes large and small type together can create a strong effect (as in Figure 21.2).

FIGURE 21.2

Proportion can add impressive effects to type

Direction refers to which direction the type is read. Type can appear vertical, horizontal, or can be manipulated to run at angles.

Leading, Kerning, and Spacing

Kerning is the width between individual letters *within* the font. Spacing is the width between letters outside of the technical parameters of the font. Leading is vertical width between lines of type and may also be referred to as line height.

Type and Color

Color adds distinction and effect to type. As with any graphic element, using a light hand is important. Too many colors might confuse your audience, whereas too few might be very sedate.

Combining Type

You can combine type on a page, or in a single word. The important rule of thumb with combination is to somehow gain *contrast*. If you use typefaces that are too similar, you stand a chance of not achieving the effect you're after.

Page Deconstruction

Let's take a look at the Design Studio's use of type.

Typefaces

- **Headers**—The headers on the Design Studio Web site are set in the Bergell typeface, which you can see in Figure 21.3. Bergell is a *decorative* typeface. There are some script-like aspects because it looks as though it could be someone's handwriting, but decorative elements separate it from a pure script (Figure 21.4).

PART

6

The Fine Art of Fonts:
Web Typography

FIGURE 21.3

The Bergell typeface

FIGURE 21.4

A close-up of decorative versus script type elements

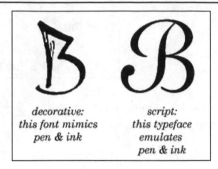

- **Body**—The body type is done in Arial (or Helvetica, or a sans serif default depending upon your type library). Figure 21.5 shows the body text as it appears on my screen in Arial font. Arial is a sans serif font with a clean, rounded look.

FIGURE 21.5

Body text from the Design Studio

As a companion Web site to my book, this site seeks to enhance both the learning within that book as well as provide auxiliary and updatable resources for the Web designer.

If there's something you'd like to see on this site, e-mail me and let me know! For more information about Web by Design, visit the Sybex Web site. For information about other Web design books and articles that I've written, visit my personal site, http://molly.com/.

- **Accents**—Accents are all done in Arial. In Figure 21.6 you can see that Arial has been used on the Flash navigation bar, as well as the main header.

FIGURE 21.6

Arial typeface on Flash navigation

Part Summary   Quiz & Answers   Tasks   Resources

Form

With the exception of the occasional use of bold or italicized fonts for emphasis, I chose to use a very light hand when it came to the Design Studio site.

Size and Direction

All of the body type is set using a normal default (size 3). Link text is set at a size 1, as is copyright information. Headers are set in Bergell at 45 points. All copy and headers are set on the vertical axis.

Leading, Kerning, and Spacing

Kerning is default to the typeface in question. Leading and spacing are as well, with the one exception being the header graphic on the main page (Figure 21.7) where the spacing and leading have been reduced to achieve the look shown in the Figure.

Color

All colors have been selected from the Design Studio palette. A color table can be found in Chapter 16.

Specifically, a brick color has been used for the headers, black for the body text, and a combination of olive and brick for links. The main header as shown in Figure 21.7 uses rust, peach, and olive with a lighting effect applied.

Type Design: Quiz

Please answer the following multiple choice questions.

1. Sub-categories of serif faces include:

    a. oldstyle

    b. Helvetica

    c. oblique

    d. a and b

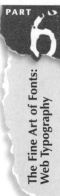

PART

**The Fine Art of Fonts:
Web Typography**

2. Sans serif type can be described as:

   a. thin with strokes

   b. rounded without strokes

   c. angular with flattened strokes

   d. rounded with decorative strokes

3. A common serif font is:

   a. Helvetica

   b. Times

   c. oblique

   d. Arial

4. A common sans serif font is:

   a. Century Schoolbook

   b. modern

   c. Helvetica

   d. Bergell

5. Decorative fonts are excellent for:

   a. body text

   b. copyrights

   c. headers

   d. very small type

Please answer true or false for the following statements.

6. Typography is seen as both practical and aesthetic.

7. A monospaced font looks like handwriting.

8. Bold should be applied to full areas of body text.

9. Italic and oblique are best used for emphasis.

10. Anti-aliasing prevents fonts from smoothing.

Write out short answers to the following questions.

11. What typefaces discussed in these past two chapters are new to you? If nothing is new, list three to five typefaces you have worked with recently.

12. Which of these do you like? Dislike? Think about your attraction or dislike of a given typeface, and write a short, journal-style entry as to why.

Answers to the quiz can be found at the end of this chapter, and on the Design Studio Web site at http://www.designstudio.net/type/.

Type Design: Task

In the following tasks you will address the typographic needs of a given client.
For this task you will need:

- A pencil and paper
- A library of fonts (look on your computer for a selection of fonts)

Read through each option and then write out an approach for each case study.

Case 1

The editor of a trend-setting, cutting-edge poetry and spoken word magazine has asked you to design a Web site. She tells you the look should be "unlike anything" that's been seen on the Web. "Go nuts!" she exclaims, when you ask her about design issues.

You're sitting down working on ideas as to how to approach this typographically. You know you want to stray away from the norm when it comes to decorative typographic elements. Another consideration, however, is that the type on the poetry pages remains legible.

Write down several typefaces that you think will do the trick.

Case 2

A young woman makes an appointment to consult with you regarding a Web site design for her business. She comes into your office and is obviously very well dressed. She hands you her business card and tells you she owns an international chain of very exclusive skin care salons.

She emphasizes her use of all natural products, claiming that beauty and health go hand in hand. Her menu of offerings is very extensive, with special treatments for the whole body that are sensual, deeply rejuvenating, and very, very expensive.

Her clientele is made up of movie starts and business magnates, world leaders, and old money. Her Web site's intent is not to sell her product or services, but rather provide another visible identity of her products and services.

What typefaces might you use to design this Web site?

Case 3

Tea Exotica specializes in select Asian exotic teas. They want a company storefront that works on the sense of mystery and danger many feel about the East.

You are certain you can address some of this mystery using typography. What are some of your ideas?

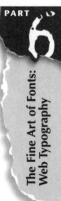

PART 6

The Fine Art of Fonts:
Web Typography

Web Typography: Review

With a foundation of typographic design concepts, you can now move into the area of typographic application.

You are already aware that the Web has limitations regarding type, but these should not prohibit you from doing the best job with the tools you have.

Main Concepts

The most important thing to remember about typographic method on the Web is that you'll probably be using at least one if not a combination of the three total available methods. These methods include:

- Graphics
- Standard HTML using the <font> tag
- Cascading style sheets

Depending upon your audience, client, and subject matter, you may have the opportunity to use any or all of these methods to accomplish effective and attractive typographic design.

Graphics

Graphics offer the best opportunity to select and manipulate typefaces as you would in print. The downside of graphic typography is that any graphic is bound to add load time to a page. You must therefore keep your file sizes as low as possible while still maintaining the integrity of your type.

Remember to anti-alias any graphic-based type that is 12 points and above for the best results. In most cases, smaller type is going to look better without anti-aliasing applied.

HTML

The <font> tag offers control of face, size, and color.

Font faces should always be "stacked." This means that you place the face you most want displayed first, then a reasonable pair from another platform next, and so forth, ending with the family name:

```
<font face="times,garamond,serif">
```

Size is limited by a range of numeric values that do not relate to points. A size 5 font (Figure 21.8) will be very different than a size 1 (Figure 21.9):

```
<font face="times,garamond,serif" size="5">
<font face="times,garamond,serif" size="1">
```

FIGURE 21.8

A size 5 font

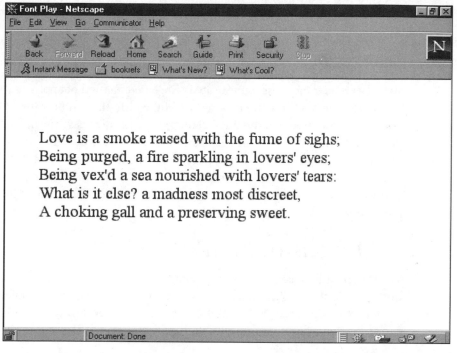

FIGURE 21.9

A size 1 font

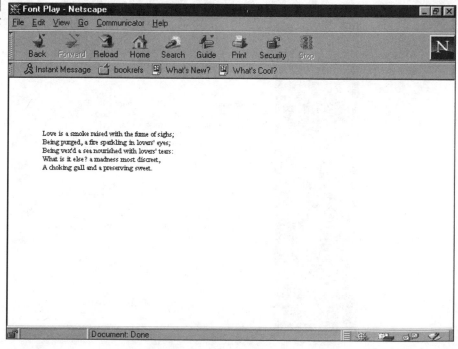

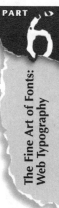

Color is set using hexadecimal or literal color names. Always use safe palette color (see color reference) and hexadecimal codes.

```
<font face="times,garamond,serif" size="5" color="#00FFFF">
```

Style Sheets

Style sheets offer the most sophisticated code-based method of applying style to type.

You can set typefaces and families, weight, width, size, and posture. Control over leading exists as well, via the line-height option. Color is easy to control with style sheets, and the distinct advantage of style sheets is that you can apply style to only one small part of a page, an entire page, or an entire site via linked style sheets.

More information on style sheets can be found in references mentioned throughout this book, as well as the resource area of the Design Studio Type Mill at http://www.designstudio.net/type/.

Page Deconstruction

The Design Studio uses graphics and font tags to achieve typeface attributes. It does not use style sheets, although style sheet examples are available throughout the site.

Here is a look at the Design Studio's typography page. Study Figure 21.10 and the code to define what I've done with type on both the graphics and in the HTML.

FIGURE 21.10

The Design Studio Type Mill page

```
<!-- Site by Molly E. Holzschlag molly@molly.com-->

<html>

<head>
<title>The Design Studio by Molly: Type Mill</title>
</head>

<body bgcolor="#FFFFFF" background="images/ds-bakr.gif" text="#000000"
link="#666633" vlink="663300" alink="#FFFFFF">

<table border="0" width="580" cellpadding="0" cellspacing="0">
<tr>

<!--begin left margin-->

<td width="125">

<img src="images/dsh.jpg" width="112" height="102" border="0" alt="The
Design Studio by Molly Header">

</td>

<td width="25">

<img src="images/clear.gif" width="25" height="1" border="0" alt="spacer">

</td>

<!--begin text area-->

<td valign=top width="320">

<img src="images/tm-hed.gif" width="300" height="100" border="0"
alt="welcome!">
<p>

<font face="arial,helvetica,sans-serif">

Everywhere you look you'll find typography. The papers on your desk all use
typefaces and typographic elements. Newspapers, magazines--even television
each make use of type. Sometimes the design is as simple as a single plain
typeface, other times intricate combinations of face, form, and color are
put to use.
<p>
```

PART

6

The Fine Art of Fonts:
Web Typography

Whether you use type to communicate specific words, as an art form in and of itself, or combine the communication and the art to create compelling designs, knowing a bit about how type is used will help you express your ideas to the people who come into contact with your work.

```
<p>

</font>

<div align="center">

<!--begin flash navigation-->

<OBJECT CLASSID="clsid:D27CDB6E-AE6D-11cf-96B8-444553540000"
        codebase="http://active.macromedia.com/flash2/cabs/swflash
.cab#version=2,0,0,11"
        align=middle border="0" width="316" height="58">
                <param name="Movie" value="images/subnav.swf">
                <param name="Loop" value="False">
                <param name="Play" value="True">
                <param name="BGColor" value="FFFFFF">
                <param name="Quality" value="high">
                <param name="Scale" value="Showall">

<!--Netscape 2.0 or above-->

<embed SRC="images/subnav.swf"pluginspage="/shockwave/download/index
.cgi?P1_Prod_Version=ShockwaveFlash" type=application/futuresplash
width="316" height="58" loop="true" quality="best">

</object>
<p>

<!--begin text navigation-->

<div align="center">

<font face="arial" size="1">

[ <a href="office.htm"> front office </a> ] [ <a href="planning
.htm">planning room</a> ] [ <a href="space.htm">space place</a> ]
<br>

[ <a href="workshop.htm">workshop</a> ] [ <a href="color.htm">color lab</a> ]
[ <a href="media.htm">multimedia center</a> ]
```

```
<br>

[ <a href="index.html">welcome</a> ] [ <a href="contact.htm">contact</a> ]
</font>
</div>

<!--begin copyright and mailto-->

<div align="center">

<font size="1">

<i>Copyright &copy; <a href="mailto:molly@molly.com">Molly E.
Holzschlag</a>, 1997</i>

</div>
</font>
</td>

<td width="25">

<img src="images/clear.gif" width="25" height="1" border="0" alt="spacer">

</td>

<!--begin navigation column-->

<td valign="top" width="50">

<img src="images/navmap3.gif" width="50" height="395" border="0"
alt="navigational image map, text navigation below" usemap="#navmap3">

</td>

</table>

<!--begin map data-->

<map name="navmap3">
<area shape="rect" coords="0,0,57,46" href="office.htm">
<area shape="rect" coords="0,48,57,98" href="planning.htm">
<area shape="rect" coords="0,100,57,160" href="space.htm">
<area shape="rect" coords="0,162,57,214" href="workshop.htm">
<area shape="rect" coords="0,216,57,275" href="color.htm">
<area shape="rect" coords="0,278,57,330" href="type.htm">
```

```
<area shape="rect" coords="0,332,58,393" href="media.htm">
<area shape="default" nohref>
</map>

</body>
</html>
```

Here's the code and a screen shot (Figure 21.11) of the Design Studio Type Mill Part Summary for you to examine as well.

FIGURE 21.11

The Design Studio Type Mill Part Summary

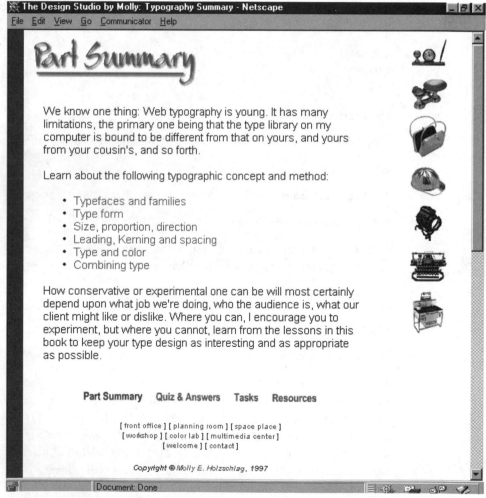

```
<!--Site by Molly E. Holzschlag molly@molly.com-->

<html>

<head>
<title>The Design Studio by Molly: Typography Summary</title>
</head>

<body bgcolor="#FFFFFF" background="../images/type-bak.gif" text="#000000"
link="#666633" vlink="663300" alink="#FFFFFF">

<table border="0" width="580" cellpadding="0" cellspacing="0">
<tr>

<!--begin text area-->

<td valign="top" width="500">

<img src="../images/clear.gif" width="15" height="1" border="0"
alt="spacer">

<img src="../images/sum-hed.gif" width="234" height="69" border="0" alt=" ">
<p>

<font face="arial,helvetica,sans-serif">
<blockquote>

We know one thing: Web typography is young. It has many limitations, the
primary one being that the type library on my computer is bound to be
different from that on yours, and yours from your cousin's, and so forth.
<p>

Learn about the following typographic concept and method:
<p>

<ul>
<li><a href="face.htm">Typefaces and families</a>
<li><a href="form.htm">Type form</a>
<li><a href="size.htm">Size, proportion, direction</a>
<li><a href="kern.htm">Leading, Kerning and spacing</a>
<li><a href="t-color">Type and color</a>
<li><a href="combine.htm">Combining type</a>
</ul>
```

PART

6

The Fine Art of Fonts:
Web Typography

How conservative or experimental one can be will most certainly depend upon what job we're doing, who the audience is, what our client might like or dislike. Where you can, I encourage you to experiment, but where you cannot, learn from the lessons in this book to keep your type design as interesting and as appropriate as possible.

```
</blockquote>
<p>

<div align="center">

<!--begin ie flash navigation-->

<object classid="clsid:D27CDB6E-AE6D-11cf-96B8-444553540000"
codebase="http://active.macromedia.com/flash2/cabs/swflash
.cab#version=2,0,0,0"
border="0" width="316" height="58">

<param name="Movie" value="../images/subnav.swf">
<param name="Loop" value="False">
<param name="Play" value="True">
<param name="BGColor" value="FFFFFF">
<param name="Quality" value="high">
<param name="Scale" value="Showall">

<!--begin netscape flash navigation-->

<embed src="../images/subnav.swf" pluginspage="/shockwave/download/index
.cgi?P1_Prod_Version=ShockwaveFlash" type=application/futuresplash
width="316" height="58" loop=false quality=high play=true>

</object>
<br>

<!--begin text navigation-->

<font face="arial" size="1">

[ <a href="../office.htm"> front office </a> ] [ <a href="../planning
.htm">planning room</a> ] [ <a href="../space.htm">space place</a> ]
<br>

[ <a href="../workshop.htm">workshop</a> ] [ <a href="../color.htm">color
lab</a> ] [ <a href="../media.htm">multimedia center</a> ]
```

```
<br>

[ <a href="../index.html">welcome</a> ] [ <a href="../contact
.htm">contact</a> ]
</font>

</div>
<p>

<!--begin copyright and mailto-->

<div align="center">

<font size="1">

<i>Copyright &copy; <a href="mailto:molly@molly.com">Molly E.
Holzschlag</a>, 1997</i>

</div>
</font>
</td>

<td width="25">

<img src="../images/clear.gif" width="25" height="1" border="0"
alt="spacer">

</td>

<!--begin navigation column-->

<td valign="top" width="50">

<img src="../images/navmap3.gif" width="50" height="395" border="0"
alt="navigational image map, text navigation below" usemap="#navmap3">

</td>

</table>

<!--begin map data-->

<map name="navmap3">
<area shape="rect" coords="0,0,57,46" href="../office.htm">
<area shape="rect" coords="0,48,57,98" href="../planning.htm">
<area shape="rect" coords="0,100,57,160" href="../space.htm">
```

```
<area shape="rect" coords="0,162,57,214" href="../workshop.htm">
<area shape="rect" coords="0,216,57,275" href="../color.htm">
<area shape="rect" coords="0,278,57,330" href="../type.htm">
<area shape="rect" coords="0,332,58,393" href="../media.htm">
<area shape="default" nohref>
</map>
</body>
</html>
```

If you wonder why I've been rather conservative with the type, layout, and overall design of the Design Studio site, it has to do with accessibility and cross-platform issues. You can refer back to the beginning of this book to review those issues. Some areas of this site use more adventuresome programming and multimedia, but for the most part I tend to design very simply, believing that less is more when it comes to the overall look and feel of *most* sites.

Web Typography: Quiz

Please answer the following multiple choice questions.

1. When working with type and graphics:

a. always use anti-aliasing

b. never use anti-aliasing

c. use anti-aliasing only on small type

d. use anti-aliasing on larger type

2. The <font> tag allows you to size fonts using:

a. the size attribute

b. point measurement

c. pixel measurement

d. all of the above

3. The <tt> tag will create type in:

a. a serif font

b. a sans serif font

c. a cursive font

d. a monospaced font

4. Which of the following uses inline style?

    a. `{ font-family: arial, helvetica, sans-serif;}`

    b. `<font face="arial,helvetica,sans-serif">`

    c. `<blockquote style="font-family: arial, helvetica, sans-serif">`

    d. none of the above

5. In style sheets, the equivalent of a decorative typeface is:

    a. cursive

    b. script

    c. line-height

    d. fantasy

Please answer true or false for the following statements.

6. Kerning can only be achieved with style sheets.

7. Leading can be achieved with both style sheets and graphics.

8. Spacing can be achieved using the `space="x"` attribute.

9. When using style sheets to color type, you should always use the literal color name, such as `"red"`.

10. Generally speaking, it's best to avoid using graphics for type.

Write out a short answer for the following question.

11. What's your preferred method of typographic design? Describe why you prefer this method over others.

Web Typography: Task

In this task, you will design a type-based graphic.

You will need:

- Photoshop
- The safe color palette (located in the color reference)
- A serif typeface (I'm going to use Century Schoolbook)

Follow these steps:

1. Open Photoshop.

2. Select File ➤ New.

3. Create a 250×150 pixel graphic at 72 DPI resolution in RGB color (see Figure 21.12).

FIGURE 21.12

Creating the graphic in Photoshop

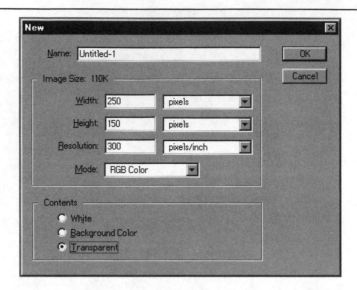

4. Select the type tool from the toolbar.

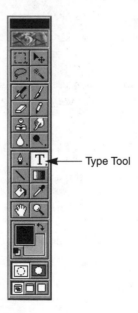

Type Tool

5. Click on your graphic field to bring up the type tool dialog box.

6. Select Century Schoolbook or a suitable serif typeface (Figure 21.13).

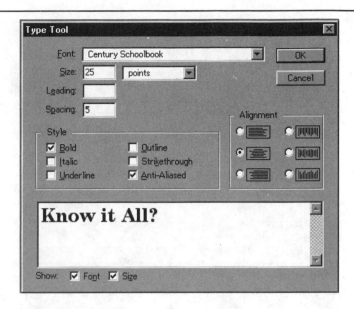

7. Set the size. I'm using 25 points (remember, if you use a font size greater than 12 points, check the anti-aliasing box).

8. Set the Spacing box to 5.

9. Select bold.

10. Type in the words **Know it All?**.

11. Click OK.

12. Move the type to the upper right of the graphic field.

13. Select the type tool again.

14. Now set the typeface to 18 points, bold (no italics), default spacing, with a leading of 16.

15. Select right alignment.

16. Type in the words **Keep an open mind, learn as much as you can, and maybe then, you will know it some** with a carriage return at each comma.

17. Click OK and you'll see the right-aligned text in Figure 21.14.

18. From the Layer menu, flatten the image.

19. Now save the image as a GIF, walking through the optimization process described in Chapter 17.

You have now set type on a graphic!

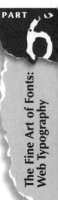

PART

6

The Fine Art of Fonts: Web Typography

FIGURE 21.14

Right-aligned text

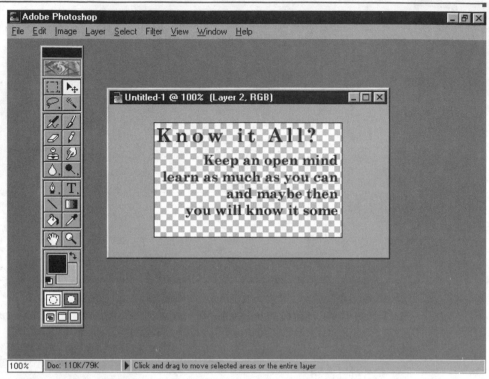

Answer Key

The following key provides the correct answers to the quizzes in this chapter.

Type Design

Multiple Choice

1. The correct answer is A. Oldstyle is a sub-category of serif typefaces.

2. The correct answer is B. Sans serif type can be described as rounded without strokes.

3. The correct answer is B. Times is a common serif typeface.

4. The correct answer is C. Helvetica is a common sans serif typeface.

Continued

5. The correct answer is C. Decorative fonts are great for headers, but should not be used for body text.

True or False

6. True. Typography is practical and aesthetic.

7. False. A monospaced font looks like the type on a typewriter.

8. False. Bold should be used to *emphasize* smaller areas of text.

9. True. Use italic and oblique for emphasis.

10. False. Anti-aliasing allows fonts to become smoother.

Short Answers

11. and **12.** These answers are wholly personal, there are no right or wrong answers.

Web Typography

Multiple Choice

1. The correct answer is D. Anti-aliasing should be applied to type that is 12 points or larger.

2. The correct answer is A. Font tags use the size attribute to control size of type.

3. The correct answer is D. The <tt> tag will create a monospaced font.

4. The correct answer is C. This code uses *inline* style.

5. The correct answer is D. Fantasy fonts are the style sheet equivalent of decorative typefaces.

True or False

6. False. The only place kerning can be applied for use on the Web is within a graphic, using Illustrator or another typesetting tool.

7. True. Leading can be achieved with graphics as well as style sheets.

8. False. There is no such thing as a space attribute.

9. False. You *can* use the literal color name, but most professionals prefer the hexadecimal equivalent.

10. False. There is no reason to not use graphics for type, as long as you are following optimization procedures and using alt tags to describe the type header clearly.

Short Answers

11. This question requires a personal answer, with no answer being right or wrong.

PART

6

The Fine Art of Fonts:
Web Typography

Next Up

The next few chapters move away from pure design and into the aspect of Web design that forces designers to think about how they must be both scientists *and* artists.

You will learn about interactivity, multimedia, and Web programming. Obviously, one book cannot delve into great depth regarding any of these issues, so you will learn specifically how to use some of these technologies to *enhance* the designs you create.

PART VII

dynamic media: multimedia and web programming

chapter 22

INTERACTIVITY

INTERACTIVITY

Interactive. The word is tossed about like so many tissues behind a mid-winter cold-sufferer. When words get overused to that extent, their meaning becomes vague and distorted.

In Chapter 3, you were briefly introduced to some of the theory behind interactivity and the Web's non-linear environment. There is a huge amount of academic thought surrounding the theory of interactivity and the results of people interacting within a non-linear space. As a Web designer, it's important to try to find a logical balance between the practice of making things interactive and the theoretical aspect of interactivity so that you can do the magic that you do.

In this chapter we'll examine:

- Interactive theory
- Interactivity and machines
- Interactivity and people
- Applications of interactivity

How does one go from lofty theories to literal practice? We'll look at some hypothetical examples in this chapter, and pull together the ideas expressed with a demonstration of functional interactivity as well as examples of progressive interactivity.

Interactive Theory

In 1996, I wrote the following statement in a book chapter about interactive Web content.

> *"Interactivity is a major reason why the Web is both a fascination and an emerging resource. Media has, until very recently, been a rather passive activity. Television, radio, newspapers, and magazines all deliver information to us in a linear fashion. All offer information that is predetermined by the content providers in form, feel, and experience. You have little control over what happens during a given television or radio program. Of course, you can turn up the volume, turn down the volume, change the program, or as some prefer, turn off the machine completely. With newspapers and magazines you can subscribe or unsubscribe, choose the articles you want to read from the pool provided, or if so inspired, write letters to the editor regarding content. These options are very limited when compared to the exciting, truly interactive environment of the World Wide Web."*
>
> From "Adding Interactive Content to Your Web Page,"
> *The Internet Unleashed,* 1997

Generally speaking, I still agree with the idealistic voice I used when writing that passage. Recently, I taught an interactive media class to graduate media students at the New School University. These students were, in general, very familiar with the Web, and they had more than a few mature ideas and opinions to offer when discussions about interactivity came up in class. These discussions, combined with my own Web experience, left me thinking about how the Web has met, and failed to meet, the vision that many of us early entrants into the Web design field so enthusiastically embraced.

So I came up with a more extrapolated notion about what interactivity really means. This is a work in progress, but it will benefit you greatly as you move from mastering static to active (and hopefully interactive) Web sites. These ideas begin with the Cycle of Interactivity, and move to a theory that states that the truly memorable interactive experience results in profound changes to both function and life.

The Cycle of Interactivity

The simplest definition of interactivity is something *acting* on another. This is vague in and of itself—which is one of the reasons interactivity is largely theoretical and up for discussion and exploration.

Try to visualize this in terms of the Web. If you go to the most basic act—linking— you find a good place to start.

Web interactivity can then be measured by the cycle of an end-user making a choice, and the medium (in this case the underlying technology of the Web) responding to that choice. Click on a link, get another page. Do this again, and the cycle repeats. The user makes a choice, and the medium responds (Figure 22.1). In fact, the Cycle of Interactivity is perfectly exemplified by the act of linking.

FIGURE 22.1

*The Cycle of
Interactivity*

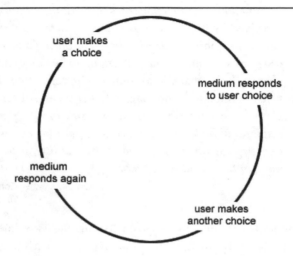

The Cycle of Interactivity

Linking was certainly the element that I, and many people were most excited about several years ago. It put choice into the hands of the end-user—choice that seemed severely lacking in other, more familiar, media such as TV. To us, it seemed that the act of linking numerous Web pages together would alone change the level of interaction between us and our computers.

To a certain degree it has, but if we're completely honest, we find that in most cases the act of linking doesn't separate us that far from the television medium. In fact, it's quite similar to the point-and-click phenomenon known as channel surfing.

This doesn't mean that hope is lost—it just means that either we haven't completely grasped the power of linking, and thus, the power of using multimedia and Web programming to enhance that power, or that we are staying in the safety zone as we design sites that meet the needs of clients.

Ultimately, the level and satisfaction of interactivity will be determined by the end-user. If a visitor becomes caught in a neverending loop of give and take with a Web site, it may in fact become frustrating rather than interesting. This can be particularly true of navigation systems that are so complex as to confuse the visitor.

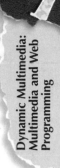

Interacting with Machines

Interactivity with machines is limited by the capacity of the machine and the programmers and designers creating for that machine. Machine-based interactivity will almost always be limited by the technology used by people, and the people who are creating that technology.

An example of machine-based interactivity is the feedback form. At one time, the thought of having an online form that could mail detailed information to the owner of a Web site was *the essence* of the Web's interactivity. Despite the fact that the end result is always the same. You type in your information, you send the form, and the site says, "thanks!" A useful process indeed, but only satisfying because it is functional, not particularly fun or interesting.

A common misperception of machine-based interactivity is defining something as interactive simply because it isn't *static*. A perfect example is the animated GIF. If I had a penny for every time I heard someone say: "Make that site more interactive. Add an animation!"

An animation on its own is not interactive. The key here is that it is *active*, but that's where the relationship ends. It has acted on you, but you have not acted back on it.

An animation can, however, be designed to be interactive. Start by linking it, and you've added the first level of interactivity. Now, link it to a site with *another* interactive option and you've increased the level of interactivity, and so forth.

Interactivity goes far beyond simple movement. It is the *engagement* of the audience, and that is the critical difference between the casual and professional definitions of interactivity.

Toward Better Interactivity

Interactive media really seems to come to life when interaction means one of the following:

1. Your input *significantly* alters the outcome of the interaction.

2. The interaction is with *people* rather than machines.

Let's say you're involved with a Web site where you can input information. Suddenly, the site is altered significantly by your input. This would be a gratifying experience on the interactive scale. An example might be if a designer developed a child's game where the child could choose from any color of virtual crayons, draw a picture with the virtual crayons, and submit that picture to the Web site for immediate incorporation of that design into the Web site. This interaction is much more expansive because the child's input alters the reality of the site.

Machines, in and of themselves, are usually limited in their interactive capabilities. But when people are interacting with other people, anything can happen. Boredom can ensue, or, as with many chat rooms, the focus can shift to flirtation rather than in-depth conversation. However, if communities are built around common ideas, the potential of defining the quality of the interactive experience does exist.

An example of this type of interactive community would be the creation of a Web designer's community, where Web designers could get together and seriously discuss information regarding design. The interactive experience is immediately heightened. Friendships are formed, sometimes with profound effect. The action of the medium on the individual is radical, and vice-versa. By building a community online you have the potential to bring the Web to life.

I think that I, as well as many others, bought into the idea that clicking on a link was the gestalt of the interactive experience. I don't believe that anymore. Linking is an *aspect* of interactivity, but it's important to separate what is interactive in terms of humans and machines.

In a nutshell, machines offer limited interactivity at best, whereas the use of machines *as a bridge* to personal or community involvement helps us view interactivity in an entirely new light. It is in personal revelation and community where the potential for unlimited interactivity and progress lies.

Methods

So am I saying that machine-based interactivity isn't important? No. But it is limited in terms of depth. Machine-based interactivity is *of definite use* to the Web designer and the end-user. You need the practical applications of interactivity, they are necessary and important.

The main point here is to ensure that you understand the differences in the depth of the interactive experience and to influence your thinking about functional (machine-based) versus progressive (community-oriented or human) interaction.

Functional Interactivity

Functional interactivity can best be thought of as any type of interactive engagement with Web media that serves a function. Whether it's sending feedback, or shopping online, the interactivity involved is a function. It may not be a mind-blowing interactive experience, but it works, and it makes the Web more versatile and life a bit easier.

In your journeys as a designer, you will find and use many functional applications. Below you will see an example of a feedback form and an example of an online shopping catalog, but the functional interactive experience is not at all limited to these things. In fact, functional interactivity can be as simple as linking to an ancillary site, or as complex as having a company send information to your pager to keep you up-to-date with airline fares.

Feedback Forms

You've seen these everywhere—forms that allow you to input your name and other relevant information. You return the feedback and get some kind of response from the server and/or the service to which you sent the information.

On the Design Studio site, you will find a functional feedback form on the Contact page (Figure 22.2). This form is built using a CGI (Common Gateway Interface) script, which you'll learn more about in Chapter 24.

FIGURE 22.2

Feedback form on the Design Studio site

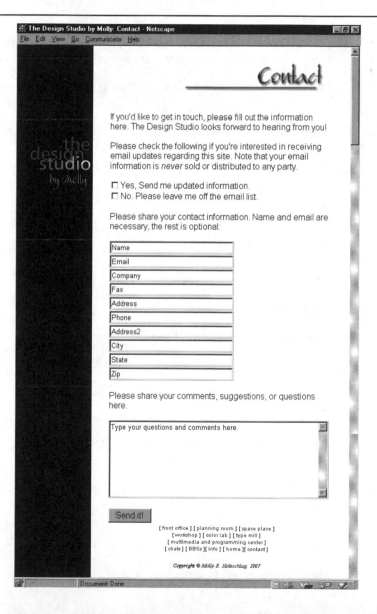

The following code shows you how the feedback form was put together using CGI scripting. This early section of the code is familiar to you. It sets up the body, header graphic and layout attributes of the page:

```
<!--Site by Molly E. Holzschlag molly@molly.com-->

<html>

<head>
<title>The Design Studio by Molly: Contact</title>
</head>

<body bgcolor="#FFFFFF" background="images/ds-bakr.gif" text="#000000"
link="#666633" vlink="663300" alink="#FFFFFF">

<table border="0" width="590" cellpadding="10" cellspacing="0">
<tr>

<!--begin left margin-->

<td width="125" valign="top">

<img src="images/clear.gif" width="1" height="250" border="0" alt="spacer">

<img src="images/dsh.jpg" width="112" height="102" border="0" alt="The
Design Studio by Molly Header ">

</td>

</td>

<td width="25">

<img src="images/clear.gif" width="25" height="1" border="0" alt="spacer">

</td>

<!--begin text area-->

<td width="300" valign="top" bgcolor="#FFFFFF">

<img src="images/con-hed.gif" width="300" height="100" border="0"
alt="contact header" align="right">
<br clear="all">

<div align="center">

<table border="0" width="300">
<tr>

<td width="300" valign="top">
```

In this section, you are introduced to the form syntax, which creates both the look and function of the input areas.

```
<form method="post" action="http://opus1.com/htbin/mailto">
<input name="from" type="hidden" value="DesignStudio@bitbucket.opus1.com">
<input name="subject" type="hidden" value="Design Studio Contact Form">
<input name="version" type="hidden" value="Form version is 2.0">
<input name="to" type="hidden" value="ybi@ybi.com">

<font face="arial">

If you'd like to get in touch, please fill out the information here. The
Design Studio looks forward to hearing from you!
<p>

Please check the following if you're interested in receiving email updates
regarding this site. Note that your email information is <i>never</i> sold
or distributed to any party.
<p>

<input type="checkbox" name="Order" value="email yes">Yes, Send me updated
information.
<br>

<input type="checkbox" name="Order" value="email no">No. Please leave me off
the email list.
<p>

Please share your contact information. Name and email are necessary, the
rest is optional:
<p>

<input type="text" name="Name" size="20"
value="Name">   <input type="text" name="Email" size="20"
value="Email"><br>
<input type="text" name="Company" size="20"
value="Company">   <input type="text" name="Fax" size="20"
value="Fax"><br>
<input type="text" name="Address" size="20"
value="Address">   <input type="text" name="Phone" size="20"
value="Phone"><br>
<input type="text" name="Address2" size="20" value="Address2"><br>
<input type="text" name="City" size="20" value="City"><br>
<input type="text" name="State" size="20" value="State"><br>
<input type="text" name="Zip" size="20" value="Zip"><br>
<p>
```

```
Please share your comments, suggestions, or questions here.
<p>

<textarea name="feedback" rows="8" cols="35" wrap="physical">Type your
questions and comments here.</textarea>
<p>

<input type="Submit" value="Send it!">
<p>

</form>

</td>
</tr>
</table>
```

At this point, the form is completed and the text-based navigation resumes. Note that in order to accommodate the input information, the image map that normally appears to the right on top-level pages of the Design Studio site has been left out. This decision was based on aesthetics rather than a technical issue: In order to have the input information appear attractive, I needed the extra space.

```
<!--begin text navigation-->
<font face="arial" size="1">
[ <a href="office.htm"> front office </a> ] [ <a href="planning
.htm">planning room</a> ] [ <a href="space.htm">space place</a> ]
<br>

[ <a href="workshop.htm">workshop</a> ] [ <a href="color.htm">color lab</a> ]
[ <a href="media.htm">multimedia center</a> ]
<br>

[ <a href="index.html">welcome</a> ] [ <a href="contact.htm">contact</a> ]

</font>
</div>
<p>

<!--begin copyright and mailto-->

<div align="center">

<font size="1">

<i>Copyright &copy; <a href="mailto:molly@molly.com">Molly E.
Holzschlag</a>, 1997</i>
```

```
</div>
</font>
</td>

</table>

</body>
</html>
```

The page ends with the standard text navigation and copyright information.

Shopping

Another very popular interactive function is online shopping. The following code uses JavaScript *and* a CGI form to carry out its function. The JavaScript calculates the total cost from the selected items, and the CGI form sends the information to the server. The sale is then made, and the user will receive his or her purchase.

Figure 22.3 shows the full page of the Buffalo Exchange's Off the Beaten Path Catalog. Here is the code from the page, beginning with site comments and identity and META tagging:

```
<!--site by desertnet designs: sales@desert.ne -->
<!--web engineer: wil gerken wil@desert.net-->
<!--art director: amy burnham-->
<!--content provided by Buffalo Exchange-->

<html>
<head>
<title>Buffalo Exchange</title>
<meta name="description" content="Buffalo Exchange is a pioneering 17-store
resale clothing recycling business which operates directly with the public,
buying, trading, consigning, and, of course, selling good, fashionable
clothing and accessories at fair prices.">
<meta name="keywords" content="resale, apparel, Levi, jeans, thrift, store,
clothing, consignment, disco, retro, designer, wear, career, casual, shoes,
footwear, environment, ecology, garment, gothic, vintage, fashion, clubwear,
styles, recycling, bargain, trade, cash, buy-sell-trade, accessories,
second-hand, overalls, shopping, re-use, 70s, 60s, 50s, leather, outfits,
rockabilly, dresses, boots, trends, textile, used, costume, buffalo">
```

FIGURE 22.3

Off the Beaten Path Catalog

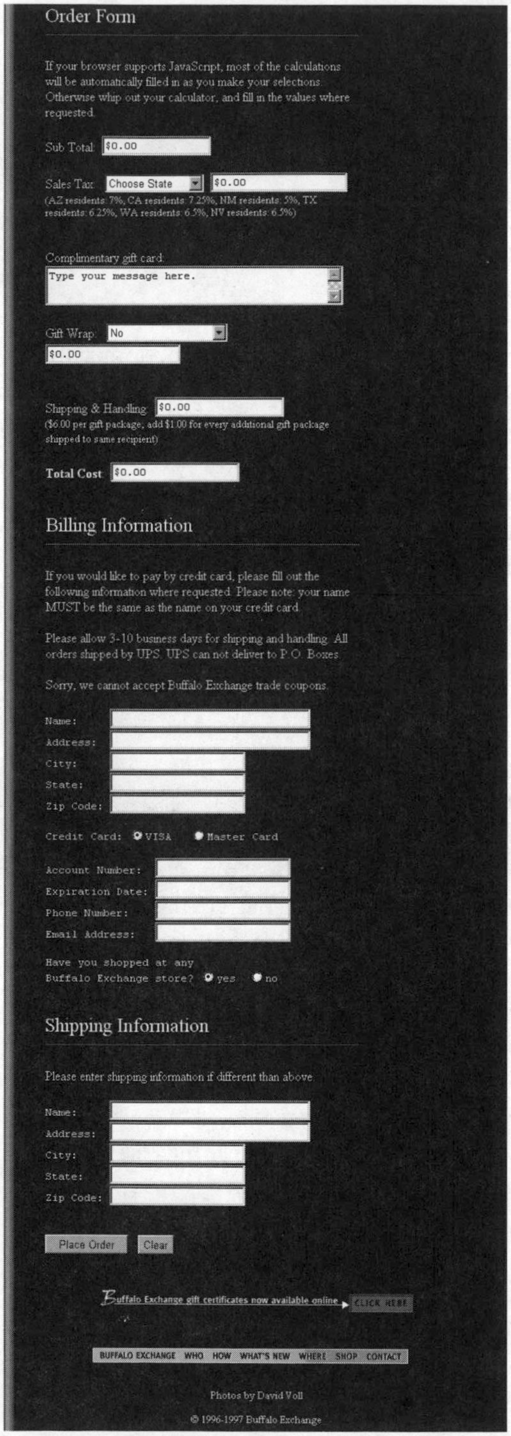

Order Form

If your browser supports JavaScript, most of the calculations will be automatically filled in as you make your selections. Otherwise whip out your calculator, and fill in the values where requested.

Sub Total: `$0.00`

Sales Tax: [Choose State ▼] `$0.00`
(AZ residents: 7%, CA residents: 7.25%, NM residents: 5%, TX residents: 6.25%, WA residents: 6.5%, NV residents: 6.5%)

Complimentary gift card:
`Type your message here.`

Gift Wrap: [No ▼]
`$0.00`

Shipping & Handling: `$0.00`
($6.00 per gift package; add $1.00 for every additional gift package shipped to same recipient)

Total Cost: `$0.00`

Billing Information

If you would like to pay by credit card, please fill out the following information where requested. Please note: your name MUST be the same as the name on your credit card.

Please allow 3-10 business days for shipping and handling. All orders shipped by UPS. UPS can not deliver to P.O. Boxes.

Sorry, we cannot accept Buffalo Exchange trade coupons.

Name:
Address:
City:
State:
Zip Code:

Credit Card: ◉ VISA ⬤ Master Card

Account Number:
Expiration Date:
Phone Number:
Email Address:

Have you shopped at any
Buffalo Exchange store? ◉ yes ⬤ no

Shipping Information

Please enter shipping information if different than above.

Name:
Address:
City:
State:
Zip Code:

[Place Order] [Clear]

Buffalo Exchange gift certificates now available online [CLICK HERE]

[BUFFALO EXCHANGE WHO HOW WHAT'S NEW WHERE SHOP CONTACT]

Photos by David Voll

© 1996-1997 Buffalo Exchange

Next, we have the JavaScript code that calculates purchases and renders a total cost:

```
<script language="JavaScript">

<!--JavaScript (c) 1996-97 DesertNet/Gordon McComb (roundDollar) .
http://desert.net/ -->
<!--Authors: Wil Gerken + Gordon McComb (roundDollar) . wil@desert.net

function roundDollar(val) {
 dollar = Math.floor(val)
 val = "" + Math.round(val * 100)
 decimal = val.substring(val.length-2, val.length)
 return(dollar + "." + decimal);
}

// Qty|Type or Comment|Price

function getPrice(dataString) {
 dataString = dataString.substring(dataString.indexOf("|")+1, dataString
.length);
 return(dataString.substring(dataString.indexOf("|")+1, dataString.length));
}

function getQty(dataString) {
 return(dataString.substring(0, dataString.indexOf("|")));
}


function calculateCost() {
 qty = 0
 qty += parseFloat(getQty(document.orderForm.A971.options[document
.orderForm.A971.selectedIndex].value));
 qty += parseFloat(getQty(document.orderForm.A972.options[document
.orderForm.A972.selectedIndex].value));
 qty += parseFloat(getQty(document.orderForm.A973.options[document
.orderForm.A973.selectedIndex].value));
 qty += parseFloat(getQty(document.orderForm.A974.options[document
.orderForm.A974.selectedIndex].value));
 qty += parseFloat(getQty(document.orderForm.A975.options[document
.orderForm.A975.selectedIndex].value));
 qty += parseFloat(getQty(document.orderForm.A976.options[document
.orderForm.A976.selectedIndex].value));
 qty += parseFloat(getQty(document.orderForm.A977.options[document
.orderForm.A977.selectedIndex].value));
 qty += parseFloat(getQty(document.orderForm.A978.options[document
.orderForm.A978.selectedIndex].value));
```

```
  qty += parseFloat(getQty(document.orderForm.A979.options[document
.orderForm.A979.selectedIndex].value));
  qty += parseFloat(getQty(document.orderForm.A9710.options[document
.orderForm.A9710.selectedIndex].value));
  qty += parseFloat(getQty(document.orderForm.A9711.options[document
.orderForm.A9711.selectedIndex].value));
  qty += parseFloat(getQty(document.orderForm.A9712.options[document
.orderForm.A9712.selectedIndex].value));
  qty += parseFloat(getQty(document.orderForm.A9713.options[document
.orderForm.A9713.selectedIndex].value));
  qty += parseFloat(getQty(document.orderForm.A9714.options[document
.orderForm.A9714.selectedIndex].value));

  subTotal = 0
  subTotal += parseFloat(getPrice(document.orderForm.A971.options[document
.orderForm.A971.selectedIndex].value));
  subTotal += parseFloat(getPrice(document.orderForm.A972.options[document
.orderForm.A972.selectedIndex].value));
  subTotal += parseFloat(getPrice(document.orderForm.A973.options[document
.orderForm.A973.selectedIndex].value));
  subTotal += parseFloat(getPrice(document.orderForm.A974.options[document
.orderForm.A974.selectedIndex].value));
  subTotal += parseFloat(getPrice(document.orderForm.A975.options[document
.orderForm.A975.selectedIndex].value));
  subTotal += parseFloat(getPrice(document.orderForm.A976.options[document
.orderForm.A976.selectedIndex].value));
  subTotal += parseFloat(getPrice(document.orderForm.A977.options[document
.orderForm.A977.selectedIndex].value));
  subTotal += parseFloat(getPrice(document.orderForm.A978.options[document
.orderForm.A978.selectedIndex].value));
  subTotal += parseFloat(getPrice(document.orderForm.A979.options[document
.orderForm.A979.selectedIndex].value));
  subTotal += parseFloat(getPrice(document.orderForm.A9710.options[document
.orderForm.A9710.selectedIndex].value));
  subTotal += parseFloat(getPrice(document.orderForm.A9711.options[document
.orderForm.A9711.selectedIndex].value));
  subTotal += parseFloat(getPrice(document.orderForm.A9712.options[document
.orderForm.A9712.selectedIndex].value));
  subTotal += parseFloat(getPrice(document.orderForm.A9713.options[document
.orderForm.A9713.selectedIndex].value));
  subTotal += parseFloat(getPrice(document.orderForm.A9714.options[document
.orderForm.A9714.selectedIndex].value));
  document.orderForm.subTotalCost.value = "$" + roundDollar(subTotal);
```

```
// Calculate Shipping Cost
shipping = 0.00
if (qty == 1) shipping = 6.00;
if (qty > 1) shipping = 6.00 + (qty-1);

document.orderForm.totalShipping.value = "$" + roundDollar(shipping);

// Calculate Gift Wrap Cost
gift = qty * parseFloat(getPrice(document.orderForm.giftWrap
.options[document.orderForm.giftWrap.selectedIndex].value));
document.orderForm.totalGiftWrap.value = "$" + roundDollar(gift);

// Calculate Tax Cost
taxRate = parseFloat(document.orderForm.StateTax.options[document
.orderForm.StateTax.selectedIndex].value);
if (taxRate == 1) taxCost = 0.00;
if (taxRate > 1) taxCost = (subTotal * taxRate) - subTotal;
document.orderForm.totalStateTax.value = "$" + roundDollar(taxCost);

// Calculate Total Cost
total = (subTotal * taxRate) + shipping + gift;
document.orderForm.totalCost.value = "$" + roundDollar(total);
}
//-->

</script>
</head>
```

The body attributes and general page layout tags follow:

```
<body background="images/bkgd.gif" bgcolor="#000000" text="#ffffff"
link="#5d3d2d" vlink="#38251b" alink="#000000">

<blockquote>
<br>

<table border="0" cellpadding="0" cellspacing="0" width="387">
<tr><td>
<img src="http://desert.net/buffalo/catalog/images/header.gif" width="387"
height="34" alt="Off the Beaten Path" usemap="#Header" border="0">
<p>

<map name="Header">
<area shape="rect" coords="326,0,386,33" href="../index.htmlx"
target="_top">
<area shape="default" nohref>
</map>
```

```
WELCOME to Buffalo Exchange's On-Line Gift Catalog where you'll find a
virtual plethora of fun and functional gifts.
<p>

Click on each individual picture to see an enlargement. Please note that
pricing does not include tax and/or shipping and handling. Just follow the
ordering instructions and above all...HAVE FUN!!
<p>

Seize the moment! Quantities are limited...offer good while supplies last.
MasterCard and VISA accepted.
<p>

</td></tr>
</table>
<p><br>
```

Here you see the CGI form that sends the accumulated information to the server. It looks very much like the more simple CGI contact form shown in the earlier example about feedback forms:

```
<form method="post" action="http://desert.net/htbin/mailto"
name="orderForm">
<input name="to" type="hidden" value="bepurchast@aol.com,webmaster@desert
.net">
<!input name="to" type="hidden" value="bigbufflo@aol.com,webmaster@desert
.net">
<input name="from" type="hidden" value="websurfer@bitbucket.opus1.com">
<input name="subject" type="hidden" value="Off The Beaten Path Order Form">
<input name="version" type="hidden" value="Buffalo OBP Order Form 2.0">
<input name="success" type="hidden" value="http://desert.net/buffalo/
catalog/success.html">
<input name="" type="hidden" value="">


<table border="0" cellpadding="0" cellspacing="0" width="387">
<tr>

<td valign="top" align="left" width="85">
<a href="1.html"><img src="images/01_image.jpg" width="72" height="72"
alt="" border="0"></a><br>
<img src="images/spacer.gif" width="85" height="1" alt=""><br>
</td>
<td valign="top" align="left">
```

```
<img src="images/01_text.gif" width="83" height="42" alt="Cocktail Shaker
$19.00/each"><br>
<select name="A971" onChange="calculateCost()">
<option value="0|0|0.00">Select Qty.
<option value="1|1|19.00">1 - $19.00
<option value="2|2|38.00">2 - $38.00
<option value="3|3|57.00">3 - $57.00
<option value="4|4|76.00">4 - $76.00
<option value="5|5|95.00">5 - $95.00
</select><br>
</td>

<td width=100% valign=bottom aln=left><img src="images/spacer.gif"
width="20" height="1" alt=""></td>

<td valign="top" align="left" width="85">
<a href="2.html"><img src="images/02_image.gif" width="72" height="72"
alt="" border="0"></a><br>
<img src="images/spacer.gif" width="85" height="1" alt=""><br>
</td>
<td valign="top" align="left">
<img src="images/02_text.gif" width="83" height="42" alt="Dishtowel $7.00/
each"><br>
<select name="A972" onChange="calculateCost()">
<option value="0|0|0.00">Select Qty.
<option value="1|1|7.00">1 - $7.00
<option value="2|2|14.00">2 - $14.00
<option value="3|3|21.00">3 - $21.00
<option value="4|4|28.00">4 - $28.00
<option value="5|5|35.00">5 - $35.00
</select><br>
</td>

</tr>
<tr>
<td valign="top" align="left" colspan="5"><img src="images/spacer.gif"
width="1" height="20" alt=""><br></td>
</tr>
<tr>

<td valign="top" align="left" width="85">
```

```
<a href="3.html"><img src="images/03_image.jpg" width="72" height="72"
alt="" border="0"></a><br>
<img src="images/spacer.gif" width="85" height="1" alt=""><br>
</td>
<td valign="top" align="left">
<img src="images/03_text.gif" width="83" height="42" alt="Flying Butterfly
$13.00/each"><br>
<select name="A973" onChange="calculateCost()">
<option value="0|0|0.00">Select Qty.
<option value="1|1|13.00">1 - $13.00
<option value="2|2|26.00">2 - $26.00
<option value="3|3|39.00">3 - $39.00
<option value="4|4|52.00">4 - $52.00
<option value="5|5|65.00">5 - $65.00
</select><br>
</td>

<td width="100%" valign="bottom" aln="left"><img src="images/spacer.gif"
width="20" height="1" alt=""></td>0


<td valign="top" align="left" width="85">
<a href="4.html"><img src="images/04_image.jpg" width="72" height="72"
alt="" border="0"></a><br>
<img src="images/spacer.gif" width="85" height="1" alt=""><br>
</td>
<td valign="top" align="left">
<img src="images/04_text.gif" width="83" height="42" alt="Pin-up trading
cards $3.00/pack"><br>
<select name="A974" onChange="calculateCost()">
<option value="0|0|0.00">Select Qty.
<option value="1|1|3.00">1 - $3.00
<option value="2|2|6.00">2 - $6.00
<option value="3|3|9.00">3 - $9.00
<option value="4|4|12.00">4 - $12.00
<option value="5|5|15.00">5 - $15.00
</select><br>
</td>

</tr>
<tr>
<td valign="top" align="left" colspan="5"><img src="images/spacer.gif"
width="1" height="20" alt=""><br></td>
```

```html
</tr>
<tr>

<td valign="top" align="left" width="85">
<a href="5.html"><img src="images/05_image.gif" width="72" height="72"
alt="" border="0"></a><br>
<img src="images/spacer.gif" width="85" height="1" alt=""><br>
</td>
<td valign="top" align="left">
<img src="images/05_text.gif" width="83" height="42" alt="Body glitter
$7.00/each"><br>
<select name="A975" onChange="calculateCost()">
<option value="0|0|0.00">Select Qty.
<option value="1|1|7.00">1 - $7.00
<option value="2|2|14.00">2 - $14.00
<option value="3|3|21.00">3 - $21.00
<option value="4|4|28.00">4 - $28.00
<option value="5|5|35.00">5 - $35.00
</select><br>
</td>

<td width="100%" valign="bottom" aln="left"><img src="images/spacer.gif"
width="20" height="1" alt=""></td>

<td valign="top" align="left" width="85">
<a href="6.html"><img src="images/06_image.gif" width="72" height="72"
alt="" border="0"></a><br>
<img src="images/spacer.gif" width="85" height="1" alt=""><br>
</td>
<td valign="top" align="left">
<img src="images/06_text.gif" width="83" height="42" alt="Verga magnets
$11.00/set"><br>
<select name="A976" onChange="calculateCost()">
<option value="0|0|0.00">Select Qty.
<option value="1|1|11.00">1 - $11.00
<option value="2|2|22.00">2 - $22.00
<option value="3|3|33.00">3 - $33.00
<option value="4|4|44.00">4 - $44.00
<option value="5|5|55.00">5 - $55.00
</select><br>
</td>
```

```
</tr>
<tr>
<td valign="top" align="left" colspan="5"><img src="images/spacer.gif"
width="1" height="20" alt=""><br></td>
</tr>
<tr>

<td valign="top" align="left" width="85">
<a href="7.html"><img src="images/07_image.gif" width="72" height="72"
alt="" border="0"></a><br>
<img src="images/spacer.gif" width="85" height="1" alt=""><br>
</td>
<td valign="top" align="left">
<img src="images/07_text.gif" width="83" height="42" alt="Forkchops $18.00/
box"><br>
<select name="A977" onChange="calculateCost()">
<option value="0|0|0.00">Pick Color
<option value="1|Black|18.00">Black
<option value="2|Dark Blue|18.00">Dark Blue
</select><br>
</td>

<td width="100%" valign="bottom" aln="left"><img src="images/spacer.gif"
width="20" height="1" alt=""></td>

<td valign="top" align="left" width="85">
<a href="8.html"><img src="images/08_image.gif" width="72" height="72"
alt="" border="0"></a><br>
<img src="images/spacer.gif" width="85" height="1" alt=""><br>
</td>
<td valign="top" align="left">
<img src="images/08_text.gif" width="83" height="42" alt="Snap hair clips
$4.00/6pr"><br>
<select name="A978" onChange="calculateCost()">
<option value="0|0|0.00">Select Qty.
<option value="1|1|4.00">1 - $4.00
<option value="2|2|8.00">2 - $8.00
<option value="3|3|12.00">3 - $12.00
<option value="4|4|16.00">4 - $16.00
<option value="5|5|20.00">5 - $20.00
</select><br>
</td>
```

```html
</tr>
<tr>
<td valign="top" align="left" colspan="5"><img src="images/spacer.gif"
width="1" height="20" alt=""><br></td>
</tr>
<tr>

<td valign="top" align="left" width="85">
<a href="9.html"><img src="images/09_image.gif" width="72" height="72"
alt="" border="0"></a><br>
<img src="images/spacer.gif" width="85" height="1" alt=""><br>
</td>
<td valign="top" align="left">
<img src="images/09_text.gif" width="83" height="42" alt="Verga gum $6.00-
$39.50"><br>
<select name="A979" onChange="calculateCost()">
<option value="0|0|0.00">Select Qty.
<option value="1|25pcs|6.00">25 - $6.00
<option value="1|50pcs|11.00">50 - $11.00
<option value="1|200pcs|39.50">200 - $39.50
</select><br>
</td>

<td width="100%" valign="bottom" aln="left"><img src="images/spacer.gif"
width="20" height="1" alt=""></td>

<td valign="top" align="left" width="85">
<a href="10.html"><img src="images/10_image.gif" width="72" height="72"
alt="" border="0"></a><br>
<img src="images/spacer.gif" width="85" height="1" alt=""><br>
</td>
<td valign="top" align="left">
<img src="images/10_text.gif" width="83" height="42" alt="Sunglasses $8.50/
each"><br>
<select name="A9710" onChange="calculateCost()">
<option value="0|0|0.00">Pick Style
<option value="1|Cateye|8.50">Cateye
<option value="1|Nerd|8.50">Nerd
<option value="1|Square|8.50">Square
</select><br>
</td>
```

```
</tr>

</tr>
<tr>
<td valign="top" align="left" colspan="5"><img src="images/spacer.gif"
width="1" height="20" alt=""><br></td>
</tr>
<tr>

<td valign="top" align="left" width="85">
<a href="11.html"><img src="images/11_image.gif" width="72" height="72"
alt="" border="0"></a><br>
<img src="images/spacer.gif" width="85" height="1" alt=""><br>
</td>
<td valign="top" align="left">
<img src="images/11_text.gif" width="83" height="42" alt="Pin-up postcard
book $8.50/each"><br>
<select name="A9711" onChange="calculateCost()">
<option value="0|0|0.00">Select Qty.
<option value="1|1|8.50">1 - $8.50
<option value="2|2|17.00">2 - $17.00
<option value="3|3|25.50">3 - $25.50
<option value="4|4|34.00">4 - $34.00
<option value="5|5|42.50">5 - $42.50
</select><br>
</td>

<td width="100%" valign="bottom" aln="left"><img src="images/spacer.gif"
width="20" height="1" alt=""></td>

<td valign="top" align="left" width="85">
<a href="12.html"><img src="images/12_image.gif" width="72" height="72"
alt="" border="0"></a><br>
<img src="images/spacer.gif" width="85" height="1" alt=""><br>
</td>
<td valign="top" align="left">
<img src="images/12_text.gif" width="83" height="42" alt="Handwoven
bedspread $13.00/each"><br>
<select name="A9712" onChange="calculateCost()">
<option value="0|0|0.00">Select Qty.
<option value="1|1|13.00">1 - $13.00
<option value="2|2|26.00">2 - $26.00
```

```
<option value="3|3|39.00">3 - $39.00
<option value="4|4|52.00">4 - $52.00
<option value="5|5|65.00">5 - $65.00
</select><br>
</td>

</tr>

</tr>
<tr>
<td valign="top" align="left" colspan="5"><img src="images/spacer.gif"
width="1" height="20" alt=""><br></td>
</tr>
<tr>

<td valign="top" align="left" width="85">
<a href="13.html"><img src="images/13_image.gif" width="72" height="72"
alt="" border="0"></a><br>
<img src="images/spacer.gif" width="85" height="1" alt=""><br>
</td>
<td valign="top" align="left">
<img src="images/13_text.gif" width="83" height="42" alt="Color drip candles
$3.50/pair"><br>
<select name="A9713" onChange="calculateCost()">
<option value="0|0|0.00">Select Qty.
<option value="1|1|3.50">1 - $3.50
<option value="2|2|7.00">2 - $7.00
<option value="3|3|10.50">3 - $10.50
<option value="4|4|14.00">4 - $14.00
<option value="5|5|17.50">5 - $17.50
</select><br>
</td>

<td width="100%" valign="bottom" aln="left"><img src="images/spacer.gif"
width="20" height="1" alt=""></td>

<td valign="top" align="left" width="85">
<a href="14.html"><img src="images/14_image.gif" width="72" height="72"
alt="" border="0"></a><br>
<img src="images/spacer.gif" width="85" height="1" alt=""><br>
</td>
<td valign="top" align="left">
```

```
<img src="images/14_text.gif" width="83" height="42" alt="Rubber ducky
$5.00/each"><br>
<select name="A9714" onChange="calculateCost()">
<option value="0|0|0.00">Select Qty.
<option value="1|1|5.00">1 - $5.00
<option value="2|2|10.00">2 - $10.00
<option value="3|3|15.00">3 - $15.00
<option value="4|4|20.00">4 - $20.00
<option value="5|5|25.00">5 - $25.00
</select><br>
</td>

</tr>
</table>
<p><br>

<input name="" type="hidden" value="">

<table border="0" cellpadding="0" cellspacing="0" width="387">
<tr>
<td valign="top" align="left">

<font size="5">Order Form<hr size="1"></font>
<p>

If your browser supports JavaScript, most of the calculations will be
automatically filled in as you make your selections. Otherwise whip out
your calculator, and fill in the values where requested.
<p>

Sub Total:  <input type="text" size="16" name="subTotalCost"
value="$0.00">
<p>

<input name="" type="hidden" value="">

Sales Tax:  
<select name="StateTax" onChange="calculateCost()">
<option value="1">Choose State
<option value="1">Other
<option value="1">Alabama
<option value="1">Alaska
<option value="1.07">Arizona
```

```
<option value="1">Arkansas
<option value="1.0725">California
<option value="1">Colorado
<option value="1">Connecticut
<option value="1">Delaware
<option value="1">Florida
<option value="1">Georgia
<option value="1">Hawaii
<option value="1">Idaho
<option value="1">Illinois
<option value="1">Indiana
<option value="1">Iowa
<option value="1">Kansas
<option value="1">Kentucky
<option value="1">Louisiana
<option value="1">Maine
<option value="1">Maryland
<option value="1">Massachusetts
<option value="1">Michigan
<option value="1">Minnesota
<option value="1">Mississippi
<option value="1">Missouri
<option value="1">Montana
<option value="1">Nebraska
<option value="1.065">Nevada
<option value="1">New Hampshire
<option value="1">New Jersey
<option value="1.05">New Mexico
<option value="1">New York
<option value="1">North Carolina
<option value="1">North Dakota
<option value="1">Ohio
<option value="1">Oklahoma
<option value="1">Oregon
<option value="1">Pennsylvania
<option value="1">Rhode Island
<option value="1">South Carolina
<option value="1">South Dakota
<option value="1">Tennessee
<option value="1.0625">Texas
```

```
<option value="1">Utah
<option value="1">Vermont
<option value="1">Virginia
<option value="1.065">Washington
<option value="1">West Virginia
<option value="1">Wisconsin
<option value="1">Wyoming
</select>  <input name="totalStateTax" value="$0.00"><br>
<font size="2">
(AZ residents: 7%,
CA residents: 7.25%,
NM residents: 5%,
TX residents: 6.25%,
WA residents: 6.5%,
NV residents: 6.5%)
</font>
<p><br>

<input name="" type="hidden" value="">

Complimentary gift card:
<textarea name="Gift Message" rows="2" cols="43" wrap="physical">Type your
message here.</textarea>
<p>

Gift Wrap:  
<select name="giftWrap" onChange="calculateCost()">
<option value="0|No|0.00">No
<option value="0|Yes|3.00">Yes - $3.00 per item
</select>  <input name="totalGiftWrap" value="$0.00"><br>
<p><br>

<input name="" type="hidden" value="">

Shipping & Handling:  <input name="totalShipping" size=19
value="$0.00"><br>
<font size="2">($6.00 per gift package; add $1.00 for every
additional gift package shipped to same recipient)</font>
<p>

<input name="" type="hidden" value="">
```

```
<b>Total Cost</b>:  <input type="text" name="totalCost" size="19"
value="$0.00">
<p><br>

<input name="" type="hidden" value="">

<font size="5">Billing Information<hr size="1"></font>
<p>
```

If you would like to pay by credit card, please fill out the following
information where requested. Please note: your name MUST be the same
as the name on your credit card.
```
<p>
```

Please allow 3-10 business days for shipping and handling. All orders
shipped by UPS. UPS can not deliver to P.O. Boxes.
```
<p>
```
Sorry, we cannot accept Buffalo Exchange trade coupons.
```
<p>

<pre>
Name:    <input type="text" name="Billing Name" value="" size="30">
Address: <input type="text" name="Billing Address" size="30" value="">
City:    <input type="text" name="Billing City" value="" size="20">
State:   <input type="text" name="Billing State" value="" size="20">
Zip Code: <input type="text" name="Billing Zip Code" value=""
size="20"><input name="" type="hidden" value="">

Credit Card: <input type="radio" name="Credit Card" value="VISA"
CHECKED>VISA   <input type="radio" name="Credit Card"
value="MasterCard">Master Card

Account Number: <input type="text" name="Credit Card Number" value=""
size="20">
Expiration Date: <input type="text" name="Expiration Date" value=""
size="20">
Phone Number:   <input type="text" name="Phone Number" value="" size="20">
Email Address:  <input type="text" name="Email" value="" size="20"><input
name="" type="hidden" value="">

Have you shopped at any
Buffalo Exchange store? <input type="radio" name="New Customer" value="Yes"
CHECKED>yes <input type="radio" name="New Customer" value="No">no
</pre>
<p>
```

```
<br>

<font size="5">Shipping Information<hr size="1"></font>
<p>

Please enter shipping information if different than above.
<p>

<input name="" type="hidden" value="">

<pre>
Name:    <input type="text" name="Shipping Name" value="" size="30">
Address: <input type="text" name="Shipping Address" size="30" value="">
City:    <input type="text" name="Shipping City" value="" size="20">
State:   <input type="text" name="Shipping State" value="" size="20">
Zip Code: <input type="text" name="Shipping Zip Code" value="" size="20">
</pre>
<p><br>

<input type="submit" value="Place Order">  
<input type="reset" value="Clear">
<img src="../images/spacer.gif" width="387" height="1" alt="">
<p>

</td>
</tr>
</table>

</form>
```

The form is complete—a *tremendous amount* of code to create what appears to be a simple page, undeniably! Other information and navigation follow:

```
<center>
<a href="../giftcert.htm"><img src="../images/giftcert_ad2.gif" width="389"
height="35" alt="Gift Certificates Available" border="0"></a>
<p><br>
<a href="http://desert.net/htbin/mapimage.exe/buffalo/menubar.map"><img
src="../images/menubar_rev.gif" width="401" height="27" border="0" ismap
usemap="#MenuBar"></a>
<p>

<map name="MenuBar">
<area shape="rect" coords="0,0,106,20" href="../index.htmlx"
target="_parent">
```

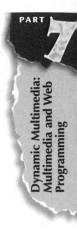

```
<area shape="rect" coords="107,0,144,20" href="../who.htm">
<area shape="rect" coords="145,0,176,20" href="../how.htm">
<area shape="rect" coords="177,0,249,20" href="../what.htm">
<area shape="rect" coords="250,0,293,20" href="../where.htm">
<area shape="rect" coords="294,0,333,20" href="../catalog/index.html">
<area shape="rect" coords="334,0,391,20" href="../contact.htm">
</map>

<font size="2">
Photos by David Voll<br>
<a href="http://desert.net/designs/" target="_parent">Site by DesertNet
Designs</a><br>
&#169; 1996-1997 Buffalo Exchange<p>
</font>
</center>
<p>

</body>
</html>
```

You can visit the Off the Beaten Path Catalog at `http://www.desert.net/buffalo/` `catalog/`.

Progressive Interactivity

I like to think that community will be the focus of online interactivity that progresses beyond the functional, hence the term progressive interactivity. Certainly, the state of chats and newsgroups provided by online services vary greatly, and in some cases have gotten very bad reputations for being like a single's bar (or worse!); or, in the case of newsgroups, a free-for-all where the good information becomes difficult to find.

> *"The notion of an 'online community' is part of the magic of the Internet."*
>
> JEFF FRENTZEN, PCWeek Online.

What I am suggesting is to harness the power of like-minded people by providing forums based around certain topics. Link this to a product or service that your client is working with and conceivably you could end up with a very powerful interactive environment.

A great example of this is Saturn Cars (`http://www.saturncars.com/`). Saturn has all kinds of message boards for car owners, and the entire Saturn brand has been created with a community feel. It's worked extremely well, being one of the more effective and memorable ad campaigns of this decade.

Web Bulletin Boards

Bulletin boards or interactive newsgroups are a seminal part of the online community. The message-by-message style of communicating with others began years ago even before the Internet went public to any significant degree.

There are a number of ways of incorporating bulletin boards (BBSs) into a Web site. One way is using an *inline-style* BBS, which involves the use of server-sided software that delivers the technology.

> *"Discussion forums are an excellent way to take full advantage of the Net's two-way interactivity and to build community around your site."*
>
> REX BALDAZO, C|NET

The Weekly Wire's Talk Back conference is an inline example. In Figure 22.4, you can see how the topics are loaded into the left frame, and the messages appear in the right window. Click on another topic, and another message appears (Figure 22.5).

FIGURE 22.4

The topics are in the left frame, messages in the right

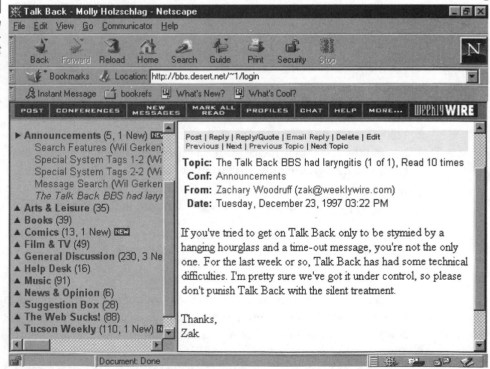

FIGURE 22.5

*Click on
another topic,
get another
message*

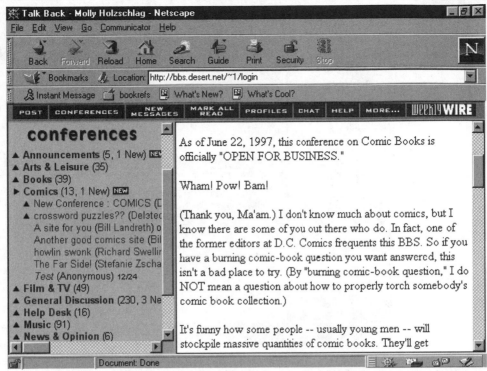

You can post your own message to the conference, and people will undoubtedly respond. This means that not only is the Web serving up the functional aspect of interactivity, but it is also providing an opportunity for the development of community.

Another type of BBS that is available is the standard *newsgroup style*, which will cause an external or integrated piece of software to run. The Design Studio offers up one such BBS. Here's the snippet of code that links you to that BBS:

```
Jump on over to the
<a href="news://forums.annex.com/designnews ">discussion newsgroup</a>
```

If you click the link to the newsgroup in Internet Explorer 3.0 and above, an external newsreader program will launch (Figure 22.6) and from there, you can answer or post messages (note that the interface is very similar to the inline example above).

In Netscape Navigator 3.0 and above, you'll launch Netscape's integrated newsreader that will read the newsgroup (Figure 22.7) and allow you to post (Figure 22.8).

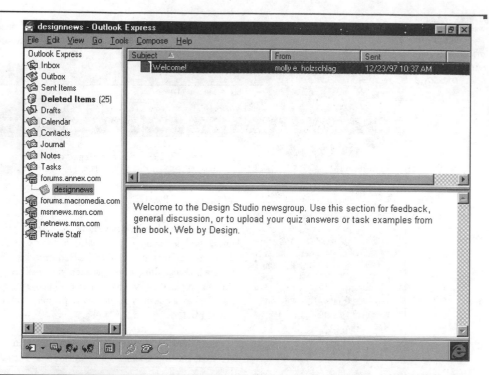

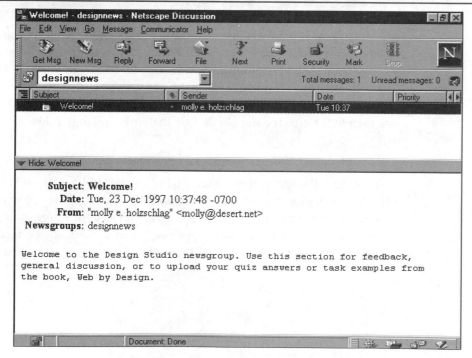

FIGURE 22.8

*Using the news-
reader to post a
message*

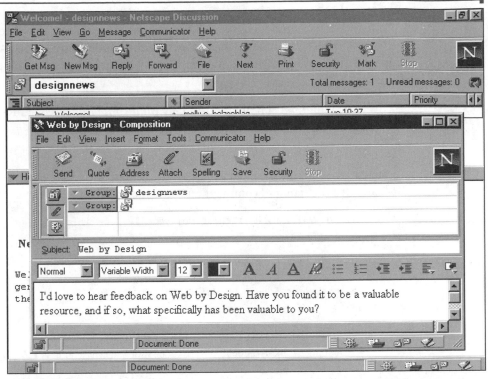

 line!

The following URLs will help you find information about popular conferencing software
for the Web.

- **Allaire Forums:** This is Web BBS conferencing based on the Cold Fusion database
  application, http://www.allaire.com/.
- **Oracle Workgroup Collaboration Forums:** http://www.oracle.com/.
- **Spinnaker:** From Searchlight Software, http://www.searchlight.com/.
- **WebBoard:** From O'Reilly and Associates, http://webboard.ora.com/.
- **David R. Woolley's guide:** For an extremely comprehensive, updated list of avail-
  able conferencing software, visit this guide, http://freenet.msp.mn.us/people/
  drwool/webconf.html.

Web Chats

Another essential component for building online community is to create Web chats. As with the BBS-style conferencing, there are inline and external chats. And, depending upon the type of browser you're using, the way those chats are handled will be different.

> *"Instead of the simple one-to-many publishing offered by most Web sites, adding chat creates a richer many-to-many experience."*
>
> JONATHAN HIRSCHMAN, C|NET

Here is the code for the Chats! page on the Design Studio site (Figure 22.9). Start with the standard comment and structure tags:

```
<!--Site by Molly E. Holzschlag molly@molly.com-->

<html>

<head>
<title>The Design Studio by Molly: Chats!</title>
</head>

<body topmargin="0" bgcolor="#FFFFFF" background="images/medi-bak.gif"
text="#000000" link="#666633" vlink="663300" alink="#FFFFFF">

<table border="0" width="580" cellpadding="0" cellspacing="0">
<tr>

<!--begin text area-->

<td valign="top" width="500">

<img src="images/clear.gif" width="15" height="1" border="0" alt="spacer">

<img src="images/chat-hed.gif" width="234" height="69" border="0" alt="front
office header">
<p>

<font face="arial">

<blockquote>
```

FIGURE 22.9

*The Chats! page on
the Design Studio*

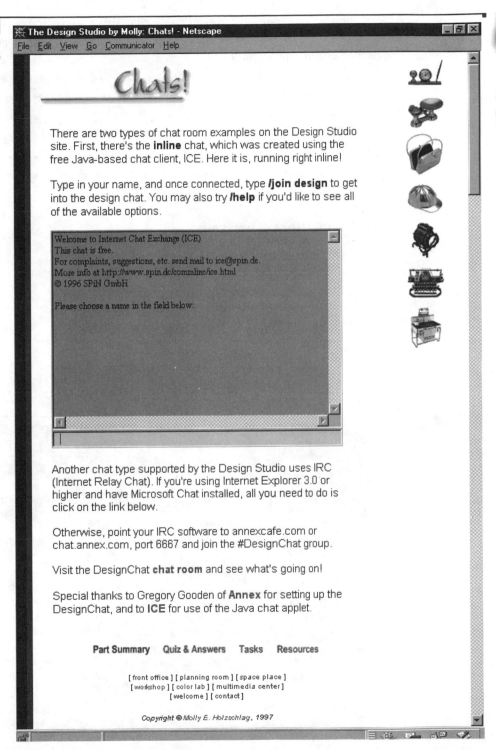

The following code demonstrates an inline chat, using a Java applet. This is viewable in both Internet Explorer (Figure 22.10) and Netscape Navigator (Figure 22.11) *as long as* the version is Java compliant.

```
There are two types of chat room examples on the Design Studio site. First,
there's the <b>inline</b> chat, which was created using the free Java-based
chat client, ICE. Here it is, running right inline!
<p>

Type in your name, and once connected, type <b>/join design</b> to get into
the design chat. You may also try <b>/help</b> if you'd like to see all of
the available options.
<p>
<APPLET CODE="EmbryoClient.class"
        CODEBASE="http://www.spin.de/classes/"
        WIDTH=400 height=295>
        <PARAM NAME="channel" VALUE="welcome!">
        <PARAM NAME="bgcolor" VALUE="CC9966">
        <PARAM NAME="fgcolor" VALUE="000000">
        <PARAM NAME="fontsize" VALUE="12">
        Please get a Java capable browser!
        </APPLET>
                    <P>
```

FIGURE 22.10

The inline chat in Internet Explorer

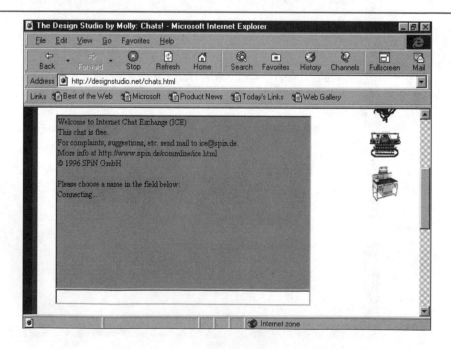

FIGURE 22.11

*The inline chat in
Netscape Navigator*

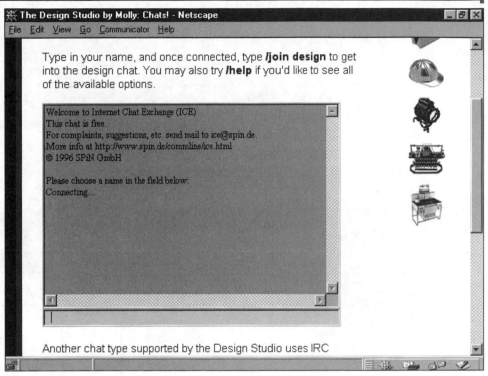

Another type of chat is the external chat. In Internet Explorer 3.0 and above, clicking on the link in the following code will start an external chat program that connects to the chat (Figure 22.12). Netscape doesn't have this feature, but with any of the many IRC chat clients available, you can simply point to the server where the chat resides, and join the group.

```
Another chat type supported by the Design Studio uses IRC (Internet Relay
Chat). If you're using Internet Explorer 3.0 or higher and have Microsoft
Chat installed, all you need to do is click on the link below.
<p>

Otherwise, point your IRC software to annexcafe.com or chat.annex.com, port
6667 and join
the #DesignChat group.
<p>
```

Visit the DesignChat <a href="mic://chat.annex.com/#designchat">chat room</a> and see what's going on!
<p>

Special thanks to Gregory Gooden of <a href="http://www
.annex.com">Annex</a> for setting up the DesignChat, and to <a
href="http://www.spin.de/commline/ice.html">ICE</a> for use of the
Java chat applet.

</blockquote>
<p>

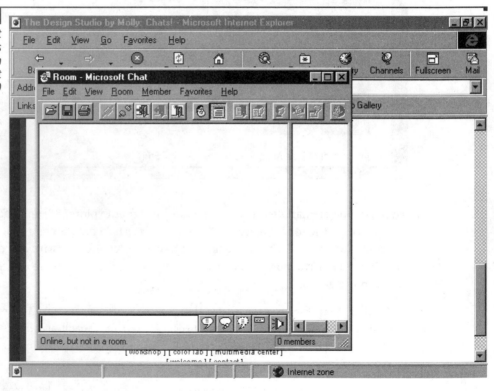

FIGURE 22.12

The external chat program is launched from Internet Explorer 4.0

The chat information is completed, and the rest of the page's code is dedicated to the standard sub-navigation, text navigation, image map, and map data.

```
<div align="center">

<!--begin ie flash navigation-->

<object classid="clsid:D27CDB6E-AE6D-11cf-96B8-444553540000"
codebase="http://active.macromedia.com/flash2/cabs/swflash
.cab#version=2,0,0,0"
border="0" width="316" height="58">

<param name="Movie" value="images/subnav.swf">
<param name="Loop" value="False">
<param name="Play" value="True">
<param name="BGColor" value="FFFFFF">
<param name="Quality" value="high">
<param name="Scale" value="Showall">

<!--begin netscape flash navigation-->

<embed src="images/subnav.swf" pluginspage="/shockwave/download/index
.cgi?P1_Prod_Version=ShockwaveFlash" type=application/futuresplash
width="316" height="58" loop=false quality=high play=true>

</object>
<br>

<!--begin text navigation-->

<font face="arial" size="1">

[ <a href="../office.htm"> front office </a> ] [ <a href="../planning
.htm">planning room</a> ] [ <a href="../space.htm">space place</a> ]
<br>

[ <a href="../workshop.htm">workshop</a> ] [ <a href="../color.htm">color
lab</a> ] [ <a href="../media.htm">multimedia center</a> ]
<br>

[ <a href="../index.html">welcome</a> ] [ <a href="../contact
.htm">contact</a> ]
</font>

</div>
```

```
<p>

<!--begin copyright and mailto-->

<div align="center">

<font size="1">

<i>Copyright &copy; <a href="mailto:molly@molly.com">Molly E.
Holzschlag</a>, 1997</i>

</div>
</font>
</td>

<td width="25">

<img src="images/clear.gif" width="25" height="1" border="0" alt="spacer">

</td>

<!--begin navigation column-->

<td valign="top" width="50">

<img src="images/navmap3.gif" width="50" height="395" border="0"
alt="navigational image map, text navigation below" usemap="#navmap3">

</td>

</table>

<!--begin map data-->

<map name="navmap3">
<area shape="rect" coords="0,0,57,46" href="office.htm">
<area shape="rect" coords="0,48,57,98" href="planning.htm">
<area shape="rect" coords="0,100,57,160" href="space.htm">
<area shape="rect" coords="0,162,57,214" href="workshop.htm">
<area shape="rect" coords="0,216,57,275" href="color.htm">
<area shape="rect" coords="0,278,57,330" href="type.htm">
<area shape="rect" coords="0,332,58,393" href="media.htm">
<area shape="default" nohref>
</map>

</body>
</html>
```

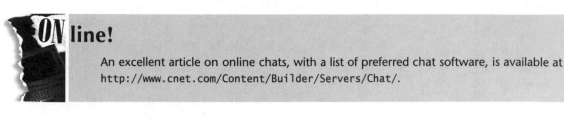

ON line!

An excellent article on online chats, with a list of preferred chat software, is available at
`http://www.cnet.com/Content/Builder/Servers/Chat/`.

Next Up

Now that you've had an introduction to the ideas and practices of interactivity, it's
time to look more closely at the methods involved in delivering that interactivity.
Whether you choose to work with more functional interactivity, or use progressive
interactivity wherever possible, the bottom line is you'll need to know about the tools
and mechanisms of its delivery.

In the following chapter, you'll be introduced to animated GIFs, Web audio and
video, and multimedia packages such as Shockwave and Flash. All of these technologies have the potential to be functional or progressive interactive media, but that
potential must be put into action by you, the designer.

chapter 23

MULTIMEDIA DESIGN

Multimedia Design

Multimedia design is the visionary spirit of a Web site. It can take static site elements such as navigation buttons and graphics and bring them to life with sound and audio. Multimedia allows for full radio shows to be delivered online to listeners, either live or in an archive. Real-time video is just around the corner, and complete multimedia packages including animation, audio, and user input bring Web pages to life.

Bandwidth is the big issue with multimedia delivery, and it is the lack of broad bandwidth that has kept multimedia from being used with greater frequency. Certain technologies discussed in this chapter are making that delivery more realistic, despite the lack of broad bandwidth for most people.

Designing with multimedia is a little like going to a buffet. You want a little of everything, but if you actually eat everything, you'll no doubt become sick. With multimedia, you have to pick what you really want, and what you really need, to deliver your message. If the activity enhances your intent, then you are well within reason to serve it up. However, I caution you to tread lightly and not burden the plate with so much that it becomes impossibly confused.

In this chapter we will examine the following multimedia technologies:

- Animated GIFs
- Downloadable audio
- Streaming audio
- Web-based phones
- Downloadable video
- Streaming video
- Macromedia Shockwave
- Macromedia Flash

You will also get some hands-on design experience by learning how to make an animated GIF, looking at the code behind streaming audio, and stepping through a Flash animation.

OFF line!

If you're interested in learning how to prepare and design multimedia, be sure to look at *The Multimedia Scriptwriting Workshop* by Douglas J. Varchol (Sybex, 1996).

Whether it comes in the form of a simple animated GIF, or packaged in a more complex application plug-in such as Shockwave or FutureSplash, multimedia design is the present tense of the Web design's future.

Animated GIFs

Animated GIFs began their lives before the Web was born. Of course, no one could know this. It took the innovative imaginations of Web designers studying applications of the GIF89a format developed in 1989 to figure out how its algorithms could be used to create animations.

Because animated GIFs are in fact, GIFs, they utilize the same compression as a standard GIF. They allow only for a maximum of 256 colors.

> *"GIF89a is still a 256-color (maximum) format. GIF allows for any number of colors between 2 and 256. The fewer colors the less data and the smaller the graphic files. If your GIF only uses 4 colors, you can reduce the palette to only 2 bits (4 color) and decrease the file size by upwards of 75%."*

> ROYALE FRAZIER, Animated GIF Guru

Animated GIFs arrived on the scene when Netscape 2.0 was released and are now fully supported by all Netscape versions above 2.0, and Internet Explorer 3.0 and above.

There are many benefits to using animated GIFs. For starters, their cross-platform compatibility factor is wide-range. No need for plug-ins and accessories here, just load it and go.

Of course, that's why designers sometimes get carried away with GIF animation. It's easy. But that doesn't always mean it's attractive, so be sure to use a soft hand when approaching GIF animation.

Other benefits of GIF animation stem from the flexibility of the GIF format itself. GIF animations can be made transparent, meaning that you can place them seamlessly over textured, design-rich background graphics. They can also be interlaced for progressive rendering.

And of course, because you can optimize GIFs down to the exact colors used in a given design, you can end up with extremely small file sizes, which makes them fast-loading.

Of course, there are a number of limitations. As you already are aware, photographs are much better compressed using JPEG format. This means the best quality GIF animations are going to be flat-color, line drawings rather than photographic in nature.

If you're thinking: "Wow! I can use a background GIF to create motion all over my page" you're not only looking for design trouble but it can't be done. Animated GIFs will only display the first frame if they are placed in the background of a page's body.

Another limitation is that animated GIFs are not interactive per se, as you learned in Chapter 22. Engaging, yes, and indeed designers can use words or images to draw you into a somewhat interactive relationship, enticing you to click on them and see where you'll end up next. Ad banners count on this, in fact. But mechanically speaking, GIFs cannot accept user input in and of themselves.

Finally, if you've ever watched a page load that contains animations, you'll notice that the motion of the animation can be interrupted by other data being sent between the browser and the server. This means your smooth, slick animation may not appear so smooth on its first load. Caching helps, but this means that someone has had to have visited your site in order for that assistance to occur.

ON line!

The following sites can offer information on animation products.

- **Alchemy Mindworkshop, GIF Construction Set:** Easy interface and a wizard for the novice animator, but it's PC only, located at `http://www.mindworkshop.com/alchemy/alchemy.html`.

- **Microsoft Image Composer and Microsoft GIF Animator:** These two programs work together to create smooth animation, located at `http://www.microsoft.com/frontpage/`.

- **GIFBuilder:** The most loved GIF animator for the Mac, located at `http://iawww.epfl.ch/Staff/Yves.Piguet/clip2gif-home/GifBuilder.html`.

- **GIF Movie Gear:** Great color palette control and optimization in this one, by Gamani Productions, located at `http://www.gamani.com/`.

GIF Animation Software

GIF animation is created by first generating the individual graphics (often referred to as *cells*) you need in a drawing program such as Photoshop or Microsoft Image Composer, and processing them through a GIF animation software program.

In this section, we'll be looking at GIF Animator, a PC-based animation program that works in tandem with Photoshop or Microsoft Image Composer to help you create GIF animations.

The GIF Animator program is unlike any other program that Microsoft has designed. There are no text pull-down menus, only buttons with tool tips. This keeps the program compact and the interface easy to use. For a quick overview of the interface, see Figure 23.1.

N OTE

While GIF Animator offers its own unique set of options, most of these options are global to other animation programs. You should have no trouble following along with the concepts described here even if you are working with different software.

FIGURE 23.1

The Microsoft GIF Animator program interface

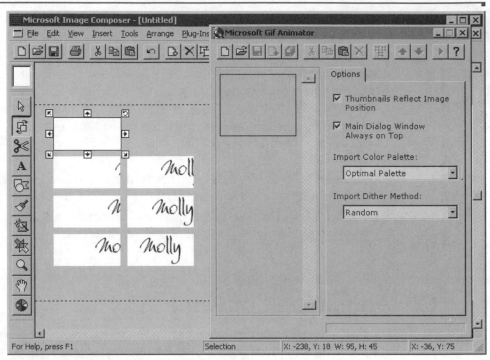

There are dialog boxes in GIF Animator that allow you to set a variety of attributes necessary for creating the GIF. The following list describes some of the options available in the Options dialog box (shown in Figure 23.2) and how to use them.

- **Thumbnails Reflect Image Position**—To make sure the animation behaves as you want, check this. The images should align to the top left of each frame.

- **Main Dialog Window Always on Top**—This makes it easier to drag and drop images from Image Composer to the Gif Animator frames.

- **Import Color Palette**—For 256 colors, make sure this is set to "Browser Palette."

- **Import Dither Method**—This dictates how the image will dither in a browser with a smaller or different palette.

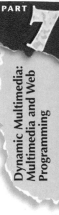

FIGURE 23.2

*Options dialog box
in Microsoft GIF
Animator*

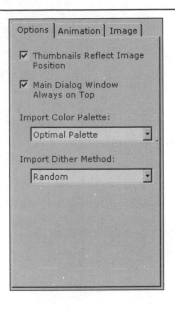

The Animation dialog box (shown in Figure 23.3) allows for these selections. They should be used as follows:

- **Animation Width, Animation Height**—Hit select all, and these values should remain constant. If they do not, you run the risk of having images that are sized incorrectly within the frames and the animation will not work perfectly.

- **Image Count**—This value should reflect the number of frames you wish to have in your image

- **Looping**—How many times should the animation play, once or more? If more than once, should it repeat forever?

The Image dialog box (shown in Figure 23.4) offers these options:

- **Image**—Width and height should be fixed, and left and right should be set at "0,0."

- **Duration**—How long should this image remain in focus? For best results, apply consistently across the majority of images for a smooth process.

- **Undraw Method**—Most animated GIFs use restore previous, although Netscape 2.0 doesn't handle this properly. Experiment for the effect you want.

- **Transparency**—You can choose one palette entry to be transparent.

- **Comment**—This is an optional feature. You can insert comments like "Created by Molly E. Holzschlag."

FIGURE 23.3

*Animation box
in Microsoft
GIF animator*

FIGURE 23.4

*Image dialog box
in Microsoft
GIF animator*

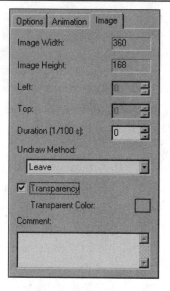

Making an Animated GIF

Using Microsoft's Image Composer 1.5 and GIF Animator, Aaron Bertrand, programming and new technologies consultant for *Web by Design*, offers up this exercise. You will be able to follow along fairly well no matter what animation program you choose to use if you do the drawing in Photoshop or in Image Composer.

1. Open Image Composer.

2. Make three squares of identical size. The best way to do this is draw a square, then use duplicate (Ctrl+D) twice. Note that the image frames must be of identical width/height or else the animation will not run as desired.

3. Draw your animation sequence on each of the three squares.

4. Enable GIF Animator by clicking Tools ➤ GIF Animator.

5. Drag each image in turn from Image Composer onto GIF Animator. A frame will be automatically created for each individual image you drag over.

6. Set up the appropriate options as set forth in the section above.

7. Save the file.

In Figure 23.5, you can see seven flattened selections, each containing a different frame (or cell) of the animation to be created. All seven frames measure 95 pixels wide by 45 pixels high.

FIGURE 23.5

Seven frames in the Molly animation sequence

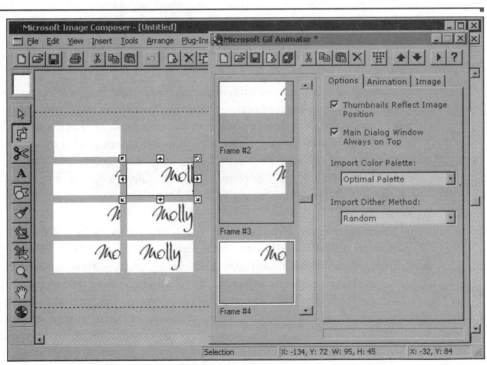

After that, it's a just a matter of drag and drop. The separate sprites (called layers in Photoshop) are moved in the desired order to the next available frame in the GIF Animator window. The attributes are set, and the file is saved as `molly.gif`.

You can see part of the sequence of the `molly.gif` animation in action below. The animation can be viewed in real-time on the Design Studio Web site at `http://www .designstudio.net/media/`.

Audio

There are two primary methods of delivering Web audio. They include a downloadable method, where end-users download the file to play on their end, and *streaming* audio, which is delivered to the browser in a somewhat steady stream of information, allowing the audio to be heard inline.

Almost all Web audio is enabled by the original MIME (Multimedia Internet Mail Extension) protocol developed fairly early on in the evolution of the Internet as an extension of the Internet mail system. Since that time, the use of MIME-style content headers has become almost universal on the Web to identify all sorts of file types, including multimedia types.

Because a browser can distinguish the types of files it receives, it can call external viewers or plug-ins. Plug-ins are an associated or *external* piece of software that renders the downloaded content. This method was the only one available for a time, but it remains popular because it is inexpensive and does not require the purchase of servers or services that provide the technology to deliver streaming audio. Of course, downloadable media is often time consuming, and many people are not patient enough to wait for the large files to download in order to hear the piece of music or speech they're interested in.

Streaming audio addresses the needs of those who are interested in providing on-demand audio that is delivered with immediacy to the end-user. There is, of course, a down side to streaming audio. First, streaming audio must be delivered by a server that has the necessary software and hardware required to stream the audio—an added expense for many. The second limitation is that streaming audio can be lower in quality than some of the downloadable options. This is usually not a significant problem with speech, but some audio designers who are accustomed to digital-quality sound feel that streaming audio is not ready for primetime when it comes to high-end music production.

Despite the limitations of audio delivery, continuous work is being done by companies interested in providing Web audio options, and many choices do exist for the designer when it comes to providing audio for clients and audiences alike.

Downloadable Audio

The following file types are representative of common downloadable audio. You'll notice that many of these file types also support video. This is because both audio and video are dealt with using the same technology.

All of these options share the disadvantage of requiring a complete download before starting the sound. The advantage is simplicity and almost universal support on browsers. For short snippets of sound or a simple tune to play as background music, selecting one of these file types is an excellent idea. They're also a good choice for small downloadable files when streaming audio is not a realistic option.

- **AIFF**—This is the Apple sound file format.
- **AU**—Audio sound file format, developed for Unix and Sun, is now available for PCs as well.
- **AVI**—Audio/Video Interface is used in Windows 3.11 and Windows 95 to provide sound and video, with the sound being primary. It may drop frames to keep the sound playing, thereby allowing the format to work on almost any Windows machine, from the least powerful to the most.
- **MIDI**—The Musical Instrument Digital Interface standard plays orchestral-style sounds from sound cards or from dedicated MIDI processors devoted to producing instrumental sounds from a score. The score describes how to produce the sound rather than capturing actual wave forms.
- **MPEG**—Motion Picture Experts Group is a platform-independent audiovisual file format designed by an industry group.
- **WAV**—Windows Audio format is the audio portion of an AVI file.

"Many of you are familiar with data compression, that software marvel that stuffs, packs, and zips files into neat little packages fractions of their original sizes. Why don't we just do that to these big bad audio files?

Because it's virtually useless, that's why. Try an experiment: take a plain WAV, AU or AIFF file and compress it with PKZip, Stuffit, or GZip. See how much good that did? If you were lucky, it shrank the file by five percent.

That's because there's really not much 'filler' in common digital audio formats—all those bits mean something. So, we have to dig deeper into the bag of tricks.

Enter MPEG, a set of standards defined by the Moving Picture Experts Group. These hard-working folks have come up with a workable solution to the problems inherent in audio and video data compression. It's not magic, but simply takes advantage of something called masking. This is the reason you raise your voice in a crowded room, and why taped sounds such as rainfall and surf can block out intrusive noises.

MPEG encoding analyzes the audio content, and uses the masking effect to disguise its handiwork as much as possible. The end result can be well over 15:1 compression while retaining acceptable (decent FM radio) sound quality."

PHIL STEVENS, Audio Engineer and Webmaster

I'm an avid musician in my spare time, and so I offer a few tastes of music on my Web site. Streaming audio isn't really a concern—for me it's just the desire to make some snippets of what I do available to anyone who is interested.

Here's a look at the code that creates links on my Poetry and Music page, located on my home site at http://www.molly.com/, to the two AU format files that are housed on my server:

```
<ul>

<li><a href="images/wrldgrow.au">World Grows Small</a> mono au 1:12 (1.59
MB).
<p>

<li><a href="images/tokens.au">Tokens</a> mono au 1:06 (1.45 MB).
<p>

</ul>
```

As you can see, it's a simple link pointing to the location and file in question. Figure 23.6 shows the links as they appear on the page.

Songs

Here are two downloadable AU files. These excerpts were taken from recordings with my music partner, Patty Sundberg, for a CD recording titled "Dancing Together." The CD has yet to be released. One day, maybe!

- World Grows Small mono au 1:12 (1.59 MB).

- Tokens mono au 1:06 (1.45 MB).

If a visitor clicks on one of these links the file will begin to download, and, if a supporting plug-in is available, the file will *spawn the application* (find and run the software necessary to play the file). Browsers handle this somewhat differently. Netscape 4.0 will automatically pop up the audio console and begin the download (Figure 23.7), and Internet Explorer 4.0 will ask if you'd like to save it to a disk, where you can listen to it later, or run it directly (Figure 23.8). If you choose to run it directly, the IE audio console will appear (Figure 23.9) and the file will begin to download.

OTE

It's important to keep your plug-ins up to date, otherwise you'll receive an error message letting you know your software has expired. At that point, you should return to the originating Web site for a fresh copy of the software.

FIGURE 23.7

Spawned console in Netscape 4.0

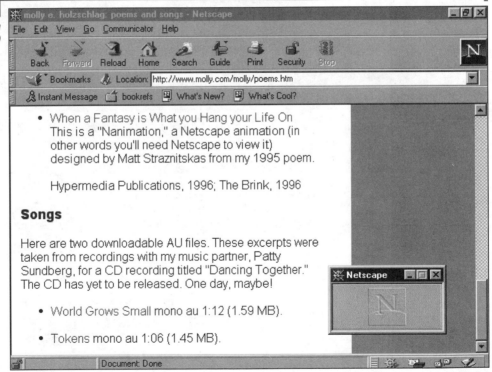

FIGURE 23.8

*Internet Explorer 4.0
offers options*

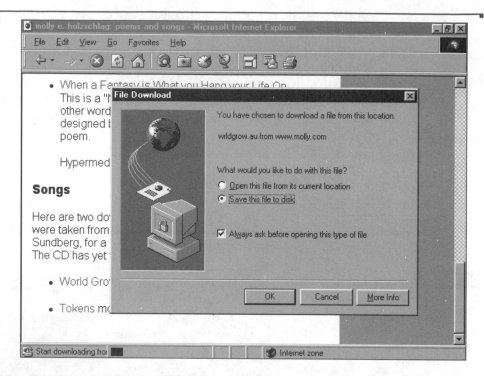

FIGURE 23.9

*Internet Explorer 4.0
audio console*

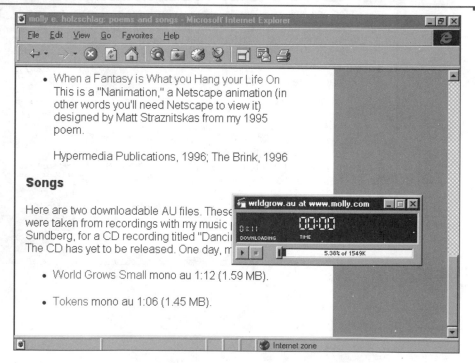

Streaming Audio

RealAudio burst on the scene in 1994 with a unique content delivery system based on UDP (User Datagram Protocol) rather than the usual TCP (Transmission Control Protocol) used for most Internet-based information transfers. What this means in human terms is that UDP sends data packets as fast as possible instead of waiting for confirmation of receipt, as would be done with TCP.

ON line!

Check out RealAudio (and RealVideo) with a visit to RealNetworks at `http://www`
`.realnetworks.com/`.

Using UDP as a delivery system, RealAudio added error-correcting information into the data packet. It also shifted some error compensation logic into the receiving end, and compressed the input using lossy compression schemes (you'll remember lossy compression from our study of JPEGs in Chapter 17). These changes made a breakthrough in audio technology delivery systems. RealAudio was able to provide what was the equivalent of AM-quality sound over relatively slow 14.4 and 28.8 modems.

Delivering streaming audio requires the recording or modification of existing digital recordings into the streaming format (RA is the RealAudio file extension). You can use the RealAudio encoder to do this. In Figure 23.10, you can see an audio file being encoded into a RealAudio file for streaming.

Once this is done, the files must be put onto a server equipped with the UDP technology so that the information can be streamed to the end-user.

As a designer, you'll need to be concerned with cost to your client as well as issues involved with sound quality. If there is a genuine need for streaming audio, that's terrific—go for it. Check the following sidebar for a list of sites that have made intelligent use of RealAudio.

The Rolling Reporter site on the Microsoft Network uses RealAudio. Part of the rationale is that some of the people visiting this site are blind, which gives them an opportunity to have audio as a way to enhance their experience of the site. Furthermore, the client provides the RealAudio server and software, making the availability of the technology ready at hand.

In Figure 23.11 you can see a RealAudio console. While it looks somewhat like an externally spawned console, it's actually not at all the same—this console is part of the RealAudio software that allows for streaming to occur as close to *real-time* as is possible.

FIGURE 23.10

Encoding RealAudio

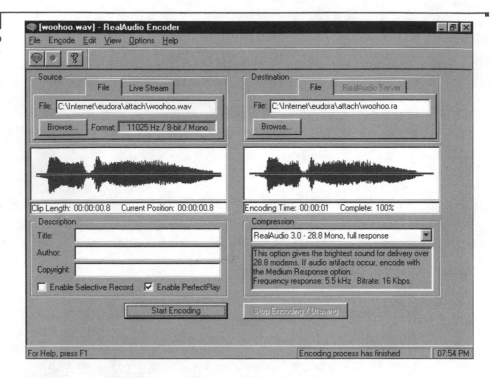

FIGURE 23.11

The RealAudio console

ONline!

Here's a short selection of Web sites that use RealAudio.

- **Timecast:** For information on schedules and shows, you can visit the listings on this Web site, `http://www.timecast.com/`.
- **C-Span:** Yes, that cable station that lets you glimpse what's going on behind closed political doors is on the Web, `http://www.timecast.com/cspan.html`.
- **National Public Radio (NPR):** Perhaps my favorite, with excellent, broad coverage of world news, arts, and culture, `http://www.npr.org/`.
- **LiveConcerts.Com:** That's right, listen to live concerts at this site, `http://www.liveconcerts.com/`.

PART 7

Dynamic Multimedia:
Multimedia and Web
Programming

Telephony

Since the time that UDP was developed, there have been widely varying results in terms of quality sound on the Web. RealAudio (and now RealVideo) are the dominant providers of streaming technology, but are no longer the only players in town.

Among the more interesting offshoots of this technology have been the development of Web phones, which use UDP and compression techniques to enable two-way communication between any two Internet users with the right software. The traditional telephone companies are not amused by this and are seeking legislation in some cases to prohibit the use of unregulated, long-distance calls made via UDP.

Advantages of this technology are lower expenses and wider geographic distribution, since the innate cost of bandwidth is very low for historical reasons and the Web is worldwide by definition. A disadvantage is the unpredictability of network traffic, which can disrupt calls or make reception so poor that listening to an ancient crystal radio set through broken headphones next to ten pneumatic hammer operators in syncopated cacophony seems like orchestra seating in Carnegie Hall by comparison.

You get what you pay for, so it is said.

NOTE

There are many vendors offering streaming technologies. One of the more interesting is ToolVox (`http://www.toolvox.com/`) which uses a complex algorithm to actually create a model of the speaker's vocal tract and then transmit that to the receiver, thereafter sending commands to tell the remote virtual voice to speak. Other vendors have increased the compression ratios of their products enough that they can use ordinary TCP to transmit the packets, which means they don't need special servers to transmit using UDP, a significant savings for small sites.

Video

Conceptually, video online operates exactly like audio. There are downloadable file types and streaming video.

Downloadable Video

A popular non-streaming format is the QuickTime (QT) `.mov` file. QuickTime was developed by Apple and offers excellent video. It also offers a virtual reality option called QuickTimeVR (QTVR). Instead of standard frame-by-frame video, QTVR is created by using a panoramic still camera. The shots are then stitched together using special software (see Figure 23.12).

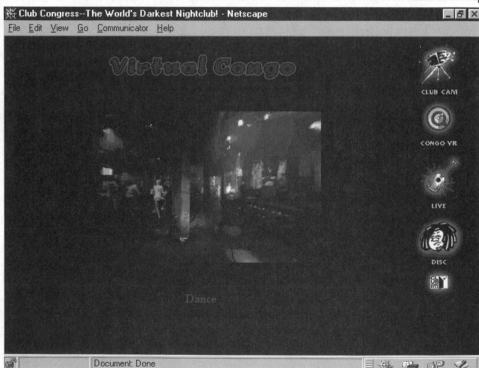

FIGURE 23.12

QuickTime Virtual Reality

Since QTVR doesn't require you to duplicate the order that the original pictures were taken in, the user can experience the illusion of movement by selecting views preferentially in a desired direction.

QuickTime is unique in the flexibility it provides, making it a favorite with video designers and especially for graphic designers, who are still very involved in the Macintosh market and for whom QuickTime is their native format. QuickTime has 50 percent of the market for video on the Web.

The latest versions of QuickTime even support a sort of streaming model with their Fast Start technology, which starts playing the movie while it's still downloading. QuickTime supports multiple *codecs* (coders/decoders, the software tools that compress and decompress files), allowing the designer to choose a favorite codec without choosing a new package. Intel's Indeo, Cinepack, MPEG, and ClearVison are all available.

A major rival to QuickTime is AVI (Audio Video Interleaved) which is the native Windows format (Figure 23.13). File sizes run larger than the equivalent QuickTime video, though, and support is not as widespread as with the Macintosh format.

FIGURE 23.13

*Audio Visual
Interleaved*

Another downloadable type of video is MPEG (Motion Picture Experts Group). Even bigger file sizes are seen in MPEG video, but it has the major advantage because it's an ISO (International Standards Organization) format and is therefore considered a Web standard rather than convention. This is a professional-quality file format designed by video specialists rather than computer hacks, and is capable of very high-quality reproduction in spite of heavy compression. But, MPEG file sizes are large enough to make download times enormous.

It's always a tradeoff, isn't it?

ON line!

More information on video file types can be found at the following sites:

- **QuickTime:** `http://quicktime.apple.com`
- **QuickTime Virtual Reality:** `http://qtvr.quicktime.apple.com`
- **Audio Video Interleave (AVI):** `http://www.microsoft.com/`
- **MPEG:** `http://drogo.cselt.stet.it/mpeg/`

Streaming Video

The triumph of hope over experience is surely exemplified in streaming video. Either that or we're so desperate for TV in our little boxes that we're willing to put up with really problematic technologies on our journey to faster, better ones. Streaming video usually sports a tiny little screen set in a huge frame, possibly to try and fool you into thinking that the picture is larger than it really is.

Unless you're lucky enough to have high speed access to the Net, the sound quality fades in and out like short wave radio, and the picture, which is painfully slow at standard access speeds, has a tendency to freeze up.

Right now, the VDOLive codec is the most popular streaming video out there on the Net although the new RealVideo/RealAudio combination in RealPlayer is making the Real products a good second choice.

Both solutions have high upfront costs, however, as they require dedicated servers to deliver their content. True Hypertext Transfer Protocol (HTTP or what most understand as the Web) servers don't do UDP or proprietary equivalents. As a result, UDP services can levy a per stream charge. If you expect your site to be popular, it's likely you're going to have to pay for every simultaneous user.

Since streaming doesn't really work well through the limited pipelines to Europe and the Far East, this means your server will sit more-or-less idle for a good part of the day.

Xing and Vosaic, other streaming video offerings, have the same problem, high cost and not enough of an audience, not to mention the fact that they all have problems with firewalls, which don't much care for UDP and proprietary equivalents as a general rule.

On the other hand, Vosaic has an interesting Java technology that doesn't use plug-ins, which may help overcome user resistance to yet another streaming video format.

VivoActive is one of the only server-less video technologies that seems to have a strong chance at success although the quality is not quite as good as the others.

And the effect of Macromedia, which is integrating streaming audio/video into Shockwave, has yet to be really felt.

Designers working with live video would do well to have a very convincing reason to do so. If you are involved with a video company, or a company interested in working out the kinks in video technology, then by all means work with online video. It's challenging, but a lot of money and interest is going into the field as we move toward technologies that will merge—like the Web and television—and broadband could become as commonplace as cable TV in people's homes.

ON line!

- **VDOLive:** Information can be found at the VDOLive Web site. `http://www.vdolive.com/`.
- **Vosaic:** `http://www.vosaic.com/`
- **VivoActive:** `http://www.vivo.com/`
- **Xing:** Pronounced "zing," this site has information at the ready. `http://www.xingtech.com/`

Live Delivery

In March of 1992, the first audiocast Internet broadcast was made over the MBone (Multicast Backbone—high speed Internet line), using a technology that allowed audio and video traffic to tunnel through regular Internet. The very first videocast was in June of that same year in Boston. Since that time the same technique has been used to provide audiovisual coverage of IETF (Internet Engineering Task Force) meetings and a host of other events of interest to the Internet experimental community.

ON line!

Information and MBone schedules can be found at `http://www.msri.org/mbone/`.

The MBone is attempting to work around the incredible inefficiency of traditional point-to-point communications for events where millions of people might want to listen and see the proceedings by distributing feeds to local distribution points so that traffic and hits on the originating server can be kept to a minimum.

In 1994, the Rolling Stones made history by broadcasting on the MBone to a large group of people. One week earlier, a small, unconventional Seattle-based band called Sky Cries Mary did the same thing, although their audience was significantly smaller and the event had much less money to promote itself, so the event went by quietly. Still, Net fans (and Sky Cries Mary fans, for that matter) will remember history the way it *really* went down.

The point? We can safely say that the popular media has been playing with the idea of live broadcast via the Web even though the number of channels available on the MBone is so extremely limited that it can only be used by common consent among experimenters.

What does this say about the future? Well, until broadband becomes available to every home, live delivery will be limited. There's also some rumination over how costs will be managed—will we as end-users have to pay for the privilege of watching what is essentially TV on our computers?

A more likely scenario is, as mentioned earlier, the merging of technologies and solutions for bandwidth. This is called *convergence* and forecasters suggest it will be here as soon as 1999.

Multimedia Packages

The combination of animation, audio, and video into an entire software package is not a new idea. In fact, most CD-ROMs are built using this type of software. The idea was brought to the Web by a company called Macromedia, which has since made quite a name and presence for itself as it expands and improves upon its line of developer tools, bringing multiple forms of media to the online world.

Macromedia Shockwave

Macromedia was formed in 1992 when three companies, Macromind, Authorware, and Pera.Comp, merged in order to take advantage of their individual strengths in the growing multimedia market.

By 1993, they had three flagship products: Director™, an animation authoring tool for creating multimedia CD-ROM content; Authorware™, an interactive information presentation tool aimed at the educational and corporate learning/presentation market; and MacroModel, a 3-D modeling and animation tool. At that time Macromedia was focused on CD-ROM, kiosk, and other non-Internet based multimedia development.

Late in 1993, Macromedia came to an agreement with an electronic game manufacturer, 3DO, to incorporate Macromedia authoring applications (Director/MacroModel) in the 3DO development tool kit.

In December of that year, they made their Initial Public Offering (IPO) and their dominance as a multimedia tool developer steadily expanded, encompassing many products clustered around the central paradigm of combined interactivity and multimedia. This paradigm provides a rich educational or entertainment experience no matter what the platform or venue. Their reach is worldwide now, and it's no accident that their Web site, `http://www.macromedia.com`, offers versions in Japanese, German, and French.

Macromedia's product emphasis has shifted slightly over time, and many of their products are now aimed directly at the Web, which was only a faint cloud of dust on the horizon when they began. Although Authorware and interactive learning are still an important part of their corporate marketing effort, a large part of what ordinary people know about Macromedia is in the entertaining "Shocked" displays made with Shockwave that either delight or irritate Web surfers. Shockwave is a complete multimedia package, allowing designers to create animation, audio, and interactive displays for use on the Web. It is estimated that 22 million people have browsers capable of viewing Shockwave content on the Web, although it is much less clear what percentage of users are actually using the viewers to enjoy Shockwave.

Director, the software used to build Shockwave content, enables the designer to create interactive animated multimedia displays using "sprites" that load into a predefined frame, much like competing technologies from other vendors, and a host of other tools. Since it's a proprietary format, the designer must use Macromedia tools to create the content, and the end-user must use Macromedia tools to render it, enabling complete control over the entire viewing experience.

ON line!

For more information on developing Shockwave applications with Director, read *Mastering Macromedia Director 6*, Second Edition, by Chuck Henderson (Sybex, 1997).

There are a rich set of tools available (in part because Macromedia can afford the up-front cost of providing them) causing developers writing more open platforms to always have to worry about competition. For the true design professional, the savings in development time can easily be worth the cost, but the tools are prohibitive in cost for many home users.

Currently Macromedia is embracing Java and JavaScript (see Chapter 24), and the latest version of Director supports it directly, allowing designers to use the sophisticated development tools available in Director as well as making access to Java-enabled browsers possible without plug-ins.

The latest versions of Director and Shockwave support streaming audio and video as well, which means that the length of time spent waiting for a complex application has been shortened considerably. This, in turn, should make streaming media more popular on the Web.

Macromedia Flash

In 1996, a San Diego software company named FutureWave released a compact graphic animation package called FutureSplash. Within several months of the FutureSplash release, large corporations such as Microsoft were jumping on this wave of the future and using it to treat their site visitors to a fun ride.

With smooth animation features, a fairly approachable interface, and compact files, FutureSplash was a product that quickly worked its way into inline support in Internet Explorer 3.0 and above, and plug-in support for Netscape.

By early 1997, Macromedia had bought the product from FutureWave, made some minor changes, and released it as Macromedia Flash. In subsequent months, audio was added to the program, and this lightweight but extremely powerful package has become quite popular with designers and site visitors alike.

In Figure 23.14 you can see the Flash interface, where you can create animated buttons with audio effects, beautiful navigation maps, and full-scale animations.

BrainBug's multimedia specialist, Michelle Carrier, loves the program and used it to create the company's Happy Holiday event on the BrainBug Web site. In Figure 23.15, you see Frosty the Snowman and the BrainBug, the little bug in the upper-left corner who is wearing a pair of reindeer ears. The stage is set for something fun. The BrainBug moves closer (Figure 23.16) and closer still (Figure 23.17), until it is so close it bumps right into the screen (Figure 23.18).

FIGURE 23.14

The Macromedia
Flash interface

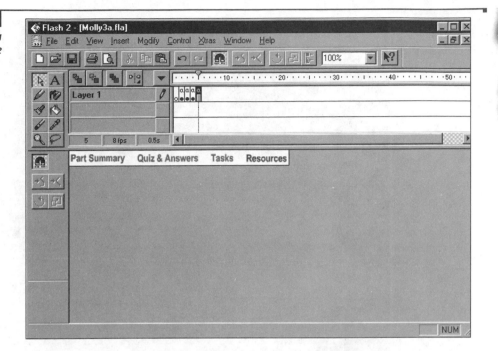

FIGURE 23.15

BrainBug Flash,
beginning of
sequence

FIGURE 23.16

*BrainBug Flash,
mid-sequence*

FIGURE 23.17

*BrainBug Flash, get-
ting closer*

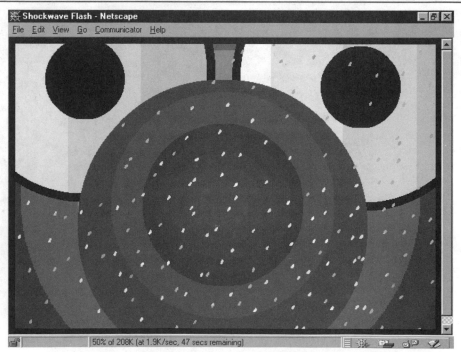

FIGURE 23.18

*BrainBug bumps the
screen!*

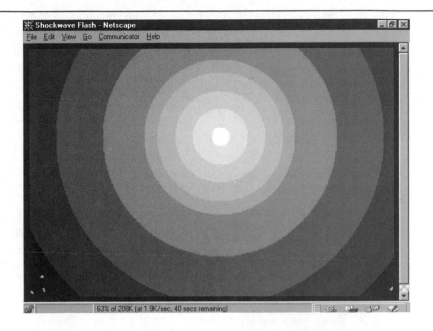

The BrainBug survives, of course, to turn around and alight on the "I" in the word BrainBug (Figure 23.20) which slowly vanishes as the Happy Holidays message is flashed on the screen.

FIGURE 23.19

*BrainBug Flash, end
of sequence*

In Internet Explorer, Flash files require the <object> tag, and work with JavaScript or VBScript (see Chapter 24) to be delivered to the screen. The <embed> tag is used to deliver the Flash animation to Netscape versions 3.0 and above, and still requires a plug-in for viewing.

Here's a look at the BrainBug Happy Holiday Flash code:

```
<html>
<head>
<title>Shockwave Flash</title>
</head>
<body bgcolor="#000000">

<center>

<!--Aftershock bbxmas.swf 3=100 4=100 2=1 5 9=57 37=0 38 40 41 29= 30= 31= -->
<object classid="clsid:D27CDB6E-AE6D-11cf-96B8-444553540000"
 codebase="http://active.macromedia.com/flash/cabs/swflash.cab"
 id=bbxmas width="100%" height="100%">
 <param name=movie value="bbxmas.swf">
 <param name=quality value=autohigh>
 <param name=bgcolor value=000000>

<script language=javascript>

<!--
function checkForFlash()
{
navigator.plugins.refresh();
if ( navigator.mimeTypes["application/x-shockwave-flash"] )
    parent.location.reload();
else
    setTimeout( "checkForFlash()", 1000 );
}
var FlashMode = 0
if (navigator.mimeTypes && navigator.mimeTypes["application/x-shockwave-
flash"] &&
 navigator.mimeTypes["application/x-shockwave-flash"].enabledPlugin) {
    FlashMode = 1;
}
if (!FlashMode && navigator.appName && navigator.appName.indexOf("Netscape")
!= - 1 && navigator.appVersion.indexOf("4.") != - 1
```

```
    && navigator.javaEnabled() && netscape.softupdate.Trigger.UpdateEnabled() &&
    document.cookie.indexOf("StartedFlashInstall") == -1) {
        var jarPath = new String("");
        if (navigator.platform.indexOf("Win32") >= 0 )
            jarPath = "http://download.macromedia.com/pub/shockwave/jars/
english/silentflash32.jar"
        else if (navigator.platform.indexOf("Win16") >=0 )
            jarPath = "http://download.macromedia.com/pub/shockwave/jars/
english/silentflash16.jar"
        else if (navigator.platform.indexOf("MacPPC") >=0 )
            jarPath = "http://download.macromedia.com/pub/shockwave/jars/
english/silentflashppc.jar"
        if (jarPath.length) {
            netscape.softupdate.Trigger.StartSoftwareUpdate (jarPath, netscape
.softupdate.Trigger.SILENT_MODE);
            document.cookie='StartedFlashInstall;path=/;'
            setTimeout("checkForFlash()", 1000);
        }
    }
//-->

</script>
<embed src="bbxmas.swf"
 name=bbxmas width=100% height=100%

 quality=autohigh bgcolor="000000"

 type="application/x-shockwave-flash" pluginspage="http://www
.macromedia.com/shockwave/download/index
.cgi?P1_Prod_Version=ShockwaveFlash">
</embed>

</object>

<!-- EndAftershock bbxmas.swf -->
</body>
</html>
```

Flash is a professional tool that can be used with relative ease and has adequate browser support. It's lighter weight than Shockwave itself, which makes it more accessible to people with only a modicum of multimedia development experience.

Next Up

Multimedia, which you've just learned about, and Web programming, which you are going to be introduced to in the next chapter, are almost inseparable. They rely upon one another not only in what they deliver, but how they deliver it. But, unlike multimedia packages which often require knowledge of graphic, multimedia, audio, and video design, Web programming requires a knowledge of true computer programming.

This is not HTML! Web programming might be logical, but it's not always easy or approachable to many. In fact, that's why I had Aaron Bertrand, who did the GIF animation work for this chapter, work with me in the next chapter to help you understand more about Web programming and how it relates to Web design. Aaron is a programmer, and I am in the strictest definition a programmer. However, Web programming is becoming as integrated into the design aspect of the Web as a simple graphic, and we, as designers, must at least understand what is available and how those scripts and languages can be used to enhance our designs.

chapter 24

WEB
PROGRAMMING

WEB PROGRAMMING

I f I had only one word to sum up the Web programming experience, I'd be hard-pressed to choose between *exciting* and *frustrating*. The excitement is drawn from the fact that Web programming is what will take the Web as we know it today to a whole new medium that, within a few years, might look very, very different from what the most imaginative of designers can postulate.

The frustration is born of trying to take the currently available programming methods and make them behave. Like unruly children, they often run wild. This is often a result of improper discipline on the parents' part. Technology and browser developers are wrapped up in impossibly complicated legal, political, and philosophical arguments that get in the way of giving stable, cross-platform, compatible tools to Web designers.

But as with most children, programming can respond well to positive input. The intelligent Web designer will learn enough about Web programming to understand where a given application is appropriate to use. Even if your forté is graphic art, you're going to benefit from having at least a basic understanding of what programming options are available to you. With a qualified, competent programmer, you can then take that unruly child and create an environment where dynamic, exciting growth can occur.

The point, which is carried throughout this book, is that *no matter the limitations*, Web designers can surpass them and create sites that not only look great, but offer functionality to their users as well as progress to the overall field of design.

The following scripting and programming techniques are discussed in this chapter:

- Common Gateway Interface (CGI)
- Active Server Pages (ASP)
- Java
- JavaScript
- VBScript
- Dynamic HTML (DHTML)
- ActiveX
- Push technologies
- XML

As with many designers, I rely on a skilled programmer to assist me when it comes to realistic applications of Web programming. I know my limitations in terms of programming, and want to save time as well as provide the best information possible. Because of this I've asked my colleague, Aaron Bertrand, Director of New Technologies at Waterworks Interactive, to work with me on this section of the book and related areas on the Design Studio. Aaron has provided countless hours of assistance with this chapter. The programming examples here are his work, or have been modified by him from public domain material. The examples all have live components, which can be found on the Design Studio Web site at http://www.designstudio.net/media/.

CGI

The Common Gateway Interface (CGI) is the grandfather method of Web programming. It's been around since the first days of the Web, and its compatibility factor remains the most consistent of all programming methods.

CGI is not in and of itself a programming language. Common Gateway Interface is a standard that allows programs and pages to interface with servers; it's the bridge between the browser and the server—the interpreter, if you will.

Let's say you call up a site with your browser. If that site uses a CGI application, what occurs next is that when the browser sends its HTML-based queries to the server, the CGI will act as an interpreter and ask the server to process a program *on the server side* and deliver the results back to the browser.

The programs residing on the server can be written in any compiled or interpreted language such as C, C++, Perl (Practical Extraction and Report Language), Fortran, and Visual Basic. The most commonly used languages for CGI are C and Perl.

"CGI takes research and time to master. Once you have gotten the basics down however, CGI programming, especially in Perl, is very easy. However, though incredibly short, the learning curve is very, very steep. That means you should be prepared to spend a solid month studying CGI before you will be ready to do real CGI work or ask answerable questions. After that month, which can sometimes seem like a year, you should be very comfortable. But you MUST dedicate the month of hair-pulling study."

FROM SELENA SOL'S CGI SCRIPT FAQ,
http://selena.mcp.com/Scripts/faq1.html

CGI is used by most Web servers including Apache, NCSA, and CERN. Common applications for CGI scripting include database storage and retrieval (although this is being replaced by advanced database servers such as Cold Fusion), logging information, guestbooks, feedback form processing, and randomization processes.

ON line!

Here's a selection of CGI resources online:

- **Yale's PC Lube and Tune:** This site provides an excellent history of CGI, http://pclt.cis.yale.edu/pclt/webapp/cgi.htm.
- **CGI tutorial for programmers:** http://www.usi.utah.edu/bin/cgi-programming/counter.pl/cgi-programming/index.html
- **CGI Forms:** http://www.usi.utah.edu/bin/cgi-forms/counter.pl/cgi-forms/index.html
- **The CGI Collection:** Hundreds of scripts available for your use, along with background information on CGI, security issues, and other support information, at http://www.itm.com/cgicollection/.

Here's an example of CGI using a Perl script modified by Aaron Bertrand for this book and the companion Web site. This script sends feedback in plain English to molly@molly.com and immediately reverts the user to some other page, in this case, the Design Studio's programming test site.

The script makes use of SendMail and Perl and, of course, can be edited to accept as many or as few input fields as required.

This is the information that you would use within the HTML:

```
<form action="/cgi-bin/mailit.pl" method="post">
<input type="text" name="comments1">
</form>
```

And this is the Perl script located on the server.

```
#!/usr/local/bin/perl
$mailprog = '/usr/lib/sendmail';
$recipient = 'molly@molly.com';

print "Content-type:text/html\n\n";
print "<html><head><title>Thanks for your feedback...</title>\n";
print "<meta http-equiv=refresh content=\"0;url=http://www.molly.com/\"\n";
print "</head><body bgcolor=#ffffff></body></html>\n";

read(STDIN, $buffer, $ENV{'CONTENT_LENGTH'});
@pairs = split(/&/, $buffer);
foreach $pair (@pairs)

{
  ($name, $value) = split(/=/, $pair);
  $value =~ tr/+/ /;
  $value =~ s/%([a-fA-F0-9][a-fA-F0-9])/pack("C", hex($1))/eg;
  $value =~ s/~!/ ~!/g;
  $FORM{$name} = $value;
}

$FORM{'email'} =~ s/\r/\n/g;
open (MAIL, "|$mailprog $recipient") || die "Can't open $mailprog!\n";
print MAIL "Subject: Feedback Form\n\n";
print MAIL "\n$FORM{'comments'}\n";
close (MAIL);
```

Figure 24.1 shows the Web page holding the script. In Figure 24.2, the script redirects to another page, in this case to http://www.molly.com/.

FIGURE 24.1

The Web page with CGI script

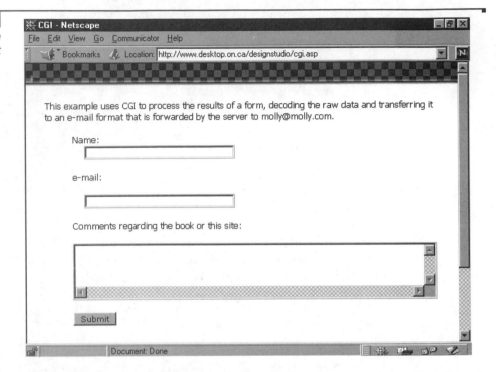

FIGURE 24.2

This CGI redirects to another page

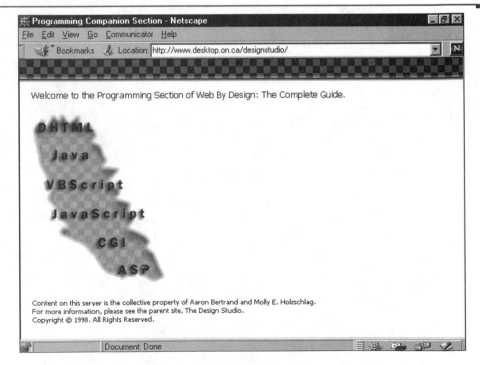

OFF line!

Looking for a good book on Perl and CGI programming? Check out *Perl CGI Programming: No experienced required*, by Erik Strom (Sybex, 1998).

ASP

ASP, or Active Server Page, is Microsoft's server-sided processing function. It is similar to CGI in that it is a component installed on a Web server which facilitates server-to-client exchanges. As with CGI, the action appears seamless—with the programmed action taking place on the server side and then being delivered to the client.

First introduced as an add-on for Windows NT in early 1996, ASP quickly became a popular way to deliver CGI-style applications. It requires NT Server, NT Workstation, or other Microsoft operating system-based servers to run. However, it *delivers* to any browser or platform, making it cross-platform and cross-browser compliant.

ASP's default language is VBScript (Visual Basic Script, see the VBScript section later in this chapter), Jscript (Microsoft's JavaScript version), Perl, and other languages on the server side to build applications dynamically.

Here is a sample which transparently displays content formatted specifically for the browser at hand.

```
<html>
<body>
<%
dim browzer
browzer=lcase(request.servervariables("http_user_agent"))
if instr(browzer,"msie 4")>0 then
      response.write("You are using IE 4.0")
elseif instr(browzer,"msie 3")>0 then
      response.write("You are using IE 3.0")
elseif instr(browzer,"msie 2")>0 then
      response.write("You are using IE 2.0")
elseif instr(browzer,"msie")>0 then
      response.write("You are using Internet Explorer")
elseif instr(browzer,"mozilla/4")>0 then
      response.write("You are using Netscape 4.0")
```

```
elseif instr(browzer,"mozilla/3")>0 then
      response.write("You are using Netscape 3.0")
elseif instr(browzer,"mozilla/2.0")>0 then
      response.write("You are using Netscape 2.0")
elseif instr(browzer,"mozilla/1.0")>0 then
      response.write("You are using Netscape 1.0")
else
      response.write("You are using an obscure browser")
end if
%>
</body>
</html>
```

In Figure 24.3, you can see that the script delivered a page that clearly states the name of the browser which is being used, in this case Internet Explorer 4.0. In Figure 24.4, the ASP script correctly pointed out that the browser being used is Netscape 4.0.

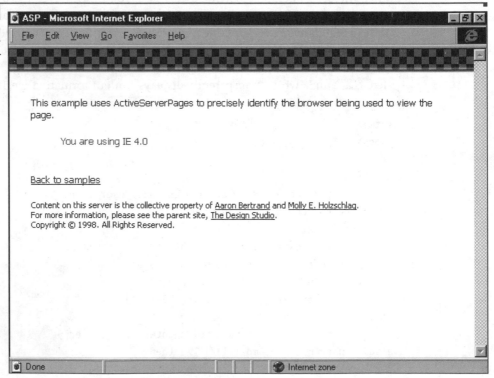

FIGURE 24.3

The script as shown with Internet Explorer

FIGURE 24.4

*The script as shown
with Netscape 4.0*

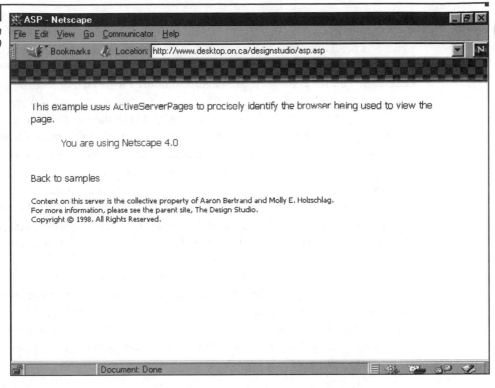

This example uses ActiveServerPages to precisely identify the browser being used to view the
page.

   You are using Netscape 4.0

Back to samples

Content on this server is the collective property of Aaron Bertrand and Molly E. Holzschlag.
For more information, please see the parent site, The Design Studio.
Copyright © 1998. All Rights Reserved.

ON line!

ASP resources on the Web include:

- **ASP 101:** A primer with detailed visual examples and a compare/contrast to CGI.,
  at http://www.vallin.com/pub/1/asp1.asp.

- **ASP Developer's Site:** Dedicated to developers, this site offers comprehensive
  developer information regarding ASP, at http://www.genusa.com/asp/.

- **ASP Developer Network:** Information and conversation for ASP developers, at
  http://www.aspdeveloper.net/.

- **Microsoft ASP:** This site offers applications and demos, at http://backoffice
  .microsoft.com/downtrial/moreinfo/iissamples.asp

- **The ASP Hole:** Huge resource for ASP developers located at http://asphole.
  stellarvision.com/.

Java

Java has been quite a buzzword in design circles for some time. The reason is because it's very powerful code, modeled after C++. Developed by Sun Microsystems, Java has been both hailed as *the* Web language, and faulted for a rash of security problems that broke out in 1996.

Interest in Java remains very strong, largely due to the fact that it is so powerful and therefore, its applications are usually only limited by the imagination of the programmer working with it. A skilled programmer can use Java to write full applications—programs that don't require a browser at all and can run stand-alone.

The most popular use of Java on the Web currently is applets. Applets are small programs that allow the addition of interactivity or animation on a Web page.

Java is portable across multiple platforms and operating systems, and Java applets are viewable in Netscape 2.0 and above, Internet Explorer 3.0 and above, and Sun's own browser, HotJava.

Aside from the fact that some people turn Java off in their browsers, preferring to avoid the technology altogether, there are some cross-browser problems with Java. Much of the problems surrounding Java are considered to be the result of in-fighting between Java development and browser companies rather than problems with the actual product development itself. For more information on Java's rather colorful history, visit `http://www.sun.com/java/`.

> *"Java is still being hurt by its lack of maturity and well-developed software tools. Still, Java is being deployed, developed, or seriously considered in applications as diverse as cellular telephones, factory control systems, and the Hubble Space Telescope . . . part of the problem is the confusion engendered by the Java Wars between Sun and Microsoft."*
>
> RICK COOK, JavaWorld

The following example doesn't use an applet or application directly, but it uses JavaScript to connect to the Java interface—accessing core Java package calls directly from JavaScript, which is described in detail in the following section.

What this means is the client-side script is using the browser's *internal* Java machine to access the built-in Java function toolkit, instead of embedding the toolkit function directly into the page.

```
<html>
<body>
<script language="javascript">
<!--
var brz=navigator.appName
if(brz=="Netscape") {
```

```
if(navigator.javaEnabled()) {
var Sizer=java.awt.Toolkit.getDefaultToolkit()
var ScrSize=Sizer.getScreenSize();
var ScrW=ScrSize.width;
var ScrH=ScrSize.height;
document.write("Screen size: ",ScrW,"x",ScrH);
}
}
//-->
</script>
</body>
</html>
```

This function will read information from the Java within the browser and deliver that information to the screen. In this case, the information called for is my screen resolution at the time of my visit to the page (Figure 24.5). In Figure 24.6, I visit using a different resolution, and the function accurately returns the information.

Unfortunately, this script is not viewable in Internet Explorer 4.0, so a report is sent to the user saying just that (Figure 24.7).

FIGURE 24.5

Screen resolution information, first visit

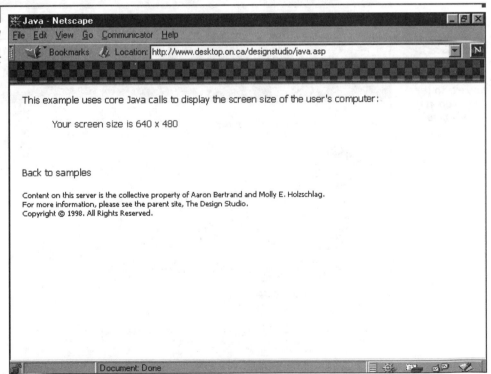

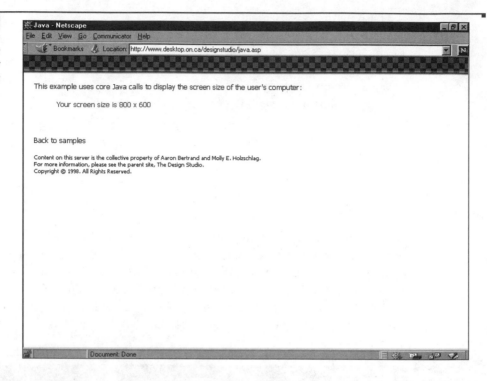

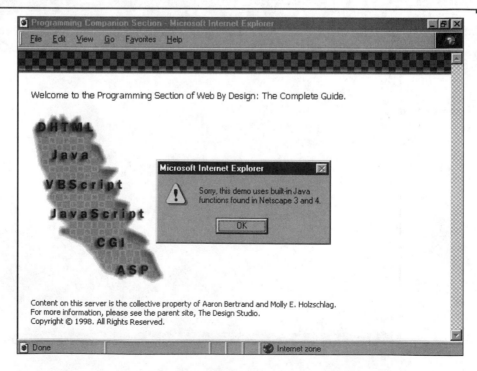

ONline!

Java resources abound online. Here are a few of them to get you started:

- **20 Questions About Java:** This easy-to-understand article by C|NET is a good place for the novice to start out, `http://www.cnet.com/Content/Features/Techno/Java20/index.html`.
- **Developer.com:** This site is geared toward professional Web developers, offering information on a variety of concerns with a healthy dose of Java. Community and products are available at `http://www.developer.com/`.
- **The Java Home Page:** Sun Microsystems offers this site with Java development, support, and services, `http://java.sun.com/`.
- **Java Applet Page:** Demonstrations of applets that you can put to work on your pages right away, `http://gserver.grads.vt.edu:80/hooked_on_java_ch3.html`.
- **Microsoft on Java:** Explanations and points-of-view from Microsoft, `http://www.microsoft.com/java/`.

JavaScript

Sun, working with Netscape, took a script that had been in development under Netscape's auspices, called LiveScript, and made it function and act more like Java. The results debuted in early December of 1995 as what we know today as JavaScript, which runs right in the HTML page to carry out a variety of client-sided functions.

JavaScript was introduced by Sun through Netscape 2.0 in a joint effort. New functions, such as New Image() and New Array() methods, layer methods (such as `moveTo`, `resizeTo`, `moveAbove`, and `moveBelow`), and new window events (like `captureEvents` and `releaseEvents`), were added in subsequent releases of JavaScript and Netscape browsers.

Microsoft has a similar script called JScript. It is, in essence, much like JavaScript version 1.0, but certain incompatibilities make JScript difficult to run in certain browsers. The following compatibility chart shows current JavaScript support.

JavaScript Version or Type	Browser
JScript (Microsoft's near JavaScript 1.0 version)	Internet Explorer 3.0 and above
JavaScript 1.0	Netscape Navigator 2.0 and above, Internet Explorer 4.0 and above
JavaScript 1.1	Netscape Navigator 3.0 and above, Internet Explorer 4.0 and above
JavaScript 1.2	Netscape Navigator 4.0 and above

You'll note that JavaScript's current 1.2 version is *not* supported by Internet Explorer 4.0. A headache for designers, indeed.

> *"Agreement must be reached. Both Netscape and Microsoft have publicly committed to supporting the standard when it is established. In the meantime, even though JavaScript is now a standardized language and will eventually be properly supported in Internet Explorer as it already is in Netscape Navigator, scripts that rely on the underlying object model (documents, windows, links, anchors, tables, forms, and the like) will continue to be browser-specific."*
>
> DAN SHAFER, Editor, C|Net's Builder.Com

JavaScript has complex syntax which is similar (like Java) to C/C++. JavaScript is best suited for programmers, although many poorly written scripts have been developed and spread around the Net. This can cause a lot of problems such as browser and even operating system lockups for Web site visitors. It's a good idea for Web designers to be sure the script they are using is compatible with the audience they are intending the pages to be viewed by, and that the scripts they use are written by competent programmers.

Here is a JavaScript example that will display the date to the browser.

```
<script language="javascript">
<!--
function aaray(date1) {
  this.length = date1
  return this
  }
Month = new aaray(12)
  Month[1] = "January";
  Month[2] = "February";
  Month[3] = "March";
  Month[4] = "April";
  Month[5] = "May";
```

```
    Month[6] = "June";
    Month[7] = "July";
    Month[8] = "August";
    Month[9] = "September";
    Month[10] = "October";
    Month[11] = "November";
    Month[12] = "December";
WeekDay = new aaray(7)
    WeekDay[1] = "Sunday";
    WeekDay[2] = "Monday";
    WeekDay[3] = "Tuesday";
    WeekDay[4] = "Wednesday";
    WeekDay[5] = "Thursday";
    WeekDay[6] = "Friday";
    WeekDay[7] = "Saturday";
function adate(theDate) {
    var wday = WeekDay[theDate.getDay() + 1]
    var munth = Month[theDate.getMonth() + 1]
    var dai = theDate.getDate();
    var trunc="th";
    if ((dai=="1") || (dai=="21")) {
        trunc="st"
    }
    if (dai=="31") {
        trunc="st"
    }
    if ((dai=="2") || (dai=="22")) {
        trunc="nd"
    }
    if ((dai=="3") || (dai=="23")) {
        trunc="rd"
    }
return wday + ", " + munth + " " + dai + trunc
}
document.write(adate(new Date()))
//-->
</script>
```

Figure 24.8 shows the date in Netscape and Figure 24.9 shows how Internet Explorer can read this JavaScript, which was written specifically using JavaScript syntax that could be interpreted by both browsers.

FIGURE 24.8

JavaScript sample as viewed in Netscape

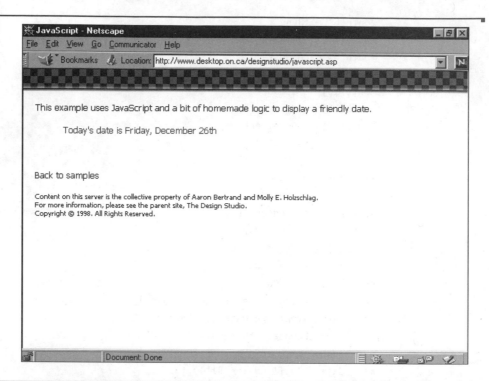

FIGURE 24.9

JavaScript sample as seen in Internet Explorer

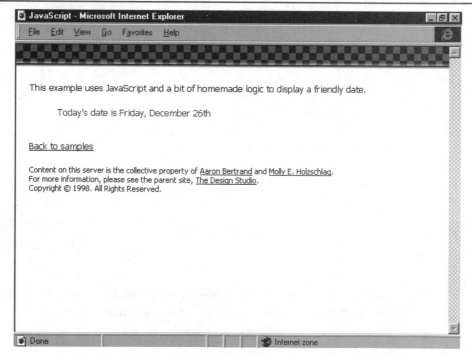

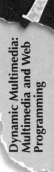

ON line!

Here are some helpful jumping-off spots to learn more about JavaScript:

- **JavaScript Resource Center:** Tips, newsgroups, and code, at `http://jrc .livesoftware.com/`.
- **A Beginner's Guide to JavaScript:** Excellent place for individuals interested in JavaScript to learn more, see `http://www.geocities.com/SiliconValley/Park/ 2554/index.html`.
- **JavaScript vs. Jscript:** A helpful article that explains the differences between the Sun/Netscape versions and implementation of JavaScript and Microsoft's JScript, `http://www.javacats.com/US/articles/Eitan_JJ.html`.
- **JavaScript World:** Source code, discussion groups, and chats, at `http://www .jsworld.com/`.
- **JavaWorld Online Magazine:** News, views, tutorials, and opinions, at `http://www .javaworld.com/`.

VBScript

Visual Basic is a programming language developed by Microsoft. A subset of that programming language is Visual Basic for Applications (VBA), and a subscript of VBA is VBScript, which was created by Microsoft in 1996. VBScript was introduced as a browser script in the Internet Explorer 3.0 browser for Windows 95 and NT platforms.

VBScript syntax is very intuitive, and unlike JavaScript, there is no case sensitivity. As mentioned in the ASP section earlier, it is the default language of ASP which makes it a great server-sided script language for those servers running ASP.

VBScript was once referred to as the "Java Killer" because of its intuitive code and excellent security. However, VBScript remains limited to Internet Explorer browser versions 3.0, 4.0, and above, with *no* support from any Netscape browser. This, of course, has kept its use extremely limited.

> *"VBScript is gaining popularity day by day, both as a way of creating exciting pages on the web, and as a means of porting desktop applications to the browser in corporate intranet situations."*
>
> PAUL LOMAX, VBScript.Com

Visual Basic programmers find the script easy to work with, and it can be a very powerful script for Internet Explorer-only sites such as corporate intranets.

This VBScript sample is similar in function to the JavaScript sample above, providing the correct date in an IE 4.0 browser (Figure 24.10).

FIGURE 24.10

VBScript sample

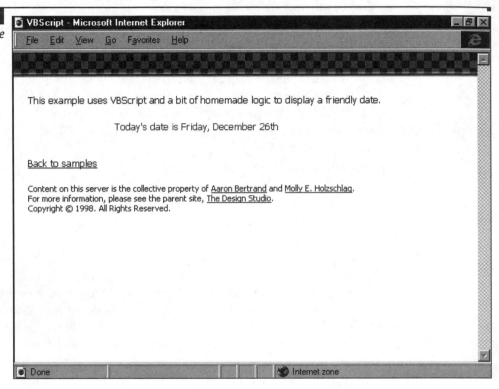

```
<script language=vbscript>
<!--
dim months(12)
        months(1) = "January"
        months(2) = "February"
        months(3) = "March"
        months(4) = "April"
        months(5) = "May"
        months(6) = "June"
        months(7) = "July"
        months(8) = "August"
```

```
        months(9) = "September"
        months(10) = "October"
        months(11) = "November"
        months(12) = "December"
munth=months(month(now))
dai=day(now)
        trunc="th"
        if right(dai,1)=1 then
          trunc="st"
        elseif right(dai,1)=2 then
          trunc="nd"
        elseif right(dai,1)=3 then
          trunc="rd"
        end if
dim days(7)
        days(1)="Sunday"
        days(2)="Monday"
        days(3)="Tuesday"
        days(4)="Wednesday"
        days(5)="Thursday"
        days(6)="Friday"
        days(7)="Saturday"
today=days(weekday(now))
document.write(today & ", " & munth & " " & dai & trunc)
-->
</script>
```

When you visit the page with Netscape, you get a warning because you cannot
view the programmed application with that browser (Figure 24.11).

ON line!

VBScript information can be found at:

- **VBScript.com**: A developer resource with book recommendations, code, discussion groups, and links to related resources, http://www.vbscript.com/.
- **Using VBScript in HTML**: A helpful tutorial that covers VBScript background, coding conventions, and applications, http://www.aspdeveloper.net/iasdocs/aspdocs/ref/vbs/vbscript/vbstutor.htm.

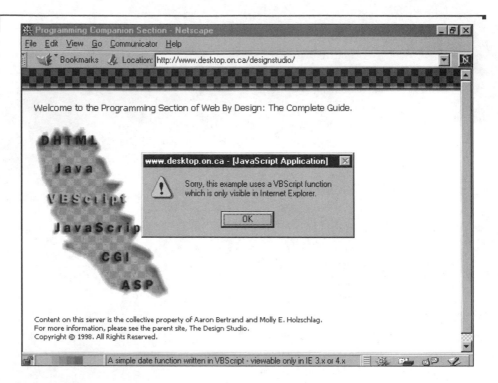

FIGURE 24.11

VBScript is not supported by any version of Netscape.

DHTML

Dynamic HTML (DHTML) is a new extension to the original Hypertext Markup Language developed to overcome the restrictive limitations of HTML. It was developed during the Internet Explorer 4.0 beta, from September 1996 until September of 1997. Netscape Navigator has a comparable but inexact version that emerged with the 4.0 release.

DHTML has been reviewed and recommended by the World Wide Web Consortium as part of the HTML 4.0 standard. Unfortunately, the current implementations in the two major browsers are very different, and no other browser supports DHTML.

> *"It may look and feel a lot like the old HTML, but it's radically different. The main difference between Dynamic HTML (DHTML) and classic HTML is that each and every tag is now an Object and can have a unique ID and properties."*
>
> VIJAY MUKHI, Dynamic HTML

Here's a look at some of the differences between Internet Explorer and Netscape implementation of DHTML.

Internet Explorer

- In Internet Explorer 4.0, every HTML element of the page is accessible to script. Take a tag, any tag. Take an <img>, <h1>, <p>. Any of these tags can accept a DHTML script.

- DHTML allows the author to alter the layout of the page and present new information based on user action or a timer without going back to the server.

- With DHTML, you can restructure the entire page and totally change/update all information within one page.

Here is an Internet Explorer 4.0 example of changing the elements of a page through user interaction *without* requiring a trip to the server.

```
<html>
<!--
Demo created by Aaron Bertrand
http://www.desktop.on.ca/
mailto:aaron@desktop.on.ca
-->
<head>
<style type="text/css">
      a { text-decoration:none }
      a:hover { text-decoration:underline;color:red }
      BODY { font-size: 9pt; font-family: "myriad web,geneva,verdana,tahoma" }
</style>
<script>
      a1="Your mouse is over the first link"
      a2="Now your mouse is over the second link"
      a3="And now it's over the third link"
      a4=""
      a5="Oh! You clicked the first link"
      a6="Oh! You cliked the second link"
      a7="Oh! You clicked the third link"
</script>
</head>
<body bgcolor="#ffffff" link="#000080">
<center>
<table border="0" cellpadding="0" cellspacing="0" width="450">
  <tr valign="middle">
   <td width="125" onmouseout="p1.innerHTML=a4" align=center>
      <a onmouseover="p1.innerHTML=a1" onclick="p1.innerHTML=a5"
href="#">Link 1</a><br>
```

```
    <a onmouseover="p1.innerHTML=a2" onclick="p1.innerHTML=a6"
href="#">Link 2</a><br>
    <a onmouseover="p1.innerHTML=a3" onclick="p1.innerHTML=a7"
href="#">Link 3</a>
  </td>
  <td width="325" align="center">
    <p id="p1">Move your mouse over a link...</p>
  </td>
  </tr>
</table>
</center>
</body>
</html>
```

In Figure 24.12, you can see the page with Internet Explorer. Watch the text change as the mouse is moved over the link (Figure 24.13), and then when the link is clicked (Figure 24.14). This change can be repeated with each of the links.

FIGURE 24.12

DHTML in Internet Explorer 4.0

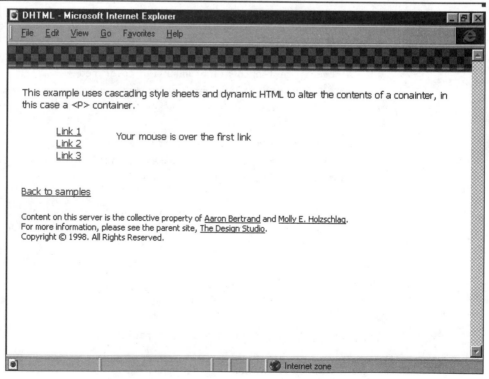

FIGURE 24.13

*DHTML reacts as
the mouse is moved
over the link.*

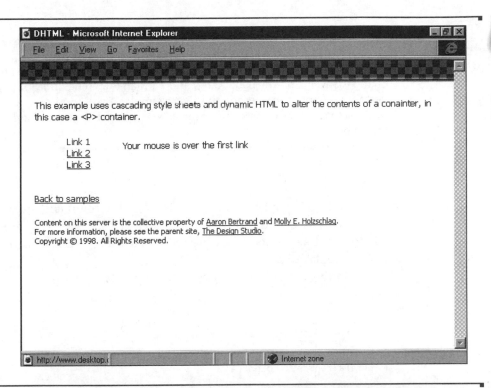

FIGURE 24.14

*DHTML reacts as
the link is clicked.*

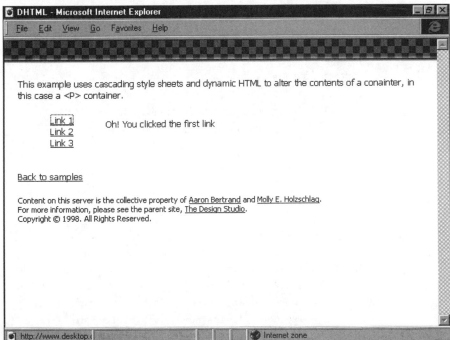

OTE

This example also uses a simple DHTML event called hover (look in the style tag). This changes any link on the page to red and adds an underline. Individual style tags on certain elements can override this. For example, if you used <a href="Wherever" style="text-decoration:none;color:black"> the changes in a and a:hover class are ignored.

Netscape 4.0

In Netscape 4.0, the implementation of DHTML is less comprehensive. One of the main issues in Netscape is that DHTML cannot access normal elements via script the way it does in IE 4.0's Document Object Model. Instead, layers are used to achieve a somewhat similar effect.

The following example works only in Netscape 4.0:

```
<html>
<!--
Demo created by Aaron Bertrand
http://www.desktop.on.ca/
mailto:aaron@desktop.on.ca
-->
<head>
<title>Netscape 4.0 and Layers</title>

<script>
function lay(num) {
        for (i=0;i<6;i++) {
                    document.layers[i].visibility='hide';
                    document.layers[num].visibility='inherit';
        }
}
function lay2() {
        for (i=0;i<6;i++) {
                    document.layers[i].visibility='hide';
        }
}
function makevis(num) {
            lay2()
            document.layers[num].visibility='inherit';
            document.layers[num+3].visibility='hide';
            document.layer0.visibility='hide';
}
```

```
function makedis(num) {
        lay2()
        document.layers[num].visibility='hide';
        document.layers[num+3].visibility='hide';
        document.layer0.visibility='inherit';
}
</script>
</head>

<body bgcolor="#ffffff" link="#000080"><font face="verdana,tahoma,arial"
size="2">

<layer width="300" height="100" visibility="inherit" name="layer0"
left="150" top="10">Move your mouse over a link...</layer>
<layer width="300" height="100" visibility="hide" name="layer1" left="150"
top="10">Your mouse is over link 1!</layer>
<layer width="300" height="100" visibility="hide" name="layer2" left="150"
top="10">Now it's over link 2!</layer>
<layer width="300" height="100" visibility="hide" name="layer3" left="150"
top="10">Is your mouse over link 3?</layer>
<layer width="300" height="100" visibility="hide" name="layer4" left="150"
top="10">You clicked link 1!</layer>
<layer width="300" height="100" visibility="hide" name="layer5" left="150"
top="10">You clicked link 2!</layer>
<layer width="300" height="100" visibility="hide" name="layer6" left="150"
top="10">You clicked link 3!</layer>

<a href="javascript:lay(4)"
  onmouseover="makevis(1)" onmouseout="makedis(1)">Link 1</a><br>
<a href="javascript:lay(5)"
  onmouseover="makevis(2)" onmouseout="makedis(2)">Link 2</a><br>
<a href="javascript:lay(6)"
  onmouseover="makevis(3)" onmouseout="makedis(3)">Link 3</a>

</body>
</html>
```

In Figure 24.15, the page is visited using Netscape. Immediately you can see that the target text is different.

When the mouse is passed over the link, the text changes (Figure 24.16). In Figure 24.17, when the link is clicked, it changes again. Comparable, but not the same as the Internet Explorer 4.0 version.

FIGURE 24.15

DHTML in Netscape

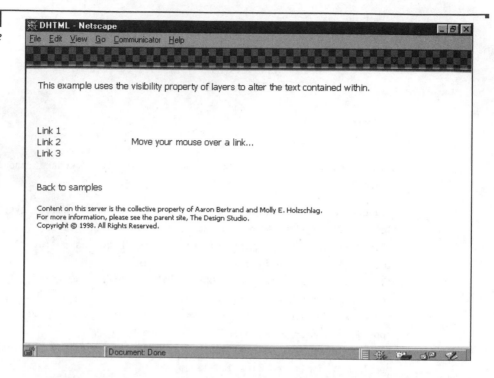

FIGURE 24.16

*DHTML reacts as
the mouse is moved
over the link.*

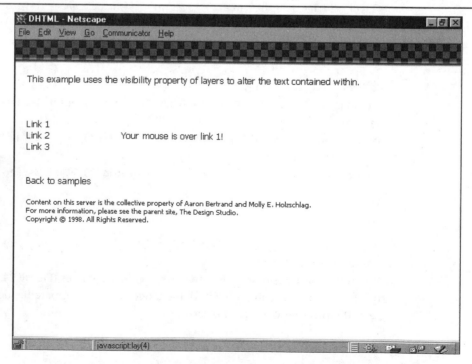

FIGURE 24.17

*DHTML reacts as
the link is clicked.*

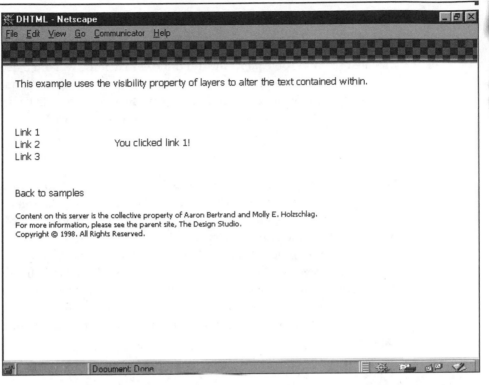

This example uses the visibility property of layers to alter the text contained within.

Link 1
Link 2   You clicked link 1!
Link 3

Back to samples

Content on this server is the collective property of Aaron Bertrand and Molly E. Holzschlag.
For more information, please see the parent site, The Design Studio.
Copyright © 1998. All Rights Reserved.

The good news is that with the stamp of approval from the W3C, DHTML is expected to eventually develop into a powerful option for Web designers. To learn more about DHTML, check out *Dynamic HTML: Master the Essentials* by Joseph Schmuller (Sybex, 1998).

ON line!

DHTML resources include:

- **Microsoft's Dynamic HTML Page:** News, views, and applications on Microsoft's DHTML implementation, http://www.microsoft.com/workshop/author/dhtml/.

- **Dynamic HTML in Netscape Communicator:** Using DHTML with Netscape products, http://developer.netscape.com/library/documentation/communicator/dynhtml/index.htm.

- **The Dynamic HTML Zone:** Macromedia's DHTML site, http://www.dhtmlzone.com/.

Other Technologies

There are still other programming languages and programming-style technologies that are used with some popularity on the Web. Their use will often depend upon who the audience is, and what support exists for the applications in question.

A short overview of three technologies with which you should be familiar is provided below, along with resources for more information on each.

ActiveX

Really a catch-all term for a number of technologies from Microsoft, ActiveX is most familiar to Web designers in terms of the ActiveX control, which can allow for the development of inline programs. These programs are then downloaded to the Web browser and executed on the client side.

If this sounds a little like the Java applets we discussed earlier, that's because ActiveX does function somewhat like applets. ActiveX works in sync with Microsoft's operating systems, which can give it great power, but only in the Windows environment.

This translates, of course, into the fact that ActiveX is not supported by Netscape browsers and therefore its use is limited to Microsoft platforms and the Internet Explorer browser.

ON line!

ActiveX information can be found at the following Web sites:

- **Developer.Com:** This ActiveX resource offers information on news, tools, and use, `http://activex.developer.com/`.

- **ActiveX.com:** C|NET's comprehensive ActiveX resource for sitebuilders, `http://www.activex.com/`.

- **Microsoft:** Information on ActiveX from Microsoft's Web site, `http://www.microsoft.com/sitebuilder/dna/tech.asp`.

Push Technology

When you fire up your browser and type in a URL, you are requesting that information be delivered to you. In essence, you are *pulling* that information from a server.

Push technology is a technique that certain Web sites employ to deliver information *to* you, without waiting for your specific request.

If this sounds kind of familiar, it should. TV and radio are essentially Push technologies. You may choose the channel, but you don't have much control over what is delivered to you. In fact, Push on the Web relies on the TV and radio model as a method of describing what it does. The familiar term *broadcasting* has been assimilated by Push and become *Webcasting.* Channels are a big buzzword, too, and in fact browsers such as Internet Explorer 4.0 come with channel interfaces built right in.

One of the oldest Internet Push examples is from Pointcast, http://www.pointcast.com/. Download the Pointcast package and news, weather, sports, stock information, entertainment, and other information can be delivered right to your desktop. Pointcast is integrated with the Web, and you can get more information on any by simply clicking on the related links.

Push can be integrated by designers and developers into existing and new sites with the use of various programming technologies, most of which have been described in this chapter.

There is debate surrounding Push and its relevance to the Web. While resources such as Pointcast are undeniably helpful to many, the idea of Web sites delivering information without much input *from* me definitely changes the *interactive* element of the Web.

I personally question whether this is a dangerous trend—one that will lead us back to comfortable models such as TV and radio—and push us away, if you will, from the challenge of non-linear, progressively interactive media. However, the Push model has already made its presence a serious one. The ultimate decision as to how (and if) to use Push technology will depend on the client, the audience, and the intent of the project in question.

ON line!

Here are some helpful Push technology sites:

- **Pointcast Home Page:** Download Pointcast, and read about the Pointcast Network at http://www.pointcast.com/.
- **Web Broadcasting:** This site lists providers and service, at http://www.thunderlizard.com/wb-links.html.

XML

Another buzz in the biz is Extensible Markup Language (XML). XML, like HTML, is a subset of Standard Generalized Markup Language (SGML).

Currently, XML 1.0 has been deemed ready to enter the review for recommendation process at the World Wide Web Consortium. The popularity or growth of XML will depend primarily upon two things: how seriously the browser developers take XML; and how important the W3C decides XML is to the Web. Microsoft is currently the only browser developer that has made a statement saying that XML will be supported in a future edition of the Internet Explorer browser.

ON line!

- **World Wide Web Consortium:** XML news and information can be found at `http://www.w3.org/XML/`.

- **XML Resources:** An overview of XML with links to other XML-related Web sites, at `http://www.sil.org/sgml/xml.html`.

- **XML from Microsoft:** White papers, draft documentation, and planning from the Microsoft Web site, `http://www.microsoft.com/standards/xml/xmlintro.htm`.

Next Up

No doubt you've noticed that interactivity, multimedia, and Web programming are rather complex and demanding areas of study. The chapters you've just studied have given you an overview of what is currently available, and how the theories as well as methods can be applied.

In the following and final chapter, we'll be reviewing each of these, looking at a few real-life applications, and challenging your design sensibilities to find out where, and how, you might apply a given technology.

THE DESIGN STUDIO MULTIMEDIA AND WEB PROGRAMMING CENTER

25

THE DESIGN STUDIO MULTIMEDIA AND WEB PROGRAMMING CENTER

Interactivity, multimedia, and Web programming—they've been around for several years respectively, but their use is still filled with problems. Cross-platform and browser compatibility are primary issues. Accessibility and expense are also considerable concerns.

Designing Web sites professionally means being able to assess an audience, meet the needs of a client, and provide the best experience for the visitors to that site. Very frequently, this means *not* taking advantage of some of the more advanced technologies that exist.

Of course, this doesn't mean you shouldn't have some understanding of what those technologies are, and what they can do for you should the opportunity to use them be reasonable. And, with progress being made in terms of browser support and better computers sitting on the home desktop, the reality of bringing advanced technologies to the general public is becoming easier and easier.

This chapter synthesizes concepts and techniques that relate to:

- Functional interactivity
- Community-based interactivity
- Inline multimedia
- Streaming media

- Multimedia packages
- CGI
- ASP
- Java and JavaScript
- VBScript
- DHTML

Examples from the Design Studio Web site (`http://www.designstudio.net/media/`), quizzes, and general review will assist you in gaining an overview of current Web programming technologies.

Interactivity: Review

Interactivity is a philosophical as well as functional issue. In this section, we'll review the main concepts pertaining to interactivity as expressed in *Web by Design*.

Main Concepts

The primary concept of interactivity is that two or more entities act on one another. In terms of a Web site, this can be as simple as clicking on a link and having a different page appear, or as complex as real-time relationships that evolve from online interaction via community-based environments.

The Cycle of Interactivity

The Cycle of Interactivity is a simple model which demonstrates the primary concept of interaction. An end-user makes a choice, the medium (in this case the Web) responds to that choice, and the cycle can be repeated as many times from that point forward as the function requires.

While this cycle is the essence of interactivity, and interaction cannot exist without it, people working with interactive media have often had broader expectations of the Web. These expectations included the idea that because the Web is non-linear, highly satisfactory interactive experiences could be developed.

This does happen sometimes, but many Web designers involved in most day-to-day Web projects don't really test the limits of interactivity from a philosophical sense, even if they are doing so with technology itself.

Interactivity, therefore, encompasses two areas. The first is the *functional*, which exists to provide a specific function on a Web site, such as a feedback form or shopping cart. The other form of interactivity, described as *progressive* interactivity, comprises community. The difference is that functional interactivity is essentially interactivity between human and machine, whereas progressive interactivity is interaction between humans via the bridge formed by the machines.

Both are essential to the Web and to the Web's evolution. Both hold practical aspects. A form is a primary way of individuals getting organized information back to a given company. Community development on a Web site can enhance that site's ability to do other things, such as sell and support a product.

Beyond that, Web designers working in both arenas are challenged to use existing technologies to design and achieve their end goal. They are also faced with the development of new technologies to achieve those desired results, which forces progress and brings about the exciting technologies that exist today, and that we will summarize in this chapter.

Functional Interactivity

The interactivity that takes place between human and machine still requires human intelligence to anticipate the needs of the end-user, and the needs of the individuals who will be interpreting that data after the interactive session has been completed.

Functional interactivity is generally and most simply the kind of interactivity necessary to bring about a result. Two examples given in Chapter 22 include forms processing and online shopping. Along with database-intensive applications such as searches (visit any common search engine for an example of this), functional interactivity is a potent contender on the Web, and designers need to examine along with their clients when, and where, function should be included on a site.

Progressive Interactivity

The fundamental concept behind progressive interactivity lies in the development of community. Whether it is through bulletin board (BBS) style conferencing or real-time chats, the idea is to build a community that is based on shared interests. This has been done successfully with many products. Refer back to Chapter 22 for more details about several methods of how to deliver community-based functions.

OTE

The designer's job is to know and understand how to use technology to create the interface for community. But it will be the client's responsibility to learn how to manage communities. An interesting article on this issue with extended resources can be found at http://www.cnet.com/Content/Builder/Business/Community/.

Page Deconstruction

Deconstructions of community-oriented interactivity on the Design Studio site can be found in Chapter 22. Aside from the functional example of the Contact page in that chapter, the Design Studio has another functional interactive form. If you visit the multimedia and programming section of the Design Studio, http://www.designstudio .net/media.html, you will encounter a demonstration of CGI. This code creates a form, which is shown in Figure 25.1.

PART

7

Dynamic Multimedia:
Multimedia and Web
Programming

FIGURE 25.1

*CGI demo on
Design Studio*

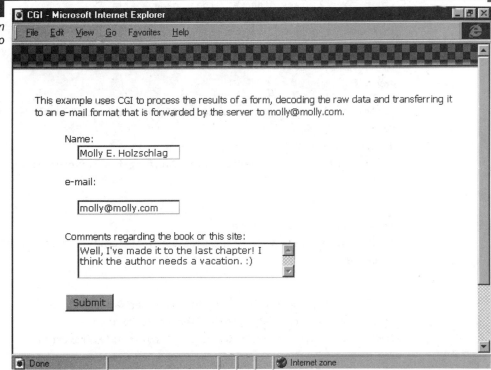

Here's a look at the code:

```html
<html>
<head>
<title>CGI</title>

<style type="text/css">

a {text-decoration:underline;color: #000080}
a:hover {text-decoration:none;color:#ff0000}

</style>

<body bgcolor="#ffffff" background="checker.gif" link="#000080"
vlink="#000080" alink="#000080" text="#000000">

<center>
```

```
<table border="0" width="97%" cellpadding="10" cellspacing="0">
<tr>
<td colspan="2"> <p>

<div style="font-size:10pt">

<font size="2" face="tahoma,verdana,geneva,arial">

This example uses CGI to process the results of a form, decoding the raw
data and transferring it to an e-mail format that is forwarded by the server
to molly@molly.com.
<p>

<form method="post" action="http://207.201.166.52/cgi-local/design.pl">
<ul>
Name:<br>   
<input type="text" style="font-size:9pt;font-family:verdana;color:#000080"
size="20">
<p>

e-mail:<br><br>   
<input type="text" style="font-size:9pt;font-family:verdana;color:#000080"
size="20">
<p>

Comments regarding the book or this site:<br>   
<textarea name="comments" style="font-size:9pt;font-
family:verdana;color:#000080" rows="3" cols="45"></textarea>
<p>

<input type="submit" value="Submit" style="font-size:9pt;font-
family:verdana;color:#000080">
<p>

</form>
</font>
</center>
</div>


</center> <p>

<font size="2" face="tahoma,verdana,geneva,arial">
<div style="font-size:10pt">
<a href="/designstudio/">Back to samples</a>
<p>

<font size="1" face="tahoma,verdana,geneva,arial">
```

```
<div style="font-size:8pt">Content on this server is the collective property
of <a href="mailto:aaron@desktop.on.ca">Aaron Bertrand</a> and <a
href="mailto:molly@molly.com">Molly E. Holzschlag</a>.
<br>
For more information, please see the parent site,
<a href="http://www.designstudio.net/">The Design Studio</a>.
<br>Copyright &copy; 1998. All Rights Reserved.
</div>

</td>
</tr>
</table>

</body>
</html>
```

This form, while created for demonstration purposes, is fully functional. If you fill it in, an e-mail containing your comments will be sent to me (see Figure 25.2). The form can be found at http://www.designstudio.net/media/.

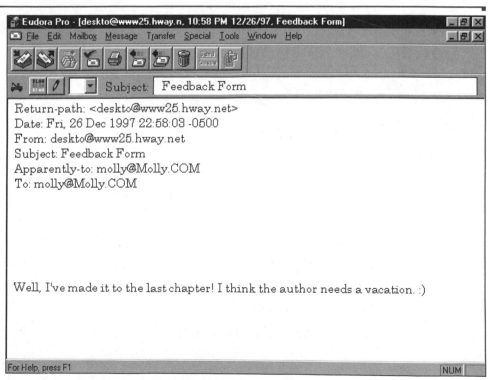

The script returns an e-mail to me

Interactivity: Quiz

Please answer the following multiple choice questions.

1. The Cycle of Interactivity includes:

    a. functional

    b. progressive

    c. user choice

    d. media choice

2. A GIF animation changes from active to interactive when:

    a. it is used as an advertisement

    b. it is used as a header

    c. the animation uses inviting and vibrant colors that attract the eye

    d. the animation is hyperlinked

3. The interactive experience can be more complete for a user when:

    a. the users input significantly alters the outcome of the interaction

    b. the interaction is with a machine

    c. the interaction is self-contained

    d. all of the above

4. An example of functional interactivity would be:

    a. a chat room

    b. a BBS

    c. a GIF animation

    d. a feedback form

5. An example of progressive interactivity is:

    a. a database search function

    b. a CGI script

    c. dynamic HTML

    d. a real-time chat

Please answer true or false for the following statements.

6. A link is interactive.

7. A hyperlinked image is interactive.

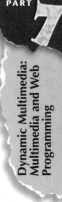

PART **7**

Dynamic Multimedia:
Multimedia and Web
Programming

8. A chat room is always static.

9. It is technically very difficult to add a chat room on the Web.

10. A virtual shopping cart is an example of functional interactivity.

Write out a short answer to the following question.

11. What do you consider a satisfying interactive experience?

Answers to the quiz can be found at the end of this chapter and on the Design Studio Web site, `http://www.designstudio.net/media/`.

Interactivity: Task

In the following tasks you will address the interactive needs of a client. Read through each option and then write out an approach for each case study.

Case 1

You've been hired to build an extranet for a government surplus agency. Within that extranet will be an area where other government agencies can check what's available on a daily basis. Speed is of the essence as surplus goods are very desirable and agencies want to get the best quality available goods.

You can deliver this through two mechanisms: a functional search, or a BBS-style conference. Which do you choose to use, and why?

Case 2

The Family Planning Project is a not-for-profit, nationwide group that seeks to educate teens and young adults about birth control and sexual health issues. On their Web site, they offer courses, quizzes, information about various issues, and product ordering information.

The project has come to you saying that something is missing from their Web site. They want to make it more interactive, but they're not sure how.

What do you recommend for them, and why?

Multimedia: Review

Multimedia on the Web is intrinsically related to interactivity and can help add functional as well as progressive interactivity to your site. Multimedia livens up a site by adding dynamic and active components. Despite the cross-platform and browser issues, multimedia is a growing area of Web design.

Main Concepts

Web multimedia includes animation, audio, video, and complete packages of combined media. The following sections provide a brief review of the multimedia options discussed in *Web by Design*.

Animated GIFs

The animated GIF is a very useful and easy-to-create media. The technology is based on the existing GIF file format and simply requires an appropriate animation tool (resources are listed in Chapter 23) to create the animation.

Audio

Web audio is available in two primary formats. The first is *downloadable* audio. This can be any number of audio formats that have been stored on your server and linked to your HTML page. The individual must have the appropriate software to run the downloaded audio file. This software is called an *external viewer* or *helper application*. When the browser is set up to accommodate the external viewer, the application is *spawned*.

The other popular format for audio is referred to as *streaming* audio. Streaming audio is based on a specific technology that allows the information to start playing as soon as it is requested by the end-user's browser.

Streaming audio can be more expensive but is growing in popularity and can often be used to enhance Web sites significantly.

Video

As with audio, video comes in the downloadable and streaming varieties. Video is especially problematic on the Web because the files are even larger than audio due to the amount of data they carry.

Advances in Web video technologies and expanding bandwidth will assist in making Web audio a realistic tool. It can be used to enhance existing sites and is especially useful on intranet or extranet sites where bandwidth is not a concern.

Multimedia Packages

The most often used and professional multimedia packages are Macromedia Shockwave and Flash.

Shockwave is a fairly compact package that allows designers to create animation and audio with interactive components using a program called Director. Shockwave requires a plug-in to be viewed. With the recent addition of streaming technologies into the Shockwave package, improvements in speed and delivery will be seen.

Macromedia Flash is an extremely compact vector-based graphic animation and audio tool. The lightweight interface and general ease-of-use makes Flash an extremely attractive choice for designers wishing to add multimedia to their sites. Flash runs without a plug-in in Internet Explorer 3.0 and above, but requires a plug-in for Netscape.

Macromedia has other packages that can create multimedia, such as Authorware, and graphics-oriented programs that can be used to work with multimedia, such as Freehand. For more information, be sure to visit Macromedia's Web site, `http://www` `.macromedia.com/`.

Page Deconstruction

The Design Studio site uses very little multimedia outside of programmed examples of animated sequences.

The one exception to this is the Flash-based sub-navigation found on the summary sections of the site.

```
Part Summary    Quiz & Answers    Tasks    Resources
```

The reason for so little multimedia on the site is simply audience. I even had concerns about using Flash, but opted to do it simply so there would be *some* aspect of multimedia used on the site. A secondary issue is that I tend to be a conservative designer when it comes to sites that will be used by people from a broad audience. As you might remember from Chapter 1, accessibility is a big issue as well, and the use of multimedia should be very well thought out before it is applied.

Multimedia: Quiz

Please answer the following multiple choice questions.

1. An animated GIF:

a. requires a plug-in to work

b. can be used to make moving backgrounds

c. should be used in abundance

d. is extremely flexible and cross-browser compatible

2. Animated GIFs:

    a. cannot be optimized

    b. cannot be made transparent

    c. can be interlaced

    d. all of the above

3. Which of the following is not specifically a GIF animation program?

    a. GIF Animator

    b. Microsoft Image Composer

    c. GIF Construction Set

    d. GIF Movie Gear

4. Which of the following is not a downloadable audio file type?

    a. AIFF

    b. WAV

    c. MPEG

    d. AVI

5. The company best-known for streaming media technology is:

    a. RealNetworks

    b. Zing

    c. QuickTime

    d. Apple

Please answer true or false for the following statements.

6. Shockwave requires a plug-in.

7. Shockwave now supports streaming media.

8. Animation can be achieved with Shockwave.

9. Flash does not support audio.

10. Flash requires a plug-in in Internet Explorer browsers.

Write out a short answer for the following question.

11. Have you used any multimedia packages? If so, which do you like or dislike, and why?

Multimedia: Task

This one is simple. Visit Macromedia's Web site at http://www.macromedia.com/ and download the appropriate demo version of Flash for your platform.

1. Open the demo (Figure 25.3).

PART

7

Dynamic Multimedia:
Multimedia and Web
Programming

FIGURE 25.3

Flash interface

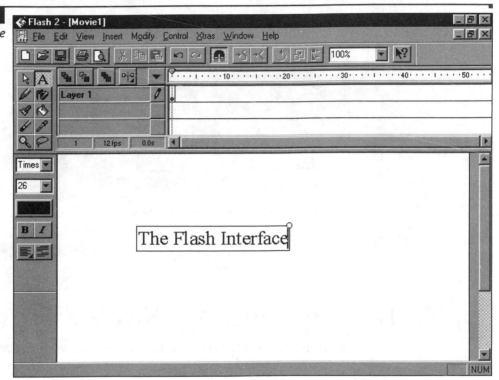

2. From the Xtras menu, choose Lessons ➤ Quick Start (Figure 25.4).

3. Move through the lessons at your own pace.

FIGURE 25.4

Opening Quick Start in Flash

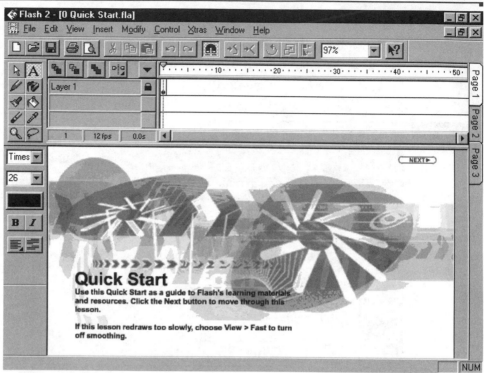

Web Programming: Review

As with multimedia, Web programming is intimately related to interactivity and adds action and liveliness to a page. Both functional and progressive interactivity can be developed with various Web programming techniques.

Main Concepts

There are a range of Web programming languages and scripts in use today, such as CGI, ASP, Java, JavaScript, VBScript, and DHTML, as well as a few that are in the works for future use.

CGI

The Common Gateway Interface (CGI) is a bridge between browser and server. It allows for full programs to be run on the server-side and then returned to the browser. These programs are typically written in Perl or C++.

General examples of processes using CGI include forms processing, shopping carts, and searches.

ASP

Active Server Pages are similar to CGI in that they work on the server-side with languages and scripts in order to deliver active pages to the browser. The languages used by ASP are typically Visual Basic or VBScript.

ASP is a Microsoft product and therefore runs best on Microsoft servers such as NT, Windows 95, and Information Servers.

Java

A complete applications language developed by Sun Microsystems, Java is loosely based on C++.

Java can be used to build stand-alone programs, and is in fact used within Netscape for certain core functions.

For the Web, the most common uses of Java are in the form of *applets*. These little applications allow for a variety of interactive or multimedia-style events such as chats or animations.

JavaScript

This script is modified from Netscape's original LiveScript by Sun Microsystems. Sun integrated Java-style syntax into the script, making it function nicely as a subset of Java.

JavaScript has the advantage of running completely on the client-side. This means that the time necessary to run the given application is decreased.

JavaScript versions have a range of browser support (see Chapter 24 for a comparison chart). One problem encountered by designers using JavaScript is the lack of consistent support in Internet Explorer versions prior to 4.0. Internet Explorer has its own script version called JScript, which is similar to but not the same as JavaScript.

VBScript

A sub-subset of Visual Basic, VBScript is quite similar in form and function to JavaScript. Some of the differences include security and stability. Furthermore, VBScript is even more browser-centric than JavaScript.

There is no support for VBScript in any browser other than Internet Explorer versions 3.0 and above. Therefore, the use of VBScript is limited to intranet and extranet sites that only use Internet Explorer.

DHTML

Dynamic HTML (DHTML) is an extension to standard HTML. The idea is to allow script functions into every available HTML tag. This conceptually moves HTML from a formatting script toward an actual programming-style language.

DHTML was developed by Microsoft during the beta sessions of Internet Explorer 4.0, and was released formally in the public beta of Internet Explorer 4.0 in September of 1997. Netscape 4.0 has some DHTML support but it is rather different functionally and syntactically than the Internet Explorer version.

DHTML is an exciting entry into the world of Web programming. It was inevitable that script functions would be integrated with HTML because coders are looking for increased functionality that puts the weight on the client-side rather than the server-side. DHTML incorporates rather than excludes other forms of Web programming, but does so in a fashion that potentially makes it a permanent structure of HTML.

Other Programming Concerns

Three other script and programming issues that are either in use or under scrutiny for use by Web designers are:

- **ActiveX**—ActiveX is not a programming language per se, but a hybrid of object-oriented programming that allows for the execution of complete programs inline. It must be integrated with a language such as VBScript in order to render within a browser.

- **Web Push (Webcasting)**—Pushing content rather than waiting for a Web visitor to come to a given site is growing in popularity. Push technology can be extremely useful, particularly when information such as stock quotes, news, and weather can be delivered to the desktop at regular intervals with no input from the individual user.

- **XML**—This is the Extensible Markup Language. A subset of SGML, XML is simply another method of marking up documents. To what extent it will become useful or used by the design community will be determined by browser developers and the World Wide Web Consortium.

Page Deconstruction

Other than the demonstration examples discussed in Chapter 24, Web programming on the Design Studio site is limited to the implementation of Java applet-based chat in the chat area.

Here's a look at the applet code:

```
<APPLET CODE="EmbryoClient.class"

    CODEBASE="http://www.spin.de/classes/"

    WIDTH="400" height="295">

    <PARAM NAME="channel" VALUE="welcome!">

    <PARAM NAME="bgcolor" VALUE="CC9966">

    <PARAM NAME="fgcolor" VALUE="000000">

    <PARAM NAME="fontsize" VALUE="12">

    Please get a Java capable browser!

</APPLET>
```

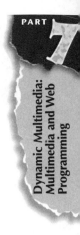

Web Programming: Quiz

Please answer the following multiple choice questions.

1. CGI stands for:
   a. Common Gateway Interleave
   b. Command Gate Interface
   c. Common Gateway Interface
   d. Commonly Gated Interface

2. ASP is:
   a. a Microsoft innovation
   b. Active Server Pages
   c. similar to CGI
   d. all of the above

3. Java is often used on the Web via:
   a. C++
   b. applications
   c. animation
   d. applets

4. JavaScript runs on:
   a. Netscape only
   b. Internet Explorer only
   c. the client-side
   d. the server-side

5. VBScript:

   a. is an excellent cross-browser script

   b. was written by Netscape

   c. was written by Apple

   d. is only available to Internet Explorer browsers

Please answer true or false for the following statements.

6. DHTML is exactly the same in IE 4.0 and Netscape 4.0.

7. ActiveX is a programming language.

8. Java is known for its security.

9. XML is fully supported by Netscape Navigator 4.0.

10. JScript is similar to JavaScript.

Write out a short answer for the following question.

11. Are you a Web programmer? If so, what are your preferred scripts and languages and how do you use them?

Web Programming: Task

Pick a language, any language. Find an application for that language (hint: use the resources in Chapter 24 or on the Design Studio site at http://www.designstudio.net/media/) and create an application.

The exercise can be as simple as adding a chat applet like the one I did to a page. If you're a more aggressive programmer, consider writing a small section of code and apply it to an existing Web site.

Answer Key

The following key provides the correct answers to the quizzes in this chapter.

Interactivity

Multiple Choice

1. The correct answer is C. The Cycle of Interactivity includes user choice.

2. The correct answer is D. A GIF animation becomes interactive when it is hyperlinked.

Continued

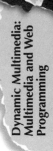

3. The correct answer is A. If a user's input significantly alters the outcome of interaction, the experience can be more complete.

4. The correct answer is D. A feedback form is functionally interactive.

5. The correct answer is D. A real-time chat would be progressive interactivity.

True or False

6. True. Although it is simple interactivity, a link is interactive because it follows the Cycle of Interactivity.

7. True. A hyperlinked image is similar to a link and is interactive.

8. False. A chat room can be active and interactive.

9. False. Chats can be extremely easy to add to a page.

10. True. A virtual shopping cart is an example of functional interactivity.

Short Answers

11. This answer is wholly personal, there is no right or wrong answer.

Multimedia

Multiple Choice

1. The correct answer is D. An animated GIF is extremely flexible and cross-browser compatible.

2. The correct answer is C. Animated GIFs can be interlaced.

3. The correct answer is B. Microsoft Image Composer can be used along *with* an animation program, but it is in and of itself not an animation program.

4. The correct answer is D. AVI is a video format. It does support audio but its primary use is video.

5. The correct answer is A. RealNetworks (including RealAudio and RealVideo) is best known for streaming media technology.

True or False

6. True. Shockwave does require a plug-in.

7. True. Shockwave now supports streaming media.

8. True. Animation can be achieved with Shockwave.

9. False. Flash does support audio.

10. False. Flash requires a plug-in for Netscape!

Continued

Short Answers

11. This answer is wholly personal, with no answer being right or wrong.

Web Programming

Multiple Choice

1. The correct answer is C. CGI is Common Gateway Interface.

2. The correct answer is D. ASP is a Microsoft innovation, it stands for Active Server Pages, and it is similar to CGI.

3. The correct answer is D. Java on the Web frequently uses applets.

4. The correct answer is C. JavaScript runs on the client-side.

5. The correct answer is D. VBScript is only supported by Internet Explorer.

True or False

6. False. DHTML is quite different in IE 4.0 and Netscape 4.0

7. False. ActiveX is a hybrid application for executable programs. It is not in and of itself a language.

8. False. Java is known for having had trouble with security.

9. False. XML is not supported by IE 4.0 or Netscape 4.0.

10. True. JScript is similar to JavaScript

Short Answers

11. This answer is wholly personal, with no answer being right or wrong.

Next Up

What's up next is that you get to apply all of the knowledge you learned in this book. I encourage you to work through the review chapters from time to time to keep your basic knowledge intact.

The Design Studio site is not only an additional resource for you, I'd like to invite you to submit your task work to the newsgroup so as to share it with other designers for feedback and critique. Also, any wisdom, new information, and improved methods of doing things that I've done on the site are welcome, too.

Most importantly, have fun. Web design is one cool profession. It demands dedication and hard work; I've never met a serious Web designer who wasn't extremely dedicated and very intent on challenging limits.

I know you will be successful in your Web design endeavors. I hope this book has played a helpful role in that success.

appendix A

HTML
REFERENCE

HTML REFERENCE

This complete HTML reference includes relevant tags and attributes for Web designers. It has been arranged alphabetically for convenient reference.

HTML Tags and Attributes

Tags	Attributes	Description
<!-- ... -->		SGML comment
<!DOCTYPE>		Public declaration
	HTML PUBLIC...	DTD conformance
<A>...</A>		Anchor
	ACCESSKEY=	Keyboard shortcut
	CHARSET=	Character encoding of link
	CLASS= ID= STYLE= TITLE=	Class(es), unique ID, style information, title
	COORDS=	Object coordinates of anchor
	DIR= LANG=	Text direction and language ID
	HREF=	Hypertext link
	NAME=	Name of hypertext link

Tags	Attributes	Description
	REL=	Forward link type
	REV=	Reverse link type
	SHAPE="rect | circle | poly | default"	Object shape of described anchor
	TABINDEX=	Explicit tabbing order
	TARGET=	Target frame name for rendering
	[events]	Core intrinsic events
<ACRONYM>...</ACRONYM>		Acronym content
	CLASS= ID= STYLE= TITLE=	Class(es), unique ID, style information, title
	DIR= LANG=	Text direction and language ID
	[events]	Core intrinsic events
<ADDRESS>...</ADDRESS>		Address content
	CLASS= ID= STYLE= TITLE=	Class(es), unique ID, style information, title
	DIR= LANG=	Text direction and language ID
	[events]	Core intrinsic events
<APPLET>...</APPLET>		Java applet
	ALIGN=	Alignment of applet
	ALT=	Alternate text description
	CODE=	Java applet name
	CODEBASE=	Location of applet
	DOWNLOAD=	Order of applet download
	HEIGHT=	Height of object
	HSPACE=	Horizontal space
	NAME=	Name of applet
	VSPACE=	Vertical space
	WIDTH=	Width of object
<AREA>		Client-side image map area description
	ALT=	Alternate text description
	COORDS=	Coordinates
	HREF=	Hypertext link
	NOHREF	No hypertext link
	SHAPE="rect | circle | poly | default"	Shape of described area
	TABINDEX=	Explicit tabbing order
	TARGET=	Target frame name for rendering
	[events]	Core intrinsic events
<B>...</B>		Bold text
	CLASS= ID= STYLE= TITLE=	Class(es), unique ID, style information, title
	DIR= LANG=	Text direction and language ID
	[events]	Core intrinsic events
<BASE>		Base URL
	HREF=	Hypertext link
	TARGET=	Target frame name for rendering

Tags	Attributes	Description
<BASEFONT>		Font setting for document
	COLOR=	Color of basefont
	FACE=	Typeface of basefont
	SIZE=	Size of basefont
<BDO>		Bi-directional override
	DIR=	Text direction required
	LANG=	Language ID
<BGSOUND>		Background sound
	LOOP=	Number of times sound repeats
	SRC=	Address of sound file
<BIG>...</BIG>		Big text
	CLASS= ID= STYLE= TITLE=	Class(es), unique ID, style information, title
	DIR= LANG=	Text direction and language ID
	[events]	Core intrinsic events
<BLOCKQUOTE>...</BLOCKQUOTE>		Block quote
	CLASS= ID= STYLE= TITLE=	Class(es), unique ID, style information, title
	DIR= LANG=	Text direction and language ID
	[events]	Core intrinsic events
<BODY>...</BODY>		Body of document
	ALINK=	Active link color
	BACKGROUND=	Location of background image
	BGCOLOR=	Background color
	CLASS= ID= STYLE= TITLE=	Class(es), unique ID, style information, title
	DIR= LANG=	Text direction and language ID
	LEFTMARGIN=	Create left margin
	LINK=	Link color
	TEXT=	Text color
	TOPMARGIN=	Create top margin
	VLINK=	Visited link color
	[events] onload, onunload	Core intrinsic events
 		Break
	CLASS= ID= STYLE= TITLE=	Class(es), unique ID, style information, title
	CLEAR=	Fixes text beside or below image
<BUTTON>...</BUTTON>		Form button
	CLASS= ID= STYLE= TITLE=	Class(es), unique ID, style information, title
	DIR= LANG=	Text direction and language ID
	DISABLED	Disables button
	NAME=	Name of button
	TABINDEX=	Explicit tabbing order

Tags	Attributes	Description
	TYPE=	Type of button
	VALUE=	Action desired
	[events] onfocus, onblur	Core intrinsic events
<CAPTION>...</CAPTION>		Table caption
	ALIGN=	Alignment of table caption
	CLASS= ID= STYLE= TITLE=	Class(es), unique ID, style information, title
	DIR= LANG=	Text direction and language ID
	VALIGN=	Vertical alignment
	[events]	Core intrinsic events
<CENTER>...</CENTER>		Centers text
	CLASS= ID= STYLE= TITLE=	Class(es), unique ID, style information, title
	DIR= LANG=	Text direction and language ID
	[events]	Core intrinsic events
<CITE>...</CITE>		Citation content
	CLASS= ID= STYLE= TITLE=	Class(es), unique ID, style information, title
	DIR= LANG=	Text direction and language ID
	[events]	Core intrinsic events
<CODE>...</CODE>		Code content
	CLASS= ID= STYLE= TITLE=	Class(es), unique ID, style information, title
	DIR= LANG=	Text direction and language ID
	[events]	Core intrinsic events
<COL>...</COL>		Column
	ALIGN=	Alignment of column
	CLASS= ID= STYLE= TITLE=	Class(es), unique ID, style information, title
	DIR= LANG=	Text direction and language ID
	SPAN=	Number of columns spanned
	VALIGN=	Vertical alignment
	WIDTH=	Width of column
	[events]	Core intrinsic events
<COLGROUP>		Column grouping
	ALIGN=	Alignment of column grouping
	CLASS= ID= STYLE= TITLE=	Class(es), unique ID, style information, title
	SPAN=	Number of column groupings spanned
	VALIGN=	Vertical alignment
	WIDTH=	Width of column grouping
<DD>		Definition data
	ALIGN=	Alignment of data
	CLASS= ID= STYLE= TITLE=	Class(es), unique ID, style information, title
	DIR= LANG=	Text direction and language ID
	[events]	Core intrinsic events

Tags	Attributes	Description
<DEL>...</DEL>		Deleted text
	CITE=	Change data
	CLASS= ID= STYLE= TITLE=	Class(es), unique ID, style information, title
	DATETIME=	ISO change date
	DIR= LANG=	Text direction and language ID
	[events]	Core intrinsic events
<DFN>...<DFN>		Definition content
	CLASS= ID= STYLE= TITLE=	Class(es), unique ID, style information, title
	DIR= LANG=	Text direction and language ID
	[events]	Core intrinsic events
<DIR>...<DIR>		Directory list
	CLASS= ID= STYLE= TITLE=	Class(es), unique ID, style information, title
	COMPACT	Compact representation
	DIR= LANG=	Text direction and language ID
	[events]	Core intrinsic events
<DIV>		Document division
	ALIGN=	Alignment of text section
	CLASS= ID= STYLE= TITLE=	Class(es), unique ID, style information, title
	DIR= LANG=	Text direction and language ID
	[events]	Core intrinsic events
<DL>...</DL>		Definition list
	ALIGN=	Alignment of list
	CLASS= ID= STYLE= TITLE=	Class(es), unique ID, style information, title
	CLEAR=	Clears list
	COMPACT	Compact representation
	DIR= LANG=	Text direction and language ID
	[events]	Core intrinsic events
<DT>		Definition term
	ALIGN=	Alignment of term
	CLASS= ID= STYLE= TITLE=	Class(es), unique ID, style information, title
	DIR= LANG=	Text direction and language ID
	[events]	Core intrinsic events
<EM>...</EM>		Emphasized text
	CLASS= ID= STYLE= TITLE=	Class(es), unique ID, style information, title
	DIR= LANG=	Text direction and language ID
	[events]	Core intrinsic events
<EMBED>...</EMBED>		Embedded object
	ALIGN=	Alignment of object
	HEIGHT=	Height of object

Tags	Attributes	Description
	HIDDEN=	Hides object
	PALETTE=	Sets color palette
	PLUGINSPAGE=	Sets plug-ins source link
	SRC=	Location of object source
	WIDTH=	Width of object
	[events]	Core intrinsic events
<FIELDSET>...</FIELDSET>		Form fieldset
	CLASS= ID= STYLE= TITLE=	Class(es), unique ID, style information, title
	DIR= LANG=	Text direction and language ID
	[events]	Core intrinsic events
<FONT>...</FONT>		Font
	COLOR=	Color of font
	FACE=	Typeface of font
	SIZE=	Size of font
<FORM>...</FORM>		Form
	ACCEPT-CHARSET=	List of supported character sets
	ACTION=	Server-side form handler
	CLASS= ID= STYLE= TITLE=	Class(es), unique ID, style information, title
	DIR= LANG=	Text direction and language ID
	ENCTYPE=	Encryption type
	METHOD="get | post"	Form data sent to server
	NAME=	Name of form
	TARGET=	Target frame name for rendering
	[events] onsubmit, onreset	Core intrinsic events
<FRAME>...</FRAME>		Frame within frameset
	BORDERCOLOR=	Color of border
	FRAMEBORDER=	Width of border
	HEIGHT=	Height of frame
	MARGINHEIGHT=	Height of margin
	MARGINWIDTH=	Width of margin
	NAME=	Name of frame
	NORESIZE	Prohibits resize
	SCROLLING="yes | no | auto"	Sets scroll
	SRC=	Location of frame source
	WIDTH=	Width of frame
<FRAMESET>...</FRAMESET>		Frameset
	BORDER=	Width of border
	BORDERCOLOR=	Color of border
	COLS=	Number of columns
	FRAMEBORDER=	Width of border

Tags	Attributes	Description
	FRAMESPACING=	Space between frames
	ROWS=	Number of rows
	[events] onload, onunload	Intrinsic events
<HEAD>...</HEAD>		Document head
	DIR= LANG=	Text direction and language ID
	PROFILE=	URL of metadata
<H1>...</H1>		Heading 1
	ALIGN=	Alignment of heading
	CLASS= ID= STYLE= TITLE=	Class(es), unique ID, style information, title
	CLEAR=	Fixes text beside or below image
	COLOR=	Color of text
	DINGBAT=	Adds defined dingbat
	DIR= LANG=	Text direction and language ID
<H2>, <H3>, <H4>, <H5>, <H6>	Same as <H1>	Headings 2 through 6
<HR>		Horizontal rule
	ALIGN=	Alignment of rule
	CLASS= ID= STYLE= TITLE=	Class(es), unique ID, style information, title
	CLEAR=	Fixes text beside or below image
	COLOR=	Color of rule
	NOSHADE=	No shading on rule
	NOWRAP	No wrapping of rule
	SIZE=	Height of rule
	WIDTH=	Width of rule
	[events]	Core intrinsic events
<HTML>...</HTML>		Document container
	DIR= LANG=	Text direction and language ID
	VERSION=	HTML standard version used
<I>...</I>		Italic text
	CLASS= ID= STYLE= TITLE=	Class(es), unique ID, style information, title
	DIR= LANG=	Text direction and language ID
	[events]	Core intrinsic events
<IFRAME>...</IFRAME>		Inline frame
	ALIGN=	Alignment of inline frame
	BORDER=	Size of border
	BORDERCOLOR=	Color of border
	FRAMEBORDER=	Width of border
	FRAMESPACING=	Space between frames
	HEIGHT=	Height of frame
	HSPACE=	Horizontal space
	MARGINHEIGHT=	Height of margin
	MARGINWIDTH=	Width of margin

Tags	Attributes	Description
	NAME=	Name of inline frame
	NORESIZE=	Prohibits resize of frame
	SCROLLING="yes | no | auto"	Sets scroll
	SRC=	Location of inline frame source
	VSPACE=	Vertical space
	WIDTH=	Width of frame
<ILAYER>...</ILAYER>	(same as LAYER tag)	Inline layer positioning (behaves like text element)
<IMG>		Image
	ALIGN=	Alignment of image
	ALT=	Alternate text description
	BORDER=	Size of image border
	CLASS= ID= STYLE= TITLE=	Class(es), unique ID, style information, title
	DIR= LANG=	Text direction and language ID
	DYNSRC=	Dynamic source
	HEIGHT=	Height of image
	HSPACE=	Horizontal space
	ISMAP	Server-side image map
	LOOP=	Number of repetitions
	LOWSRC=	Location of low-resolution image
	NAME=	Name of image
	SRC=	Location of image source
	USEMAP=	Client-side image map
	VSPACE=	Vertical space
	WIDTH=	Width of image
	[events]	Core intrinsic events
<INPUT>...</INPUT>		Form input
	ACCEPT=	Accept input
	ALT=	Alternate text description
	CHECKED	Loads checkboxes already selected
	CLASS= ID= STYLE= TITLE=	Class(es), unique ID, style information, title
	DIR= LANG=	Text direction and language ID
	DISABLED	Disables input
	MAX=	Maximum number of input characters
	MAXLENGTH=	Maximum length of field
	NAME=	Name of form
	SIZE=	Size of field
	SRC=	Location of added images
	TABINDEX=	Explicit tabbing order
	TYPE=" button | checkbox | file | hidden | image | password | radio | reset | submit | text"	Type of input method

Tags	Attributes	Description
	USEMAP=	Client-side image map
	VALUE=	Sets default value
	[events] onfocus, onblur, onselect, onchange Core intrinsic events	
<INS>...</INS>		Inserted text
	CITE=	Change data
	CLASS= ID= STYLE= TITLE=	Class(es), unique ID, style information, title
	DATETIME=	ISO change date
	DIR= LANG=	Text direction and language ID
	[events]	Core intrinsic events
<ISINDEX>		Document is a searchable index—Obsolete, use <FORM> instead
	ACTION=	URL
	CLASS= ID= STYLE= TITLE=	Class(es), unique ID, style information, title
	DIR= LANG=	Text direction and language ID
	PROMPT=	Prompt text
<KBD>...</KBD>		Keyboard
	CLASS= ID= STYLE= TITLE=	Class(es), unique ID, style information, title
	DIR= LANG=	Text direction and language ID
	[events]	Core intrinsic events
<KEYGEN>...</KEYGEN>		Form-generated security key
	NAME=	Required
	CHALLENGE=	Public key challenge string
<LABEL>...</LABEL>		Form field label
	ACCESSKEY=	Keyboard shortcut
	CLASS= ID= STYLE= TITLE=	Class(es), unique ID, style information, title
	DIR= LANG=	Text direction and language ID
	DISABLED	Disables labeling
	FOR=	Field ID
	[events] onfocus, onblur	Core intrinsic events
<LAYER>...</LAYER>		Layer positioning element (behaves like structure)
	Note: Style sheets can also be used to control positioning of layer elements in a manner similar to but not the same as the W3C DOM and CSS-Positioning methods.	
	ABOVE=	Relative stacking order
	BACKGROUND=	Background image
	BELOW=	Relative stacking order
	BGCOLOR=	Background color
	CLIP="n,n,n,n"	Coordinates of viewable area
	HEIGHT=	Height of layer

Tags	Attributes	Description
	LEFT=	Horizontal position of layer in layer
	PAGEX=	Horizontal position of layer in page
	PAGEY=	Vertical position of layer in page
	SRC=	Source of content
	TOP=	Vertical position of layer in layer
	VIEW="hidden | inherit | show"	Define layer visibility
	WIDTH=	Horizontal size of layer
	Z-INDEX=	Absolute stacking order
	onmouseover, onmouseout, onfocus, onblur, onload	Intrinsic events
<LEGEND>		Form fieldset legend
	ACCESSKEY=	Keyboard shortcut
	ALIGN=	Alignment of legend
	CLASS= ID= STYLE= TITLE=	Class(es), unique ID, style information, title
	DIR= LANG=	Text direction and language ID
	[events]	Core intrinsic events
<LI>...</LI>		List item
	ALIGN=	Alignment of items
	CLASS= ID= STYLE= TITLE=	Class(es), unique ID, style information, title
	DIR= LANG=	Text direction and language ID
	TYPE=	Numbering or bullet style
	VALUE="number"	Reset sequence number
	[events]	Core intrinsic events
<LINK>		Link
	CLASS= ID= STYLE= TITLE=	Class(es), unique ID, style information, title
	DIR= LANG=	Text direction and language ID
	HREF=	Hypertext link
	MEDIA=	Supported media list
	NAME=	Name of link
	REL=	Forward link type (application dependent)
	REV=	Reverse link type (application dependent)
	TARGET=	Target frame name for rendering
	TYPE=	Media type
<MAP>...</MAP>		Client-side image map
	CLASS= ID= STYLE= TITLE=	Class(es), unique ID, style information, title
	NAME=	Name of image map
<MENU>...</MENU>		Menu list
	COMPACT	Compact representation
	CLASS= ID= STYLE= TITLE=	Class(es), unique ID, style information, title
	DIR= LANG=	Text direction and language ID
	[events]	Core intrinsic events

Tags	Attributes	Description
<META>		Metadata
	CONTENT=	Content description
	DIR= LANG=	Text direction and language ID
	HTTP-EQUIV=	Server response
	NAME=	Name of document
	TITLE=	Title of document
	URL=	URL of document
<NOBR>...</NOBR>		Inhibits line breaking
<NOEMBED>		Inhibits embedding
<NOFRAMES>...</NOFRAMES>		No frames alternate document body
<NOLAYER>...</NOLAYER>		Inhibits layers
<NOSCRIPT>...</NOSCRIPT>		Noscript data
<OBJECT>...</OBJECT>		Object
	ALIGN=	Alignment of object
	BORDER=	Width of border
	CLASS= ID= STYLE= TITLE=	Class(es), unique ID, style information, title
	CLASSID=	Class identifier
	CODE=	Type of script
	CODEBASE=	Object code base
	CODETYPE=	Media type
	DATA=	Data type
	DECLARE=	References object name
	DIR= LANG=	Text direction and language ID
	DISABLED	Disables object
	HEIGHT=	Height of object
	HSPACE=	Horizontal space
	NAME=	Name of object
	SHAPES=	Name of shaped hyperlink
	STANDBY=	Standby message
	TABINDEX=	Explicit tabbing order
	TYPE=	Media type
	USEMAP=	Image map
	VSPACE=	Vertical space
	WIDTH=	Width of image
	[events]	Core intrinsic events
<OL>...</OL>		Ordered list
	ALIGN=	Alignment of list
	CLASS= ID= STYLE= TITLE=	Class(es), unique ID, style information, title
	COMPACT	Compact representation
	DIR= LANG=	Text direction and language ID

Tags	Attributes	Description
	START=	Starting number
	TYPE=	Numbering style
	[events]	Core intrinsic events
<OPTION>...</OPTION>		Form option
	CLASS= ID= STYLE= TITLE=	Class(es), unique ID, style information, title
	DIR= LANG=	Text direction and language ID
	DISABLED	Disables option
	SELECTED=	Option selected at default
	VALUE=	Value to be returned
	[events]	Core intrinsic events
<P>...</P>		Paragraph
	ALIGN=	Alignment of paragraph
	CLASS= ID= STYLE= TITLE=	Class(es), unique ID, style information, title
	DIR= LANG=	Text direction and language ID
	WIDTH=	Width of paragraph
	[events]	Core intrinsic events
<PARAM>...</PARAM>		Parameter
	NAME=	Name of parameter
	TYPE=	Internet media type
	VALUE=	Sets value
	VALUETYPE=	Interprets value
<PRE>...</PRE>		Preformatted text
<Q>...</Q>		Inline quote
	CLASS= ID= STYLE= TITLE=	Class(es), unique ID, style information, title
	DIR= LANG=	Text direction and language ID
	[events]	Core intrinsic events
<S>...</S>		Strikeout text
	CLASS= ID= STYLE= TITLE=	Class(es), unique ID, style information, title
	DIR= LANG=	Text direction and language ID
	[events]	Core intrinsic events
<SAMP>...<SAMP>		Sample text
	CLASS= ID= STYLE= TITLE=	Class(es), unique ID, style information, title
	DIR= LANG=	Text direction and language ID
	[events]	Core intrinsic events
<SCRIPT>...</SCRIPT>		Script data
	LANGUAGE=	Script language
	SRC=	URL of script source
	TYPE=	Internet content type
	[events]	Core intrinsic events

Tags	Attributes	Description
<SELECT>...</SELECT>		Form selection list
	ALIGN=	Alignment of list
	CLASS= ID= STYLE= TITLE=	Class(es), unique ID, style information, title
	DIR= LANG=	Text direction and language ID
	DISABLED	Disables list
	HEIGHT=	Height of object
	NAME=	Names of object
	SIZE=	Size of object
	TABINDEX=	Explicit tabbing order
	WIDTH=	Width of object
	[events] onfocus, onblur, onselect, onchange	Core intrinsic events
<SMALL>...</SMALL>		Small text
	CLASS= ID= STYLE= TITLE=	Class(es), unique ID, style information, title
	DIR= LANG=	Text direction and language ID
	[events]	Core intrinsic events
<SPAN>...</SPAN>		Generic text container
	ALIGN=	Alignment of container
	CLASS= ID= STYLE= TITLE=	Class(es), unique ID, style information, title
	DIR= LANG=	Text direction and language ID
	[events]	Core intrinsic events
<STRIKE>...</STRIKE>		Strikeout text
	CLASS= ID= STYLE= TITLE=	Class(es), unique ID, style information, title
	DIR= LANG=	Text direction and language ID
	[events]	Core intrinsic events
<STRONG>...</STRONG>		Strong text
	CLASS= ID= STYLE= TITLE=	Class(es), unique ID, style information, title
	DIR= LANG=	Text direction and language ID
	[events]	Core intrinsic events
<STYLE>...</STYLE>		Style sheet definition
	DIR= LANG=	Text direction and language ID
	MEDIA=	Supported media list
	TYPE=	Internet content type
<SUB>...</SUB>		Subscript text
	CLASS= ID= STYLE= TITLE=	Class(es), unique ID, style information, title
	DIR= LANG=	Text direction and language ID
	[events]	Core intrinsic events
<SUP>...</SUP>		Superscript text
	CLASS= ID= STYLE= TITLE=	Class(es), unique ID, style information, title
	DIR= LANG=	Text direction and language ID
	[events]	Core intrinsic events

Tags	Attributes	Description
<TAB>		Tab value
	ALIGN=	Alignment of tab
	INDENT=	
<TABLE>...</TABLE>		Table
	ALIGN=	Alignment of table
	BACKGROUND=	Location of background image
	BGCOLOR=	Background color
	BORDER=	Size of border
	BORDERCOLOR=	Color of border
	BORDERCOLORDARK=	Dark color for 3-D border
	BORDERCOLORLIGHT=	Light color for 3-D border
	CELLPADDING=	Space between table cell edge and content
	CELLSPACING=	Space between cell borders
	CLASS= ID= STYLE= TITLE=	Class(es), unique ID, style information, title
	COLS=	Number of columns
	DIR= LANG=	Text direction and language ID
	FRAME=	External border around table
	HEIGHT=	Height of table
	NOWRAP	Prohibits text wrapping
	WIDTH=	Width of table
	[events]	Core intrinsic events
<TBODY>...</TBODY>		Table body
	ALIGN=	Alignment of table body
	BGCOLOR=	Background color
	CLASS= ID= STYLE= TITLE=	Class(es), unique ID, style information, title
	DIR= LANG=	Text direction and language ID
	VALIGN=	Vertical alignment
	[events]	Core intrinsic events
<TD>...</TD>		Table cell
	ALIGN=	Alignment of table cell
	AXIS=	Abbreviated cell name
	AXES=	AXIS values
	BACKGROUND=	Location of background image
	BGCOLOR=	Background color
	BORDERCOLOR=	Border color
	BORDERCOLORDARK=	Dark color for 3-D border
	BORDERCOLORLIGHT=	Light color for 3-D border
	CLASS= ID= STYLE= TITLE=	Class(es), unique ID, style information, title
	COLSPAN=	Number of columns spanned
	DIR= LANG=	Text direction and language ID
	HEIGHT=	Height of table cell

Tags	Attributes	Description
	NOWRAP	Prohibits text wrap
	ROWSPAN=	Number of rows spanned
	VALIGN=	Vertical alignment
	WIDTH=	Width of table cell
	[events]	Core intrinsic events
<TEXTAREA>...</TEXTAREA>		Form input text area
	ALIGN=	Alignment of text field
	CLASS= ID= STYLE= TITLE=	Class(es), unique ID, style information, title
	COLS=	Width of text input field
	DATAFLD=	Field of data
	DATASRC=	Location of data source
	DIR= LANG=	Text direction and language ID
	DISABLED	Disables text field
	ERROR=	Error message
	NAME=	Name of text field
	READONLY	Read-only
	ROWS=	Height of text input field
	TABINDEX=	Explicit tabbing order
	WRAP=	Wrap text
	[events] onfocus, onblur, onselect, onchange Core intrinsic events	
<TFOOT>...</TFOOT>		Table footer
	ALIGN=	Alignment of footer
	BGCOLOR=	Background color
	CLASS= ID= STYLE= TITLE=	Class(es), unique ID, style information, title
	DIR= LANG=	Text direction and language ID
	VALIGN=	Vertical alignment
	[events]	Core intrinsic events
<TH>...</TH>		Table cell heading
	ALIGN=	Alignment of heading
	AXIS=	Abbreviated cell name
	AXES=	AXIS values
	BACKGROUND=	Location of background image
	BGCOLOR=	Background color
	BORDERCOLOR=	Border color
	BORDERCOLORDARK=	Dark color for 3-D border
	BORDERCOLORLIGHT=	Light color for 3-D border
	CLASS= ID= STYLE= TITLE=	Class(es), unique ID, style information, title
	COLSPAN=	Number of columns spanned
	DIR= LANG=	Text direction and language ID
	HEIGHT=	Height of table cell

Tags	Attributes	Description
	NOWRAP	Prohibits text wrap
	ROWSPAN=	Number of rows spanned
	VALIGN=	Vertical alignment
	WIDTH=	Width of table cell
	[events]	Core intrinsic events
<THEAD>...</THEAD>		Table header
	ALIGN=	Alignment of header
	BGCOLOR=	Background color
	CLASS= ID= STYLE= TITLE=	Class(es), unique ID, style information, title
	DIR= LANG=	Text direction and language ID
	VALIGN=	Vertical alignment
	[events]	Core intrinsic events
<TITLE>...</TITLE>		Document title
	DIR= LANG=	Text direction and language ID
<TR>...</TR>		Table row
	ALIGN=	Alignment of table row
	BGCOLOR=	Background color
	BORDERCOLOR=	Border color
	BORDERCOLORDARK=	Dark color for 3-D border
	BORDERCOLORLIGHT=	Light color for 3-D border
	CLASS= ID= STYLE= TITLE=	Class(es), unique ID, style information, title
	DIR= LANG=	Text direction and language ID
	HEIGHT=	Height of table row
	NOWRAP	Prohibits text wrap
	VALIGN=	Vertical alignment
	VSPACE=	Vertical space
	[events]	Core intrinsic events
<TT>...</TT>		Monospaced text
	CLASS= ID= STYLE= TITLE=	Class(es), unique ID, style information, title
	DIR= LANG=	Text direction and language ID
	[events]	Core intrinsic events
<U>...</U>		Underline text
	CLASS= ID= STYLE= TITLE=	Class(es), unique ID, style information, title
	DIR= LANG=	Text direction and language ID
	[events]	Core intrinsic events
<UL>...</UL>		Unordered list
	ALIGN=	Alignment of list
	CLASS= ID= STYLE= TITLE=	Class(es), unique ID, style information, title
	COMPACT	Compact representation
	DIR= LANG=	Text direction and language ID

Tags	Attributes	Description
	SRC=	Location of list source
	TYPE="disk|square|circle"	Bullet style
	WRAP=	Wrap text
	[events]	Core intrinsic events
<VAR>...</VAR>		Variable content
	CLASS= ID= STYLE= TITLE=	Class(es), unique ID, style information, title
	DIR= LANG=	Text direction and language ID
	[events]	Core intrinsic events
<WBR>		Conditional break

appendix B

CROSS-BROWSER REFERENCE

CROSS-BROWSER REFERENCE

This cross-browser reference includes both tags and attributes and corresponding relevant browser support.

Legend

[nc] = non-conforming (browser doesn't support tag or attribute)

[xx] = obsolete (attribute is considered to be outdated)

* = supported (browser supports tag or attribute)

MSIE = Microsoft Internet Explorer

MS = Microsoft

NSNC = Netscape Navigator / Communicator

NS = Netscape

Lynx = Lynx (text-based browser)

HTML Version = World Wide Web Consortium standard version

Author = author of tag

W3C = World Wide Web Consortium

Cross-Browser Tag and Attribute Support Table

Tag / Attribute	MSIE	NSNC	Lynx	HTML Version	Author
<!--...-->	*	*	*	2	W3C
<!DOCTYPE>	*	*	*	2	W3C
HTML...	*	*	*	2	W3C
<A>	*	*	*	2	W3C
...</A>					
accesskey=	4			4	W3C
charset=	4			4	W3C
class=		*3/4	*	3/4	W3C
coords=	4			4	W3C
dir=				4	W3C
href=	*	*	*	2/4	W3C
hreflang=				4	W3C
id=	*3/4	*3/4	*	3/4	W3C
lang=	*3/4	*3/4	*	3/4	W3C
language=	*3/4			[nc]	MS
md=			*	3	W3C
methods=	*2/4	*	*	2	W3C
name=	*	*	*	2/4	W3C
rel=	*	*2/4	*	2/4	W3C
rev=		*2/4	*	2/4	W3C
shape=			*	3/4	W3C
style=	*3/4	4		4	W3C
tabindex=	*3/4	4*		4	W3C
target=	*3/4	*2/4	*	4	W3C
title=	*2/4	*2/4	*	2/4	W3C
urn=	*2/4	*2/4	*	2	W3C
onfocus, onblur	*	*			
{event}=	*3/4	*		4	W3C
<ABBR>				4	W3C
...</ABBR>				4	W3C
class=				4	W3C
dir=				4	W3C
id=				4	W3C
lang=				4	W3C
style=				4	W3C
title=				4	W3C
{event}=				4	W3C
<ACRONYM>			*	3	W3C
...</ACRONYM>					
class=			*	3	W3C
dir=					W3C
id=			*	3	W3C
lang=			*	3	W3C
style=			*	3	W3C
title=			*	3	W3C
{event}=				3	W3C
<ADDRESS>	*	*	*	2/4	W3C
...</ADDRESS>					
align=	*3/4			[nc]	
class=		*3/4	*	3/4	W3C

Tag / Attribute	MSIE	NSNC	Lynx	HTML Version	Author
clear=		*3/4	*	3	W3C
dir=				4	W3C
id=	*	*3/4	*	3/4	W3C
lang=		*3/4	*	3/4	W3C
nowrap		*	*	3	W3C
style=	*3/4	4		4	W3C
title=	*3/4			4	W3C
{event}=	*3/4			4	W3C
<APP>	4			[nc]	SM
...</APP>					
align=	4			[nc]	SM
class=	4			[nc]	SM
height=	4			[nc]	SM
src=	4			[nc]	SM
width=	4			[nc]	SM
<APPLET>	*3/4	*2/4	*	3+/4	W3C
...</APPLET>					
align=	*3/4	*2/4		3+	W3C
alt=	*3/4	*2/4	*	3+	W3C
archive=				4	W3C
code=	*3/4	*2/4	*	3+	W3C
codebase=	*3/4	*2/4	*	3+	W3C
download=	*3/4			[nc]	MS
height=	*3/4	*2/4	*	3+	W3C
hspace=	*3/4	*2/4	*	3+	W3C
name=	*3/4	*2/4	*	3+	W3C
object=		4		4	W3C
title=	*3/4			3	MS
vspace=	*3/4	*2/4	*	3+	W3C
width=	*3/4	*2/4	*	3+	W3C
<AREA>	*	*	*	3+/4	W3C
...</AREA>	[nc]				
accesskey=					
alt=		*2/4	*	3+/4	W3C
coords=	*2/4	*2/4	*	3+/4	W3C
href=	*2/4	*2/4	*	3+/4	W3C
id=	*3/4	*3	*	3	W3C
name=	*3/4		*	3	W3C
nohref=	*2/4	*2/4	*	3+/4	W3C
shape=	*2/4	*2/4	*	3+/4	W3C
style=	*3/4	4		3	W3C
tabindex=	4	4*		4	W3C
target=	*3/4	*2/4		4	W3C
title=	*3/4	*2/4		3	W3C
{event}=	*3/4			3	W3C
<AU>			*	3	W3C
...</AU>					
class=			*	3	W3C
id=			*	3	W3C
lang=			*	3	W3C

Tag / Attribute	MSIE	NSNC	Lynx	HTML Version	Author
<B>	*	*	*	2/4	W3C
...</B>					
class=		*3/4	*	3/4	W3C
dir=				4	W3C
id=	*3/4	*3/4	*	3/4	W3C
lang=		*3/4	*	3/4	W3C
style=	*3/4	4		4	W3C
title=	*3/4	4		4	W3C
{event}=	*3/4			4	W3C
<BANNER>			*	3	W3C
...</BANNER>					
class=			*	3	W3C
id=			*	3	W3C
lang=			*	3	W3C
<BASE>	*	*2/4	*	2/4	W3C
...</BASE>	[nc]				
href=	*	*2/4	*	2/4	W3C
target=	*3/4	*2/4	*	4	W3C
title=	*3/4			[nc]	MS
<BASEFONT>	*	*	*	3+/4	W3C
...</BASEFONT>					
color=	*3/4	*2/4	*	3+/4	W3C
face=	*3/4	*2/4	*	4	W3C
id=	*3/4	*3/4	*	3	W3C
size=	*	*24	*	3+	W3C
title=	*3/4				MS
<BDO>				4	W3C
...</BDO>					
dir=				4	W3C
lang=				4	W3C
<BGSOUND>	*	*2/4		[nc]	MS
loop=	*	*2/4			
src=	*	*2/4			
id=	*				
title=	*				
<BIG>	*	*	*	3+/4	W3C
...</BIG>					
class=		*3/4	*	3/4	W3C
dir=				4	W3C
id=	*3/4	*3/4	*	3/4	W3C
lang=		*3/4	*	3/4	W3C
style=	*3/4	4		4	W3C
title=	*3/4			4	W3C
{event}=	*3/4			4	W3C
<BLINK>		*2/4		NS	[nc]
...</BLINK>					
<BLOCKQUOTE>	*	*	*	2	W3C
...</BLOCKQUOTE>					
cite=				4	W3C
class=				4	W3C
dir=				4	W3C

Tag / Attribute	MSIE	NSNC	Lynx	HTML Version	Author
id=	3/4	*3/4		4	W3C
lang=				4	W3C
style=	*3/4	4		4	W3C
title=	*3/4			4	W3C
{event}=	*3/4			4	W3C
<BODY>	*	*	*	2/4	W3C
...</BODY>					
align=	*3/4			4	W3C
alink=	*	*		3+/4	W3C
background=	*	*		3+/4	W3C
bgcolor=	*	*		3+/4	W3C
bgproperties= fixed	*3/4			[nc]	MS
class=				4	W3C
dir=				4	W3C
id=	*3/4	*3/4		4	W3C
lang=				4	W3C
leftmargin=	*			[nc]	MS
link=	*3/4	*2/4		3+/4	W3C
scroll=	*3/4			[nc]	MS
style=	*3/4	4		4	W3C
text=	*3/4	*2/4		3+/4	W3C
title=	*3/4			4	W3C
topmargin=	*3/4			[nc]	MS
vlink=	*3/4	*2/4		3+/4	W3C
{event}=	*3/4			4	W3C
 	*	*	*	2/4	W3C
class=	*	*3/4		3	W3C
clear=	*	*2/4		3	W3C
none				3+	W3C
dir=				4	W3C
id=	*	*3/4		3	W3C
lang=		*3/4		3	W3C
style=	*3/4	4		4	W3C
title=	*3/4			4	W3C
<BQ>			*	3	W3C
...</BQ>					
<BUTTON>	*3/4			4	W3C
...</BUTTON>					
accesskey=	*3/4			[nc]	MS
class=	4			4	W3C
dir=				4	W3C
disabled	*3/4			4	W3C
id=	4			4	W3C
lang=				4	W3C
name=				4	W3C
style=	4			4	W3C
tabindex=	4			4	W3C
title=	*3/4			4	W3C
type=	4			4	W3C
value=	4			4	W3C
{event}=	*3/4			4	W3C

Tag / Attribute	MSIE	NSNC	Lynx	HTML Version	Author
<CAPTION> ...</CAPTION>	*	*	*	3	W3C
align=	*	*	*	3+/4	W3C
class=				4	W3C
dir=				4	W3C
id=	*	*3/4	*	3/4	W3C
lang			*	3/4	W3C
style=	*3/4	4		4	W3C
title=	*3/4			4	W3C
valign=	*2/4	*	*	3+	W3C
{event}=	*3/4			4	W3C
<CENTER> ...</CENTER>	*	*	*	3+	W3C
class=				4	W3C
dir=				4	W3C
id=	*3/4	*3/4	*	3	W3C
lang=				4	W3C
style=	*3/4	4		4	W3C
title=	*3/4			4	W3C
{event}=	*3/4			4	W3C
<CITE> ...</CITE>	*	*	*	2/4	W3C
class=		*3/4	*	3/4	W3C
dir=				4	W3C
id=	*3/4	*3/4	*	3/4	W3C
lang=		*3/4	*	3/4	W3C
style=	*3/4	4		4	W3C
title=	*3/4			4	W3C
{event}=	*3/4			4	W3C
<CODE> ...</CODE>	*	*	*	2	W3C
class=		*3/4	*	3	W3C
dir=				4	W3C
id=	*3/4	*3/4	*	3	W3C
lang=		*3/4	*	3	W3C
style=	*3/4	4		4	W3C
title=	*3/4			4	W3C
{event}=	*3/4			4	W3C
<COL> ...</COL>	4			4	W3C
align=	4			4	W3C
char=				4	W3C
charoff=				4	W3C
class=				4	W3C
dir=				4	W3C
id=	4			4	W3C
span=	4			4	W3C
style=	4			4	W3C
title=	4			4	W3C
valign=	4			4	W3C
width=	4			4	W3C
{event}=	4			4	W3C

Tag / Attribute	MSIE	NSNC	Lynx	HTML Version	Author
<COLGROUP> ...</COLGROUP>	*3/4			4	W3C
align=	4			4	W3C
char=				4	W3C
charoff=				4	W3C
class=				4	W3C
id=	4			4	W3C
span=	4			4	W3C
style=	4			4	W3C
title=	4			4	W3C
valign=				4	W3C
width=	4			4	W3C
<COMMENT> ...</COMMENT>	*		*	[nc]	
title=	*				
<CREDIT> ...</CREDIT>			*	3	W3C
<DD> ...</DD>	*	*	*	2/4	W3C
align=	4			3	W3C
class=	4	3		4	W3C
dir=				4	W3C
id=	4	3		3	W3C
lang=		3		3	W3C
style=	4	4		3	W3C
title=	4			3	W3C
{event}=	4				
<DEL> ...</DEL>			*	3	W3C
cite=				4	W3C
class=			*	3/4	W3C
datetime=				4	W3C
dir=				4	W3C
id=			*	3/4	W3C
lang=			*	3/4	W3C
style=			*	3/4	W3C
title=			*	3/4	W3C
{event}=				3/4	W3C
<DFN> ...<DFN>	*	*	*	3/4	W3C
class=			*	3/4	W3C
dir=				4	W3C
id=	*3/4		*	3/4	W3C
lang=			*	3/4	W3C
style=	4			4	W3C
title=	4			4	W3C
{event}=	4			4	W3C
<DIR> ...<DIR>	*	*	*	2	W3C
class=				4	W3C
compact	*	*	*	2	W3C

Tag / Attribute	MSIE	NSNC	Lynx	HTML Version	Author
dir=				4	W3C
id=	4	*3/4		4	W3C
lang=				3/4	W3C
style=	4	4		4	W3C
title=	4			4	W3C
{event}=	4			4	W3C
<DIV> ...**</DIV>**	*	*	*	3/4	W3C
align=	4	*	*	3/4	W3C
justify				3	W3C
class=		*3/4	*	3/4	W3C
clear=		*	*	3	W3C
{measurement}			*	3	W3C
datafld=	4			[nc]	
dataformats=	4			[nc]	
datasrc=	4			[nc]	
dir=				4	W3C
id=	4	*3/4	*	3/4	W3C
lang=		*3/4	*	3/4	W3C
nowrap		*3/4	*	3	W3C
style=	4	4		4	W3C
title=	4			4	W3C
{event}=	4			4	W3C
<DL> ...**</DL>**	*	*	*	2/4	W3C
align=	4				
class=		3	*	3/4	W3C
clear=		*	*	3	W3C
compact	*	*	*	2/4	W3C
dir=				4	W3C
id=	4	*3/4	*	3/4	W3C
lang=		*3/4		3/4	W3C
style=	4	4		4	W3C
title=	4			4	W3C
{event}=	4			4	W3C
<DT> ...**</DT>**	*	*	*	2/4	W3C
align=	4			3	W3C
class=				4	
dir=				4	
id=	4		*	3	W3C
lang=				4	W3C
style=	4			4	W3C
title=	4			4	W3C
{event}=	4			4	W3C
<EM> ...**</EM>**	*	*	*	2/4	W3C
class=			*	3/4	W3C
dir=				4	W3C
id=	*3/4			3/4	W3C
lang=				3/4	W3C
style=	4			4	W3C

Tag / Attribute	MSIE	NSNC	Lynx	HTML Version	Author
title=	4			4	W3C
{event}=	4			4	W3C
<EMBED> ...**</EMBED>**	*3/4	*		[nc]	NS
accesskey=	4				
align=	4	*			
height=	4				
hidden=	4				
id=	4				
palette=	4				
pluginspage=	4				
src=	4				
style=	4				
title=	4				
width=	4				
{event}=	4				
<FIELDSET> ...**</FIELDSET>**	4			4	W3C
class=				4	W3C
dir=				4	W3C
id=				4	W3C
lang=				4	W3C
style=				4	W3C
title=				4	W3C
{event}=				4	W3C
<FIG> ...**</FIG>**			*	3	W3C
align=			*	3	W3C
class=			*	3	W3C
clear=			*	3	W3C
height=				3	W3C
id=				3	W3C
imagemap=				3	W3C
lang=				3	W3C
md=				3	W3C
noflow				3	W3C
src=				3	W3C
units=				3	W3C
width=				3	W3C
<FN> ...**</FN>**			*	3	W3C
class=			*	3	W3C
dir=				4	W3C
id=			*	3	W3C
lang=			*	3	W3C
<FONT> ...**</FONT>**	*3/4	*	*	3+	W3C
color=	*	*	*	3+	W3C
face=	*			4	W3C
id=					
size=	*	*	*	3+	W3C
style=					W3C

Tag / Attribute	MSIE	NSNC	Lynx	HTML Version	Author
title=					W3C
{event}=					W3C
<FORM> ...</FORM>	*	*	*	2/4	W3C
acceptcharset=				4	W3C
action=	*	*	*	2/4	W3C
class=				4	W3C
dir=				4	W3C
enctype=	*	*	*	2/4	W3C
id=	4			4	W3C
lang=				4	W3C
method=	*	*	*	2/4	W3C
get | post	*	*	*	2/4	W3C
name=	4				
script=				3	W3C
style=	4			4	W3C
target=	4				W3C
title=	4			4	W3C
{event}=	4			4	W3C
<FRAME> ...</FRAME>	*	*	*	4	W3C
bordercolor=	*	*3/4			
class=				4	W3C
dir=				4	W3C
frameborder=	*3/4	4		4	W3C
framespacing	*3/4	*			
height=	4				W3C
id=	4			4	W3C
marginheight=	*3/4	*		4	W3C
marginwidth=	*3/4	*		4	W3C
method=				4	W3C
name=	*3/4	*2/4	*	4	W3C
noresize=	*3/4	*		4	W3C
scrolling=	*3/4	*2/4		[nc]	MS
src=	*3/4	*2/4	*	4	W3C
style					W3C
target=	*	*	*	4	W3C
title=	4			4	W3C
width=	4				W3C
{event}=	4			4	W3C
<FRAMESET> ...</FRAMESET>	*3/4	*2/4	*	4	W3C
border=	4				
bordercolor=	4				
cols=	4	*		4	W3C
frameborder=	4				
framespacing=	4				
id=	4				W3C
rows=	4	*		4	W3C
title=	4				W3C
{event}=	4			4	W3C
<HEAD> ...</HEAD>	*	*	*	2/4	W3C
id=	4				W3C
dir=				4	W3C

Tag / Attribute	MSIE	NSNC	Lynx	HTML Version	Author
lang=				4	W3C
profile=				4	W3C
style=	4				W3C
title=	4			4	W3C
<H1> ...</H1>	*	*	*	2/4	W3C
align=	*	*	*	3	W3C
justify				3	W3C
class=				3/4	W3C
clear=	*	*		3	W3C
color=	*			[nc]	
dingbat=			*	3	W3C
dir=				4	W3C
id=			*	3/4	W3C
lang=			*	3/4	W3C
md=			*	3	W3C
nowrap			*	3	W3C
seqnum=				3	W3C
skip=				3	W3C
style=				4	W3C
title=				4	W3C
<H2>, <H3>, <H4>, <H5>, <H6> Same as <H1>					
<HR>	*	*	*	2	W3C
align=	*	*	*	3	W3C
class=				4	W3C
clear=				3	W3C
color=	4			[nc]	MS
id=	4			3/4	W3C
md=				3	W3C
noshade=	*	*	*	3+/4	W3C
nowrap				3	W3C
size=	4	*	*	3+	W3C
src=	4			3	W3C
style=	4			4	W3C
title=	4			4	W3C
width=	*	*	*	3+	W3C
{event}=	4			4	W3C
<HTML> ...</HTML>	*	*	*	2/4	W3C
dir=				4	W3C
lang=				4	W3C
profile=					
TITLE=	4				
version=				4	W3C
<I> ...</I>	*	*	*	2/4	W3C
class=			*	3/4	W3C
dir=				4	W3C
ID=	*3/4		*	3/4	W3C
lang=			*	3/4	W3C
style=	4			4	W3C
title=	4			4	W3C
{event}=	4			4	W3C

Tag / Attribute	MSIE	NSNC	Lynx	HTML Version	Author
<IFRAME> ...**</IFRAME>**	*3/4	*		4	W3C
align=	*3/4			4	W3C
border=	4	*			
bordercolor=	4				
frameborder=	*	4		4	W3C
framespacing=	4				
height=	4				W3C
hspace=	4				W3C
id=	4				W3C
marginheight=	4			4	W3C
marginwidth=	4				W3C
name=	4	*		4	W3C
noresize=	*	4		4	W3C
scrolling=	4			4	W3C
src=	4			4	W3C
style=	4				
title=	4				
vspace=	4				
width=	4			4	W3C
{event}=	4			4	W3C
<ILAYER> ...**</ILAYER>**		4		[nc]	NS
<IMG>	*	*	*	2	W3C
align=	*	*	*	2	W3C
alt=	*	*	*	2/4	W3C
border=	*	*		3+/4	W3C
class=				3/4	W3C
controls=	*			[nc]	
dir=				4	W3C
datafld=	4			[nc]	
datasrc=	4			[nc]	
dynsrc=	4			[nc]	
height=	*	*		2/4	W3C
hspace=	*3/4	*		3+/4	W3C
id=	*3/4			3/4	W3C
ismap=	*	*	*	2/4	W3C
lang=				3/4	W3C
loop=	4			[nc]	
lowsrc=	4	*		[nc]	
md=				3	W3C
name=	4				
src=	*	*	*	2/4	W3C
style=	4			4	W3C
title=	4			4	W3C
units=				3	W3C
usemap=	*	*	*	3+/4	W3C
vrml=	4				
vspace=	*	*		3+/4	W3C
width=	*	*		2	W3C
{event}=	4			4	W3C
<INPUT> ...**</INPUT>**	*	*	*	2/4	W3C
accesskey=	4			[nc]	MS
accept=				4	W3C

Tag / Attribute	MSIE	NSNC	Lynx	HTML Version	Author
align=	*	*		3/4	W3C
alt=				4	W3C
checked=	*	*	*	3/4	W3C
class=				3/4	W3C
datafld=	4			[nc]	
datasrc=	4			[nc]	
dir=				4	W3C
disabled=	4			3/4	W3C
error				3	W3C
id=	4			3/4	W3C
lang=				3/4	W3C
language=	4				
max=	*	*		3	W3C
maxlength=	*	*	*	2/4	W3C
md=				3	W3C
min=	*	*		3	W3C
name=	*	*	*	2/4	W3C
readonly=	4			4	W3C
size=	*	*	*	2/4	W3C
src=				2/4	W3C
style=	4			4	W3C
tabindex=	4	4*		4	W3C
title=	4			4	W3C
type=	*	*	*	2/4	W3C
usemap=				4	W3C
value=	*	*	*	2	W3C
{event}=	4			4	
<INS> ...**</INS>**			*	3/4	W3C
cite=				4	W3C
class=			*	3/4	W3C
datetime=				4	W3C
dir=					W3C
id=				3	W3C
lang=				3	W3C
style=					W3C
title=					W3C
{event}=					W3C
<ISINDEX>	*	*	*	2/4	W3C
Note: Use <FORM> instead, if possible.					
action=					
class=				4	W3C
dir=				4	W3C
id=				4	W3C
lang=				4	W3C
prompt=	*	*		4	W3C
style=				4	W3C
title=				4	W3C
<KBD> ...**</KBD>**	*	*	*	2/4	W3C
class=			*	3/4	W3C
dir=				4	W3C
id=	*3/4		*	3/4	W3C
lang=			*	3/4	W3C
style=	4			4	W3C

Tag / Attribute	MSIE	NSNC	Lynx	HTML Version	Author
title=	4			4	W3C
{event}=	4			4	W3C
<KEYGEN> ...</KEYGEN>		*		[nc]	NS
<LABEL> ...</LABEL>	*3/4			4	W3C
accesskey=	4			4	W3C
class=				4	W3C
dir–				4	W3C
disabled				4	W3C
for=	4			4	W3C
id=	4			4	W3C
lang=				4	W3C
style=	4			4	W3C
title=	4			4	W3C
{event}=	4			4	W3C
<LAYER> ...</LAYER>		4		[nc]	NS
<LEGEND> ...</LEGEND>	4			4	W3C
accesskey=	4			4	W3C
align=				4	W3C
class=				4	W3C
dir=				4	W3C
id=	4			4	W3C
lang=				4	W3C
style=	4			4	W3C
title=	4			4	W3C
{event}=	4			4	W3C
<LI> ...</LI>	*	*	*	2	W3C
align=	4				
class=				4	W3C
dir=				4	W3C
id=	4			4	W3C
lang=				4	W3C
style=	4			4	W3C
title=	4			4	W3C
type=	*	*	*	3+/4	W3C
value=	4			3+/4	W3C
{event}=	4			4	W3C
<LINK> ...</LINK>	* [nc]	*	*	2/4	W3C
class=				4	W3C
dir=				4	W3C
href=	*	*	*	2/4	W3C
hreflang=				4	W3C
id=				4	W3C
lang=				4	W3C
media=				4	W3C
methods=	*	*	*	2	W3C
name=	*			2	W3C
rel=	*	*	*	2/4	W3C
rev=	*	*	*	2/4	W3C
style=				4	W3C

Tag / Attribute	MSIE	NSNC	Lynx	HTML Version	Author
target=	*			4	W3C
title=	*	*	*	2/4	W3C
type=	*			4	W3C
urn=	*	*	*	2	W3C
<LISTING> ...</LISTING>	*	*	*	2	W3C
align=	4				
class=		*		3	W3C
id=	*3/4		*	3	W3C
lang=				3	W3C
style=	4				W3C
title=	4				W3C
{event}=	4				W3C
<MAP> ...</MAP>	*3/4	*	*	3+/4	W3C
class=				4	W3C
id=	4			4	W3C
name=	*	*	*	3+/4	W3C
style=	4			4	W3C
title=	4			4	W3C
{event}=	4			4	W3C
<MARQUEE> ...</MARQUEE>	*		*	[nc]	MS*
align=	*				
behavior=	*				
bgcolor=	*				
datafld=	4				
dataformats=	4				
datasrc=	4				
direction=	*				
height=	*				
hspace=	*				
id=	4				
loop=	*				
scrollamount=	4				
scrolldelay=	4				
style=	4				
title=	4				
vspace=	*				
width=	*				
{event}=	4				
$...$				3	W3C
<MENU> ...</MENU>	*	*	*	2/4	W3C
compact	*	*	*	2/4	W3C
dir=				4	W3C
id=	4			4	W3C
lang=				4	W3C
style=	4			4	W3C
title=	4			4	W3C
{event}=	4			4	W3C
<META> ...</META>	* [nc]	*	*	2/4	W3C
content=	*	*	*	2/4	W3C

Tag / Attribute	MSIE	NSNC	Lynx	HTML Version	Author
dir=				4	W3C
httpequiv=	*	*	*	2/4	W3C
lang=				4	W3C
name=	*	*	*	2/4	W3C
scheme=				4	W3C
title=	4				W3C
url=	4				
<NEXTID>	*	*	*	2	W3C
n=	*	*	*	2	W3C
<NOBR>	*	*			NS
...</NOBR>					
id=	4			4	W3C
style=	4			4	W3C
title=	4			4	W3C
<NOEMBED>		*		[nc]	NS
<NOFRAMES>	*3/4	*2/4	*	4	W3C
...</NOFRAMES>					
id=	4	*		4	MS
style=	4			4	MS
title=	4			4	MS
<NOLAYER>		4		[nc]	NS
...</NOLAYER>					
<NOSCRIPT>	*3/4	*3/4	*		W3C
...</NOSCRIPT>					
title=	4			4	W3C
<NOTE>			*	3	W3C
...</NOTE>					
class=			*	3	W3C
clear=			*	3	W3C
id=			*	3	W3C
lang=			*	3	W3C
md=				3	W3C
src=			*	3	W3C
<OBJECT>	*3/4		*	4	W3C
...</OBJECT>					
accesskey=	4			4	MS
align=	*3/4			4	W3C
border=	*3/4			4	W3C
class=	*3/4			4	W3C
classid=	4			4	W3C
code=	4				
codebase=	4			4	W3C
codetype=	4			4	W3C
data=	*3/4			4	W3C
datafld=	4				
datasrc=	4				
declare=				4	W3C
dir=				4	W3C
disabled	4				
height=	*3/4			4	W3C
hspace=				4	W3C
id=	4			4	W3C
lang=				4	W3C
name=	*3/4			4	W3C

Tag / Attribute	MSIE	NSNC	Lynx	HTML Version	Author
shapes=				4	W3C
standby=				4	W3C
style=	4			4	W3C
tabindex=	4			4	W3C
title=	4			4	W3C
type=	*3/4			4	W3C
usemap=				4	W3C
vspace=				4	W3C
width=	*3/4			4	W3C
{event}=	4			4	W3C
<OL>	*	*	*	2/4	W3C
...</OL>					
align=	4				
class=			*	3/4	W3C
clear=			*	3	W3C
compact			*	2	W3C
continue			*	3	W3C
dir=				4	W3C
id=	4		*	3/4	W3C
lang=			*	3/4	W3C
seqnum=	*	*	*	3	W3C
start=	*3/4	*	*	3+/4	W3C
style=	4			4	W3C
title=	4			4	W3C
type=	*	*	*	2/4	W3C
{event}=	4			4	W3C
<OPTION>	*	*	*	2/4	W3C
...</OPTION>					W3C
class=				4	W3C
dir=				4	W3C
disabled				4	W3C
id=	4			4	W3C
lang=				4	W3C
name=	*	*	*	2/4	W3C
selected=	*	*	*	2/4	W3C
style=				4	W3C
title=	4			4	W3C
value=	*	*	*	2/4	W3C
<OVERLAY>			*	3	W3C
<P>	*	*	*	2/4	W3C
...</P>					
align=	*	*	*	3+	W3C
justify				3	W3C
class=				3/4	W3C
clear=		*		3	W3C
dir=				4	W3C
id=	4			3/4	W3C
lang=				3/4	W3C
style=	4			4	W3C
title=	4			4	W3C
width=	4			2	W3C
{event}=	4			4	W3C

Tag / Attribute	MSIE	NSNC	Lynx	HTML Version	Author
<PARAM>	*3/4	*		3+	W3C
...</PARAM>					
data=	4				
datafld=	4				
datasrc=	4				
name=	4	*		3+/4	W3C
object=	4				
ref=	4				
title=	4				
type=				4	W3C
value=	4	*		3+/4	W3C
valuetype=				4	W3C
<PERSON>			*	3	W3C
...<PERSON>					
class=			*	3	W3C
id=			*	3	W3C
lang=			*	3	W3C
<PLAINTEXT>	*	*	*	2	W3C
id=	4				W3C
style=	4				W3C
title=	4				W3C
{event}=	4				W3C
<PRE>	*	*	*	2/4	W3C
...</PRE>					
class=				3/4	W3C
clear=				3	W3C
dir=					W3C
id=	*3/4			3/4	W3C
lang=				3/4	W3C
style=	4			4	W3C
title=	4			4	W3C
width=	4			2/4	W3C
{event}=	4			4	W3C
<Q>	4		*	3/4	W3C
...</Q>					
cite=				4	W3C
class=			*	3/4	W3C
dir=				4	W3C
id=	*3/4		*	3/4	W3C
lang=			*	3/4	W3C
style=	4			4	W3C
title=	4			4	W3C
{event}=	4			4	W3C
<RANGE>				3	W3C
class=				3	W3C
from=				3	W3C
id=				3	W3C
until=				3	W3C
<S>	*	*	*	2	W3C
...</S>					
class=		*3/4	*	3/4	W3C
dir=				4	W3C
id=	*3/4	*3/4	*	3/4	W3C
lang=		*3/4	*	3/4	W3C
style=	4			4	W3C
title=	4			4	W3C
{event}=	4			4	W3C
<SAMP>	*	*	*	2/4	W3C
...<SAMP>					
class=			*	3/4	W3C
dir=				4	W3C
id=	*3/4		*	3/4	W3C
lang=			*	3/4	W3C
style=	4			4	W3C
title=	4			4	W3C
{event}=	4			4	W3C
<SCRIPT>	*	*		3+/4	W3C
...</SCRIPT>					
{event}=	4				
for=	4				
id=	4				
in=	4				
language=	*	*		4	W3C
library=	4				
src=	*	*		4	W3C
title=	4			4	W3C
type=				4	W3C
<SELECT>	*	*	*	2/4	W3C
...</SELECT>					
accesskey=	4			[nc]	MS
align=	4			3	W3C
class=		*3/4		3/4	W3C
datafld=	*			[nc]	
datasrc=				[nc]	
dir=				4	W3C
disabled	4			3/4	W3C
height=				3	W3C
id=	4	*3/4		4	W3C
lang=		*3/4		3/4	W3C
language=	4				
md=				3	W3C
multiple	*	*		2/4	W3C
name=	*	*		2/4	W3C
readonly=	4				
size=	*	*		2/4	W3C
style=	4	4		4	W3C
tabindex=	4	4*		4	W3C
title=	4			4	W3C
units=				3	W3C
width=				3	W3C
{event}=	4			4	W3C
<SERVER>		*		[nc]	NS
<SMALL>	*	*	*	3/4	W3C
...</SMALL>					
class=		3	*	3/4	W3C
dir=				4	W3C
id=	*3/4	3	*	3/4	W3C
lang=		3	*	3/4	W3C

Tag / Attribute	MSIE	NSNC	Lynx	HTML Version	Author
style=	4	4		4	W3C
title=	4			4	W3C
{event}=	4			4	W3C
<SPACER>		*3/4		[nc]	NS
<SPAN> ...</SPAN>	*3/4	4		4	W3C
align=				4	W3C
class=				4	W3C
datafld=	4			[nc]	
dataformats=	4			[nc]	
datasrc=	4			[nc]	
dir=				4	W3C
id=	4	3		4	W3C
style=	4	4		4	W3C
title=	4			4	W3C
{event}=	4			4	W3C
<SPOT>				3	W3C
id=				3	W3C
<STRIKE> ...</STRIKE>	*	*	*	3+/4	W3C
class=		*3/4	*	4	W3C
dir=				4	W3C
id=	4	*3/4	*	4	W3C
lang=		*3/4	*	4	W3C
style=	4	4		4	W3C
title=	4			4	W3C
{event}=	4			4	W3C
<STRONG> ...</STRONG>	*	*	*	2/4	W3C
class=		3	*	3/4	W3C
dir=				4	W3C
id=	*3/4	3	*	3/4	W3C
lang=		3	*	3/4	W3C
style=	4	4		4	W3C
title=	4			4	W3C
{event}=	4			4	W3C
<STYLE> ...</STYLE>	*3/4	4	*	3+/4	W3C
dir=				4	W3C
lang=				4	W3C
media=				4	W3C
title=	4			4	W3C
type=	4		*	4	W3C
_{...}	*	*	*	3/4	W3C
class=		3	*	3/4	W3C
dir=				4	W3C
id=	3/4	3	*	3/4	W3C
lang=		3	*	3/4	W3C
style=	4	4		4	W3C
title=	4			4	W3C
{event}=	4			4	W3C
^{...}	*	*	*	3/4	W3C

Tag / Attribute	MSIE	NSNC	Lynx	HTML Version	Author
class=		3	*	3/4	W3C
dir=				4	W3C
id=	3/4	3	*	3/4	W3C
lang=		3	*	3/4	W3C
style=	4	4		4	W3C
title=	4			4	W3C
{event}=	4			4	W3C
<TAB>			*	3	W3C
align=			*	3	W3C
dp=			*	3	W3C
id=			*	3	W3C
indent=			*	3	W3C
<TABLE> ...</TABLE>	*	*	*	3+/4	W3C
align=	[ck}	*	*	3+/4	W3C
class=		3		3/4	W3C
background=	*3/4	4*			
bgcolor=	*3/4	4		4	W3C
border=	*	*	*	3+/4	W3C
bordercolor=	*3/4			[nc]	MS
bordercolordark=	*3/4		[nc]		MS
bordercolorlight=	*3/4			[nc]	MS
cellpadding=	4	*		3+/4	W3C
cellspacing=	4	*		3+/4	W3C
class=		*3/4		3/4	W3C
clear=				3	W3C
cols=	4			4	W3C
colspec=				3	W3C
datasrc=	4			[nc]	
dir=				4	W3C
dp=				3	W3C
frame=	4			4	W3C
height=	4				
id=	4	*3/4		3/4	W3C
lang=		*3/4		3/4	W3C
noflow				3	W3C
nowrap	*	*		3	W3C
rules=	4			4	W3C
style=	4	4		4	W3C
title=	4			4	W3C
units=				3	W3C
width=	4			3+/4	W3C
{event}=	4			4	W3C
<TBODY> ...</TBODY>	*3/4	4		4	W3C
align=	4			4	W3C
bgcolor=	4				
char=					
charoff=					
class=				4	W3C
dir=				4	W3C
id=	4			4	W3C
lang=				4	W3C
style=	4			4	W3C
title=	4			4	W3C
valign=	4			4	W3C
{event}=	4			4	W3C

Tag / Attribute	MSIE	NSNC	Lynx	HTML Version	Author
`<TD>` ...`</TD>`	*	*	*	3+/4	W3C
abbr=				4	W3C
align=	*3/4*	*		3+/4	W3C
decimal				3	W3C
justify				3	W3C
axis=				3/4	W3C
axes=				3	W3C
background=	4				
bgcolor=	4	4		4	W3C
bordercolor=	4				
bordercolordark=	4				MS
bordercolorlight=	4				MS
char=				4	W3C
charoff=				4	W3C
class=				4	W3C
colspan=	*	*		3+/4	W3C
dir=				4	W3C
dp=				3	W3C
height=	4			3+	W3C
id=	4	3		3/4	W3C
lang=		3		3/4	W3C
nowrap	*	*		3+	W3C
rowspan=	4	*		3+	W3C
style=	4	4		4	W3C
title=	4			4	W3C
valign=	*	*		3+/4	W3C
width=	4			3+	W3C
{event}=	4			4	W3C
`<TEXTAREA>` ...`</TEXTAREA>`	*	*	*	2/4	W3C
accesskey=	4			[nc]	MS
align=	4			3	W3C
class=		*3/4		3/4	W3C
cols=	*	*	*	2	W3C
datafld=	*			[nc]	MS
datasrc=	*			[nc]	MS
dir=				4	W3C
disabled	4			3/4	W3C
error=				3	W3C
id=	4	3	*	3/4	W3C
lang=		*3/4	*	3/4	W3C
name=	*	*	*	2/4	W3C
readonly=	4			4	W3C
rows=	*	*	*	2/4	W3C
style=	4	4		4	W3C
tabindex=	4	4*		4	W3C
title=	4			4	W3C
wrap=		*		[nc]	NS
{event}=	4			4	W3C
`<TFOOT>` ...`</TFOOT>`	*3/4	4		4	W3C
align=	4			4	W3C
bgcolor=	4			[nc]	MS
char=				4	W3C
charoff=				4	W3C
dir=				4	W3C
id=	4			4	W3C
lang=				4	W3C
style=	4			4	W3C
title=	4			4	W3C
valign=	4			4	W3C
{event}=	4			4	W3C
`<TH>` ...`</TH>`	*	*	*	3+/4	W3C
abbr=				4	W3C
align=	*	*	*	3+/4	W3C
decimal				3	W3C
justify				3	W3C
axes=				3	W3C
axis=				3/4	W3C
background=	*	*		[nc]	
bgcolor=	*	*		4	W3C
bordercolor=	4			[nc]	MS
bordercolordark=	4			[nc]	MS
bordercolorlight=	4			[nc]	MS
char=				4	W3C
charoff=				4	W3C
class=				4	W3C
colspan=	*	*		3+/4	W3C
dir=				4	W3C
dp=				3	W3C
height=	*	*		3+	W3C
id=	4	3		3	W3C
lang=		3		3	W3C
nowrap	*	*		3+	W3C
rowspan=	*	*		3+	W3C
style=	4	4		4	W3C
title=	4			4	W3C
valign=	*	*		3+	W3C
width=	*	*		3+	W3C
{event}=	4			4	W3C
`<THEAD>` ...`</THEAD>`	*3/4	4		4	W3C
align=	4			4	W3C
bgcolor=	4			[nc]	MS
char=				4	W3C
charoff=				4	W3C
class=				4	W3C
dir=				4	W3C
id=	4			4	W3C
lang=				4	W3C
style=	4			4	W3C
title=	4			4	W3C
valign=	4			4	W3C
{event}=	4			4	W3C
`<TITLE>` ...`</TITLE>`	*	*	*	2/4	W3C
dir=				4	W3C
lang=				4	W3C

Tag / Attribute	MSIE	NSNC	Lynx	HTML Version	Author
<TR> ...</TR>	*	*	*	3+/4	W3C
align=	4*			3+/4	W3C
justify				3	W3C
bgcolor=	4	4		4	W3C
bordercolor=	4			[nc]	MS
bordercolordark=	4			[nc]	MS
bordercolorlight=	4			[nc]	MS
char=				4	W3C
charoff=				4	W3C
class=		*		3/4	W3C
dir=				4	W3C
dp=				3	W3C
height=	4			3+	W3C
id=	4	*		3/4	W3C
lang=		*		3/4	W3C
nowrap		*		3	W3C
style=	4	4		4	W3C
title=	4			4	W3C
valign=	*	*	*	3/4	W3C
vspace=	*	*		[nc]	NS
{event}=	4			4	W3C
<TT> ...</TT>	*	*	*	2/4	W3C
class=		*	*	3/4	W3C
dir=				4	W3C
id=	3/4	*	*	3/4	W3C
lang=		*	*	3/4	W3C
style=	4	4		4	W3C
title=	4			4	W3C
{event}=	4			4	W3C
<U> ...</U>	*	*	*	3/4	W3C
class=		*	*	3/4	W3C
dir=				4	W3C
id=	*	*	*	3/4	W3C
lang=		*	*	3/4	W3C
style=	4	4		4	W3C
title=	4			4	W3C
{event}=	4			4	W3C

Tag / Attribute	MSIE	NSNC	Lynx	HTML Version	Author
<UL> ...</UL>	*	*	*	2/4	W3C
align=	4		*		
class=		3	*	3/4	W3C
clear=				3	W3C
compact	*	*	*	2/4	W3C
dingbat=		*		3	W3C
dir=				4	W3C
id=	4	3		3/4	W3C
lang=		3		3/4	W3C
md=				3	W3C
plain				3	W3C
src=	4			3	W3C
style=	4	4		4	W3C
title=	4			4	W3C
type=	4	*	*	3+/4	W3C
wrap=				3	W3C
{event}=	4			4	W3C
<VAR> ...</VAR>	*	*	*	3+/4	W3C
class=		*	*	3/4	W3C
dir=				4	W3C
id=	*	*	*	3/4	W3C
lang=		*	*	3/4	W3C
style=	*	*		4	W3C
title=	4			4	W3C
{event}=	4			4	W3C
<WBR>	*	*		[nc]	NS
id=	4	3			
style=	4	4			
title=	4				
<XMP> ...</XMP>	*	*	*	2	W3C
id=	4	3		3	W3C
style=	4	4		3	W3C
title=	4			3	W3C
{event}=	4			4	W3C

ON line!

For the latest official information on HTML 4.0, consult the World Wide Web Consortium at http://www.w3.org/.

For current browser capabilities, visit these Web sites:

- **Lynx:** http://www.crl.com/~subir/lynx.html
- **Microsoft Internet Explorer:** http://www.microsoft.com/ie/
- **Netscape Navigator:** http://www.netscape.com/

HTML 4.0 Escaped Entities

Character Entity	Alternate Character Entity	Character
&quot;	&#34;	" (double quote mark)
&amp;	&#38;	& (ampersand)
&gt;	&#62;	> (greater than)
&lt;	&#60;	< (less than)

HTML 4.0 Named Colors

Black	= #000000	K = (Black)
Navy	= #000080	
Blue	= #0000FF	B = (Blue)
Green	= #008000	
Teal	= #008080	
Lime	= #00FF00	G = (Green)
Aqua	= #00FFFF	C = (Cyan)
Maroon	= #800000	
Purple	= #800080	
Olive	= #808000	
Gray	= #808080	
Silver	= #C0C0C0	
Red	= #FF0000	
Fuchsia	= #FF00FF	M = (Magenta)
Yellow	= #FFFF00	Y = (Yellow)
White	= #FFFFFF	

HTML 4.0 Character Entities

Portions copyright International Organization for Standardization 1986

Permission to copy in any form is granted for use with conforming SGML systems and applications as defined in ISO 8879, provided this notice is included in all copies.

Name	Value	Description
&AElig;	&#198;	capital AE diphthong (ligature)
&Aacute;	&#193;	capital A, acute accent
&Acirc;	&#194;	capital A, circumflex accent
&Agrave;	&#192;	capital A, grave accent
&Alpha;	&#913;	Greek capital letter alpha, Unicode: 0391
&Aring;	&#197;	capital A, ring
&Atilde;	&#195;	capital A, tilde
&Auml;	&#196;	capital A, dieresis or umlaut mark
&Beta;	&#914;	Greek capital letter beta, Unicode: 0392

Name	Value	Description
&Ccedil;	&#199;	capital C, cedilla
&Chi;	&#935;	Greek capital letter chi, Unicode: 03A7
&Dagger;	&#8225;	double dagger, Unicode: 2021
&Delta;	&#916;	Greek capital letter delta, Unicode: 0394
&ETH;	&#208;	capital Eth, Icelandic
&Eacute;	&#201;	capital E, acute accent
&Ecirc;	&#202;	capital E, circumflex accent
&Egrave;	&#200;	capital E, grave accent
&Epsilon;	&#917;	Greek capital letter epsilon, Unicode: 0395

Name	Value	Description
&Eta;	&#919;	Greek capital letter eta, Unicode: 0397
&Euml;	&#203;	capital E, dieresis or umlaut mark
&Gamma;	&#915;	Greek capital letter gamma, Unicode: 0393
&Iacute;	&#205;	capital I, acute accent
&Icirc;	&#206;	capital I, circumflex accent
&Igrave;	&#204;	capital I, grave accent
&Iota;	&#921;	Greek capital letter iota, Unicode: 0399
&Iuml;	&#207;	capital I, dieresis or umlaut mark
&Kappa;	&#922;	Greek capital letter kappa, Unicode: 039A
&Lambda;	&#923;	Greek capital letter lambda, Unicode: 039B
&Mu;	&#924;	Greek capital letter mu, Unicode: 039C
&Ntilde;	&#209;	capital N, tilde
&Nu;	&#925;	Greek capital letter nu, Unicode: 039D
&OElig;	&#338;	Latin capital ligature oe, Unicode: 0152
&Oacute;	&#211;	capital O, acute accent
&Ocirc;	&#212;	capital O, circumflex accent
&Ograve;	&#210;	capital O, grave accent
&Omega;	&#937;	Greek capital letter omega, Unicode: 03A9
&Omicron;	&#927;	Greek capital letter omicron, Unicode: 039F
&Oslash;	&#216;	capital O, slash
&Otilde;	&#213;	capital O, tilde
&Ouml;	&#214;	capital O, dieresis or umlaut mark
&Phi;	&#934;	Greek capital letter phi, Unicode: 03A6
&Pi;	&#928;	Greek capital letter pi, Unicode: 03A0
&Prime;	&#8243;	double prime, seconds, inches, Unicode: 2033
&Psi;	&#936;	Greek capital letter psi, Unicode: 03A8
&Rho;	&#929;	Greek capital letter rho, Unicode: 03A1
&Scaron;	&#352;	Latin capital letter s with caron, Unicode: 0160
&Sigma;	&#931;	Greek capital letter sigma, Unicode: 03A3
&THORN;	&#222;	capital THORN, Icelandic
&Tau;	&#932;	Greek capital letter tau, Unicode: 03A4
&Theta;	&#920;	Greek capital letter theta, Unicode: 0398
&Uacute;	&#218;	capital U, acute accent
&Ucirc;	&#219;	capital U, circumflex accent
&Ugrave;	&#217;	capital U, grave accent
&Upsilon;	&#933;	Greek capital letter upsilon, Unicode: 03A5
&Uuml;	&#220;	capital U, dieresis or umlaut mark
&Xi;	&#926;	Greek capital letter xi, Unicode: 039E
&Yacute;	&#221;	capital Y, acute accent
&Yuml;	&#376;	Latin capital letter y with diaeresis, Unicode: 0178
&Zeta;	&#918;	Greek capital letter zeta, Unicode: 0396
&aacute;	&#225;	small a, acute accent
&acirc;	&#226;	small a, circumflex accent
&acute;	&#180;	acute accent
&aelig;	&#230;	small ae diphthong (ligature)
&agrave;	&#224;	small a, grave accent
&alefsym;	&#8501;	alef symbol, first transfinite cardinal, Unicode: 2135
&alpha;	&#945;	Greek small letter alpha, Unicode: 03B1
&amp;	&#38;	ampersand, Unicode: 0026
&and;	&#8869;	logical and, wedge, Unicode: 2227
&ang;	&#8736;	angle, Unicode: 2220
&aring;	&#229;	small a, ring
&asymp;	&#8776;	almost equal to, asymptotic to,

Name	Value	Description
		Unicode: 2248
&atilde;	&#227;	small a, tilde
&auml;	&#228;	small a, dieresis or umlaut mark
&bdquo;	&#8222;	double low9 quotation mark, Unicode: 201E
&beta;	&#946;	Greek small letter beta, Unicode: 03B2
&brvbar;	&#166;	broken (vertical) bar
&bull;	&#8226;	bullet, black small circle, Unicode: 2022
&cap;	&#8745;	intersection, cap, Unicode: 2229
&ccedil;	&#231;	small c, cedilla
&cedil;	&#184;	cedilla
&cent;	&#162;	cent sign
&chi;	&#967;	Greek small letter chi, Unicode: 03C7
&circ;	&#710;	modifier letter circumflex accent, Unicode: 02C6
&clubs;	&#9827;	black club suit, shamrock, Unicode: 2663
&cong;	&#8773;	approximately equal to, Unicode: 2245
&copy;	&#169;	copyright sign
&crarr;	&#8629;	downwards arrow with corner leftwards, carriage return, Unicode: 21B5
&cup;	&#8746;	union, cup, Unicode: 222A
&curren;	&#164;	general currency sign
&dArr;	&#8659;	downwards double arrow, Unicode: 21D3
&dagger;	&#8224;	dagger, Unicode: 2020
&darr;	&#8595;	downwards arrow, Unicode: 2193
&deg;	&#176;	degree sign
&delta;	&#948;	Greek small letter delta, Unicode: 03B4
&diams;	&#9830;	black diamond suit, Unicode: 2666
&divide;	&#247;	divide sign
&eacute;	&#233;	small e, acute accent
&ecirc;	&#234;	small e, circumflex accent
&egrave;	&#232;	small e, grave accent
&empty;	&#8709;	empty set, null set, diameter, Unicode: 2205
		em space, Unicode: 2003
		en space, Unicode: 2002
&epsilon;	&#949;	Greek small letter epsilon, Unicode: 03B5
&equiv;	&#8801;	identical to, Unicode: 2261
&eta;	&#951;	Greek small letter eta, Unicode: 03B7
&eth;	&#240;	small eth, Icelandic
&euml;	&#235;	small e, dieresis or umlaut mark
&exist;	&#8707;	there exists, Unicode: 2203
&fnof;	&#402;	Latin small f with hook, function, florin, Unicode: 0192
&forall;	&#8704;	for all, Unicode: 2200
&frac12;	&#189;	fraction onehalf
&frac14;	&#188;	fraction onequarter
&frac34;	&#190;	fraction threequarters
&frasl;	&#8260;	fraction slash, Unicode: 2044
&gamma;	&#947;	Greek small letter gamma, Unicode: 03B3
&ge;	&#8805;	greaterthan or equal to, Unicode: 2265
&gt;	&#62;	greaterthan sign, Unicode: 003E
&hArr;	&#8660;	left right double arrow, Unicode: 21D4
&harr;	&#8596;	left right arrow, Unicode: 2194
&hearts;	&#9829;	black heart suit, valentine, Unicode: 2665
&hellip;	&#8230;	horizontal ellipsis, three dot leader, Unicode: 2026
&iacute;	&#237;	small i, acute accent
&icirc;	&#238;	small i, circumflex accent

Name	Value	Description
¡	¡	inverted exclamation mark
ì	ì	small i, grave accent
ℑ	ℑ	blackletter capital I, imaginary part, Unicode: 2111
∞	∞	infinity, Unicode: 221E
∫	∫	integral, Unicode: 222B
ι	ι	Greek small letter iota, Unicode: 03B9
¿	¿	inverted question mark
∈	∈	element of, Unicode: 2208
ï	ï	small i, dieresis or umlaut mark
κ	κ	Greek small letter kappa, Unicode: 03BA
⇐	⇐	leftwards double arrow, Unicode: 21D0
λ	λ	Greek small letter lambda, Unicode: 03BB
⟨	〈	leftpointing angle bracket, bra, Unicode: 2329
«	«	angle quotation mark, left
←	←	leftwards arrow, Unicode: 2190
⌈	⌈	left ceiling, apl upstile, Unicode: 2308,
“	“	left double quotation mark, Unicode: 201C
≤	≤	lessthan or equal to, Unicode: 2264
⌊	⌊	left floor, apl downstile, Unicode: 230A,
∗	∗	asterisk operator, Unicode: 2217
◊	◊	lozenge, Unicode: 25CA
‎	‎	lefttoright mark, Unicode: 200E RFC 2070
‹	‹	single leftpointing angle quotation mark, Unicode: 2039
‘	‘	left single quotation mark, Unicode: 2018
<	<	lessthan sign, Unicode: 003C
¯	¯	macron
—	—	em dash, Unicode: 2014
µ	µ	micro sign
·	·	middle dot
−	−	minus sign, Unicode: 2212
μ	μ	Greek small letter mu, Unicode: 03BC
∇	∇	nabla, backward difference, Unicode: 2207
		nobreak space
–	–	en dash, Unicode: 2013
≠	≠	not equal to, Unicode: 2260
∋	∋	contains as member, Unicode: 220B
¬	¬	not sign
∉	∉	not an element of, Unicode: 2209
⊄	⊄	not a subset of, Unicode: 2284
ñ	ñ	small n, tilde
ν	ν	Greek small letter nu, Unicode: 03BD
ó	ó	small o, acute accent
ô	ô	small o, circumflex accent
œ	œ	Latin small ligature oe, Unicode: 0153
ò	ò	small o, grave accent
‾	‾	overline, spacing overscore, Unicode: 203E
ω	ω	Greek small letter omega, Unicode: 03C9
ο	ο	Greek small letter omicron, Unicode: 03BF
⊕	⊕	circled plus, direct sum, Unicode: 2295
∨	⊦	logical or, vee, Unicode: 2228
ª	ª	ordinal indicator, feminine
º	º	ordinal indicator, masculine
ø	ø	small o, slash
õ	õ	small o, tilde

Name	Value	Description
⊗	⊗	circled times, vector product, Unicode: 2297
ö	ö	small o, dieresis or umlaut mark
¶	¶	pilcrow (paragraph sign)
∂	∂	partial differential, Unicode: 2202
‰	‰	per mille sign, Unicode: 2030
⊥	⊥	up tack, orthogonal to, perpendicular, Unicode: 22A5
φ	φ	Greek small letter phi, Unicode: 03C6
π	π	Greek small letter pi, Unicode: 03C0
ϖ	ϖ	Greek pi symbol, Unicode: 03D6
±	±	plusorminus sign
£	£	pound sterling sign
′	′	prime, minutes, feet, Unicode: 2032
∏	∏	nary product, product sign, Unicode: 220F
∝	∝	proportional to, Unicode: 221D
ψ	ψ	Greek small letter psi, Unicode: 03C8
"	"	quotation mark, apl quote, Unicode: 0022
⇒	⇒	rightwards double arrow, Unicode: 21D2
√	√	square root, radical sign, Unicode: 221A
⟩	〉	rightpointing angle bracket, ket, Unicode: 232A
»	»	angle quotation mark, right
→	→	rightwards arrow, Unicode: 2192
⌉	⌉	right ceiling, Unicode: 2309,
”	”	right double quotation mark, Unicode: 201D
ℜ	ℜ	blackletter capital R, real part symbol, Unicode: 211C
®	®	registered sign
⌋	⌋	right floor, Unicode: 230B,
ρ	ρ	Greek small letter rho, Unicode: 03C1
‏	‏	righttoleft mark, Unicode: 200F RFC 2070
›	›	single rightpointing angle quotation mark, Unicode: 203A
’	’	right single quotation mark, Unicode: 2019
‚	‚	single low9 quotation mark, Unicode: 201A
š	š	Latin small letter s with caron, Unicode: 0161
⋅	⋅	dot operator, Unicode: 22C5
§	§	section sign
­	­	soft hyphen
σ	σ	Greek small letter sigma, Unicode: 03C3
ς	ς	Greek small letter final sigma, Unicode: 03C2
∼	∼	tilde operator, varies with, similar to, Unicode: 223C
♠	♠	black spade suit, Unicode: 2660
⊂	⊂	subset of, Unicode: 2282
⊆	⊆	subset of or equal to, Unicode: 2286
∑	∑	nary summation, Unicode: 2211
⊃	⊃	superset of, Unicode: 2283
¹	¹	superscript one
²	²	superscript two
³	³	superscript three
⊇	⊇	superset of or equal to, Unicode: 2287
ß	ß	small sharp s, German (sz ligature)
τ	τ	Greek small letter tau, Unicode: 03C4
∴	∴	therefore, Unicode: 2234
θ	θ	Greek small letter theta, Unicode: 03B8

Name	Value	Description
ϑ	ϑ	Greek small letter theta symbol, Unicode: 03D1
		thin space, Unicode: 2009
þ	þ	small thorn, Icelandic
˜	˜	small tilde, Unicode: 02DC
×	×	multiply sign
™	™	trade mark sign, Unicode: 2122
⇑	⇑	upwards double arrow, Unicode: 21D1
ú	ú	small u, acute accent
↑	↑	upwards arrow, Unicode: 2191
û	û	small u, circumflex accent
ù	ù	small u, grave accent
¨	¨	umlaut (dieresis)
ϒ	ϒ	Greek upsilon with hook symbol, Unicode: 03D2
υ	υ	Greek small letter upsilon, Unicode: 03C5
ü	ü	small u, dieresis or umlaut mark
℘	℘	script capital P, power set, Weierstrass p, Unicode: 2118
ξ	ξ	Greek small letter xi, Unicode: 03BE
ý	ý	small y, acute accent
¥	¥	yen sign
ÿ	ÿ	small y, dieresis or umlaut mark
ζ	ζ	Greek small letter zeta, Unicode: 03B6
‍	‍	zero width joiner, Unicode: 200D
‌	‌	zero width nonjoiner, Unicode: 200C

NUMERIC ORDER

Name	Value	Description
"	"	quotation mark, apl quote, Unicode: 0022
&	&	ampersand, Unicode: 0026
<	<	less-than sign, Unicode: 003C
>	>	greater-than sign, Unicode: 003E
		no-break space
¡	¡	inverted exclamation mark
¢	¢	cent sign
£	£	pound sterling sign
¤	¤	general currency sign
¥	¥	yen sign
¦	¦	broken (vertical) bar
§	§	section sign
¨	¨	umlaut (dieresis)
©	©	copyright sign
ª	ª	ordinal indicator, feminine
«	«	angle quotation mark, left
¬	¬	not sign
­	­	soft hyphen
®	®	registered sign
¯	¯	macron
°	°	degree sign
±	±	plus-or-minus sign
²	²	superscript two
³	³	superscript three
´	´	acute accent
µ	µ	micro sign

Name	Value	Description
¶	¶	pilcrow (paragraph sign)
·	·	middle dot
¸	¸	cedilla
¹	¹	superscript one
º	º	ordinal indicator, masculine
»	»	angle quotation mark, right
¼	¼	fraction one-quarter
½	½	fraction one-half
¾	¾	fraction three-quarters
¿	¿	inverted question mark
À	À	capital A, grave accent
Á	Á	capital A, acute accent
Â	Â	capital A, circumflex accent
Ã	Ã	capital A, tilde
Ä	Ä	capital A, dieresis or umlaut mark
Å	Å	capital A, ring
Æ	Æ	capital AE diphthong (ligature)
Ç	Ç	capital C, cedilla
È	È	capital E, grave accent
É	É	capital E, acute accent
Ê	Ê	capital E, circumflex accent
Ë	Ë	capital E, dieresis or umlaut mark
Ì	Ì	capital I, grave accent
Í	Í	capital I, acute accent
Î	Î	capital I, circumflex accent
Ï	Ï	capital I, dieresis or umlaut mark
Ð	Ð	capital Eth, Icelandic
Ñ	Ñ	capital N, tilde
Ò	Ò	capital O, grave accent
Ó	Ó	capital O, acute accent
Ô	Ô	capital O, circumflex accent
Õ	Õ	capital O, tilde
Ö	Ö	capital O, dieresis or umlaut mark
×	×	multiply sign
Ø	Ø	capital O, slash
Ù	Ù	capital U, grave accent
Ú	Ú	capital U, acute accent
Û	Û	capital U, circumflex accent
Ü	Ü	capital U, dieresis or umlaut mark
Ý	Ý	capital Y, acute accent
Þ	Þ	capital THORN, Icelandic
ß	ß	small sharp s, German (sz ligature)
à	à	small a, grave accent
á	á	small a, acute accent
â	â	small a, circumflex accent
ã	ã	small a, tilde
ä	ä	small a, dieresis or umlaut mark
å	å	small a, ring
æ	æ	small ae diphthong (ligature)
ç	ç	small c, cedilla
è	è	small e, grave accent
é	é	small e, acute accent
ê	ê	small e, circumflex accent
ë	ë	small e, dieresis or umlaut mark
ì	ì	small i, grave accent
í	í	small i, acute accent
î	î	small i, circumflex accent

Name	Value	Description
ï	ï	small i, dieresis or umlaut mark
ð	ð	small eth, Icelandic
ñ	ñ	small n, tilde
ò	ò	small o, grave accent
ó	ó	small o, acute accent
ô	ô	small o, circumflex accent
õ	õ	small o, tilde
ö	ö	small o, dieresis or umlaut mark
÷	÷	divide sign
ø	ø	small o, slash
ù	ù	small u, grave accent
ú	ú	small u, acute accent
û	û	small u, circumflex accent
ü	ü	small u, dieresis or umlaut mark
ý	ý	small y, acute accent
þ	þ	small thorn, Icelandic
ÿ	ÿ	small y, dieresis or umlaut mark
Œ	Œ	Latin capital ligature oe, Unicode: 0152
œ	œ	Latin small ligature oe, Unicode: 0153
Š	Š	Latin capital letter s with caron, Unicode: 0160
š	š	Latin small letter s with caron, Unicode: 0161
Ÿ	Ÿ	Latin capital letter y with diaeresis, Unicode: 0178
ƒ	ƒ	Latin small f with hook, function, florin, Unicode: 0192
ˆ	ˆ	modifier letter circumflex accent, Unicode: 02C6
˜	˜	small tilde, Unicode: 02DC
Α	Α	Greek capital letter alpha, Unicode: 0391
Β	Β	Greek capital letter beta, Unicode: 0392
Γ	Γ	Greek capital letter gamma, Unicode: 0393
Δ	Δ	Greek capital letter delta, Unicode: 0394
Ε	Ε	Greek capital letter epsilon, Unicode: 0395
Ζ	Ζ	Greek capital letter zeta, Unicode: 0396
Η	Η	Greek capital letter eta, Unicode: 0397
Θ	Θ	Greek capital letter theta, Unicode: 0398
Ι	Ι	Greek capital letter iota, Unicode: 0399
Κ	Κ	Greek capital letter kappa, Unicode: 039A
Λ	Λ	Greek capital letter lambda, Unicode: 039B
Μ	Μ	Greek capital letter mu, Unicode: 039C
Ν	Ν	Greek capital letter nu, Unicode: 039D
Ξ	Ξ	Greek capital letter xi, Unicode: 039E
Ο	Ο	Greek capital letter omicron, Unicode: 039F
Π	Π	Greek capital letter pi, Unicode: 03A0
Ρ	Ρ	Greek capital letter rho, Unicode: 03A1
Σ	Σ	Greek capital letter sigma, Unicode: 03A3
Τ	Τ	Greek capital letter tau, Unicode: 03A4
Υ	Υ	Greek capital letter upsilon, Unicode: 03A5
Φ	Φ	Greek capital letter phi, Unicode: 03A6
Χ	Χ	Greek capital letter chi, Unicode: 03A7
Ψ	Ψ	Greek capital letter psi, Unicode: 03A8
Ω	Ω	Greek capital letter omega, Unicode: 03A9
α	α	Greek small letter alpha, Unicode: 03B1
β	β	Greek small letter beta, Unicode: 03B2
γ	γ	Greek small letter gamma, Unicode: 03B3

Name	Value	Description
δ	δ	Greek small letter delta, Unicode: 03B4
ε	ε	Greek small letter epsilon, Unicode: 03B5
ζ	ζ	Greek small letter zeta, Unicode: 03B6
η	η	Greek small letter eta, Unicode: 03B7
θ	θ	Greek small letter theta, Unicode: 03B8
ι	ι	Greek small letter iota, Unicode: 03B9
κ	κ	Greek small letter kappa, Unicode: 03BA
λ	λ	Greek small letter lambda, Unicode: 03BB
μ	μ	Greek small letter mu, Unicode: 03BC
ν	ν	Greek small letter nu, Unicode: 03BD
ξ	ξ	Greek small letter xi, Unicode: 03BE
ο	ο	Greek small letter omicron, Unicode: 03BF
π	π	Greek small letter pi, Unicode: 03C0
ρ	ρ	Greek small letter rho, Unicode: 03C1
ς	ς	Greek small letter final sigma, Unicode: 03C2
σ	σ	Greek small letter sigma, Unicode: 03C3
τ	τ	Greek small letter tau, Unicode: 03C4
υ	υ	Greek small letter upsilon, Unicode: 03C5
φ	φ	Greek small letter phi, Unicode: 03C6
χ	χ	Greek small letter chi, Unicode: 03C7
ψ	ψ	Greek small letter psi, Unicode: 03C8
ω	ω	Greek small letter omega, Unicode: 03C9
ϑ	ϑ	Greek small letter theta symbol, Unicode: 03D1
ϒ	ϒ	Greek upsilon with hook symbol, Unicode: 03D2
ϖ	ϖ	Greek pi symbol, Unicode: 03D6
		en space, Unicode: 2002
		em space, Unicode: 2003
		thin space, Unicode: 2009
‌	‌	zero width non-joiner, Unicode: 200C
‍	‍	zero width joiner, Unicode: 200D
‎	‎	left-to-right mark, Unicode: 200E RFC 2070
‏	‏	right-to-left mark, Unicode: 200F RFC 2070
–	–	en dash, Unicode: 2013
—	—	em dash, Unicode: 2014
‘	‘	left single quotation mark, Unicode: 2018
’	’	right single quotation mark, Unicode: 2019
‚	‚	single low-9 quotation mark, Unicode: 201A
“	“	left double quotation mark, Unicode: 201C
”	”	right double quotation mark, Unicode: 201D
„	„	double low-9 quotation mark, Unicode: 201E
†	†	dagger, Unicode: 2020
‡	‡	double dagger, Unicode: 2021
•	•	bullet, black small circle, Unicode: 2022
…	…	horizontal ellipsis, three dot leader, Unicode: 2026
‰	‰	per mille sign, Unicode: 2030
′	′	prime, minutes, feet, Unicode: 2032
″	″	double prime, seconds, inches, Unicode: 2033
‹	‹	single left-pointing angle quotation mark, Unicode: 2039
›	›	single right-pointing angle quotation mark, Unicode: 203A
‾	‾	overline, spacing overscore, Unicode: 203E

Name	Value	Description
⁄	⁄	fraction slash, Unicode: 2044
ℑ	ℑ	blackletter capital I, imaginary part, Unicode: 2111
℘	℘	script capital P, power set, Weierstrass p, Unicode: 2118
ℜ	ℜ	blackletter capital R, real part symbol, Unicode: 211C
™	™	trade mark sign, Unicode: 2122
ℵ	ℵ	alef symbol, first transfinite cardinal, Unicode: 2135
←	←	leftwards arrow, Unicode: 2190
↑	↑	upwards arrow, Unicode: 2191
→	→	rightwards arrow, Unicode: 2192
↓	↓	downwards arrow, Unicode: 2193
↔	↔	left right arrow, Unicode: 2194
↵	↵	downwards arrow with corner leftwards, carriage return, Unicode: 21B5
⇐	⇐	leftwards double arrow, Unicode: 21D0
⇑	⇑	upwards double arrow, Unicode: 21D1
⇒	⇒	rightwards double arrow, Unicode: 21D2
⇓	⇓	downwards double arrow, Unicode: 21D3
⇔	⇔	left right double arrow, Unicode: 21D4
∀	∀	for all, Unicode: 2200
∂	∂	partial differential, Unicode: 2202
∃	∃	there exists, Unicode: 2203
∅	∅	empty set, null set, diameter, Unicode: 2205
∇	∇	nabla, backward difference, Unicode: 2207
∈	∈	element of, Unicode: 2208
∉	∉	not an element of, Unicode: 2209
∋	∋	contains as member, Unicode: 220B
∏	∏	n-ary product, product sign, Unicode: 220F
∑	∑	n-ary sumation, Unicode: 2211
−	−	minus sign, Unicode: 2212
∗	∗	asterisk operator, Unicode: 2217
√	√	square root, radical sign, Unicode: 221A
∝	∝	proportional to, Unicode: 221D
∞	∞	infinity, Unicode: 221E
∠	∠	angle, Unicode: 2220

Name	Value	Description
∩	∩	intersection, cap, Unicode: 2229
∪	∪	union, cup, Unicode: 222A
∫	∫	integral, Unicode: 222B
∴	∴	therefore, Unicode: 2234
∼	∼	tilde operator, varies with, similar to, Unicode: 223C
≅	≅	approximately equal to, Unicode: 2245
≈	≈	almost equal to, asymptotic to, Unicode: 2248
≠	≠	not equal to, Unicode: 2260
≡	≡	identical to, Unicode: 2261
≤	≤	less-than or equal to, Unicode: 2264
≥	≥	greater-than or equal to, Unicode: 2265
⊂	⊂	subset of, Unicode: 2282
⊃	⊃	superset of, Unicode: 2283
⊄	⊄	not a subset of, Unicode: 2284
⊆	⊆	subset of or equal to, Unicode: 2286
⊇	⊇	superset of or equal to, Unicode: 2287
⊕	⊕	circled plus, direct sum, Unicode: 2295
⊗	⊗	circled times, vector product, Unicode: 2297
∧	⊥	logical and wedge, Unicode: 2227
⊥	⊥	up tack, orthogonal to, perpendicular, Unicode: 22A5
∨	⊦	logical or vee, Unicode: 2228
⋅	⋅	dot operator, Unicode: 22C5
⌈	⌈	left ceiling, apl upstile, Unicode: 2308,
⌉	⌉	right ceiling, Unicode: 2309,
⌊	⌊	left floor, apl downstile, Unicode: 230A,
⌋	⌋	right floor, Unicode: 230B,
⟨	〈	left-pointing angle bracket, bra, Unicode: 2329
⟩	〉	right-pointing angle bracket, ket, Unicode: 232A
◊	◊	lozenge, Unicode: 25CA
♠	♠	black spade suit, Unicode: 2660
♣	♣	black club suit, shamrock, Unicode: 2663
♥	♥	black heart suit, valentine, Unicode: 2665
♦	♦	black diamond suit, Unicode: 2666

INDEX

Note to the Reader: First level entries are in **bold**. Page numbers in **bold** indicate the principal discussion of a topic or the definition of a term. Page numbers in *italic* indicate illustrations.